S0-CJP-777

ENCYCLOPEDIA OF THE GLOBAL ECONOMY

ENCYCLOPEDIA OF THE Global Economy

A Guide for Students and Researchers

VOLUME 1

David E. O'Connor

GREENWOOD PRESS
Westport, Connecticut • London

Library of Congress Cataloging-in-Publication Data

O'Connor, David E. (David Edward)
Encyclopedia of the global economy : a guide for students and researchers / David E. O'Connor.
p. cm.
Includes bibliographical references and index.
ISBN 0–313–33584–2 (set : alk. paper)—ISBN 0–313–33585–0 (v. 1 : alk. paper)—ISBN 0–313–33586–9 (v. 2 : alk. paper)
1. International economic relations—Encyclopedias. 2. Globalization—Economic aspects—Encyclopedias. 3. Economic history—Encyclopedias. I. Title.
HF1359O28 2006
330.03—dc22 2005025481

British Library Cataloguing in Publication Data is available.

Library of Congress Catalog Card Number: 2005025481
ISBN: 0–313–33584–2 (set)
0–313–33585–0 (vol. 1)
0–313–33586–9 (vol. 2)

First published in 2006

Greenwood Press, 88 Post Road West, Westport, CT 06881
An imprint of Greenwood Publishing Group, Inc.
www.greenwood.com

Printed in the United States of America

The paper used in this book complies with the Permanent Paper Standard issued by the National Information Standards Organization (Z39.48–1984).

10 9 8 7 6 5 4 3 2 1

Every reasonable effort has been made to trace the owners of copyrighted materials in this book, but in some instances this has proven impossible. The author and publisher will be glad to receive information leading to more complete acknowledgments in subsequent printings of the book and in the meantime extend their apologies for any omissions.

Contents

List of Entries

Guide to Related Topics

Economic Growth and Sustainable Economic Development

Advanced Economies
Brain Drain
Bretton Woods System
Business Cycle
Capital Flight
Capital Formation
Capital Markets
Competitiveness
Corporate Social Responsibility
Corruption
Democracy
Developing Countries
Development Economics
Development Plan
Digital Divide
Economic Freedom
Economic Growth
Emerging Market Economies
Energy Resources
Entrepreneurship
Environmental Degradation
Factors of Production
Financial Contagion
Foreign Aid
Foreign Direct Investment
Good Governance
Gross Domestic Product
Gross National Income
Group of Eight
Group of Seventy-Seven
Group of Twenty
Human Development
Industrial Revolution
Informal Economy
Information and Communications Technologies
International Financial Institutions
International Trade
Keynes, John Maynard
Kuznets, Simon
Least Developed Countries
Multilateral Environmental Agreements
Newly Industrialized Economies
Offshoring
Population
Poverty
Production Sharing
Quality of Life
Race to the Bottom
Rostow, Walt W.
Sachs, Jeffrey D.
Sen, Amartya K.
Solow, Robert M.
Sustainable Consumption
Sustainable Economic Development
Transition Countries
Transnational Corporations
Unsustainable Debt

Economic History

Basic Economic Questions
Bretton Woods System
Capitalism
Command Economy
Commercial Revolution
Communism

Democratic Socialism
Deng Xiaoping
Development Economics
Development Plan
Economic System
General Agreement on Tariffs and Trade
Global Culture
Hayek, Friedrich A.
Industrial Revolution
Joseph, Keith S.
Keynes, John Maynard
Kuznets, Simon
Lewis, William A.
Malthus, Thomas R.
Market Economy
Mercantilism
Mun, Thomas
Myrdal, Karl G.
Nyerere, Julius K.
Pigou, Arthur C.
Ricardo, David
Rostow, Walt W.
Schumpeter, Joseph A.
Smith, Adam
Solow, Robert M.
Third World Socialism
United Nations System
Ward, Barbara M.

Economic Systems

Advanced Economies
Basic Economic Questions
Capitalism
Command Economy
Communism
Democratic Socialism
Deng Xiaoping
Developing Countries
Economic System
Emerging Market Economies
Factors of Production
Global Economy
Hayek, Friedrich A.
Joseph, Keith S.
Least Developed Countries
Market Economy
Marx, Karl H.
Newly Industrialized Economies
Nyerere, Julius K.
Pigou, Arthur C.
Smith, Adam
Third World Socialism
Transition Countries

Finance and Banking

African Development Bank Group
Asian Development Bank
Bank for International Settlements
Bretton Woods System
Capital Flight
Capitalism
Capital Markets
Corruption
Democracy
European Bank for Reconstruction and Development
Exchange Rates
External Debt
Financial Contagion
Foreign Aid
Foreign Direct Investment
Foreign Exchange Market
Global Financial Architecture
Globalization
Good Governance
Group of Eight
Group of Seventy-Seven

Group of Twenty
Heavily Indebted Poor Countries (HIPC) Initiative
Inflation
Inter-American Development Bank Group
International Bank for Reconstruction and Development
International Development Association
International Finance Corporation
International Financial Institutions
International Investment Agreements
International Monetary Fund
Microfinance Institutions
Offshore Financial Centers
Organization for Economic Cooperation and Development
Poverty
South-South Cooperation
Terms of Trade
Transnational Corporations
Unsustainable Debt
World Bank Group
World Trade Organization
Yunus, Muhammad

Global Issues

Balance of Payments
Balance of Trade
Brain Drain
Capital Flight
Cartel
Civil Society Organizations
Competitiveness
Corporate Social Responsibility
Corruption
Digital Divide
Dumping
Energy Resources
Environmental Degradation
External Debt
Financial Contagion
Foreign Aid
Foreign Direct Investment
Global Culture
Global Financial Architecture
Globalization
Heavily Indebted Poor Countries (HIPC) Initiative
Inflation
Informal Economy
Localization
Maquiladoras
Multilateral Environmental Agreements
New Protectionism
Non-Governmental Organizations
Offshore Financial Centers
Offshoring
Organization of Petroleum Exporting Countries
Population
Poverty
Privatization
Production Sharing
Protectionism
Race to the Bottom
Supply Chains
Sustainable Consumption
Terms of Trade
Transnational Corporations
Unsustainable Debt

Globalization

Advertising
Annan, Kofi
Bretton Woods System
Capital Flight
Capital Markets
Civil Society Organizations

Commercial Revolution
Consumers International
Democracy
Digital Divide
Environmental Degradation
Exports
Financial Contagion
Foreign Direct Investment
Foreign Exchange Market
General Agreement on Tariffs and Trade
Global Culture
Global Economy
Globalization
Imports
Information and Communications Technologies
International Financial Institutions
International Investment Agreements
International Trade
Localization
Maquiladoras
Mercantilism
Moore, Mike
New Protectionism
Non-Governmental Organizations
Offshoring
Production Sharing
Protectionism
Race to the Bottom
Supply Chains
Transnational Corporations
World Trade Organization

Institutions and Organizations

African Development Bank Group
Annan, Kofi
Asian Development Bank
Bank for International Settlements
Bretton Woods System
Capital Markets
Civil Society Organizations
Consumers International
European Bank for Reconstruction and Development
Foreign Exchange Market
General Agreement on Tariffs and Trade
Group of Eight
Group of Seventy-Seven
Group of Twenty
Inter-American Development Bank Group
International Centre for Settlement of Investment Disputes
International Co-operative Alliance
International Development Association
International Finance Corporation
International Financial Institutions
International Labor Organization
International Monetary Fund
Moore, Mike
Multilateral Investment Guarantee Agency
Organization for Economic Cooperation and Development
Organization of Petroleum Exporting Countries
Regional Development Banks
Stiglitz, Joseph E.
United Nations System
Wolfensohn, James D.
World Bank Group
World Economic Forum
World Health Organization
World Intellectual Property Organization
World Trade Organization
Yunus, Muhammad

International Trade

Absolute Advantage
Balance of Payments
Balance of Trade
Bhagwati, Jagdish

People

Poverty and Income Distribution

Emerging Market Economies
Export Processing Zone
External Debt
Foreign Aid
Global Economy
Good Governance
Gross Domestic Product
Gross National Income
Group of Eight
Group of Seventy-Seven
Group of Twenty
Heavily Indebted Poor Countries (HIPC) Initiative
Human Development
Informal Economy
International Labor Organization
Least Developed Countries
Malthus, Thomas R.
Maquiladoras
Microfinance Institutions
Millennium Development Goals
Myrdal, Karl G.
Newly Industrialized Economies
Non-Governmental Organizations
Organization for Economic Cooperation and Development
Peace Corps of the United States
Pigou, Arthur C.
Population
Purchasing Power Parity
Quality of Life
Race to the Bottom
Sachs, Jeffrey D.
Sen, Amartya K.
Soto, Hernando de
South-South Cooperation
Supply Chains
Sustainable Economic Development
Third World Socialism
Unsustainable Debt
Ward, Barbara M.
Yunus, Muhammad

Production and Output

Advanced Economies
Basic Economic Questions
Brain Drain
Business Cycle
Capital Flight
Capital Formation
Capital Markets
Cartel
Competitiveness
Corporate Social Responsibility
Developing Countries
Digital Divide
Economic Freedom
Economic Growth
Economic Sectors
Emerging Market Economies
Energy Resources
Entrepreneurship
Environmental Degradation
Export Processing Zone
Factors of Production
Foreign Direct Investment
Global Economy
Good Governance
Gross Domestic Product
Industrial Revolution
Informal Economy
Information and Communications Technologies
International Centre for Settlement of Investment Disputes
International Co-operative Alliance
International Investment Agreements
International Labor Organization
Least Developed Countries
Localization
Maquiladoras
Multilateral Environmental Agreements
Multilateral Investment Guarantee Agency
Offshoring
Privatization

Production Sharing
Purchasing Power Parity
Race to the Bottom
Schumacher, Ernst F.
Schumpeter, Joseph A.
Supply Chains
Sustainable Consumption
Transition Countries
Transnational Corporations
World Economic Forum

Regionalism

African Development Bank Group
Andean Community
Asian Development Bank
Asia-Pacific Economic Cooperation
Association of Southeast Asian Nations
Caribbean Community
Central American Common Market
Economic Community of West African States
European Bank for Reconstruction and Development
European Free Trade Association
European Union
Free Trade Area of the Americas
Inter-American Development Bank Group
International Commodity Agreements
International Investment Agreements
MERCOSUR
Multilateral Environmental Agreements
North American Free Trade Agreement
Organization for Economic Cooperation and Development
Organization of Petroleum Exporting Countries
Regional Development Banks
Regional Trade Agreements
South-South Cooperation

Figures and Tables

Figures

Tables

Author's Note

This two-volume reference text offers a wide variety of information on the people, events, history, and institutions of the global economy. A couple of clarifications at the beginning of this study will help smooth the path. First, the terms "countries" and "economies" are often used interchangeably. For example, for reasons of convenience, the book makes references to developing countries, or developing economies. In fact, countries and economies are distinct terms. In 2004, there were 192 countries in the world and 208 economies. There are more "economies" mainly because a number of largely autonomous territories or regions within countries are counted as separate economies by multilateral organizations such as the World Bank and International Monetary Fund. The Hong Kong SAR and Macao are each counted as separate economies by the World Bank, yet each is a region within the People's Republic of China. Similarly, Puerto Rico and the U.S. Virgin Islands are counted as economies, separate from the United States.

A second clarification involves Chinese Taipei. At the conclusion of the Chinese Civil War in 1949, millions of Nationalists fled to the island of Formosa—today called Taiwan—to escape communist rule. The status of Chinese Taipei has been a matter of dispute since 1949. At the heart of the debate is whether Chinese Taipei is sovereign country or a province of the People's Republic of China. The political and economic issues surrounding this debate are complex. The term Chinese Taipei, which is the preferred citation by the World Trade Organization (WTO), is used throughout this reference book for reasons of consistency. Other common names include the Taiwan Province of China, which is used by the IMF; Taiwan, China, which is used by the World Bank; and the Republic of China, or simply Taiwan, which are used in many basic reference texts.

Preface

The global economy is the international network of individuals, businesses, governments, multilateral organizations, and civil society groups, which collectively make decisions about the production, consumption, and distribution of goods and services. Since the 1850s, the global economic pendulum has swung between two poles, economic integration and economic isolation. The globalization process promotes economic integration. The two modern phases of globalization occurred from 1850 to 1914, and 1946 to the present. The pillars of modern economic globalization include the free cross-border movements of goods and services, foreign direct investment, financial capital, labor, and technology. On a broader level, globalization also embraces international flows of ideas, political and social values, language, and other aspects of culture. The most significant reversal in the global pendulum occurred from 1914 to 1945. During this period of retrenchment, the globalization juggernaut was knocked back on its heels by two devastating world wars and a prolonged global depression.

The *Encyclopedia of the Global Economy* consists of two related volumes. The book examines the key people, institutions, current issues, and historical events that shaped the global economy. Alphabetized entries on topics in the global economy dominate Volume 1 of the two-volume set. Volume 1 is heavily illustrated with dozens of photographs and graphs, and nearly 100 tables. Photographs, graphs, and tables are carefully integrated into the running narrative. Key documents and statistical data related to the global economy comprise Volume 2. Relevant documents, and timely statistical data, are gleaned from the world's most respected, authoritative sources. This reference work provides a wealth of information on the global economy for researchers, teachers, high school and college students, and concerned citizens.

Volume 1 of the *Encyclopedia of the Global Economy* consists of 168 encyclopedic entries on key international topics. It also includes several reference features. Reference features in both volumes include a list of Common Abbreviations, which untangles the web of multilateral organizations, government agencies, programs, and concepts that dot the literature of international economics. An extensive Timeline of Key Events in the Global Economy, 1776–2009, provides an historical sketch of major economic, political, scientific, and cultural forces that have shaped the global economy. The timeline also establishes an historical grounding for important issues and events. Additional information at the back of each volume provides opportunities for quick reference and further research. A comprehensive Glossary of Selected Terms facilitates informed reading and analysis of economic literature. A list of Key Global Economy Web Sites encourages further research by unlocking a treasure chest of international sites and links to primary documents, statistical data, and other information. The Selected Bibliography familiarizes readers with core literature in global economics.

Volume 1 entries offer in-depth information and analysis of the people, institutions, issues, and historic trends in the global economy. Entries explore the lives and contributions of dozens of individual movers and shakers, past and present. Centuries ago, Adam Smith and David Ricardo rebelled against prevailing mercantilist thought by extolling the virtues of free markets and free trade. Today, the echoes of Smith and Ricardo influence world leaders such as UN Secretary-General Kofi Annan, former WTO Director-General Mike Moore, and other proponents of globalization. Entries trace the evolution of development economics, from W. W. Rostow's defense of linear development, to Hernando de Soto's policies of economic inclusion, to Jeffrey Sachs' prescription for an end to poverty in our time. Still others have shaped the structure of economic systems, including Karl H. Marx, the revolutionary; Deng Xiaoping, the reformer; Julius K. Nyerere, the idealist; and Keith S. Joseph, architect of the capitalist counterrevolution.

Entries examine the structure and function of key institutions in the global economy. They spotlight major multilateral organizations such as the World Bank, International Monetary Fund (IMF), and World Trade Organization—the Big Three organizations that oversee the economic and financial system in the rules-based global economy. The United Nations and its specialized agencies, such as the World Health Organization and World Intellectual Property Organization, are also examined. Other entries focus on the grassroots activism of civil society organizations (CSOs) and non-governmental organizations (NGOs), modern-day gadflies that demand transparency, accountability, and inclusion in global decision making. Many multilateral institutions in today's global economy support the liberalization of international trade and cross-border investment. Some of globalization's strongest support comes from regional trade and investment agreements, such as the European Union (EU), North American Free Trade Agreement (NAFTA), and Southern Common Market (MERCOSUR). Other key supporters of global integration are the regional development banks, including the African Development Bank Group, Asian Development Bank, European Bank for Reconstruction and Development, and the Inter-American Development Bank Group.

Entries analyze current issues in the global economy. Many controversial issues involve obstacles to economic development in the world's poorer regions. Development issues in the third world concern the brain drain, capital flight, corporate social responsibility, corruption, cultural homogenization, digital divide, extreme poverty, foreign aid, population, the race to the bottom, supply chains, terms of trade, and unsustainable debt. The advanced economies face growing concerns about dumping, energy dependence, offshore financial centers, offshore outsourcing, and unsustainable consumption. The advanced countries also face mounting pressure for a more equitable distribution of the world's resources and wealth. Spearheading demands for economic and social justice are thousands of CSOs and NGOs, the G77, and other voices from the global South. Economic problems related to environmental degradation, cracks in the global financial architecture, and financial contagion, are a constant reminder of the precarious nature of humankind's interdependence.

Entries also analyze historical movements, events, and trends in the global economy. Entries on mercantilism, commercial revolution, and the Industrial Revolution provide an historical backdrop for the first age of globalization, which began in the mid-1800s. Entries examine the major economic systems, including capitalism, communism, democratic socialism, third world socialism, and the unique transition economies of eastern and central Europe and central Asia. Economic history is also woven into the biographies, the institutions, and issues associated with the rise of the global economy. Each entry is crossed-referenced and includes a list of additional readings to facilitate in-depth research. A comprehensive general Index, which provides quick access to a specific subject, is also cross-referenced to related topics.

Volume 2 of the *Encyclopedia of the Global Economy* is packed with rich primary documents and statistical data. About sixty primary documents are organized under ten headings: population; poverty reduction; economic growth and sustainable development; international trade; regional integration in the global trading system; foreign direct investment and corporate social responsibility; global labor markets and labor rights; the environment and sustainable development; consumer rights and sustainable consumption; and quality of life and economic justice. Documents represent the views of major multilateral organizations such as the World Bank, International Monetary Fund (IMF), World Trade Organization (WTO), Organization for Economic Cooperation and Development, and specialized agencies, programs, and funds within the United Nations System; non-governmental organizations such as Oxfam International, Greenpeace, WorldWatch, and World Vision; think-tanks and research institutions such as the Institute for Liberty and Democracy, New Economic Foundation, Population Reference Bureau, World Resources Institute, Fraser Institute, Institute for Management Development, Kauffman Foundation; other advocacy groups such as Public Citizen, Consumers International, Fair Labor Association, and the Group of 77; and regional associations such as the Asia-Pacific Economic Cooperation, European Union, and North American Free Trade Agreement. Each primary document is prefaced with an introductory statement and is cross-referenced with related Volume 1 entries.

Timely statistical data presented in Volume 2 describe current realities and historical trends in the global economy. Statistical data is organized in tabular form under ten headings: population; global output; advanced economies; least developed economies; income distribution, poverty, and external debt; quality of life indicators; transnational corporations and foreign direct investment; international trade; regional development banks; global energy consumption and production; and global competitiveness and freedom. Global data sources include the *World Development Indicators* and *Global Economic Prospects* (World Bank), *World Economic Outlook* (IMF), *International Trade Statistics* (WTO),

World Investment Report and *Least Developed Countries Report* (United Nations Conference on Trade and Development), *Human Development Report* (United Nations Development Program), *State of the World Population* (United Nations Population Fund), *United Nations Literacy Decade* (United Nations Educational, Scientific, and Cultural Organization), *International Energy Outlook*, and *International Energy Annual* (U.S. Energy Information Administration). Also included are annual reports and statistical bulletins published by the regional development banks, and by other influential groups such as the World Economic Forum, Freedom House, Transparency International, Fortune, the Institute for Management Development, the Kauffman Foundation, and the Organization of Petroleum Exporting Countries.

The *Encyclopedia of the Global Economy* invites readers to explore and analyze the international organizations, global issues, and personalities that have molded today's dynamic global economy. In-depth entries, complemented by authoritative documents and data, enable readers to analyze global economic topics from a variety of perspectives and to form opinions on complex issues, policies, and practices in the global arena. The globalization juggernaut has strengthened the economic web among nations and has improved the quality of life for billions of people. At the same time, globalization has widened the income and technological gap between the world's richest and poorest citizens, and aggravated tensions between the global North and South. Globalization, as a process, is neither good nor bad. Instead, it is a means to an end; a way to improve people's standard of living and quality of life. To fulfill the promise of globalization, the global community must first recognize that global prosperity and social justice are in everyone's best interest.

Acknowledgments

I would like to recognize the following individuals for their contributions to this publication: John Thomas Ridyard, for the production of the book's charts, graphs, and diagrams, and for related technical and research assistance; Professor Subhash C. Jain, Executive Director of the Center for International Business Education and Research (CIBER) at the University of Connecticut, for his expertise and constructive counsel; the Government Publications research staff at the Homer Babbidge Library, University of Connecticut, for its research support; Linda Mathes, Jane White, Jan Nuhn, and Peter Salesses of the Edwin O. Smith High School Library Media Center for technical and research assistance; Marcia Goldstein, Permissions Coordinator for the Greenwood Publishing Group, and Anne Ortega of the Copyright Clearance Center, for their assistance in obtaining primary documents; Nicholas Philipson, Senior Editor of Business and Economics at Greenwood, for his contributions to the structure and scope of the *Encyclopedia of the Global Economy*; and Mark Kane at Greenwood and Jane McGraw at Capital City Press for their skillful preparation of the manuscript for publication.

I also thank the following multilateral and intergovernmental organizations for their assistance in providing primary documents and authoritative statistical data for the encyclopedia: the African Development Bank, Asia-Pacific Economic Cooperation group, Association of Southeast Asian Nations, Asian Development Bank, European Bank for Reconstruction and Development, European Union, Group of Seventy-Seven, Inter-American Development Bank, International Monetary Fund, the NAFTA Secretariat, Organization for Economic Cooperation and Development, Organization of Petroleum Exporting Countries, World Bank, World Trade Organization, and a number of specialized programs and funds within the United Nations System—the International Labor Organization; UN Conference on Trade and Development; UN Development Program; UN Educational, Scientific and Cultural Organization; UN Environment Program; and UN Population Fund.

A number of think-tanks, research organizations, civil society organizations, non-governmental organizations, and business groups contributed to this work, including: Babson College and the Kauffman Foundation, Consumers International, Fair Labor Association, Fortune, Fraser Institute, Freedom House, Grameen Bank, Greenpeace, Institute for Liberty and Democracy, Institute for Management Development, International Chamber of Commerce, International Co-operative Alliance, New Economics Foundation, Nike, Oxfam International, Public Citizen, Transparency International,

World Resources Institute, World Economic Forum, World Vision, and WorldWatch. The following U.S. government agencies provided a variety of timely economic data: U.S. Bureau of Economic Analysis, U.S. Commerce Department, and U.S. Energy Information Administration/U.S. Department of Energy.

Common Abbreviations

ACP	African, Caribbean, and Pacific (countries)
ADB	Asian Development Bank
ADB Group	African Development Bank Group
ADF	African Development Fund
ADF	Asian Development Fund
AFTA	ASEAN Free Trade Area
AIA	ASEAN Investment Area
APEC	Asia-Pacific Economic Cooperation
ASEAN	Association of Southeast Asian Nations
ATC	Agreement on Textiles and Clothing
B2B	business to business (transactions)
B2C	business to consumer (transactions)
BIS	Bank for International Settlements
BIT	bilateral investment treaty
BOP	balance of payments
CACM	Central American Common Market
CAFTA	Central American Free Trade Agreement
CARICOM	Caribbean Community and Common Market
CCP	Chinese Communist Party
CDF	Comprehensive Development Framework
CEE	Central and Eastern Europe
CET	common external tariff
CFE	Common Fund for Commodities
CI	Consumers International
CIS	Commonwealth of Independent States
COMECON	Council for Mutual Economic Assistance
COMESA	Common Market for Eastern and Southern Africa
CPI	consumer price index
CPI	Corruption Perceptions Index
CRS	corporate social responsibility
CSME	CARICOM Single Market and Economy
CSO	civil society organization
DAC	Development Assistance Committee
DDA	Doha Development Agenda

DSB	Dispute Settlement Body (WTO)
DTT	double taxation treaty
EBRD	European Bank for Reconstruction and Development
EC	European Community
ECA	export credit agency
ECB	European Central Bank
ECOSOC	Economic and Social Council (UN)
ECOWAS	Economic Community of West African States
EEA	European Economic Area
EEC	European Economic Community
EFTA	European Free Trade Association
EME	emerging market economies
EMU	European Monetary Union
EP	European Parliament
EPZ	export processing zone
ESCB	European System of Central Banks
EU	European Union
EUR	euro
EUROPOL	European Police Office
FAO	Food and Agriculture Organization (UN)
FDI	foreign direct investment
FSU	Former Soviet Union
FTA	free trade area
FTAA	Free Trade Area of the Americas
G8	Group of Eight
G7	Group of Seven
G77	Group of Seventy-Seven
G20	Group of Twenty
GATS	General Agreement on Trade in Services
GATT	General Agreement on Tariffs and Trade
GDP	gross domestic product
GFA	global financial architecture
GNI	gross national income
GNP	gross national product
HDI	Human Development Index
HIPC	Heavily Indebted Poor Countries (Initiative)
IBC	international business corporation
IBRD	International Bank for Reconstruction and Development
ICA	international commodity agreement
ICA	International Co-operative Alliance
ICFTU	International Confederation of Free Trade Unions

ICP	International Comparison Program
ICPD	International Conference on Population and Development
ICSID	International Centre for Settlement of Investment Disputes
ICT	information and communications technologies
IDA	International Development Association
IDB	Inter-American Development Bank (Group)
IFC	International Finance Corporation
IFI	international financial institution
IIC	Inter-American Investment Corporation
ILD	Institute for Liberty and Democracy
ILO	International Labor Organization
IMD	Institute for Management Development
IMF	International Monetary Fund
INGO	international non-governmental organization
IPA	investment promotion agency
IPR	intellectual property rights
ISO	International Standards Organization
IT	information technology
ITDG	Intermediate Technology Development Group
ITO	International Trade Organization
LDCs	least developed countries
LLDCs	Landlocked developing countries
MAI	Multilateral Agreement on Investment
M&As	mergers and acquisitions
MDGs	Millennium Development Goals
MEA	multilateral environmental agreement
MERCOSUR	Southern Common Market
METI	Ministry of Economy, Trade and Industry
MFA	Multi-Fiber Agreement
MFI	microfinance institution
MFN	most favored nation
MIGA	Multilateral Investment Guarantee Agency
MIF	Multilateral Investment Fund
MITI	Ministry of International Trade and Industry
MNC	multinational corporation
NAFTA	North American Free Trade Agreement
NBER	National Bureau of Economic Research
NEP	New Economic Policy
NGO	non-governmental organization
NIE	newly industrialized economies
NTF	Nigeria Trust Fund

OA	official aid
OAS	Organization of American States
ODA	official development assistance
OECD	Organization for Economic Cooperation and Development
OFC	offshore financial center
OPEC	Organization of Petroleum Exporting Countries
PCT	Patent Cooperation Treaty
PPI	producer price index
PPP	purchasing power parity
PRB	Population Reference Bureau
PRGF	Poverty Reduction and Growth Facility
PTA	preferential trade agreement (arrangement)
PVO	private and voluntary organization
R&D	research and development
RDB	regional development bank
RMC	regional member country
RTA	regional trade agreement
SAP	structural adjustment program
SAR	Special Administrative Region
SDR	Special Drawing Rights
SDT	special and differential treatment
SIDS	small island developing states
SME	small and medium size enterprises
SOE	state owned enterprise
TI	Transparency International
TNC	transnational corporation
TRIPS	Trade-Related Aspects of Intellectual Property
TRQ	tariff rate quota
TVE	township and village enterprise
UN	United Nations
UNCTAD	United Nations Conference on Trade and Development
UNDP	United Nations Development Program
UNEP	United Nations Environment Program
UNESCO	United Nations Educational, Scientific and Cultural Organization
UNFCCC	United Nations Framework Convention on Climate Change
UNFPA	United Nations Population Fund
UNICEF	United Nations Children's Fund
USAID	United States Agency for International Development
VER	voluntary export restraint
VIE	voluntary import expansion
VRA	voluntary restraint agreement

WEF	World Economic Forum
WFP	World Food Program (UN)
WHA	World Health Assembly
WHO	World Health Organization
WIPO	World Intellectual Property Organization (UN)
WTO	World Trade Organization
WWW	World Wide Web

Timeline of Key Events in the Global Economy, 1776–2009

1776 Adam Smith publishes *An Inquiry into the Nature and Causes of the Wealth of Nations*, a treatise that underpins the free enterprise system

1798 Thomas R. Malthus publishes *An Essay on the Principle of Population as It Affects the Future Improvement of Society*, a major treatise on the consequences of unbridled population growth

1817 David Ricardo publishes *Principles of Political Economy and Taxation*, defending free trade based on the theory of comparative advantage

1848 Karl H. Marx and Friedrich Engels publish *The Communist Manifesto*, a fundamental treatise on communism

1850s First modern "age" of globalization begins (1850s to 1914)

1867 The first of three volumes of Marx's *Das Kapital* is published

1883 The Paris Convention creates protections for industrial property rights

1886 The Berne Convention creates protections for copyrights

1895 The International Co-operative Alliance (ICA) is founded

1914 World War I breaks out in Europe, paralyzing global trade and investment

The first modern "age" of globalization ends

1917 Russian Bolsheviks stage a successful communist revolution in Russia under the leadership of Vladimir I. Lenin

1919 The League of Nations is formed

The International Labor Organization (ILO) is formed to protect workers' rights

1920 Arthur Pigou publishes *The Economics of Welfare*, marking the birth of welfare economics

1921 The New Economic Policy restores some private enterprise in the USSR

1922 The Union of Soviet Socialist Republics (USSR) is formally established as the world's first communist country

1928 Joseph Stalin introduces the five-year plan to dictate the use of productive resources in the Soviet Union

1929 The Stock Market Crash signals the beginning of the Great Depression in the United States

1930 Most of the industrialized world sinks into a global economic depression

The Smoot-Hawley Tariff is passed in the United States, severely restricting foreign trade, and touching off trade wars

The Bank for International Settlements (BIS) is founded to promote international financial stability and cooperation
World population hits 2 billion people
1939 World War II erupts in Europe, crippling the global economy
1941 The Freedom House is founded in the United States
1942 Joseph A. Schumpeter publishes *Capitalism, Socialism, and Democracy*, stressing the role of innovation and creative destruction in economic growth
1944 The Bretton Woods Conference is held in New Hampshire, creating the Bretton Woods institutions—the International Monetary Fund (IMF) and the World Bank
The fixed exchange rate system is established
Friedrich August von Hayek publishes *The Road to Serfdom*, a passionate defense of capitalism and laissez-faire economics
1945 The United Nations is created at the San Francisco Conference to promote world peace, economic development, and human rights
The United Nations Educational, Scientific, and Cultural Organization (UNESCO) is founded
World War II ends in Europe (May) and Asia (September)
1946 The Bretton Woods System goes into effect
The International Labor Organization (ILO) joins the UN system
The iron curtain divides the East from the West, and the Cold War begins
The second modern "age" of globalization begins (1946–present)
1947 The General Agreement on Tariffs and Trade (GATT) negotiations begin
The Organization of European Economic Cooperation (OEEC) is founded
1948 The Marshall Plan provides massive U.S. aid to war-torn Europe
The World Health Organization (WHO) is formed to advance human health, the physical and mental well-being of all people
Delegates to the Havana Conference support the International Trade Organization (ITO), but governments do not ratify the agreement
1949 The People's Republic of China is established under Mao Zedong
1951 The European Coal and Steel Community (ECSC) Treaty begins European economic integration
Japan creates the Ministry of International Trade and Industry (MITI) to support export industries
1956 The International Finance Corporation (IFC) joins the World Bank Group
1957 The Rome Treaties create the European Economic Community (EEC) and the European Atomic Energy Community (Euratom)
1959 The Inter-American Development Bank begins operations
Fidel Castro establishes communism in Cuba
1960 The European Free Trade Association (EFTA) is formed
The Organization of Petroleum Exporting Countries (OPEC) is founded

The Central American Common Market (CACM) is founded
Consumers International (CI) is founded as a federation of consumer organizations and advocate for consumer rights in the global economy
The International Development Association (IDA) joins the World Bank Group
W. W. Rostow's *The Stages of Economic Growth: A Non-Communist Manifesto* popularizes linear development theory
The U.S. embargo of Cuba is established
1961 The Organization for Economic Cooperation and Development (OECD) is founded to replace the OEEC
The Peace Corps of the United States, an agency within the federal government, is created to foster mutual understanding and economic development throughout the world
1964 The African Development Bank (ADB) is founded
The G77 is formed to promote a new and just world economic order
1965 Mexico establishes the Border Industrialization Program, later renamed the Maquiladora Program, to attract U.S. investment
1966 The Asian Development Bank (ADB) is founded
The International Centre for Settlement of Investment Disputes (ICSID) joins the World Bank Group
1967 The Association of Southeast Asian Nations (ASEAN) is founded
Julius K. Nyerere commits Tanzania to *ujamaa* socialism, a type of African socialism based on traditional tribal communalism
The World Intellectual Property Organization (WIPO) is founded, and enters into force in 1970
1968 Karl Gunnar Myrdal publishes *Asian Drama: An Inquiry into the Poverty of Nations*, which rekindles debate about development strategies in the third world
1969 The Internet, originally called ARPANET, is invented by the U.S. Department of Defense as an "inter-networking of networks"
1971 The Generalized System of Preferences is implemented
The World Economic Forum (WEF) is founded (originally called the European Management Forum until its name changed in 1987 to the WEF)
1972 The United Nations Environment Program (UNEP) is formed
The African Development Fund (ADF) joins the African Development Bank Group
The Freedom House begins its annual freedom rankings of countries
1973 The Bretton Woods System collapses, and a flexible exchange rate system replaces the fixed exchange rate system
The Caribbean Community and Common Market (CARICOM) is formed

Some OPEC members place an oil embargo on Western countries in retaliation for Western support for Israel in the Yom Kippur War

E. F. Schumacher publishes *Small is Beautiful: Economics as if People Mattered* to defend localized production and appropriate technology

1975 The Economic Community of West African States (ECOWAS) is founded

The G7, comprised of leading industrialized nations, is formed

World population climbs to 4 billion people

1976 The Nigeria Trust Fund (NTF) joins the African Development Bank Group

1978 Deng Xiaoping adopts a gradualist approach to initiating market-oriented economic reforms in China

1983 Muhammad Yunus formally establishes the Grameen Bank in Bangladesh

1985 United Nations Guidelines for Consumer Protection is adopted

Mikhail Gorbachev introduces perestroika to restructure the Soviet economy, and glasnost to open the Soviet political system

1986 The Uruguay Round (1986–1994) of trade negotiations commences

1987 The Montreal Protocol is established to reduce emissions of ozone-depleting substances into the Earth's atmosphere

1988 The Multilateral Investment Guarantee Agency (MIGA) joins the World Bank Group

The U.S.-Canada Free Trade Agreement is created

1989 Poland becomes the first Soviet bloc nation to elect a noncommunist government

The Asia-Pacific Economic Cooperation (APEC) group is founded

The Inter-American Investment Corporation joins the Inter-American Development Bank Group

Hernando de Soto publishes *The Other Path: The Invisible Revolution in the Third World*, which supports inclusion of the poor in the formal economy

Tim Berners-Lee invents the World Wide Web

1990 A Human Development Index is introduced by the UNDP to measure progress toward sustainable economic development

The European Bank for Reconstruction and Development (EBRD) is founded, and begins operations in 1991

1991 MERCOSUR, the Southern Common Market, is formed

The Union of Soviet Socialist Republics is dissolved

The Council on Mutual Economic Assistance (COMECON) is disbanded

Transition economies begin an epic transformation toward market-based economies and democracy

1992 The Rio Conference generates *Agenda 21*, a plan for global development; it approves the UN Framework Convention on Climate Change

The Commonwealth of Independent States (CIS) is formed

1993 The Maastricht Treaty creates the European Union (EU)
The Andean Free Trade Area is formed
The Multilateral Investment Fund joins the Inter-American Development Bank Group

1994 The European Economic Area (EEA) creates a single market for EU and EFTA nations (only Switzerland votes not to join the EEA)
The Marrakesh Treaty is approved at the conclusion of the Uruguay Round; it creates the World Trade Organization to replace GATT
The Western Hemisphere is introduced to the idea of a free trade area for the thirty-four democracies of North and South America
The North American Free Trade Agreement (NAFTA) takes effect
The International Conference on Population takes place in Cairo, Egypt

1995 The World Trade Organization (WTO) officially replaces GATT
James D. Wolfensohn becomes World Bank president, the first of two five-year terms of office in the World Bank's top spot
About 25,000 non-governmental organizations (NGOs) operate globally
The Trade-Related Aspects of Intellectual Property (TRIPS) agreement is implemented

1996 The Heavily Indebted Poor Countries (HIPC) Initiative is launched by the IMF and World Bank
The Helms-Burton Act strengthens the U.S. embargo on Cuba

1997 Hong Kong becomes a Special Administrative Region (SAR) of China
Kofi Annan begins his first term as UN secretary-general
The East Asian financial crisis begins (1997–1998), destabilizing the global economy and illustrating the dangers of financial contagion
The Kyoto Protocol targets greenhouse gases and global warming

1998 The G8 is formed, by including Russia alongside the G7 countries
The ILO announces its *Declaration of Fundamental Principles and Rights at Work*
The Russian financial crisis begins (1998–1999), another example of financial contagion

1999 Macao is returned to China by Portugal
The Poverty Reduction and Growth Facility (PRGF) is established
The so-called Millennium Round of trade negotiations flops at the WTO's ministerial conference in Seattle, Washington
The Treaty of Amsterdam paves the way for a European Union enlargement
The euro is introduced as the EU's common currency, beginning a three-year phase-in period
The Global Compact is adopted by the United Nations
The Global Sullivan Principles is introduced by the Rev. Leon H. Sullivan

The "banana war" trade dispute erupts between the United States and European Union

The G20 is created to promote the inclusion of key developing countries in global decision making

Sustainable consumption is formally added to the UN Guidelines for Consumer Protection

2000 Foreign direct investment inflows peak at $1.4 trillion

The UN Millennium Summit adopts the UN Millennium Development Goals (MDGs)

The *Global Entrepreneurship Monitor (GEM)* is launched

The World Resources Institute publishes *World Resources 2000–2001*, which warns against continued abuse of natural ecosystems by human populations

The World Bank introduces the gross national income (GNI) per capita, a new measurement of economic well-being

China moves from low-income status to lower middle-income status

The G77 adopts the Havana Program of Action, a sign of improved South-South communication and consensus

World population hits 6 billion people

2001 The Summit of the Americas is held in Quebec City to lay the groundwork for the creation of a thirty-four-nation Free Trade Area of the Americas (FTAA)

The United States and the European Union quietly settle the banana war

The September 11 terrorist attacks on the United States jolt international markets

The Ministry of Economy, Trade and Industry (METI) replaces MITI in Japan

The Doha Development Round of trade negotiations begins, a WTO trade round stressing economic development in the world's poorer regions

Argentina defaults on $81 billion in government bonds, the largest default in history

2002 The euro replaces the national currencies of twelve EU countries in the euro zone

Hong Kong SAR is named the world's freest economy by leading think-tanks

About 3,000 export processing zones operate in the global economy

2003 The third annual World Social Forum attracts over 100,000 participants from 156 countries

The UN Convention Against Corruption is drafted by the United Nations

The WTO's 2003 ministerial meeting in Cancun, Mexico, makes little progress in implementing the Doha Development Agenda

Official Development Assistance (ODA) and Official Aid (OA) hits $76 billion

62,000 transnational corporations control 927,000 foreign affiliates in the global economy
Foreign direct investment (FDI) inflows tumble to $560 billion, less than half of the $1.4 trillion in FDI inflows during the 2000 peak year
2,265 bilateral investment treaties (BITS) and 2,361 double taxation treaties (DDTs) define the rules of cross-border investment

2004 The International Monetary Fund creates two classifications for economies; advanced economies, and other emerging market and developing countries
The U.S. trade deficit hits a record $617 billion
The nominal gross domestic product (GDP) of the United States reaches $11.7 trillion; the U.S. remains the world's largest economy
Freedom House reports that 119 democracies exist in the world
A European Union enlargement adds ten countries to the EU
The value of world exports hits $11 trillion
Foreign exchange (forex) trading hits $1.9 trillion per day
Global GDP hits $42 trillion (exchange rate method), or $56 trillion (PPP method)
More than half a trillion dollars is spent on advertising in the global economy
A catastrophic tsunami rips through Western Asia and East Africa; billions of dollars in humanitarian aid flows to the effected regions
Wal-Mart is the world's largest corporation, measured by total revenues and by total employees

2005 The proposed Free Trade Area of the Americas fails to gain formal approval by the January target date
World oil prices spike at more than $70 per barrel
France and the Netherlands reject the proposed European Union Constitution
The average annual growth rate for the world economy is 3.8 percent between 1996 and 2005
The Kyoto Protocol, which limits greenhouse gas emissions, enters into force after Russia signs the multilateral environmental treaty
The external debt of emerging market and developing countries reaches $3 trillion
The UN's Millennium Ecosystem Assessment proposes global policy changes to reverse environmental degradation
The United Nations is comprised of 191 member countries
208 economies operate in the global economy
The UN proclaims 2005 the Year of Microcredit
About 300 regional trade agreements (RTAs) operate in the global economy

About 1.1 billion people live in extreme poverty
Jeffrey Sachs publishes *The End of Poverty: Economic Possibilities for Our Time*, a comprehensive blueprint for economic development
About 50,000 NGOs operate globally
World population hits 6.5 billion people

2008 China is scheduled to host the 2008 Summer Olympics

2009 The controversial Three Gorges Dam in China is scheduled for completion

A 

ABSOLUTE ADVANTAGE

An absolute advantage exists when a nation or other economic region is able to produce a good or service more efficiently than a second nation or region. Adam Smith, who penned *An Inquiry into the Nature and Causes of the Wealth of Nations* (1776), used the principle of absolute advantage to defend regional specialization and free trade in global markets. There are two main ways to measure a region's absolute advantage.

First, a region has an absolute advantage if it can produce the same quantity of a product as another region while using fewer resources in the process. Resources, or factors of production, include natural resources, human resources, and capital goods. Economists often measure a region's absolute advantage in terms of labor inputs used in the production of a good. Consider the production of wheat by farmers in Australia and South Africa, as shown in Table 1. In this hypothetical example, Australia enjoys an absolute advantage over South Africa in the production of wheat. Measured in terms of labor inputs, Australia is able to produce 10,000 bushels of wheat per day with 100 workers, while South Africa needs 200 workers to produce the same amount of daily output.

Second, a region has an absolute advantage if it can produce a greater quantity of a product than another region using the same amount of resources. Consider the production of coffee by farmers in Brazil and China. Table 2 shows that Brazil enjoys an absolute advantage over China in the production of coffee beans. Brazil's absolute advantage stems from its ability to produce 1,000 bushels of coffee beans per day with ten laborers, while China can produce just 500 bushels of coffee beans per day with ten laborers.

Nations or other regions achieve an absolute advantage in the production of a good in different ways. In some cases, the absolute advantage stems from conscious policies or business practices. For example, a nation that invests heavily in education is likely to create a skilled labor force. This type of investment in human resources may result in the nation's absolute advantage in the production of sophisticated manufactured goods, such as computers and software, and commercial services in the realms of banking and finance, insurance, consulting, and so on. Complementing a skilled work force are society's investment in capital goods, research and development (R&D), a solid economic infrastructure, and other forces that contribute to a stable business climate. In today's global economy many of the advanced economies of the world have pumped significant amounts of money into public education, infrastructure construction, and so on. Predictably, these advanced economies also have an

TABLE 1 **Absolute Advantage: Daily Production of Wheat**

	Australia		South Africa	
Product	Number of Workers	Output (bushels of wheat)	Number of Workers	Output (bushels of wheat)
Wheat	100	10,000	200	10,000

TABLE 2 **Absolute Advantage: Daily Production of Coffee Beans**

	Brazil		China	
Product	Number of Workers	Output (bushels of coffee beans)	Number of Workers	Output (bushels of coffee beans)
Corn	10	1,000	10	500

absolute advantage over most developing economies in the production of many types of consumer goods, capital goods, and commercial services.

A nation's absolute advantage in the production of a certain product might also be derived from its supply of natural resources, such as large tracts of arable land, plentiful rainfall and sunlight, expansive forests, or generous mineral deposits. Because the earth's natural resources are unevenly distributed, production advantages vary from one geographic region to another. For example, some Middle East nations such as Saudi Arabia, Kuwait, and the United Arab Emirates harbor large reserves of crude oil. Not surprisingly, nations with large reserves of oil have chosen to specialize in the production of this valuable primary energy source. The major oil-producing nations have an absolute advantage in the production of oil over countries such as Japan, France, and Germany, which have scant oil reserves. A similar argument can be made for nonpetroleum commodities. For instance, favorable soil conditions and climate give other nations an absolute advantage in the production of certain agricultural goods such as cocoa from Ghana, coffee from Brazil, cotton from China, natural rubber from Indonesia, sugar from Cuba, timber from Canada, and wheat from the United States.

The concept of absolute advantage underscores the economic benefits associated with specialization. First, specialization channels scarce resources into a nation's most productive areas at a moment in time. This is not to say that a nation's economic future is eternally bound to a single commodity or a narrow range of productive activity, however. Dynamic economies that support innovation, entrepreneurship, business formation, and other forward-looking endeavors can alter their competitive advantages over time. Many development economists even caution against overspecialization, viewing most "one-crop economies" as economically unstable. Second, specialization promotes international trade. Specialization requires nations to import items that are not produced domestically and to export their surpluses. Specialization promotes economic integration in the global economy. Economists generally agree that open trade is an engine of global growth.

British economist David Ricardo took the free trade argument one step further. Ricardo popularized the theory of comparative advantage in his classic *The Principles of Political Economy and Taxation* (1817). Comparative advantage extols the benefits of free trade between two countries even when one country has an absolute advantage in the production of both traded products.

See also **Comparative Advantage; International Trade; Ricardo, David; Smith, Adam; Terms of Trade.** ***See also in Volume 2,*** **Document 19.**

Further Reading

Bhagwati, Jagdish N. *Free Trade Today*. Princeton, NJ: Princeton University Press, 2003.

Irwin, Douglas A. *Free Trade under Fire*. Princeton, NJ: Princeton University Press, 2003.

Ricardo, David. *The Principles of Political Economy and Taxation*. New York: E. P. Dutton & Company, Inc., 1911.

United Nations Conference on Trade and Development. *Trade and Development Report 2004*. New York and Geneva: United Nations, 2004.

World Bank. *Global Economic Prospects 2004*. Washington, DC: World Bank, 2004.

World Trade Organization. *International Trade Statistics 2004*. Geneva: WTO, 2004.

ADVANCED ECONOMIES

The advanced economies are the richer, more industrialized countries of the world. Advanced economies are often referred to as the developed economies or developed countries. In 2004 the International Monetary Fund (IMF) revised the global classification of countries, from three to two categories. In the past the three categories included advanced economies, developing countries, and countries in transition. The new IMF categories include advanced economies versus other emerging market economies and developing countries. As a term of convenience, the advanced economies are often referred to as the global North, mainly due to their geographic concentration in the northern hemisphere. The developing countries are often referred to as the global South. A list of the world's twenty-nine advanced economies is shown in Table 3.

TABLE 3 **The World's Advanced Economies by Subgroup, 2004**

Major Advanced Economies	Other Advanced Economies		
Canada	Australia	Hong Kong SAR*	New Zealand
France	Austria	Iceland	Norway
Germany	Belgium	Ireland	Portugal
Italy	Cyprus	Israel	Singapore*
Japan	Denmark	Korea*	Spain
United Kingdom	Finland	Luxembourg	Sweden
United States	Greece	Netherlands	Switzerland
			Taiwan*

*The newly industrialized economies (NIEs). Taiwan is also called Chinese Taipei.
Source: International Monetary Fund, *World Economic Outlook, April 2004*, 178.

The advanced economies benefit from a virtuous cycle that supports and strengthens sustainable economic development. The virtuous cycle is based on sustained investment in productive capital, capital deepening, and economic growth. The advanced economies maintain the virtuous cycle by nurturing a pro-development environment. Economic factors conducive to economic development include capital formation, which stems from significant saving and investing in capital goods; human capital development, which is derived from education, training, and other investments in the labor force; and innovation, which is supported by research and development (R&D), economic freedom, and entrepreneurial activity. Political factors that favor sustainable development include public infrastructure investments in roads and highways, airports and seaports, water and sanitation systems, courts and the justice system, and domestic security systems; social programs, which attend to the needs of the poor, the elderly, and others in need; and good governance, which includes honest and competent public officials, solid democratic institutions, and the rule of law.

The bullet train system is part of Japan's sophisticated economic infrastructure.
Courtesy of CORBIS

Advanced economies have highly sophisticated economic sectors, which include the services-producing sector, goods-producing sector, and agricultural sector. The size and sophistication of these economic sectors translates into high per capita gross national income (GNI). High productivity in these sectors is also a pillar of economic growth and development. High GNI alone does not satisfy the requirements for advanced economy status, however. High-income countries that lack the size or sophistication to be categorized as advanced economies include Bahrain, Greenland, Kuwait, Liechtenstein, Malta, Monaco, Qatar, Slovenia, and the United Arab Emirates. Using the traditional exchange rate, or Atlas method of comparing cross-border GNIs, people in high-income countries earn a per capita income roughly sixty times higher than people in the low-income countries, twenty times higher than the average income of people in lower middle-income countries, and seven times higher than upper middle-income countries. Even adjusting for purchasing power parity (PPP), the per capita income in high-income countries is fourteen times higher than those in the low-income countries, five times higher than those in lower middle-income countries, and three times higher than upper middle-income countries. The per capita GNI comparisons for 2004 are shown in Table 4.

Most business activity in advanced economies deals with the production and consumption of services. Lesser amounts of output are produced in the goods-producing and agricultural sectors. The services-producing sector includes

TABLE 4 **Per Capita Gross National Income: Global Averages, 2004**

Country Classification by Income	GNI per Capita (exchange rate method)	GNI per Capita (PPP method)
Low income	$510	$2,260
Lower middle income	$1,580	$5,640
Upper middle income	$4,770	$10,090
High income	$32,040	$30,970

Source: World Bank, *Data and Statistics*, 2005.

transportation and public utilities, wholesale and retail trade, real estate, banking and other financial services, computer data processing services, government, and others. The goods-producing industries include manufacturing, construction, and mining. Agriculture consists of farming, dairying, livestock and poultry, forestry, fishing, and shellfish industries. Today's focus on services represents a dramatic shift during the twentieth century, a shift marked by a steady decline in agriculture and industry as a percentage of gross domestic product (GDP) and the rise of service-based economies. By the early 2000s, over 70 percent of GDP in the high-income countries consisted of services, as shown in Figure 1. By contrast, the GDP in low-income countries was more evenly dispersed between agriculture (24 percent), industry (30 percent), and services (46 percent).

Most people living in the advanced economies enjoy a high standard of living and quality of life. In part, this is a result of a relatively high per capita GNI in developed countries. High per capita income enables people to buy a wide variety of consumer goods. It also gives people access to recreation and leisure activities, higher education, health care, and so on. Another important feature of living in the advanced countries is the ability of government to provide services to support a high quality of life. Government is financially able to provide essential public goods and services, including infrastructure and social services necessary to the public well-being. One internationally recognized measure of quality of life is the Human Development Index (HDI), which is reported annually by the United Nations Development Program (UNDP). The HDI captures key ingredients involved in expanding people's choices to live happy and productive lives. The index focuses on the core areas of life expectancy, access to education, and GDP per capita. The advanced economies claim the top spots in the 2002 HDI. Life expectancy in the high-income countries is seventy-eight years compared to seventy years

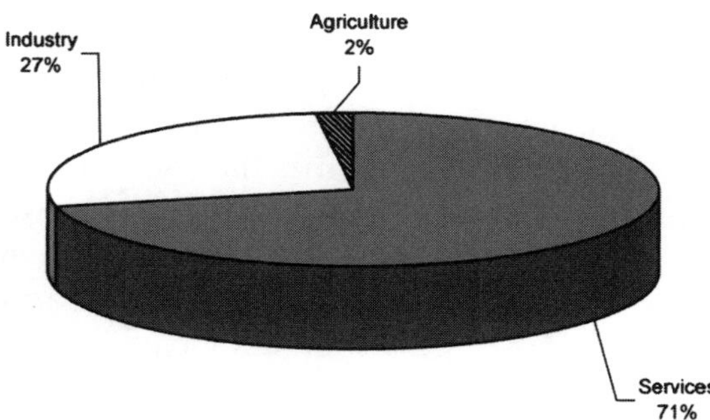

FIGURE 1 **Structure of Output: High-Income Countries, 2003**

Source: World Bank, *2005 World Development Indicators*, Table 4.2.

in the middle-income countries and fifty-nine years in the low-income countries. The adult literacy rate in high-income countries is 99 percent compared to 90 percent in middle-income countries and 64 percent in low-income countries. The GDP per capita, using the PPP method, shows the high-income countries ($28,741) topping the middle-income ($5,908) and low-income ($2,149) countries by a wide margin.

See also **Developing Countries; Emerging Market Economies; Gross Domestic Product; Gross National Income; Human Development; Least Developed Countries; Quality of Life.** ***See also in Volume 2,*** **Documents 16, 50.**

Further Reading

Baily, Martin N. *A Radical Transformation of the European Economy: The New Economy in the U.S., Europe and Japan.* Washington, DC: Institute for International Economics, 2004.

International Monetary Fund. *World Economic Outlook, April 2004.* Washington, DC: IMF Publications, 2004.

Isaak, Robert A. *The Globalization Gap: How the Rich Get Richer and the Poor Get Left Further Behind.* Paramus, NJ: Prentice Hall Financial Times, 2004.

United Nations Development Program. *Human Development Report 2004: Cultural Liberty in Today's Diverse World.* New York: Oxford University Press, 2004.

World Bank. *2004 World Development Indicators.* New York: Oxford University Press, 2004.

ADVERTISING

Advertising is a paid announcement by a business. It is designed to inform consumers about a good or service and to persuade people to buy the product. Business advertising highlights product differentiation, as businesses accent the unique features or benefits of the advertised product. The features of a product represent its composition, design, ingredients, components, or other physical attributes. The benefits highlight what the product can do for the buyer, including ways to improve one's health, appearance, comfort, performance, and so on. Advertising is also used for purposes other than selling products. Political candidates advertise to influence voters' electoral decisions. Charitable and other nonprofit organizations advertise to bring attention to issues or to raise funds.

Business advertising can be local, national, or international in scope. In the United States, advertising agencies are often used to devise advertising campaigns for large firms. Ad agencies employ a number of advertising appeals and techniques to garner the consumer's attention, to create brand loyalties, and to shape tastes and preferences. An advertising appeal represents the general direction of an advertisement or an ad campaign. Leading ad appeals include humor, sex appeal, rational appeal, and a variety of emotional appeals. Several time-honored ad techniques include the bandwagon approach, which asks consumers to join the crowd by purchasing a good; cardstacking, which lists the positive features or benefits of a good; the demonstration, which shows how a good works or how it meets a need; product comparison, which shows the superiority of one good over a substitute; and the testimonial, which relies on a personal endorsement of a good, sometimes by a celebrity.

Advertising in the global economy is big business. Estimates of global spending on advertising vary greatly. One of the world's leading sources of advertising data, Universal McCann, estimated that more than half a trillion dollars was spent on advertising in the global economy in 2004—about one-half of this total ($264 billion) in the United States. This dollar figure included both measured media expenditures and estimates of additional unmeasured advertising expenditures. Other big spenders on advertising were Japan, Germany, and the United Kingdom. By 2005 China had also become a top advertising country. Table 5 shows the top ten global advertisers in 2002, ranked by measured media, as reported by *Advertising Age.*

Advertisers seek to create brand loyalty. Brand names are a key ingredient in differentiating one product from a similar competing good. Brand names and brand loyalty stem from consistency in product quality over time, as well as from the advertising blitz that follows these goods through the global economy. Marketing specialists nurture brand loyalties in the global marketplace in a number of ways. First, marketers create a positive image for the product, often connecting the product with mainstream beliefs or values involving the family, personal freedom, or independence. In the long run, however, the product's image is most influenced by its performance. Second, marketers create a positive image for the company, perhaps publicizing positive achievements in worker satisfaction, environmental protection, or overall corporate social responsibility. In an age of instant global communications the image of being a good corporate citizen is essential. Third, marketers often cater to the local culture by adapting products to better meet local needs, employing local managers and financing local community projects. In recent years the highly respected *Business Week* magazine and Interbrand consultants have teamed up to rank the world's most valuable brands. To be considered for world brand ranking companies must do significant business in global markets and have sufficient marketing data to determine the value of the brand name on the company's future sales. Based on the *Business Week*/Interbrand research, the world's most valuable brand in 2004 was Coca-Cola, followed by Microsoft, IBM, GE, Intel, Disney, McDonald's, Nokia, Toyota, and Marlboro.

TABLE 5 Global Advertising Spending, 2002 Rankings ($ millions)

Rank	Corporation	Ad Spending ($ millions)	Corporate Headquarters	Home Country
1	Procter & Gamble	$4,479	Cincinnati	United States
2	Unilever	$3,315	London/Rotterdam	United Kingdom/Netherlands
3	General Motors	$3,218	Detroit	United States
4	Toyota Motor	$2,405	Toyota City	Japan
5	Ford Motor	$2,387	Dearborn	United States
6	Time Warner	$2,349	New York	United States
7	DaimlerChrysler	$1,800	Stuttgart/Auburn Hills	Germany/United States
8	L'Oreal	$1,683	Paris	France
9	Nestle	$1,547	Vevey	Switzerland
10	Sony	$1,513	Tokyo	Japan

Source: *Advertising Age, 2nd Annual Guide to Advertising & Marketing, 2004 Edition*, 16.

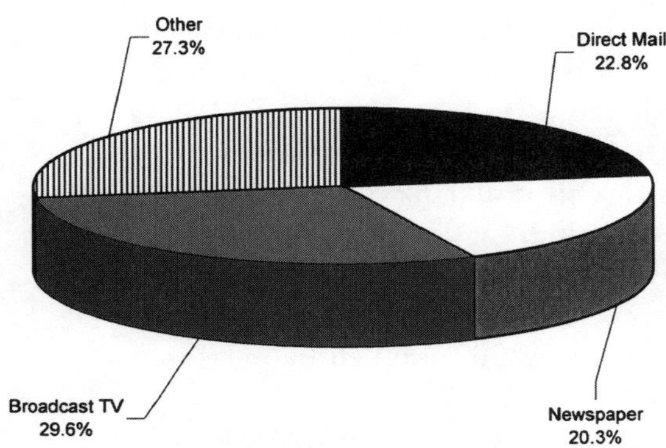

FIGURE 2 **U.S. Advertising Spending by Media, 2004**

Source: *Advertising Age*, June 27, 2005, S-21.

The United States is the world's largest consumer society. Throughout the twentieth century the growth in advertising has paralleled the growth of consumer spending. According to *Advertising Age*, U.S. spending on the production and airing of advertisements was $264 billion in 2004. Roughly one-half of this $264 billion represented measured media, while the remainder was based on estimates. In 2004 nearly three-quarters of all ad spending was on just three forms of media—television, direct mail, and newspapers—as shown in Figure 2. The remainder was spent on ads that appeared in other forms of media including radio, the Yellow Pages, magazines, business publications, the Internet, outdoor displays, or others. Predictably, fierce competition in America's consumer industries generated the most spending on advertising. In 2004 the top ten ad spenders in the U.S. economy were General Motors ($4.0 billion), Procter & Gamble ($3.92 billion), Time Warner ($3.28 billion), Pfizer ($2.96 billion), SBC Communications ($2.69 billion), DaimlerChrysler ($2.46 billion), Ford Motor ($2.46 billion), Walt Disney ($2.24 billion), Verizon Communications ($2.20 billion), and Johnson & Johnson ($2.18 billion).

Advertising provides basic information to consumers about products. Thus, it helps fulfill two of the four basic consumer rights named by President John F. Kennedy in his historic 1962 "Consumer Bill of Rights for Americans"—the right to be informed and the right to choose. Other core consumer rights included the right to product safety and the right to be heard. The 1985 "United Nations Guidelines for Consumer Protection" adapted these basic rights for a global audience. Over time, many countries have instituted laws and regulations to protect consumer rights. In the United States, for example, the Federal Trade Commission (FTC) and the Federal Communications Commission (FCC) provide some oversight of the advertising industry and investigate questionable ad claims. Other federal agencies, such as the Consumer Product Safety Commission (CPSC), investigate products and product claims with an eye toward protecting the public welfare. Advertisers are also self-policing. The American Advertising Federation, a professional association of advertisers, developed a set of principles to promote truth and good taste in advertising. Truth in advertising is important in today's consumption-oriented market economies. Expanded Internet access during the 1990s and early 2000s opened the floodgate to information about products and companies. Greater Internet use prompted businesses to market their wares on company websites. At the same time, the Internet created new avenues for consumers to comparison shop and, thus, make informed buying decisions. In the United States alone, consumers spent $8.2 trillion on finished goods and services in 2004, about two-thirds of the nation's total gross domestic product (GDP). The fact that businesses around the world were willing to shell out over half a trillion dollars on advertising in 2004 is one indication that the business community values advertising's power of persuasion.

See also **Consumers International; Sustainable Consumption.** ***See also in Volume 2,*** **Document 49.**

Further Reading

Advertising Age. 100 Leading National Advertisers: 48th Annual Advertiser Profile Edition. New York: Advertising Age, June 23, 2003.

———. *2nd Annual Guide to Advertising & Marketing.* New York: Advertising Age, March 8, 2004.

Berger, Warren. *Advertising Today.* New York: Phaidon Press, Inc., 2004.

De Mooij, Marieke. *Global Marketing and Advertising: Understanding Global Paradoxes.* 2d ed. Thousand Oaks, CA: SAGE Publications, 2005.

Lewis, Herschell G., Carol Nelson, and Rance Crain. *Advertising Age Handbook of Advertising.* New York: McGraw-Hill/Contemporary Books, 2000.

Lindstrom, Martin, and Patricia B. Seybold. *Brandchild: Remarkable Insights into the Minds of Today's Global Kids & Their Relationships with Brands.* Rev. ed. Dover, NH: Kogan Page, 2004.

"The Top 100 Brands." *Business Week*, August 2, 2004, 68–71.

AFRICAN DEVELOPMENT BANK GROUP

The African Development Bank Group (ADB Group) is a regional development bank that serves the continent of Africa. It is one of four major regional development banks currently operating in the global economy. Today, the ADB Group is comprised of three institutions: the African Development Bank (ADB), which was founded in 1964 and began operations in 1966; the African Development Fund (ADF), which was founded in 1972 and began operations in 1974; and the Nigeria Trust Fund (NTF), which was established by the government of Nigeria in 1976. The ADB Group is headed by a Board of Governors, which sets the bank's general policies. The Board of Governors, in turn, selects a Board of Directors, which, in conjunction with the bank's management, conducts the bank's business. The ADB Group's permanent headquarters is located in Abidjan, Cote d'Ivoire, but was temporarily relocated to Tunis, Tunisia, in the early 2000s.

The ADB Group, like other regional development banks, is owned and operated by member countries to support the development efforts of regional member countries (RMCs). Today, the ADB Group consists of seventy-seven member countries—fifty-three regional member countries located on the continent of Africa and twenty-four nonregional member countries located in Asia, Europe, North America, and South America. The bank's mission, as stated in Article 1 of the Agreement Establishing the Bank, is to "contribute to the economic development and social progress of its regional members—individually and jointly." Today, the overarching goals of poverty reduction and sustainable economic development reflect this mission statement.

Agricultural and rural development is an important poverty-reduction strategy in Cote d'Ivoire and other African countries.

Courtesy of Getty Images: Connie Coleman

To break the vicious cycle of poverty in Africa, the ADB Group extends development loans to RMCs, encourages investment in the private and public sectors, and supplies technical assistance. In recent years, the bank's resources have focused on achieving several key objectives. First, at the country level the bank's efforts emphasize agricultural and rural development, including the construction of roads, irrigation systems, and other elements of an economic infrastructure; investments in human capital, including education and health care services; and reforms to create an attractive environment for entrepreneurship, business formation, and domestic and foreign investment. Second, on a broader regional level the bank has given high priority to programs that support good governance and the rule of law; gender equity, especially in the realms of education, health needs, and employment; environmental protection, including efforts to prevent resource depletion, land degradation, and the loss of bio-diversity; and regional cooperation, including the reduction of tariffs and other barriers to trade and investment among RMCs. Loan and grant approvals in 2003 reflected these bank priorities. The top three categories—finance, transport, and water supply and sanitation—accounted for one-half of all bank operations. Other major categories of loan and grant approvals included agriculture and rural development, education, power, and poverty reduction and microfinance, as shown in Figure 3.

Today the three institutions of the ADB Group address a variety of development needs of African countries. The African Development Bank, for example, extends loans on a non-concessional basis to the more creditworthy RMCs. Non-concessional loans are made at prevailing interest rates. In 2003, total ADB loans and grants to RMCs totaled $745 million. The African Development Fund (ADF), on the other hand, provides development loans with concessional terms to the low-income RMCs. Concessional loans are often interest free, have longer repayment periods of forty to fifty years, and include financial grants to the poorer RMCs. Low-income RMCs not eligible for loans through the normal ADB channels obtain these "soft loans" from the ADF. In 2003 total ADF soft loans and grants to poorer RMCs was $998 million. The Nigeria Trust Fund (NTF) also extends loans on highly favorable concessional terms to low-income

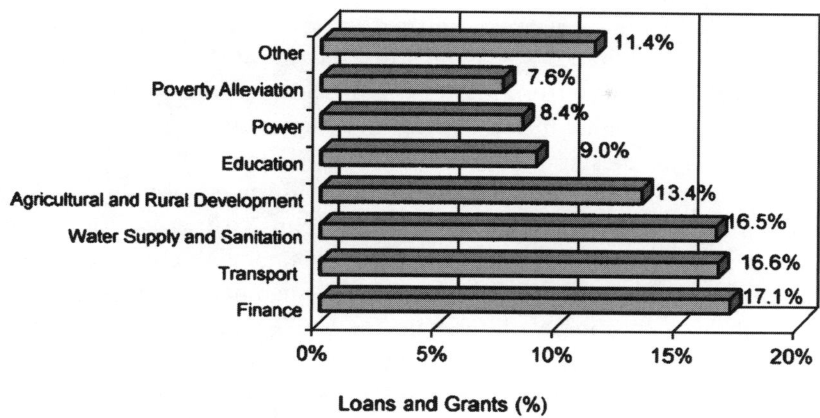

FIGURE 3 **African Development Bank Loan and Grant Approvals, 2003**
Source: ADB Group, *Compendium of Statistics on Bank Operations 2004*, vol. 27, 4.

RMCs to stimulate economic development. In 2003 the NTF offered $23 million in new loans to poorer RMCs.

Since the commercial operations of the ADB Group began in 1966 the bank has approved $36 billion in loans and other assistance to African countries, as shown in Table 6. In addition, the ADB Group has coordinated its development projects with a variety of outside groups, resulting in an additional $46 billion in co-financed projects within RMCs. In 2003 the five largest recipients of ABD Group loans and grants were Tunisia ($196 million), Morocco ($177 million), South Africa ($106 million), Ethiopia ($102 million), and Burkina Faso ($79 million).

The ADB Group raises funds in four main ways. First, operating capital is raised through subscriptions or assigned contributions by RMCs and nonregional member countries. By paying subscriptions, the seventy-seven members of the ADB Group become shareholders in the bank. In the early 2000s the largest shareholder was Nigeria (9.3 percent of the total shares), followed by the United States (6.6 percent of the total shares). RMCs control 60 percent of all shares, and the nonregional members control the remaining 40 percent. Member countries are often asked to contribute additional funds to the bank

TABLE 6 **Summary of ADB Group Operations, 1967 to 2003 (total approvals)**

Institutions of the ADB Group	Number of Projects	Amount ($ millions)
African Development Bank (1967–2003)	934	$20,912
African Development Fund (1974–2003)	1,881	$14,553
Nigeria Trust Fund (1976–2003)	70	$296
Total ADB Group (1967–2003)	2,885	$35,761

Source: African Development Bank Group, *Compendium of Statistics on Bank Group Operations*, 2004, vol. 27, 6, 18, 32, 46.

through a General Capital Increase. In the fifth General Capital Increase (GCI-5), for example, the United States pledged to pay about $5 million to the ADB for eight consecutive years, from 2000 to 2007. Second, the bank collects interest payments on past loans. Interest rates vary, depending on the income status of the RMC. The interest rate charged by the ADB to middle-income RMCs is comparable to prevailing market interest rates in the economy. The ADF, on the other hand, normally extends interest-free loans to low-income countries. Third, the bank negotiates replenishments, or financial commitments from donor countries, to bolster bank coffers. Replenishments usually span three years and are a main source of revenue for the ADF. In the Ninth Replenishment (2002–2004) donor countries pledged an additional $2.4 billion to support the ADF's concessional lending to Africa's poorest countries. Fourth, the bank borrows money in global capital markets. The ADB borrows money by selling bank bonds to international investors. Traditionally, the security of ADB bonds has enabled the bank to borrow on favorable terms.

Regional and sub-regional development banks are a major source of development loans and other development assistance in the global economy. The four main regional development banks are the African Development Bank Group, Asian Development Bank, European Bank for Reconstruction and Development, and Inter-American Development Bank Group. Smaller, sub-regional development banks also dot the economic landscape and include the Caribbean Development Bank, Central American Bank for Regional Integration, East African Development Bank, and West African Development Bank.

See also **Asian Development Bank; European Bank for Reconstruction and Development; Inter-American Development Bank Group; Regional Development Banks.** ***See also in Volume 2,*** **Document 7.**

Further Reading

African Development Bank. *African Development Report 2004*. New York: Oxford University Press, 2004.

———, Statistics Division. *Compendium of Statistics on Bank Group Operations: 2004*, vol. 27. Tunis, Tunisia: ADB Group, 2004.

Gardner, Robert K. A. *The African Development Bank, 1964–1984: An Experiment in Economic Cooperation and Development*. Abidjan, Cote d'Ivoire: African Development Bank Group, 1984.

Mule, Harris M., and E. Philip English. *The Multilateral Development Banks: The African Development Bank*. Boulder, CO: Lynne Rienner Publishers, 1996.

World Bank. *African Development Indicators 2004*. Washington, DC: World Bank Publications, 2004.

ANDEAN COMMUNITY

The Andean Community is a five-nation sub-regional organization that promotes regional integration, economic development, and social progress. The Andean Community is comprised of five South American nations: Bolivia, Colombia, Ecuador, Peru, and Venezuela, along with the many institutions of the Andean Integration System (AIS). The AIS consists of certain organizational bodies, such as the General Secretariat and the Andean Parliament, along with specialized bodies to support labor rights, business formation, justice, and others. The five countries of the Andean Community have a combined population of 120 million people and a combined gross domestic product (GDP) of $260 billion. The overarching goal of the Andean Community is to improve the standard of living and the quality of life for people in the region. In recent years the Andean Community has also been outward looking, seeking to cement mutually beneficial economic relations with other multilateral organizations in the global economy including the Asia-Pacific Economic Cooperation (APEC), European Union (EU), and Southern Common Market (MERCOSUR).

The Andean Community has overseen the region's evolution from a free trade area (FTA), to a customs union, and finally to a common market. The process of regional integration began in 1969 when several South American countries signed the Cartagena Agreement, also called the Andean Pact. This agreement opened the doors to further negotiations, which, in 1993, culminated in the creation of the Andean Free Trade Area (FTA) among four countries: Bolivia, Colombia, Ecuador, and Venezuela. A free trade area is an economic region in which tariffs and non-tariff barriers to trade are eliminated. The elimination of trade barriers has increased trade among Andean nations. From 1999 to 2001, for example, intra-Andean Community exports increased from $3.9 billion to $5.7 billion, a 44 percent jump in just three years. This trade expansion is shown in Table 7. The rise in intra-Andean Community trade occurred in spite of the Brazilian financial crisis of the late 1990s and the global economic slowdown of the early 2000s. The Andean FTA was unique in that the elimination of trade barriers applied to all goods, without the numerous "exceptions" that appear in other FTAs. In addition, the Andean FTA was viewed as merely the first step toward a more ambitious regional integration scheme—the creation of an Andean common market. In 1997 Peru became a member of the Andean FTA. Full integration of Peru into the Andean FTA is scheduled to occur in 2005.

The second step in Andean integration was the creation of the Andean Customs Union in 1995. A customs union maintains free trade among member nations but also applies a uniform tariff on goods entering the region from non-member countries. This uniform tariff is called the common external tariff (CET). Originally, just three member nations agreed to the CET, including Columbia, Ecuador, and Venezuela. In 2002, however, the Santa Cruz Declaration solidified support for the CET among the five member nations. The CET went into effect on January 1, 2004, for Bolivia, Colombia, Ecuador, and Venezuela, with the expectation that Peru would adopt the CET at a later date.

TABLE 7 **Intra-Andean Community Exports, 1999 to 2001 ($ millions)**

Countries	1999	2000	2001
Bolivia	$294	$304	$351
Colombia	$1,634	$2,167	$2,744
Ecuador	$445	$663	$779
Peru	$347	$446	$518
Venezuela	$1,220	$1,595	$1,288
Total	$3,940	$5,175	$5,680

Source: Andean Community (General Secretariat), "Key Andean Community Indicators," 2002.

The third and final step in Andean integration is the creation of an Andean common market. A common market is a higher form of regional integration. It includes an FTA for goods and services, a common external tariff, and the free movement of all factors of production among member nations. Nations of the Andean Community have agreed, in principle, to create a true common market by the close of 2005. Under a common market arrangement, there would be free movement of merchandise and commercial services, financial capital, foreign direct investment, and labor across national borders. In addition, the creation of a common market will advance the Andean Social Agenda, which strives to improve peoples' quality of life. Key elements in the Andean Social Agenda are efforts to reduce poverty, improve the quality of public education, reinvigorate the study of the region's cultural heritage, promote job creation and labor rights, and strengthen democracy and respect for human rights in the region.

See also **Regional Trade Agreements.**

Further Reading

Lengyel, Miguel F., and Vivianna Ventura Dias, eds. *Trade Policy Reforms in Latin America*. New York: Palgrave Macmillan, 2004.

Schiff, Maurice, and Alan L. Winters. *Regional Integration and Development*. Washington, DC: World Bank Publications, 2003.

Schott, Jeffrey J. *Free Trade Agreements: US Strategies and Priorities*. Washington, DC: Institute for International Economics, 2004.

Secretary General of the Andean Community. *How to Do Business in the Andean Community: Trade and Investment Guide*. Peru: Andean Community, 1999.

ANNAN, KOFI

Kofi Annan (1938–) is a prominent statesman and seventh secretary-general of the United Nations (UN). Annan revitalized the United Nations during the late 1990s and early 2000s in all realms of UN activity—peacekeeping, economic development, and human rights. Annan is also a vocal supporter of globalization and its potential to improve people's quality of life worldwide. Annan was born in Kumasi, Ghana. Born to a family of privilege and position, Annan attended the best local schools as a youth. He began his college studies at the University of Science and Technology in Kumasi but completed his bachelor's degree at Macalester College in St. Paul, Minnesota (1961). The following year Annan joined the UN system. In 1971 Annan enrolled in the MIT Sloan School of Management, from which he earned a master's degree in 1972. Most of Annan's professional career has been spent in the service of the United Nations. In December 1996 Annan was elected UN secretary-general. He began his first five-year term of office on January 1, 1997. On January 1, 2002, he began a second term as the UN's top official.

During his tenure as UN secretary-general, Annan pursued a vigorous campaign to extend the benefits of globalization to developing countries. In 1999 Annan introduced the Global Compact, which challenged transnational corporations (TNCs) to support and defend workers' rights, human rights, and the natural environment. Under Annan's leadership, the 2000 UN Millennium Summit adopted the Millennium Development Goals (MDGs). The MDGs rallied the international community around a series of measurable development objectives in the realms of poverty reduction, educational attainment, gender equity, and health care. In 2001 Annan issued a Call to Action to deal with the HIV/AIDS epidemic, a global pandemic that had caused more than 20 million deaths by the early 2000s. In 2001 Kofi Annan and the United Nations also shared the Nobel Peace Prize in recognition of their role in creating a more peaceful and secure world.

Annan encouraged the creation of partnerships to coordinate balanced development throughout the world. Annan argued that only through global partnerships could people muster the energy and resources to promote sustainable economic development. He proposed partnerships consisting of multilateral institutions such as the United Nations and its specialized agencies, programs, and funds; TNCs, the primary architects and beneficiaries of globalization; civil society organizations such as labor unions, think-tanks, private foundations, and non-governmental organizations; and governments. Annan argued that the globalization process was desirable and irreversible but, as of yet, incomplete. To deliver on the promises of globalization, Annan passionately challenged stakeholders to tackle problems associated with gross economic and technological inequality, policies of exclusion, and the marginalization of the world's poorest peoples.

See also **Corporate Social Responsibility; Globalization; Millennium Development Goals; United Nations System. *See also in Volume 2,* Document 52.**

Further Reading

Annan, Kofi. *We the Peoples: The Nobel Lecture Given by the 2001 Nobel Peace Laureate Kofi Annan*. New York: Ruder Finn Press, Inc., 2002.

———, and Sadako Ogata. *The Turbulent Decade: Confronting the Refugee Crises of the 1990s*. New York: W. W. Norton & Company, 2005.

Tessitore, John. *Kofi Annan*. Morongo Valley, CA: Sagebrush Press, 2000.

United Nations. *Basic Facts about the United Nations*. Lanham, MD: Bernan Press, 2004.

ASIAN DEVELOPMENT BANK

The Asian Development Bank (ADB) is a regional development bank that serves Asia and the Pacific region. It is one of four major regional development banks currently operating in the global economy. The ADB was founded in 1966. The main operations of the ADB are conducted by the bank and its Special Funds, which include the Asian Development Fund (ADF), Technical Assistance Special Fund, Japan Special Fund, and ADB Institute Special Fund. The ADB also administers other funds and grants to support bank goals. A Board of Governors, which convenes once each year at the annual meeting, is the bank's highest decision-making body. The Board of Governors elects a twelve-member Board of Directors to conduct the day-to-day operations of the bank. The ADB headquarters is located in Manila, the Philippines.

The ADB is owned and operated by member countries. Since its founding in 1966 the ADB has expanded from thirty-one member countries to sixty-three members—forty-five countries located within the Asia and Pacific region and eighteen countries from outside the region. Most of the regional members are low-income or middle-income developing countries, often referred to as Developing Member Countries (DMCs). According to the Agreement Establishing the Asian Development Bank, the purpose of the bank is "to foster economic growth and co-operation in the region of Asia and the Far East . . . and to contribute to the acceleration of the process of economic development of developing member countries in the region, collectively and individually." In 1999 the ADB sharpened its central mission to emphasize poverty reduction in the region.

Traditional agriculture is a feature of many developing economies in Asia.
Courtesy of CORBIS

With poverty reduction as the centerpiece of the ADB's mission, the bank's main operations—development loans, public and private investments, and technical assistance—are designed to address the causes of poverty. In recent years the ADB's development strategy has stressed economic growth; infrastructure building, including transportation and communications; human resources development, including education and health care; gender equity; environmental protection; good governance; regional cooperation, including the reduction of trade barriers; social development; and private sector development, including support for small- and medium-sized firms and microcredit. The 2003 distribution of ADB loans is shown in Table 8.

The institutions of the ADB are sensitive to the different development needs of its Developing Member Countries. The ADB, for example, makes loans from the bank's ordinary capital resources (OCRs) to members deemed capable of repaying the loan, plus interest, on schedule. The bank evaluates the creditworthiness of a member country by its per capita income and current external debt burden. These non-concessional loans carry interest rates comparable to prevailing market interest rates. In 2003 total ADB loans topped $4.7 billion. The ADF, sometimes called the ADB's "soft window," offers loans with concessional terms—lower interest rates and longer repayment schedules, perhaps

TABLE 8 **Sectoral Distribution of Asian Development Bank Loans, 2003 ($ millions)**

Sectors	ADB Loans ($ millions)	ADF Loans ($ millions)	Total ADB and ADF Loans ($ millions)	Percent of ADB/ADF Loans
Agriculture and natural resources	153	239	392	6.4
Energy	673	84	757	12.4
Finance	447	36	483	7.9
Social infrastructure	667	453	1,131	18.5
Transport and communications	2,436	142	2,578	42.2
Multi-sector	140	326	466	7.6
Other	200	100	300	4.9
Total	4,726	1,379	6,105	99.7*

*Numbers do not equal 100 percent due to rounding.
Source: Asian Development Bank, *Annual Report 2003*, 166.

forty to fifty years. Concessional loans are reserved for the poorer countries that already suffer from higher external debt burdens. In 2003 ADF loans totaled $1.4 billion. The ADB's smaller Special Funds also supply concessional loans to the poorer member countries.

From 1966 to 2003 the ADB and ADF approved more than 2,000 loans worth $105 billion, as shown in Table 9. In addition, the ADB marshaled $41 billion in co-financed projects. The ADB supports co-financing when at least one other external financier, such as a national government, World Bank, or other multilateral organization, is involved in the project. Since 1966 nearly two-thirds of all ADB and ADF loans have flowed to just five countries, including Indonesia ($19.4 billion), China ($13.6 billion), Pakistan ($13.5 billion), India ($13.3 billion), and Bangladesh ($7.3 billion). In 2003 the five largest recipient countries were India ($1,532 million), China ($1,488 million), Pakistan ($693 million), Bangladesh ($286 million), and Indonesia ($187 million).

The funding for ADB and ADF operations is derived from four main sources. First, ordinary capital resources (OCR) is raised through country subscriptions. Subscriptions represent the assigned monetary contribution that each regional and nonregional member country pays into the ADB. By paying their subscriptions, member countries become shareholders, or owners, of the bank. In the early 2000s the two largest shareholders in the ADB were the United States and Japan, each owning 15.8 percent of all subscribed capital. Other major stockholders were China (6.5 percent), India (6.4 percent), and Australia (5.9 percent). Regional ADB members own 63 percent of all subscribed capital and 65 percent of the voting power within the bank. Nonregional members own the remaining 37 percent of the subscribed capital and 35 percent of the voting power. Today, the total subscribed capital of the ADB is $52 billion. Second, the ADB raises funds through borrowing in global capital markets. The bank borrows by selling

TABLE 9 **Summary of ADB and ADF Operations, 1966 to 2003 ($ billions)**

Institutions	Amount of Loans	Percent of Total Loans
Asian Development Bank	76.3	72.6
Asian Development Fund	28.8	27.4
Total loans	105.1	100.0

Source: Asian Development Bank, *Annual Report 2003*, 6.

bank bonds to a variety of investors such as foreign banks and governments. ADB bonds, which carry an AAA rating, are typically viewed as an attractive investment. Third, the bank earns interest from loan repayments and profits from its other investments.

Finally, additional funds are solicited regularly by the ADF from donor countries. These donations are called replenishments. Since the ADF began making concessional loans in 1973, nine four-year replenishments have been negotiated. By 2003, the cumulative replenishments to the ADF totaled $24 billion. The largest donor countries were Japan ($11.9 billion), the United States ($2.9 billion), Germany ($1.6 billion), Canada ($1.3 billion), and Australia ($1.1 billion). The most recent replenishment, ADF 9, committed donor countries to a total of $7 billion in new funds between 2005 and 2008. Donor countries have also contributed money to the ADB's Special Funds.

Regional and sub-regional development banks are a major source of development loans and other development assistance in the global economy. The four main regional development banks are the African Development Bank Group, Asian Development Bank, European Bank for Reconstruction and Development, and Inter-American Development Bank Group. Smaller, sub-regional development banks also dot the economic landscape and include the Caribbean Development Bank, Central American Development Bank for Regional Integration, East African Development Bank, and West African Development Bank.

See also **African Development Bank Group; European Bank for Reconstruction and Development; Inter-American Development Bank Group; Regional Development Banks.** ***See also in Volume 2,*** **Document 32.**

Further Reading

Asian Development Bank. *ADB Annual Report 2003*. Manila: Asian Development Bank, 2004.

———. *Asian Development Outlook 2004*. New York: Oxford University Press and the Asian Development Bank, 2004.

———. *Key Indicators 2004: Poverty in Asia, Measurement, Estimates, and Prospects*. Asian Development Bank, 2004.

Brooks, Douglas H., and Hall Hill, eds. *Managing FDI in a Globalizing Economy: Asian Experiences*. New York: Palgrave Macmillan, 2004.

ASIA-PACIFIC ECONOMIC COOPERATION

Asia-Pacific Economic Cooperation (APEC) is the world's largest forum designed to promote economic growth, regional cooperation, and free trade and investment. APEC countries hail from four continents: Asia, Australia, North America, and South America. APEC was founded in 1989 by twelve countries: Australia, Brunei Darussalam, Canada, Indonesia, Japan, the Republic of Korea, Malaysia, New Zealand, the Philippines, Singapore, Thailand, and the United States. In 2004 APEC's membership stood at twenty-one countries, more commonly referred to as "Member Economies." The new member economies that joined APEC during the 1990s included Chile, Chinese Taipei,

Hong Kong SAR (Special Administrative Region of China), Mexico, Papua New Guinea, the People's Republic of China, Peru, Russia, and Vietnam. APEC's Secretariat is located in Singapore and is headed by an executive director. By the early 2000s, 2.6 billion people lived in APEC member economies. APEC economies had a combined gross domestic product (GDP) of $19.2 trillion.

APEC is a unique multilateral organization. Its uniqueness stems from its mandate to promote economic growth, sustainable economic development, and international trade and investment through voluntary, nonbinding agreements instead of negotiated treaties. APEC cultivates dialogue, debate, and decisions by consensus rather than by a formal vote. The most important forum for APEC is its annual Economic Leaders' Meeting, which is hosted by a different APEC member economy each year. The most important outcome of a Leaders' Meeting is the Leaders' Declaration. These annual declarations state the organization's goals, policies, or other initiatives for the coming year. A Ministerial Meeting usually precedes the Leaders' Meeting. The intent of the Ministerial Meeting is to discuss vital trade and development issues and to make concrete recommendations to heads of state and other dignitaries who attend the Leaders' Meeting. Other, more specialized APEC meetings are held on a regular basis. For example, Sectoral Ministerial Meetings concentrate on specific areas of economic activity such energy, finance, human resources development, technology, or tourism. The APEC Business Advisory Council offers recommendations on how to support entrepreneurship, business formation, investment, and other topics related to a sound business climate. The conclusions of these lower-level meetings are presented to the APEC leaders for formal consideration and action. Because APEC is not a donor institution its annual budget is small in comparison with many other important multilateral organizations. In 2004, for example, member economies supplied just $3.4 million to fund APEC's Secretariat and the projects it oversees. Since the late 1990s Japan has also contributed a few million dollars per year to cover certain program expenses.

The main goals of APEC have been remarkably consistent since the organization's founding in 1989. These goals were eloquently stated in the APEC Economic Leaders' Declaration of 1994, often called the Bogor Declaration. In the Bogor Declaration APEC leaders pledged to increase regional economic cooperation, support an open multilateral trading system, reduce barriers to trade and investment, and share the benefits of growth and sustainable development with the peoples of the region. The Bogor Declaration also solidified member economies' commitment to market economies and to narrowing the income gap between the region's rich and poor economies. A decade later the Leaders' Declaration of 2004, called the Santiago Declaration, also stressed the importance of human security and good governance as a means to improving economic growth and development in the Asia and Pacific regions. The Santiago Declaration called on APEC member economies, individually and collectively, to combat terrorism by supporting all antiterrorist conventions and by taking steps to cut off terrorist access to the international financial system.

Economic progress in the APEC region has been impressive since 1989. First, trade liberalization in the form of lower tariffs stimulated foreign trade. From 1989 to the early 2000s the value of exports from APEC countries more than doubled. Second, foreign direct investment (FDI) in APEC countries soared during the 1990s and early 2000s, tripling during the period. Third, the APEC region witnessed a significant increase in real gross national product (GNP). Fourth, measurable improvements in the region's "social advancement" were recorded. Notable achievements included lower poverty and infant mortality rates and higher employment rates, educational attainment, and life expectancy.

See also **Regional Trade Agreements. *See also in Volume 2,* Document 25.**

Further Reading

Downing, Sandra L. *Asia Pacific Economic Cooperation Apec: Current Issues and Background*. Huntington, NY: Nova Science, 2003.

Ravenhill, John, ed. *Asia Pacific Economic Cooperation: The Construction of Pacific Rim Regionalism*. New York: Cambridge University Press, 2001.

Ruland, Jurgen, Eva Manske, and Werner Draguhn. *Asia-Pacific Economic Cooperation (Apec): The First Decade*. London: Curzon Press, 2002.

Yamazawa, Ippei, ed. *Asia Pacific Economic Cooperation: Challenges and Tasks for the Twenty-first Century*. New York: Routledge, 2000.

Yong Deng. *Promoting Asia-Pacific Economic Cooperation: Perspectives from East Asia*. New York: Palgrave Macmillan, 1997.

ASSOCIATION OF SOUTHEAST ASIAN NATIONS

The Association of Southeast Asian Nations (ASEAN) is a regional association of ten countries designed to foster regional economic growth, cultural development, social progress, and peace among its members. The Asean Declaration, more commonly referred to as the Bangkok Declaration, established ASEAN in 1967. This founding document declared that ASEAN "represents the collective will of the nations of Southeast Asia to bind themselves together in friendship and cooperation and, through efforts and sacrifices, secure for their peoples and posterity the blessings of peace, freedom and prosperity." ASEAN's five original members were Indonesia, Malaysia, the Philippines, Singapore, and Thailand. Since ASEAN's founding, five additional countries have joined the association, including Brunei Darussalam (1984), Vietnam (1995), Laos and Myanmar (1997), and Cambodia (1999). In 1999 ASEAN negotiated a Joint Statement on East Asia Cooperation with Japan, the Republic of Korea, and the People's Republic of China to widen the spirit of cooperation throughout the East Asia region. In 2003 the ASEAN region had a population of about 500 million people, a combined gross domestic product (GDP) of $686 billion, and an average per capita GDP of $1,266.

ASEAN has a multi-tiered organizational structure. At the top of the power pyramid is the Meeting of the ASEAN Heads of State. The first Heads of State meeting took place in 1976. An annual ASEAN Summit and an annual ASEAN Ministerial Meeting also discuss issues of critical concern to the region. Regular sectoral meetings discuss more specialized topics such as agriculture and forestry, energy, the environment, poverty, and social welfare. ASEAN maintains a permanent headquarters in Jakarta, Indonesia, and diplomatic missions in fifteen capital cities around the world. The chief official of the association is the secretary-general, who has a five-year term of office. The secretary-general and his staff are responsible for coordinating ASEAN's activities and programs and overseeing work of the association's fifteen missions, twenty-nine committees, 122 working groups, and communications with numerous agencies, nongovernmental organizations, and related groups.

The Bangkok Declaration identified a series of goals for the association. First, member countries pledged to promote economic growth and social progress in the region. To stimulate economic growth and prosperity, ASEAN approved a number of agreements to build economic relationships and use scarce resources wisely. For example, member countries have liberalized trade and investment among association members. In 1977 ASEAN adopted a Preferential Trading Arrangement (PTA) to reduce tariffs in intraregion trade. Additional trade agreements were concluded in the following years, including the 1988 Enhanced PTA Program, the 1992 Framework Agreement on Enhancing Economic Cooperation, and the 1997 ASEAN Vision 2020, which promised the creation of a "highly competitive ASEAN Economic Region in which there is a free flow of goods, services and investments." The creation of the ASEAN Free Trade Area (AFTA) in 1993 was one important step toward the goal of regional economic integration. Between 1993 and 2003 the average tariff for ASEAN-6 nations—Brunei Darussalam, Indonesia, Malaysia, the Philippines, Singapore, and Thailand—dropped from 12.8 percent to just 1.5 percent on listed items. AFTA stimulated trade within the region and helped the ASEAN-6 nations more than double their exports, as shown in Table 10. ASEAN negotiated separate trade agreements with the People's Republic of China, Japan, and India in the early 2000s.

The liberalization of investment also progressed during the 1990s and early 2000s. Following closely on the heels of ASEAN Vision 2020, the association approved the 1998 Framework Agreement on the ASEAN Investment Area (AIA). This framework liberalized investment by reducing barriers to foreign

TABLE 10 **ASEAN-6 Exports and Imports, 1993 to 2003 ($ billions)**

ASEAN-6 Nations	1993 Exports	Imports	2003 Exports	Imports
Brunei Darussalam	$0.5	$0.9	$3.2	$1.4
Indonesia	$36.8	$28.3	$61.1	$32.6
Malaysia	$46.3	$44.4	$99.4	$80.1
Philippines	$11.4	$17.6	$36.2	$37.5
Singapore	$74.0	$85.2	$143.5	$127.3
Thailand	$37.6	$46.9	$80.5	$75.8
Total ASEAN-6	$206.6	$223.3	$423.8	$354.6

Source: Association of Southeast Asian Nations, *ASEAN Statistical Yearbook 2004*, 56–57.

investment, outlawing discriminatory practices against foreign firms or output produced by foreign firms, expanding cross-border flows of skilled labor, increasing the transparency of rules and policies, and encouraging flows of technology among association members. Under the provisions of the AIA most investment restrictions on goods-producing and agricultural industries will be phased out by 2020. By 2001 the cumulative value of foreign direct investment (FDI) inflows into the ASEAN region totaled $282 billion. In recent years most FDI inflows have come from the European Union (EU), the United States, Japan, and other ASEAN countries. Current negotiations are focused on expanding the more liberalized investment rules to the services-producing industries such as health care, insurance, telecommunications, and banking and finance.

A second major ASEAN goal identified in the Bangkok Declaration is to promote peace in the region. Many of the principles underlying this pledge of peaceful relations among association members are found in the 1976 Treaty of Amity and Cooperation. In this treaty, members agreed to respect each nation's sovereignty and territorial integrity. The treaty also reaffirmed earlier commitments to peaceful methods of conflict resolution. More recently, the 1994 ASEAN Regional Forum (ARF) was established to expand the use of diplomacy, rather than armed conflict, to reconcile differences. Parties to the ARF included all ten members of ASEAN plus Australia, Canada, the European Union, India, Japan, Mongolia, New Zealand, Papua New Guinea, Russia, and the United States. In 2003 the Declaration of ASEAN Concord II, also called the Bali Concord II, created the ASEAN Security Community (ASC), which committed members to "rely exclusively on peaceful processes in the settlement of intraregional differences."

A third ASEAN goal outlined in the Bangkok Declaration is to promote and expand regional cooperation in a variety of other areas of common interest, such as science and technology, education, transportation and communications, and culture and cultural studies. Concrete progress has been achieved in these areas. For example, in 1996, the Framework for Elevating Functional Cooperation to a Higher Plane was approved to create specific plans of regional action in the areas of social development, culture and information, science and technology, the environment, drug control, and international crime. Calls for additional cooperation were made in later documents including ASEAN Vision 2020 and the Bali Concord II of 2003. Association members have also strengthened their bonds by designing regional transportation networks, communications systems, and power grids.

See also **Regional Trade Agreements. *See also in Volume 2,* Document 23.**

Further Reading

Association of Southeast Asian Nations. *ASEAN Annual Report 2003–2004*. Manila, Philippines: ASEAN, 2004.

———. *The Asean Declaration*. Declaration of the ASEAN Ministerial Meeting. Bangkok, Thailand, August 8, 1967.

———. *ASEAN Statistical Yearbook 2004*. Manila, Philippines: ASEAN, 2004.

———. *ASEAN Vision 2020*. Declaration of the ASEAN Heads of State. Kuala Lumpur, Malaysia, December 15, 1997.

———. *Declaration of ASEAN Concord II* (*Bali Concord II*). Declaration of ASEAN Heads of State. Bali, Indonesia, October 7, 2003.

Gill, Ranjit. *Asean towards the 21st Century: A Thirty-Year Review of the Association of Southeast Asian Nations*. London: Asean Academic Press, 1997.

B

BALANCE OF PAYMENTS

The balance of payments (BOP) is a record of one country's transactions with the rest of the world in a given period of time. These transactions involve individuals, business firms, the government, and other groups. Governments collect BOP data regularly, and it is typically reported quarterly and annually. When a transaction causes money to enter a country, this money is called an inflow. Inflows appear on the country's BOP as a positive number, or credit. When a transaction causes money to exit a country, this is called an outflow. Outflows appear on the country's BOP as a negative number, or debit. Theoretically, the combined credits and debits shown on a country's BOP statement should be equal during each reporting period. International transactions are counted in both countries, once as an outflow from a country and once as in inflow to a second country—a process referred to as the double entry accounting system. The main categories of transactions include the country's current account, capital account, and financial account. Often the data for the capital and financial accounts are combined. Table 11 summarizes the BOP for the United States in 2003.

The current account deals with a country's international trade in merchandise and services, net investment income, and unilateral transfers. In 2003, for example, the United States had a merchandise trade deficit of $547.6 billion. Merchandise includes items such as machinery, consumer goods, and automobiles. This massive merchandise trade deficit occurred because the value of goods imported by the United States ($1,260.7 billion) was greater than the value of goods the United States exported ($713.1 billion) to other countries. The $547.6 billion merchandise trade deficit is recorded as a debit because it represents an outflow of U.S. dollars to other countries. In that same year, however, the United States recorded a trade surplus in services totaling $51 billion. Commercial services include items such as wholesale and retail trade, tourism, consulting, engineering, and transportation. The trade surplus in services occurred because the value of U.S. services exports ($307.4 billion) was greater than the value of the services the United States imported ($256.4 billion) from other countries. The $51 billion trade surplus in services is recorded as a credit because it represents an inflow of foreign currencies into the U.S. economy. Net investment income was also a credit in the U.S. balance of payments. Investment income represents the interest and dividends payments that cross national borders. In 2003, about $33 billion more investment income flowed into the United States than flowed out of the country. Net unilateral transfers, which consist mainly of U.S. foreign aid, gifts by Americans to foreigners, and other one-way transfers out of the country, were a $67 billion debit in 2003. The sum of these four components of the U.S. current account in 2003 showed a current account deficit of $530.7 billion.

TABLE 11 **U.S. Balance of Payments, 2003 ($ billions)**

Categories of Transactions	Debit (−) or Credit (+)	Summary
Current account		
Merchandise trade balance	−$547.6	
Services trade balance	+$51.0	
Net investment income	+$33.3	
Net unilateral transfers	−$67.4	
Summary of current account	−$530.7	−$530.7
Capital account	−$3.1	−$3.1
Financial account	+$545.8	+545.8
Statistical discrepancy	−$12.0	−$12.0
Sum of the U.S. balance of payments	0	0

Source: Bureau of Economic Analysis, "International Economic Accounts, Table 1," November 1, 2004.

The capital account includes a variety of capital transfers between countries. For example, money or other property that migrant or temporary workers carry across a national border represents a capital outflow from the country of departure and an inflow to the country the worker is entering. Inflows and outflows of capital can also result from cross-border sales or purchases of patents, copyrights, and undeveloped properties. In 2003, the capital account in the United States recorded a $3.1 billion deficit, thus it shows as a debit (−$3.1).

The financial account records the cross-border sale or purchase of assets. Some of the main categories of traded assets include corporate stocks and bonds, government securities, and long-term foreign direct investment (FDI)—including money spent on mergers and acquisitions (M&As) and greenfield investments. M&As occur when two existing firms are legally joined under a single ownership. Greenfield investments involve the construction of entirely new production facilities. In 2003 the United States had a $545.8 billion surplus in its financial account. This surplus resulted from foreign investors' willingness to buy $829.2 billion worth of U.S. financial and physical assets, while U.S. investors purchased just $283.4 billion in foreign assets. A statistical discrepancy results mainly from unreported cross-border transactions and inconsistencies in accounting procedures in the global economy. The sum total of all three BOP components, minus the $12 billion statistical discrepancy, summarizes the U.S. BOP in 2003.

The BOP receives significant media attention in the United States because of the growing current account deficits. From 1946 to 2005 the U.S. current account has been in surplus thirty times, mainly in the 1940s, 1950s, and 1960s, and in deficit thirty times during more recent decades. In fact, the U.S. current account has been in surplus just three times since 1980. Massive merchandise trade deficits during the early 2000s, including a trade deficit of over half a trillion dollars in 2003, is the largest reason for the current account deficit. Economists offer some perspective on the size of a nation's current account deficit by relating its size to the size of the nation's gross domestic product (GDP). In 2003 the U.S. current account deficit was 4.8 percent of GDP. This figure is calculated by dividing the current account deficit ($530.7 billion) by the

TABLE 12 **Current Account Positions of Selected Economies, 2002 to 2005 (% GDP)***

Economies	2002	2003	2004	2005
Australia	−4.4	−5.9	−5.3	−4.9
Canada	2.0	2.0	2.9	2.4
Japan	2.8	3.2	3.4	3.2
United Kingdom	−1.7	−1.9	−2.0	−1.9
United States	−4.5	−4.8	−5.4	−5.1
Euro area**	0.8	0.3	0.8	0.9
Newly industrialized Asian economies***	5.8	7.6	6.8	6.5
All advanced economies	−0.8	−0.8	−0.8	−0.8
All low- and medium-income economies	1.2	0.5	−0.1	−0.1

*2004 and 2005 data based on estimates.
**Euro area includes Austria, Belgium, Finland, France, Germany, Greece, Ireland, Italy, Luxembourg, the Netherlands, Portugal, and Spain.
***NIEs include the Hong Kong SAR, Singapore, South Korea, and Chinese Taipei.
Source: International Monetary Fund, *World Economic Outlook, September 2004*, 15; World Bank, *Global Economic Prospects 2004*, 283.

gross domestic product ($11,004 billion). Using this yardstick, the U.S. current account deficit is significantly higher than that of most advanced and developing economies, as shown in Table 12.

Economic historians often identify four stages in the evolution of a nation's balance of payments position. The first stage is the young debtor nation stage. During this early stage the nation is saddled with a current account deficit due to high imports and low exports and capital and financial account surpluses due to high foreign investment. The second stage is the mature debtor stage. This stage is marked by a small current account deficit mainly because of the high exodus of investment income as foreign investors collect interest and dividend payments on their earlier capital investments. This stage also witnesses an expansion of exports, however, and the resulting merchandise trade surplus tends to balance the outflow of investment income to other countries. The inflow and outflow of money in capital and financial accounts is roughly in balance. The third stage is young creditor nation. During this stage trade surpluses rise, which creates an inflow of money and a current account surplus. The growing nation's foreign investments also rise, which creates an outflow of money and a capital account deficit. The fourth stage is the mature creditor nation. During this stage the nation's imports and trade deficits rise, an occurrence partially offset by large inflows of investment income. The result is a current account that is balanced or slightly in surplus. Mature creditor nations also invest heavily in foreign economies and provide a stable environment in which foreign enterprises can invest. Mutually beneficial investment opportunities promote balance in the capital account.

The United States has progressed through these four BOP stages over the past couple of centuries. During the past quarter century, however, the U.S. economy has moved out of the mature creditor nation stage. Huge current account deficits have necessitated heavy U.S. borrowing from foreign creditors, mainly from mature creditor nations. The International Monetary Fund (IMF) estimated that by the early 2000s the United States was borrowing about one-tenth of all savings in the global economy. As a result, the United States had become a debtor nation.

See also **Balance of Trade; International Trade.**

Further Reading

International Monetary Fund. *Balance of Payments Statistics Yearbook 2003.* Washington, DC: IMF, 2003.

McCombie, J. S. L., and A. P. Thirlwall. *Essays on Balance of Payments Constrained Growth: Theory and Evidence.* New York: Routledge, 2004.

Miller, Norman C. *Balance of Payments and Exchange Rate Theories.* Northampton, MA: Edward Elgar Publishing, 2003.

Thirlwall, A. P. *Trade, the Balance of Payments and Exchange Rate Policy in Developing Countries.* Northampton, MA: Edward Elgar Publishing, 2004.

BALANCE OF TRADE

The balance of trade is the difference between the value of a nation's total imports and total exports in a given period of time. The balance of trade, sometimes called the trade balance, measures trade in merchandise and in commercial services. It is unusual for a nation's balance of trade to settle at a break-even point where the value of its imports and exports are equal. Instead, nations typically incur a trade imbalance. One type of trade imbalance is called a negative balance of trade, more commonly referred to as a trade deficit. A trade deficit occurs when the value of a country's imports is greater than the value of its exports. The second type of trade imbalance is called a favorable balance of trade, or trade surplus. A trade surplus occurs when the value of a nation's exports is greater than the value of its imports.

U.S. trade imbalances have shifted from consistent trade surpluses during the 1950s and 1960s to consistent trade deficits since the 1970s. The average annual trade surplus during the 1950s and 1960s was $3 billion. During the 1970s the trend toward trade deficits was firmly established as the United States

Global exports of goods and services hit $11 trillion in 2004.
Courtesy of CORBIS

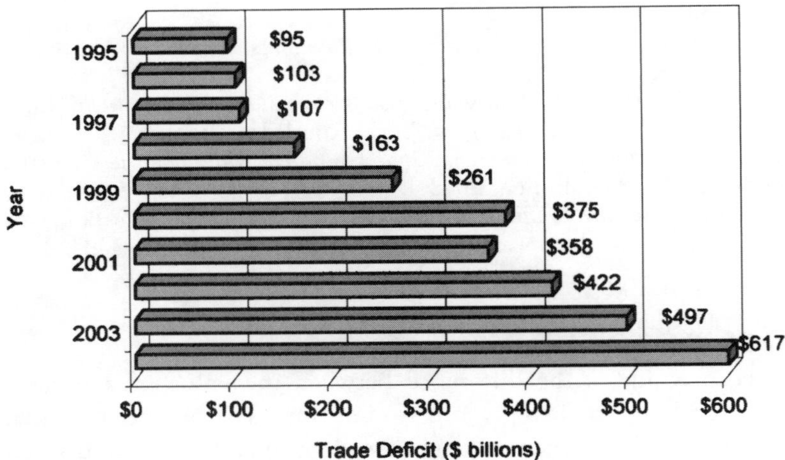

FIGURE 4 **U.S. Trade Deficit in Goods and Services, 1995 to 2004 ($ billions)**

Source: Economic Report of the President, 2004, "Table B-103," 406; and U.S. Census Bureau, *United States Department of Commerce News, March 11, 2005*, "Exhibit 1," 4.

recorded seven trade deficits during the decade. Still, on average, U.S. trade was in deficit by just $8 billion per year. The U.S. economy recorded its last trade surplus in 1975. Trade deficits continued to grow. During the 1980s, the U.S. trade deficit averaged $85 billion per year. During the 1990s, the trade deficit averaged $105 billion per year. From 2000 to 2004, the annual trade deficit averaged $454 billion per year. The growth of the U.S. trade deficit over the past decade is shown in Figure 4.

The overall balance of trade is divided into two branches: trade in merchandise and trade in commercial services. Trade in merchandise refers to the import or export of physical items, or goods. The main categories of merchandise exchanged in the global trading system are capital goods, industrial supplies and materials, consumer goods, automotive goods and parts, and foods, beverages, and animal feeds. In 2004 the United States exported $807.6 billion in merchandise to other countries and imported $1,473.1 billion in merchandise from other countries. Thus, the United States incurred a $665.5 billion merchandise trade deficit. The United States fared better in its global exchanges of commercial services. Trade in commercial services refers to the import or export of productive activities rather than physical goods. Major categories of commercial services were travel, passenger fares, other transportation, royalties and fees, wholesale and retail trade, financial services, and a host of other professional services. In 2004 the United States exported $339.6 billion in commercial services to other countries and imported just $291.2 billion in services from abroad. Thus, the United States had a trade surplus in services of $48.4 billion in 2004. In 2004 the overall U.S. trade deficit totaled $617.1 billion because the large merchandise trade deficit ($665.5 billion) was only partially offset by the more modest trade surplus in services ($48.4 billion). To put it another way, the United States imported a total of $1,764 billion in goods and services and was able to export just $1,147 billion in goods and services, thus accounting for the $617 billion trade deficit. Table 13 shows the trading partners with whom the United States had the largest trade surpluses and trade deficits in 2003.

TABLE 13 **Largest U.S. Trade Imbalances in 2004 ($ billions)**

Top U.S. Trade Surpluses		Top U.S. Trade Deficits	
Country	Amount of Surplus	Country	Amount of Deficit
Netherlands	$11.7	China	$162.0
Australia	$6.7	Japan	$75.6
Hong Kong SAR	$6.5	Canada	$65.8
Belgium	$4.4	Germany	$45.9
Singapore	$4.3	Mexico	$45.1

Source: International Trade Administration, *Industry, Trade, and the Economy: Data and Analysis*, tables 10 and 11.

Over the past quarter century the annual U.S. trade deficits have risen. This fact reflects the widening gap between U.S. merchandise imports and exports. During the 1990s, for example, the United States imported $174 billion more in merchandise each year than it was able to export. Between 2000 and 2004 the average annual trade deficit in merchandise had swelled to $515 billion. The United States maintained steady trade surpluses in services during this same period of time, a factor that moderated the rapid declines in the merchandise trade balance. The average annual trade surplus in commercial services was $68 billion during the 1990s and $60 billion during the early 2000s.

Economists often disagree about the main causes for the persistent and growing U.S. trade deficits. Still, there are a variety of credible explanations, each offering some insight into U.S. trade imbalances. One explanation of U.S. trade deficits is America's economic growth rate, which has consistently outpaced much of the world. The United States is the world's largest economy with an insatiable appetite for consumer goods. Its staggering gross domestic product (GDP) hit $11.7 trillion in 2004, and its per capita GDP rose to $41,400. Prolonged periods of economic growth since World War II have stimulated consumer spending on both domestic and foreign products. Irregular or sluggish economic growth in other world regions, however, hurt American exports to many foreign markets. The prolonged Japanese recession of the 1990s, the East Asian Financial Crisis of 1997–1998, and the slow economic growth in the European Union during the early 2000s all dimmed U.S. prospects for export expansion.

A second explanation for U.S. trade deficits involves trade restrictions imposed by foreign countries. Countries with higher trade barriers, including tariffs and non-tariff barriers, limit the entry of some U.S. exports. In the past, for example, contentious trade barriers reduced the sale of American-made products in Japan. Today, China's trade barriers help account for its $162 billion trade surplus with the United States. By the early 2000s the average U.S. tariff was 4.1 percent, while the average tariff in China was 15.1 percent. Trade negotiations between the United States and China, along with China's admission to the World Trade Organization in 2001, instigated a phase-in of tariff and import quota reductions during the early 2000s. China agreed to reduce its automobile tariff from 100 to 80 percent by 2007. China also initiated reforms to soften its strict trading rights rules, which had limited the ability of foreign firms to import or export goods. It also agreed to amend its own distribution rights, which had restricted the ability of foreign firms to set up wholesale and retail operations, repair services, and other service-oriented businesses.

A third explanation for U.S. trade deficits is the growing competitiveness of foreign producers. The post–World War II recovery of major European and Asian economies created formidable competitors in the global marketplace. By the 1960s and 1970s keen competition among the advanced economies such as Germany, Japan, and the United Kingdom caused the United States to lose its global grip on key industries such as automobiles, motorcycles, and electronics. In fact, in 2003 Germany bumped the United States from its perch as the world's leading exporter of merchandise. Other competitors, such as the Newly Industrialized Economies (NIEs) of Asia, also laid claim to larger shares of global markets. In the developing world, outward-looking economies such as China and Mexico capitalized on foreign investment and a large pool of low-wage labor to improve their competitive edge. By the early 2000s about one-half of all manufacturing in Mexico was generated by the duty-free, export-oriented maquila industries, which contributed to Mexico's $45 billion trade surplus with the United States in 2004.

A fourth explanation for U.S. trade deficits is the strength of the U.S. dollar. Since 1973 the flexible exchange rate system has allowed currencies to appreciate or depreciate in international markets. A currency appreciates in value when demand for the currency is strong and depreciates when demand is weak. The U.S. dollar, which has served as the bedrock for the global economy since World War II, has generally gained in value relative to other currencies because of strong demand for the dollar. The high demand for dollars results mainly from significant investments by foreigners in U.S. assets. This is because the purchase of U.S. assets, such as corporate stocks and bonds, government securities, and developed properties, requires U.S. dollars. What does this mean for U.S. trade deficits? As the value of the U.S. dollar appreciates against foreign currencies, U.S. exports become more expensive in foreign markets. This discourages foreigners from buying American-made exports. The dollar's appreciation also causes foreign imports to the United States to become less expensive. This encourages Americans to buy more foreign goods.

Finally, a variety of negative external factors has contributed to short-term U.S. trade deficits. For example, higher oil prices in the early 2000s aggravated the U.S. trade imbalance. From 1999 to 2005 the price of crude oil jumped from $11 to $70 per barrel. Heavy U.S. imports of oil, about 11.5 million barrels per day, added billions of dollars to the U.S. trade deficit during the period. The U.S. Department of Energy predicted that U.S. oil imports would jump to over 20 million barrels per day by 2025, sparking concerns about future trade imbalances. Other external shocks, including terrorism or the resurgence of rampant protectionism, could also reduce the flow of U.S. exports in the multilateral trading system.

See also **Balance of Payments; Exports; Imports; International Trade.**

Further Reading

Mann, Catherine. *Is the US Trade Deficit Sustainable?* Washington, DC: Institute for International Economics, 1999.
O'Connor, David E. *Demystifying the Global Economy.* Westport, CT: Greenwood Press, 2002.
Preeg, Ernest H. *The Trade Deficit, the Dollar, and the U.S. National Interest.* Indianapolis, IN: Hudson Institute, 2000.
United Nations Conference on Trade and Development. *Trade and Development Report, 2004.* Geneva, Switzerland: UNCTAD, 2004.
World Trade Organization. *World Trade Report 2004.* Geneva: WTO, 2004.

BANK FOR INTERNATIONAL SETTLEMENTS

The Bank for International Settlements (BIS) is an international organization with two main functions—to promote international monetary and financial cooperation among central banks, and to serve as a bank for central banks and international organizations. To achieve these goals, the BIS provides an international forum for central banks to meet and discuss issues related to monetary and financial stability, share economic data and other research, and generate policies to strengthen the global financial architecture. The BIS regularly conducts meetings, seminars, and workshops, and publishes volumes of statistical data and scholarly research to advance global economic security. It also serves member central banks by holding gold and other reserves and stabilizing today's international financial system. The BIS headquarters is located in Basel, Switzerland. BIS also maintains representative offices in the Hong Kong SAR and Mexico City.

The three most important decision-making groups within the BIS include the General Meeting of member central banks, Board of Directors, and Management Committee. The General Meeting is held annually, and is attended by central bank representatives from each member country. Voting power is determined by the number of BIS shares owned by each central bank. In 2004, fifty-five institutions had voting rights at the General Meeting. Important decisions made at the General Meeting involve the distribution of BIS dividends and profits, approval of the annual budget, and choice of outside auditors to scrutinize BIS financial records. The Board of Directors, a second important decision-making group, consists of up to twenty-one members. The first twelve include the Governors of central banks from six countries—Belgium, France, Germany, Italy, the United Kingdom, and the United States—plus an appointed representative from each of these same six countries. In 2004 just five additional central bank Governors were elected to the Board; hence the Board was comprised of seventeen members. The Board of Directors meets at least six times each year. It has primary responsibility for most of the bank's financial matters and for the bank's administration. Most administrative duties are, in turn, delegated to the bank's third main decision-making group—Management. Management coordinates the daily bank operations, and is headed by a General Manager.

The BIS is the world's oldest international financial organization. It began operations in 1930, in large measure to coordinate Germany's reparations payments to the victorious allied countries after World War I. The bank's mission soon grew to include stability in global financial markets and cooperation among the world's central banks. Over time the bank's role expanded. It adapted to new financial challenges in the global economy. For example, from 1945 to the early 1970s, the bank worked to support the Bretton Woods System. The bank promoted the fixed exchange rate system. It also supported the work of the World Bank, International Monetary Fund (IMF), and General Agreement on Tariffs and Trade (GATT). By the 1990s the BIS, along with other multilateral institutions, worked to defuse global financial crises in East Asia, Latin America, and elsewhere.

Today, the BIS is intimately involved in global economic and financial stability. As a bank for central banks, the BIS provides numerous services including the effective management of gold reserves and foreign exchange reserves, acceptance of deposits from member central banks, and the provision of emergency infusions of capital during financial crises. In 2004, 140 central banks and other institutions stored a portion of their foreign reserves at the BIS. These reserves totaled SDR 133 billion, or 6 percent of all foreign exchange reserves in the world. The International Monetary Fund's SDR, or Special Drawing Rights, is the unit of account used by the BIS. In recent years the BIS has helped member central banks invest their assets in secure, yet profitable ways. The bank also keeps track of economic and financial data in the global economy. For example, in its *Triennial Central Bank Survey of Foreign Exchange and Derivatives Market Activity*, the BIS measured cross-border financial flows conducted through the foreign exchange market, or forex. Forex is comprised of thousands of international investors such as central banks, commercial and investment banks, transnational corporations, and others. The *Triennial Survey 2004* reported that $1.9 trillion in national currencies and other financial instruments changed hands each day on the highly speculative forex, making it the largest financial market in the world.

The goal of fostering communication and cooperation among central banks around the world took a step forward when the Basel Committee was founded in 1974. The Basel Committee, which meets four times per year, discusses supervision of central banks and works closely with national authorities in the interest of global banking stability. In 2004 the Basel Committee issued a set of guidelines, the *International Convergence of Capital Measurement and Capital Standards: A Revised Framework* (*Basel II*), to strengthen global financial system. *Basel II* established three categories of banking reform including minimum capital requirements, increased supervision, and greater transparency. The recommendations outlined in Basel II are scheduled to be implemented beginning in 2006.

See also **Bretton Woods System; Capital Markets; Exchange Rates; Foreign Exchange Market; Global Financial Architecture.**

Further Reading

Baker, James C. *The Bank for International Settlements: Evolution and Evaluation.* Westport, CT: Quorum Books, 2002.

Bank for International Settlements. *74th Annual Report (1 April 2003–31 March 2004).* Basel, Switzerland: Author, 2004.

———. *Triennial Central Bank Survey of Foreign Exchange and Derivatives Market Activity in April 2004.* Basel, Switzerland: Author, 2004.

Toniolo, Gianni, Michael D. Bordo, Forest Capie, and Angela Redish, eds. *Central Bank Cooperation at the Bank for International Settlements, 1930–1973.* New York: Cambridge University Press, 2005.

BASIC ECONOMIC QUESTIONS

The basic economic questions are the universal questions that all economies, past and present, answer. These universal questions include: what to produce and in what quantity? how to produce goods and services? for whom to produce? How an economy answers these basic questions helps to distinguish one economic system from another. There are many ways to classify economies. Economists often consider how the basic economic questions are answered by traditional economies, pure market economies, and pure command economies. In reality, there are no pure economies operating in the global economy. Instead, all economies are "mixed economies." Today, most economies lean toward the market economy model, while a few lean toward the command economy model.

Labor-intensive production is common in many developing countries.

Courtesy of Getty Images: D. Falconer/PhotoLink

The "what to produce and in what quantity" question deals with decisions that individuals, firms, and countries make about which goods and services should be produced. A good is any object that satisfies a person's wants or needs. A service is any productive activity that satisfies a want or need. In a market-oriented economy such as the United States or Japan, individuals are mainly responsible for answering the "what to produce" question. This is because consumers cast their "dollar votes" for or against certain goods and services through their buying decisions. Today, consumers value automobiles and the skills of auto mechanics, so consumers' dollar votes are cast in favor of this good and this productive service. Dollar votes are no longer cast for horse-drawn carriages or blacksmiths, however, because newer technologies have rendered this good and productive service obsolete. In command-oriented economies, such as the Cuba or North Korea, government economic planners dictate the answer to the "what to produce" question. Government planners create central plans, often called a five-year plan, to allocate scarce resources. In command economies government-determined goals are more important than the individual's wants or needs.

The "how to produce goods and services" question concerns the employment of society's factors of production—natural resources, human resources, and capital goods. Business firms answer the "how to produce" question in market-oriented economies. In the highly industrialized market economies, such as the United States, business firms determine the most efficient mix of resources to use in production. Often, firms employ sophisticated capital goods—such as precision tools, robots, computers, and software—to increase productivity in their plants. Firms in market economies also employ other needed resources, including human and natural resources. Production in the United States and other highly industrialized market-oriented economies is capital-intensive, or heavily reliant on capital goods and technology to produce products. The "how to produce" question in command-oriented economies is largely determined by the central planners. These planners control society's factors of production and allocate natural, human, and capital resources to meet government objectives. In today's global economy production in the few command-oriented economies tends to be labor-intensive, or heavily reliant on human labor. This is mainly due to the low development status of countries such as Cuba and North Korea rather than their commitment to a centrally planned economy, however.

The "for whom to produce" question concerns the distribution of society's output. In effect, this question deals with who will receive the goods and services that are produced. In the market-oriented economies, the "for whom to produce" question is determined mainly by an individual's income and the prevailing prices of goods and services. People with higher incomes are better able to purchase goods and services than people with lower incomes. As a result, higher income groups have a higher standard of living than people with lower incomes. During the twentieth century, all industrialized market-oriented economies instituted programs to influence income distribution. The government adjusts the distribution of income through public transfer payments, which supplement the income of the needy. Transfer payments improve people's access to necessary goods and services, and, thus, elevates their standard of living. Examples of public transfer payments in the U.S. economy include Temporary Assistance to Needy Families, food stamps, Medicare and Medicaid, and Social Security payments. In command-oriented economies the "for whom to produce" question is determined by the government. Government planners set the wage rates for workers and the prices of most goods. By controlling wages and prices the government's heavy hand determines each person's share of national output. In command economies the government also provides some low-cost or no-cost services, such as health care and housing, to support a minimum standard of living.

See also **Command Economy; Economic System; Market Economy.**

Further Reading

Black, John. *A Dictionary of Economics.* 2d ed. New York: Oxford University Press, 2003.

Heilbroner, Robert, and Lester Thurow. *Economics Explained.* New York: Touchstone, 1998.

O'Connor, David E. *The Basics of Economics.* Westport, CT: Greenwood Press, 2004.

———, and Christopher Failles. *Basic Economic Principles: A Guide for Students.* Westport, CT: Greenwood Press, 2000.

BHAGWATI, JAGDISH

Jagdish Bhagwati (1934–) is a prominent Indian-born academic economist and one of the world's most recognized supporters of globalization. Bhagwati was born and raised in India. He earned his advanced academic degrees at Western universities, however, including Cambridge and Oxford in the United Kingdom, and MIT in the United States. After teaching economics at the Indian Statistical Institute and the Delhi School of Economics for much of the 1960s, Bhagwati accepted teaching positions in the United States, first at MIT (1968–1980) and then Columbia University (1980–2001). Bhagwati has written hundreds of scholarly articles and about forty books. Among his most influential books are: *Protectionism* (1988), *The World Trading System at Risk* (1991), *The Wind of the Hundred Days: How Washington Mismanaged Globalization* (2001), *Free Trade Today* (2002), and *In Defense of Globalization* (2004). Professor Bhagwati also founded the prestigious *Journal of International Economics* in 1971.

Bhagwati's central message is that the benefits of globalization outweigh its costs. In Bhagwati's view, there are five interrelated components of globalization, including the liberalization of international trade, foreign direct investment, cross-border financial flows, technology transfers, and immigration. He contends that each of these components of globalization promotes economic growth and development, higher living standards, and a better quality of life for people in the advanced economies and in developing economies. The liberalization of international trade, investment, and other cross-border economic contacts also advance the social agendas for countries in the developing world. For instance, Bhagwati believes that greater wealth and prosperity gained through international trade enables governments to build better schools, health care facilities, and other elements of an economic infrastructure, all of which benefit traditionally marginalized peoples. Further, greater contact with western countries spreads ideas such as gender equity and opposition to the exploitation of child laborers. Bhagwati is quick to point out that globalization has resulted in some market failures, such as pollution, worker dislocation and unemployment, and the weeding out of less efficient local businesses. Yet, he argues that it is wiser to address these types of specific market failures than to abandon the benefits of connectivity in the global marketplace.

Much of Bhagwati's attention is devoted to supporting free trade in an open multilateral trading system. In *Free Trade Today*, Bhagwati identified five benefits of free trade, including its positive impact on the economies of scale, consumer choice, productivity, technology sharing, and productive investment.

He maintains that in a true multilateral trading system the benefits of trade extend to rich and poor countries alike.

Bhagwati is also attentive to the question of "how to" promote free trade. He opposes "aggressive unilateralism," which bullies other countries into reducing their trade barriers. Bullying tactics might include threats of trade sanctions, intimidation, or even war. He also opposes the use of "reciprocity in preferential trade agreements" (PTAs), which includes regional and bilateral trade agreements. Bhagwati argues that PTAs, by definition, extend certain trade advantages to member countries at the expense of non-member countries. He contends that the rapid expansion of bilateral and regional trade agreements has eroded the impact of most-favored-nation (MFN) status, a basic principle of the General Agreement on Tariffs and Trade (GATT) and the World Trade Organization (WTO). Under MFN, a trade concession granted to one country is automatically granted to other WTO member countries. Bhagwati also fears the aggressive expansion of PTAs in recent years has rekindled the fires of protectionism, an inward looking set of trade policies that paralyzed the global trading system during the 1930s.

As an alternative to aggressive unilateralism and reciprocity in PTAs, Bhagwati favors trade policies based on "conventional unilateralism" and "reciprocity in multilateral trade negotiations." Under conventional unilateralism a country voluntarily reduces its own trade barriers. Under reciprocal multilateral trade negotiations (MTN), such as those conducted under the auspices of the WTO, MFN principles apply. The MFN status of WTO members guarantees equal benefits and nondiscrimination. In *Free Trade Today* Bhagwati summarized his views more colorfully by arguing "that both conventional unilateralism and MTN [multilateral trade negotiations] reciprocity have a useful role to play in freeing trade, whereas both aggressive unilateralism and PTAs are a pox on the world trading system."

Bhagwati's widely respected views have influenced policies of governments and multilateral organizations and shaped public opinion. His work has encouraged free trade, competitive markets, and other market-drive reforms in his native India and in other countries. Over the past decade, the General Agreement on Tariffs and Trade (GATT), United Nations, and World Trade Organization (WTO) have also solicited Bhagwati's advice on matters of global concern. Bhagwati's articles, which appear regularly in leading newspapers such as the *Financial Times*, *The New York Times*, and *Wall Street Journal*, have spread the gospel of globalization to millions of readers. He has also sought to expand the voices of traditionally marginalized peoples by supporting NGO participation in global decision making.

See also **Global Economy; Globalization; International Investment Agreements; International Trade; Regional Trade Agreements; World Trade Organization.**

Further Reading

Bhagwati, Jagdish. *Free Trade Today*. Princeton, NJ: Princeton University Press, 2002.
———. *In Defense of Globalization*. New York: Oxford University Press, 2004.

———. *The World Trading System at Risk*. Princeton, NJ: Princeton University Press, 1991.

Stiglitz, Joseph E. *Globalization and Its Discontents*. New York: W.W. Norton & Company, 2003.

Wolf, Martin. *Why Globalization Works*. New Haven, CT: Yale University Press, 2004.

BRAIN DRAIN

The brain drain refers to the migration of skilled professionals from one country to another country for an extended period of time. Implied in this definition is that the exodus of this professional elite has a direct, negative impact on the sending country and a corresponding positive impact on the receiving country. The brain drain is sometimes called human capital flight. The term human capital refers to human labor that has been enhanced by knowledge and skills acquired through education or training. Thus, human capital flight highlights the loss of skilled labor from an economy. It is commonly assumed that the brain drain applies only to the departure of skilled professionals from poorer, developing countries to greener pastures in the advanced countries. The brain drain, however, is also a concern for some advanced countries. In fact, the term brain drain was first used by the British Royal Academy to describe the immediate post–World War II migration of scientists and researchers from the United Kingdom to the United States. Today, heated discussions about the brain drain have focused on the loss of skilled professionals from countries in the developing world. These discussions often pit countries of the global South, which incur a net loss of professionals through emigration, against the countries of the global North, which incur a net gain through immigration. Categories of skilled professionals involved in cross-border migrations include scientists and researchers, information technologies (IT) technicians, physicians and other medical personnel, educators, and business managers or consultants.

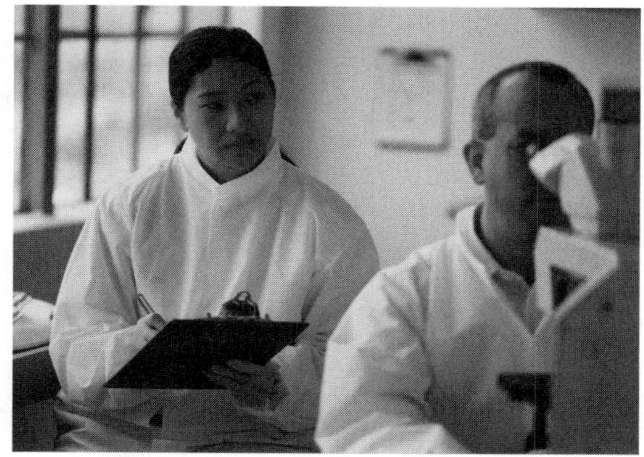

The brain drain depletes the supply of human capital in some developing and transition economies.

Courtesy of Getty Images: Ryan McVay

Measuring the brain drain in today's global economy is a tricky business. Credible organizations such as the World Bank, International Monetary Fund (IMF), and the International Organization for Migration have only recently initiated scholarly research on the brain drain and its impact, both positive and negative, on the global economy. The research relies mainly on data from the U.S. Census and the Organization for Economic Cooperation and Development's Continuous Reporting System on Immigration. This data tends to concentrate on immigrants with a tertiary education—formal education beyond the high school level. While incomplete, the data sheds some light on the main motivations for emigration, the most popular destinations, the direct and indirect impact of cross-border migrations, and the types of enticements needed to lure skilled professionals back to their homelands.

Skilled professionals are motivated to uproot themselves and their families by a number of push-pull factors. In the developing and transition economies the "push" factors are compelling and include relatively poor wages or salaries; a poor quality of life, marked by limited educational opportunities, inadequate health care, and the lack of basic services such as clean water and sanitation systems; unemployment and underemployment; an underdeveloped economic and IT infrastructure; government corruption and cronyism; and political instability and civil conflict. The "pull" factors focus on a wide variety of economic and social opportunities that are readily accessible in a different country. Pull factors attract skilled professionals from high-income and low-income countries to the advanced countries. Pull factors include attractive wages and salaries, thus a higher standard of living; increased access to education, particularly for advanced degrees; the availability of extensive social services; a solid economic and technological infrastructure; higher social and economic mobility; and a stable and secure political environment. Some governments in advanced economies also recruit talented foreign professionals. Germany, for example, loosened its immigration policies to recruit thousands of IT specialists, mainly from Eastern European countries. The United States relaxed its H1B Specialty Occupation Visas to attract additional university-educated specialists from other countries.

A relatively small number of advanced economies attract most of the world's skilled immigrants, including Australia, Canada, France, Germany, and the United States. The IMF estimates that over 90 percent of all inflows of skilled professionals migrating to advanced countries select one of these five nations. The world's leading country of destination is the United States. The OECD reported that the United States had attracted roughly 1 million skilled professionals, many in the field of information technology, from the early 1990s to the early 2000s. A sizable proportion of these skilled workers came from India, China, and Russia. Recent data suggest that migrations of professionals from the world's poorer regions to the United States and other advanced countries is one way because only a small percentage of these people return to their homelands. The migration of professionals from one advanced economy to another tends to be more temporary, however. It is not unusual for professionals from Canada or the United Kingdom to work in the United States for a number of years and then return to their homelands. This temporary migration is often called "brain circulation" rather than "brain drain" to emphasize the mutual benefits to sending and recipient countries. The brain drain among developing countries also occurs. In recent years professionals from Eritrea, Ethiopia, Somalia, and Sudan were pushed from the Horn of Africa to escape the carnage of bloody civil war or domestic unrest. Professionals from India, on the other hand, were often "pulled" to jobs in the oil-rich countries of the Middle East such as Bahrain, Kuwait, Qatar, and the United Arab Emirates.

The impact of the brain drain on countries, particularly developing and transition countries, is difficult to assess. On the one hand, the migration of significant numbers of skilled professionals from poorer nations is a major impediment to economic growth in less developed regions. The depletion of a nation's talent pool affects some countries more than others. For example, over half of all college-educated professionals from Jamaica and Haiti—two of the Western Hemisphere's poorest countries—live and work in the United States or United Kingdom. The brain drain from other Latin American countries, including the Dominican Republic, El Salvador, Guatemala, Guyana, and Mexico, depletes these countries' human capital. The United States also attracts disproportionately high percentages of highly educated people from Africa. Table 14 shows some of the disparities in scientific research and the application of research to business activity in selected high-, middle-, and low-income countries.

On the flip side there are benefits derived from the exodus of human capital. First, significant remittances return to professionals' homelands. Remittances are monetary sums that are earned by workers in one country but sent to relatives, friends, business associates, or others in the home country. According to the International Organization for Migration, total remittances by skilled and unskilled workers in the global economy surpassed $100 billion in 2003. Remittances stimulate consumer demand for goods, provide seed money for business investments, and otherwise support business activity in developing countries. Second, the availability of sophisticated information and communications technologies encourage professionals to network with one another, within

TABLE 14 **Global Disparities on Research and Patents in Selected Countries**

Countries by Income Status	Patents Granted to Residents (per million people) 2000	Research and Development (R&D) Spending (% of GDP) 1996–2002	Researchers in R&D (per million people) 1990–2001
High-income countries			
Australia	68	1.5%	3,439
Germany	205	2.5%	3,153
Japan	884	3.1%	5,321
Middle-income countries			
China	5	1.1%	584
Hungary	18	0.9%	1,440
Mexico	1	0.4%	225
Low-income countries			
Moldova	47	0.6%	329
Nicaragua	1	0.1%	73
Uganda	0	0.8%	24

Source: United Nations Development Program, *Human Development Report 2004*, 180–183.

nations and between nations. Networking between expatriates and their colleagues back home promotes positive transfers of knowledge to developing countries. Further, globalization has relaxed many barriers to cross-border travel and the movement of labor. In time, the brain drain from the developing world might be replaced with the brain circulation—the return of skilled nationals to their land of origin. This influx of human capital could be a significant step toward sustainable economic development.

The brain drain has been a tender topic in relations between the global North and global South for many years. To lure expatriates back to their homelands and retain professionals already residing in developing countries, national governments must create a suitable economic and social climate in which to nurture their talents. Key ingredients in this new environment include real opportunity for social and economic advancement, substantial investment in R&D, guarantees for security of person and property, and provision of public goods to satisfy vital social needs in education, health and nutrition, communications and transportation, and information.

See also **Capital Flight; Capital Formation; Developing Countries; Factors of Production; Sustainable Economic Development.**

Further Reading

International Monetary Fund. "How Extensive Is the Brain Drain?" *Finance and Development*, June 1999.

International Organization for Migration. *The International Organization for Migration*. New York: United Nations Publications, 2003.

Khadria, Binod. *The Migration of Knowledge Workers: Second Generation Effects on India's Brain Drain*. Thousand Oaks, CA: SAGE Publications, 2000.

Masey, Douglas S., and J. Edward Taylor. *International Migration: Prospects and Policies in a Global Market*. New York: Oxford University Press, 2004.

Organization for Economic Cooperation and Development. "The Brain Drain: Old Myths, New Realities." *OECD Observer*, May 2002.

United Nations. *International Migration Report 2002*. New York: United Nations Publications, 2003.

BRETTON WOODS SYSTEM

The Bretton Woods System refers to the institutions and operation of the international monetary system from 1946 to 1973. The Bretton Woods System takes its name from Bretton Woods, New Hampshire, which hosted the groundbreaking Bretton Woods Conference from July 1–20, 1944. At this conference representatives from forty-four countries met to discuss the creation of three multilateral institutions: the International Monetary Fund (IMF), International Bank for Reconstruction and Development (World Bank), and International Trade Organization (ITO).

Conference proceedings were dominated by the United States and the United Kingdom. Harry Dexter White, U.S. Secretary of the Treasury, headed the American delegation, and John Maynard Keynes led the British team. The final Bretton Woods Agreement was successful in establishing the IMF and World

Bank, but set aside ITO negotiations for a later date. The Bretton Woods Agreement also established overarching goals for the post–World War II era. These goals included the reconstruction of Allied and Axis economies, long-run economic growth and stability, and world peace. Shortly after the San Francisco Conference of 1945 established the United Nations (UN), the IMF and World Bank joined the UN system as autonomous specialized agencies.

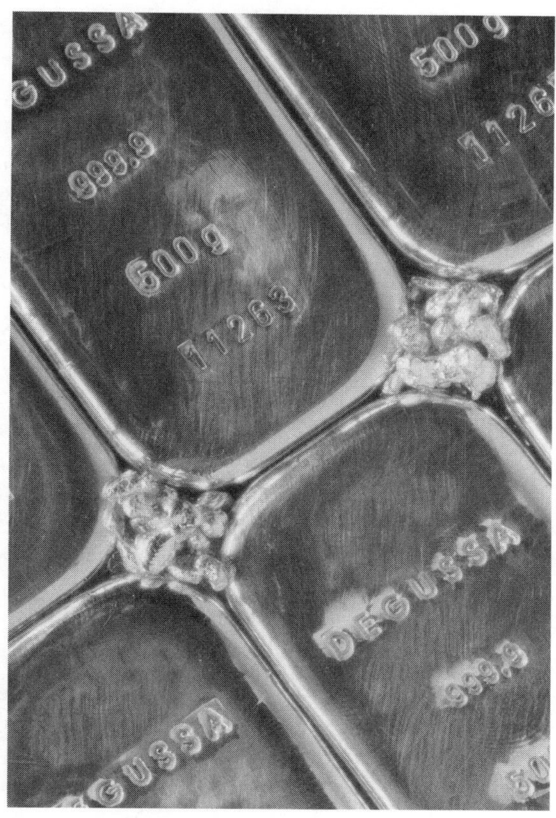

The Bretton Woods System pegged national currencies to gold and the U.S. dollar from 1946 to 1973.

Courtesy of Getty Images: PhotoLink

The Bretton Woods System was based on multilateral cooperation rather than the traditional bilateral agreements that dominated the pre-war era. Multilateral cooperation through supranational institutions, such as the IMF and World Bank, was necessarily balanced with national interests, however. The IMF promoted economic stability and worked to create an orderly, predictable environment for international trade. Delegates to the conference agreed that a fixed exchange rate system would best support a stable global trading system. Under the fixed exchange regime, the value of national currencies was "pegged" to the U.S. dollar, a practice that permitted only small fluctuations in currency values. The value of the U.S. dollar, in turn, was set at $35 per ounce of gold. Soon, the noncommunist countries of the world recognized the U.S. dollar as the dominant, international currency against which all other currencies would be measured. The IMF also held reserves, partly paid in gold and partly in national currencies, which were contributed by member nations through subscriptions. Subscriptions were used to stabilize currencies and assist struggling nations with their balance of payments deficits. The IMF, with supranational authority, also reminded nations of their responsibilities to avoid protectionist trade measures and to support one another in times of financial crisis. The IMF's headquarters is located in Washington, DC.

The second major Bretton Woods institution was the World Bank. Originally, the World Bank consisted of a single institution, the International Bank for Reconstruction and Development (IBRD). Its primary mission was to make loans to support the post-war recovery of European and Asian nations. The

World Bank's initial pool of loanable funds was derived from subscriptions, which were assigned in rough proportion to each member nation's economic clout. This meant that the United States was assigned the largest subscription quota. In 1947 the government of France received the World Bank's first loan, a tidy $250 million. During the 1950s World Bank lending gradually shifted from post-war reconstruction to economic development in the third world. In later decades four complementary institutions were added to IBRD to form the World Bank Group. These institutions were the International Finance Corporation (1956), International Development Association (1960), International Centre for Settlement of Investment Disputes (1966), and Multilateral Investment Guarantee Agency (1988). The World Bank's headquarters is located in Washington, DC.

The Bretton Woods Conference also laid the groundwork for a third multilateral institution, the International Trade Organization (ITO). The ITO's mission was to promote free trade in the post-war global trading system. Despite being shelved at the Bretton Woods Conference, high-level negotiations continued at separate conferences in London, Geneva, and finally in Havana. In 1948 delegates from fifty-four countries signed the ITO Charter, also called the Havana Charter. In several leading countries enthusiasm for yet another multilateral institution had cooled, however, by the late 1940s. In the United States, Congress failed to ratify the Havana Charter, and by 1950 the idea of an ITO was abandoned. The provisional General Agreement on Tariffs and Trade (GATT), which had provided a forum for multilateral trade negotiations since 1947, now took center stage in global free trade efforts. GATT, an agreement rather than a multilateral institution, was less threatening to many nations. From 1947 to 1994, eight trade rounds were conducted under the auspices of GATT. Delegates to GATT's eighth and final trade round founded the World Trade Organization (WTO) in 1994. The WTO commenced operations in January 1995.

The Bank for International Settlements (BIS) was another multilateral organization that supported the Bretton Woods System from 1946 to 1973. The BIS headquarters is in Basel, Switzerland. The BIS was established in 1930 to promote international monetary and financial cooperation among central banks and to serve as a bank for the world's central banks. Its founding was instigated by the global depression, which began in some countries during the late 1920s and continued into the 1930s. The BIS accepts deposits from member central banks to create a reserve of funds. These reserves are loaned to central banks to meet local banking needs and to avert financial crises. Cooperation between the BIS, IMF, World Bank, and GATT advanced their mutual goals.

The Bretton Woods System collapsed in 1973, but signs of its demise were present by the 1960s. One major weakness was an over-reliance on the United States to promote economic growth and stability in the global arena. During the post-war years foreign countries relied on open U.S. markets to sell their exports, extensive U.S. aid programs such as the Marshall Plan to fund their reconstruction, and a continuous flow of U.S. loans to jump-start development.

These significant outflows of money, plus massive expenditures for the Vietnam War and Great Society Programs during the 1960s, increased American debt. In the United States these stresses showed up in the form of inflation, sluggish growth, and large federal budget deficits. In the global economy there was also an oversupply of U.S. dollars stashed in foreign central banks as foreign reserves. Complicating U.S. economic woes was its pledge to convert U.S. dollars into gold on request by foreign governments. U.S. gold supplies dwindled as foreign governments cashed in their dollars for gold. In 1971 President Richard Nixon ordered an end to the conversion of dollars into gold, a policy that weakened confidence in the U.S. dollar and in the Bretton Woods System. The economic turmoil in the U.S. economy by the early 1970s, coupled with the U.S. refusal to convert foreign-held dollar reserves into gold, doomed the fixed exchange rate system. In 1973 a flexible exchange rate system was introduced to replace the fixed exchange rate system.

Despite the collapse of the gold standard and the introduction of a flexible exchange rate system, the Bretton Woods institutions survived the traumas of the early 1970s. Institutions such as the IMF, World Bank, BIS continued their work to promote international trade, economic growth and stability, and global peace. GATT organized additional multinational trade rounds, including the Tokyo Round (1973–1979) and the Uruguay Round (1986–1994). The WTO was born in 1995, joining the IMF and World Bank as one of the Big Three global institutions to guide economic relations among nations. The spirit of a multilateralism is, in large measure, the legacy of the Bretton Woods System.

See also **Bank for International Settlements; Exchange Rates; General Agreement on Tariffs and Trade; International Monetary Fund; World Bank Group.** ***See also in Volume 2,*** **Documents 17, 18.**

Further Reading

Battilossi, Stefano, and Youssef Cassis. *European Banks and the American Challenge: Competition and Cooperation in International Banking under Bretton Woods.* New York: Oxford University Press, 2002.

Eichengreen, Barry, and Michael D. Bordo, eds. *A Retrospective on the Bretton Woods System: Lessons for International Monetary Reform.* Chicago: University of Chicago Press, 1993.

James, Harold. *International Monetary Cooperation since Bretton Woods.* New York: Oxford University Press, 1996.

Kirshner, Orin, Edward M. Bernstein, and Institute for Agriculture and Trade Policy. *The Bretton Woods-GATT System: Retrospect and Prospect after Fifty Years.* Armonk, NY: M. E. Sharpe, 1995.

Stevenson, Jonathon. *Preventing Conflict: The Role of the Bretton Woods Institutions.* Washington, DC: International Institute for Strategic Studies, 2000.

BUSINESS CYCLE

A business cycle is a recurring, but irregular pattern of upswings and downswings in economic activity. The upswings are normally called expansions and the downswings are called contractions. Economists endeavor to predict business

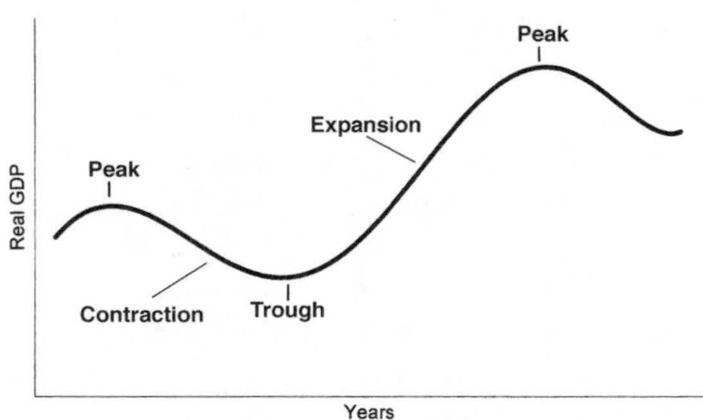

FIGURE 5 **The Business Cycle Model**

cycles at the national and international levels, with varying degrees of success. In the advanced economies, sophisticated data collection methods enable economists to make reasonable predictions about changes in the nation's business cycle. Economic data in the developing world is less reliable.

A country-specific business cycle illustrates the short-term increases and decreases in the nation's real gross domestic product (GDP) over time. The two main phases of a country's business cycle are the expansion phase, in which real GDP rises, and the contraction phase, in which real GDP falls. There are also two points on the business cycle. The peak represents highest real GDP for that particular business cycle, while the trough represents the lowest point. Figure 5 illustrates the phases and points along the business cycle model. A contraction that lasts for at least two quarters, or six months, is called a recession. A prolonged recession is called a depression. While changes in the real GDP are pivotal to identifying a country's position on a business cycle, economists often consider other economic data before declaring an economy to be in expansion or recession. Other key indicators include changes in unemployment, investment, consumer confidence, and consumer spending.

A business cycle for the entire global economy also seeks to measure global trends in real output, employment, and investment. The concept of a global business cycle is the source of some grumbling among economists. Some economists question whether sufficient data exists to determine global economic upswings or downswings. Others track national business activity, mainly business activity in the advanced economies, to chart global cycles. The International Monetary Fund (IMF) notes a number of limitations in determining global business cycles, including limited or unreliable economic data, gross regional differences in economic growth rates, and conflicting measurements of GDP.

The twentieth century has witnessed numerous business cycles within nations and in the global arena. The century's most dramatic cycle occurred during the late 1920s and early 1930s. In the United States, the world's largest economy, real GDP peaked in 1929 and then contracted during the early 1930s, as shown in Table 15. At about the same time other industrialized countries were also ravaged by falling national output, investment, and aggregate spending; massive banking failures and panic runs on financial institutions; deflation; and generalized despair. The six industrialized nations listed in the Table 15 produced over 80 percent of the world's total output in the early 1930s.

Based on recent IMF research economists are able to make certain generalizations about modern business cycles. First, the duration of the average business cycle is about six years, one year of contraction followed by five years of expansion. Second, the modern business cycle records a 3 percent dip in national

TABLE 15 **Fall in Global Output during the Great Depression**

Country	Share of World Output (1931 percent)	Business Cycle Peak	Business Cycle Trough	Output Loss (percent)
United States	42.4%	1929	1933	−29.4%
United Kingdom	13.1%	1930	1931	−0.5%
Germany	9.5%	1928	1932	−26.3%
France	7.9%	1932	1935	−10.4%
Italy	5.4%	1928	1933	−13.7%
Japan	5.1%	1930	1933	−14.9%

Source: International Monetary Fund, *World Economic Outlook, April 2002*, 110.

output during the contraction and a real GDP growth rate of 3 percent for each of the five years of expansion. Hence, the real GDP at the end of a business cycle is, on average, significantly higher than at its beginning. Third, recessions are shorter and milder today than in the past. For example, recessions that occurred in the industrialized countries during the 1919–1938 period caused an average real GDP decline of 8.1 percent. Average GDP declines resulting from post–World War II recessions recorded output losses of just 2.1 percent from 1950–1972, and 2.5 percent from 1973–2000.

Recessions also tend to be more synchronized today than in the past. Synchronization refers to the simultaneous occurrence of recessions in the industrialized countries. For example, in the *World Economic Outlook 2002*, IMF sources identified three periods of global recession over the past thirty years: 1975, 1981, and 1991. During these years, growth in the world's real GDP dropped significantly, measured on a purchasing power parity (PPP) basis, but never fell below a 1 percent growth rate. PPP measures the actual buying power of a currency within different economies. A U.S. dollar, for example, buys more goods in India, where the costs of living are relatively low, and fewer goods in the United States, where the costs of living are relatively high. The IMF noted that the magnitude of the real GDP decline during these years, led by dips in national output in the world's advanced economies, was sufficient to meet the global standard for a recession. In addition, the IMF considered global changes in real per capita GDP. Real per capita GDP, also measured on a PPP basis, dipped to about zero in 1975 and into negative numbers in 1982 and 1991. The most recent global slowdown in 2001 was not considered a global recession mainly because the real GDP and real per capita GDP were both positive based on PPP calculations. Yet, this 2001 economic slowdown was highly synchronized, as economic activity in many industrialized countries stalled during the period.

A business cycle illustrates short-term increases and decreases in real GDP. Changes in real GDP over time are often used to calculate a nation's economic growth rate. For example, if a nation's real GDP in 2004 was $100 billion, and its real GDP grew to $105 billion in 2005, the economic growth rate for the year is 5 percent ($5 billion increase in real GDP, divided by the original $100 billion real GDP in 2004). The concept of economic growth also considers other factors—factors that expand the nation's potential GDP. These factors include investments in capital goods, research and development (R&D), human capital, entrepreneurship, and innovation. When viewing economic growth as a long-term process, economists often disregard the temporary blips in an economy's business cycle and instead focus on the long-term growth trend. How big is the global economy? According to IMF estimates global output grew from $30 trillion in 1996 to $42 trillion in 2005, measured by the traditional exchange rate (Atlas) method. Measured by the PPP method, global output grew from $36 trillion to $56 trillion during the same period. World Bank estimates generated similar results.

Another theory of the global business cycle is the Kondratiev wave. The Kondratiev wave, sometimes called the Kondratiev cycle, theorized that the industrialized nations of the world progress through a series of extended business cycles, each encompassing fifty or more years of business activity. At the beginning of each Kondratiev wave, economic growth is sparked by a flurry of new technologies, new products, and high consumer confidence and spending. A generalized prosperity accompanies this technology-driven growth spurt. During the period of expansion, aggregate demand and the inflation rate also rise. According to the Kondratiev wave theory prosperity wanes as markets mature, competition stiffens, and production is shifted to low-wage countries. The downward slide in business activity is pitted with recessions and depressions that cripple economic growth and stability and cause living standards in the industrialized countries to decline. During these contractions deflation occurs as business failures, rising unemployment, and lower wages reduce aggregate demand. Adherents of the Kondratiev wave claim that the global economy has already witnessed four complete cycles since the birth of the Industrial Revolution in the late 1700s. They also contend that a fifth wave is currently underway—this one sparked by the explosion of information and communications technologies (ICTs).

See also **Economic Growth; Gross Domestic Product; Information and Communications Technologies; Kuznets, Simon.**

Further Reading

Barker, David K. *The K Wave: Profiting from the Cyclical Booms and Busts in the Global Economy*. New York: Irwin Professional Publishing, 1995.

Diebold, Francis X., and Glenn D. Rudebusch. *Business Cycles*. Princeton, NJ: Princeton University Press, 1999.

International Monetary Fund. *World Economic Outlook, April 2002*. Washington, DC: IMF Publications, 2002.

———. *World Economic Outlook, September 2004*. Washington, DC: IMF Publications, 2004.

Krugman, Paul R. *The Return of Depression Economics*. New York: W. W. Norton & Company, 2000.

Lakshman, Achuthan, and Anirvan Banerji. *Beating the Business Cycle*. New York: Currency, 2004.

CAPITAL FLIGHT

Capital flight refers to certain outflows of funds from a country. Generally, capital flight focuses on excessive cross-border transfers of financial capital, rather than the normal purchases of foreign securities, properties, or other assets that investors make to diversify their investment portfolios. Capital flight is a burning issue in today's global economy mainly because it drains scarce financial capital from developing countries. In doing so, capital flight puts a damper on domestic investment and long-term economic growth. In addition, only a small cadre of wealthy and well-connected individuals derive financial benefits from these outflows. Capital flight includes the outflow of financial capital through legal and illegal means. There is much debate about the causes, the magnitude, the economic effects, and the prospects for the reversal of capital flight in the global economy.

Current research suggests that capital flight results from a variety of economic and political factors. First, economists generally agree that capital takes flight when a country's macroeconomic performance is weak. Signs of macroeconomic instability include a high inflation rate, high unemployment rate, high budget deficits, and low or negative economic growth. These types of macroeconomic instability reduce investor confidence in the domestic economy, which prompts the rich to seek more secure foreign investments. One recent International Monetary Fund (IMF) study demonstrated the correlation between macroeconomic instability and high rates of capital flight for countries in several world regions. Table 16 illustrates this compelling correlation for countries in central Europe and Latin America. Note that in the years when there was "intense capital flight," real economic growth in each region was sluggish or negative, and budget deficits and inflation rates were high. During the periods of "capital flight reversal," on the other hand, macroeconomic conditions had improved in each category.

A second factor that causes capital flight is the threat of currency devaluation. A formal devaluation reduces one currency's value relative to other world currencies. Thus devaluations could decrease the value of an investment portfolio virtually overnight. To avoid this type of financial calamity, the rich transfer assets to foreign banks, offshore financial centers (OFCs), or other safe havens. Third, the absence of good governance speeds capital outflows. Unfair tax systems, poorly defined private property rights, political corruption and cronyism, and arbitrary enforcement of business rules and regulations contribute to a poor domestic investment climate. Fourth, international crime sparks

TABLE 16 **Capital Flight and Macroeconomic Stability, 1990s**

World Region	Average for Years of Intense Capital Flight	Average during Period of Capital Flight Reversal
Central Europe	1990–1992	1993–1998
Capital flight (US $ per capita)	−$16.0	$73.0
Real GDP growth rate	−6.0%	4.0%
Budget deficit (% of GDP)	−3.4%	−2.0%
Inflation rate	36.0%	19.0%
Latin America	1982–1991	1992–1998
Capital flight (US $ per capita)	−$45.0	−$3.0
Real GDP growth rate	2.0%	4.0%
Budget deficit (% of GDP)	−3.2%	−1.2%
Inflation rate	73.0%	29.0%

Source: Prakash Loungani and Paolo Mauro, International Monetary Fund (Research Department), *Capital Flight from Russia*, 8.

illegal cross-border capital flows. At the top of list of financial crimes is money laundering, an illegal practice used to grease the wheels of global crime syndicates as well as global terrorism.

The channels by which financial capital travels through the global economy are numerous and sophisticated. Legal financial channels include banks, securities dealers, and other legitimate financial intermediaries. It is not illegal, or unethical, to diversify one's portfolio by saving in foreign banks or investing in foreign securities markets. It is only when excessive transfers are made through legal financial channels, or these legal channels are used to support tax avoidance or other illegal activity, that capital flight occurs.

Capital outflows through illegal channels are often disguised. Illegal channels manipulate financial data, falsify records, and employ other shady business practices. One common technique of deception is misrepresenting the true value of an exported good. By understating the value of an export at the country of departure, an exporter can sell the good at a higher market price in the country of entry—and then pocket the difference. The excess cash earned "off the books" is then stashed in a foreign bank or, better yet, in an anonymous offshore account. Another illegal channel for capital outflows involves phony advance payments for an import. Under this scheme a fake business is established to pay for an import before it is shipped. Once the payment is made to a foreign bank or firm, the fake business dissolves without a trace. The payment, an outflow of financial capital, remains in the foreign account. At times funds are simply carried in suitcases, boxes, or other containers across national borders. Illegal schemes transfer huge sums of money secretly from one nation to another. These funds support international crime. Historically, they have also bolstered the personal assets of corrupt political figures throughout the developing world including Ferdinand Marcos in the Philippines, the Duvalier family in Haiti, and Saddam Hussein in Iraq.

The economic impact of capital flight on poorer developing countries and transition countries is often significant. The most apparent negative effect of capital flight is the stress it puts on domestic savings in poorer regions. Capital flight drains scarce financial capital from countries and slows domestic investment. Investment in capital goods is a prerequisite for sustained economic growth in all economies. Investment in private and public capital is critical in the developing world, as poorer nations play catch-up with the advanced economies.

Yet, in some of the world's poorest, least stable countries investment is thwarted by capital flight.

A recent World Bank study compared the outflows of financial capital from five world regions, as shown in Table 17. The study concluded that in selected countries from two world regions, sub-Saharan Africa and the Middle East, about 40 percent of all private domestic savings was channeled into foreign investments outside of the region. It was also estimated that financial outflows resulted in a 16 percent loss in national output for countries in these regions. Capital flight on this scale severely impedes progress toward sustainable development. Lesser impacts on national output were recorded for Latin America, South Asia, and East Asia.

TABLE 17 **Impact of Capital Flight on Selected World Regions, 1990**

World Region	Capital Flight per Worker ($ US)	Capital Flight Ratio (% outflows)	Estimated Output Loss (% loss)
Sub-Saharan Africa	$696	40%	16%
Latin America	$1,923	10%	4%
South Asia	$90	5%	2%
East Asia	$627	6%	2%
Middle East	$2,322	39%	16%

Source: Paul Collier, Anke Hoeffler, and Catherine Pattillo, "Flight Capital as a Portfolio Choice," *The World Bank Economic Review*, vol. 15, no. 1, 59.

Another negative economic consequence of capital flight is the diminished quality of life for people. Quality of life refers to people's income status as well as the overall conditions under which people live. When capital flight reduces national savings and investment it also stymies job creation and entrepreneurship. Starved for funds, domestic firms cannot expand, and entrepreneurial activity is crushed. The stream of tax revenues into government coffers also slows because interest, dividends, and other profits earned on foreign investments are beyond the reach of local authorities. Lower government revenues translate into fewer public services, such as public education, health care, water and sanitation, and fewer public goods, such as roads, airports, seaports, courts, and other components of a modern infrastructure. The loss of public services and goods hits hardest on the poorest citizens of developing countries, which widens the already large income gap between the rich and the poor. Lower government tax revenues also limit the ability of poorer nations to service high foreign debt obligations.

The reversal of capital flight is a front-burner issue in today's global economy. Proposals to reduce or eliminate capital flight are often viewed as an important step in reforming the global financial architecture. The most important prerequisite for the reversal of capital flight is to establish macroeconomic stability and financial reforms within developing countries. Stable currencies, profitable investment opportunities, sound financial institutions, secure property rights, and fair tax codes would provide incentives for people to save and invest within the domestic economy. Second, good governance is essential to slowing financial outflows. Good governance, which relies on transparency and competency in public affairs, is another way to reduce capital flight. Good governance insists on rules-based economic activity, such as the enforcement of contracts and legal remedies to financial disputes. It also negates the pillage of the public till by self-seeking dictators and other well-connected public officials. Third, some countries have imposed capital controls to limit financial outflows. Capital controls are sometimes initiated after crises such as the East Asian Financial Crisis and the Russian Financial Crisis of the late 1990s. Finally, recent proposals have stressed international cooperation to reverse capital flight. Already, governments and international financial institutions (IFIs) have organized to combat the most egregious forms of capital flight such as money laundering. Global cooperation combats international crime, tax avoidance, and terrorism. The repatriation of funds looted from developing nations by corrupt political figures is another type of international cooperation. Proposals to prevent banks and other financial institutions from luring foreign funds out of the world's poorer economies are also under discussion.

See also **Brain Drain; Capital Formation; Capital Markets; Developing Countries; Economic Growth; International Financial Institutions; Offshore Financial Centers; Sustainable Economic Development.** ***See also in Volume 2,*** **Document 58.**

Further Reading

Ajayi, S. Ibi, and Mohsin S. Khan. *External Debt and Capital Flight in Sub-Saharan Africa*. Washington, DC: International Monetary Fund, 2000.

Chisholm, Andrew. *An Introduction to Capital Markets: Products, Strategies, Participants*. New York: John Wiley & Sons, 2002.

Epstein, Gerald A. *Capital Flight and Capital Controls in Developing Countries*. Northampton, MA: Edward Elgar Publishers, 2005.

Obstfeld, Maurice, and Alan M. Taylor. *Global Capital Markets: Integration, Crisis, and Growth*. New York: Cambridge University Press, 2004.

CAPITAL FORMATION

Capital formation is the process of increasing the amount of capital goods in a country. Capital goods, also called physical capital, are tangible items designed to produce other products. The total amount of capital goods in a country is called its capital stock. Capital goods are produced by the private sector and by the public sector. Private sector capital goods include business computers and software, heavy industrial and farm equipment, office and factory buildings, department stores, delivery vehicles, and taxicabs. Capital goods produced or provided by the government include many elements of the nation's infrastructure, such as roads and highways, dams, canals, airports, seaports, and water and sewage systems. Also included are public buildings such as schools and universities, libraries, public hospitals and clinics, municipal offices, courts and prisons, and police and fire stations. Capital provided by the government is often called social capital.

Capital formation is a primary goal of countries throughout the global economy. Capital formation increases the productivity of labor, a prerequisite for increasing the per capita gross national income (GNI), people's standard of living, and sustainable economic development. The advanced economies have high rates of productivity and correspondingly high living standards due, in part, to consistent investment in and expansion of their capital stock over time. Development economists stress the need for developing countries to expand the amount of productive capital per worker, a process called capital deepening. Capital deepening is essential for raising worker productivity in all three economic sectors—agricultural, goods-producing, and services-producing.

Investments in sophisticated harvesting equipment increase a country's capital stock and improve the productivity of its labor force.
Courtesy of Getty Images: PhotoLink

The process of capital formation requires a ready pool of savings. When people save money they sacrifice some present consumption. Gross domestic saving and the productive investment of these savings are the foundations of capital formation. Gross domestic saving is the sum of savings by individuals, businesses, and government in an economy. The *Economic Report of the President* reported that U.S. gross savings topped $1.5 trillion in 2002. A nation's gross savings finances gross investment. The private sector and the public sector invest in the U.S. economy. In 2002 U.S. gross investment also topped $1.5 trillion, mostly the result of business investments. Businesses invested more than $1 trillion in 2002, mainly on computers and other information processing equipment ($400 billion), industrial and transportation equipment ($301 billion), and nonresidential production facilities such as factories, retail outlets, and mines ($269 billion). Hundreds of billions of dollars were also invested by individuals and firms in residential structures, mainly single-family houses.

Gross saving and investment in the global economy varies by world region and development status. The World Bank reported that sub-Saharan Africa and South Asia, two of the world's poorest regions, recorded the lowest gross domestic savings rates. In 2002 gross savings in sub-Saharan Africa was 17 percent of GDP, while in South Asia gross savings represented 20 percent of GDP. The highest rates of gross domestic savings appeared in the East Asia and Pacific region, which hit 37 percent of GDP during the same time period. Gross domestic savings and capital formation for countries in the global economy are shown in Table 18. While the high-income countries averaged gross savings and capital formation of just 19 percent of GDP, this represented trillions of dollars in productive investment. Conversely, the higher rates of gross savings and investment in some poorer regions represented relatively small amounts of money.

Countries in the developing world face a series of obstacles to achieving the virtuous cycle of savings, productive investment, and sustainable economic growth. One major obstacle is poverty, a problem complicated by rapidly rising populations in the world's poorer regions. To save money people must sacrifice present consumption, a difficult proposition with so many mouths to feed. Another obstacle is the flight of scarce financial and human resources from poorer

TABLE 18 **Gross Domestic Savings and Capital Formation, 2002 (% GDP)**

Income Status	Gross Domestic Savings	Gross Capital Formation
Low income	19%	20%
Lower middle income	28%	25%
Upper middle income	25%	19%
High income	19%	19%

Source: World Bank, *2004 World Development Indicators*, 214–217.

regions. Capital flight and the brain drain sap resources from developing economies. Capital flight occurs when the rich from developing nations transfer savings to safer, more profitable investments abroad. The brain drain occurs when human capital exits developing countries for greener pastures, mainly in the advanced countries. A third obstacle is the dearth of foreign direct investment (FDI). FDI in the form of mergers and acquisitions (M&As) and greenfield investments provide foreign financial capital, technology transfers, and access to global markets for a handful of developing countries. Yet in many poorer countries uncertain property rights, underdeveloped economic and technological infrastructures, and an unstable investment climate pose risks that many foreign investors are unwilling to accept. A fourth obstacle to capital formation is poor governance. Government corruption, favoritism, discriminatory tax codes, and the inability to enforce contracts or other business obligations weaken incentives to save and invest in some poorer countries. Finally, foreign aid is inadequate to meet the needs of many of the world's poorest economies. Foreign aid from other governments, multilateral development organizations, and private foundations supplement the shallow pool of domestic savings and helps jump-start the virtuous cycle of development. In recent decades foreign aid as a percentage of most rich countries' GDP has declined.

The process of capital formation is enhanced by proactive, pro-development policies. One development policy is to attract foreign investment. Responsible foreign direct investment (FDI) infuses new physical capital, financial capital, technology, and management skills into host economies, and links local enterprises with profitable global opportunities. Joint ventures with foreign firms generate similar benefits to the host country. A second policy is to solicit outside help to reduce the digital divide. The digital divide is the technological gap that isolates the global South from the benefits of globalization. External technical assistance might come from transnational corporations (TNCs), multilateral development institutions, the World Trade Organization, private foundations, non-governmental organizations (NGOs), think-tanks, the Peace Corps, and other channels. A third policy is to expand incentives to keep financial and human resources within the developing country. Key incentives include private property rights, a sound social infrastructure, strong capital markets, and a stable macroeconomy. Finally, policies must nurture good governance and the rule of law. At its most basic level, governments must protect society's productive resources and infrastructure from the devastation of recurrent civil wars and domestic violence. Good governance also promotes transparency, competence, and ethical behavior in government. These conditions are enhanced by the development of democratic institutions and an independent media.

See also **Brain Drain; Capital Flight; Digital Divide; Economic Growth; Foreign Aid; Foreign Direct Investment; Good Governance; Population; Sustainable Economic Development. *See also in Volume 2,* Document 55.**

Further Reading

Diamond, Walter H., Dorothy B. Diamond, and Charles C. Luetke. *A State by State Guide to Investment Incentives and Capital Formation in the United States*. 2d ed. Norwell, MA: Kluwer Law International, 2004.

Economic Report of the President: 2004. Washington, DC: United States Government Printing Office, 2004.

Ito, Takatoshi, and Andrew K. Rose, eds. *Growth and Productivity in East Asia*. Chicago: University of Chicago Press, 2004.

World Bank. *2004 World Development Indicators*. New York: Oxford University Press and the World Bank, 2004.

———. *World Development Report 2005: A Better Investment Climate for Everyone*. Washington, DC: Author, 2004.

CAPITALISM

Capitalism is a type of economic system based on the private ownership and control of the factors of production—natural resources, human resources, and capital goods. A capitalist economy relies on decentralized private sector decision making by individuals and firms. Thus, the private sector is mainly responsible for answering the basic economic questions of what, how, and for whom to produce. Key institutions of capitalism include private property rights, profit incentives, competition, and economic freedom. Capitalism is often referred to as the free enterprise system, or mixed market system. Over the past two decades most economies in the global economy have made a discernable shift away from command economic systems, and toward capitalism.

The most important treatise on the virtues and functioning of capitalism is Adam Smith's book, *An Inquiry into the Nature and Causes of the Wealth of Nations* (1776). In this landmark book Smith extolled the benefits of a free-market economy—an economy based on individual decision making and the pursuit of one's own "self-interest." In Smith's view, individuals and firms are best able to determine how to allocate scarce resources to satisfy their consumption or production needs. Decentralized private sector economic decision making became the cornerstone of laissez-faire capitalism, which dominated economic policymaking in some major industrialized countries for nearly a century. Laissez-faire capitalism rejected most types of government intervention in the economy. Included in fundamental laissez-faire principles was free trade in global markets. Smith's support for free trade was an open challenge to the powerful mercantilists of the late 1700s. The mercantilists favored protectionist trade policies and active government intervention to support domestic businesses.

Laissez-faire capitalism dominated the global economy from the mid-1800s to the outbreak of the global depression of the 1930s. Rapid industrialization in the advanced capitalist economies such as Germany, the United Kingdom, and the United States, increased per capita national output and improved the standard of living for millions of people. Under these favorable economic conditions, governments tended to support capitalism.

By the early 1900s laissez-faire capitalism had also greased the wheels of global economic integration and interdependence. Free trade, exuberant foreign direct investment (FDI), and investment in capital markets were the threads that stitched the global economy together. The rise of global capitalism was hastened by the imperialist policies of the world's major powers. Imperialism is a process by which one country wrestles political power away from another country, kingdom, tribe, or other political entity. Imperialism was driven by a number of forces, including the quest for military power, national prestige, and profit. Profits could be made from the global exploitation of natural and human resources, the creation of new trade routes and markets for national output, and other entrepreneurial business activities. Imperialism brought many of the poorer regions of the world under the control of the industrialized nations, mainly the major European powers. Some economic historians refer to the period of time between the mid-1800s and the outbreak of World War I in 1914 as the first "great age" of globalization.

Laissez-faire capitalism, which seemed so secure during the pre–World War I era, was severely shaken by World War I, the global depression of the 1930s, and World War II. World War I (1914–1918) struck at the heart of Europe, the epicenter of the capitalist revolution during the nineteenth and early twentieth centuries. The destruction of business enterprises, massive death toll, toppled governments, and other nightmares of the war unraveled the economic web that the Europeans had so carefully woven. The United States and some other nations retreated into isolationism after the war. By the early 1930s most countries had erected formidable trade barriers, such as tariffs and import quotas, to restrict imports. These misguided attempts to protect domestic firms and jobs during the early years of the global depression only worsened the economic crisis. Capitalism was also threatened by the growing power of the world's first communist nation, the Union of Soviet Socialist Republics (USSR), which was established at the close of World War I. During the global depression of the 1930s, the weaknesses inherent in laissez-faire capitalism were magnified. Throughout the global economy unemployment rates rose, businesses failed, and national output plummeted. As the global depression dragged on, people's suffering compelled nations to seek new answers to the basic economic questions.

Almost overnight the United States and other industrialized countries reinvented capitalism to meet the challenges of the deepening global depression. In the United States the basic institutions of capitalism, such as private property rights, profit incentives, and competitive markets were protected. Yet, Congress passed a flurry of new laws in the 1930s, collectively called New Deal legislation, which would irrevocably change American capitalism. The New Deal expanded the government's role in four key areas. First, the government increased its provision of public goods such as highways and bridges, sewage systems, dams, national parks and recreation areas, and public buildings. Second, the government assumed greater responsibility for people's economic well-being by expanding social programs for the needy. Third, the government increased regulations on business activity. New laws and regulations were designed to prevent fraud in securities markets, reduce risky investments by commercial banks, and guarantee workers a minimum wage. Fourth, the government assumed a more active role in stabilizing the economy through monetary and fiscal policies. Stabilization policies were given a theoretical boost in the United States and elsewhere with the publication of *The General Theory of Employment, Interest, and Money* (1936) by the British economist John Maynard Keynes.

Capitalism proved to be a resilient economic system. It weathered the storm of two world wars, a global depression, and the emergence of major contenders—communism and socialism—during the twentieth century. In the immediate post–World War II era some of the nations of the West, such as the United States and later Japan, clung to many of the capitalist principles that had propelled their economies into positions of global dominance during the 1800s and early 1900s. In these economies most production and consumption decisions relied on the market mechanism, an informal system of price signals.

World events had altered capitalism in significant ways during the global depression and World War II, however. Throughout the world contending economic systems arose to challenge capitalism. Many Western European countries, including economic powerhouses such as France, the United Kingdom, and West Germany, adopted democratic socialism, a type of economic system in which the government owns and controls some of the most important industries and provides an extensive array of social welfare programs to the people. In Eastern and Central Europe, communism, under the oppressive thumb of the Soviet Union, became entrenched. In Asia violent revolution brought communism to China, the world's most populous country.

The prolonged post–World War II ideological battle between the West, headed by the United States, and the East, headed by the Soviet Union, dissipated with the collapse of USSR in 1991. The Cold War struggle that pitted capitalism against communism was put to rest. Over the past couple of decades capitalism's resurgence was apparent throughout the global economy. The former communist countries of eastern and central Europe are currently transitioning toward capitalism. The former democratic socialist economies of western and northern Europe, and most third world socialist economies, have taken a decided turn toward free enterprise. Since 1978 economic reforms in the People's Republic of China have also steered the Chinese economy down a market-oriented path.

It is tempting to conclude, as some economists have done, that the triumph of capitalism has, indeed, occurred. Yet, significant challenges remain before victory is declared. Among the more visible challenges for the twenty-first century are the vast income gaps between the wealthier economies of the global North and the poorer economies of the global South; the weaknesses in the global financial architecture that invite financial crises such as the Asian

Financial Crisis of 1997–1998; the absence of good governance and the rule of law in many countries around the world; and the unsustainable debt faced by the severely indebted countries. The resilience of capitalism is well documented. These challenges and others will surely test the world's resolve to create a global economy where markets and social justice can co-exist.

See also **Business Cycle; Command Economy; Communism; Democratic Socialism; Emerging Market Economies; Globalization; Hayek, Friedrich A.; Market Economy; Smith, Adam; Third World Socialism; Transition Countries.** ***See also in Volume 2,*** **Documents 13, 55.**

Further Reading

Ebenstein, William, Edwin Fogelman, and Alan Ebenstein. *Today's ISMS: Socialism, Capitalism, Fascism, Communism, and Libertarianism.* 11th ed. Paramus, NJ: Prentice Hall, 1999.

Friedman, Milton. *Capitalism and Freedom.* Chicago: University of Chicago Press, 1963.

Fulcher, James. *Capitalism: A Very Short Introduction.* New York: Oxford University Press, 2004.

Gilpin, Robert. *The Challenge of Global Capitalism: The World Economy in the 21st Century.* Princeton, NJ: Princeton University Press, 2002.

Radice, Hugo. *Political Economy of Global Capitalism.* New York: Routledge, 2004.

Soto, Hernando de. *The Mystery of Capital: Why Capitalism Triumphs in the West and Fails Everywhere Else.* New York: Basic Books, 2000.

CAPITAL MARKETS

Capital markets are institutions that channel surplus money into medium- and long-term productive investments—investments that last at least one year. Domestic capital markets include institutions such as commercial banks, stock and bond markets, and insurance companies. Some capital markets are designed to supply investment capital mainly to borrowers in global markets. Examples include the international bond market, the Eurodollar market, and international financial institutions (IFIs) such as regional development banks and the World Bank. Further, transnational corporations (TNCs) are a major component of today's capital markets. TNCs are the source of most foreign direct investment (FDI). Well-functioning capital markets are essential to productive investment in individual countries and in the larger global economy. As the wellspring of investment funds, capital markets enable business firms and governments to raise needed money for private sector and public sector investment. Productive investments, in turn, promote economic growth, job creation, capital formation, and higher living standards for the peoples of the world.

Access to capital markets in the global economy is uneven. The advanced economies of the global North typically have highly sophisticated domestic capital markets, which have evolved over time. In the United States 19,000 depository institutions amassed over $9 trillion in assets by the early 2000s. About 80 percent of these assets were held by commercial banks, and the remainder was held by savings banks, savings and loan associations, and credit unions. Other features of U.S. capital markets were sophisticated stock exchanges, such as the NASDAQ Stock Market and New York Stock Exchange; active computerized bond markets for corporate and government securities; multibillion dollar insurance corporations and pension funds; and a variety of smaller institutions such as venture capital funds.

Key reasons for the stability of domestic capital markets in the advanced economies are transparency in rules-based financial dealings, effective regulation and supervision of financial institutions, accurate and timely reporting of financial information, and a modern information and communications technologies (ICT) infrastructure. In addition, investors from the advanced economies are generally perceived to be creditworthy, and are better connected to international capital markets. This connectivity gives investors from the rich countries easy access to funds in global capital markets.

The Paris bourse (stock exchange). In 1999 the Paris bourse joined several other European stock exchanges to form Euronext, Europe's largest stock exchange.

Courtesy of Getty Images: Neil Beer

The Eurodollar market is one popular source of funding for well-connected investors. Eurodollars are U.S. dollars deposited at any foreign bank. Wealthy individuals, corporations, central banks, and governments make these dollar-denominated deposits. In the Eurodollar market, foreign banks loan U.S. dollars to investors such as TNCs. Interest rates on these loans are generally lower than rates in the United States because Eurodollar loans are not regulated, and the Eurodollar deposits are not subject to Federal Deposit Insurance Corporation (FDIC) fees or Federal Reserve System reserve requirements. Governments and corporations can also sell bonds in the international bond market to raise needed capital for public and private investments.

Capital markets in most emerging market and developing economies are less sophisticated than those in the advanced economies. Underdeveloped domestic capital markets stem from a number of factors related to the history and development status of countries. For example, poorer countries have a low gross national income (GNI) per capita, which reduces people's ability to save money. Low domestic savings retards the development of depository institutions such as banks. Other limitations include capital flight, as domestic funds are whisked away to more secure institutions abroad; poor management, due to limited experience in forming viable financial institutions; and the absence of good governance and the rule of law. These factors reduce the creditworthiness of investors from the global South, and limit their access to funds in global capital markets.

IFIs are able to pick up some of the slack by extending development loans to emerging market and developing countries. For example, regional development banks provide billions of dollars in development loans to regional member countries. The four main regional development banks include the African Development Bank Group (ADB Group), the Asian Development Bank (ADB), the Inter-American Development Bank Group (IDB), and the European Bank for Reconstruction and Development (EBRD). The World Bank Group also provides a variety of development loans to support government and private development through the International Bank for Reconstruction and Development (IBRD), the International Development Association (IDA), and the International Finance Corporation (IFC).

In recent years capital markets have been at the center of a firestorm in the global economy. Core concerns include how to promote efficient capital markets in the developing countries, and how to level the playing field for poorer borrowers in global financial markets. Often, the reform of capital markets is lumped together with other reforms in the global financial architecture—the sum total of all types of financial transfers between nations. Several major proposals for reforming capital markets and the overall global financial architecture are under discussion. First, uniform rules for borrowing, and TNC investment, are essential. Second, corruption and cronyism in developing countries must be curtailed. Third, additional funds are required to deal with liquidity crises in poorer nations. Fourth, external debt rescheduling and other debt relief is necessary for heavily indebted countries. Fifth, additional development loans to poorer countries are needed to complement the work of the World Bank and other IFIs.

Microfinance, a nontraditional source of development financing, is another promising source of development funds. Microfinance, also called microcredit, is a means by which the poor obtain small loans, called microloans, to start or expand a small business. Microfinance institutions accept deposits and grant loans, some as small as $50–100, to support entrepreneurship. Thus, microfinance institutions represent a more grassroots capital market. Microloans are made to poor people who are routinely excluded from traditional financing by banks because they do not meet established lending criteria, such as income level and collateral requirements. Microfinance is not a new idea in the realm of development financing, however. The Grameen Bank of Bangladesh has made microloans to the poor of Bangladesh since 1983. Under the direction of its founder, Muhammad Yunus, the Grameen Bank has made nearly 4 million microloans to local entrepreneurs—mainly women. Since the 1970s major international organizations, such as the United Nations and regional development banks, have recognized the importance of microfinance, and have developed programs to expand microcredit in the global economy. Today, thousands of microfinance institutions operate in the global economy, some offering related services such as insurance.

See also **Capital Flight; Capital Formation; Global Financial Architecture; International Financial Institutions; Microfinance Institutions; Regional Development Banks; Yunus, Muhammad.** ***See also in Volume 2,*** **Documents 8, 55.**

Further Reading

Birdsall, Nancy. *What Role for Regional Development Banks in Financing for Development?* Washington, DC: Institute for International Economics, 2003.

Fabozzi, Frank J., and Franco Modigliani. *Capital Markets: Institutions and Instruments.* 3d ed. Old Tappan, NJ: Prentice Hall, 2002.

International Monetary Fund. *World Economic Outlook and International Capital Markets.* Washington, DC: IMF, 1998.

Litan, Robert, Michael Pomerleano, and V. Sundararajan. *The Future of Domestic Capital Markets in Developing Countries.* Washington, DC: The Brookings Institution Press, 2003.

Yunus, Muhammad. *Banker to the Poor: Micro-Lending and the Battle against World Poverty.* Washington, DC: Public Affairs, 2003.

CARIBBEAN COMMUNITY

The Caribbean Community is a multilateral organization of fifteen nations that promotes economic development and social progress in the Caribbean region. It supports regional integration and positive external relations with other multilateral institutions, trade blocs, and national governments. The Caribbean Community members are Antigua and Barbuda, the Bahamas, Barbados, Belize, Dominica, Grenada, Guyana, Haiti, Jamaica, Montserrat, St. Kitts and Nevis, Saint Lucia, St. Vincent and the Grenadines, Suriname, and Trinidad and Tobago.

The Treaty of Chaguaramas established the Caribbean Community in 1973. Its original name was Caribbean Community and Common Market, or CARICOM. Its four founding members were Barbados, Jamaica, Guyana, and Trinidad and Tobago. Under the Treaty of Chaguaramas, signatory nations pledged to strengthen economic integration, promote balanced development, coordinate foreign policies, and advance cultural and technological development with the region. Since 1973 eleven full members and five associate members have joined the Caribbean Community. Associate members include the British Virgin Islands (1991), Turks and Caicos Islands (1991), Anguilla (1999), the Cayman Islands (2002), and Bermuda (2003). CARICOM was restructured in 2002 through a series of amendments, or protocols, which were added to the Treaty of Chaguaramas. Today, the organization is simply called the Caribbean Community. The highest authority in the Caribbean Community is The Conference of Heads of Government, more commonly called The Conference. The Caribbean Community's headquarters is located in Georgetown, Guyana.

Plans to amend CARICOM began to take shape by the late 1980s. The Conference was determined to further integrate the Caribbean region into a single market. This determination was based mainly on the rising power of other regional economic blocs and the tidal wave of globalization that threatened to swallow the region. In 1989 the CARICOM Heads of State committed themselves to the Grand Anse Declaration. This Declaration spearheaded negotiations to amend CARICOM's structure and mission. The final 2002 treaty revisions created the Caribbean Community. An important part of the Caribbean Community is the CARICOM Single Market and Economy (CSME).

At the heart of the CSME is the goal of creating a single economic region. The "single market" refers to the free cross-border flows of merchandise and commercial services, workers, financial capital, and real capital. In the early 2000s all tariffs, import quotas, and other trade barriers were dropped within the CSME. Many travel restrictions on workers in service industries were lifted, permitting individuals to work and take up residence in any CSME country. Policies to permit flows of money, including the purchase of corporate stocks throughout the region, were also being developed. The free movement of products, people, and resources was designed to increase production efficiency, global competitiveness, and economic development.

The CSME's goal of a "single economy" refers to the coordination of national economic policies in the interest of regional economic stability and growth. Challenges facing the single economy include the creation of uniform tax codes, business and environmental regulations, a common currency, and other policies that support balanced development. Even before the CSME was officially enacted in 2002, the spirit of regional cooperation was manifest in the Caribbean Community's response to sagging tourism after the September 11, 2001, terrorist attacks on the United States. It was agreed that member nations would unite to promote travel to "the Caribbean" rather than to engage in cutthroat competition to attract scarce tourist dollars.

The Caribbean Community has expanded the political and economic clout of the region. It coordinates the regional response to drug trafficking, HIV/AIDs and other health issues, inadequate educational systems, and poverty. In legal matters, cases are referred to its Caribbean Court of Justice. The Caribbean Community represents regional interests in negotiations and debates that involve the proposed Free Trade Area of the Americas (FTAA) and major multilateral institutions such as the World Trade Organization (WTO), the Organization of American States (OAS), and the United Nations. As an organization representing fifteen countries and 14 million people, its voice is magnified in other negotiations with regional trade blocs such as the European Union, powerful transnational corporations, and non-member national governments. The Caribbean Community also formulates and articulates a unified foreign policy. The Caribbean Community has two affiliated institutions: the Caribbean Development Bank and the University of the West Indies.

See also **Regional Trade Agreements.**

Further Reading

Benn, Denis, and Kenneth Hall. *The Caribbean Community: Beyond Survival.* Concord, MA: Ian Randle Publishers, 2002.

CARICOM Secretariat. *CARICOM Single Market and Economy.* Georgetown, Guyana: CARICOM, 2004.

Hall, Kenneth. *Integrate or Perish: Perspectives of Heads of Government of the Caribbean Community and Commonwealth of Caribbean Countries 1963–2002.* Concord, MA: Ian Randle Publishers, 2003.

International Business Publications. *Caribbean Community and Common Market Business Law Handbook.* Cincinnati, OH: International Business Publications, 2004.

United Nations. *Trade between Caribbean Community (CARICOM) and Central American Common Market (CACM) Countries: The Role to Play for Ports and Shipping Services.* New York: United Nations, 2003.

CARTEL

A cartel is a formal agreement or organization that coordinates the production decisions of independent producers or suppliers of a similar or identical product in order to influence the product's global supply and price. Producers, in this context, can be business firms or governments. Cartels limit the supply of the product by assigning each member a production quota, which sets a maximum quantity of output for each member. If the market price for the product falls, the cartel lowers each member's production quota to decrease the global supply. Lower supply makes the product scarce, which tends to boost its price. Conversely, if the market price for the product rises too quickly, endangering economic stability, the cartel increases each member's production quota. An expanded supply tends to stabilize the product's price. Cartels have been at the center of many controversies over the past century mainly because their collusive, anticompetitive behaviors create artificially high prices for certain goods. By forming powerful producer cartels, suppliers increase their market power—the ability to raise prices without losing significant demand for their output. Today the world's two most recognized and powerful producer cartels are the Organization of Petroleum Exporting Countries (OPEC) and DeBeers.

OPEC is a producer cartel comprised of major oil-producing nations. The original five OPEC countries founded the organization in September 1960, largely to counterbalance the powerful oil companies that dictated oil prices to the oil-producing nations. OPEC's founding nations were Iran, Iraq, Kuwait, Saudi Arabia, and Venezuela. Today, OPEC consists of eleven member nations, the original five plus Algeria, Indonesia, Libya, Nigeria, Qatar, and the United Arab Emirates. The first major demonstration of OPEC's market power came in the fall of 1973, when OPEC cut production after the Yom Kippur War. This production cut was politically motivated, largely meant to punish the United States and other western nations for their support of Israel in the war. The impact of the production cut caused a fourfold increase in oil prices and sent a clear message throughout the global economy—OPEC collusion could influence the global price of the world's most precious primary energy resource.

Since the 1970s OPEC's market power in global oil markets has had its peaks and valleys. OPEC, like other producer cartels, was susceptible to internal conflicts, cheating, and external competition, all of which eroded its market power. For instance, economic slumps in certain advanced economies during the late

1970s and early 1980s reduced the demand for oil. As oil prices plummeted, member nations resorted to cheating on their production quotas. Armed conflict between OPEC nations also undermined the cartel's unity. The prolonged Iran-Iraq War of the 1980s, along with the Iraqi invasion of neighboring Kuwait in 1991 and subsequent Gulf War in 1992, created discord within the cartel as well as regional devastation. In addition, non-OPEC oil producers have stepped up production, chipping away at OPEC's global dominance. By 2003 the Former Soviet Union (FSU), Mexico, Norway, and other non-OPEC producers supplied more than 60 percent of the world's daily oil needs, as shown in Table 19. By the late 1990s OPEC oil ministers announced a target price range for crude oil that ranged from $22 to $28 per barrel—a price range that was discarded in January 2005. Global price spikes exceeding $60 per barrel in 2005 illustrated the volatility of global oil markets.

The DeBeers diamond cartel is another major producer cartel operating in today's global economy. The company headquarters is located in Johannesburg, South Africa. DeBeers is often described as a "marketing" or "selling" cartel rather than a production cartel. Through its Central Selling Organization (CSO), DeBeers coordinates the sale of diamonds mined by many different producers around the world. Today the CSO controls roughly 70 percent of the global rough diamond market by purchasing uncut stones from major diamond producers and then selling them in mixed batches to preferred clients called "sightholders." The bundling and sale of diamonds takes place in London, in a distribution system called the "London mix." In this way DeBeers is able to control the type and quantity of diamonds released for sale to sightholders and, thus, to the global marketplace. Complementing DeBeers' influence on the supply side of the diamond market is effective advertising that for decades has shaped consumer demand for diamonds. DeBeers created the catchy "Diamonds Are Forever" slogan in the 1940s to stimulate demand and to discourage the creation of a second-hand diamond market. DeBeers' influence on both sides of the market—supply and demand—kept diamond prices artificially high for decades. The cartel's success in maintaining high prices explains why major producers from Botswana, Namibia, Russia, South Africa, and elsewhere continue to sell their diamonds exclusively to DeBeers.

TABLE 19 **Global Daily Oil Production, 1970 to 2003 (millions of barrels per day)**

Producers	1970	1980	1990	2000	2003
OPEC	23.5	27.2	24.5	30.7	29.8
FSU	7.1	12.1	11.5	7.9	10.2
Other non-OPEC	17.4	24.6	30.9	38.0	39.1
Total	48.0	63.9	66.9	76.6	79.1
OPEC (% of global market)	49.0%	42.6%	36.6%	40.0%	37.8%
Non-OPEC (% of global market)	51.0%	57.4%	63.4%	60.0%	62.2%

Source: World Bank, *Global Economic Prospects 2004*, Table A2.13, 274.

In recent years there have been a variety of challenges to DeBeers' dominance of the global diamond market. First, Israeli diamond sellers have grabbed a significant market share (perhaps as large as 20 percent) of the global rough diamond market. Thus, Israeli diamond suppliers have become a major competitor to DeBeers. Second, high quality substitute goods, including artificially produced diamonds, have entered the market. U.S. firms using patented production processes have produced flawless diamond crystals that are virtually indistinguishable from mined diamonds. Third, new diamond mines have been established to cash in on the profitable diamond market. The entry of new firms into a profitable industry is characteristic of free-market economics. For DeBeers, however, this entry of additional firms has flooded the global diamond market. Fourth, legal challenges to DeBeers have shaken the cartel's air of invincibility. In July 2004 DeBeers pleaded guilty to anticompetitive business practices in the United States, and was fined $10 million by the U.S. government. Other legal challenges are expected from diamond-producing nations who wish to cut and polish a percentage of their own stones rather than export all output for sale in the London mix. In the early 2000s DeBeers announced that its marketing strategy would henceforth concentrate on increasing the demand for diamonds rather than manipulating the supply of diamonds in global markets.

Producer cartels have existed in other industries. Among the most successful was the aluminum cartel that dominated global production and sales of aluminum during the early twentieth century. A series of cartel agreements, which began in the 1890s and were renegotiated during the first half of the twentieth century, strengthened the collusion among the world's top aluminum producers. The cartel members laid claim to exclusive sales in certain geographic regions, guaranteed each member a fixed market share, and set prices. The first truly global aluminum cartel was established in 1901, the result of an agreement that included the Aluminum Company of America (Alcoa) and Europe's four largest producers. Combined, these five companies controlled about 90 percent of the world's total output of aluminum. The cartel's price fixing schemes resulted in a 50 percent increase in aluminum's price during the early century. The demise of the cartel occurred during the post–World War I period when an aluminum glut forced members to dump excess aluminum on global markets for a fraction of its former price. In 1931 the aluminum cartel reunited. To avoid antitrust charges in the United States, Alcoa was represented in the cartel by its Canadian subsidiary, the Royal Aluminum Company. Once again, aluminum prices were propped up by the cartel even as the global depression ravaged other industries throughout the world. By the mid-1930s Alcoa had control of virtually all bauxite resources needed in the production of aluminum, and manufactured 100 percent of all primary aluminum in the United States. It wasn't until after World War II that the U.S. government clamped down on the Alcoa monopoly, and new competitors such as Reynolds and Kaiser entered the market.

Cartels are sometimes confused with international commodity agreements (ICAs). Contrary to producer cartels, which coordinate the behaviors of producers, ICAs organize both producers and consumers of certain commodities into a single group. The goal of ICAs is to ensure an adequate supply of a commodity at a reasonable price. During the twentieth century, a number of important ICAs were negotiated, including the following: International Sugar Agreement (ISA) in 1954; International Tin Agreement (ITA) in 1954; International Coffee Agreement (ICoA) in 1962; International Cocoa Agreement (ICCA) in 1972; and International Natural Rubber Agreement (INRA) in 1980. By 2005, just three ICAs remained: the ICoA; the ICCA; and the ISA.

See also **Energy Resources; International Commodity Agreements; Organization of Petroleum Exporting Countries; Terms of Trade.** ***See also in Volume 2,*** **Document 44.**

Further Reading

Akiyama, Takamasa, John Baffes, Donald Larson, and Panos Varangis. *Commodity Market Reforms: Lessons of Two Decades*. Washington, DC: World Bank Publications, 2001.

Amuzegar, Jahangir. *Managing the Oil Wealth: OPEC's Windfalls and Pitfalls*. Rev. ed. New York: I. B. Tauris, 2001.

Holloway, Steven K. *The Aluminum Multinationals and the Bauxite Cartel*. New York: St. Martin's Press, 1988.

Organization of Petroleum Exporting Countries. *OPEC Annual Statistical Bulletin 2003*. Austria: Ueberreuter Print und Digimedia, 2004.

CENTRAL AMERICAN COMMON MARKET

The Central American Common Market (CACM) is a five-nation multilateral trade organization. The General Treaty on Central American Economic Integration established the CACM in 1960. The CACM's founding members included El Salvador, Guatemala, Honduras, and Nicaragua. Costa Rica joined in 1962. The General Treaty on Central American Economic Integration outlined an ambitious five-year plan to create a Central American free trade area (FTA), a customs union, and eventually a common market. The notion that these goals could be met within a five-year period was bolstered by their success in negotiating earlier treaties, such as the Multilateral Treaty of Central American Free Trade and Economic Integration (1958), and the Central American Agreement on the Equalization of Import Duties and Charges (1959).

During the 1960s, the CACM made significant progress in reducing intraregion trade barriers, and by instituting a common external tariff (CET), a uniform tariff that is levied on imports from non-member nations. The elimination of tariffs and other trade barriers within the CACM resulted in a tenfold increase in intraregion trade during the decade. Thus, a solid groundwork for a Central American FTA was laid by the mid-1960s. Also during the 1960s, the CACM took giant steps toward forming a customs union by successfully implementing a CET. The daunting task of creating a common market remained.

The CACM's plan to create a common market has been pitted with detours, false starts, and dead ends since the 1960s. In fact, the goal of forming a true common market never materialized. A common market is a higher form of economic integration. It is based on a functioning free trade region, the CET, and free cross-border movements of all factors of production—natural resources, human resources, and capital goods. To create a common market, the CACM solicited the support and cooperation of the larger Latin American Free Trade Association. This Association consisted of Mexico and most of the economies of South America. Negotiations stalled during the 1970s, and in 1980 the dysfunctional Latin American Free Trade Association dissolved.Its successor organization, the Latin American Integration Association, refocused its energies on creating a Latin American FTA rather than a common market.

The inability of the CACM to maintain its free trade area and customs union during the turbulent 1970s and 1980s was largely the result of intraregional tensions and conflicts during the period. For instance, open warfare between El Salvador and neighboring Honduras erupted in 1969. At the root of this war was unbalanced economic development in the region, which favored El Salvador and Guatemala over some of their Central American neighbors. The growing development gap between El Salvador and Honduras, coupled with a widening Honduran trade deficit with El Salvador, boiled over into armed conflict. This conflict was not the only violence in the region, however. Prolonged and bloody civil wars in El Salvador and Nicaragua during the 1970s and 1980s, rampant government corruption, capital flight, protectionist trade policies, and intense competition among some Central American economies for limited export markets eroded popular support for regional integration. By the early 1990s the coffin had been nailed shut on proposals for a Central American common market.

In 1993, however, the five original CACM economies rekindled the idea of economic integration by forging a new Central American Free Trade Zone. Under the provisions of this agreement, tariffs and other trade barriers among member nations were once again eliminated. In addition, members of the new agreement became more outward-looking, seeking new economic alliances. The most significant outward-looking initiative was the successfully negotiated U.S.-Central America Free Trade Agreement, or CAFTA, which was signed in Washington, DC, in May 2004. Soon thereafter, the Dominican Republic (DR), the largest Central American economy, also joined into the Agreement. With the entry of the Dominican Republic, the DR-CAFTA region created the second largest U.S. export market in Latin America, second only to Mexico. The Office of the U.S. Trade Representative reported that two-way trade between the United States and the DR-CAFTA nations totaled $32 billion in 2003. Before CAFTA is implemented it must receive the formal approval of the U.S. Congress and the elected assemblies of each participating country. These national legislatures will consider CAFTA in 2005.

See also **Regional Trade Agreements.**

Further Reading

Danielson, Anders, and Geske Dijkstra, eds. *Towards Sustainable Development in Central America and the Caribbean*. New York: Palgrave Macmillan, 2001.

De Alonso, Irma T., ed. *Trade, Industrialization, and Integration in Twentieth-Century Central America*. Westport, CT: Praeger Publishers, 1994.

Hufbauer, Gary C. *Trade Policy, Standards, and Development in Central America*. Washington, DC: World Bank, 2001.

International Business Publications. *Central American Common Market Investment and Business Guide*. Cincinnati, OH: Author, 2001.

Melmed-Sanjak, Jolyne, Carlos E. Santiago, and Alvin Magid, eds. *Recovery or Relapse in the Global Economy: Comparative Perspectives on Restructuring in Central America*. Westport, CT: Praeger Publishers, 1993.

CIVIL SOCIETY ORGANIZATIONS

Civil society organizations (CSOs) refer to a variety of non-governmental and nonprofit groups, or citizens' associations, that work to improve society and the human condition. CSOs are built on foundations of free association and free speech. CSOs coordinate the activities and empower members of civil society—individuals volunteering their energy and skills to work collectively for the public good. Through CSOs, people express viewpoints, share information, and advocate for change. The views expressed by CSOs may be based on ethical, cultural, political, scientific, religious, or charitable considerations.

CSO activities address local, national, or international issues. CSOs with a global reach include international non-governmental organizations (INGOs), labor unions, business forums, community-based organizations, research centers, philanthropic foundations, student organizations, professional associations, think-tanks, faith-based groups, and others. Many CSOs are household names, such as Amnesty International, Corporate Watch, Friends of the Earth, Greenpeace, Oxfam International, Save the Children, and World Vision. Excluded from the list of CSOs are governments and all government agencies, political parties, business firms, and the media. The definition of civil society is still the subject of some debate. Yet there is little debate that CSOs have made an impact on policymakers within individual countries and throughout the global community.

CSOs have expanded during the twentieth century. Yet the past two decades have witnessed the largest increase in the number and clout of CSOs. According to the Center for Civil Society and the Center for the Study of Global Governance, the first hard data on INGOs dates back to 1924 when 639 INGOs operated globally. By the early 2000s, the number of INGOs had jumped to about 48,000. During the 1990s and early 2000s, the INGOs and other elements of civil society increased their connectivity by forging alliances with other INGOs, civil society groups, multilateral organizations, and governments. Sophisticated information and communications technologies (ICTs) enabled CSOs to make strategic alliances with one another, disseminate information to a global audience, and rally global support for their causes. These alliances magnified the voices of traditionally marginalized peoples and aided the fundraising efforts of international nonprofit groups. Recently, the Center for Civil Society reported the single largest source of operating funds of the international nonprofits are donations by individuals, foundations, and corporations. Other major revenue sources include government grants, membership fees, and charges for services. Not counted in the official revenue figures for the nonprofits is the monetary value of volunteers' time.

CSOs and INGOs have become involved in many different issues and problems in the global arena. Nearly one-half of all INGOs listed in the authoritative *Global Civil Society 2003* are concerned with economic development, research, or science. Other important categories include social services, law and advocacy, culture, health, education, and the environment. High visibility protests during the late 1990s and early 2000s propelled CSOs and INGOs into the international limelight. A massive CSO presence at the World Trade Organization's (WTO) ministerial conference in Seattle, Washington (1999) jump-started a wave of similar protest around the world. Tens of thousands of demonstrators converged on Seattle to challenge the globalization juggernaut. Protesters also criticized the pro-globalization policies of multilateral institutions including the WTO, World Bank, and the International Monetary Fund (IMF). In Seattle, the coalition of demonstrators expressed concerns about the negative impact of globalization on worker and human rights. Other concerns included environmental decay, unethical corporate behavior, and the global poverty gap. They also condemned the skewed power structure of multilateral institutions that favored the advanced economies over poorer regions. Bolstered by their success in Seattle, CSO protests spread to meetings of the World Bank, IMF, World Economic Forum, and other organizations.

In the early 2000s CSOs embarked on a new strategy to bring attention to global issues and problems—the social forum. A social forum is a mass meeting of CSOs designed to examine global issues, and discuss appropriate policy responses to these issues. The three main types of social forums are the World Social Forum, regional social forum, and thematic social forum. The first World Social Forum was hosted by Porto Alegre, Brazil in 2001. Since this time, four additional World Social Forums have convened; the second and third also hosted by Porto Alegre, and the fourth hosted by Mumbai, India. In 2003, the third World Social Forum held in Porto Alegre attracted 100,000 participants from 156 countries. The 2003 agenda addressed poverty reduction, environmental degradation, and human rights issues. In 2004, the Social Forum held in Mumbai, India, attracted similar numbers of participants. The fifth World Social Forum (2005), again held in Porto Alegre, produced the *Porto Alegre Manifesto*. The *Porto Alegre Manifesto* supported a dozen major initiatives in the realms of economic justice, world peace, and good governance. Between 2002 and 2004 a dozen regional social forums were scheduled in Africa, Asia and the Pacific, Europe, North America, and South America. During this same period of time, eight thematic social forums were held to focus on single topics such as health care, education, women, foreign debt, and human rights. Social forums have successfully mobilized and energized CSOs in recent years, and are likely to play a significant role in global policymaking in the years to come.

Today, multilateral organizations involve CSOs in policy debates and the decision-making process. In 1999, Kofi Annan, secretary-general of the United Nations, set the tone for inclusion by calling INGOs and NGOs "indispensable partners" in policy debates. In recent years, the World Bank, IMF, and WTO have also been more aggressive in seeking the advice and expertise of INGOs and other elements of civil society. For example, the World Bank reported that in 2002 nearly 70 percent of its projects involved CSO participation, more than triple its 1990 percentage. In addition, the World Bank has established a variety of funding mechanisms to provide grants to CSOs. Since the mid-1980s the World Bank has contributed about $4 billion to CSOs in sixty developing countries. CSOs are an effective partner to multilateral organizations. CSOs bring new information and fresh perspectives to policy debates. They assist in identifying people's needs, and in delivering social services, development assistance, and emergency aid. They monitor the operation of government and demand transparency in public policymaking, thus supporting the universal goal of good governance and the rule of law. CSOs give a voice to traditionally marginalized peoples by elevating grassroots concerns to a global stage.

See also **Corporate Social Responsibility; Non-Governmental Organizations.**

Further Reading

Edwards, Michael. *Civil Society*. Malden, MA: Polity Press, 2004.
Kaldor, Mary, Helmut Anheier, and Marlies Glasius. *Global Civil Society 2003*. New York: Oxford University Press, 2003.
Keane, John, and Ian Shapiro, series eds. *Global Civil Society?* New York: Cambridge University Press, 2003.
Van Rooy, Alison. *The Global Legitimacy Game: Civil Society, Globalization and Protest*. New York: Palgrave Macmillan, 2004.
Van Til, Jon. *Growing Civil Society: From Nonprofit Sector to Third Space*. Bloomington, IN: Indiana University Press, 2000.

COMMAND ECONOMY

A command economy is a highly centralized economic system in which the government owns or controls the factors of production. In a command economy, the government answers the basic economic questions of what, how, and for whom to produce. A command economy represents one extreme along a continuum of economic systems, an extreme that represents total government control over economic decision making. A pure market economy, on the other hand, represents the opposite extreme along the economic continuum. In pure market economy, the private sector, rather than the government, answers the basic economic questions. Both the command economy and the market economy are considered economic models because, in reality, neither exists in its pure form. Instead, the world's economies tend to lean toward the command model or market model, but are a mixture of each.

For thousands of years command economies governed the use of resources for many advanced civilizations. In northern Africa, the Old Kingdom in Egypt (2660 BC to 2180 BC) employed a command economy headed by a pharaoh.

The pharaoh owned all land and other precious natural resources. Peasants worked the land and paid taxes to the government. The pharaoh also required peasants to work on public projects such as temples, canals, and pyramids, and to serve in the army, illustrating his control over labor resources.

Over time feudal systems evolved in different world regions. The feudal system embraced command structures in economic decision making. In China, the Chou Dynasty (1122 BC to 256 BC) established a complex feudal economy. Under Chinese feudalism, the emperor owned the land, but entrusted nobles to govern geographic areas within the empire. In exchange for these grants of land a noble owed allegiance and tribute payments to the emperor. Peasants farmed plots of land in exchange for their allegiance and payments to the nobles. For centuries this hierarchical system permitted Chou emperors to maintain peace throughout the sprawling empire, to build magnificent palaces and an economic infrastructure, and to develop other features of an advanced civilization.

In Europe, a similar feudal system took root by the eighth century AD. During the coming centuries, kings granted tracts of land called fiefs to trusted nobles called vassals, in exchange for their loyalty, military service, and tax payments. In theory, the king owned all of the land but in reality, each vassal, called a lord, commanded his own fief. Lords dictated the conditions of life to the peasants, called serfs, who were tied to the land. The command economies in ancient Egypt and China, and in Medieval Europe, severely restricted the individual's economic freedom, but created an orderly process by which society could allocate scarce resources.

In more modern times, communist economies, which closely resemble the command model, reshaped the global economy. The expansion of communist economies, especially during the post–World War II period, brought large regions of Eastern and Central Europe, East Asia, and Central Asia under communist control. In these nations, the Communist Party and legions of central planners dictated the use of society's resources. This type of central planning solidified the economy's command structure. Central planners created five-year plans to coordinate economic activity around the government's goals. At the close of World War II, a strong Soviet presence in Eastern Europe created a ring of satellite nations to buffer the Soviet Union from the Western democracies. Under the watchful eye of Joseph Stalin, the communist governments in the Eastern bloc nations mimicked the command structure of the Soviet economy. State planners in Bulgaria, Czechoslovakia, East Germany, Hungary, Poland, and Romania dictated resource use for the next forty-five years. Meanwhile, in East Asia, the People's Republic of China was born in 1949, the crowning achievement of the communist revolutionary Mao Zedong. During Mao's rule, farmland was collectivized into people's communes. Other factors of production, such as the factories and mines, were also brought under the government's control. Cumbersome Chinese planning bureaucracies, modeled on the equally cumbersome Soviet planning structures, implemented a series of five-year plans during the 1950s, 1960s, and 1970s.

The collapse of communist regimes during the late 1980s and early 1990s was, in large measure, the result of the crumbling command economies in these nations. Command economies rejected private property rights and profit incentives, which, in turn, discouraged essential growth factors such as entrepreneurship, individual initiative, and product innovation. The breakup of the Soviet Union in 1991, the transitioning of twenty-eight countries in Europe and central Asia toward democracy and capitalism, and the gradual introduction of market principles into the Chinese economy ended the reign of command economies in most world regions. Today, remnants of command economies can still be found in Cuba and North Korea.

See also **Basic Economic Questions; Communism; Democratic Socialism; Economic System; Emerging Market Economies; Third World Socialism; Transition Countries.**

Further Reading

Biel, Timothy L. *The Age of Feudalism*. San Diego, CA: Lucent Books, 1994.

Gregory, Paul R., ed. *Behind the Façade of Stalin's Command Economy: Evidence from the Soviet State and Party Archives*. Stanford, CA: Hoover Institution Press, 2001.

Lawrance, Alan. *China under Communism*. New York: Routledge, 1998.

Maisels, Charles K. *Early Civilizations of the Old World: The Formative Histories of Egypt, the Levant, Mesopotamia, India and China*. New York: Routledge, 2001.

Pipes, Richard. *Communism: A History*. New York: Modern Library, 2001.

COMMERCIAL REVOLUTION

The commercial revolution refers to the dramatic increase in international trade, and the underlying forces that supported these commercial relationships, during the late fifteenth century through the eighteenth century. The term "revolution" implies an abrupt change in the economic status quo. Yet, the dramatic changes spawned by the commercial revolution spanned several centuries. The seeds of the commercial revolution were planted as early as the twelfth and thirteenth centuries. This early period was marked by the rise of an urban merchant class, which profited handsomely from foreign trade. Trade brought wealth, power, and prestige to trading cities such as Venice and Florence in Italy, Bruges and Antwerp in Flanders, Lubeck and Hamburg in Germany, and London in England. In the absence of strong national governments, these trading cities were the political and economic hubs of Europe.

The commercial revolution received a boost during the fourteenth and fifteenth centuries when many European towns joined the Hanseatic League. The Hanseatic League was an organization of towns and cities dedicated to mutual protection and profitable trade in items such as grains, timber, precious metals, furs, and cloth. At the height of its power, League membership swelled to about 150 cities. The League supported trade fairs as a means of expanding its growing web of commercial contacts. Predictably, important European trade fairs emerged in existing trading cities, which stretched from London to Novgorod, Russia. For centuries, trade fairs remained an important conduit for international commerce in raw materials, intermediate goods, and finished products.

The Hanseatic League declined during the sixteenth and seventeenth centuries as stronger nation-states and powerful commercial competitors evolved.

The commercial revolution supported aggressive European exploration and conquest of Asia, Africa, and the Americas. From the late 1400s to the 1700s, European nations competed for profitable overseas markets, expanded their colonial empires, and looted established civilizations. The growth of trade with other world regions increased the wealth and power of the commercial class of merchants, sometimes called the mercantile class. The new wealth garnered from international trade enabled the mercantile class to forge strong and mutually beneficial alliances with the budding manufacturing class and, more importantly, with the monarchs. Over time, the mercantile class overwhelmed the fading feudal aristocracy, whose wealth and position was tied to the land. The commercial successes of the mercantile class changed the concept of wealth in much of Europe. Land and estates, which for centuries had measured wealth, was supplanted with specie—gold and silver—that could be gained through trade.

The commercial revolution had a profound impact on the global economy. First, it strengthened the foundations of capitalism including private property rights, profit incentives, competition, and economic freedom. Private property rights refer to people's ability to own and control private assets. During the commercial revolution, individual ownership of financial and real assets encouraged entrepreneurs to invest in new businesses engaged in global commerce. Profit incentives represent the financial motivation for creating a business. During the commercial revolution, profit incentives stimulated business activity and foreign trade. In the process, it also challenged entrenched Catholic Church doctrine, which condemned most types of profits as sinful. Competition occurred within and between trading towns and cities. Later, the playing field expanded to include intense economic rivalries between nations for global markets. Finally, economic freedom expanded the choices available to individuals and firms. The commercial revolution encouraged international trade, which opened the doors of opportunity to aspiring entrepreneurs. Even serfs, who for centuries had been the muscle of the feudal system, gradually left the farms seeking opportunities in the bustling towns and cities.

Second, the commercial revolution supported the rise of financial institutions and the birth of global capital markets. The creation of financial institutions, including banks and stock exchanges, was necessary to carry on the business of trade. The banks that formed during the early stages of the commercial revolution bore little resemblance to modern banks. During the fourteenth and fifteenth centuries, for example, banks were limited to money transfers between merchants and currency conversions. These early banks were typically clustered in well-protected cities in Italy, Germany, Spain, England, the Netherlands, and other countries. Early banks also operated under the watchful eye of the Catholic Church, which forbade charging or receiving interest payments for the use of money. Undaunted, innovative merchants established banks and money exchanges to convert currencies. Merchants also issued letters of credit, which enabled them to purchase goods or settle debts with a written promise of payment. Letters of credit were more convenient than the transport of bulky coins. Letters of credit also reduced the danger of theft on the dangerous highways and seaways of commerce. Banks gradually expanded their financial services during the sixteenth and seventeenth centuries to accept deposits from savers and extend interest-bearing loans to borrowers. The first national banks, such as the Bank of Amsterdam and the Bank of England, were also created to supply long-term credit to support business enterprises.

The commercial revolution sparked the creation of joint-stock companies and formal stock exchanges. A joint-stock company received its start-up capital from the sale of stock, or shares, to investors. The issuance of stock also spread the business risks over a larger number of investors. Investors willingly purchased stocks expecting to earn handsome returns on their investments. Investors' profits were dependent on the financial success of the joint-stock company, however. By the early 1600s most of the great trading nations of Europe had authorized the creation of joint-stock companies, such as the British East India Company (1600), the Dutch East India Company (1602), the French Royal West Indian Company (1664), and the Hudson Bay Company (1670). Stock exchanges, such as the Amsterdam stock exchange, were soon established to facilitate the buying and selling of stocks in joint-stock companies. Economic historians often view the joint-stock company as the birth of the modern corporation. Over time, monarchs gave their heavily regulated joint-stock companies exclusive rights to trade with colonial possessions and other dependent territories, mainly to support the powerful mercantile class and encourage continued inflows of specie into the country.

The commercial revolution spawned an awakening in Europe, an awakening that permitted an outward-looking merchant class to seize economic opportunities available in the global economy. But mercantilist doctrine, which supported government-sponsored monopolies, extensive business regulations, and high trade barriers, also stifled true global integration and interdependence. Later, economists Adam Smith, David Ricardo, and others challenged the mercantilists' worldview, and instigated a new era of economic integration built on free trade.

See also **Global Economy; International Trade; Mercantilism; Mun, Thomas.**

Further Reading

Brenner, Robert. *Merchants and Revolution: Commercial Change, Political Conflict, and London's Overseas Traders, 1550–1653*. New York: Verso, 2003.

Chaudhuri, K. N. *The English East India Company: The Study of an Early Joint Stock Company, 1600–1640*. New York: Routledge, 2000.

Lopez, Robert S. *The Commercial Revolution of the Middle Ages, 950–1350*. New York: Cambridge University Press, 1976.

Wallerstein, Immanuel. *The Modern World-System II: Mercantilism and the Consolidation of the European World-Economy, 1600–1750*. Orlando, FL: Academic Press, 1980.

COMMUNISM

Communism is a type of economic system based on government ownership and control of the factors of production—natural resources, human resources, and capital goods. A communist economy relies on centralized public sector decision making. Thus, central planners within the government answer the basic economic questions of what, how, and for whom to produce. Modern communism is based on the theories of Karl Marx, a German-born philosopher, economist, historian, and revolutionary. The twentieth-century applications and adaptations of Marxist thought, often called Marxism, reshaped the economic landscape of the global economy.

Market-oriented reforms in China increased agricultural output and promoted economic growth in recent decades.

Courtesy of Getty Images: PhotoLink

Communist economies during much of the twentieth century were inward-looking, choosing to isolate themselves from most forms of connectivity in the global economy. For instance, communist confiscations of business firms in Russia, China, Cuba and elsewhere, terminated many economic or financial contacts with outside firms. Government-imposed restrictions on international trade and foreign investment also limited most cross-border flows from noncommunist nations. From 1949 to 1991 the Soviet Union stressed economic cooperation and economic integration only among the COMECON countries. COMECON, the Council for Mutual Economic Assistance, was a type of economic alliance to promote economic, scientific, and technical cooperation among member nations. Its original members included Bulgaria, Czechoslovakia, Hungary, Poland, Romania, and the Soviet Union. Over time, additional nations joined, including Albania (1949–1961), East Germany (1950–1990), Mongolia (1962), Cuba (1972), and Vietnam (1978). As the dominant economic and military partner in this economic alliance, the Soviet Union's inward-looking policies thwarted most outside contacts. COMECON, and the Union of Soviet Socialist Republics, formally disbanded in 1991.

The theoretical underpinnings of modern communism are found in the writings of Karl Marx, the acknowledged founder of communism. Many of the basic principles of modern communism are explained in *The Communist Manifesto* (1848), co-authored by Marx and lifelong friend Friedrich Engels. A more exhaustive treatment of Marxist theory is outlined in Marx's three-volume tome, *Das Kapital*. The first volume of *Das Kapital* was published in 1867. The final two volumes were published in 1883, shortly after Marx's death. During the twentieth century the writings of Marx fueled the fires of revolution in Russia, China, Cuba, and elsewhere. During much of the twentieth century, communism posed a formidable challenge to capitalism in the global economy.

Marxism is built on several core principles, including theory of surplus value, dialectical materialism, and the inevitability of communism. First, surplus value is the gap between the monetary value of the worker's output and the monetary value of the worker's wage. In Marx's view, the capitalists, who owned the factories and other businesses, confiscated this surplus value to enrich themselves. The common workers were doomed to lives of poverty. Marx's second principle, dialectical materialism, explains how history progresses from one stage to the next. Marx believed that all history was a history of class struggle between exploited and exploiter classes. He predicted that the injustices during the capitalist stage would eventually boil over into revolution, pitting the proletariat, or propertyless laboring class, against the bourgeoisie, or capitalist owners of society's wealth. The proletariat's victory would create a new stage in humankind's evolutionary history, called socialism. Third, the inevitability of communism, theorized that perfect communism was the natural culmination of past class conflicts. Marx believed that, under socialism, classes would be eliminated through the abolition of all private property, private profits, and other capitalist baggage. The gradual perfection of socialism would then lead to the ultimate goal—communism. Under communism people would be willing to work for the common good and to distribute society's output according to people's need. The government, itself viewed as an instrument of oppression, would eventually "wither away" during the transition.

The Soviet Union, People's Republic of China, Cuba, and other countries adapted communism to support revolutions and to organize economic activity during the twentieth century. The first communist government was formed in Russia. Russian revolutionaries, under the leadership of Vladimir I. Lenin and Leon Trotsky, brought communism to Russia in 1917. The Bolsheviks, one branch of the Russian communist movement, had long favored violent revolution as a means of creating a communist state in Russia. As a tight-knit band of professional revolutionaries, the Bolsheviks were also quick to seize opportunities. In the fall of 1917, Lenin and Trotsky pounced on the teetering Russian provisional government, a government that had just been formed in the spring of that year. The provisional government was unable to bring victory against Germany in World War I, or quell the chaos caused by wartime shortages of food and other essential goods. A disciplined Bolshevik assault on the weakened provisional government put the Bolsheviks in the driver's seat with Lenin at the wheel. Communism had arrived, but with a Leninist twist. While Lenin accepted the traditional Marxist proposition that the urban proletariat would be in the vanguard of the revolution, he also stressed the importance of the peasantry in transforming the agricultural sector along communist lines. Thus, Marx's vision of revolution by an urban proletariat was adapted to include a revolutionary rural peasantry.

The Russian brand of communism vacillated between the theoretical and the practical during the 1920s. Under war communism (1917–1921), Russia's resources were mobilized to win a fierce civil war. During this period, the communists expropriated domestic and foreign-owned banks, manufacturers, mines, railroads, and other industries. Crops were confiscated. Forced labor was instituted. By the close of the civil war Russia's economy was in shambles. To jump-start economic activity during the post-war years, Lenin immediately introduced the New Economic Policy (NEP) in 1921, a program of small-scale private enterprise. Under the NEP, the government permitted peasants to own and farm private plots of land, and to sell their surpluses—the amount left over after an assigned quota had been delivered to the government—on the open market. The positive results of the NEP were felt almost immediately. Production of most goods and services rose to pre-war levels, and the economy stabilized under the watchful eye of the Bolshevik leadership, the Red Army, and the Cheka (secret police).

Joseph Stalin jockeyed for power after Lenin's death in 1924. Under Stalin's tyrannical rule from 1927 to 1953, the Soviet economy was redesigned to stamp out the remnants of private enterprise. He created a command economy built on a foundation of public ownership of the means of production and central planning. Entire villages were absorbed into massive state-owned farms. Millions of rich peasants, or kulaks, were slaughtered, many dying of famine or disease in the countryside or in Siberian slave labor camps. Smaller industries were again expropriated. Stalin also introduced the five-year plan to the Soviet economy. Five-year plans, which began in 1928, established priorities for national production and set specific production targets, called production quotas, for state-owned industries. Gosplan, the state planning agency, created and implemented the five-year plans. The concept of centralized decision making was transplanted by the Soviet Union into the communist-occupied countries of Eastern Europe after World War II. These occupied countries, called the Eastern bloc, included Bulgaria, Czechoslovakia, East Germany, Hungary, Poland, and Romania.

The Soviet economy began to unravel by the late 1960s and 1970s. By the mid-1980s, the Soviet economy was in crisis. Premier Mikhail Gorbachev attempted to rescue the faltering economy with a series of economic and political reforms. Economic reforms were packaged under the banner of perestroika. Perestroika restructured the Soviet economy along more market-oriented lines to promote economic growth and modernization. Under perestroika, limited private enterprise was encouraged, many wage and price controls were lifted, subsidies to state-owned enterprises (SOEs) were reduced, commercial contacts in the global economy were expanded, and individual plant managers were empowered to make many production decisions. Gorbachev also introduced national campaigns to reduce corruption, alcoholism, and other drags on the fragile economy. Political reforms, under the heading of glasnost, were also instituted to support a more open political process and individual freedoms.

The inherent weaknesses of the communist system overwhelmed the Soviet Union. Severely limiting the effectiveness of Gorbachev's reforms were bloated and corrupt government bureaucracies, obsolete capital goods, low worker productivity, weak incentives, and the lack of entrepreneurial skills and business expertise. International stresses also weakened the faltering Soviet economy. Government coffers were drained by the unsuccessful Soviet invasion of Afghanistan from 1980 to 1989, and by an ongoing arms race with the United States. Festering resentments by people in certain Soviet republics and in the Soviet-occupied Eastern bloc nations also boiled over into the streets. By 1991, the Baltic republics of Lithuania, Latvia, and Estonia had declared their independence from the Soviet Union. Poland, under the leadership of Lech Walesa and the Solidarity Movement, openly challenged the communists' monopoly on political power in the Eastern bloc. By the early 1990s, communism in the Soviet Union and Eastern Europe had collapsed. The Soviet Union was formally dissolved on December 26, 1991, and the fifteen former Soviet "republics" became independent countries soon thereafter.

Communism came to China in 1949, the result of decades of armed struggle between the Chinese Communist Party (CCP), headed by Mao Zedong, and the Kuomintang Party (KMT), headed by Chiang Kai-shek. During the bloody Chinese civil war, Mao skillfully built alliances, especially with the peasantry. Mao promised land reform to the peasants, an attractive pledge in a country where large landlords dominated the agricultural sector and dictated the conditions of life for millions of tenant farmers. In 1949 the KMT or Nationalists, weakened by corruption, military defeats, and sagging popular support, fled to the island of Taiwan. Chiang Kai-shek established a separate Chinese government on Taiwan, the Republic of China. Meanwhile, on the Chinese mainland, Mao and the CCP triumphantly established the People's Republic of China in October 1949.

Chinese communism, often called Maoism, wavered between the pragmatic and the dogmatic from 1949 to Mao's death in 1976. Under Maoism, the CCP held a monopoly on political power, and permitted no opposition to policies emanating from Beijing, the nation's capital. Under its "people's democratic dictatorship," the CCP controlled the government and dictated China's economic course. The path toward communism was pitted with unrealistic "leaps" and painful retrenchments throughout the 1950s, 1960s, and 1970s, however. Unrealistic economic goals, faulty five-year plans, and widespread resistance to change, disrupted production in agriculture, industry, and commerce.

Collectivization was the centerpiece of the government's agricultural policy from the 1950s to 1970s. The first step in the collectivization process was to rid the countryside of rich landlords and to redistribute land to the peasants in small private plots. This goal was achieved between 1949 and 1952. The second step was to introduce cooperative enterprise into the countryside. In 1953, small "collective farms" were created by government decree. The land on these collectives was still privately owned, but worked by several families called mutual-aid teams. Soon, larger "cooperatives" were formed, with land, tools, draft animals, and other possessions owned by the cooperative enterprise rather than by individual peasants. Finally, in 1958, the "people's communes" were introduced, marking a radical leap toward communism. Almost overnight over 100 million households were absorbed into people's communes. Now, the CCP leadership in each commune dictated the allocation of resources, including labor, to build the region's infrastructure, work the farms, and attend to other business activity in industry and commerce. Communes also controlled education and law enforcement, and administered punishments for counterrevolutionary activity or dissent. All private property and private incentives were banned.

The negative reaction to the communes in the countryside was swift. Some peasants refused to plant or harvest crops without an incentive system, while others sabotaged farms and other businesses, destroyed their herds, or otherwise disrupted production. Widespread opposition by the peasants, and a serious drought, reduced crop yields. Faced with the specter of famine, the government restored limited incentives, including small private plots of land, to the peasantry from 1959 to 1961. The functioning of the commune system, with its limited and uncertain incentive system, fluctuated greatly during the 1960s and 1970s. Selective implementation of government policies by local CCP officials, the economic chaos caused by the Great Proletariat Cultural Revolution during the 1960s and early 1970s, and internal power struggles, added to the confused state of Chinese agriculture and industry during the period.

Reform in China's industrial sector followed a similar course during the Maoist era. The 1950s witnessed the systematic dismantling of private enterprise, and the rapid rise of state-owned enterprises (SOEs). To coordinate the government's expropriation of private firms in industry and commerce, China embarked on its first five-year plan in 1953. By the end of this five-year plan in 1957, virtually all of the country's industrial and commercial firms were in the government's hands. Buoyed by its success in reigning in privately owned firms, the government's second five-year plan (1958–1962) promised a Great Leap Forward to double the nation's industrial production. Under this plan, peasants in the people's communes were expected to contribute to China's rapid industrialization by constructing and operating "backyard furnaces" to increase China's production of steel and other heavy industrial products.

Inadequate capital goods, the lack of technical expertise, and nonexistent private incentives transformed the "great leap" into an economic freefall. By the early 1960s, the government was forced to retrench in the industrial sector, just as it had already done in agriculture. The crippled Chinese economy was given another negative jolt by the excesses of the Great Proletarian Cultural Revolution in the 1960s and 1970s. The Cultural Revolution was meant to be a purification campaign to identify and punish counterrevolutionaries. Youthful militants, called the Red Guard, purged scientists, engineers, party officials, and other well-educated professionals to stamp out lingering capitalist ideas among China's elite. These purges destroyed important elements of China's human capital, however, a tragedy that rippled through China's already stumbling economy. After Mao's death in 1976, reform-minded leadership began a series of cautious, methodical experiments in free-market, incentive-based enterprises—China's first steps toward a market-oriented economy.

Communism came to Cuba in 1959 through revolution. Under the leadership of Fidel Castro, Cuba's dictatorship was toppled and the Republic of Cuba was established. Castro instituted a series of socialist reforms, including the expropriation of private enterprises and the elimination of dissent. He also introduced Soviet style central planning to dictate the use of Cuba's resources. In response to Castro's aggressive seizure of private assets, including American-owned plantations and other businesses, the United States slapped a total embargo on the Cuba in the early 1960s. This embargo halted U.S. trade, foreign investment, and other economic ties with Cuba. Castro turned to the Soviet Union for economic and military assistance, which the USSR generously supplied to its new friend in the Western Hemisphere.

Cuba instituted economic reforms during the 1990s, particularly after the collapse of its most important benefactor, the Soviet Union, in 1991. In 1993, the Castro dictatorship dismantled its cumbersome central planning agency, the Central Planning Board, in favor of more specialized planning ministries. This reshuffling within government was designed to promote tourism, industrial development, agricultural development, foreign direct investment, and other economic activity. During the 1990s Castro also legalized many small-scale private enterprises, mainly in the services-producing sector. In agriculture, some large state-owned farms were divided into smaller producer cooperatives. These cooperatives were required to sell a portion of their output to the state for a set price, but were encouraged to sell the remainder for profit in farmers' markets. The Cuban government also courted foreign investment and legalized the use of the U.S. dollar in most types of transactions.

By the early 2000s, the Castro regime had reversed course and abandoned some of the market reforms of the 1990s. The government reasserted its control over state-owned enterprises and cracked down on fledgling private sector business activity. In November 2004, Castro banned the use of U.S. dollars in Cuba and required citizens to convert dollars into pesos. Today, the vast majority of Cuba's human, capital, and natural resources remain firmly under the government's thumb. In addition, the communists retain a monopoly on political power, ruthlessly suppressing dissenting viewpoints.

See also **Capitalism; Command Economy; Democratic Socialism; Economic System; Emerging Market Economies; Marx, Karl H.; Third World Socialism; Transition Countries.**

Further Reading

Burki, Shahid J., and Danile P. Erikson, eds. *Transforming Socialist Economies: Lessons for Cuba and Beyond*. New York: Palgrave Macmillan, 2005.

Busky, Donald. *From Utopian Socialism to the Rise and Fall of the Soviet Union: Communism in History and Theory*. Westport, CT: Praeger, 2002.

Ebenstein, William, Edwin Fogelman, and Alan O. Ebenstein. *Today's ISMS: Socialism, Capitalism, Fascism, Communism, and Libertarianism*. 11th ed. Paramus, NJ: Prentice Hall, 1999.

Marx, Karl, and Friedrich Engels. *The Communist Manifesto*. New York: Washington Square Press, 1964.

Pipes, Richard. *Communism: A History*. New York: Modern Library, 2001.

Schwartz, Benjamin, John K. Fairbanks, and Conrad Brandt. *A Documentary History of Chinese Communism*. New York: Routledge, 2004.

COMPARATIVE ADVANTAGE

A comparative advantage exists when a nation or economic region is able to produce a product at a lower opportunity cost compared to another nation or region. Key to understanding comparative advantage is that mutually beneficial trade between two nations can take place even if one country enjoys an absolute advantage in the production of both traded products.

Sophisticated capital resources, such as a robotized assembly plant, influence a country's comparative advantage.
Courtesy of CORBIS

The theory of comparative advantage has been the single most influential justification for free trade since the early 1800s. Robert Torrens introduced the theory of comparative advantage in his *Essay on the External Corn Trade* (1815). But it was David Ricardo who popularized the theory in his book, *The Principles of Political Economy and Taxation* (1817). The theory of comparative advantage is a natural complement to the earlier theory of absolute advantage, which Adam Smith defended in his famous *An Inquiry into the Nature and Causes of the Wealth of Nations* (1776). Smith explained that trade between two nations was mutually beneficial when one nation was superior in the production of one good, and a second nation was superior in the production of a different good. Smith argued that each nation should specialize in its area of superiority, and then trade its surpluses with the other nation. Torrens and Ricardo expanded on the theory of absolute advantage by arguing that specialization and trade should occur even if one nation is superior in the production of both traded products.

There are different ways to measure one country's comparative advantage over a second country. One way is to compare different rates of output generated by the two countries. Using the hypothetical data shown in Table 20, the United States has an absolute advantage in the production of both flashlights and disposable cameras over Mexico. That is, using the same resources, the United States is able to produce 100 flashlights (compared to just fifty flashlights in Mexico), or 100 disposable cameras (compared to just twenty in Mexico). It is important to remember that the United States is able to produce 100 flashlights or 100 disposable cameras—but not both at the same time. Similarly, Mexico is able to produce fifty flashlights or twenty disposable cameras,

TABLE 20 Comparative Advantage: Output of Flashlights and Cameras

	United States	Mexico	United States Advantage
Flashlights	100	50	2:1
Cameras	100	20	5:1

but not both at the same time. This either-or situation stems from the fact that there are fixed resources. Thus, if the United States produces 100 flashlights, zero disposable cameras are produced. If Mexico produces fifty flashlights, zero disposable cameras are produced. For simplicity's sake, in most measurements of comparative advantage, it is assumed that labor is the sole cost of production.

Despite the U.S. advantage in both products, it is still mutually beneficial for each nation to specialize in the production of the product that it produces "most best." That is, each country should produce the product in which it has the greatest advantage, or at least the lesser disadvantage. Table 20 shows that the United States is able to produce twice as many flashlights as Mexico, a two-to-one advantage; and five times as many disposable cameras as Mexico, a five-to-one advantage. Hence, from an economic perspective, the United States should specialize in the production of disposable cameras, where it enjoys the greatest advantage, and Mexico should specialize in the production of flashlights, where it has the lesser disadvantage. In reality, both countries would likely produce some flashlights and cameras, but would tend to devote more resources to products in which they enjoyed a comparative advantage.

Another way to illustrate the theory of comparative advantage is to compare the relative input costs, measured in labor hours, needed to produce two goods from different countries. This second measurement is concerned with the amount of an input (labor hours) needed to produce a good, rather than with the quantity of output generated by each nation. Table 21 shows the amount of labor it would take to produce a single unit of cocoa and soybeans in Ghana and Sierra Leone. This hypothetical example shows that Ghana has an absolute advantage in both cocoa and soybean production. In Ghana, one unit of cocoa can be produced using just two hours of labor, compared to four hours of labor in Sierra Leone. Similarly, Ghana produces one unit of soybeans in two hours, while Sierra Leone requires ten hours of labor to produce the same quantity.

While the labor inputs required in the production of cocoa and soybeans favors Ghana, Ghana enjoys the greatest advantage over Sierra Leone in the production of soybeans. That is, Ghana is five times as efficient as Sierra Leone as measured in labor hours needed to produce soybeans. According to the theory of comparative advantage, Ghana should specialize in the production of soybeans. Sierra Leone, on the other hand, has its least disadvantage in the production of cocoa, and, thus, should specialize in cocoa.

TABLE 21 Comparative Advantage: Labor Inputs in the Production of Cocoa and Soybeans

	1 Unit of Cocoa	1 Unit of Soybeans
Ghana	2 hours of labor	2 hours of labor
Sierra Leone	4 hours of labor	10 hours of labor

The theory of comparative advantage supports national and regional specialization. Specialization promotes the most efficient utilization of the world's scarce resources and generates maximum global output. Yet there are certain assumptions that complicate the application of comparative advantage in the global trading system. First, the theory assumes that resources within nations are easily transferable from one industry to a second industry. For example, if Ghana specializes in the production of soybeans, it is assumed that the workers, capital goods, and land previously used in cocoa production are effortlessly transferred to soybean production. Second, transportation costs are not accounted for in the theory of comparative advantage. Production efficiency might be maximized through specialization, but the added costs of transporting raw materials, intermediate goods, or finished products may reduce or eliminate any cost advantage. Third, a variety of impediments to international trade, such as tariffs or import quotas, may upset the cross-border exchanges of goods and services. Because trade barriers restrict exports, stockpiles of surplus commodities could rot in warehouses or storage bins. Fourth, comparative advantage does not consider the terms of trade for goods exchanged between nations. If specialization creates an oversupply of certain goods, such as coffee or sugar, the value of these commodities declines relative to other goods such as computers or software. Arriving at fair terms of trade has been a contentious issue in the global economy in recent decades and has contributed to North-South tensions. Fifth, comparative advantage discourages diversification in an economy. In extreme cases, regional specialization could result in the creation of a "one-crop economy," which places the nation at the mercy of sudden global shifts in demand or catastrophic losses in supply through drought, infestation, or other blight.

See also **Absolute Advantage; International Trade; Ricardo, David; Smith, Adam; Terms of Trade.** ***See also in Volume 2,*** **Document 19.**

Further Reading

Cline, William R. *Trade Policy and Global Poverty*. Washington, DC: Institute for International Economics, 2004.

Hall, Peter A., and David W. Soskice. *Varieties of Capitalism: The Institutional Foundations of Comparative Advantage*. New York: Oxford University Press, 2001.

Johansson, B., and Charlie Karlsson. *Regional Policies and Comparative Advantage*. Northampton, MA: Edward Elgar Publishers, 2002.

Keuschnigg, Mirela. *Comparative Advantage in International Trade: Theory and Evidence*. New York: Springer-Verlag Telos, 1999.

Ricardo, David. *The Principles of Political Economy and Taxation*. New York: E. P. Dutton & Company, 1911.

COMPETITIVENESS

Competitiveness refers to the factors that influence economic performance in a nation's macroeconomy and microeconomy. A nation's macroeconomic performance deals with growth and stability in the overall economy. Thus, competitiveness indicators in the macroeconomy focus on changes in the gross domestic product (GDP), price levels, and employment. Countries that are highly competitive on the macroeconomic level tend to have solid private and public sector economic institutions that support sustained economic growth, price stability, and full employment. Countries that are less competitive lack the resources and institutions to meet their macroeconomic goals. A nation's microeconomic performance deals with the productivity of business enterprises and the efficient allocation of resources. Thus, competitiveness indicators in the microeconomy deal with the quality of the labor force, capital goods, research and development (R&D), entrepreneurial skills, and infrastructure. Highly competitive countries invest heavily in human and real capital, information and communications technologies (ITCs), innovation and entrepreneurship, and infrastructure to create a hospitable business environment. Less competitive economies make fewer investments in their productive resources, social and physical infrastructure, and other institutions. The competitiveness gap between the more competitive economies and the less competitive economies is one of the main causes of the growing income gap between the rich and poor nations of the global economy.

There are a number of ways to measure the "competitiveness of nations." One of the most recognized competitiveness rankings appears in the *IMD World Competitiveness Yearbook* (*WCY*), an annual publication of the International Institute for Management Development (IMD). The IMD is a nonprofit foundation that specializes in manager training to improve companies' competitiveness in global markets. The IMD collects economic data on sixty of the world's leading economies, and evaluates each economy's performance based on stated criteria. In the *IMD World Competitiveness Yearbook 2004*, 323 competitiveness criteria were used to determine countries' competitiveness ranking. The four main categories of criteria included economic performance, government efficiency, business efficiency, and infrastructure. The first category, economic performance, includes the economy's size and growth, international trade and investment, employment picture, and price stability. The second category, government efficiency, includes responsible macroeconomic policies, a sound central bank, and a competent legal system capable of maintaining an open and competitive business environment. The third category, business efficiency, includes high productivity, skilled labor, sound capital markets, innovative management, and pro-business social values. The fourth category, infrastructure, is broadly defined to include the nation's basic infrastructure, such as roads, bridges, airports, and seaports; sophisticated technological and scientific infrastructures; and a social infrastructure to advance education and health care. According to the IMD's rankings, the United States is the world's most competitive country, as shown in Table 22.

Another highly regarded ranking of global competitiveness is the *Global Competitiveness Report*, an annual publication of the World Economic Forum (WEF). The WEF is a nonprofit foundation dedicated to improving the state of the world through constructive dialogue among government, business, and academic leaders. WEF collects economic data from over 100 countries. This data is used to assess the competitiveness of nations in two broad areas: growth competitiveness and business competitiveness. The first category, growth competitiveness, assesses the quality of each nation's macroeconomic environment, public institutions, and technological infrastructure. A separate index is used to rank economies on each of these subsets. In the *Global Competitiveness Report 2004–2005*, Finland ranked first and the United States second in the growth competitiveness index. The second category, business competitiveness, evaluates the microeconomic factors that contribute to high productivity and sustainable growth. Key microeconomic categories include the sophistication of business management techniques and company strategies, and the quality of the national business environment under which firms compete. The WEF's 2004–2005 *Report* ranked the United States first and Finland second in business competitiveness. The advanced economies dominated the top twenty positions in both indexes, claiming eighteen of the top twenty spots in the growth competitiveness index, and all twenty top spots in the business competitiveness index. Table 23 shows the top five and the bottom five nations in each index.

TABLE 22 **World Competitiveness Scoreboard, 2004**

Top Five Countries		Bottom Five Countries	
Rank	Country	Rank	Country
1	United States	56	Mexico
2	Singapore	57	Poland
3	Canada	58	Indonesia
4	Australia	59	Argentina
5	Iceland	60	Venezuela

Source: International Institute for Management Development, *IMD World Competitiveness Yearbook 2004*, 5.

In today's global economy, discussions about nations' competitiveness are most often linked to their ability to fully participate in the global trading system. Since the 1990s, the "trade not aid" theme has represented mainstream thought in development economics. Recently, the United Nations Conference on Trade and Development (UNCTAD) identified a series of conditions necessary for improved trade competitiveness for the world's poorer nations. First, UNCTAD stressed the need for an adequate transportation and communications infrastructure. Included in this category is the need for roads and highways, seaports and airports, railways, telecommunications systems, and information and communications technologies (ICTs). ICTs are necessary in all nations' connectivity and are particularly crucial to the landlocked countries. Second, UNCTAD identified a need for trade finance. Trade finance refers to the ability to obtain the necessary financial capital to produce a product prior to its sale. Trade finance can be obtained through traditional channels, such as bank loans, or through loans from regional development banks or

TABLE 23 **Growth Competitiveness and Business Competitiveness Indexes, 2004**

Growth Competitiveness Index			
Top Five Countries		Bottom Five Countries	
1	Finland	100	Paraguay
2	United States	101	Ethiopia
3	Sweden	102	Bangladesh
4	Chinese Taipei	103	Angola
5	Denmark	104	Chad
Business Competitiveness Index			
Top Five Countries		Bottom Five Countries	
1	United States	99	Ethiopia
2	Finland	100	Nicaragua
3	Germany	101	Bolivia
4	Sweden	102	Chad
5	Switzerland	103	Angola

Source: World Economic Forum, *Global Competitiveness Report 2004–2005*, 13, 18.

national governments. Prepayments by buyers is yet another option. Third, UNCTAD noted that nations must strive to keep workers' wage increases in line with increases in worker productivity. When wage rates outpace productivity gains, the higher wages tend to push price levels higher. Higher priced goods are less attractive in global markets. Fourth, UNCTAD stresses the need for nations to maintain a stable currency and stable exchange rates. Rapid swings in exchange rates destabilize trade relations among nations. Currency appreciation increases the price of a nation's exports in foreign markets and thus discourages exports. Currency depreciation, on the other hand, may temporarily decrease the price of a nation's exports in foreign markets, but may also lead to competitive devaluations by other exporting nations. UNCTAD concludes that raising productivity is the key to raising the competitiveness of nations. Higher productivity is particularly important as the poorer nations transition from labor-intensive agricultural economies to more capital-intensive industrial and service economies.

A country's competitiveness bears directly on its prospects for sustainable economic growth and development. In today's global economy, the most competitive economies are the rich nations, well positioned to reap the benefits of international trade, foreign direct investment (FDI), and other advantages of global connectivity. As a result, people in the advanced economies continue to enjoy high living standards and a high quality of life. Noncompetitive economies are generally the poorest nations, wracked by poverty and excluded from most of globalization's benefits. Today multilateral institutions work to improve the competitiveness of poorer nations as a means toward the world's primary development goal—poverty reduction. The World Bank, International Monetary Fund, and regional development banks provide a variety of loans, grants, and technical assistance to developing and transition economies to build and maintain necessary economic infrastructure and institutions for development. The World Trade Organization (WTO) promotes free trade and inclusion of economies in the global trading system. Improving competitiveness enables nations to join in globalization's feast.

See also **Advanced Economies; Developing Countries; Economic Growth; International Trade; Sustainable Economic Development; World Economic Forum.** ***See also in Volume 2*, Documents 10, 13, 14, 15, 16.**

Further Reading

Dutta, Soumitra, Bruno Lanvin, and Fiona Paua. *The Global Information Technology Report 2003–2004: Towards an Equitable Information Society*. New York: Oxford University Press, 2004.

Garelli, Stephanie. *IMD World Competitiveness Yearbook 2004*. Lausanne, Switzerland: International Institute for Management Development, 2004.

Porter, Michael E., Klaus Schwab, Xavier Sala-I-Martin, and Augusto Lopez-Claros. *The Global Competitiveness Report 2004–2005*. New York: Palgrave Macmillan, 2004.

United Nations Conference on Trade and Development. *Trade and Development Report, 2004*. New York: United Nations, 2004.

World Bank. *Doing Business in 2005: Obstacles to Growth*. Washington, DC: World Bank Publications, 2004.

CONSUMERS INTERNATIONAL

Consumers International (CI) is an independent, nonprofit federation of consumer groups and non-governmental organizations (NGOs). CI is dedicated to protecting and promoting consumers' interests in the global economy. Originally called the International Organization of Consumers Unions, CI was founded in 1960 to unify the voices of consumers worldwide. By the early 2000s, CI membership included over 250 organizations spread across 115 countries.

CI's highest decision-making body is the General Assembly, which meets once every three years at its World Congress. The General Assembly represents CI's full members and establishes the federation's policies and priorities for the coming years. The General Assembly also elects a president and a council to coordinate the activities of CI. Many responsibilities are delegated to CI's staff of seventy individuals, all of whom are under the direction of a director-general. CI's headquarters is located in London, United Kingdom. Its three regional offices are located in Santiago, Chile; Kuala Lumpur, Malaysia; and Harare, Zimbabwe.

CI visibility and influence have expanded over time. Today, it is a powerful voice, lobbying for consumer reforms in national economies and in the dynamic global economy. In its *Consumers International Annual Report 2003,* CI states that the "challenge is to consider what market economies can do for consumers, and what they cannot do, and what governments and consumer organizations must do to provide the necessary countervailing power." Countervailing power, in this context, refers to the ability of governments and consumer groups to overcome the enormous economic and political power of transnational corporations (TNCs) and other power brokers in the global economy. CI, in cooperation with the United Nations and numerous non-governmental organizations, has taken the lead in the global consumer movement. It has endeavored to form consumer organizations to meet growing consumer needs in the poorer world regions. CI also sponsors high-profile annual events such as World Consumer Rights Day, which has been held on March 15 since 1983. In 2005, this global consumer celebration focused on the dangers of genetically modified organisms in crops and foods and the right to a safe food supply.

Over the past decade CI championed a variety of global consumer concerns, many of which were connected with the changing global economy. By the early 2000s, CI's efforts were focused mainly on the issues of food safety, the availability of basic services, health care, environmental protection, consumer education, sustainable consumption, and corporate social responsibility. In recent years CI has also channeled its consumer protection efforts to meet the special needs of different world regions. In the early 2000s, for example, CI stressed the availability of food and clean water in Africa; fairer trade practices in the Americas; and farmers' rights, ownership of traditional knowledge, and intellectual property rights in Asia and the Pacific region.

CI assists member organizations reform national consumer policies. It also participates in global decision making. It is active in deliberations within the United Nations system and the World Trade Organization (WTO), and in

TABLE 24 **Consumers International Program Spending, 2003**

Categories of CI Spending	Percent of Total Spending
Food programs, biotechnology	33
International networking, World Congress	24
Trade and economics programs	17
Utilities, including clean water projects	9
Sustainable consumption	6
Others (governance, capacity building, etc.)	11

Source: Consumers International, *Consumers International Annual Report 2003*, 29–30.

regional policy forums of the Economic Community of West African States (ECOWAS), the Organization for Economic Development and Co-operation (OECD), and the Association of Southeast Asian Nations (ASEAN). CI helped devise, and currently supports, the implementation of the United Nations Guidelines for Consumer Protection, originally established in 1985. These UN guidelines expanded on the four consumer rights named in President John F. Kennedy's historic Consumer Bill of Rights for Americans more than a score of years earlier. President Kennedy's March 15, 1962, statement included the right to product safety, the right to be informed, the right to choose, and the right to be heard. The UN guidelines added the right to redress, the right to consumer education, the right to a healthy environment, and the right to the satisfaction of basic needs. In 1999 sustainable consumption was added to the UN guidelines. More recently, at its seventeenth World Conference in 2003, CI examined a variety of twenty-first-century issues such as the growth of e-commerce, cross-border retailing, genetically modified foods, and corporate power in the global economy.

Membership fees and project grants fund most of CI's activities and programs. In 2003, CI's income totaled $5.7 million. The biggest contributors were government development agencies (44.5 percent of CI's total income), followed by the European Union (25 percent), and international institutions (8.5 percent). The remaining 22 percent of CI's income came from non-governmental organizations (NGOs), private foundations, and others. The income generated from membership fees, about $1.9 million, was spent on the general operations of CI—salaries, office expenses, travel, and publications. About three-quarters of the $3.8 million in project funds was spent on food programs, international networking, and trade and economics, as shown in Table 24.

See also **Advertising; Sustainable Consumption.** ***See also in Volume 2,*** **Documents 45, 46, 47, 48, 49.**

Further Reading

Consumers International. *Consumer Charter for Trade: Consumers Internationals' Recommendations for Cancun and the Future of the Doha Development Agenda*. London: Author, 2003.

———. *The Consumer Guide to Competition: A Practical Handbook*. London: CI, 2003.

———. *Consumers International Annual Report 2003*. London: Author, 2004.

———. *Consumers International 17th World Congress*. London: Author, 2003.

Coskun, Samli. *International Consumer Behavior*. Westport, CT: Quorum Books, 1995.

Stearns, Peter N. *Consumerism in World History: The Global Transformation of Desire*. New York: Routledge, 2001.

CORPORATE SOCIAL RESPONSIBILITY

Corporate social responsibility refers to the responsibilities that corporations, including transnational corporations (TNCs), have to workers and their families, consumers, investors, host governments, and indigenous peoples. At the heart of corporate social responsibility (CSR) is the understanding that harmonious relations among businesses, workers, governments, and other stakeholders are in everyone's best interests. Implied in the concept of CSR is that governments in advanced and developing countries create a positive business environment in which companies, including TNCs, can profitably operate. Good governance, the provision of a sound infrastructure, and macroeconomic stability, help cement the working relationship between TNCs and the host country.

Strip mining degrades local ecosystems and is a type of unsustainable production.
Courtesy of Getty Images: Annie Reynolds/PhotoLink

The concept of CSR has changed over time. During the early years of the Industrial Revolution in Europe and the United States, major corporations had a narrow view of CSR. That is, corporations existed to earn profits, a portion of which were reinvested in the firm and the remainder distributed in the form of dividends to the company's stockholders. During the twentieth century, however, corporations were obliged to expand their view of good corporate citizenship. In part the concept of CSR was broadened to accommodate a flurry of new laws and regulations designed to protect workers, consumers, investors, and the environment. The growth of civil society organizations (CSOs), including international nongovernmental organizations (INGOs), also caused corporations to re-examine their internal policies and act in more socially responsible ways. By the 1970s and 1980s corporations and a number of international organizations devised voluntary "codes" to guide business conduct in domestic and global markets. Over time, these codes defined what it meant to be a socially responsible corporation.

One type of code is the "corporate code of conduct." A corporate code of conduct is written and implemented by individual corporations. Under a corporate code of conduct, the firm establishes standards to govern its treatment of workers, its dealings with indigenous peoples, and its use of the natural environment. Nearly all corporations today have adopted a corporate code of conduct. Nike, for example, strengthened its code of conduct after the firm suffered the ill effects of a global consumer boycott in the late 1990s. Nike responded to criticisms of sweatshop working conditions in the overseas plants of its subcontractors by pledging to strictly enforce its code. The Nike code promises a safe and healthy workplace, fair compensation, freedom of association, and limits on required work hours.

A second type of code is the "code of conduct for multinationals." Individuals or organizations outside of the corporate structure devise this type of code. The standards of behavior outlined in these codes resemble the "corporate codes" penned by the corporations themselves. One of the most recognized codes is the Guidelines for Multinational Enterprises, which was produced by the Organization for Economic Cooperation and Development (OECD). Thirty-seven governments endorsed this code, including the thirty OECD countries and seven non-OECD countries. Its recommendations represent best practice for companies in the global economy. For example, the Guidelines oppose business practices that result in environmental degradation, child and forced labor, workplace discrimination, and bribery and other forms of corruption. The Guidelines support human rights, transparency, honesty in advertising and marketing, consumer safety and privacy, technology transfers, functional worker associations, and respect for local laws and cultures. The Guidelines are widely supported by businesses and labor groups.

Other important corporate codes have surfaced in the global economy. The Tripartite Declaration of Principles Concerning Multinational Enterprises and Social Policy, a document produced by the International Labor Organization (ILO), stresses partnerships among businesses, labor, and government. Key principles in this Declaration are the promotion of human rights and sustainable development; full employment in a secure and nondiscriminatory environment; human capital development for workers and management; workplace reforms, including improved wages and benefits, working conditions, and abolition of child labor; and freedom of association, including the right to form unions, bargain collectively, and resolve disputes with management.

The United Nations' Global Compact, which was introduced in 1999 by UN secretary-general Kofi Annan, identified nine core principles to promote CSR. Since this time 1,200 companies have signed the Compact. The first category of principles, human rights, asks corporations to respect human rights and avoid any complicity in business activity that involves human rights abuses. The second category, labor rights, supports workers' right to unionize, and calls for the abolition of compulsory labor, child labor, and workplace discrimination. The third category, environmental protection, calls on business to use the natural environment wisely and to develop and employ environmentally friendly technologies. In 2004 a tenth principle, anti-corruption, was added to the original list. In 1999, the Reverend Leon H. Sullivan introduced the Global Sullivan Principles of Corporate Social Responsibility. This document promoted human rights, equal opportunity, freedom of association, fair pay, a safe workplace, fair competition, and an improved quality of life for all peoples in the global economy.

Corporate social responsibility has been a hot topic in the modern era of globalization. INGOs and other elements of civil society openly confront TNCs for not living up to their civic responsibilities. There is still considerable debate over the success of voluntary codes on business behaviors. Supporters of voluntary codes argue that effective monitoring of TNCs ensures compliance with international standards. Intense surveillance, by INGOs and CSOs, the International Standards Organization (ISO), and other groups, reinforces laws and regulations approved by national legislatures. Critics counter that voluntary codes are toothless, and cannot prevent the abuse of the marginalized, voiceless element in the world's poorest economies. Critics note that low-skilled workers in the global supply chain continue to languish in sweatshops as TNCs implement cost-cutting strategies to pad corporate profits.

See also **Corruption; Foreign Direct Investment; Good Governance; International Labor Organization; Non-Governmental Organizations; Production Sharing; Race to the Bottom; Supply Chains; Transnational Corporations.** ***See also in Volume 2,*** **Documents 29, 30, 31, 33, 34, 35, 36, 37, 38, 52, 53.**

Further Reading

Benioff, Marc, and Karen Southwick. *Compassionate Capitalism: How Corporations Can Make Doing Good an Integral Part of Doing Well.* Franklin Lakes, NJ: Career Press, 2004.

Hopkins, Michael. *The Planetary Bargain: Corporate Social Responsibility Matters.* Washington, DC: Earthscan Publications, 2003.

Korten, David C. *When Corporations Rule the World.* 2d ed. San Francisco, CA: Berrett-Koehler, 2001.

Kotler, Philip, and Nancy Lee. *Corporate Social Responsibility: Doing the Most Good for Your Company and Your Cause.* New York: John Wiley & Sons, 2004.

McIntosch, Malcolm, Ruth Thomas, Deborah Leipziger, and Gill Coleman. *Living Corporate Citizenship: Strategic Routes to Socially Responsible Business.* Paramus, NJ: Financial Times Management, 2003.

Schwartz, Peter, and Blair Gibbs. *When Good Companies Do Bad Things.* New York: John Wiley & Sons, Inc., 1999.

CORRUPTION

Corruption is the abuse of the public trust for personal gain. Corruption occurs when public officials or private sector business people intentionally circumvent existing laws and ethical conduct to improve their own well-being. The activities commonly associated with corruption are manifest in a tangled web of improprieties among public officials, government agencies, private businesses, or other special interest groups. Corruption has been a problem in the global economy for many years. Only recently, however, has this sensitive topic been addressed as a serious obstacle to poverty reduction and sustainable economic development. Today, efforts to curb corruption are being undertaken by governments, multilateral organizations, civil society organizations, and others.

Greed, the quest for power, and other personal ambitions cause corruption and poor governance. Governance is a general term that encompasses the way a country is governed—the operation of its public institutions, the formation and implementation of its laws, policies, and practices. Good governance refers to the honest, competent operation of a country by its leadership and civil service. The absence of good governance breeds corruption, however. Bribery, the most common form of public corruption, runs rampant in many developing countries. Bribery flourishes when public officials put their personal interests ahead of the public good. Examples of bribery abound. Bribery occurs when exporters illegally pay customs officials to falsify records; when contractors offer kickbacks to government agencies to obtain lucrative building contracts; when businesses offer payoffs to legislators in exchange for favorable laws, regulations, or government subsidies; and when individuals slip money to poorly paid civil servants for a variety of petty favors.

So pervasive is bribery in some countries that businesses view it as just another cost of production. Resource-rich developing countries are particularly vulnerable to corruption, mainly because the prospects for ill-gotten gains are so high. Domestic and foreign businesses offer payoffs to local officials to obtain mining, drilling, or other resource-extraction rights for resources such as gold, oil, or diamonds. Further, cronyism, a type of favoritism based on social class, ethnicity, race, gender, or other determinant, sways public policies in many countries. The absence of clearly defined, fair, and enforceable laws and regulations encourages cronyism in levying taxes, awarding contracts, hiring civil servants, and so on.

The negative effects of corruption, particularly in the developing world, are staggering. Today, development economists are united in their view that corruption saps poorer countries of scarce resources and thus retards poverty reduction efforts and the prospects for sustainable economic development. First, corruption reduces a country's ability to build a functional economic and social infrastructure. This is because tax revenues, foreign aid, and loans or grants from multilateral organizations is funneled into corrupt officials' pockets rather than to the intended public projects such as schools, health care facilities, roads, water and sewage treatment plants, and other infrastructure. Transparency International (TI), the world's leading anti-corruption non-governmental organization, estimated that bribery in the developing world siphons about $400 billion per year from the public till. Some of the most corrupt world leaders in recent decades, such as Ferdinand Marcos (Philippines), the Duvaliers (Haiti), and Saddam Hussein (Iraq), all looted the national treasury for personal benefit.

Corruption reduces a country's growth potential. Rampant bribery, intimidation, and cronyism stifles legitimate business start-ups, investment, research and development, and innovation; weakens entrepreneurship; retards capital formation; and discourages long-term global connections with the outside world, including foreign direct investment (FDI) and international trade. This type of unstable business environment, in turn, encourages the brain drain of human capital and capital flight of financial assets from the country. Sluggish or negative economic growth limits a country's ability to raise people's living standards and quality of life.

Corruption weakens the flow and effectiveness of foreign assistance. Donor countries, and multilateral development organizations such as the World Bank and regional development banks, are hesitant to provide development assistance through loans or grants to the world's most corrupt regimes. In extreme cases development assistance is discontinued. Since 1998, the World Bank has ceased making loans to resource-rich Turkmenistan due to state corruption and the slow implementation of reforms.

Development economists agree that corruption in the global economy will not dissipate overnight. In many countries, the culture of corruption is embedded in the inadequate salaries of civil servants, the institutional scheming of policymakers, and in the self-serving business practices of firms. Still, the world has awakened to the need for anti-corruption initiatives as a way to promote the global community's overarching goal of poverty reduction. NGO's, such as TI, took the lead in the global war on corruption in the mid-1990s. Today TI's annual Corruption Perceptions Index (CPI), which examines 146 of the world's 208 economies, is the most authoritative ranking of corrupt regimes. The most and least corrupt countries named in the CPI 2004 are shown in Table 25.

TI's Corruption Perceptions Index (CPI) 2004 ranked 146 countries on a scale of one to ten, one representing very corrupt and ten representing very clean. The CPI is based on the perceptions of business people and country analysts, and consists of eighteen separate surveys administered throughout the world. Country data from at least three of these surveys was required for a country to be ranked. In its 2004 CPI ranking, TI found that corruption was rampant in sixty countries, countries that scored a three or below. All of these

TABLE 25 **Transparency International Corruption Perceptions Index 2004**

Least Corrupt			Most Corrupt		
Rank	Country	CPI 2004 Score	Rank	Country	CPI 2004 Score
1	Finland	9.7	133	Angola	2.0
2	New Zealand	9.6		Congo (DR)	2.0
3	Denmark	9.5		Cote d'Ivoire	2.0
	Iceland	9.5		Georgia	2.0
5	Singapore	9.3		Indonesia	2.0
6	Sweden	9.2		Tajikistan	2.0
7	Switzerland	9.1		Turkmenistan	2.0
8	Norway	8.9	140	Azerbaijan	1.9
9	Australia	8.8		Paraguay	1.9
10	Netherlands	8.7	142	Chad	1.7
11	United Kingdom	8.6		Myanmar	1.7
12	Canada	8.5	144	Nigeria	1.6
13	Austria	8.4	145	Bangladesh	1.5
	Luxembourg	8.4		Haiti	1.5

Source: Transparency International, *Global Corruption Report 2004*, 4–5.

countries were developing or transition countries. Countries that scored nine or higher were viewed as very clean countries. Only the top seven countries achieved this level, as shown in Table 25. Of the top twenty-five countries listed in the CPI ranking just three were developing countries—Chile (twenty), Barbados (twenty-one), and Malta (twenty-five).

TI's efforts to place corruption at the center of the global agenda snowballed during the late 1990s and early 2000s. The World Bank, International Monetary Fund (IMF), regional development banks, Organization for Economic Co-operation and Development (OECD), G8 industrial nations, numerous NGOs, and others jumped on the anti-corruption bandwagon. In 2003, 114 nations signed the UN Convention Against Corruption (UNCAC). By November 2004, ten countries had ratified the agreement. The UNCAC stresses the transnational nature of corruption. The Convention pledged to fight global corruption through strategies of prevention, criminalization, international cooperation, and asset recovery. Multilateral organizations have conducted research on corruption and on the effectiveness of anti-corruption policies. One recent OECD study concluded that fighting corruption is possible when all stakeholders—local governments, NGOs and CSOs, multilateral organizations, international financial institutions (IFIs), donor governments, and businesses—are willing partners in the process. Today, many of the anti-corruption programs of multilateral organizations provide financial and technical assistance to strengthen good governance and transparency in public policy.

See also **Corporate Social Responsibility; Good Governance; Sustainable Economic Development.** ***See also in Volume 2,*** **Documents 52, 53, 58.**

Further Reading

Asian Development Bank. *Effective Prosecution of Corruption.* Manila: Author, 2004.

Paolo, Mauro. *Why Worry about Corruption?* Washington, DC: International Monetary Fund, 1997.

Transparency International. *Global Corruption Report 2005, Special Focus: Corruption in Construction and Post-Conflict Reconstruction.* London: Pluto Press, 2005.

———. *Global Corruption Report 2004, Special Focus: Political Corruption.* London: Pluto Press, 2004.

World Bank. *World Development Report 2005: A Better Investment Climate for Everyone.* Washington, DC: World Bank, 2004.

D 

DEMOCRACY

Democracy is a type of political system in which political authority is derived from the people. In a functional democracy the adult citizenry is responsible for the government's decisions, either directly or indirectly. Direct democracy means that adult citizens debate and cast their votes on important policy issues. The traditional New England town meeting is an example of direct democracy. Indirect democracy means that adult citizens freely elect representatives to positions of authority in government. Senators and congresspersons are examples of elected representatives within the U.S. government. The concept of democracy, and adult participation, has changed over time. For example, in 1900, none of the world's "democracies" allowed women to vote in national elections. A century later, policies of exclusion from the political process based on gender, race, and so on is expressly forbidden in the world's democracies. The Freedom House, the world's most authoritative voice on the subject of democracy and freedom, reported that 119 of the world's 192 nations were classified as democracies in 2004. Table 26 shows the growth of democracy during the twentieth century. Note that in 1900 no democracies were listed, mainly because universal suffrage did not apply to women at the turn of the century.

The growth of democracy over the past century has promoted growth and prosperity in the global economy. Democracy, which is built on an educated and informed citizenry, supports good governance. Good governance is the fair and competent execution of pubic affairs by public officials. Good governance is the linchpin that discourages corruption, cronyism, and inefficient resource use in an economy. Good governance is a common feature in the advanced economies. The absence of good governance in many developing countries impedes their growth and development. Democracies embrace transparency and the right to be informed about economic issues and policies. Institutions such as a free press and an impartial judiciary also support good governance.

Democracy is compatible with capitalism. Informed decision making by individuals is the bedrock of democracy. Under indirect democracy, citizens cast their vote for or against candidates. Political candidates who best represent the values or views of the electorate are elected to public office. Similarly, capitalism rests on informed economic decision making by individuals and businesses. Individuals, for example, cast their "dollar votes" for or against certain products. Products that best meet consumers' wants or needs are purchased, and products that do not satisfy consumers' needs eventually fade away. Businesses shop for productive resources in much the same way that individuals shop for

TABLE 26 **Growth of Democracy in the World, 1900 to 2000 (population in millions)**

Democracies	1900	1950	2000
Number of countries	0	22	120
Percent of countries	0	14.3%	62.5%
Population	0	743	3,439
Population (% of global population)	0	31%	58.2%

Source: Freedom House, *Democracy's Century: A Survey of Political Change in the 20th Century*, 3.

TABLE 27 **Freedom in the World, 2004**

Freedom	Free	Partly Free	Not Free	Totals
Number of countries	89	54	49	192
Percent of countries	46%	28%	26%	100%
Population (billions)	2.8	1.2	2.4	6.4
Population (%)	44%	19%	37%	100%

Source: Freedom House, *Freedom in the World 2005*, 4.

products. Businesses look for the best mix of human, natural, and capital resources to use in the production process. Decentralized decision making and freedom of choice are common features of a democratic political system and a capitalist economic system.

Connected with the rise of democracies in the world is the rise of "freedom." Democracy and freedom are similar but not identical terms. Freedom extends beyond the existence of democratic institutions and the electoral process. The concept of freedom includes the political freedoms found in functional democracies, and the safeguards of people's civil and human rights. According to the Freedom House, there were eighty-nine liberal democracies that vigorously protect people's civil rights and liberties in 2004. These liberal democracies were labeled "free" countries. The remaining thirty democracies showed some weakness in protecting people's human or civil rights and were classified as "partly free." In 2003, about three-quarters of all countries were classified as free or partly free, as shown in Table 27. One hundred percent of the countries in western Europe were either free or partly free in 2004. The percent of free or partly free countries in other world regions included the Americas (94 percent), central and eastern Europe and the Former Soviet Union (70 percent), Asia and the Pacific (72 percent), sub-Saharan Africa (67 percent), and the Middle East and North Africa (34 percent). Research conducted by the Freedom House has consistently shown a direct relationship between freedom and economic growth, regardless of countries' development status.

See also **Capitalism; Economic Freedom; Good Governance.** ***See also in Volume 2,*** **Documents 34, 51, 58.**

Further Reading

Freedom House. *Democracy's Century: A Survey of Global Political Change in the 20th Century*. New York: Author, 1999.

Halperin, Morton H., Joseph T. Siegle, and Michael M. Weinstein. *The Democracy Advantage: How Democracies Promote Prosperity and Peace*. New York: Routledge, 2004.

Karatnycky, Adrian. *Freedom in the World 2005: The Annual Survey of Political Rights and Civil Liberties*. New York: Freedom House, 2005.

Paehlke, Robert C. *Democracy in Dilemma: Environment, Social Equity, and the Global Economy*. Cambridge: MIT Press, 2004.

Yi Feng. *Democracy, Governance, and Economic Performance*. Cambridge: MIT Press, 2005.

DEMOCRATIC SOCIALISM

Democratic socialism is a type of economic system in which core socialist beliefs guide national economic policy, and democratic institutions govern the nation. Democratic socialism is most concerned with creating an environment conducive to social and economic justice. Democratic socialism became a major player in the global economy during the post–World War II period by claiming electoral victories in many advanced countries. Democratic socialism is sometimes referred to as the "third way" to distinguish it from capitalism, which leans heavily toward the market model, and communism, which leans heavily toward the command model.

Democratic socialism in the post-war world was non-Marxist and gradualist, preferring to work within existing political institutions rather than toppling them from without. Its stronghold was in Scandinavia, Western Europe, and several regions of the British Commonwealth such as Australia and New Zealand. Democratic socialism in these regions embraced policies to bring the commanding heights of the economy under government control, create consensus-based economic plans, and construct comprehensive social-welfare programs. Further, democratic socialism invited open discussion of economic and political issues, guaranteed free elections, and protected the civil and human rights of citizens.

Once the electorate handed the reigns of power to the democratic socialist governments, the new leadership moved to nationalize elements of the economy's commanding heights. The commanding heights of an economy represent key industries including transportation, communications, energy, health care, and finance. Nationalization occurs when the government assumes ownership of an important firm or industry, but compensates the previous owner. Nationalized businesses were organized and managed in different ways. Most were restructured as public corporations, run by a government-appointed board of directors. Others were jointly owned and operated by public and private interests, or operated as appendages of certain government agencies. Democratic socialists supported nationalization to guarantee an adequate quantity and quality of essential goods and services. Nationalization also gave the government some control over prices and employment. In the post-war United Kingdom, several key industries were nationalized, including coal and steel, railways, docks and harbors, some public utilities, and the health care system. Similarly, in France, the government nationalized some public utilities, mining, banking, and insurance.

Another pillar of the democratic socialist agenda was indicative planning. Indicative planning is a collaborative economic planning process that gives a meaningful voice to labor leaders, business leaders, academicians, and public officials. Indicative plans establish national production goals, targets for inflation and unemployment, guidelines for public expenditures, and so on. The overriding goal of planning was to improve the standard of living and quality of life for the people, not to meddle in the affairs of private firms. France pioneered indicative planning at the close of World War II. By the 1960s, most other European countries, socialist and non-socialist alike, adopted some form of economic planning. Not surprisingly, developing countries mimicked this European planning model even after these poorer countries achieved independence.

The final cornerstone of democratic socialist policy was the welfare state. In a welfare state, government programs redistribute some of society's wealth to promote people's economic well-being. By the 1950s, Sweden was the world's preeminent welfare state. It created an extensive network of mutually supporting social-welfare programs, which, over time, were woven into the fabric of Swedish society. Included were national health care, national accident insurance, unemployment insurance, job training programs, paid childbearing and childraising leaves, subsidized higher education and housing, paid vacations, and retirement and other pensions.

Challenges to democratic socialism stiffened over the past quarter century. For example, by the late 1970s and 1980s, many governments moved to denationalize or privatize state-owned businesses. Privatization is the process of selling state-owned enterprises to individuals or firms. In the vanguard of privatization was Britain's Conservative Prime Minister Margaret Thatcher, who privatized telecommunications, coal, and some railways. In France, Prime Minister Jacques Chirac initiated privatization in many large industrial corporations, banks, and insurance companies by the late 1980s. At roughly the same time, enthusiasm for economic planning was waning. Led by Great Britain, most advanced countries shifted toward market-oriented solutions to economic problems. The welfare state concept was also under siege by the 1980s and 1990s. Many European nations dismantled elements of people's cradle-to-grave security blankets during this period. Even in Sweden critics argued that heavy taxes, which financed the welfare state, were a disincentive to work, save, and invest. In the early 1990s, Swedish voters bumped the socialists out of office in favor of a more conservative administration. Soon, market reforms capped certain taxes on investment income, privatized some industries, and nurtured entrepreneurial activity. While elements of the social safety net remained in Sweden and other former socialist countries, it was clear by the 1990s that the economic pendulum had swung decisively toward the free market.

See also **Capitalism; Command Economy; Communism; Democracy; Economic System; Emerging Market Economies; Joseph, Keith S.; Market Economy; Myrdal, Karl G.; Pigou, Arthur C.; Third World Socialism.**

Further Reading

Albritton, Robert, John R. Bell, and Shannon Bell, eds. *New Socialisms: Futures beyond Globalization.* New York: Routledge, 2004.

Ebenstein, William, Edwin Fogelman, and Alan O. Ebenstein. *Today's ISMS: Socialism, Capitalism, Fascism, Communism, and Libertarianism.* 11th ed. Paramus, NJ: Prentice-Hall, 1999.

Fitzpatrick, Tony. *After the New Social Democracy: Social Welfare for the 21st Century.* Manchester, UK: Manchester University Press, 2003.

Muravchik, Joshua. *Heaven on Earth: The Rise and Fall of Socialism.* San Francisco: Encounter Books, 2002.

Webb, Sidney, and Beatrice Webb. *The Decay of Capitalist Civilization.* New York: Harcourt, Brace and Company, 1923.
Yergin, Daniel, and Joseph Stanislaw. *The Commanding Heights: The Battle for the World Economy.* Rev. ed. New York: Free Press, 2002.

DENG XIAOPING

Deng Xiaoping (1904–1997) was an important Chinese revolutionary, leader, and reformer. Deng received his early education in local schools in China, and continued his studies in France and the Soviet Union during the 1920s. Later in the 1920s, he returned to his homeland to support the fledgling Chinese Communist Party (CCP). Deng endured the prolonged and costly civil war between the communists and the ruling Kuomintang. In 1949, the communists, headed by Mao Zedong, claimed victory over the Kuomintang. For the next five decades Deng helped mold China's economic future. Deng is widely viewed as the chief architect of China's gradualist economic reforms—reforms that eventually established China as a more market-oriented and globally connected powerhouse in Asia.

Deng assumed a number of key leadership roles in the newly formed People's Republic of China during the 1950s. He was often caught in the shifting tides of Maoist dogma and irrational CCP policies. In the mid-1950s, Deng sat comfortably as the secretary-general of the CCP and a member of the ruling Politburo. During the Great Proletarian Cultural Revolution of the 1960s, however, he was publicly disgraced, tossed out of the CCP, and forced to work as a manual laborer. By the early 1970s, he regained favor within the CCP hierarchy and steadily rebuilt his power base. In 1978, two years after Mao's death, Deng emerged as China's leader.

Deng immediately set a new course for China's economic development. High on the economic agenda was the implementation of the Four Modernizations, reforms necessary to upgrade industry, agriculture, science and technology, and national defense. Deng slowly introduced policies to restore private incentives, encourage entrepreneurship, and rejoin the global economy. He established a dual-track economy to test the viability of market-oriented economic reforms. One track was the state-planned sector, a sector dominated by central planners and production quotas. The other track was a series of experiments in free-market economics. The household responsibility system was introduced on this second track. The household responsibility system enabled peasants to lease agricultural land from the government for farming. Farmers were required to sell a portion of their output to the state at a fixed price. The remainder could be sold at a market price for private profit. The success of the household responsibility system paved the way for additional market reforms, including profit-oriented township and village enterprises (TVEs), private entrepreneurship, joint ventures between foreign and domestic businesses, free trade zones, and numerous regional development zones. Deng often referred to his gradualist approach to economic reform as "crossing the river by feeling the stones." His gradualism created a hybrid economy which, by the 1990s, the Chinese labeled a "socialist market economy with Chinese characteristics."

Largely through the market-oriented, outward-looking policies of Deng Xiaoping, China has claimed a dominant position in today's global economy. Since the 1990s, China has attracted more foreign direct investment (FDI) than any other country in the developing world. China was the world's second largest producer in 2004, ranked by gross domestic product (GDP) on a purchasing power parity (PPP) basis (seventh largest producer when ranked by the traditional Atlas method of calculating GDP). In 2004 China was the fourth largest exporter and third largest importer of goods and services in the entire global economy.

Economic problems remain, many of them connected with China's failed centrally planned economy. Weaknesses in China's economy include dysfunctional state-owned enterprises (SOEs), massive nonperforming loans in the state-run banking system, uneven regional development, pervasive corruption, and an authoritarian political system. Yet Deng's vision for a more globally connected, prosperous China has gradually taken root in the world's most populous country.

See also **Capitalism; Communism; Purchasing Power Parity; Transition Countries.**

Further Reading

Chi Fulin, ed. *China's Economic Reform at the Turn of the Century*. Beijing, China: Foreign Languages Press, 2000.

Deng Rong. *Deng Xiaoping and the Cultural Revolution: A Daughter Recalls the Critical Years*. New York: Doubleday, 2005.

Deng Xiaoping. *Selected Works of Deng Xiaoping: 1975–1982*. Baltimore: University Press of the Pacific, 2001.

Marti, Michael E. *China and the Legacy of Deng Xiaoping: From Communist Revolution to Capitalist Evolution*. Dulles, VA: Brasseys, Inc., 2002.

Misra, Kalpana. *From Post-Maoism to Post-Marxism: The Erosion of Official Ideology in Deng's China*. New York: Routledge, 1998.

Stewart, Whitney. *Deng Xiaoping: Leader in a Changing China*. Minneapolis, MN: Lerner Publications, 2001.

DEVELOPING COUNTRIES

Developing countries are the poorer, less industrialized countries in the global economy. In 2004 the International Monetary Fund (IMF) revised its classification of economies to include two main categories: the advanced economies, and other emerging market and developing countries. Prior to 2004 the IMF and other multilateral organizations identified three categories of countries: advanced, developing, and countries in transition. The developing countries are often referred to as the global South, mainly due to the geographic concentration of poorer countries in the southern hemisphere. The twenty-nine advanced economies comprise the global North. The remaining 179 economies in the world are classified as emerging market and developing countries.

The term least developed countries (LDCs) is reserved for the fifty poorest developing countries. As a group, the LDCs have the lowest average gross national incomes (GNIs) in the global economy. They are also most likely to

Volatile prices for many commodities, such as coffee, create economic instability in some developing countries.
Courtesy of Getty Images: T. O'Keefe/PhotoLink

be trapped in the vicious cycle of poverty. Low savings and investment rates, sluggish or negative economic growth per capita, and a deteriorating quality of life characterize the cycle of poverty. Between 1990 and 2000 about 40 percent of all LDCs experienced negative growth in their real per capita GDPs. Table 28 compares "all developing countries" with LDCs in a number of economic categories.

Unique histories and cultures dot the developing world. Yet most developing countries share several common characteristics. One common feature is a relatively low gross national income (GNI). GNI measures the nation's total income by adding up annual spending by households, businesses, and the government. The GNI per capita is the GNI divided by the country's population. The World Bank introduced the GNI per capita in 2000 to replace a similar measurement, the gross national product (GNP) per capita. Today, the World Bank and other international institutions classify countries by their GNI per capita. The four categories of countries include low-income, lower middle-income, upper

TABLE 28 **Developing Countries and the Least Developed Countries, 2002**

Comparisons	Least Developed Countries	All Developing Countries
Per capita GDP	$281	$1,195
Population (millions)	700	5,019
Population growth rate	2.4%	1.5%
Urban population (2000)	27%	41%
Under-five mortality (per 1000)	161	89
Life expectancy (2000–2005)	50	63
Televisions (per 1000)	50	183
Cellular subscribers (per 1000)	6	75
Internet users (per 1000)	12	73
ODA per capita*	$31	$11
Total ODA* ($ billions)	$16.4	$45.0
FDI inflows** ($ billions)	$5.2	$162.1

*Official development assistance.
**Foreign direct investment (FDI).
Source: United Nations Conference on Trade and Development, *The Least Developed Countries Report 2004*, 321, 327–28, 332, 347–48.

TABLE 29 **Classification of Economies by Income Status, 2004**

Classification*	GNI per Capita	Average GNI per Capita (Exchange Rate Method)	Number of Economies	Average GNI per Capita (PPP Method)
Low income	$825 or less	$510	59	$2,260
Lower middle income	$826–$3,255	$1,580	54	$5,640
Upper middle income	$3,256–$10,065	$4,770	40	$10,090
High income	$10,066 or more	$32,040	55	$30,970
World		$6,280	208	$8,760

*Classifications are based on the exchange rate (Atlas) method.
Source: World Bank, *World Development Indicators* database, July 15, 2005.

middle-income, and high-income countries, as shown in Table 29. The low-income and middle-income countries are generally called developing countries. Income status is not a definitive statement of a country's development status, however. While the GNI per capita is a useful tool for cross-border statistical comparisons, there are limitations to using this measurement of economic well-being. For instance, GNI per capita does not include unreported business activity in the informal sector, or account for unreliable data collection methods, skewed income distribution within countries, or regional differences in purchasing power.

A second common characteristic of developing countries is high population growth. World population grew dramatically during the twentieth century, and according to United Nations estimates will reach nearly 9 billion people by 2050. Table 30 traces world population growth from 1950 to 2050. The burst in world population that occurred over the past half century is often called the population explosion. The great majority of population growth since 1950 took place in the developing world. Demographic trends indicate that nearly all population growth between 2000 and 2050 will occur in the global South. As a result, the population of the developing world will swell by an additional 3 billion people. Population growth creates a number of development challenges for poorer countries including unemployment and underemployment; internal migrations to overcrowded urban areas; degradation of local ecosystems;

TABLE 30 **Population Explosion, 1950 to 2050**

Year	World Population (millions)	Developed Countries (millions)	Developed Countries (% of world population)	Developing Countries (millions)	Developing Countries (% of world population)
1950	2,519	813	32.3%	1,706	27.7%
2000	6,071	1,194	19.7%	4,877	80.3%
2050	8,919	1,220	13.7%	7,699	86.3%

Source: United Nations Department of Economic and Social Affairs, *World Population to 2300*, 14.

intense competition for resources such as fresh water, farmland, and mineral rights; and reduced saving and investment in private and public capital goods.

A third feature of many developing countries is limited natural resources. Limited natural resources might result from exploitation during a country's colonial period, few natural endowments, or current resource mismanagement. The scarcity of natural resources, and the desire to specialize in the production of goods in which a comparative advantage exists, steer some developing countries toward one-crop economies. In a one-crop economy, producers supply one or a few primary commodities, such as foods, beverages, agricultural raw materials, or minerals. One-crop economies are inherently unstable, as volatile commodity prices in global markets lead to periods of boom and bust. The mismanagement of resources, past and present, further erodes countries' ability to break the vicious cycle of poverty. Self-serving colonial regimes in the past, and widespread government corruption today, have squandered precious resources and retarded the growth process. Inefficient practices such as overgrazing, overfarming, and overtimbering have also raised havoc with fragile ecosystems. As a result, deforestation, desertification, and other forms of environmental decay wrack many developing countries. In addition, landlocked developing countries (LLDCs) and small island developing states (SIDS) are often cut off from essential resources by political borders or their remote location.

Finally, developing countries typically face high external debt obligations. External debt, also called foreign debt, is the money owed by one country to foreign creditors including governments, commercial banks, and multilateral organizations. The IMF calculated that the total external debt of developing and emerging market economies increased by $850 billion between 1996 and 2005, and topped $3 trillion by 2005. Developing countries accumulated the lion's share of external debt ($2,259 billion), and the transition economies of central and eastern Europe and the Commonwealth of Independent States (CIS) accounted for the remainder ($788 billion). In 2005 these poorer economies owed more than $475 billion in debt service payments to foreign creditors. The World Bank identified fifty-two "severely indebted" countries in 2005, twenty-eight of which were low-income, developing countries. Severely indebted countries were saddled with unsustainable external debt, a debt that could not be serviced without crippling the domestic economy and public services.

In recent years the topic of sustainable economic development in poorer world regions has become a front-burner issue for governments, multilateral organizations, non-governmental organizations, and others. In 2000 the UN General Assembly adopted the UN Millennium Declaration, which pledged to reduce global poverty and improve people's quality of life. The accompanying Millennium Development Goals (MDGs) outlined an agenda for global development, with specific targets to achieve by 2015. Of the eight MDGs, poverty reduction became the centerpiece of the global development agenda. The fact that 1.1 billion people lived on $1 or less per day in the early 2000s, and nearly 3 billion people lived on $2 or less, underscored the need for a global response to poverty. The seven other MDGs support poverty reduction. Other goals include universal public education, gender equity, reduced child mortality, improved maternal health, disease prevention, environmental protection, and the expansion of global partnerships in the economic development process. The MDGs have become a rallying point for development efforts by the United Nations System, World Bank, International Monetary Fund, regional multilateral development banks, national governments, and others in the global economy.

Developing countries often draft a development plan to plot a strategy for sustainable growth and development. Development plans can be based on a command or a market model. A development plan based on the command model relies on government decision making. A development plan based on the market model puts most decision making into the hands of individuals and businesses. All development plans establish goals and set national priorities for development. At the heart of most development plans are policies to increase long-term productivity and growth, and improve the quality of people's lives. One common priority is to nurture the transition from traditional subsistence agriculture into industry and commercial services. By 2003, 88 percent of all output produced in low-income and middle-income countries was categorized as services (53 percent of GDP) or industrial (35 percent of GDP). The remaining 12 percent was agricultural output, according to the World Bank. A second priority is capital formation—the expansion of a nation's capital stock. A third priority is human capital development and entrepreneurship. Human resources are often viewed as the wellspring of innovation and business creation. A fourth priority is trade expansion. Failed import substitution policies have given way to more successful export promotion policies in recent decades. Export promotion encourages efficient production based on a nation's comparative advantage, and the export of surplus output ranging from basic commodities to high-tech capital goods.

See also **Advanced Economies; Corruption; Development Economics; Development Plan; Emerging Market Economies; External Debt; Gross Domestic Product; Gross National Income; Least Developed Countries; Lewis, William A.; Millennium Development Goals; Myrdal, Karl G.; Population; Poverty; Quality of Life; Sen, Amartya K.; South-South Cooperation; Sustainable Economic Development; Third World Socialism; Ward, Barbara M. *See also in Volume 2*, Documents 1, 2, 3, 5, 6, 11, 12, 20, 21, 50, 51, 54, 55, 56, 57, 59.**

Further Reading

International Monetary Fund. *World Economic Outlook April 2005*. Washington, DC: Author, 2005.

Miller, Margaret J. *Implementing the Millennium Development Goals*. Washington, DC: World Bank, 2003.

O'Connor, David E. *Demystifying the Global Economy*. Westport, CT: Greenwood Publishing Group, 2002.

Sachs, Jeffrey D. *The End of Poverty: Economic Possibilities for Our Time*. New York: Penguin Press, 2005.

United Nations Conference on Trade and Development. *Least Developed Countries Report 2004*. Geneva, Switzerland: United Nations, 2004.

United Nations Economic and Social Affairs Department. *World Population to 2300.* New York: United Nations Publications, 2004.
World Bank. *2004 World Development Indicators.* Washington, DC: Author, 2004.

DEVELOPMENT ECONOMICS

Development economics is a specialized field of study in economics that deals with sustainable economic development. Development economics investigates a broad range of economic, political, and cultural topics that pertain to the nature and causes of economic growth and the quality of people's lives. Development economics, broadly defined, applies to sustainable economic development in all countries, advanced, emerging market, and developing alike. Yet, over the past half century, most of the work of development economists has focused on the prospects for sustainable development in the world's poorer regions.

Development economics straddles traditional lines between macroeconomics, microeconomics, and international economics. On the macroeconomic level, it deals with a country's gross domestic product (GDP), unemployment and underemployment rates, price levels, gross savings, investment, and capital formation. On the microeconomic level, it probes the issues of productivity, wage rates, income distribution, access to technology and knowledge, and the uses of society's factors of production—natural resources, human resources, and capital goods. It also delves into the role of government in providing public goods such as schools and infrastructure; social services such as health care and financial assistance to the needy; and honest, competent leadership that protects the rule of law. Development economics is also vitally connected with issues of connectivity in the global economy. Relevant topics include international trade, foreign direct investment, global capital markets, and economic assistance from national governments and multilateral organizations. Finally, development economics delves into social and cultural issues, institutions, and policies. Topics include population growth, the work ethic, entrepreneurial attitudes, and a host of other social or cultural norms that affect a country's prospects for development.

Development economics gained popular acceptance as a legitimate field of study after World War II. The spread of independence movements after the war forced government leaders and economists to consider the impact of decolonization on developing countries. Some early development theories during the 1950s and 1960s stressed linear development. Linear development models outlined uniform, sequential, and predictable stages of economic development. Walt W. Rostow was the leading advocate of the linear theory of development. In his book, *The Stages of Economic Growth: A Non-communist Manifesto* (1960), Rostow identified five developmental stages. The first stage, the "traditional society," was characterized by subsistence agriculture and primitive barter exchanges. Second, the "preconditions for take-off" was a transitional period that witnessed the rise of saving and investment, entrepreneurship, commerce, and national governments. Public investments in education and infrastructure also emerged during this transitional period. Third, the "take-off" was marked by industrialization, technological change, and still higher rates of savings and investment. As a result, higher productivity and economic growth became the norm during the nation's take-off stage. Fourth, the "drive to maturity" widened the circle of enterprises that employed advanced capital and technology in production. A highly educated work force, pro-growth social values, and expanded international trade also supported rapid industrialization and economic growth. Fifth, the "age of mass consumption" witnessed the triumph of capital-intensive production. During this stage businesses produced a wide variety of capital goods and consumer goods, and households purchased the comforts of life.

Other early development theorists stressed the primacy of saving and investment in attaining economic development without relying on a linear framework. During the 1950s and 1960s, economic development was viewed mainly through the narrow lens of national output and economic growth. William A. (Sir Arthur) Lewis, a British economist, argued that the transition from a traditional subsistence agricultural economy to a modern economy was founded on productive investments in sophisticated capital goods, the infusion of foreign capital through foreign direct investment (FDI), and entrepreneurial business activity. Lewis believed that sustained capital formation, and the use of surplus labor from the bloated agricultural sector, would increase business productivity, profits, and savings for re-investment. At about the same time, American economist Robert M. Solow argued that the main drivers of economic growth were new technologies and knowledge. Solow's widely respected views stressed the need for sustained investment in research and development, education, and the application of new technologies to production in all economic sectors—agricultural, industrial, and services.

In the 1970s and 1980s other strands of development economics emerged. The dependency theory, for example, was widely acknowledged, especially among development economists and intellectuals in the third world. According to the dependency theory, developing countries were hopelessly dependent on the more powerful advanced countries for their economic survival. As a result, the poorer countries were relegated to an inferior, and static, position in the global economy. Dependency theorists often argued that discriminatory trade practices by the rich countries, abuses by powerful transnational corporations (TNCs), limited access to international capital markets, and other barriers explained the slow pace of economic development in the third world. To counter the power of the world's leading capitalist countries, dependency theorists supported external debt forgiveness for the poorest developing countries, greater self-reliance, government controls over foreign investment, and inclusion in global decision making—particularly in multilateral organizations such as the World Bank and International Monetary Fund (IMF). In more extreme cases, dependency theorists supported aggressive nationalization or expropriation of domestic and foreign businesses, the collectivization of agriculture, and the creation of state-owned enterprises (SOEs) to replace private sector business activity.

A new direction in development theory emerged in the mid-1980s, one based on laissez-faire principles of government noninterference in the economy. Under the banner of a neoclassical revolution, development economists argued that government intervention in economic activity usually resulted in government failures, particularly the misallocation of resources. The neoclassicals opposed state planning and SOEs, which misallocated resources and distorted prices. They also opposed restrictive trade barriers, which thwarted prospects for global connectivity. Over the past twenty years the neoclassical economists have favored policies to promote good governance and the rule of law, enforceable private property rights, privatization, liberalized trade and investment, and market-determined prices. Today, the World Bank, IMF, World Trade Organization, and other multilateral organizations share the neoclassicals' support for free-market answers to development questions.

Over the past fifty years the field of development economics has adapted to changes in the global economy, to different political currents, to world events, and to the expanded perception of sustainable economic development. Early development economists typically measured economic development by changes in national output. Today's version of sustainable economic development is more comprehensive. It measures sustained economic growth and improvements in people's quality of life such as higher adult literacy rates, longer life expectancies, better diet and nutrition, greater access to new technologies, increased consumption, and better social services. Not surprisingly, competing theories of economic development have risen and fallen over time. Today, the linear development model so popular in the 1950s and 1960s has been largely discarded by economists in today's fast-paced, technologically connected global environment.

As time marched on, development economists emphasized different aspects of growth and development in their prescriptions for prosperity. Early economists focused on savings, investment in capital goods, and technology. Later economists added to and refined earlier work in the field. In time, other theorists stressed investment in human capital through public education, health care, nutrition, and access to economic opportunity. In the 1990s and early 2000s the groundbreaking work of Peruvian economist Hernando de Soto sought to expand opportunities by extending property rights to the poor. He argued that the inclusion of people from the informal sector, and their productive assets, was the key to capital formation and prosperity for all people. Today, another dominant theme in development economics is the need to infuse information and communications technologies (ICTs) into developing economies. ICTs are viewed as essential to a country's ability to leapfrog into the twenty-first century. A technology-driven approach to economic development is possible only if the global community initiates development policies to bridge the digital divide.

See also **Developing Countries; Economic Growth; Foreign Aid; Lewis, William A.; Myrdal, Karl G.; Poverty; Rostow, Walt W.; Sachs, Jeffrey D.; Schumacher, Ernst F.; Schumpeter, Joseph A.; Sen, Amartya K.; Solow, Robert M.; Soto, Hernando de; Sustainable Economic Development; Ward, Barbara M.**

Further Reading

Harrison, Graham, ed. *Global Encounters: The International Political Economy, Development and Globalization*. New York: Palgrave Macmillan, 2005.

Lewis, Arthur (Sir). *The Theory of Economic Growth*. London: Unwin Hyman, 1955.

Lynn, Stuart R. *Economic Development: Theory and Practice for a Divided World*. Paramus, NJ: Prentice-Hall, 2002.

Rostow, W. W. *The Stages of Economic Growth: A Non-communist Manifesto*. London: Cambridge University Press, 1960.

Sen, Amartya K. *Development as Freedom*. New York: Anchor Books, 2000.

Soto, Hernando de. *The Mystery of Capital: Why Capitalism Triumphs in the West and Fails Everywhere Else*. Rev. ed. New York: Basic Books, 2003.

Wilson, Ernest J., III. *The Information Revolution and Developing Countries*. Cambridge, MA: MIT Press, 2004.

DEVELOPMENT PLAN

A development plan is a country's strategy to promote sustainable economic development. A national development plan is formulated by the federal government, sometimes in conjunction with business interests, labor organizations, or elements of civil society. To promote sustainable development, the plan establishes a series of medium- and long-term goals, or targets, in areas such as saving and investment, production and consumption, wages and income, and international trade. During the post–World War II period, development plans, some simple and others comprehensive, were devised and implemented in the global economy. National economic planning was a key feature in the post-war reconstruction of Western European democracies. Planning was also used extensively in the communist countries, taking the form of rigid five-year plans. Several types of development plans were devised to meet the development needs of the newly independent countries of Africa, Asia, and the Middle East. Overly ambitious medium-term development plans established by developing countries often fell short of their goals.

A number of development plan models competed for supremacy during the post–World War II era. One leading contender was the command model, which stressed public sector decision making by national authorities. Under the command model the federal government dictated the answers to the basic economic questions of what, how, and for whom to produce. Central planning was used to advance national goals, such as rapid industrialization or regional development. Five-year plans dominated the allocation of natural, human, and capital resources in the communist economies of eastern and central Europe and in third world communist nations such as Cuba, North Korea, North Vietnam, and Mongolia. The leading advocate of strong centralized development planning during the post-war period was the Soviet Union, itself a centrally planned communist economy.

A second planning model was the market model, which focused on decentralized private sector decision making. Under a market model, the private sector, rather than government, answered the basic economic questions. Market principles include private property, profit incentives, and economic freedoms. During the post–World War II period the United States was the foremost market economy, but shunned national economic planning. Japan, on the other hand, rebuilt its post-war market economy with the assistance of the Ministry of International Trade and Industry (MITI), a quasi-public planning agency. From 1951 to 2001, MITI represented the interests of government, labor, business, and academia. MITI planned the modernization of Japan's economy and offered a variety of incentives, such as tax breaks, grants, and low-interest bank loans to support export industries. In 2001 the newly created Ministry of Economy, Trade and Industry (METI) replaced MITI. Japan's emphasis on national planning gave rise to similar planning agencies in other market economies in Asia. In 1961 South Korea established its Economic Planning Board to promote industrialization and export industries. The Economic Planning Board initiated a series of five-year economic development plans to jump-start entrepreneurial activity and exports. Most noncommunist developing countries did not experience the same level of success as South Korea, however. In fact, the development plans in most developing countries wilted under the weight of extreme poverty, poor governance, unstable macroeconomic conditions, unsustainable external debt, and other economic problems.

During the post-war years successful independence movements added many new countries to the global economy. Most of these newly independent developing countries opted for a mixed economy approach to economic planning. Many development plans were loosely based on socialist principles. The turn toward socialism in the developing world mirrored a similar post-war movement toward socialism in the European democracies. During the 1950s, 1960s, and 1970s, the third world socialists adopted policies to nationalize key industries, invest in essential infrastructure, and redistribute some of society's wealth to the poor. Economic goals and targets for economic performance varied from nation to nation. In socialist Tanzania, President Julius K. Nyerere instituted *ujamaa*, a largely unsuccessful plan based on the forced collectivization of agriculture. In contrast, socialist India allowed agriculture to remain in the hands of private landowners, many of whom represented the privileged elite.

Development plans are intended to promote sustainable economic development. Development plans had a shaky record of success during the second half of the twentieth century, however. Some economists blamed economic conditions within developing countries for the failure of planning. These experts argued that widespread poverty, overpopulation, inadequate domestic savings and investment, civil conflict, rampant corruption, and other economic woes disrupted the flow of multi-year plans. Other experts blamed external factors such as ill-advised policies of multilateral organizations, inadequate foreign aid, discriminatory trade policies, and global shocks from oil-price spikes, commodity gluts, terrorism, and natural disasters. In most cases development plans were unable to rally national support for sustainable development.

See also **Communism; Democratic Socialism; Developing Countries; Lewis, William A.; Myrdal, Karl G.; Nyerere, Julius K.; Sustainable Economic Development; Third World Socialism.**

Further Reading

Johnson, Chaimers A. *Miti and the Japanese Miracle: The Growth of Industrial Policy, 1925–1975*. Stanford, CA: Stanford University Press, 1983.

Quaddus, Muhammed A., and M. A. B. Siddique. *A Handbook of Sustainable Development Planning: Studies in Modeling and Decision Support*. Northampton, MA: Edward Elgar Publishing, 2005.

Sacquet, Anne-Marie. *World Atlas of Sustainable Development: Economic, Social and Environmental Data*. London: Anthem, 2005.

World Bank. *Global Economic Prospects: Trade, Regionalism, and Development 2005*. Washington, DC: Author, 2004.

Zetter, Roger, and Mohamed Hamza. *Market Economy and Urban Change: Impacts in the Developing World*. Washington, DC: Earthscan Publications, 2004.

DIGITAL DIVIDE

The digital divide refers to the gap in information and communications technologies (ICTs) between the "haves" and the "have-nots." ICTs are technologies that collect, store, retrieve, and disseminate information. ICTs include computers and software, the Internet and World Wide Web, fiber optics and satellite communications, and a variety of microelectronics products. Economists distinguish between the international digital divide and the digital divide that exists within nations. The international digital divide highlights the glaring technological chasm between the advanced economies and the developing economies. At issue is the exclusion of many developing countries from the benefits of global connectivity. Similarly, the digital divide within nations tends to widen existing economic and social gaps between the privileged class, which has access to ICTs, and the marginalized poor.

The advanced economies are the main beneficiaries of technological connectivity in today's global economy. ICTs stimulate innovation, entrepreneurship, business formation, job creation, and business competitiveness. Using ICTs, well-connected firms scan the planet for low-cost factors of production, conduct business with suppliers and consumers, and advertise their wares. By the early 2000s, business-to-business (B2B) and business-to-consumer (B2C) electronic commerce (e-commerce) accounted for trillions of dollars in sales in the global economy. Ready access to ICTs in the advanced economies accelerate the pace of research and development (R&D) and create millions of service-based jobs in banking and finance, insurance, telecommunications, wholesale and retail trade, and transportation. In addition, a strong ICT infrastructure attracts foreign direct investment, enhances prospects for international

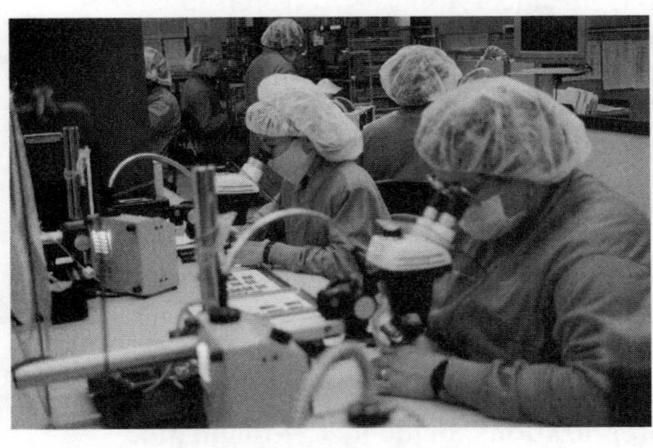

The digital divide threatens to widen the development gap between the rich countries and the poor countries.

Courtesy of Getty Images: John A. Rizzo

trade, and facilitates other profitable cross-border transactions. The infusion of ICTs into the fabric of business activity promotes economic growth and sustainable development. The advanced economies copped the top twenty-five spots in *The Economist*'s 2005 e-readiness rankings. E-readiness measures the e-business environment in sixty-five major economies. In 2005 Denmark topped the e-readiness ranking, followed by the United States, Sweden, Switzerland, and the United Kingdom. Table 31 shows key indicators of the digital divide by income status and world region.

The lack of ICTs in the poorer regions of the world restricts their global reach. As a result, the widening digital divide impedes economic growth and development in the global South. Table 31 illustrates the depth of the ICT disadvantage that poorer regions face. For example, in the early 2000s there were 467 personal computers per 1,000 people in the high-income countries, compared to just twenty-eight personal computers per 1,000 people in the low- and middle-income countries, a seventeen-to-one advantage for high-income countries. The high-income countries also held a seven-to-one advantage in Internet users, and people from high-income countries pay significantly less money for their Internet service than people living in poorer world regions. The lack of ICTs and a supportive technological infrastructure discourage foreign direct investment (FDI), international trade, and other commercial contacts with businesses in poorer nations. Weak global connections deny many developing countries access to foreign capital goods, new technologies, innovative management techniques, credit, and profitable global markets. Exclusion from the ICT revolution places individuals, businesses, and nations on the fringes of the global economy. Among the most important twenty-first century challenges is to bridge the digital divide, and level the playing field for global business activity.

Global efforts to close the international digital divide, and the digital divide within nations are underway. The United Nations, Organization for Economic Cooperation and Development (OECD), Group of 8 (G8) major industrialized countries, World Bank, IMF, and others have researched the problem and made

TABLE 31 **Digital Divide Indicators by Income Status and World Region, 2002–2003**

Regions	Personal Computers (per 1000 people) 2002	Internet Users (per 1000 people) 2002	Internet Monthly Price (20 hours) 2003	Internet Price as a % of Monthly GNI 2003
Low- and middle-income countries	28	50	$41	115%
East Asia and Pacific	26	44	$31	66%
Europe and Central Asia	73	87	$26	40%
L. America and Caribbean	67	92	$33	32%
Mid-East and North Africa	38	37	$31	30%
South Asia	7	14	$30	59%
Sub-Saharan Africa	12	16	$64	269%
High-income countries	467	364	$23	1.6%

Source: World Bank, *2004 World Development Indicators*, 296.

recommendations for corrective action. In 2002 the G8 Digital Opportunities Task Force outlined the most comprehensive plan to integrate ICTs into poorer countries' development strategies. The G8 plan of action pledged to help developing countries create national e-strategies, improve connectivity, develop human resources, encourage business enterprise and entrepreneurship, promote inclusion, coordinate multilateral initiatives, and adapt technologies to meet local needs and circumstances. Individual governments also pledged support for bridging the digital divide. Japan's $15 billion commitment toward this goal is the most significant global response. The Peace Corps of the United States, an agency within the federal government, also targeted the digital divide as a major twenty-first century initiative. Transnational corporations (TNCs) have aggressively expanded mobile phone networks in the developing world. The use of mobile phones has already revolutionized business practices in some developing countries. Mobile phones link small businesses with low-cost suppliers, prospective employees, and customers. Low-cost mobile phone service is also well suited to regions in which poverty and illiteracy are the norm.

See also **Advanced Economies; Developing Countries; Globalization; Information and Communications Technologies; Sustainable Economic Development.** ***See also in Volume 2,*** **Document 54.**

Further Reading

Cohen, Daniel, Pietro Garibaldi, and Stefano Scarpetta. *The Ict Revolution: Productivity Differences and the Digital Divide.* New York: Oxford University Press, 2004.

James, Jeffrey. *Bridging the Global Digital Divide.* Northampton, MA: Edward Elgar Publishing, 2003.

Kehal, Harbhajan S., and Varinder P. Singh. *Digital Economy: Impacts, Influences and Challenges.* Hershey, PA: Idea Group Publishing, 2004.

Servon, Lisa J. *Bridging the Digital Divide: Technology, Community, and Public Policy.* Malden, MA: Blackwell Publishers, 2002.

Warschauer, Mark. *Technology and Social Inclusion: Rethinking the Digital Divide.* Cambridge, MA: MIT Press, 2003.

DUMPING

Dumping is an illegal trade practice that occurs when a company from one nation sells its output in a second country at a price lower than its production costs, or lower than the price charged in its own domestic market. Under the World Trade Organization's (WTO) Anti-Dumping Agreement, countries can defend domestic industries against dumping with prescribed anti-dumping measures.

Exporting companies dump products in foreign markets at artificially low prices for two main reasons. First, dumping is used to reduce or eliminate unsold inventories of certain goods. This often happens when the exporting country is in recession and domestic demand for output is low. Reluctant to fire workers or close plants, exporting companies continue to produce goods at a loss for overseas markets. Second, exporters dump products in foreign markets to undercut competitors in the second country. In this respect dumping involves predatory pricing and is designed to gain a foothold in the second country. Whichever the motive, dumping threatens the survival of some firms and jeopardizes job security for workers in the targeted country.

The WTO's Anti-Dumping Agreement established the world's most recognized guidelines for anti-dumping actions. Before a government can retaliate against an exporter for alleged dumping, the government must satisfy three requirements. First, the government must prove that dumping has taken place. Proof of dumping may involve a price comparison with prevailing market prices in the exporter's home country, or with the market price of the exported product in a third country. Second, the government must calculate the magnitude of the dumping. This calculation is normally expressed as the difference between the normal market price of the product in the exporter's home country and the market price in the second country. Third, the government must prove that the dumping has damaged domestic producers, or at least has the potential to damage domestic producers.

It may appear that existing rules and procedures to identify and deal with dumping are in place, but the application of existing regulations is subject to interpretation. There are many gray areas in determining what constitutes dumping, and in what constitutes an appropriate response to dumping. The WTO's Anti-Dumping Agreement was the culmination of a quarter century of debate and litigation, first under the General Agreement on Tariffs and Trade (GATT) and later under the WTO. Yet, even today, the issue of dumping remains a challenge to the stability of the global trading system. One celebrated anti-dumping action involved U.S. retaliatory duties on Russian and Japanese steel during the late 1990s and early 2000s. Cases of dumping that make the headlines represent just the tip of the iceberg, however. Between 1995 and 2002 nearly 2,000 formal anti-dumping actions were initiated, as shown in Figure 6. By volume, the majority of anti-dumping actions were initiated by developing countries.

Dumping, and resulting anti-dumping actions, create instability in the global trading system. When exporters dump their wares in foreign countries, they disrupt normal pricing mechanisms, threaten domestic producers, and invite retaliation by foreign governments. Anti-dumping actions also pose a significant obstacle to international trade. By the early 2000s, anti-dumping actions were used by governments in the advanced and developing countries as a type of trade barrier, a loophole in the WTO's prohibitions against other forms of trade protectionism. Anti-dumping actions included exorbitant tariffs on disputed products. Tariffs topping

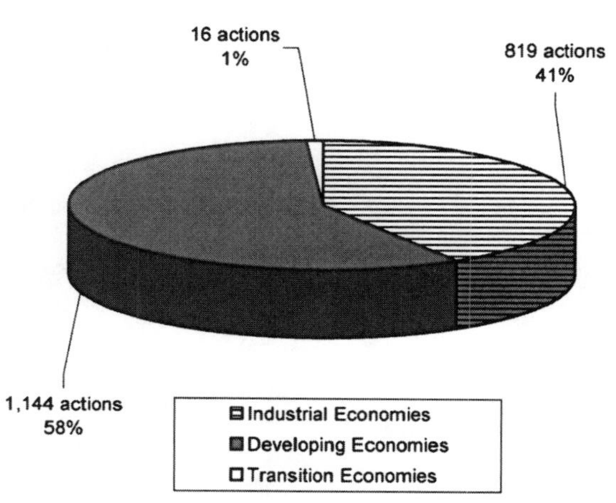

FIGURE 6 **Total Anti-Dumping Actions, 1995 to 2002**

TABLE 32 Anti-Dumping Tariffs in Selected Countries, 2002

Countries by Development	Provisional Duties	
	Low	High
Developing countries		
Argentina	163%	328%
Brazil	54%	64%
China	28%	50%
India	64%	91%
Mexico	269%	345%
Peru	75%	330%
Advanced countries		
Australia	6%	16%
Canada	40%	41%
European Union	33%	45%
Israel	4%	10%
Korea	47%	56%
United States	30%	49%

Source: World Bank, *Global Economic Prospects 2004*, 87.

300 percent of the value of disputed items were not uncommon, as shown in Table 32. Some economists see aggressive anti-dumping actions as a form of disguised protectionism, which can not only disrupt international trade but can also reward production inefficiency in domestic markets.

See also **Exports; Imports; International Trade; Protectionism; Tariffs; World Trade Organization.**

Further Reading

Czako, Judith, Johann Human, and Jorge Miranda. *A Handbook on Anti-Dumping Investigations*. New York: Cambridge University Press, 2003.

Durling, James P., and Matthew R. Nicely. *Understanding the WTO Anti-Dumping Agreement*. London: Cameron May, 2002.

Lindsey, Brink, and Danile J. Ikenson. *Antidumping Exposed: The Devilish Details of Unfair Trade Law*. Washington, DC: Cato Institute, 2003.

Van Bael, Bellis. *Anti-dumping and Other Trade Protection Laws of the EC*. 4th ed. Norwell, MA: Kluwer Law International, 2004.

World Bank. *Global Economic Prospects 2004*. Washington, DC: Author, 2004.

E

ECONOMIC COMMUNITY OF WEST AFRICAN STATES

The Economic Community of West African States (ECOWAS) is a fifteen-member multilateral organization designed to promote economic integration, sustainable growth and development, and regional political stability in West Africa. The Treaty of Lagos (Nigeria) established ECOWAS on May 28, 1975. The organization's original fifteen members included Benin, Burkina Faso, Cote d'Ivoire, Gambia, Ghana, Guinea, Guinea-Bissau, Liberia, Mali, Mauritania, Niger, Nigeria, Senegal, Sierra Leone, and Togo. Cape Verde joined ECOWAS in 1977, and Mauritania withdrew from the organization in 2002. The principal institutions of ECOWAS include the Authority of Heads of State and Government, the Council of Ministers, the Community Parliament, the Social and Economic Council, the Community Court of Justice, the Mediation and Security Council, and the Executive Secretariat.

ECOWAS's original mission centered on regional economic integration and shared development. During the organization's early years, there was also a drive for greater self-reliance by the newly independent West African nations, nations that were anxious to distance themselves from their colonial past. In the early 1990s, revisions in the ECOWAS agreement established specific regional economic goals, including the creation of a common market and a unified currency. In addition, a series of protocols were enacted to support conflict resolution and regional stability. In recent years ECOWAS's peacekeeping protocols have been tested repeatedly in nations such as Liberia, Guinea-Bissau, Sierra Leone, and Cote d'Ivoire. The creation of the Mechanism for Conflict Prevention, Management, Resolution, Peacekeeping and Security in 1999 formalized the organization's commitment to regional harmony.

Recent high-level ECOWAS meetings have accelerated plans for regional integration. The Bamako (Mali) Declaration of 2000, for example, pledged support for free cross-border movements of goods, investments, and people; monetary integration; human resources development; and intraregional infrastructure development. To jump-start the implementation of these goals, five member nations—Gambia, Ghana, Guinea, Nigeria, and Sierra Leone—agreed to fast-track the process. This group initiated formal discussions to create a single ECOWAS currency, the Eco, an initiative scheduled for implementation in 2005. Under the leadership of Nigeria, the region's largest country, the group also planned to create a West African free trade area (FTA) and construct intraregional infrastructure projects such as highways, telecommunications systems, railroad and shipping lines, and electricity grids.

Progress toward regional economic development and stability in ECOWAS countries has been pitted with obstacles. Over the past thirty years, ECOWAS members have dealt with extreme poverty, poor governance, civil unrest and international conflict, rapid population growth, unstable commodity prices, high external debt, and the lack of a sophisticated physical and technological infrastructure. Oil-rich Nigeria remained ECOWAS' dominant member nation, accounting for over half of the region's total population and gross domestic product (GDP) in the early 2000s.

See also **African Development Bank Group; Regional Trade Agreements.**

Further Reading

Economic Community of West African States. *Readings and Documents on ECOWAS: Selected Papers and Discussions from the 1976 Economic Community of West African States Conference.* Indianapolis, IN: Macmillan, 1983.

International Business Publications USA. *Economic Community of West African States Business Law Handbook.* 3d ed. Cincinnati, OH: Author, 2001.

Jaye, Thomas. *Issues of Sovereignty, Strategy and Security in the Economic Community of West African States (Ecowas) Intervention in the Liberian Civil War.* Lewiston, NY: Edwin Mellen Press, 2003.

Schiff, Maurice, and Alan L. Winters. *Regional Integration and Development.* Washington, DC: World Bank Publications, 2003.

World Bank. *Global Economic Prospects: Trade, Regionalism, and Development 2005.* Washington, DC: Author, 2004.

ECONOMIC FREEDOM

Economic freedom is the ability of individuals and businesses to freely choose how to use their private property in an economy. Consumers exercise freedom of choice in determining which goods or services to purchase. Workers express economic freedom by preparing for and securing gainful employment in an occupation, and by freely changing jobs or careers. Savers and investors freely select savings or investment instruments best suited to their financial situations. Businesses exercise freedom of enterprise to employ the best mix of resources in a production process. Economic freedom is embodied in the free enterprise system, or capitalism.

One of the world's most widely recognized measures of economic freedom is *Economic Freedom of the World* (*EFW*) an annual report published by a consortium of economic think-tanks including the Fraser Institute in Canada, the Cato Institute in the United States, and the Hong Kong Center for Economic Research (Hong Kong SAR). In the *EFW* the policies and institutions of individual countries are evaluated, and a freedom ranking is compiled. The *EFW* considers five main categories of data to assess a country's degree of economic freedom: size of government; legal structure and property rights; access to sound money; freedom to trade; and regulation of credit, labor, and business. Generally, a country's freedom ranking is enhanced when policies and institutions support personal choice, individual initiative, good governance, macroeconomic stability, voluntary exchange, private property rights, and competitive

The Hong Kong Special Administrative Region (SAR) is the freest economy in the world.
Courtesy of CORBIS

markets. A country's freedom ranking falls when excessive government intervention, or a negative business environment, limits personal freedoms and distorts market incentives to work, save, invest, or produce.

In *Economic Freedom of the World: 2004 Annual Report*, 123 economies were ranked by level of economic freedom. A nation's ranking is expressed in the freedom index, which is derived from a variety of reliable data. The absence of reliable data excludes many of the world's 208 economies from the ranking. A summary of the highest and lowest ranking countries in the world, measured by degree of economic freedom, are shown in Table 33. Index numbers approaching ten indicate high levels of economic freedom, while index numbers approaching zero indicate low levels of economic freedom.

TABLE 33 **Economic Freedom Rankings, 2002**

Rank	Highest Economic Freedom	*EFW* Index	Rank	Lowest Economic Freedom	*EFW* Index
1	Hong Kong	8.7	114	Russia	5.0
2	Singapore	8.6	115	Burundi	4.9
3	New Zealand	8.2	115	Congo, Rep. of	4.9
3	Switzerland	8.2	117	Guinea-Bissau	4.8
3	United Kingdom	8.2	118	Algeria	4.6
3	United States	8.2	118	Venezuela	4.6
7	Australia	7.9	120	Central African Rep.	4.5
7	Canada	7.9	121	Congo, Dem. Rep.	4.4
9	Ireland	7.8	122	Zimbabwe	3.4
9	Luxembourg	7.8	123	Myanmar	2.5

Source: Fraser Institute, *Economic Freedom of the World: 2004 Annual Report*, 11.

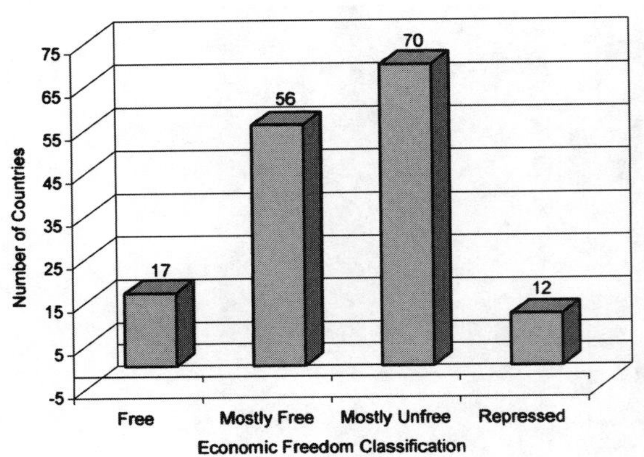

FIGURE 7 **Economic Freedom in the Global Economy, 2005**

Source: Heritage Foundation, *Wall Street Journal, 2005 Index of Economic Freedom*, 2.

Another leading measure of economic freedom in the global economy is the *Index of Economic Freedom*, an annual publication of the Heritage Foundation and *Wall Street Journal*. The *2005 Index of Economic Freedom* evaluated economic conditions in 161 countries against fifty criteria. The fifty criteria were categorized under ten headings, which include trade policy, fiscal burden of government, government intervention in the economy, monetary policy, capital flows and foreign investment, banking and finance, wages and prices, property rights, regulation, and informal market activity. Like the *EFW* ranking, the *Index of Economic Freedom* analyzed factors that affect economic growth. High country rankings in the *Index of Economic Freedom* are earned when countries support free trade, responsible and non-intrusive government policies, healthy financial institutions, and well-defined private property rights. In 2005, the Hong Kong SAR earned the highest freedom ranking. Rounding out the top ten countries were Singapore, Luxembourg, Estonia, Ireland, New Zealand, the United Kingdom, Denmark, Iceland, and Australia, respectively. The ten lowest ranking countries were Venezuela (146), Uzbekistan (147), Iran (148), Cuba (149), Laos (150), Turkmenistan (151) and Zimbabwe (151), Libya (153), Myanmar (154), and North Korea (155). The global summary of economic freedom in 2005 is shown in Figure 7.

Research by credible think-tanks and foundations suggest that economic freedom is an important determinant of investment, economic growth, and per capita income. Researchers at the Fraser Institute, Cato Institute, Heritage Foundation, and elsewhere have identified a series of causal relationships between economic freedom and the overall performance of economies. *Economic Freedom of the World: 2004 Annual Report* argued persuasively that there was a direct causal relationship between high levels of economic freedom and positive economic growth rates. EFW also correlated high freedom rankings with high per capita incomes, high life expectancies, high adult literacy, low infant mortality, low corruption, greater political rights and civil liberties, and low rates of business activity in the extralegal or informal sector. The *2005 Index of Economic Freedom* arrived at similar conclusions. The study of economic freedom and its impact on the wealth of nations is still in its infancy. The topic will likely provide fertile ground for further research in the coming years.

See also **Capitalism; Competitiveness; Democracy; Economic Growth; Entrepreneurship; Hayek, Friedrich A.; Market Economy; Smith, Adam.** ***See also in Volume 2,*** **Documents 10, 13.**

Further Reading

Gwartney, James, and Robert Lawson. *Economic Freedom of the World: 2004 Annual Report.* Vancouver, Canada: The Fraser Institute, 2004.
Miles, Marc, Edwin J. Feulner, Mary Anastasia O'Grady, Ana Isabel Eiras, and Aaron Schavey. *2005 Index of Economic Freedom.* Washington, DC: Heritage Books, 2005.
Piano, Aili, and Arch Puddington. *Freedom in the World 2004: The Annual Survey of Political Rights and Civil Liberties.* New York: Freedom House, 2004.
World Economic Forum. *The Global Competitiveness Report: 2004.* New York: Oxford University Press, 2004.
Ying Huang, Robert E. McCormick, and Lawrence J. McQuillan. *U.S. Economic Freedom Index: 2004 Report.* San Francisco, CA: Pacific Research Institute, 2004.

ECONOMIC GROWTH

Economic growth occurs when the value of a nation's output increases over time. Economic growth is mainly concerned with long-term trends in national output, rather than with annual fluctuations in business activity. Economic growth is typically measured at the national level, but can also be calculated for groups of nations, such as world regions or regional trade blocs, or for the entire global economy. Economic growth is sometimes confused with a broader term, economic development. Economic development deals with economic growth and with measurable improvements in people's quality of life. Economic growth and sustainable economic development are important goals for all countries.

The two most widely used measurements of economic growth are real gross domestic product (GDP) and real GDP per capita. The first measure, real GDP, calculates the dollar value of newly produced national output each year, after adjusting the data for inflation. The real GDP is a convenient measure of economic growth, enabling cross-border comparisons of total output and, thus, the overall size of an economy. Using the traditional exchange rate (Atlas) method of calculating GDP, the real GDP of the United States was $10.4 trillion in 2002, while the real GDP of Switzerland was $267 billion. This means that the size of the U.S. economy was nearly forty times the size of the Swiss economy in the early 2000s. The second measure, real GDP per capita, calculates the inflation-adjusted GDP, divided by the nation's population. The real GDP per capita is a better indicator of people's standard of living because it states the value of national output per person. In 2002 the GDP per capita in the United States was $36,006, while the GDP per capita in Switzerland was $36,687. Based on real GDP per capita, the standard of living for people in the United States and Switzerland was roughly the same. The International Monetary Fund (IMF) reported an increase in global output over the past decade. From 1996 to 2005, the real GDP for the global economy increased from $29.9 trillion to $40.7 trillion, using the exchange rate (Atlas) method of calculation. Using the purchasing power parity (PPP) method, the real GDP in the global economy jumped from $35.7 trillion to $59.6 trillion during the decade. World Bank data are similar but not identical to the IMF calculations. Neither the real

GDP, nor the GDP per capita accounts for the distribution of income or wealth in a country, or the amount of unreported business activity in the informal sector.

The economic growth rate is expressed as a percentage increase or decrease in real GDP over time. Table 34 shows the annual growth rate for the major categories of countries, and for the entire global economy over the past two decades. Note that the ten-year averages record positive growth for the advanced economies, and for the emerging market and developing economies.

The determinants of economic growth are varied and often complementary. At the heart of long-term economic growth is higher productivity. Productivity measures the amount of output that is produced per unit of input, such as labor inputs or capital inputs. Economists typically measure productivity gains in terms of labor inputs. Key economic factors that support the growth of national output and productivity include heavy investment in the factors of production, including capital goods, human resources, and natural resources; and investment in research and development (R&D), information and communications technologies (ICTs), and entrepreneurship and innovation. The maintenance of formal economic institutions such as capital markets, and informal institutions such as profit incentives, is also critical. Good governance, the honest and competent administration of government, creates a pro-growth environment. Key government responsibilities include the building and maintenance of an economic infrastructure, legal protections for property rights and the sanctity of contracts, and responsible macroeconomic policies. Democratic political institutions, based on broad citizen participation, a free media, and an independent judiciary, also support a pro-growth national agenda.

Economic growth is illustrated by an outward shift in a nation's production possibilities curve (PPC), as shown in Figure 8. A PPC shows the range of possible production choices for a nation at a moment in time. In the following illustration the inner PPC, AB, shows the original range of output for two types of goods, investment goods and consumption goods. At point A, all of the nation's resources are devoted to investment goods; hence, zero consumption goods are produced. At point B, all resources are used to produce consumption goods; hence, no investment goods are produced. In reality, a nation would likely

TABLE 34 **Economic Growth in the Global Economy, 1987 to 2006***

Country Classification	Real Gross Domestic Product		GDP per Capita	
	1987–1996	1997–2006	1987–1996	1997–2006
Advanced economies	3.0%	2.7%	2.3%	2.1%
Emerging market and developing economies	3.9%	5.3%	2.1%	3.9%
World	3.3%	3.9%	2.6%	2.9%

*IMF data for 2005 and 2006 are estimates.
Source: International Monetary Fund, *World Economic Outlook, April 2005*, 201.

choose to produce at a point between A and B, perhaps at point C. Economic growth is represented by a shift of the curve AB to YZ. Note that at every point along the curve YZ, more investment goods and consumption goods are produced. The outward shift of the PPC from AB to YZ illustrates economic growth.

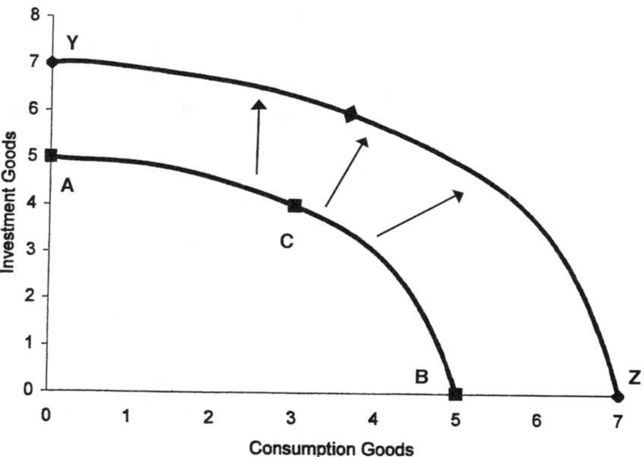

FIGURE 8 **Economic Growth: An Illustration**

The benefits of economic growth are readily observable. First, economic growth improves people's standard of living. Today, the most common standard of living measure is the gross national income (GNI) per capita. Most people who live in countries with a high GNI per capita are able to satisfy their economic needs for food, clothing, and housing. They also consume many types of luxury goods such as automobiles, personal computers, televisions, artwork, vacations, and a wide variety of consumer durables. Second, economic growth improves people's quality of life. A higher quality of life implies a higher standard of living plus other improvements in the human condition, including access to education, health care, personal security, infrastructure, and social programs. Third, economic growth fuels the virtuous cycle of development. Economic growth promotes national savings, and productive investment in R&D, private and social capital, human capital, and entrepreneurship.

The costs of economic growth are also apparent. One cost is environmental degradation, an inevitable result of production. The severity of degradation varies widely among regions, yet the drive to increase national output fouls the air, water, and land with pollutants. This drive sometimes creates wastelands due to strip-mining and aggressive timbering, overgrazing, and overplanting. Toxic emissions into the atmosphere cause global warming, ozone depletion, acid rain, and other harmful effects on the global commons. A second cost of economic growth is resource depletion. Resource depletion occurs when resources are used in production but not replaced. Nonrenewable resources, including petroleum and natural gas, are in finite supply. They are consumed in the production process and cannot be reclaimed for further use. The authoritative *World Resources 2000–2001*, a co-publication of the World Resources Institute, World Bank, and the United Nations, reported severe global resource depletion of some basic resources such as fresh water, soil, and forests. A third cost of economic growth is a decline in some people's quality of life. For instance, the widening digital divide creates unequal economic opportunities in the global economy. People in the advanced countries receive far more benefit from global economic growth than do people in the world's poorest regions.

See also **Business Cycle; Capital Formation; Competitiveness; Environmental Degradation; Gross Domestic Product; Quality of Life; Schumacher, Ernst F.; Schumpeter, Joseph A.; Solow, Robert M.; Sustainable Economic Development.** ***See also in Volume 2,*** **Documents 3, 5, 9, 12, 13, 14, 15, 16, 51.**

Further Reading

Easterly, William. *The Elusive Quest for Growth: Economists' Adventures and Misadventures in the Tropics*. Cambridge, MA: MIT Press, 2002.

Helpman, Elhanan. *The Mystery of Economic Growth*. Cambridge, MA: Belknap Press, 2004.

Jones, Charles I. *Introduction to Economic Growth*. 2d ed. New York: W.W. Norton & Company, 2002.

Sykes, Michael, ed. *Understanding Economic Growth*. New York: Palgrave Macmillan and the Organization for Economic Cooperation and Development, 2004.

World Bank. *Doing Business in 2005: Obstacles to Growth*. Washington, DC: Author, 2004.

———. *Responsible Growth for the New Millennium: Integrating Society, Ecology, and the Economy*. Washington, DC: Author, 2004.

ECONOMIC SECTORS

The economic sectors are the three main areas of production in a country—the services-producing sector, goods-producing (industrial) sector, and agricultural sector. Production and output data for most economies in the global economy are classified under one of these three general categories. Classifying production is a complicated process because the distinction between services-producing and goods-producing industries is often blurred.

A stone quarry is a type of goods-producing enterprise.
Courtesy of Getty Images: Martial Colomb

The services-producing sector consists of industries that supply productive activities in the economy. Categories of services include transportation, such as railways and airlines; telecommunications; public utilities, such as water and electricity; wholesale and retail trade; finance, such as banking and securities trading; insurance; education; tourism; broadcasting, such as television and radio; and a wide variety of services related to business operations, health care, social welfare, and personal care. Government services at the federal, state, and local levels are also included in the services-producing sector. In the high-income countries most jobs and national output stem from the services-producing sector. By the early 2000s, services accounted for at least 70 percent of the gross domestic product (GDP) in many advanced economies, including Austria, Belgium, Denmark, France, Greece, Hong Kong SAR, the Netherlands, Sweden, Switzerland, the United Kingdom, and the United States. Conversely, services accounted for a far lower percentage of GDP in poorer nations. Services represented less than 30 percent of GDP in the Central African Republic, Democratic Republic of Congo, Guinea-Bissau, Laos, Sierra Leone, and Turkmenistan.

The goods-producing, or industrial sector, consists of industries that supply tangible items. Tangible items include final goods, intermediate goods, and natural resources. Final goods are items ready for immediate consumption by households or businesses. Intermediate goods are semi-finished items that require further processing, or are components of another good. Natural resources are gifts of nature such as petroleum and minerals. In the United States the goods-producing sector includes manufacturing, construction, and mining. Other classification schemes list construction under services. In the advanced economies, the goods-producing sector is capital-intensive. Capital-intensive production relies heavily on sophisticated machinery and equipment, which increase the productivity of labor. In many developing countries the goods-producing sector is primarily labor-intensive. Labor-intensive production relies on physical labor rather than real capital. The lack of capital goods helps explain why national output, and the productivity of labor are relatively low in the poorer regions of the world.

The agricultural sector of an economy is comprised of farms, dairies, poultry and livestock farms, forestry, and the fishing and shellfish industries. In the advanced economies, production in the agricultural sector is highly mechanized and efficient. Hence, most advanced economies achieve food self-sufficiency with just a small percentage of their work force devoted to agriculture. In addition, agriculture represents a small percent of GDP in many advanced economies (2 percent or less in Japan, Norway, Sweden, Switzerland, the United Kingdom, and the United States). In the developing world, however, the agricultural sector is labor-intensive and productivity is relative low. As a consequence, a larger percentage of the labor force is employed in the agricultural sector, and more of the nation's output is agricultural. Subsistence agriculture is still the norm in some of the poorest developing countries. Agriculture represents more than 50 percent of GDP in Afghanistan, the Central African Republic, the Democratic Republic of

TABLE 35 **Structure of Global Output by Sector, 2003**

Classification of Country	Agriculture (% of GDP)	Industry (% of GDP)	Services (% of GDP)
Low income	24	27	49
Lower middle income	11	37	52
Upper middle income	6	35	59
High income	2	27	71

Source: World Bank, *2005 World Development Indicators*, Table 4.2, 186–188.

Congo, Guinea-Bissau, Laos, Myanmar, and Sierra Leone. Table 35 shows the structure of output, by economic sector, for different classifications of countries. Note that as countries' income status rises, agriculture as a percent of GDP decreases, and services as a percent of GDP increases.

See also **Advanced Economies; Basic Economic Questions; Developing Countries; Economic System.**

Further Reading

Duesterberg, Thomas J., and Ernest H. Preeg, eds. *U.S. Manufacturing: The Engine for Growth in a Global Economy*. Westport, CT: Praeger Publishers, 2003.

Fingleton, Eamonn. *In Praise of Hard Industries: Why Manufacturing, Not the Information Economy, Is the Key to Future Prosperity*. New York: Houghton Mifflin, 1999.

Triplett, Jack E., and Barry P. Bosworth. *Productivity in the U.S. Services Sector: New Sources of Economic Growth*. Washington, DC: Brookings Institution Press, 2004.

Van Loon, Gary W. *Agricultural Sustainability: Strategies for Assessment*. Thousand Oaks, CA: SAGE Publications, 2004.

World Bank. *Agricultural Growth and the Poor: An Agenda for Development*. Washington, DC: Author, 2005.

———. *2004 World Development Indicators*. Washington, DC: Author, 2004.

ECONOMIC SYSTEM

An economic system represents all economic activity in a country. Economic systems are comprised of tangible economic institutions such as businesses, financial institutions, and labor unions. They are also comprised of intangibles such as profit incentives, the work ethic, and other economic values. All economic systems answer the three basic economic questions of what, how, and for whom to produce. How a society responds to these basic questions distinguishes one type of economic system from another. Economists often identify three types of economic systems as models—the traditional economy, command economy, and market economy. In reality, all economies are "mixed economies" because they incorporate certain elements from these models into their economic system.

A traditional economy is a type of economic system that relies on custom or tradition to answer the basic economic questions. The institutions and practices in traditional economies are passed from one generation to the next without significant modification. Today, the few remaining traditional economies are generally isolated from other groups by deserts, jungles, frozen tundra, or other natural barriers. They produce goods that satisfy basic survival needs for food, clothing, and shelter. The economic status quo is reinforced by the use of primitive capital goods and the absence of technology and entrepreneurship. Further, a rigid division of labor often uses gender, age, and skills to define one's status and role in society. Primitive communalism, reinforced with kinship ties, often influences the distribution of scarce goods. Examples include the Mbuti Pygmies of Central Africa, the Kavango tribes of Namibia, the Nigritos of the Philippines, and the Saharias of central India.

A river market in Thailand illustrates many features of a free market economy.
Courtesy of Getty Images: Mark Downey

A command economy is a type of economic system in which the government dictates the answers to the basic economic questions. Economic decision making is placed in the hands of a central authority. During the twentieth century, the fascist economies of Italy and Germany, and the communist economies of the Soviet Union and eastern bloc satellite countries, were fashioned along command principles. The fascists adopted the corporate state, or corporativism, to tighten the government's control over businesses, labor, and other economic institutions. Under fascism, government control over the economy relied on strategic alliances between the government and private enterprises. The communists, on the other hand, seized control of business enterprises, and instituted central planning to dictate how resources would be used. Hence, the government owned and controlled society's productive enterprises. Fascism and communism, two antagonistic systems, adapted the command economy model to further their horrific economic and political agendas. The collapse of fascism at the close of World War II, and the demise of communism during the late 1980s and early 1990s, generally discredited the command model. Today, elements of a command economy can still be found in Cuba and North Korea.

A market economy is a type of economic system that rests on private sector decision making. Individuals and firms answer the basic economic questions. The government's economic role is relegated to maintaining a proper business climate, and providing security from internal or external threats. At the heart of a market economy are the institutions of private property, profit incentives, voluntary exchange, and a host of marketplace freedoms. Consumers, for example, have the freedom of choice—the ability to spend their money as they wish. In doing so, consumers answer the basic question of what to produce. Producers have the freedom of enterprise. Freedom of enterprise encourages businesses to use scarce resources in efficient and profitable ways. The market mechanism, guided by self-interest, permits the forces of supply and demand to determine prices and allocate resources in free and competitive markets. Capitalist economies adopted the core principles of the market economy model during the 1800s and 1900s. Today, capitalist economies include the United States, Japan, United Kingdom, and most other advanced economies. In addition, market reforms are currently being implemented in many emerging market and developing countries.

See also **Basic Economic Questions; Capitalism; Command Economy; Communism; Democratic Socialism; Emerging Market Economies; Market Economy; Third World Socialism.**

Further Reading

Ebenstein, William, Edwin Fogelman, and Alan O. Ebenstein. *Today's ISMS: Socialism, Capitalism, Fascism, Communism and Libertarianism.* 11th ed. Paramus, NJ: Prentice-Hall, 1999.

Fulcher, James. *Capitalism: A Very Short Introduction.* New York: Oxford University Press, 2004.

Lindblom, Charles E. *The Market System: What It Is, How It Works, and What to Make of It.* New Haven, CT: Yale University Press, 2001.

Pendergast, Sara, and Tom Pendergast, eds. *Worldmark Encyclopedia of National Economies.* Vols. 1–4. Farmington Hills, MI: Gale Group, 2002.

Pipes, Richard. *Communism: A History.* New York: Modern Library, 2001.

EMBARGO

An embargo is a type of economic sanction that a government or other political entity imposes on another country. A comprehensive economic embargo halts all trade, investment, and other commercial contacts between two countries. More selective embargoes can also stop trade in a specific good or type of technology. In recent years arms embargoes have been widely used to reduce the availability of munitions to governments that sponsor terrorism, violate people's human rights, or otherwise impose their will on other peoples. Many embargoes are politically motivated, designed to pressure another government to change a domestic or international policy. During the past few decades embargoes have been initiated by individual countries, such as the United States; multilateral organizations, such as the United Nations (UN); producer cartels, such as the Organization for Petroleum Exporting Countries (OPEC); and regional trade blocs, such as the European Union (EU).

The comprehensive U.S. embargo on Cuba is among the world's most contentious economic sanctions. The embargo began in 1960 in response to Fidel Castro's successful ouster of a U.S.-backed government in Cuba. The embargo stopped virtually all trade, investment, and other business dealings between the United States and Cuba. The U.S. embargo on Cuba was strengthened in 1996 when Congress passed the Cuban Liberty and Democratic Solidarity Act, also called the Helms Burton Act. Under the Helms Burton Act, the United States pledged to extend the existing embargo to any company, foreign or domestic, caught trafficking U.S. properties that had been confiscated by the Castro regime. The Helms-Burton Act created a firestorm of protest throughout the world, and its enforcement was suspended repeatedly by President Bill Clinton during the late 1990s and by President George W. Bush in the early 2000s. The U.S. embargo has crippled economic development in Cuba, but has failed to weaken the resolve or authority of the Cuban dictator Castro. In 2004, the UN General Assembly approved a resolution condemning the U.S. embargo of Cuba by a 179 to 4 vote—the thirteenth official UN condemnation of the embargo. Over the years, other U.S. embargoes were imposed on countries that sponsor terrorism, including Iran, Iraq, Libya, and Sudan.

UN embargoes support the organization's peacekeeping and humanitarian functions. For example, UN Resolution 661, which was approved in August 1990, slapped a comprehensive trade embargo on Iraq. The UN embargo was designed to end Iraq's illegal occupation of neighboring Kuwait. The failure of UN sanctions prompted a military response early in 1991. After a UN coalition force liberated Kuwait in early 1991, the embargo was resumed to help ensure Iraqi compliance with the conditions of peace. Shortly thereafter, modifications in the embargo permitted Iraq to export limited qualities of oil on the condition that oil revenues were used for humanitarian purposes, a concession referred to the oil-for-food agreement. The UN embargo on Iraq during the 1990s and early 2000s yielded uncertain benefits. Corruption in the oil-for-food program, and certain confrontational postures by Iraqi dictator Saddam Hussein, led to a U.S. invasion of Iraq in March 2003. Soon after Hussein's regime collapsed, the UN embargo was lifted. Other UN embargoes were previously placed on Rhodesia (1970s) and South Africa (1980s) to pressure white minority governments to end racist domestic policies, and on Serbia (1990s) in response to horrific human rights violations.

The sting of an economic embargo was felt by the United States and other advanced economies during the 1970s. In 1973, the Arab members of the Organization of Petroleum Exporting Countries (OPEC) imposed an oil embargo on the United States, Japan, and several Western European countries to punish certain advanced economies for their support for Israel during the Yom Kippur War. The United States and the Netherlands, each staunch supporters of Israel, bore the brunt of the oil embargo. Shortages of gasoline, home heating oil, and other petroleum-based products caused hardships for consumers and businesses. The embargo was lifted in March 1974. The embargo provided a rallying point for OPEC. By flexing its collective muscle in 1973–1974, the OPEC cartel was able to quadruple oil prices in global markets during the period.

See also **Organization of Petroleum Exporting Countries; Protectionism.** ***See also in Volume 2,*** **Document 44.**

Further Reading

Haney, Patrick J., and Walt Vanderbush. *The Cuban Embargo: The Domestic Politics of an American Foreign Policy*. Pittsburgh, PA: University of Pittsburgh Press, 2005.

Naylor, R. T. *Economic Warfare: Sanctions, Embargo Busting, and Their Human Cost*. Boston, MA: Northeastern University Press, 2001.

Ratcliff, William, and Roger Fontaine. *A Strategic Flip-Flop in the Caribbean: Lift the Embargo on Cuba*. Stanford, CA: Hoover Institution Press, 2000.
United Nations Conference on Trade and Development. *Trade and Development Report, 1995 with Overview: Embargo*. New York: United Nations, 1995.

EMERGING MARKET ECONOMIES

Emerging market economies are countries that have made significant strides toward capitalism and sustainable economic development. The term emerging market economies has been used for decades. The International Monetary Fund's (IMF's) 2004 reclassification of world economies brought new attention to the term emerging market economies. The IMF's classification of economies during much of the 1990s and early 2000s identified three main categories of economies: advanced economies, developing economies, and transition economies. The IMF's 2004 reclassification scheme eliminated the transition economy category. Today, the two categories of economies include advanced economies, and "other emerging market and developing countries." In 2004 there were twenty-nine advanced economies. The remaining 179 economies in the world were classified as other emerging market and developing countries.

The emerging market economies (EMEs) are countries that successfully implement market-oriented economic reforms, and make steady gains in economic growth and development. There is no definitive economic, geographic, or political line that separates the EMEs from other developing countries. Yet, there are some generally recognized characteristics that help make the distinction. First, EMEs are generally classified as lower middle-income or upper middle-income countries. By World Bank standards for 2004, this meant that EMEs' gross national income (GNI) per capita was between $825 and $10,065. Most low-income countries were classified as developing economies. Second, EMEs are growth-oriented. Economic growth, in this context, is typically measured by sustained increases in the country's real gross domestic product (GDP) per capita. According to the United Nations Conference on Trade and Development (UNCTAD), EMEs such as Malta, Chile, Malaysia, and China recorded high annual GDP per capita growth, topping 4 percent from 1975 to 2002. Third, some EMEs are transitional countries, shifting from closed or static economies to open market-based economies. The former communist countries of eastern and central Europe, such as Hungary, Poland, and Russia, illustrate this type of transition. Other countries not previously part of the communist world, such as India, South Africa, and Mexico, are also transitioning. Fourth, EMEs are active participants in the global economy. They liberalize trade, court foreign direct investment (FDI), develop sophisticated capital markets, and stabilize the value of their currencies. They tend to be members of, and solicit technical assistance from, multilateral organizations such as the World Bank, IMF, and regional development banks. China, Malaysia, and Thailand, for example, embrace globalization as a key element in their economic development. The May 2004 enlargement of the European Union (EU) also reflects the outward-looking mentality of nine European EMEs, including the Czech Republic,

Estonia, Hungary, Latvia, Lithuania, Malta, Poland, the Slovak Republic, and Slovenia (the tenth accession country, Cyprus, is classified as an advanced economy). Finally, EMEs support good governance and the rule of law. EMEs institute political reforms to democratize the political system, establish and enforce business codes to protect market institutions, and guarantee transparency in public and private sector business activities. Examples include the EU accession countries, Chile, and Argentina.

Under the IMF's 2004 reclassification of economies, vast quantities of economic data is merged beneath the general heading of emerging market and developing economies. Table 36 compares and contrasts the advanced economies with the emerging market and developing countries.

EMEs exist in all world regions. Emerging Europe, for example, includes most of the former communist nations of eastern and central Europe, such as the Czech Republic, Hungary, and Poland. It also includes several countries that were "republics" within the former Soviet Union, such as Estonia, Latvia, and Lithuania. Since the early 1990s, the twenty-eight countries of eastern and central Europe, and central Asia were commonly called the transition countries. Their economic transition was from centrally planned communist economies to market-oriented economies. Their political transition was from single-party totalitarian regimes to democracy. Emerging Asia includes several of the world's largest emerging market economies, such as China and India. Measured by purchasing power parity (PPP), China and India accounted for more than 19 percent of total world output in 2004—more than the twelve-country European Monetary Union (EMU), and nearly triple the output of Japan. Other major emerging market economies exist in Africa, such as South Africa, and the Americas, such as Argentina, Brazil, Chile, and Mexico.

TABLE 36 **Advanced Economies, Emerging Market and Developing Countries, 2003**

Comparisons	Advanced Economies	Emerging Market and Developing Countries
Number of countries*	29	146
Population (% of world)	15.4%	84.6%
World GDP (% of world)**	55.5%	44.5%
GDP growth rate	2.1%	6.1%
Output per capita (% growth)	1.6%	4.8%
Total exports (% of world)	73.4%	26.6%
Median inflation rate	2.2%	4.5%
External debt ($ billions)	n/a	$2,724
Debt service ($ billions)	n/a	$438

*175 economies are included. Excluded from the comparison are countries that are not IMF members or that have insufficient or unreliable economic data. World Bank data identify 179 emerging market and developing economies.
**GDP data based on purchasing power parity (PPP).
Source: International Monetary Fund, *World Economic Outlook, September 2004*, 191, 199, 210, 260.

The EMEs and developing countries face similar types of economic and political challenges. The main difference between the two groups is one of degree—the EMEs recording significant gains in economic freedom and development and the developing economies victimized by extreme poverty, poor quality of life, sluggish or negative economic growth, and corrupt or repressive governments. The progress of EMEs toward sustainable economic development is sometimes pitted with obstacles. For example, extreme poverty confronts EMEs such as India and Indonesia. Financial crises in East Asia, Russia, and Brazil during the late 1990s threw many EMEs into an economic tailspin. The lethargic pace of democratic reforms in China, and questionable electoral practices in Russia, are also challenges to the process of development. Still, the economic and political progress of EMEs far outpace that of other developing countries such as Liberia, Somalia, and Sudan in Africa; Cambodia, Myanmar, and North Korea in Asia; Azerbaijan, Tajikistan, and Uzbekistan in Central Asia; and Haiti and Cuba in the Americas.

See also **Advanced Economies; Developing Countries; Economic System; Transition Countries**

Further Reading

Das, Dilip K. *Financial Globalization and the Emerging Market Economies.* New York: Routledge, 2004.

Feldstein, Martin. *Economic and Financial Crises in Emerging Market Economies.* Chicago, IL: University of Chicago Press, 2003.

Hacker, R. Scott, B. Johansson, and Charlie Karlsson. *Emerging Market Economies and European Economic Integration.* Northampton, MA: Edward Elgar Publishing, 2005.

Kapstein, Ethan B., Branko Milanovic, and the Institute for Employment Research. *Income and Influence: Social Policy in Emerging Market Economies.* Kalamazoo, MI: W.E. Upjohn Institute, 2003.

Koodko, Grzegorz W. *Emerging Market Economies: Globalization and Development.* Brookfield, VT: Ashgate Publishing, 2003.

ENERGY RESOURCES

Energy resources fuel most production in the global economy. There are five main categories of energy resources, including oil, natural gas, coal, nuclear, and other sources. The "other" category includes electricity generated from renewable energy sources including hydroelectric, geothermal, solar, and wind power. "Other" energy resources also include fuels that can be burned such as wood, biomass, and alcohol fuels. In 2005 energy produced from the big three fossil fuels—oil, natural gas, and coal—accounted for about 85 percent of all energy consumed in the global economy, as shown in Figure 9. In its *International Energy Outlook 2004*, the U.S. Department of Energy projected that the consumption of oil and natural gas would show small percentage gains between 2005 and 2025, increasing to 39.4 percent and 25.1 percent of global consumption, respectively. The three remaining energy sources would show modest declines, including coal (22.5 percent of global energy consumption), nuclear (4.9 percent), and other (8.1 percent).

The functioning of the global economy is dependent on an adequate supply of energy at a reasonable price. Not surprisingly, there are a host of controversial issues related to the production and consumption of the world's energy resources. Production issues are mainly concerned with the supply side of the market. One production issue is the dominant position of nonrenewable fossil fuels in the global economy. Nonrenewable natural resources such as oil, natural gas, and coal cannot be reused once they have fueled electric generators, furnaces, or motor vehicles. Fossil fuels are also in finite supply. Eventually they will run out. Many people believe that additional research and development should be devoted to alternative, renewable energy sources as a way to conserve fossil fuels and to minimize the pollutants that fossil fuels create.

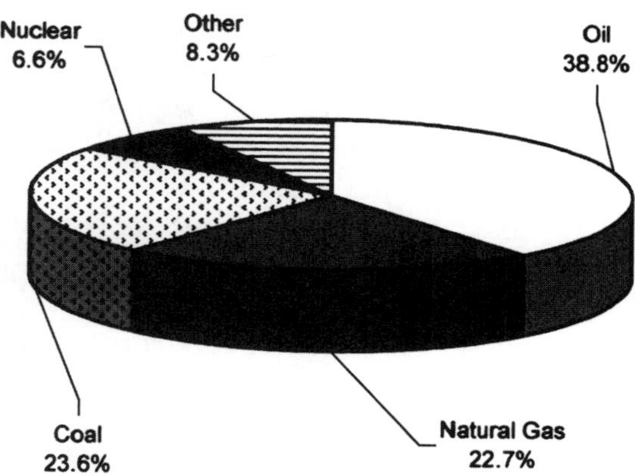

FIGURE 9 **Global Energy Consumption by Source, 2005**

Source: U.S. Department of Energy, *International Energy Outlook 2004*.

Offshore oil platforms supplement onshore production of petroleum, the world's most important energy resource.

Courtesy of Getty Images: Doug Menuez

A second production issue deals with the use of nuclear power to generate electricity. At issue is the lack of global safeguards, such as containment domes, and unresolved questions about how to store toxic wastes from existing nuclear facilities. In the United States, people living on the east coast narrowly escaped nuclear disaster when the Three-Mile Island (Pennsylvania) nuclear facility malfunctioned in 1979. The 1986 nuclear meltdown at the Chernobyl nuclear plant in the Ukraine resulted in massive radiation poisoning of people and the destruction of other resources. The fact that many nuclear power plants are aging is another cause for concern.

A third global production issue concerns interruptions in energy flows. Interruptions in global energy supplies are not a new threat to the global economy. In 1973–1974, the Arab members of the Organization of Petroleum

Exporting Countries (OPEC) placed an oil embargo on the United States and other industrialized countries. The oil embargo was a politically motivated response to the U.S. support for Israel during the Yom Kippur War in 1973. The cessation of oil exports from the Arab members of OPEC to countries in the industrialized world disrupted business activity and contributed to economic recession in the United States and elsewhere. By the early 2000s, another danger—global terrorism—also threatened cross-border flows of valuable energy resources. As a result, the global community prepared to defend its energy resources from terrorist groups, such as Al Qaeda.

Energy consumption, which represents the demand side of the market, spawns other global concerns. One important issue is the consumption gap between the industrialized economies and the transition and developing economies. The lopsided consumption of energy resources has, historically, favored the industrialized countries. The large energy requirements of rich nations stems from their need to power major industries, and to satisfy households' needs for gasoline, heating oil, and other goods. By the early 2000s the World Bank reported that people in the high-income countries consumed roughly ten times the energy, per person, as people in the low-income countries, and four times the energy, per person, as people living in the middle-income countries.

While total energy consumption in the global economy is also skewed in favor of the richer industrialized countries, the consumption gap is shrinking. The Department of Energy's *International Energy Outlook 2004* reported that in 1975, the industrialized countries consumed 62 percent of all energy resources, compared to just 21 percent for Eastern Europe and the Soviet Union, and 17 percent for developing countries. By 2005 the distribution gap had narrowed, with shares diminishing for the industrialized countries (52 percent) and eastern and central Europeans (13 percent), and doubling for the developing countries (35 percent). In addition, the Department of Energy projected that by 2025, the total amount of energy consumed by the industrialized countries (45 percent) and developing countries (43 percent) would be nearly the same. Figure 10 shows the progressive increases in global energy consumption over a fifty-year period.

Energy production and consumption decisions affect people's quality of life in both positive and negative ways. On the positive side, increased production and use of energy spurs economic growth and development, and, thus expands the quantity and quality of consumption and investment goods in the global economy. On the negative side, the by-products of large-scale energy production and

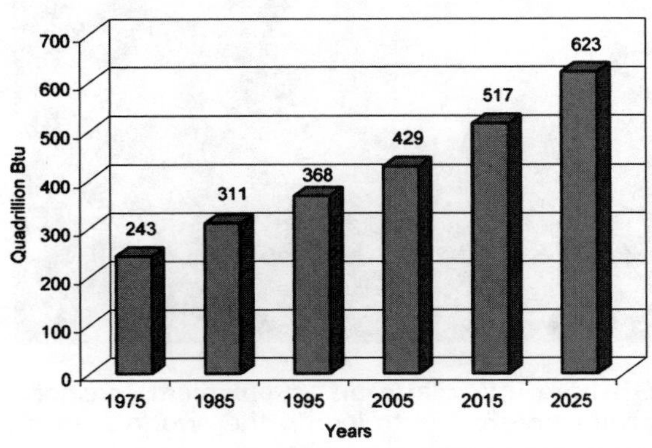

FIGURE 10 **World Energy Consumption, 1975–2025 (quadrillion btu)**

Source: Energy Information Administration, U.S. Department of Energy, *International Energy Outlook 2004*, 1.

consumption pollute local environments; upset natural balances in the atmosphere, oceans, and other realms of the global commons; and perpetuate tensions between the nations of the global North and South. The use of energy will continue to grow as economies develop and the world's population expands to 9 billion by 2050. Today, policymakers are challenged to expand the use of renewable energy resources, value energy conservation, protect the global commons, and promote sustainable energy consumption.

See also **Environmental Degradation; Factors of Production; Organization of Petroleum Exporting Countries; Sustainable Consumption.** ***See also in Volume 2,*** **Documents 43, 44.**

Further Reading

Boyle, Godfrey. *Renewable Energy.* 2d ed. New York: Oxford University Press, 2004.

Cavanagh, John, et al. *Alternatives to Economic Globalization: A Better World Is Possible.* San Francisco, CA: Berrett-Koehler Publishers, 2004.

Doig, Alison, Simon Dunnett, Tim Jackson, Smail Khennas, and Yacob Mulugetta. *Energy for Rural Livelihoods: A Framework for Sustainable Decision Making.* Rugby, UK: ITDG Publishing, 2005.

Energy Information Administration, U.S. Department of Energy. *International Energy Outlook 2004.* Washington, DC: Author, 2004.

Schrattenholzer, Leo, and Asami Miketa. *Achieving a Sustainable Global Energy System.* Northampton, MA: Edward Elgar Publishing, 2005.

ENTREPRENEURSHIP

Entrepreneurship represents the actions of entrepreneurs in developing new products, processes, or businesses. Entrepreneurs are innovators and risk-takers. They tend to see commercial opportunities, and seize the initiative to transform commercial ideas into commercial enterprises. Entrepreneurs are sometimes individuals who start a new business, a process called venture initiation. Entrepreneurs might also be innovators within an existing business enterprise, such as scientists, engineers, or managers. Entrepreneurs operating within an existing business are sometimes called intrapreneurs. Intrapreneurs adapt or improve existing products, or introduce new product lines to the firm. Entrepreneurship is an agent of growth and change in an economy. Because of the vital role of entrepreneurship in business activity and production, it is sometimes viewed as a factor of production, joining human resources, natural resources, and capital goods.

In recent years the role of entrepreneurship in the global economy has received additional attention by development economists and policymakers. Renewed interest in entrepreneurship was sparked by the launch of the *Global Entrepreneurship Monitor (GEM)*, an annual publication of Babson College and the London School of Business. The *Global Entrepreneurship Monitor 2003* measured entrepreneurial activity in forty-one advanced and developing economies. One *GEM* measurement of entrepreneurship is the Total Entrepreneurial Activity (TEA) Index. The TEA Index evaluates the entrepreneurial performance of thirty-one GEM countries based on business start-ups and

Entrepreneurs in Ecuador conduct business activity in the formal and informal sectors of the economy.
Courtesy of Getty Images: PhotoLink

the competitiveness of these business ventures. Based on the TEA Index, the top ten countries in 2003 were Uganda, Venezuela, Argentina, Chile, New Zealand, Brazil, the United States, Australia, China, and Iceland. The lowest-ranked GEM countries were South Africa, Sweden, Slovenia, Belgium, the Netherlands, Hong Kong, Italy, Japan, Croatia, and France. *GEM 2003* also offered a more comprehensive global assessment of entrepreneurial activity, which included business start-ups, and innovation and growth within existing firms. A summary of this classification, which identifies five groups of countries, is shown in Table 37. Group A represents countries with the highest levels of entrepreneurial activity, while Group E countries have the lowest levels of entrepreneurial activity.

The financing of entrepreneurship in the global economy combines informal and formal mechanisms. Today, informal methods dominate the financing of global entrepreneurial activity. Informal financing taps the personal assets of entrepreneurs, their families, and their friends to start a business. *GEM 2003* reported that $360 billion in informal investments were made in 2003 to support new business ventures. In the same year and additional $32 billion in traditional venture capital was invested in start-up firms. Venture capital, also called risk capital, is money invested in new and promising businesses, mainly by venture capital firms called venture capitalists. The $32 billion in venture capital funding represented only 8 percent of the $392 billion in total funding for entrepreneurs in 2003. In recent years, venture capital funding for entrepreneurial activities has declined. In sixteen advanced economies tracked by *GEM*, for example, venture capital investment dropped from $120 billion in 2000 to just $30 billion in 2002. Yet, historically, venture capitalists were instrumental in launching some of today's technological giants such as Microsoft, Intel, and Google.

There are different motivations and support structures for entrepreneurship in the global economy. *GEM 2003* reports that "opportunity entrepreneurship" is prevalent in richer countries, and among wealthier people. Opportunity entrepreneurship is based on personal choice, and often utilizes the higher

TABLE 37 **Classification of Countries by Entrepreneurial Activity, 2003**

Group	Number of Countries	Countries [41 GEM Countries]
A	5	Chile, South Korea, New Zealand, Uganda, Venezuela
B	4	Brazil, China, India, Mexico
C	15	Argentina, Australia, Canada, Denmark, Finland, Hong Kong SAR, Hungary, Iceland, Ireland, Slovenia, Spain, Singapore, Thailand, United Kingdom, United States
D	9	Belgium, Germany, Greece, Israel, Italy, Norway, South Africa, Sweden, Switzerland
E	7	Chinese Taipei, Croatia, France, Japan, the Netherlands, Poland, Russia

Source: Paul D. Reynolds, William D. Bygrave, and Erkko Autio, *GEM 2003 Global Report*, 12.

educational level and personal assets of individual entrepreneurs to jump-start an enterprise. "Necessity entrepreneurship" is more common in the world's poorer regions, and among poorer people in general. Necessity entrepreneurship is based on the need for additional household income to purchase the necessities of life such as for food, clothing, and housing. Among the more important factors that encourage entrepreneurship in both the rich and poor nations are personal contacts with other entrepreneurs; a younger labor force; fewer burdensome government regulations and taxes on businesses; less central planning by government; more cultural acceptance of business risk-taking; and less government support for a safety net of social programs.

Entrepreneurship has a major impact on economic growth and development in countries, regardless of their income status. First, entrepreneurship creates new firms, and makes existing firms more innovative and competitive. *GEM 2003* reported that in 2003 entrepreneurial activity in just forty GEM countries accounted for 192 million business start-ups. In addition, 37 million "entrepreneurial firms" instituted innovations in production methods or product line. Second, entrepreneurship creates new jobs. In 2003, 297 million people were involved in new business start-ups, and an additional 57 million were owner-managers of existing entrepreneurial firms. In *GEM* countries, entrepreneurs represented between 2 percent and 15 percent of the entire labor force. Third, evidence continues to mount pointing to a positive correlation between increased entrepreneurship and higher rates of economic growth over time. *GEM* research shows that necessity entrepreneurship in the world's poorer regions boosts economic growth at an even faster rate than opportunity entrepreneurship does in the wealthier nations. Table 38 shows some of the leading entrepreneurial countries measured by business and job creation.

Entrepreneurship has taken center stage in the realm of development economics in recent years. Since the 1990s, prominent development economists such as Hernando de Soto have stressed policies of inclusion to promote sustainable economic development in the world's poorer regions. At the heart

TABLE 38 **Global Entrepreneurship: Business Start-ups and Jobs, 2003**

Country	Persons Involved in Business Start-ups (millions)	Number of Start-ups (millions)	Owner-Managers of Entrepreneurial Firms (millions)	Number of Entrepreneurial Firms (millions)
India	106.9	85.4	10.0	8.0
China	99.5	56.3	28.2	19.1
United States	20.5	11.1	5.0	2.4
Brazil	14.8	8.6	2.2	1.3
Thailand	7.8	5.0	0.9	0.4
Mexico	7.3	3.9	1.5	0.9
South Korea	4.7	2.8	1.9	1.1
Venezuela	3.9	2.0	0.5	0.3
Argentina	3.8	2.0	0.4	0.2
Uganda	3.0	1.7	0.5	0.4
40 GEM countries	297.4	192.3	56.7	37.1

Source: Paul D. Reynolds, William D. Bygrave, and Erkko Autio, *GEM 2003 Global Report*, 16.

of Soto's message is that entrepreneurial activity in countries' informal sector must be harnessed, and brought into the formal economy. Soto and other like-minded economists believe that the merger of the extralegal and legal sectors would vastly accelerate capital formation—the process of expanding a nation's total amount of productive capital. Private property rights for the poor, the reduction of excessive business regulations and taxes, and access to credit are key incentives for entrepreneurs to join the formal economy. Major multilateral organizations, such as the World Bank and International Monetary Fund, and numerous private foundations and national governments have voiced support for reforms to bring entrepreneurs into the formal sector.

See also **Capital Formation; Economic Growth; Factors of Production; Informal Economy; Sustainable Economic Development.** ***See also in Volume 2,*** **Documents 8, 13, 14, 16, 55.**

Further Reading

Harper, David A. *Foundations of Entrepreneurship and Economic Development.* New York: Routledge, 2003.

Kuemmerle, Walter. *Case Studies in International Entrepreneurship: Managing and Financing Ventures in the Global Economy.* New York: McGraw Hill/Irwin, 2004.

Reynolds, Paul D., William D. Bygrave, and Erkko Autio. *GEM 2003 Global Report.* Babson Park, MA: Babson College and the London Business School, 2003.

Smart, Alan, and Josephine Smart. *Petty Capitalists and Globalization: Flexibility, Entrepreneurship, and Economic Development.* New York: SUNY Press, 2005.

Soto, Hernando de. *The Mystery of Capital: Why Capitalism Triumphs in the West and Fails Everywhere Else.* Rev. ed. New York: Basic Books, 2003.

ENVIRONMENTAL DEGRADATION

Environmental degradation refers to a wide variety of human-induced and naturally occurring stresses on the natural environment. Environmental degradation disrupts the balance of nature in all types of ecosystems—grasslands, forests, agrosystems (areas used for agriculture), freshwater systems, and coastal systems. Environmental degradation also affects the global commons such as the atmosphere and the oceans. Over time, natural factors such as climate, terrain, and amount of sunlight and water affect ecosystems. These factors, in turn, determine what types of life ecosystems can sustain, whether human, plant, animal, or insect. While ecosystems are dynamic, abrupt changes caused by humans have tested the limits of ecosystems to adapt and survive. Rising human population, industrialization, urbanization, permanent agriculture and animal domestication, aquaculture and commercial fishing, and mass consumption have contributed to environmental degradation.

The Millennium Ecosystem Assessment (MA) underscored the perils of environmental degradation in today's global economy. UN Secretary-General Kofi Annan commissioned the MA in June 2001, and its conclusions were published in 2005. The MA, a $24 million international study program, involved representatives from the UN, private and public sectors, civil society, indigenous groups, and scientific community. The MA explored the causes and scope of ecosystem change in the world and the implications of these changes on a sustainable future. The MA concluded that ecosystem changes have improved the material well-being of many people. The MA also warned that economic development had severely strained natural ecosystems, more so in the past fifty years than in any other comparable time period. The study also concluded that the deterioration of ecosystems is proceeding in an unsustainable manner and that global policy changes are necessary to reverse environmental degradation.

Land degradation takes many forms, and is often the result of poor choices by people. Unwise uses of the land include overfarming, overgrazing, and deforestation (the process of stripping timber from regions to satisfy business or

Deforestation in the Amazon region of Brazil alters local ecosystems and degrades the natural environment.

Courtesy of Getty Images: L. Hobbs

personal needs). Stresses on the land are often the result of rising population in rural and urban areas. Land degradation is especially severe in heavily populated regions of the developing world where population growth has far outpaced that of the advanced countries. The landmark *World Resources: 2000–2001*, a co-publication of the World Resources Institute, World Bank, and United Nations, documented the severity of land degradation. The report noted that about two-thirds of the world's croplands had experienced some degradation, and that half of the world's forests had been lost to agriculture, timbering, or other development. Land degradation also results from abusive acts such as strip-mining and the creation of toxic waste dumps. Reckless uses of land, and of ecosystems supported by the land, also accelerate other destructive natural processes such as desertification. Desertification is the transformation of fertile land to desert. Drought, wind erosion, and proximity to existing deserts are partly to blame for this transformation. Human actions such as intensive farming, herding, and logging accelerate the desertification process. In recent decades desertification has swallowed hundreds of thousands of square miles of land in the Sahel region of Africa, an area located on the southern fringe of the world's largest desert, the Sahara. Desertification is also evident in the countries of southern Africa, which border the Namib and Kalahari deserts.

The degradation of the atmosphere is a second global concern. Degradation of the atmosphere stems mainly from toxic emissions from business enterprises, motor vehicles, and aircraft. For example, destructive chlorofluorocarbons (CFCs), which consist of chlorine, fluorine, and carbon atoms, have depleted large areas of the earth's ozone layer, and thus exposed people to the sun's dangerous ultraviolet (UV) radiation. CFCs are used in aerosol spray cans, air conditioners, styrofoam packaging, and other commonly consumed items. In addition, the burning of fossil fuels such as petroleum and coal, spew carbon dioxide, methane, and nitrous oxide into the atmosphere. Over time, heavy concentrations of these gases trap the earth's heat, preventing it from radiating back into space—a process called the greenhouse effect. Many scientists believe that the greenhouse effect has caused global warming, the gradual warming of the earth's surface. The costs of global warming could be staggering. The melting of the polar ice caps, for example, could have a devastating impact on many low-lying coastal regions of the world.

The degradation of the seas is a third area of concern. Oceans cover about 70 percent of the earth's surface, and are an important feature of the global commons. The oceans, long viewed as limitless in their potential to satisfy basic human needs, have also succumbed to human-induced stresses. Oceans are used as convenient catch basins for industrial effluent, human sewage, and toxic runoff of pesticides, fertilizers, and other chemicals. Oceans have also been over harvested by highly mechanized deepsea fishing and by intensive small-scale coastal fishing. The stock of fish in the Mediterranean Sea, North Atlantic, North Pacific, and other regions of the world has been reduced or depleted, a fact recognized by many global watchdogs including the UN's Food and Agriculture Organization (FAO).

A number of major multilateral environmental agreements (MEAs) were negotiated during the 1980s and 1990s to create environmental safeguards in the local and global arenas. Effective implementation of these accords has lagged in some cases. The most successful MEA is the Montreal Protocol of 1987, which banned CFCs and other substances harmful to the earth's ozone. Compliance with the ban by the advanced countries has already yielded positive results in the ozone's recovery. The United Nations Framework Convention on Climate Change (UNFCCC), an environmental agreement emanating from the Rio Earth Summit of 1992, has been less successful. The UNFCCC called for reductions in greenhouse gases, the main villain in global warming. A follow-up agreement, the Kyoto Protocol of 1997, established specific targets for the reduction of gaseous emissions from the industrialized countries. In the early 2000s, two major advanced countries, the United States and Australia, withdrew from the Kyoto Protocol. In February 2005, the Kyoto Protocol entered into force without U.S. participation.

The most recognized international authority in combating environmental degradation is the United Nations Environment Program (UNEP), which was founded as an autonomous program within the United Nations System in 1972. In 1997, the Nairobi Declaration affirmed that the UNEP was the UN's most important voice in environmental matters. The UNEP coordinates global environmental programs, monitors compliance with existing MEAs, and implements sound environmental policies. Its concerns about the quality of the natural environment are shared by other UN programs and specialized agencies, including the United Nations Development Program, United Nations Population Fund, World Health Organization, and Food and Agriculture Organization. As the UN's chief environmental authority, the UNEP also consults with non-governmental organizations (NGOs), national governments, and multilateral organizations such as the World Bank and International Monetary Fund. The UNEP lacks an effective dispute settlement mechanism to investigate complaints and force compliance with MEAs, however. Some experts contend that a stronger organization, armed with the authority to challenge environmentally unfriendly policies or practices, is necessary in today's global economy.

See also **Factors of Production; Multilateral Environmental Agreements; Race to the Bottom; Sustainable Economic Development; United Nations System.** ***See also in Volume 2,*** **Documents 28, 30, 39, 40, 41, 42, 43, 52, 53.**

Further Reading

Sayer, Jeffrey, and Bruce Campbell. *The Science of Sustainable Development: Local Livelihoods and the Global Environment.* New York: Cambridge University Press, 2003.

Steffen, W. L., et al. *Global Change and the Earth System: A Planet under Pressure.* New York: Springer-Verlag, 2004.

Vogler, John. *The Global Commons: Environmental and Technological Governance.* 2d ed. New York: John Wiley & Sons, 2000.

World Resources Institute. *World Resources 2000–2001, People and Ecosystems: The Fraying Web of Life.* Washington, DC: World Resources Institute, United Nations Development Program, United Nations Environment Program, World Bank, 2000.

Worldwatch Institute. *State of the World 2004*. New York: W.W. Norton & Company, 2004.

EUROPEAN BANK FOR RECONSTRUCTION AND DEVELOPMENT

The European Bank for Reconstruction and Development (EBRD) is a regional development bank that serves twenty-seven countries from regions within Europe and Asia. EBRD identifies five clusters of borrowing countries including central Europe and the Baltic states (nine countries), southeastern Europe (six countries), eastern Europe and the Caucasus (six countries), central Asia (five countries), and Russia. EBRD was founded in May 1990, and began its commercial operations in June 1991. It is one of four major regional development banks currently operating in the global economy. Its sixty member countries, the European Community, and the European Investment Bank, own EBRD by virtue of their purchase of shares in the bank. The largest shareholders are the United States, France, Germany, Italy, Japan, and the United Kingdom. Combined, these six countries own about one-half of all subscribed capital. Each member country has voting power in proportion to its ownership of bank shares. At the top of EBRD's power structure is its board of governors, which represents the bank's members. The board of governors delegates most of its authority to a board of directors, however. The board of directors conducts bank operations from its headquarters in London, United Kingdom.

Of EBRD's sixty member countries, twenty-seven are eligible to borrow money from the bank. These countries are called "countries of operations." The most recent addition to the bank was Serbia and Montenegro (formerly the Federal Republic of Yugoslavia), which joined in 2001. Nonregional EBRD members hail from Asia and the Pacific, Europe, the Middle East, North America, and Northern Africa. According to EBRD's Establishing Agreement, the purpose of the bank is to promote regional economic development and to "foster the transition toward open market-oriented economies and to promote private and entrepreneurial initiative in the central and eastern European countries committed to and applying the principles of multiparty democracy, pluralism and market economics." The break-up of the Soviet Union in December 1991 hastened the growth in EBRD. The fifteen republics of the Former Soviet Union (FSU) became independent countries and joined EBRD. By 2005 there was some discussion about ending EBRD operations in countries that had successfully transitioned from communism to capitalism.

EBRD promotes regional economic development through its lending operations, policy advice, and technical assistance. Private sector projects account for 72 percent of the EBRD's operations. Public sector projects account for the remaining 28 percent of the bank's business activity. In 2003, EBRD financially supported 119 projects valued at $3.7 billion. These loans stimulated an additional $5.3 billion in related investments. The main categories of bank operations included lending for financial institutions (33 percent), which included loans to banks and equity funds to support business lending; infrastructure

(19 percent), which included loans for municipal water and waste treatment facilities, roads, and other transport; energy (16 percent), which included loans to increase the efficiency and environmental integrity of primary fuel production, especially the production of oil, coal, and natural gas; manufacturing (14 percent), which included loans for heavy industries such as aircraft, steel, cement, and bricks; and others (18 percent), which included loans for agribusiness, tourism, telecommunications, information technology, and media. From 1991 to 2003 EBRD approved 1,017 loans with a value of 22.7 billion euros. The top five recipient countries during this period of time were Russia, which received 5.2 billion euros (22.8 percent of all borrowing from the bank); Poland, which received 2.8 billion euros (12.5 percent of all borrowing); Romania, which received 2.4 billion euros (10.4 percent of all borrowing); Hungary, which received 1.5 billion euros (6.7 percent of all borrowing); and the Ukraine, which received 1.3 billion euros (5.6 percent of all borrowing). The bank's annual commitments for 2003, and the cumulative impact of this lending, are shown in Table 39.

EBRD raises most of its funds by borrowing in global capital markets. Like other development banks, EBRD borrows by selling bank bonds and other securities to international investors such as central banks, commercial banks, insurance companies, and pension funds. EBRD also raises funds through capital subscriptions, interest payments and other profits from its business operations, and donations from governments and organizations. Unlike other regional development banks, the EBRD does not fund commercial operations from its pool of subscribed capital. Instead, the EBRD's subscribed capital of 20 billion euros serves as a type of collateral to back the integrity of bank bonds—bonds that currently carry the highest AAA rating. In 2003, the EBRD earned a tidy 378 million euros from its commercial operations. Over the years, it has also solicited billions of euros in donations from member governments and the European Community. Donations finance technical assistance to promote a sound business climate, environmental protection, hazardous waste cleanup, entrepreneurship, microenterprises, applied technology, and modern business practices in marketing, finance, and other fields. A number of special funds have been established to deal with nuclear waste treatment and disposal.

Regional and sub-regional development banks are a major source of development loans and other development assistance in the global economy. The four main regional development banks are the African Development Bank Group, Asian Development Bank, European Bank for Reconstruction and Development, and Inter-American Development Bank Group. Smaller, sub-regional development banks also dot the economic landscape and include

TABLE 39 **Financial Commitments of EBRD, 1991 to 2003 (euro millions)**

European Bank for Reconstruction and Development	2003	Cumulative (1991–2003) (euro in millions)
Number of projects	119	1,017
EBRD financing (euro)	3,721	22,668
Additional resources mobilized (euro)	5,307	45,822

Source: European Bank for Reconstruction and Development, *Annual Report 2003*, 4.

the Caribbean Development Bank, Central American Bank for Regional Integration, East African Development Bank, and West African Development Bank.

See also **African Development Bank Group; Asian Development Bank; Emerging Market Economies; Inter-American Development Bank Group; Regional Development Banks; Transition Countries.**

Further Reading

Bronstone, Adam. *The European Bank for Reconstruction and Development.* Manchester, UK: Manchester University Press, 1999.

European Bank for Reconstruction and Development. *Annual Report 2003: Annual Review and Financial Report.* London: Author, 2004.

———. *Building Prosperity.* London: Author, 2004.

———. *A Guide to EBRD Financing.* London: Author, 2004.

———. *Transition Report 2004: Infrastructure.* London: Author, 2004.

EUROPEAN FREE TRADE ASSOCIATION

The European Free Trade Association (EFTA) is an intergovernmental organization that consists of four nations, Iceland, Liechtenstein, Norway, and Switzerland. Its mission is to promote free trade among member states, economic cooperation with the European Union (EU), and economic contacts with other regions of the world. The Stockholm Convention, also called the EFTA Convention, established the EFTA on January 4, 1960. The EFTA Convention is a statement of member states' goals and obligations. Primary goals listed in the EFTA Convention included "sustained expansion of economic activity, full employment, increased productivity and regional use of resources, financial stability, and continuous improvement in living standards." Its founding members were Austria, Denmark, Norway, Portugal, Sweden, Switzerland, and the United Kingdom (UK). Since 1960, three nations have joined the EFTA, including Finland (1961), Iceland (1970) and Liechtenstein (1991); and six member states have left the Association, including Denmark and the UK (1973), Portugal (1986), and Austria, Finland, and Sweden (1995). In 2001 the Vaduz Convention updated the original Stockholm Convention.

The EFTA's organizational structure consists of several institutions, each with its own set of responsibilities. Much of the Association's decision-making authority rests with the EFTA Council, and the Standing Committee of the EFTA States. The EFTA Council deals with issues within the four-nation Association, and between the Association and non-member countries. The Standing Committee of the EFTA States deals specifically with EFTA relations with the European Union (EU). The EFTA headquarters, including the secretariat, is located in Geneva, Switzerland. The EFTA Court, the Association's highest judicial authority, interprets and clarifies legal issues. The EFTA Surveillance Authority monitors compliance with existing rules within the Association and its EU neighbors. A profile of the EFTA and its members is shown in Table 40.

The Agreement on a European Economic Area was originally approved on May 2, 1992, and went into effect on January 1, 1994. The creation of the

TABLE 40 **Profile of the European Free Trade Association, 2002**

Economic and Social Indicators	Iceland	Liechtenstein	Norway	Switzerland
Population	288,400	33,900	4,552,300	7,316,100
Life expectancy (F)	82.3	n/a	81.5	83.0
Life expectancy (M)	78.5	n/a	76.5	77.4
GDP (euro billions)	9.0	n/a	202.5	284.4
GDP per capita (euro)	31,430	n/a	44,620	38,710
Inflation rate	5.3%	0.6%	0.8%	0.6%
Unemployment rate	3.3%	1.4%	3.9%	2.8%
Exports (euro billions)	2.4	n/a	63.0	93.1
Imports (euro billions)	2.4	n/a	36.8	88.7
Total trade (euro billions)	4.8	n/a	99.8	181.8

Source: EFTA, *Annual Report of the European Free Trade Association 2003*, 11.

EEA set the stage for expanded regional economic cooperation between the EFTA and EU. By May 2004 the European Economic Area (EEA) consisted of the twenty-five EU countries and three EFTA countries—Iceland, Liechtenstein, and Norway. The fourth EFTA country, Switzerland, rejected EEA participation, favoring bilateral agreements with the EU instead. The EEA established a single market promising free cross-border flows of goods, services, capital, and persons—also called the four freedoms. The EEA Agreement also guaranteed "equal conditions of competition, and the respect of the same rules" within the region. By 2002, about 70 percent of all EFTA members' trade was with EU nations. The single or internal market created by the EEA also extended into other areas of cooperation including education, research and technological development, the environment, and social policy.

Participation in the EEA promotes regional cooperation, but does not tie the three EFTA member states into other EU commitments. For example, EU member nations subscribe to a unified foreign policy and security policy, which EFTA members are free to reject. The EU is also a customs union, which sets uniform tariffs and other trade restrictions on imports from non-member nations—restrictions that EFTA members are not bound to follow. Further, the EFTA maintains its own decision-making institutions, such as the EFTA Council and the Standing Committee of the EFTA States.

Today, the EFTA is an outward-looking association. In the most recent revision of the EFTA agreement—the Vaduz Convention (2001)—member states strengthened protections for intellectual property rights; liberalized investment and trade in services; expanded opportunities for cross-border migrations of workers and their families; and agreed to recognize professional certificates from member countries. In addition, the EFTA continues to build trade relationships with countries in other parts of the world. The EFTA negotiated free trade agreements with Macedonia and Mexico in 2000, Croatia and Jordan in 2001, Singapore in 2002, Chile in 2003, and Tunisia in 2004. Negotiations with other regional trade blocs, including MERCOSUR, were also under way in 2005.

See also **European Union; Regional Trade Agreements.**

Further Reading

Abrams, Richard K., and Peter K. Cornelius. *The Impact of the European Community's Internal Market on the EFTA*. Washington, DC: International Monetary Fund, 1990.

Blanchet, Therese, Resto Pipponen, and Maria Westman-Clement. *The Agreement on the European Economic Area*. New York: Oxford University Press, 1994.

European Free Trade Association. *Annual Report of the European Free Trade Association 2003*. Geneva, Switzerland: Author, 2003.

European Free Trade Association Court. *The EFTA Court: Legal Framework, Case Law, and Composition, 1994–2003*. Printed in Germany: Author, 2004.

Redmond, John. *The 1995 Enlargement of the European Union*. Brookfield, VT: Ashgate Publishing, 1997.

EUROPEAN UNION

The European Union (EU) is a unique intergovernmental organization that coordinates economic, foreign, security, and judicial policies among its twenty-five member nations. The Maastricht Treaty on European Union, which entered into force on November 1, 1993, created the EU. The Maastricht Treaty, and the later Treaties of Amsterdam (1999) and Nice (2003), established the world's most integrated regional organization. Table 41 summarizes the successive "enlargements" of the EU over the past half century. To be eligible for EU membership, a country must have a stable democracy, a market economy, demonstrated respect for human rights, and a public bureaucracy capable of administering EU rules and regulations.

The process of writing a formal European Union Constitution began in 2002. On October 29, 2004, the European Council, consisting of the heads of state or government from the twenty-five member countries, approved the proposed EU Constitution. Ratification of the EU Constitution requires unanimous approval of member states by referendum or by an affirmative vote in national

TABLE 41 **European Union Membership, 1957 to 2005**

Year	Membership	Institutions*	Total Membership
1957	Belgium, France, Germany, Italy, Luxembourg, Netherlands	European Economic Community (EEC)	6
1973	First enlargement adds Denmark Ireland, United Kingdom	European Communities (EC)	9
1981	Second enlargement adds Greece	European Communities (EC)	10
1986	Third enlargement adds Spain, Portugal	European Communities (EC)	12
1995	Fourth enlargement adds Austria, Finland, Sweden	European Union (EU)	15
2004	Fifth enlargement adds Cyprus, Czech Republic, Estonia, Latvia, Lithuania, Hungary, Malta, Poland, Slovenia, Slovakia	European Union (EU)	25
2007**	Sixth enlargement adds Bulgaria, Romania	European Union (EU)	27

*European Economic Community (EEC) was changed to European Communities (EC) in 1967. The EC was comprised of the EEC, the European Coal and Steel Community (ECSC), and the European Atomic Energy Community (EURATOM). The EC was changed to the European Union (EU) in 1993.
**Anticipated enlargement.

legislatures, however. Most EU members ratified the EU Constitution in 2005. France and the Netherlands rejected the EU Constitution in national referendums in 2005.

The EU rests on three "pillars" of European integration. The first pillar is economic integration and cooperation within the region. Economic integration is based on several key principles. The first is the EU's single market, which guarantees the free cross-border flows of goods, services, capital, and people. Second, the EU maintains a coordinated stabilization policy to guard against inflation or other financial instability. Stabilization policy is orchestrated by the European System of Central Banks (ESCB), which consists of the Central Banks of member states and an independent European Central Bank (ECB). Third is the EU's common trade policy, which creates uniform import and export regulations for all member countries. Fourth is the EU's common currency, the euro. The euro was introduced in 1999, and, on January 1, 2002, became the official legal tender for twelve of the EU's fifteen member states. Fifth is enhanced EU cooperation in key regional issues related to agriculture, the environment, energy, education and training, employment and social policy, technology, and competitive markets. By treaty, individual member states have surrendered considerable sovereignty to EU decision-making bodies in order to support economic integration.

The second and third pillars of the European integration also call for regional cooperation, but permit member states more room for independent action. The EU's second pillar is a unified foreign policy and security policy for the region. The Common Foreign and Security Policy (CFSP), which was established in 1993, enables the EU to stand united on matters of global concern. The main decision-making authority behind the CFSP is the European Council, which is comprised of nations' heads of state. Other EU bodies, such as the European Commission and European Parliament, have certain participation rights but do not determine the EU's foreign policy stance. Under the CFSP, the EU sent diplomatic missions, foreign aid, observers, and peacekeeping troops to troubled regions during the 1990s and early 2000s. Recent initiatives helped stabilize Bosnia and Herzegovina, Kosovo, Macedonia, and Congo-Brazzaville.

The EU's third pillar is the regional system of justice. Under the Justice and Home Affairs (JHA) policy, the EU coordinates its response to terrorism, drug trafficking, illegal immigration, and other international criminal activity. At the top of judicial system is the European Court of Justice, often compared to the Supreme Court in the United States. The European Court of Justice consists of a panel of judges, one judge from each member state. The Court operates independently, and is not beholden to national governments or other EU institutions. Its main function is to guarantee uniform interpretation and implementation of EU laws, regulations, or other directives by all EU citizens, businesses, governments, and EU bodies. In addition, the most important intelligence-gathering and law enforcement body in the justice system is the European Police Office (EUROPOL). EUROPOL, which began operations in 1999, cooperates with law enforcement officials in member states, the United States, and other regions. After the September 11, 2001, terrorist attacks on the United States, EUROPOL created a special unit designed to combat terrorism.

Five major EU institutions support the three pillars of European integration. These institutions include the European Parliament, Council of the European Union, European Commission, Court of Justice, and Court of Auditors. First, the European Parliament (EP) consists of representatives that are elected directly by the people every five years. The EP can approve or amend the EU's budget and censure EU officials. Through the power of "codecision," the EP shares significant power with the Council of the European Union in forming EU legislation. The number of elected members to the EP will increase from 626 to 732 in 2007 after all planned enlargements are finalized. Second, the Council of the European Union consists of representatives of each member state's government. The Council of the European Union makes EU laws, and, thus, is the EU's principal decision-making body. Draft versions of EU laws are often submitted to the Council of the European Union by the heads of state who sit in the European Council. Most decisions require a majority vote. Third, the European Commission, which consists of twenty appointed Commissioners and a staff of 22,000, conducts much of the day-to-day operations of the EU. The European Commission drafts legislation, monitors compliance with EU rules, and attends to the EU's administrative functions. Fourth, the Court of Justice, which consists of one judge from each member state, interprets EU laws and regulations and ensures uniformity in the application of EU legislation. Fifth, the European Court of Auditors, which consists of skilled financial managers, guarantees the integrity of the EU budget.

The adoption of the euro is often considered the crowning achievement of the European Union. On January 1, 2002, the euro became the single currency for twelve EU countries, also known as the European Monetary Union (EMU) or euro zone. EMU countries include Austria, Belgium, Finland, France, Germany, Greece, Ireland, Italy, Luxembourg, the Netherlands, Portugal, and Spain. By February 28, 2002, all pre-existing national paper currencies and coins were permanently withdrawn from circulation in the euro zone. Today, people use euros to buy products, make bank deposits, pay taxes, buy stocks and bonds, and so on. The euro is widely used in the three pre-enlargement EU countries not in the EMU, which include Denmark, Sweden, and the United Kingdom. Most of the ten 2004 enlargement countries have expressed strong interest in joining the EMU. EU rules require a two-year waiting period, and satisfactory economic performance, before new members can participate in the EMU. The European System of Central Banks (ESCB) is responsible for maintaining stability of the euro. Euro paper notes are printed in seven denominations: 5, 10, 20, 50, 100, 200, and 500 euro. Euro coins are minted in eight denominations: 1, 2, 5, 10, 20, and 50 euro cents, and in 1 and 2 euro coins. The official abbreviation for the euro is "EUR," just as the official abbreviation for the U.S. dollar is "DOL."

The EU is a major player in the global economy in terms of total output, international trade, and foreign direct investment (FDI). In 2003 the combined gross domestic product (GDP) of the EU-25 (the fifteen long-standing EU members plus the ten recent accession countries) was about $11 trillion. This sum was almost identical to the GDP of the United States, the world's largest economy. In that same year EU-15 countries accounted for $5.8 trillion in merchandise trade, $2.9 trillion in merchandise imports and another $2.9 trillion in merchandise exports. Ranked by merchandise trade, the EU-15's $2.9 trillion in merchandise exports placed it second in the world behind the twenty-one-member Asia-Pacific Economic Cooperation (APEC), whose merchandise exports topped $3.1 trillion. EU merchandise exports far outpaced other major regional organizations including the North American Free Trade Agreement (NAFTA), which recorded $1.2 trillion in export earnings; the Association of Southeast Asian Nations (ASEAN, $451 billion); and the Southern Common Market (MERCOSUR, $106 billion). According to the *World Investment Report 2004*, a publication of the United Nations Conference on Trade and Development (UNCTAD), the EU-15 dominated foreign direct investment (FDI) in 2003. One-half of all transnational corporations were headquartered in EU-15 countries, and EU-15 countries accounted for more than 50 percent of the world's total FDI inflows and outflows. Table 42 compares the EU, United States, and Japan by landmass, population, and gross domestic product (GDP).

The EU is outward-looking, and willingly assumes a leadership role in global affairs. Through its Common Foreign and Security Policy (CFSP) the EU supports humanitarian and peacekeeping initiatives throughout the world. The EU cooperates with multilateral organizations such as the World Trade Organization to liberalize trade and support other features of globalization. The EU reaches out to the world's poorer regions to support trade initiatives and other assistance. The Cotonou Agreement, which took effect on April 1, 2003, committed billions of euros to promote growth, stability, and a higher quality of life in seventy-seven African, Caribbean, and Pacific (ACP) countries. The EU poured hundreds of millions of euros into war-torn Afghanistan and Iraq during the early 2000s, and into the tsunami-ravaged regions of western Asia and eastern Africa in 2005. In 2004, EU countries also funneled $43 billion in official development assistance (ODA) to the developing world, which represented more than half of all foreign aid granted to the world's poorer regions.

TABLE 42 **The European Union, United States, and Japan, 2003**

Region or Country	Size of Area (1000 sq. km)	Population (millions)	Gross Domestic Product ($ billions)	GDP per Capita ($)
European Union				
EU-25	3,893	455	$11,017	$24,027
EU-15	3,154	380	$10,522	$27,511
Euro-zone	2,456	307	$8,209	$26,595
United States	9,631	293	$11,000	$37,756
Japan	378	128	$4,301	$33,720

Source: European Commission Delegation, *The European Union and World Trade: 2004*, 1–3.

See also **European Free Trade Association; Regional Trade Agreements.** ***See also in Volume 2,*** **Documents 20, 46.**

Further Reading

European Commission. *The European Union: A Guide for Americans*. Washington, DC: Delegation of the European Commission to the United States, 2004.

———. *Portrait of the European Union*. Luxembourg: European Communities, 2004.

Leonard, Dick. *Guide to the European Union*. 9th ed. Princeton, NJ: Bloomberg Press, 2005.

O'Brennan, John. *The Eastern Enlargement of the European Union*. New York: Routledge, 2005.

Reid, T. R. *The United States of Europe: The New Superpower and the End of American Supremacy*. New York: Penguin Press, 2004.

EXCHANGE RATES

Exchange rates state the value of one currency compared to a second currency. Four pieces of information are included in published exchange rates: the country, the name of the currency, the U.S. equivalent, and the currency per U.S. dollar, as shown in Table 43. The "U.S. equivalent" expresses the value of a foreign currency in terms of the U.S. dollar. For instance, on January 20, 2005, the Canadian dollar was worth about eighty-one cents, and the Chinese yuan about twelve cents compared to the U.S. dollar, while one British pound was worth $1.87 in U.S. currency. The "currency per U.S. dollar" states how many units of a foreign currency it would take to equal $1. The exchange rates for January 20, 2005, show it would take about eleven Mexican pesos or 103 Japanese yen to equal $1, but it would take just seventy-seven euro cents to equal $1. Exchange rates also measure the relative value of Japanese yen to British pounds, Canadian dollars to the EMU euro, and so on. Exchange rates are published daily in major newspapers such as the *Wall Street Journal* and the *New York Times*.

The flexible exchange rate system provides investment opportunities for investors and influences international trade.
Courtesy of CORBIS

In today's flexible exchange rate system, also called the floating exchange rate system, the forces of supply and demand are mainly responsible for determining exchange rates. Every day, national currencies are bought and sold by thousands of financial institutions around the world. Collectively, these financial institutions are called the foreign exchange market. Investors buy or sell currencies much like they trade stocks, bonds, or other securities. Much of the currency trade on foreign exchange markets is highly speculative—short term and risky. Investors earn

TABLE 43 **Exchange Rates, January 20, 2005**

Country	Currency	U.S. Equivalent	Currency per U.S. Dollar
Canada	dollar	0.8110	1.2330
China	yuan	0.1208	8.2781
India	rupee	0.0228	43.8020
Japan	yen	0.0097	103.3300
Mexico	peso	0.0886	11.2880
United Kingdom	pound	1.8731	0.5343
EMU nations*	euro	1.2973	0.7708

*The Economic and Monetary Union (EMU) consists of the twelve European nations of the euro zone.
Source: "Exchange Rates, January 20, 2005," *Wall Street Journal*, January 21, 2005, B5.

profits from slight changes in exchange rates. When the demand for a currency is high, the exchange rate tends to rise. High demand for a currency might result from strong demand for a nation's exports, robust economic growth, or a positive investment climate. Positive economic performance strengthens investors' confidence in an economy and its currency, causing the currency to appreciate in value. Economists say that a currency gains strength, or becomes stronger, when it appreciates over time. When the demand for a currency is low, however, the exchange rate tends to fall. Large trade deficits, an unstable investment climate, recession, and other negative performance indicators weaken the demand for a currency. Sagging demand, in turn, causes a currency to depreciate, or weaken relative to other currencies. Periodically a national government, through its central bank, buys or sells its currency to influence the currency's value, a process called "managed float."

A value of one country's currency might also be "pegged" to another country's currency. Often, pegging is designed to stabilize the value of the second currency in global markets. China's yuan, for example, was pegged to the U.S. dollar from 1995 to 2005. During this period of time the pegged value was 8.28 yuan to $1 U.S. In July 2005 China announced its intension to end the yuan's fixed peg to the U.S. dollar. China's decision to end the fixed peg, and initiate a managed float system, was viewed as a positive step toward building a more globally integrated and market-based economy.

Exchange rates are used in many types of international transactions. This is because an exchange rate is the means by which one currency is converted into an equivalent amount of another. International trade relies on exchange rates to ensure that exporters receive proper payment for the goods or services they sell to importers in other countries. To facilitate currency conversions all countries hold cash reserves of foreign currencies, called foreign reserves. A country's stash of foreign reserves consists mainly of hard currencies, or currencies that are commonly accepted throughout the world. Leading hard currencies include the U.S. dollar, EMU euro, British pound, and the Japanese yen. Many countries in the developing world use only hard currencies in international exchanges because of the uncertain value of their local currencies in global markets. Some currencies in the world's poorer regions are considered non-convertible due to monetary instability.

Changes in exchange rates affect international trade, tourism, and other cross-border transactions in the global economy. Consider the following example. In early 2002 the exchange rate between the Japanese yen and the American dollar was 132.4 yen to $1 U.S. Thus, in 2002 a $10 American-made razor would sell for about 1,324 yen in Japan ($10 × 132.4 = 1,324). Since 2002 the Japanese yen appreciated against the U.S. dollar. On January 20, 2005 it took just 103.3 yen to equal $1. Thus, in 2005 the same $10 American-made razor would sell for just 1,033 yen in Japan ($10 × 103.3 = 1,033 yen). The drop in the razor's price in Japan from 1,324 yen to just 1,033 yen was caused by the stronger Japanese yen, or, from a different perspective, by the weaker U.S. dollar. As a general rule, when a currency strengthens, this movement discourages exports, which become more expensive in foreign markets. At the same time the stronger currency encourages imports, which become less expensive in domestic markets. Conversely, when a currency weakens, this movement encourages exports, which become less expensive in foreign markets, and discourages imports, which become more expensive in domestic markets.

See also **Bretton Woods System; Foreign Exchange Market; International Trade.**

Further Reading

Bigman, David, and Teizo Taya, eds. *Floating Exchange Rates and the State of the World Trade and Payments*. Chevy Chase, MD: Beard Books, 2002.

Rogoff, Kenneth S. *Evolution and Performance of Exchange Rate Regimes*. Washington, DC: International Monetary Fund, 2004.

Sarno, Lucio, and Mark P. Taylor. *The Economics of Exchange Rates*. New York: Cambridge University Press, 2003.

Shamah, Shani B. *A Foreign Exchange Primer*. New York: John Wiley & Sons, 2003.

Thirlwall, A. P. *Trade, the Balance of Payments and Exchange Rate Policy in Developing Countries*. Northampton, MA: Edward Elgar Publishers, 2004.

EXPORT PROCESSING ZONE

An export processing zone (EPZ) is an industrial area that offers special incentives to attract foreign direct investment (FDI), and that is involved in the production of export products. EPZs are established under different models. One model confines the EPZ to a specific area within the country. Other models apply FDI incentives to export-oriented firms that operate anywhere in the country.

The number of EPZs has grown exponentially over the past quarter century. The International Labor Organization (ILO), a specialized agency within the UN System, reported that the number of EPZs grew from seventy-nine in 1975 to 3,000 in 2002, and that the number of countries with at least one EPZ increased from 25 to 116 during the same period. The ILO also estimated that the number of workers employed in EPZs hit 42 million by the early 2000s.

EPZs are called by different names throughout the global economy, including maquiladoras (Mexico), special economic zones (China), free zones (Ireland), industrial free zones (Ghana), free trade zones (Chile), special export processing zones (Philippines), free economic zones (Russia), and a dozen other names. The rapid expansion of EPZs has been controversial in recent years, mainly the result of allegations of labor and environmental abuses by transnational corporations (TNCs) operating within these special regions. Table 44 presents a regional overview of EPZs in the global economy.

Countries establish EPZs to promote sustainable economic development, a goal that includes economic growth and an improved quality of life for people. Governments, mainly in the developing world, offer foreign TNCs a variety of incentives to locate in their countries. Incentive packages often include temporary exemptions from local taxes, the duty-free import of essential resources and export of finished or semi-finished goods, tax credits for investment in new capital goods, exemptions from local production and labor laws, and "one-stop-shop" service—a service that cuts through the usual red tape and licensing hassles connected with many other business operations. Governments also commit local tax revenues to build a modern economic and technological infrastructure within EPZs. Coupled with other incentives, a modern communications, transportation, and information technology infrastructure improves the overall business environment for firms.

TNCs and other firms operating in EPZs produce a variety of goods and services for export. Traditionally, EPZs were the domain of goods-producing firms that used low-skilled labor to assemble merchandise for export. Examples of goods include textiles, clothing and footwear, food products, animal feeds, electronic items, toys, and pharmaceuticals. In recent years EPZs have also attracted TNCs that produce commercial services. Examples include firms in telemarketing, business consulting, tourism, banking, insurance, engineering, information technologies, and product repair. The export of goods and services from EPZs represented a significant portion of many nations' overall exports, including at least 80 percent of total exports from global heavyweights such as Argentina, China, Malaysia, Mexico, and the Philippines.

TABLE 44 **Export Processing Zones, 2002–2003**

World Region	Number of EPZs*	Total Employment (2002–2003)
North Africa	16	440,515
Sub-Saharan Africa	50	431,348
Indian Ocean	2	127,509
Middle East	38	691,397
South Asia**	163	36,824,231
Mexico and Central America	81	2,241,821
South America	40	311,143
Caribbean	92	226,130
Central and Eastern Europe	93	245,619
Pacific	14	13,590
Europe	67	50,830
North America	368	330,000
Total	1,024	41,934,133

*Roughly 2,000 other EPZs appear under different names such as industrial parks, duty-free areas, bonded zones, and hi-tech industrial development zones.

**The South Asia region includes China, which accounted for an estimated 30,000,000 workers in EPZs, nearly 75 percent of the world's total.

Source: International Labor Organization, *ILO Database on Export Processing Zones* (2003), 1–13.

Host governments establish EPZs to support sustainable economic development. First, EPZs attract foreign direct investment (FDI). FDI enhances capital formation and capital deepening. Capital formation increases the nation's total amount of capital goods, while capital deepening increases the amount of capital per worker. The growth of a capital base is a prerequisite for gains in productivity and growth. Second, EPZs promote jobs creation and human capital development. Responsible TNCs invest in worker training programs and the development of local management. Third, EPZs encourage technology transfers. FDI infuses sophisticated technology into the host country, which allows poorer countries to bypass expensive research and development (R&D). Fourth, EPZs boost manufacturing. The rise of manufacturing supports economic modernization and expands total national output. Fifth, EPZs expand connectivity. Export-oriented firms operating in EPZs create profitable links between the domestic economy and foreign enterprises. Finally, EPZs generate export earnings. Export earnings bolster reserves of hard currencies such as the U.S. dollar, EMU euro, and Japanese yen. Hard currencies are needed for many types of international transactions.

The economic value of EPZs to a country's economic development is a hotly debated issue. Supporters of EPZs argue that most TNCs act responsibly. They note that TNCs and other firms operating in EPZs create tens of millions of jobs at competitive wage rates; invest in greenfield projects, which supports capital formation; expand the manufacturing base, which diversifies the economy; generate export earnings through trade; and create pockets of prosperity, which jump-start economic development. Critics of EPZs argue that TNC business practices in EPZs are highly exploitative, and result in a "race to the bottom." In particular, critics argue that TNCs exploit workers—mainly young women—in assembly plants. Exploitation is manifest in low wages, lax safety codes, abusive bosses, and the denial of basic worker rights—including the right to form labor unions. Critics also argue that business operations in EPZs contribute to uneven development within countries, widen existing income gaps between the rich and the poor, and degrade the natural environment.

See also **Exports; Foreign Direct Investment; International Labor Organization; International Trade; Maquiladoras; Race to the Bottom; Supply Chains; Sustainable Economic Development; Transnational Corporations.**

Further Reading

Guangwen Meng. *The Theory and Practice of Free Economic Zones: A Case Study of Tianjin/The People's Republic of China*. New York: Peter Lang Publishing, 2003.

International Confederation of Free Trade Unions. *Export Processing Zones—Symbols of Exploitation and a Development Dead-End*. Brussels, Belgium: Author, 2003.

International Labor Organization. *ILO Database on Export Processing Zones*. Geneva, Switzerland: Author, 2003.

Raman, Thothathri, and Parag Diwan. *Free Trade Zones to Special Economic Zones (SEZs)*. New Delhi, India: Pentagon Press, 2004.

Salzinger, Leslie. *Genders in Production: Making Workers in Mexico's Global Factories*. Berkeley, CA: University of California Press, 2003.

EXPORTS

An export is any resource, intermediate good, or final good or service that producers in one country sell to buyers in another country. Imports, on the other hand, are goods or services that are purchased from another country. International trade involves the export and import of merchandise and commercial services. The major categories of merchandise exports include capital goods, such as heavy machinery and equipment; industrial supplies and materials; automotive vehicles and auto parts; agricultural products, including animal feeds; and petroleum. The main categories of commercial services include travel, passenger fares, the transport of goods, financial services and insurance, and business and professional services.

The World Trade Organization (WTO) reported that exports of merchandise and commercial services hit $11 trillion in 2004. Merchandise exports accounted for 81 percent of total exports, while commercial services comprised the remaining 19 percent. From 1994 to 2004, the total value of exports passing through the global trading system roughly doubled, from $5.4 trillion to $11 trillion, as shown in Figure 11 (data includes significant re-exports).

In 2004 the lion's share of global exports were produced in three world regions. Western Europe led the pack with $5.1 trillion in exports (46.8 percent of world exports), followed by $2.8 trillion from Asia (25.7 percent of world exports), and $1.7 trillion from North America (15.6 percent of world exports). The remaining $1.3 trillion, or 11.9 percent of world exports, was spread across developing Africa, Central and Eastern Europe, Latin America, and the Middle East. Table 45 lists the world's six leading exporting countries. Combined, these six countries accounted for about 40 percent of the world's total exports in 2004.

In recent decades trade liberalization encouraged nations to import and export products in the global trading system. Economists generally agree that international trade, an important pillar of globalization, contributes to economic growth and sustainable development. Trade expansion is particularly important in developing countries, which often lack the global connectivity to share in globalization's benefits. Export earnings are used for a number of development purposes. Export earnings can be re-invested in businesses, saved for future investments, or stored as foreign reserves. Nearly two centuries ago economist David Ricardo popularized the theory of comparative advantage, which supported free trade. Ricardo's theory encouraged regional specialization to

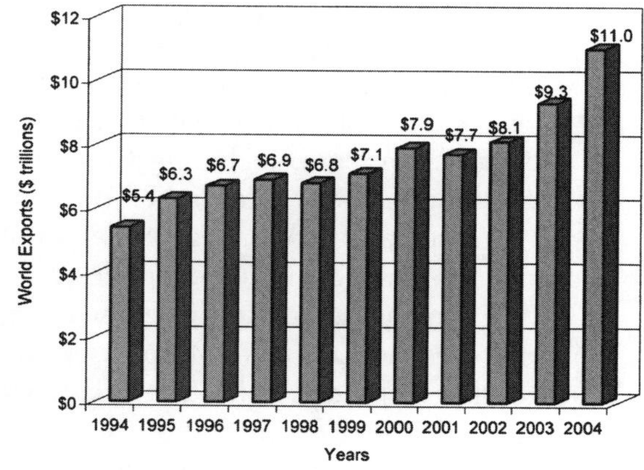

FIGURE 11 **Growth of World Exports, 1994 to 2004 ($ trillions)**

Source: World Trade Organization, *World Trade 2004, Prospects for 2005*, 15, 17.

TABLE 45 **World's Leading Exporting Countries, 2004 ($ billions)**

Rank	Country	Merchandise Exports ($ billions)	Commercial Services ($ billions)	Total Exports ($ billions)	Percent of World's Exports
1	United States	$819.0	$319.3	$1,138.3	10.1%
2	Germany	$914.8	$126.1	$1,040.9	9.3%
3	Japan	$565.5	$93.8	$659.3	5.9%
4	China	$593.4	$58.9	$652.3	5.8%
5	France	$451.0	$108.4	$559.4	5.0%
6	United Kingdom	$345.6	$169.2	$514.8	4.6%

Source: World Trade Organization, *World Trade 2004, Prospects for 2005*, 15, 17.

promote efficiency, and the export of surplus output to other countries. Since this time, mainstream economists have used Ricardo's theory of comparative advantage to support free trade—the freedom to import and export goods and services without fear of trade barriers. The World Trade Organization (WTO) supports the free flow of exports in today's global economy. Regional trade blocs, such as the Asia-Pacific Economic Cooperation (APEC), European Union (EU), North American Free Trade Agreement (NAFTA), and the Southern Common Market (MERCOSUR) have also reduced or eliminated restrictions on exports among member nations. In 2003 the world's largest RTAs, measured by intraregional exports, were APEC ($2,266 billion), the EU ($1,795 billion), and NAFTA ($651 billion).

Over the past half century, "export promotion" has accelerated economic growth and development in a number of countries. Export promotion is a trade strategy designed to increase the export of goods by offering incentives, such as tax breaks and subsidies, to export industries. Japan's miraculous economic recovery during the post–World War II period was due in large measure to aggressive export promotion policies. Japan's Ministry of International Trade and Industry (MITI), a quasi-public institution, arranged low-interest loans, government subsidies and grants, and tax breaks to support export industries. Today, Japan's economy ranks second only to the United States in terms of real gross domestic product (GDP). The meteoric rise of several other East Asian economies, including Chinese Taipei, the Hong Kong SAR, Singapore, and South Korea, also relied on export promotion. Today, these four newly industrialized economies (NIEs) of Asia are counted as among the world's twenty-nine advanced economies.

Export issues are hotly debated in today's global economy. One current issue involves restrictions on exports through anti-dumping measures. Dumping is an illegal trade practice that occurs when a firm from one country sells a product in another country at a price below production costs, or below the market price in the exporter's own economy. Governments enact anti-dumping measures, including high tariffs, to raise the price of dumped items. Since the mid-1990s, governments have initiated thousands of formal anti-dumping actions to restrict imports of products ranging from Russian steel to Vietnamese catfish.

A second export issue is instability in the global commodities trade. The commodities trade is mainly concerned with the export of primary products, such as coffee, cocoa, sugar, timber, or minerals from developing countries. The specialized production and export of commodities by developing countries is inherently unstable. Fluctuations in the global supply of or demand for a commodity affect the commodity's price, contributing to periods of feast or famine in commodity-dependent economies. A third export issue concerns voluntary quotas, a type of backdoor trade barrier. Governments negotiate voluntary quotas, often called voluntary restraint agreements (VRAs), to restrict the quantity of a good that can be exported from one country to another country. The World Trade Organization (WTO) specifically forbids VRAs, but these export restrictions lingered in the global trading system until 2005. One leading example was the VRA that limited the export Chinese textiles and clothing to the United States, a VRA that remained in effect until early 2005. A fourth export issue is economic localization. Localization favors economic self-reliance, a return to small-scale community-based production, and sustainable consumption. Localization is, in large measure, a grassroots rejection of globalization. Localization rejects an over-reliance on international trade, foreign investment, and other types of global connectivity.

See also **Absolute Advantage; Balance of Payments; Balance of Trade; Comparative Advantage; Dumping; Export Processing Zone; Import Quotas; Imports; International Trade; Localization; Mercantilism; Protectionism; Ricardo, David; Tariffs; Terms of Trade; Voluntary Quotas.**

Further Reading

Garnaut, Ross G., et al. *Sustaining Export-Oriented Development: Ideas from East Asia*. New York: Cambridge University Press, 1995.

Helleiner, Gerald K. *Non-Traditional Export Promotion in Africa: Experience and Issues*. New York: Palgrave Macmillan, 2002.

Rhee, Chase C. *Principles of International Trade (Import and Export): The First Step toward Globalization*. Bloomington, IN: 1st Books Library, 2003.

United Nations Conference on Trade and Development. *Trade and Development Report, 2004*. New York: Author, 2004.

World Trade Organization. *World Trade Report 2004*. Geneva, Switzerland: WTO Secretariat, 2004.

EXTERNAL DEBT

External debt, also called foreign debt, is money owed by a nation to a foreign government or commercial bank, a multilateral organization, or other creditor. Nations borrow money from foreigners to finance public goods such as infrastructure projects, schools, and military goods. Borrowed money is also used to support social services in areas such as health care and nutrition. By 2005 the combined foreign debt of emerging market economies and developing economies topped $3 trillion, an $850 billion increase over the 1996 total. Figure 12 shows the regional distribution of external debt in 2005.

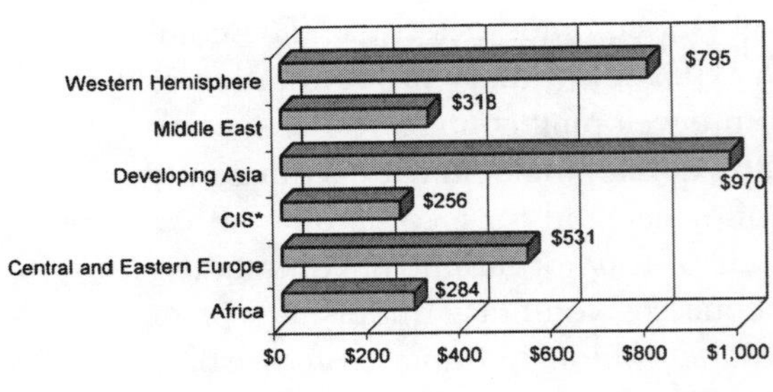

FIGURE 12 **External Debt by World Region, 2005 ($ billions)**

International creditors expect repayment of borrowed money, plus interest, as stated in the terms of the loan. Private lenders, such as commercial banks, extend loans at prevailing market interest rates. A private financial institution is designed to earn a profit from its investments. Thus, banks and other private lenders are more inclined to extend loans to creditworthy debtor nations. Multilateral organizations, such as the World Bank and the regional development banks, make development loans to member countries regardless of income status. Loans to the poorest countries, or least developed countries (LDCs), are often made on a concessional basis. A concessional loan typically carries a low interest rate and lengthy repayment schedule, perhaps as long as fifty years. Some concessional loans are interest free. The International Development Association (IDA), one of five institutions within the World Bank Group, extends concessional loans to LDCs.

External debt is a pressing economic problem for many poorer countries. At issue is the impact of debt servicing on the economic health of emerging market and developing countries. Debt servicing involves making scheduled loan repayments to foreign creditors. Annual debt-servicing obligations for the emerging market and developing countries climbed from $312 billion in 1996 to $475 billion in 2005, an increase of about 50 percent during the decade. All world regions except Africa and the Middle East faced higher debt-servicing payments in 2005 than in 1996. Debt-servicing drains scarce funds from the public till, and, thus, reduces the government's ability to provide basic public goods and services. The World Bank identified fifty-two "severely indebted" emerging market and developing economies in 2005—twenty-eight low-income countries, ten lower middle-income countries, and fourteen upper middle-income countries. Today, debt rescheduling and debt forgiveness are often complementary pieces of a debt relief package.

The severity of the external debt crisis instigated a number of debt relief efforts in recent years. The two categories of debt relief include debt rescheduling and debt forgiveness. Under debt rescheduling, creditors renegotiate the terms of the loan. Normally, the interest rate is reduced and the repayment schedule is lengthened. Debt rescheduling permits debtor nations to repay loans in more manageable installments. Under debt forgiveness, creditors erase a portion of a nation's external debt. Debt forgiveness is reserved for LDCs that have accumulated unsustainable debt—debt that cannot be repaid without horrific consequences for the nation and its people.

Over the past decade, multilateral organizations, such as the International Monetary Fund (IMF) and the World Bank, have supported debt relief programs. In 1996 the World Bank and IMF jointly sponsored the Heavily Indebted Poor Countries (HIPC) Initiative. The HIPC Initiative coordinates bilateral and multilateral debt relief measures. To be eligible to receive HIPC debt relief assistance, LDCs must be burdened with unsustainable debt, and must participate in IMF or World Bank reform programs. For example, under 1999 adjustments to the HIPC Initiative, debt relief was more directly linked with broader social goals such as poverty reduction and the expansion of health care, education, and other social policies. By 2004, twenty-seven countries had met eligibility requirements for debt relief, assistance that carried a $32 billion price tag for creditor governments, multilateral organizations, and others. Ten additional severely indebted countries will likely receive debt relief when eligibility requirements are met. In total, the HIPC Initiative expects to provide $55 billion in debt relief to thirty-seven severely indebted countries over time.

Other voices in the global community aggressively support debt forgiveness to eliminate the external debt woes of the world's poorest countries. Jubilee 2000, an influential non-governmental organization (NGO) during the 1990s, rallied millions of people under the debt forgiveness banner. Jubilee 2000 and other NGOs maintained that debt forgiveness was a key feature in peoples' struggle for global economic justice. The Jubilee 2000 platform also called for reforms in the global financial architecture and greater accountability of transnational corporations (TNCs), especially in their dealings with local economies and peoples. Today, Jubilee 2000 is called Jubilee Research. Jubilee Research is associated with the New Economics Foundation in London, England.

Default is another policy option for heavily indebted countries. Default occurs when a government refuses to make scheduled payments on its debts. In 1998 Russia, a transition country still swimming in massive Soviet-era debt, defaulted on some debt obligations. Subsequent negotiations enabled the Russian government to repay a portion of its debts to foreign creditors. Similarly, Argentina defaulted on $81 billion in government bonds in December 2001. By early 2005, after years of wangling between Argentina's government and its bondholders, most of Argentina's foreign creditors reluctantly agreed to a bond swap—the exchange of old bonds for new bonds. The new bonds were worth only about one-third the value of the old bonds, however. Default is considered a last resort action. It denies foreign creditors, such as banks and securities dealers, a legitimate return on investments. Default is also ruinous to a government's ability to borrow money in global capital markets, to attract direct foreign investment, and to maintain macroeconomic stability.

See also **Developing Countries; Heavily Indebted Poor Countries (HIPC) Initiative; International Monetary Fund; Least Developed Countries; Poverty; Unsustainable Debt; World Bank Group.** ***See also in Volume 2,*** **Documents 5, 6, 56.**

Further Reading

Birdsall, Nancy, John Williamson, and Brian Deese. *Delivering on Debt Relief: From IMF Gold to a New Aid Architecture*. Washington, DC: Institute for International Economics, 2002.

Garlake, Teresa. *Global Debt: The Impact on Our Lives*. Austin, TX: Raintree, 2003.
International Monetary Fund. *External Debt Statistics: Guide for Compilers and Users*. Washington, DC: International Monetary Fund, 2003.
Rieffel, Lex. *Restructuring Sovereign Debt: The Case for Ad Hoc Machinery*. Washington, DC: Brookings Institution Press, 2003.

F

FACTORS OF PRODUCTION

Factors of production are resources used to produce goods or services, and are often called productive resources. The three main factors of production are natural resources, human resources, and capital goods. Some economists list entrepreneurship as a fourth factor of production. At the microeconomic level, firms use the factors of production to produce goods efficiently and profitably. At the macroeconomic level, national output, employment, and sustainable economic development are heavily dependent on the efficient use of society's productive resources. The factors of production are unevenly distributed in the global economy.

Natural resources are the gifts of nature used in production. Natural resources include minerals such as bauxite, uranium, and nickel; primary energy sources such as oil, natural gas, and coal; water bodies such as oceans, rivers, and lakes; wildlife such as animals, fish, and insects; natural vegetation such as forests and plants; and naturally occurring forces such as wind and sunlight. Natural resources provide many of the raw materials needed to produce goods and services. Some nations, such as the United States, are well-endowed with a wide variety of natural resources such as mineral deposits, navigable rivers, and arable land. Other nations may be rich in a single resource such as oil or timber. Still others lack essential natural resources. Resource-poor Japan acquires natural resources through international trade and foreign direct investment, but poorer, land-locked countries have limited access to essential natural resources.

Human resources are people who are engaged in production. Human resources include assembly line workers, miners, and contractors in the goods-producing sector; teachers, doctors, and engineers in the services-producing sector; and farmers, loggers, and ranchers in the agricultural sector. Education, training, apprenticeships, and other investments in human resources create a skilled workforce, often referred to as human capital. Human capital development increases the productivity of labor. The advanced economies finance comprehensive public education, and support higher education and worker training programs to create human capital. The emerging market and developing countries value human capital, but have fewer resources to support its development. In addition, the dearth of financial incentives, uncertain property rights, and low quality of life contribute to a brain drain in many poorer countries. The brain drain, which involves a migration of professionals and other skilled workers from poorer nations to greener pastures in richer countries, depletes the stock of human capital in poorer regions.

A wind turbine is a capital good, whereas the wind that powers the turbines is a natural resource.
Courtesy of CORBIS

Capital goods are items used to produce other products, rather than to satisfy an immediate consumption need. Capital goods include bulldozers, cement mixers, and automated assembly lines in the goods-producing sector; communications satellites, subway trains, and engineering design software in the services-producing sector; and mechanical harvesters, fishing boats, and fertilizers in the agricultural sector. Investment in new capital goods is a prerequisite for capital formation, the increase in a nation's capital stock. Capital formation in the advanced economies has sharpened their competitive edge over other emerging market and developing economies. For instance, U.S. investment in information processing equipment, such as computers and software, improved the product quality in information technology (IT) firms. Sophisticated IT also increased the productivity and connectivity of firms using this technology. Similarly, capital formation in the newly industrialized economies (NIEs), including Chinese Taipei, the Hong Kong SAR, Singapore, and South Korea, accelerated their economic development over the past several decades. Low domestic savings, poorly developed capital markets, and capital flight slowed capital formation in many poorer nations.

Entrepreneurship is the process of transforming innovative business ideas into viable commercial enterprises. Entrepreneurs develop new products, production methods, or business ventures. Entrepreneurship is often considered a fourth factor of production, joining natural resources, human resources, and capital goods. Entrepreneurial activity involves risk-taking, and a visionary zeal to succeed. Entrepreneurs such as Thomas A. Edison and Henry Ford helped create the modern industrial age. Similarly Steven Jobs, co-founder of Apple Computer, and Bill Gates of Microsoft fame, helped jump-start a global information revolution. The widely respected *Global Entrepreneurship Monitor 2003* (*GEM 2003*) makes a compelling link between entrepreneurship, business and jobs creation, and economic growth. *GEM 2003* also concluded that entrepreneurship supported economic development in all classifications of countries—low-income, middle-income, and high-income.

See also **Brain Drain; Capital Flight; Capital Formation; Command Economy; Development Economics; Economic Growth; Economic Sectors; Energy Resources; Entrepreneurship; Market Economy; Sustainable Economic Development.** ***See also in Volume 2,*** **Documents 10, 16, 43, 44, 59.**

Further Reading

Hartman, Laura P., Denis G. Arnold, and Richard E. Wokutch, eds. *Rising above Sweatshops: Innovative Approaches to Global Labor Challenges.* Westport, CT: Praeger Publishers, 2003.

Ito, Takatoshi, and Andrew K. Rose, eds. *Growth and Productivity in East Asia.* Chicago: University of Chicago Press, 2004.

Marquardt, Michael J. *Advances in Developing Human Resources: Developing Human Resources in the Global Economy.* San Francisco, CA: Berrett-Koehler Publishers, 2000.

Reynolds, Paul D., William D. Bygrave, and Erkko Autio. *GEM 2003 Global Report.* Babson Park, MA: Babson College and the London Business School, 2003.

World Resources Institute. *World Resources 2002–2004: Decisions for the Earth.* Washington, DC: WRI, United Nations Development Program, United Nations Environment Program, World Bank, 2003.

Worldwatch Institute. *State of the World: 2004.* New York: W. W. Norton & Company, 2004.

FINANCIAL CONTAGION

Financial contagion refers to the spread of a financial crisis from one country or region to other countries or regions. Economic interdependence—an underpinning of globalization—increases the danger of financial contagion. International trade, foreign direct investment (FDI), and the cross-border flows of financial capital expand economic interdependence in the global economy. Economic interdependence is generally viewed as favorable because it creates a mutually supporting web of economic opportunities. However, the liberalization of financial investment regimes in today's global economy has also been a source of financial instability. Advanced technologies capable of instantaneous cross-border transfers of assets, such as stocks or bonds, have created greater volatility in global financial markets. A series of financial crises during the 1990s demonstrated the negative side of financial interdependence. Financial crises originating in Mexico, Brazil, Russia, and Thailand destabilized global financial markets. By the late 1990s and early 2000s, the specter of financial contagion instigated renewed calls for sweeping reforms in the global financial architecture.

The East Asian Financial Crisis of 1997–1998 was the world's most serious bout with financial contagion. The seeds of the East Asian crisis were sown in Thailand. In the first half of the 1990s, investment opportunities in Thailand caught the eye of foreign investors. Highly speculative investment in Thailand during this period laid the groundwork for the coming financial nightmare. Foreign and domestic investments in stocks and other securities, developed and undeveloped real estate, and other assets created a whirlwind of profitable financial transactions. Higher profits on speculative investments fueled the demand for Thai assets, which raised asset prices to unreasonably high levels. Beneath the glitter of the investment boom were serious weaknesses in the Thai financial system, however. Inadequate banking supervision, poor assessment models for credit risk, and excessive borrowing in global capital markets spelled disaster for Thailand's financial sector. Complicating the country's financial picture were governance problems, including public corruption, the lack of transparency, and inadequate economic data for policy decisions.

Short-term, speculative investments invite periods of boom and bust. In Thailand, the bottom fell out of the speculative boom in 1997. Shaken investors stampeded to sell their holdings of Thai securities, properties, and other assets. The panic selloff of Thai assets, a type of herd behavior, is characteristic of speculative investment. The financial meltdown weakened Thailand's currency, the baht, and threw the overextended banking system and securities market into chaos. In addition, property values plummeted, business activity slumped, and unemployment increased. Fears of a regional financial meltdown caused asset selloffs in other East Asian countries. Within a few months similar instability ravaged the economies of Indonesia, South Korea, and other East Asian nations. Table 46 shows the consequences of the regional financial crisis on the gross domestic product (GDP) of several leading East Asian nations in 1998.

Soon the financial contagion was knocking at the doors of Tokyo, New York City, and London. The financial crisis, which slowed business activity and dimmed consumer confidence in East Asia, also reduced Japanese, American, and European exports to traditional Asian markets. In addition, global securities markets, such as the New York Stock Exchange, dipped under the weight of the East Asian financial collapse. On a global level, the East Asian crisis slowed global economic growth in the late 1990s.

The IMF, Asian Development Bank (ADB), World Bank, and the United States orchestrated a massive bailout to prevent a total collapse of major East Asian economies. The IMF—the multilateral organization most responsible for global financial stability—took the lead in this rescue mission. The IMF coordinated global efforts to raise \$125 billion to shore up faltering economies in the region, as shown in Table 47. The IMF was widely

TABLE 46 **East Asian Financial Crisis and Real GDP, 1995 to 2000**

	Real Gross Domestic Product (% change)					
Countries	1995	1996	1997	1998	1999	2000
Hong Kong SAR	3.9	4.5	5.0	−5.3	3.0	10.5
Indonesia	8.2	8.0	4.5	−13.1	0.8	4.8
Korea	8.9	6.8	5.0	−6.7	10.9	9.3
Malaysia	9.8	10.0	7.3	−7.4	6.1	8.3
Philippines	4.7	5.8	5.2	−0.6	3.4	4.0
Singapore	8.0	7.7	8.5	−0.1	6.9	10.3
Thailand	9.2	5.9	−1.4	−10.5	4.4	4.6

Source: International Monetary Fund, *World Economic Outlook, April, 2002*, 158, 165.

criticized for its failure to foresee the financial catastrophe that blighted the region. Since the late 1990s, the IMF, other multilateral organizations, governments, non-governmental organizations (NGOs), and others have cooperated to reform the global financial architecture. High on the reform agenda was stricter supervision of banks and securities markets, heightened surveillance of countries' macroeconomic policies and performance, and technical support for good governance in both business and government.

TABLE 47 **Asian Financial Crisis Bailout, 1997–1998 ($ billions)**

Assistance	Thailand	Korea	Indonesia	Totals
IMF	$4.0	$21.1	$15.0	$40.1
Multilateral	$2.7	$14.2	$10.0	$26.9
Bilateral	$10.5	$23.1	$24.7	$58.3
Total aid	$17.2	$58.4	$49.7	$125.3

Source: International Monetary Fund, "Recovery from the Asian Crisis and the Role of the IMF," *IMF Issues Brief*, 2000.

See also **Capital Markets; Global Financial Architecture; Globalization; International Financial Institutions; International Monetary Fund.**

Further Reading

Blustein, Paul. *The Chastening: Inside the Crisis That Rocked the Global Financial System and Humbled the Imf*. Cambridge, MA: Public Affairs/Perseus, 2003.

Goodhart, C. A. E., and Gerhard Illing. *Financial Crises, Contagion, and the Lender of Last Resort*. New York: Oxford University Press, 2002.

Gul, Ferdinand A., and Judy S. L. Tsui, eds. *The Governance of East Asian Corporations: Post Asian Financial Crisis*. New York: Palgrave Macmillan, 2005.

International Monetary Fund. *Global Financial Stability Report: Market Developments and Issues, April 2004*. Washington, DC: Author, 2004.

Noble, Gregory W., and John Ravenhill, eds. *The Asian Financial Crisis and the Architecture of Global Finance*. New York: Cambridge University Press, 2000.

FOREIGN AID

Foreign aid is a grant of money, technical assistance, food, capital equipment, or other assistance from one country to another. In most cases richer countries extend foreign aid to poorer countries. The three main categories of foreign aid are development assistance, humanitarian and emergency assistance, and military assistance. Foreign aid is derived from a number of sources. Bilateral aid travels between two governments. Multilateral aid travels from international organizations to national governments or other agencies. Individuals, and groups such as private foundations, corporations, private voluntary organizations, colleges and universities, and other elements of civil society, also supply foreign aid to needy regions.

Foreign aid is categorized by its intended purpose. Development assistance directly supports economic growth and sustainable economic development. Development assistance targets infrastructure projects, good governance, and long-term investments in education and health care. Humanitarian and emergency assistance responds to national or regional crises such as natural disasters, civil conflict, or war. Humanitarian and emergency assistance consists of food, medical personnel and supplies, and temporary shelter. For example, in 2004–2005, billions of dollars in humanitarian and emergency assistance flowed from the global community to nations ravaged by a catastrophic tsunami in western Asia. Military assistance promotes stability in a region. Military assistance supports peacekeeping efforts, internal security, and the transport of emergency supplies to stricken regions. Military assistance does not include money, materials, or personnel that are directly involved in invasions or other military campaigns.

Foreign aid is a hot issue in the global economy. The foreign aid debate centers on the amount, uses, and effectiveness of foreign aid. Much of the world's foreign aid comes from the countries that comprise the Organization for Economic Cooperation and Development (OECD). Within the OECD is the Development Assistance Committee (DAC), which coordinates assistance from the richer countries. The two types of DAC assistance are official development assistance (ODA) and official aid (OA). In 2003, ODA and OA accounted for $76 billion in foreign aid, which was spread across 188 countries and territories. ODA includes food aid, emergency relief, capital projects, technical aid, and peacekeeping activities. ODA also includes contributions to multilateral institutions, including the specialized agencies and programs within the UN System, and the World Bank. ODA recipients include 154 countries and territories in the developing world. In 2003, ODA topped $69 billion. Official aid (OA), which has many of the same functions as ODA, targets thirty-four other emerging market economies, especially those in central and eastern Europe and the countries of the Former Soviet Union (FSU). OA totaled $7 billion in 2003. The top recipients of ODA and OA are shown in Table 48.

The OECD's Development Assistance Committee coordinates the distribution of ODA and OA. In 2003 about one-half of the $76 billion in ODA and OA was dispersed among three project categories: economic infrastructure; production; and education, health and population. Other categories included debt relief, program assistance, emergency aid, social infrastructure, and multi-sector projects. Ranked by world region, the top recipient of bilateral ODA in 2003 was sub-Saharan Africa ($15.3 billion), followed by Other Asia and Oceania ($8.5 billion), South and Central Asia ($7.2 billion), Latin America and the Caribbean ($5.4 billion), the Middle East and North Africa ($5.2 billion), and Europe ($3.2 billion). About $9 billion was unspecified. Ranked by countries' income classification, the highest percent of bilateral ODA was allocated to lower middle-income countries (38.2 percent), followed by the least developed countries (33.3 percent), other low-income countries (24.2 percent), and upper middle-income countries (4.3 percent).

TABLE 48 **Top Recipients of ODA and OA, 2003 ($ millions)**

Rank	Country	Amount
1	Congo, Dem. Rep.	$2,760
2	China	$2,028
3	India	$1,680
4	Indonesia	$1,596
5	Pakistan	$1,420
6	Serbia and Montenegro	$1,387
7	Egypt	$1,268
8	Mozambique	$1,232
9	Afghanistan	$1,110
10	Russia (OA)	$1,108

Source: Organization for Economic Cooperation and Development, Development Assistance Committee, *Aid from DAC Members: Total DAC Countries*, December 2, 2004.

In real terms the official flow of foreign aid to poorer regions has not kept pace with income growth in the rich countries. Measured as a percent of gross national income (GNI), DAC assistance has declined over the past few decades. In 2003, the average ODA granted by DAC member nations was 0.25 percent, one-quarter of one percent of GNI. Five nations met the unofficial target of 0.7 percent of GNI, including Denmark, Luxembourg, the Netherlands, Norway, and Sweden. Other nations, including the United States, fell below the 0.25 percent average. The largest ODA contributors by dollar amount and percent of GNI in 2003 are shown in Table 49.

There are different measurements of foreign aid. The narrowest measure considers just the official flows of ODA and OA. The U.S. Agency for International Development (USAID) uses a broader measure of foreign aid, which includes other types of government and private assistance. In 2000, for example, U.S. ODA totaled $9.9 billion. U.S. ODA included allocations to the USAID, the Peace Corps, most multilateral organizations, and some State Department and Defense Department programs. The other types of government assistance, which totaled $12.7 billion, raised the total U.S. government aid package to $22.6 billion ($9.9 billion plus $12.7 billion). Other government assistance included contributions to the International Monetary Fund (IMF) and other international agencies, certain security assistance to countries, and official aid (OA) to countries in central and eastern Europe, Israel, and elsewhere.

The USAID measurement of foreign aid also includes private aid sources. Combined, private sources added another $33.6 billion to the total of U.S. foreign aid in 2000. Private sources include cross-border aid from private foundations, corporations, private and voluntary organizations (PVOs), colleges and universities, religious groups, and individual remittances. First, foundations, such as the Rockefeller Foundation and the Bill and Melinda Gates Foundation, donated about $1.5 billion for education, health care, and other humanitarian causes. In 2005 the Seattle-based Bill and Melinda Gates Foundation was the world's largest charitable organization with an endowment of $29 billion. Second, corporations, with the pharmaceutical firms in the lead, contributed

TABLE 49 **Official Development Assistance, 2003 ($ billions)**

Largest ODA Donors by Total Contributions			Largest ODA Donors by Percent of GNI		
Rank	Country	Total ODA ($ billions)	Rank	Country	ODA as a % of GNI
1	United States	$16.3	1	Norway	0.92
2	Japan	$8.9	2	Denmark	0.84
3	France	$7.3	3	Luxembourg	0.81
4	Germany	$6.8	4	Netherlands	0.80
5	U. Kingdom	$6.3	5	Sweden	0.79
Total (all DAC)		$69.0	DAC average		0.25

Source: Organization for Economic Cooperation and Development, Development Assistance Committee, *Statistical Annex of the 2004 Development Co-operation Report*, 2004.

TABLE 50 **U.S. Foreign Assistance to Developing Countries, 2000 ($ billions)**

Type of Assistance	Amount ($ billions)	Percent of Total Assistance
Official development assistance	$9.9	18%
Other government assistance	$12.7	22%
Private assistance	$33.6	60%
Foundations	($1.5)	
Corporations	($2.8)	
PVOs	($6.6)	
Colleges, universities	($1.3)	
Religious congregations	($3.4)	
Individual remittances	($18.0)	
Total U.S. assistance	$56.2	100%

Source: U.S. Agency for International Development, *Foreign Aid in the National Interest*, 2003.

$2.8 billion. Other significant corporate contributors included the following industries: computers and office equipment, telecommunications, foods and beverages, and retail and wholesale trade. Third, private and voluntary organizations (PVOs), such as CARE, World Vision, and Save the Children, contributed $6.6 billion in humanitarian and community development work. Fourth, colleges and universities contributed an estimated $1.3 billion through scholarships to foreign students. Fifth, religious congregations contributed $3.4 billion to relief and development work through overseas ministries, foundations, and other organizations. Sixth, individual remittances—the money sent to foreign homelands by immigrants to the United States—added $18 billion to aid outflows. According to the USAID, U.S. foreign aid totaled $56 billion, as shown in Table 50.

The uses and effectiveness of foreign aid are widely debated. The debate tends to raise more questions than answers, however. One issue is whether foreign aid promotes sustainable economic development, or a culture of dependency. A second issue concerns the applicability of foreign aid models. For instance, the massive infusion of money into Europe under the Marshall Plan during the late 1940s and early 1950s was successful in reconstructing a continent ravaged by World War II. This model has been less successful in many regions of the developing world, however. A third issue involves the dissemination of foreign aid. Today, foreign aid is dispersed to governments, multilateral organizations, private companies, non-governmental organizations, and other elements of civil society. A fourth issue is the absence of good governance in many recipient countries. The lack of good governance, marked by a lack of transparency and a weak system of justice, invites corruption, cronyism, and other abuses of the public trust—including the misallocation of foreign aid. Finally, coordination issues plague the effectiveness of foreign aid. The OECD's Development Assistance Committee assists in the dispersal of ODA and OA. Yet, private aid flows are sometimes disrupted by organizational redundancies and ineffective delivery systems. These types of issues raise legitimate concerns among donors about the impact of their contributions on long-term economic development and on people's quality of life.

See also **Advanced Economies; Developing Countries; Organization for Economic Cooperation and Development; Peace Corps of the United States; Poverty; Sustainable Economic Development; United Nations System; World Bank Group.** ***See also in Volume 2,*** **Documents 5, 9, 10, 59.**

Further Reading

Burnell, Peter, and Oliver Morrissey. *Foreign Aid in the New Global Economy.* Northampton, MA: Edward Elgar Publishing, 2004.

Lancaster, Carol. *Transforming Foreign Aid: United States Assistance in the 21st Century.* Washington, DC: Institute for International Economics, 2000.

Radelet, Steven. *Challenging Foreign Aid: A Policymaker's Guide to the Millennium Challenge.* Washington, DC: Center for Global Development, 2003.

Sogge, David. *Give and Take: What's the Matter with Foreign Aid?* New York: Zed Books, 2002.

U.S. Agency for International Development. *Foreign Aid in the National Interest: Promoting Freedom, Security, and Opportunity.* Washington, DC: Author, 2003.

FOREIGN DIRECT INVESTMENT

Foreign direct investment (FDI) is a cross-border investment that results in one company gaining ownership or control of productive facilities in another country. FDI is long term in nature. The two types of FDI are mergers and acquisitions (M&As), and greenfield investments. M&As represent a legal joining of two existing companies under a single ownership. M&As are the dominant type of FDI in the advanced countries. The 1998 "merger of equals" between auto giants Daimler-Benz (Germany) and Chrysler (United States) illustrates this process. Greenfield investments occur when transnational corporations (TNCs) construct new production facilities, such as factories or retail stores, in a foreign country. The construction of Hyundai Motor's (South Korea) $1.1 billion auto manufacturing plant in Alabama—a plant that opened in May 2005—was a greenfield investment. A TNC, also called a multinational corporation, is comprised of a parent company and its foreign affiliates. Foreign affiliates are businesses in which a TNC has controlling interest. By the early 2000s, greenfield investments were fast becoming the preferred type of FDI in the developing world. In recent years liberalized FDI regimes in some countries also encouraged foreign investment in real estate and other properties. FDI, international trade, and cross-border financial flows are the three pillars of globalization.

FDI grew rapidly during the 1990s, peaked in 2000, and declined during the early 2000s. FDI is measured by inflows of FDI into a country, and by outflows of FDI out of a country. In its *World Investment Report 2004*, the United National Conference on Trade and Development (UNCTAD) summarized global FDI trends. According to UNCTAD the global inflows of FDI from 1992 to 1997 averaged just $311 billion per year, but jumped to $1.4 trillion in 2000, as shown in Figure 13. A global slump during the early 2000s interrupted the FDI growth trend, and FDI inflows plummeted to $560 billion in 2003—a decline of 60 percent from its 2000 peak. In 2003 the advanced economies received 65 percent of all FDI inflows, compared to 31 percent in the developing countries and 4 percent in the transition countries of eastern and central Europe. The top FDI recipient was Luxembourg ($88 billion), followed by China ($53 billion), France ($47 billion), the United States ($30 billion), and Belgium ($29 billion). Global FDI outflows followed a similar pattern, peaking at over $1 trillion in 2000 and declining thereafter. In 2003

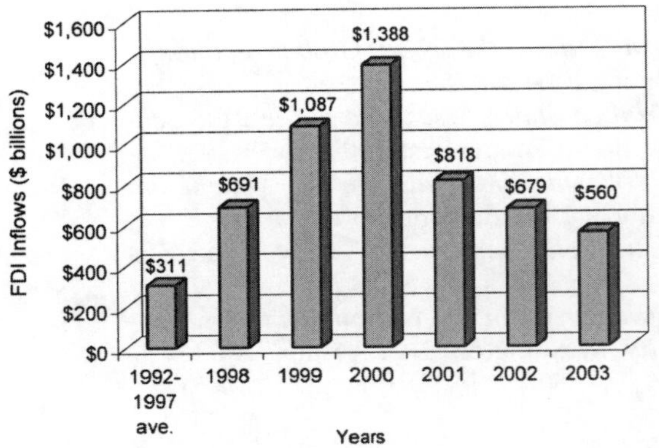

FIGURE 13 **World Foreign Direct Investment Inflows, 1992 to 2003 ($ billions)**

Source: United Nations Conference on Trade and Development, *World Investment Report 2004*, 367–371.

the advanced economies accounted for 93 percent of all FDI outflows, compared to 6 percent for the developing countries and 1 percent for the transition countries. The largest FDI outflows in 2003 came from the United States ($152 billion), Luxembourg ($96 billion), France ($57 billion), the United Kingdom ($55 billion), and Belgium ($37 billion).

FDI, a pillar of globalization, creates a more integrated and interdependent global economy. In 2003, there were 62,000 TNCs with over 927,000 foreign affiliates. Cementing the economic relationship between parent company and foreign affiliates were foreign assets worth $30.3 trillion, 54 million employees, and $3 trillion in exports by affiliates. A summary of selected TNC indicators is shown in Table 51. The liberalization of trade and investment also encouraged production sharing in recent years. Production sharing occurs when a business produces a good in stages in a number of different locations around the world. Production sharing is motivated by a firm's desire to minimize production costs. Technological advances in communications and transportation support production sharing.

The rapid expansion of FDI during the 1990s was fueled by new telecommunications technologies, changes in financial regulations, trade and investment liberalization, and the perceived financial benefits to TNCs and host countries. Advanced telecommunications allowed TNCs to tap a broader pool of financial resources in global financial markets, money that was used to fund M&As and greenfield investments. Many countries relaxed regulations governing banks and other financial institutions. These regulatory changes reduced restrictions on cross-border financial transactions; permitted mergers of banks with insurance and investment companies; and encouraged economies of scale through consolidation in the banking industry. The trend toward trade and investment liberalization stimulated FDI by increasing cross-border mobility of

TABLE 51 **Transnational Corporations: Selected Indicators, 1982 to 2003 ($ billions)**

Indicator	Dollar Values at Current Prices			
	1982	1990	2000	2003
FDI inflows	$59	$209	$1,388	$560
FDI outflows	$28	$242	$1,187	$612
Sales of foreign affiliates	$2,717	$5,660	$15,680	$17,580
Total assets of foreign affiliates	$2,076	$5,883	$21,102	$30,362
Employment of foreign affiliates (in thousands)	19,232	24,197	45,587	54,170
Exports of foreign affiliates	$717	$1,194	$3,572	$3,077

Source: United Nations Conference on Trade and Development, *World Investment Report 2004*, 9; *World Investment Report 2003*, 3; and *World Investment Report 2001* (Overview), 2.

natural, human, and capital resources, and the output produced by these resources. In the vanguard of trade liberalization were the General Agreement on Tariffs and Trade (1947–1994) and the World Trade Organization (1995–present). Supporting investment liberalization were bilateral investment treaties (BITS) and double taxation treaties (DTTs). BITS are formal agreements between two countries designed mainly to promote mutually beneficial investment opportunities. UNCTAD reported that 2,265 BITS were in effect by 2003. DTTs establish guidelines for taxing wealth or income generated by overseas investments. By 2003, 2,316 DTTs had been negotiated in the global economy. The five largest non-financial TNCs, ranked by foreign assets, are shown in Table 52.

Responsible FDI benefits both the TNC and the host economy. Through FDI, TNCs gain access to low-cost natural and human resources in the global economy. Lower production costs, in turn, increase the competitiveness of TNCs in the global marketplace. TNCs also gain access to foreign markets. By producing goods or services in foreign countries, TNCs' foreign affiliates circumvent import restrictions, and reduce shipping costs to these markets. Historically, many TNCs set up shop in the United States and other advanced countries to gain a foothold in profitable markets in the richer countries.

Host countries also derive benefits from FDI. Responsible FDI expands the nation's capital stock, infuses new technology into the economy, and supports human capital development by improving the skills of workers and management. FDI advances the competitiveness and connectivity of firms by expanding their access to credit, and linking them with other participants in the global economy. Many countries enact policies to attract FDI. The International Labor Organization (ILO), a specialized agency within the UN System, reported that 116 countries operated 3,000 export processing zones (EPZs) to bring FDI to their shores. Countries also establish investment promotion agencies (IPAs) to compete for FDI. Countries use tax breaks, subsidies, infrastructure improvements, and other incentives to sweeten the investment climate for TNCs.

Irresponsible FDI can also inflict heavy costs on a nation. Irresponsible FDI is exploitative. It uses a country's resources for short-term gain, but contributes little to the country's long-term development. Signs of irresponsible FDI are the wanton

TABLE 52 **Largest Non-financial Transnational Corporations, by Foreign Assets, 2002**

Rank	TNC	Home Country	Industry	Foreign Assets ($ billions)
1	General Electric	United States	Electrical	$229
2	Vodafone	United Kingdom	Telecommunications	$208
3	Ford Motor	United States	Motor vehicles	$165
4	British Petroleum	UK/Netherlands	Petroleum	$126
5	General Motors	United States	Motor vehicles	$108

Source: United Nations Conference on Trade and Development, *World Investment Report 2004*, 276.

destruction of forests, the pollution of rivers and lakes, and other forms of environmental degradation. The abuse of labor in sweatshops, or in other substandard workplaces, is another sign of irresponsible FDI. A sweatshop is typically an industrial workplace characterized by excessive work hours, unsafe or unhealthy working conditions, abusive bosses, and the absence of worker associations.

During the 1980s and 1990s, cases of irresponsible FDI by TNCs or their subcontractors raised the ire of non-governmental organizations (NGOs), governments, and multilateral organizations. Today, most TNCs have a well-defined "corporate code of conduct" to protect overseas laborers. The International Labor Organization (ILO), Organization for Economic Cooperation and Development (OECD), and other groups have also devised recognized "codes of conduct for multinationals." Despite these codes, cost-cutting pressures on major TNCs endanger the quality of workers' lives, especially workers at the bottom of the supply chain. Labor advocates such as the ILO, the International Confederation of Free Trade Unions (ICFTU), and Oxfam International monitor global labor conditions with an eye toward stopping exploitative, race-to-the-bottom corporate policies.

See also **Competitiveness; Corporate Social Responsibility; Export Processing Zone; Global Economy; Globalization; Maquiladoras; Multilateral Investment Guarantee Agency; Offshoring; Production Sharing; Race to the Bottom; Supply Chains; Transnational Corporations.** ***See also in Volume 2,*** **Documents 5, 9, 11, 15, 28, 29, 30, 32, 36.**

Further Reading

Organization for Economic Cooperation and Development. *New Horizons for Foreign Direct Investment*. Paris: Author, 2002.

Oxelheim, Lars, and Pervez Ghauri. *European Union and the Race for Foreign Direct Investment in Europe*. New York: Pergamon, 2003.

United Nations Conference on Trade and Development. *World Investment Report 2004*. New York: United Nations, 2004.

World Bank. *World Development Report 2005: A Better Investment Climate for Everyone*. Washington, DC: Author, 2004.

Xiaolan Fu. *Exports, Foreign Direct Investment and Economic Development in China*. New York: Palgrave Macmillan, 2005.

FOREIGN EXCHANGE MARKET

The foreign exchange market, also called the forex market, is a network of commercial banks, investment banks, brokerage houses, and other financial institutions that buy and sell currencies for profit. The currencies that are traded are called foreign exchange, or, more simply, forex (fx). The process of trading foreign exchange is called forex trading. In 2004 the daily turnover in the forex market was $1.9 trillion, a significant jump from daily trading of $1.2 trillion in 2001. This means that six days of business activity on the forex market was roughly equivalent to value of all goods and services that flowed through the global trading system for an entire year.

The forex market represents the institutions and practices of banks, brokerage firms, securities dealers, and other participants in forex trading. Commercial banks assume a central role in forex trading through "interbank" or "direct dealing" transactions. Many large commercial banks operate globally, and keep at least one forex trading station open at all times. Forex markets operate nonstop, twenty-four hours per day, seven days per week. A sophisticated electronic transfer system called SWIFT (Society for Worldwide Interbank Financial Telecommunications) records all financial transactions. The most authoritative accounting of forex trading is the Bank for International Settlements (BIS), located in Basel, Switzerland. In its *Triennial Central Bank Survey of Foreign Exchange and Derivatives Market Activity in April 2004*, BIS reported growth in forex trading by banks, asset managers, and other dealers. Most forex trading is short term and highly speculative. In 2004 about 95 percent of all forex trading was speculative, and 80 percent of all trades lasted for less than one week.

The U.S. dollar has been the world's dominant currency since World War II.

Courtesy of Getty Images: PhotoLink

The foreign exchange market is spread across all populated continents. In 2004, however, one-half of all forex trading took place in just two countries, the United Kingdom and the United States, as shown in Figure 14. The dominant financial center in the United Kingdom was London, and the dominant financial center in the United States was New York City. Other important countries in the global forex market were Japan, Singapore, Germany, the Hong Kong SAR, and Australia.

The modern foreign exchange market has changed significantly since its inception in 1946. Under the Bretton Woods System from 1946 to 1973, the main role of the foreign exchange market was currency conversion for purposes of trade. Under Bretton Woods, the process of converting currencies was relatively simple due to the prevailing fixed exchange rate system. Under the fixed exchange rate system, the value of national currencies was "pegged" to the U.S. dollar, the world's dominant currency, or to gold. The U.S. dollar was also fixed to gold, with its value equal to one thirty-fifth of an ounce of gold. Because national currencies were not permitted to fluctuate beyond a very narrow range,

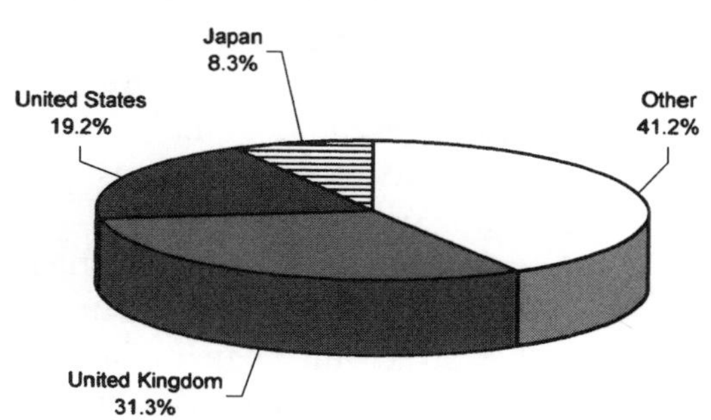

FIGURE 14 **Foreign Exchange Trading by Nation, 2004**

Source: Bank for International Settlements, *Triennial Central Bank Survey of Foreign Exchange and Derivatives Market Activity in April 2004*, 1, 13.

the foreign exchange market easily converted major currencies. Major currencies were often called "hard currencies" because they held their value over time. Most international trade was conducted with hard currencies. Pegging currencies to the U.S. dollar and to gold stabilized the post-war global financial system. Yet, over time, destabilizing cracks in the fixed exchange rate system appeared. For example, a nation could officially devalue its currency to gain a competitive edge in foreign trade. Nations could also cash in their reserves of U.S. dollars for gold, which, by the early 1970s, had put a severe strain on U.S. gold supplies.

The foreign exchange market was transformed in 1973, when a flexible exchange rate system replaced the crumbling fixed exchange rate system. Countries tinkered with different exchange rate models during the mid-1970s. In 1978 the International Monetary Fund (IMF) stepped in, and mandated a full implementation of flexible exchange rates. Under the flexible exchange rate system, also called the floating exchange rate system, the forces of supply and demand determine the value of national currencies. When the demand for a country's currency rises, the currency tends to appreciate in value compared to other currencies. When a currency appreciates in value, economists say that it has gained strength in global markets. When the demand for a country's currency falls, however, the currency depreciates or weakens relative to other currencies. By adopting the flexible exchange rate system, the global community opened the door to a new foreign exchange market. In the new forex market, the buying and selling of national currencies for profit supplanted currency conversion as the market's primary business.

Over the past three decades, governments have occasionally intervened in the forex market to stabilize their currencies or the currency of another country. For example, in the mid-1990s, the U.S. government, through the Federal Reserve System (Fed), purchased billions of U.S. dollars to prop up the dollar's value in international markets. More than a dozen other governments supported the Fed's actions by purchasing dollars in the foreign exchange market. Other industrialized countries, often in cooperation with one another, have also traded in the forex market to stabilize the global financial system. Periodic government intervention in the forex market is often called managed float. In addition, the value of one currency might be "pegged" to a different currency. From 1995 to 2005, China's yuan was pegged to the U.S. dollar at a rate of 8.28 yuan to $1 U.S. Pegging is often used to stabilize the value of a currency in global markets.

In recent years the IMF and other multilateral organizations have labored to reform the global financial architecture to support monetary stability. Reforms included structural changes in countries' banking and securities industries. Recent global financial crises, such as the East Asian Financial Crisis of 1997–1998, underscored some of the lingering vulnerabilities in the global financial and economic system.

See also **Bank for International Settlements; Bretton Woods System; Exchange Rates; Financial Contagion; Global Financial Architecture; International Monetary Fund.**

Further Reading

Bank for International Settlements. *Triennial Central Bank Survey of Foreign Exchange and Derivatives Market Activity in April 2004*. Basel, Switzerland: Author, 2004.
Ghosh, Dilip K., and Mohamed Ariff. *Global Financial Markets: Issues and Strategies*. Westport, CT: Praeger Publishers, 2004.
Goldstein, Morris, and Philip Turner. *Controlling Currency Mismatches in Emerging Markets*. Washington, DC: Institute for International Economics, 2004.
Gotthelf, Philip. *Currency Trading: How to Access and Trade the World's Biggest Market*. New York: Wiley, 2002.
Ishii, Shogo. *Exchange Arrangements and Foreign Exchange Markets: Developments and Issues*. Washington, DC: International Monetary Fund, 2003.

FREE TRADE AREA OF THE AMERICAS

The Free Trade Area of the Americas (FTAA) is a proposed free trade area for thirty-four democracies in the Western Hemisphere. A free trade area reduces or eliminates trade barriers such as tariffs and import quotas among member nations. In addition, the proposed FTAA would liberalize foreign direct investment (FDI), permitting transnational corporations greater cross-border investment opportunities throughout the hemisphere. If enacted, the FTAA would extend from Canada to Chile. The thirty-four nations of the proposed FTAA are shown in Table 53.

Initial discussions to create a single free trade area for the Western Hemisphere's thirty-four democracies began at the Summit of the Americas in 1994. At the Summit of the Americas—a meeting hosted by the city of Miami, Florida—the heads of state and government of the thirty-four democratic governments pledged support for a FTAA. In 1998 the Second Summit of the Americas, held in Santiago, Chile, initiated formal negotiations to create the free trade area. The Santiago summit also stressed the need for balanced and sustainable development throughout the thirty-four nation region. In 2001 the Third Summit of the Americas, held in Quebec City, Canada, brought the heads of state and government together to endorse a draft version of the FTAA agreement. The draft version of the agreement proposed a free trade region that would "generate economic growth and prosperity." The deadline for a final

TABLE 53 **Proposed Free Trade Area of the Americas**

Region	Number of Countries	Proposed Membership of the FTAA
Caribbean	12	Antigua and Barbuda, Bahamas, Barbados, Dominica, Dominican Republic, Grenada, Haiti, Jamaica, Saint Kitts and Nevis, Saint Lucia, St. Vincent and the Grenadines, Trinidad and Tobago
Central America	7	Belize, Costa Rica, El Salvador, Guatemala, Honduras, Nicaragua, Panama
North America	3	Canada, Mexico, United States
South America	12	Argentina, Bolivia, Brazil, Chile, Colombia, Ecuador, Guyana, Paraguay, Peru, Suriname, Uruguay, Venezuela

FTAA agreement was set for January 2005. Government leaders also pledged to cooperate in the remedy of other hemispheric problems including drug trafficking, poverty, environmental degradation, and violations of worker and human rights. In 2004 the thirty-four heads of state and government met in Monterrey, Mexico, to reaffirm their support for the FTAA. In Monterrey, leaders also reaffirmed their commitment to economic growth, poverty reduction, social development, and democratic governance. Despite proclamations of support for the FTAA, the final version of the FTAA agreement was not formally adopted by the January 2005 target date.

The proposed Free Trade Area of the Americas stirred considerable debate during the 1990s and early 2000s. FTAA supporters viewed its creation as the next logical step in the Western Hemisphere's economic integration. That is, the FTAA would extend the benefits of economic interdependence beyond the borders of existing regional trade blocs such as the Andean Community, which consists of Bolivia, Colombia, Ecuador, Peru, and Venezuela; the Caribbean Community, which consists of fifteen nations located in the Caribbean, Central America, and South America; Dominican Republic–Central American Free Trade Agreement (DR–CAFTA), which consists of Costa Rica, Dominican Republic, El Salvador, Guatemala, Honduras, and Nicaragua; MERCOSUR, which consists of Argentina, Brazil, Paraguay, Uruguay, and associate members Bolivia and Chile; and the North American Free Trade Agreement (NAFTA), which consists of Canada, Mexico, and the United States. The most apparent benefits of an FTAA agreement were the expansion of trade and FDI, job creation, economic growth, and global connectivity.

Opponents of the FTAA stressed the potential economic and social costs of an expanded free trade and investment regime. FTAA opponents argued that earlier regional free trade agreements, especially NAFTA, had opened a Pandora's box of economic woes for workers, the environment, and people's quality of life. Opponents claim that the liberalization of international trade and FDI in the Americas had revived sweatshop production methods in some Latin America and Caribbean countries. Further, opponents argued that lax or nonexistent environmental safeguards invited environmental abuse by transnational corporations (TNCs). To FTAA opponents, the low-wage, low-skill assembly work in Mexican maquiladoras, many of which border the United States, illustrated the failure of NAFTA to improve people's quality of life. Opponents also noted that a growing competitiveness in global markets only reinforced the dreaded race to the bottom, as TNCs cut production costs at the expense of indigenous peoples and the environment.

See also **Maquiladoras; North American Free Trade Agreement; Race to the Bottom; Regional Trade Agreements; Supply Chains.** ***See also in Volume 2,*** **Documents 26, 27, 28.**

Further Reading

Estevadeordal, Antoni, Dani Rodrik, Alan M. Taylor, and Andres Velasco. *Integrating the Americas: FTAA and Beyond*. Cambridge, MA: Harvard University Press, 2004.

Franko, Patrice M., and George A. Fauriol. *Toward a New Security Architecture in the Americas: The Strategic Implications of the FTAA*. Washington, DC: Center for Strategic and International Studies, 2000.

Lengyel, Miguel F., and Vivianne Ventura Dias. *Trade Policy Reforms in Latin America*. New York: Palgrave Macmillan, 2004.

Schott, Jeffrey J. *Free Trade Agreements: US Strategies and Priorities*. Washington, DC: Institute for International Economics, 2004.

Vizentini, Paulo, and Marianne Wiesebron, eds. *Free Trade for the Americas? The US Push for the FTAA Agreement*. New York: Zed Books, 2004.

G

GENERAL AGREEMENT ON TARIFFS AND TRADE

The General Agreement on Tariffs and Trade (GATT) was a multilateral agreement that established rules for international trade from 1948 to 1994. GATT's overriding goal was to promote free trade among nations. In 1947, twenty-three countries met in Geneva, Switzerland, to negotiate the first set of trade rules and tariff reductions. The result of these initial trade negotiations was the General Agreement on Tariffs and Trade. GATT, which took effect on January 1, 1948, consisted of 45,000 tariff concessions. History refers the 1947 negotiations as the first GATT trade round. From 1948 to 1994, four directors-general have led GATT: Sir Eric Wyndham-White (1948–1968), Olivier Long (1968–1980), Arthur Dunkel (1980–1993), and Peter Sutherland (1993–1994).

GATT's twenty-three founding countries, headed by the United States and the United Kingdom, assumed that GATT would soon be absorbed into a new International Trade Organization (ITO)—an institution that was also under negotiations during the late 1940s. The ITO was intended to be the third pillar of the Bretton Woods System, joining the newly formed World Bank and International Monetary Fund (IMF) in maintaining an orderly and prosperous post–World War II global economy. Negotiations to create the ITO stalled at the Bretton Woods Conference in July 1944 but continued in a series of conferences in London, Geneva, and, finally, Havana, Cuba. In 1948 delegates from fifty-four countries signed the Havana Charter, also called the ITO Charter. Yet, by the late 1940s, interest in another multilateral organization had waned in some industrialized countries, most notably the United States. The U.S. Congress shelved the Havana Charter in 1950. Without U.S. participation, plans for an ITO were abandoned.

Multilateral trade negotiations continued despite the collapse of the proposed ITO. The original GATT agreement became a rallying point for non-communist countries that supported trade expansion as a means of achieving economic growth and development. Under the auspices of GATT, a series of eight multilateral trade negotiations took place from 1947 to 1994, as shown in Table 54. Multilateral trade negotiations were called trade rounds. Early trade rounds concentrated on reducing tariffs on merchandise. A tariff is a tax on an imported good. Tariffs discourage imports by raising their price. Later trade rounds, especially the Tokyo Round and the Uruguay Round, expanded trade negotiations to reduce trade barriers on merchandise and services. Later trade rounds also responded to changes in the global economy. The Uruguay Round (1986–1994) involved 123 nations. The Uruguay Round tackled issues related to tariff and non-tariff trade barriers, subsidies, dumping, trade in services, intellectual property rights, and other issues in the global trading system.

Successive trade rounds expanded the scope of the original GATT agreement. Yet, through the years, the main GATT principles provided an anchor for an orderly evolution of the global trading system. The most fundamental GATT principle was embodied in the most-favored-nation (MFN) clause. MFN required that a trade concession granted to one country automatically applied to other GATT members. The second principle—national treatment—required that foreign and domestic output be treated in a fair and equal manner within nations. In practice this meant that imported goods, once appropriate tariffs had been paid, could not be penalized through the imposition of additional taxes or regulations. The third principle—the reporting of trade barriers—supported transparency in the global trading system. Under this principle, nations were required to justify the imposition of tariffs, import quotas, or other trade restrictions. Combined, GATT principles provided a global framework for the progressive reduction of trade barriers. The rapid expansion of GATT membership during the 1960s, 1970s, 1980s, and early 1990s indicated that many of the newly independent third world countries saw advantages in a more open and inclusive global trading system.

Over time, the GATT agreement was often viewed as one of the three primary gatekeepers of the global economy. The GATT agreement expanded global trade, the World Bank promoted global development, and the IMF stabilized the global financial system. Yet GATT, by design, was not founded as a multilateral institution. GATT lacked the organizational structures of the World Bank or IMF. Unlike the World Bank and IMF, GATT was never recognized as specialized agency within the United Nations system. GATT also

TABLE 54 **GATT/WTO Trade Rounds, 1947 to 2005**

Name of Trade Round and/or Host Country	Year(s)	Number of Participating Countries	Main Trade Topics
Geneva, Switzerland	1947	23	tariffs
Annecy, France	1949	13	tariffs
Torquay, United Kingdom	1951	38	tariffs
Geneva, Switzerland	1956	26	tariffs
The Dillon Round	1960–61	26	tariffs
The Kennedy Round	1964–67	62	tariffs, dumping
The Tokyo Round	1973–79	102	tariffs, non-tariff barriers tariffs, non-tariff
The Uruguay Round	1986–94	123	barriers, services, intellectual property, dispute settlement, foreign investment, patents, copyrights, World Trade Organization, others
Doha Development Round	2001–	148	agricultural subsidies, tariffs, non-tariff barriers, services, foreign investment, economic development, competition, environment

Source: World Trade Organization, *Understanding the WTO*, 3d ed., 15, 77–79.

lacked the authority to effectively arbitrate trade disputes and, if necessary, enforce its decisions on unwilling member nations.

During the Uruguay Round, lengthy negotiations addressed the need for a more powerful international organization to maintain the trend toward trade liberalization into the twenty-first century. The final GATT meeting took place in Marrakesh, Morocco in the spring of 1994. On April 15, 1994, delegates from many of the 123 participating nations signed the Marrakesh Declaration, which established the World Trade Organization (WTO). On January 1, 1995, the WTO officially replaced GATT as the world's leading advocate for free trade—and enforcer of trade rules—in the global economy. Many existing trade rules which had been created under the GATT system were renamed GATT 1994, and absorbed into Article 1 of the WTO charter.

See also **Bretton Woods System; Global Economy; Globalization; International Trade; Protectionism; World Trade Organization.** ***See also in Volume 2,*** **Documents 17, 18.**

Further Reading

Hoekman, Bernard, and Michael Kostecki. *The Political Economy of the World Trading System: From Gatt to Wto*. 2d ed. New York: Oxford University Press, 2001.

Mathis, James H. *Regional Trade Agreements in the GATT/WTO*. New York: Cambridge University Press, 2002.

Moore, Mike. *A World without Walls: Freedom, Development, Free Trade and Global Governance*. New York: Cambridge University Press, 2003.

Nader, Ralph, William Greidner, and Margaret Atwood. *The Case against Free Trade: Gatt, Nafta and the Globalization of Global Power*. Berkeley, CA: North Atlantic Books, 1993.

Zeiler, Thomas W. *Free Trade, Free World: The Advent of the Gatt*. Chapel Hill, NC: University of North Carolina Press, 1999.

GLOBAL CULTURE

Global culture refers to the standardization of people's attitudes and beliefs, behaviors, social norms, and institutions around the world. Economic globalization, which rests on cross-border flows of goods and services, capital, people, and ideas, created concerns about the homogenization of global culture on a Western—mainly American—model. Many indigenous cultures viewed cultural homogenization as a prelude to the disintegration of traditional values and lifestyles. Some claimed that the spread of Western ideas was an expression of cultural imperialism, the process of subjugating local cultures by a dominant outside culture. Economists cannot measure with any precision the extent of cultural homogenization in today's global economy, but signs of a global culture abound.

Changes in people's values and beliefs, lifestyles, and consumption habits along Western lines are indications of an emerging global culture. Western values, steeped in individualism, civil and human rights, and the freedom of choice, have spawned institutions compatible with these values—democratic government, an impartial judiciary, an independent media, and so on. Today, these institutions are models for political reform worldwide. Similarly, the institutions and practices of capitalism have molded the economic life of peoples throughout the global economy. Private property, profit incentives, freedom of contract, and other capitalist institutions, influence most global production, consumption, and distribution decisions.

Western lifestyles that are forward-looking, fast-paced, urban, consumption-oriented, and technology-driven have made inroads into virtually all societies. Rising living standards and rising expectations stoke the fires of mass consumption and the birth of consumer societies. The media reinforces the Western lifestyle, and creates brand loyalties to the icons of capitalism—McDonald's, Nokia, IBM, Disney, Nike, Starbucks, Levi, Coca-Cola, Microsoft, and others. Access to credit cards, e-commerce, and other conveniences facilitate consumption, especially by the growing urban middle class. And, increasingly, communication in the English language has become the global norm.

Technological advances in transportation, and in information and communications technologies (ICTs), also support the spread of Western culture to other world regions. Technology is the lubricant that facilitates economic and cultural globalization. Communications satellites, computers and the Internet, cell phones, television and radio, high-speed rail transport and supersonic airplanes, and other technological marvels, connect people with greater ease and at a lower cost than at any other time in human history. Advanced technologies also support the pillars of economic globalization including international trade, foreign direct investment (FDI), and cross-border financial flows. The technologies that create global connectivity shape peoples' preferences in clothing, entertainment, foods, and other products.

While Western influences on local cultures are apparent in many parts of the world, the degree of cultural penetration is uneven. Western cultural influences are most observable in urban areas, particularly among the younger and more educated population. The educated class is more technologically savvy, and is less tied to traditional values and lifestyles. Signs of Western culture are less apparent in remote, rural regions, where living standards are generally low and modern ICTs are less accessible. The impact of Western culture is also less apparent in countries where religious fundamentalism is powerful, such as Iran, and in countries that have been shunned for political reasons, such as Cuba and North Korea.

Grassroots movements to slow economic and cultural globalization gained some momentum during the late 1990s and early 2000s. The anti-globalization movement is comprised of non-governmental organizations (NGOs), labor and human rights activists, environmentalists, and others who believe that the economic, social, and cultural costs of globalization outweigh the benefits. Massive anti-globalization protests in Seattle (1999), Davos (2001), Genoa (2001), and elsewhere, are one manifestation of the growing discontent with policies that place corporate profits above the interests of local communities and peoples.

The localization movement also rejects cultural homogenization and economic globalization. Localization favors small-scale community-based production. Local production is adaptable to local needs and sensitive to the local culture and environment. Supporters of localization believe that many pro-globalization actions, by governments, multilateral organizations, and transnational corporations (TNCs), have been destructive to the economies and cultures of the global South.

On the global level, efforts to protect local cultures, including the cultural identity of indigenous peoples, have a mixed record of success. Since the 1990s, multilateral organizations such as the United Nations and World Bank have supported policies of inclusion to expand the voice of local peoples in decisions that affect their lives. The Rio Declaration on Environment and Development, which was approved by world leaders at the Rio Earth Summit in 1992, pledged to support the "identity, culture and interests" of local cultures and indigenous peoples. Following on the heels of the Rio Earth Summit, the United Nations' General Assembly approved A Decade of the World's Indigenous Peoples (1995–2004) to acknowledge and build respect for the world's 300 million indigenous peoples, such as the Mayas of Guatemala, Inuit of the polar region, Aborigines of Australia, and Maori of New Zealand. In 2000, the United Nations Millennium Declaration included a specific plea for tolerance and respect for the "diversity of belief, culture and language" of the world's peoples.

Not all global initiatives have been successful. For more than a decade, a UN Working Group labored on a UN Declaration on the Rights of Indigenous Peoples. The draft version of this document languishes in political limbo in 2005. Conflicts between local peoples and TNCs, particularly TNCs in the extractive industries such as oil, natural gas, and mining, was another sign of global discord. Local peoples, often excluded from the decision-making process, have routinely been uprooted to make way for economic development projects. The United Nations Development Program (UNDP) reported that the forced relocation of indigenous peoples was particularly acute in developing countries such as Colombia, Ghana, Guyana, Indonesia, Malaysia, Peru, and the Philippines.

See also **Advertising; Globalization; Quality of Life; Transnational Corporations.**
***See also in Volume 2*, Document 57.**

Further Reading

Crane, Diana, Nobuko Kawashima, and Kenichi Kawasaki. *Global Culture: Media, Arts, Policy, and Globalization*. New York: Routledge, 2002.

Mathews, Gordon. *Global Culture: Searching for Home in the Cultural Supermarket*. New York: Routledge, 2000.

Nederveen, Pieterse. *Globalization and Culture*. Lanham, MD: Rowman & Littlefield, 2003.

Tomlinson, John. *Globalization and Culture*. Chicago: University of Chicago Press, 1999.

United Nations Development Program. *Human Development Report 2004: Cultural Liberty in Today's Diverse World*. New York: United Nations, 2004.

GLOBAL ECONOMY

The global economy is the international network of individuals, businesses, governments, and multilateral organizations that collectively make decisions about the production, consumption, and distribution of goods and services. There are 208 individual "economies" within the global economy. The world's largest economy is the United States. In 2004 the gross domestic product (GDP) of the United States was $11.7 trillion. Among the world's smallest economies are Kiribati, and Sao Tome and Principe, each with a 2004 GDP of less than $100 million. The GDP measures the value of all newly produced final goods and services in an economy each year.

Global capitalism has created unprecedented prosperity in some countries, especially in the world's twenty-nine advanced economies. The remaining 179 economies are categorized as other emerging market and developing economies. The benefits of global capitalism have eluded some countries in this broad group, especially the world's fifty least developed countries (LDCs). The World Bank reported a 2004 global gross domestic product of $41 trillion, using the traditional exchange rate (Atlas) method of calculating GDP. Using the purchasing power parity (PPP) method, global GDP stood at $56 trillion in 2004. A snapshot of key indicators of the global economy is shown in Table 55.

TABLE 55 **The Global Economy at a Glance, 2003–2004**

Global Economic Indicators	Year	Economic Performance
World output		
Real GDP (exchange rates)	2004	$41 trillion
Real GDP (purchasing power parity)	2004	$56 trillion
Country classifications		
Advanced economies (number)	2004	29 economies
Developing economies and other emerging market economies	2004	179 economies
World trade		
World merchandise trade (exports)	2004	$8.9 trillion
World trade in services (exports)	2004	$2.1 trillion
Total trade (exports)	2004	$11.0 trillion
World merchandise trade (imports)	2004	$9.2 trillion
World trade in services (imports)	2004	$2.1 trillion
Total trade (imports)	2004	$11.3 trillion
Foreign Direct Investment (FDI)		
Foreign direct investment (inflows)	2003	$560 billion
Foreign direct investment (outflows)	2003	$612 billion
Transnational corporations (number)	2003	62,000
TNC foreign affiliates (number)	2003	927,000
Foreign exchange market		
Forex trading (daily volume)	2004	$1.9 trillion

Source: International Monetary Fund, *World Economic Outlook, September 2004*, 193–96, 199; United Nations Conference on Trade and Development, *World Investment Report 2004*, xvii, 9; World Trade Organization, *World Trade 2004, Prospects for 2005*, April 14, 2005, 13–14; Bank for International Settlements, *Triennial Central Bank Survey of Foreign Exchange and Derivatives Market Activity in April 2004*, 9.

The global economy is highly integrated and interdependent. Among the key players in the global economy are transnational corporations (TNCs) and other business firms with a global reach; international financial institutions (IFIs) such as the World Bank and regional multilateral development banks; multilateral organizations that monitor global economic activity such as the International Monetary Fund (IMF) and the World Trade Organization (WTO); national governments, and groups of governments such as the Organization for Economic Cooperation and Development (OECD), G8, G20, and G77; and thousands of non-governmental organizations (NGOs) and civil society organizations (CSOs). The United Nations, through its specialized agencies and programs, also promotes sustainable economic development and economic justice in the global economy.

Technological advances stimulate cross-border business activity and global interdependence. During the 1800s, the application of steam power to railroads and ships sped the transport of resources, goods, real capital, and people to distant locations. Early communications systems, such as the telegraph and telephone, also prompted cross-border transactions. Today, innovative information and communications technologies (ICTs) create a more integrated world linked by computers, the Internet, communications satellites, cell phones, and so on. ICTs permit people to store, process, and transmit enormous quantities of information. Similarly, transportation technologies such as supersonic airplanes, supertankers, automobiles, and high-speed rail transport, have advanced the connectivity of peoples in ways unimagined just a few decades ago. Global connectivity, enabled by technological advances, is most apparent in the expansion of international trade, foreign direct investment (FDI), and cross-border financial flows.

International trade is the cross-border exchange of goods or services. International trade occurs when individuals, businesses, governments, or others import or export goods or services. An import is a product that is purchased from another country. An export is a product sold to buyers in another country. The World Trade Organization (WTO) reported that total exports of merchandise and commercial services reached $11 trillion in 2004, about double the $5.4 trillion in total exports in 1994. About 81 percent of total exports in 2004 was merchandise ($8.9 trillion), and the remaining 19 percent consisted of commercial services ($2.1 trillion). International trade enables one country to specialize in the production of goods that it can produce more efficiently than another country. That is, specialization and trade encourage a country to produce goods in which it enjoys a comparative advantage. The efficient use of scarce resources increases the global supply of goods and services. International trade also expands the range of consumption choices for buyers. Imports from other countries increase the availability of goods that could not be produced efficiently by domestic producers. A number of multilateral agreements and institutions have facilitated trade expansion since World War II, including the General Agreement on Tariffs and Trade (GATT), the International Monetary Fund (IMF), and the World Trade Organization (WTO). The end of the Cold War and the rise of transition economies in eastern and central Europe during the 1990s and early 2000s opened new doors to international trade.

Transnational corporations (TNCs) are a second important feature of today's global economy. TNCs, sometimes called multinational corporations (MNCs), are businesses that own and operate production facilities in more than one country. A TNC consists of a parent company and its foreign affiliates. TNCs foster connectivity in the global economy. TNCs invest heavily in foreign countries, a process called foreign direct investment (FDI). The two types of FDI include greenfield investments, and mergers and acquisitions. Greenfield investments involve the building of entirely new production facilities, such as factories or office buildings, in another country. Mergers and acquisitions (M&As) involve the purchase of controlling interest in a foreign firm. In its *World Investment Report 2004*, the United Nations Conference on Trade and Development (UNCTAD) reported total inflows of FDI in excess of half a trillion in 2003. In addition, the foreign affiliates of TNCs employed 54 million workers, exported $3 trillion in goods and services, and owned $30 trillion in productive assets.

Cross-border financial flows are a third component of the global economy. Cross-border financial flows consist of short-term investments in stocks, bonds, other securities, and national currencies. Stock trading occurs on established stock exchanges such as the NASDAQ Stock Market and New York Stock Exchange in the United States; Shanghai Stock Exchange in China; London Stock Exchange in the United Kingdom; and Sao Paolo Exchange in Brazil. Highly speculative currency trading occurs on the foreign exchange market. The foreign exchange market is a complex network of commercial banks, investment banks, brokerage firms, and other financial institutions that buy and sell national currencies for profit. In its *Triennial Central Bank Survey of Foreign Exchange and Derivatives Market Activity in April 2004*, the Bank for International Settlements (BIS) reported a daily turnover of $1.9 trillion in the foreign exchange market in 2004. Cross-border financial flows are enhanced by sophisticated ICTs, which speed financial transactions throughout the global economy. Financial transactions occur twenty-four hours per day, seven days per week.

Multilateral organizations are key institutions of the global economy. Multilateral organizations are institutions designed to deal with global issues. Most multilateral organizations are comprised of representatives selected by member governments. Multilateral organizations have grown in size and power, especially since World War II. Today, the Big Three multilateral organizations in the global economy—the IMF, the World Bank, and WTO—monitor economic relations between countries. The IMF promotes currency stability and macroeconomic stability in nations. The World Bank extends loans and grants to fund development projects in the emerging market and developing economies. The WTO oversees trade relations and supports free trade. Other important multilateral organizations include the specialized agencies and programs of the United Nations System, regional development banks, and regional trade agreements (RTAs). Grassroots organizations, including thousands of international non-governmental organizations (NGOs) and civil society organizations (CSOs), coordinate global action to support a more stable global financial architecture and responsible foreign investment. NGOs and CSOs protect human and worker rights, the environment, and the cultural identity of indigenous peoples.

In recent years governments have supported global integration and interdependence by liberalizing trade and investment regimes. Trade liberalization promotes free trade. Trade liberalization policies reduce or eliminate trade barriers, such as tariffs and import quotas. Trade liberalization is enhanced by membership in the WTO, which guarantees most-favored-nation (MFN) status to member countries, and in regional trade agreements (RTAs) such as the North American Free Trade Agreement (NAFTA). Liberalized investment regimes attract foreign direct investment (FDI). Export processing zones (EPZs) attract FDI by offering investment incentives, including tax breaks, to TNCs. By 2002, governments in 116 countries had established 3,000 EPZs to entice TNCs to set up shop in their countries. In addition, by 2003, 2,265 bilateral investment treaties (BITs), and 2,316 double taxation treaties (DTTs), were successfully negotiated in the global economy. BITs are formal agreements between countries that foster mutually beneficial investment opportunities. DTTs establish fair tax regimes for individuals and firms that profit from overseas investments. Finally, liberalized financial investments in stocks, bonds, and other investment instruments increased capital flows between nations. Advanced ICTs solidified links among brokerage firms, banks, and other institutions in global capital markets.

See also **Bretton Woods System; Capital Markets; Foreign Direct Investment; Foreign Exchange Market; Global Culture; Globalization; Information and Communications Technologies; International Financial Institutions; International Investment Agreements; International Trade; Transnational Corporations. *See also in Volume 2,* Documents 9, 54.**

Further Reading

Anderson, Sarah, John Cavanagh, and Thea Lee. *Global Economy: Field Guide*. New York: New Press, 2005.

O'Connor, David E. *Demystifying the Global Economy: A Guide for Students*. Westport, CT: Greenwood Press, 2002.

Poot, Jacques. *On the Edge of the Global Economy*. Northampton, MA: Edward Elgar Publishers, 2005.

Radice, Hugo. *Political Economy of Global Capitalism*. New York: Routledge, 2005.

Rivoli, Pietra. *The Travels of a T-Shirt in the Global Economy: An Economist Examines the Markets, Power, and Politics of World Trade*. New York: John Wiley & Sons, 2005.

GLOBAL FINANCIAL ARCHITECTURE

The global financial architecture (GFA) is the structures and practices of international financial institutions and other multilateral organizations, governments, businesses, and others, involved in economic or financial transactions in the global economy. The global financial architecture is intimately connected with the three pillars of globalization—international trade, foreign direct investment, and cross-border financial flows. The GFA is also intertwined with the operations of international financial and regulatory institutions such as the International Monetary Fund (IMF), World Bank Group, and World Trade Organization (WTO). The current challenge is to create the GFA that promotes global economic stability and sustainable economic development for the peoples of the world.

Cracks in the global financial architecture became more visible during the 1990s when a series of financial crises shook the global economy. Financial crises in Mexico (1994–1995), East Asia (1997–1998), Brazil and South America (1998–1999), and Russia and eastern Europe (1998–1999), underscored the need for GFA reform. An undercurrent of anti-globalization sentiment also intensified the call for financial reform. Grassroots organizations, including non-governmental organizations (NGOs) and other civil society organizations (CSOs), blossomed during the 1990s and early 2000s. These reform-minded organizations rallied around themes of poverty reduction, fair trade, environmental protection, human and worker rights, and other quality-of-life issues. In 1999, mass demonstrations by NGOs and CSOs disrupted the WTO's Ministerial Conference in Seattle, Washington. The demonstrators' main targets were transnational corporations, and the "Big Three" institutions of the global economy—the IMF, World Bank, and WTO. The success of these demonstrations sparked similar events around the world, and prompted serious discussions about how to strengthen the GFA. Multilateral organizations, governments, NGOs and CSOs, and concerned individuals, were involved in these discussions. While no blueprint for GFA reform exists, a number of recommendations have surfaced.

One recommendation to reform the GFA is to strengthen international financial institutions (IFIs). The main IFIs include the World Bank Group, IMF, and regional development banks. Stronger IFIs would have the authority to devise and enforce uniform financial practices and rules of conduct for countries and businesses. Steps to reform and strengthen IFIs are underway. In 1999, the IMF and World Bank initiated financial sector assessment programs to identify structural weaknesses in countries' financial systems. The IMF introduced codes to facilitate economic data collection, fiscal transparency, and good practice in monetary policy. The IMF, World Bank, and other institutions, enacted internal reforms to expand transparency, and promote inclusion of NGOs, CSOs, local governments, and local peoples in the decisions that affect their lives. Policy coordination between IFIs, the United Nations system, the WTO, and other stakeholders was also on the reform agenda. The most significant manifestation of international cooperation was the adoption of the United Nations Millennium Development Goals (MDGs) in 2000. Today, the MDGs give focus to IFIs' global development efforts. The overarching MDG is poverty reduction.

A second recommendation is to strengthen the domestic financial sector in countries. Broadly speaking, the financial sector consists of a country's capital markets. Capital markets are financial institutions capable of channeling money from savers or investors into productive investments. Included in the financial sector are commercial banks and other depository institutions; securities markets such as stock and bond markets; insurance companies; and other financial intermediaries. Financial sector reform includes comprehensive bank surveillance by the IMF, regional development banks or central banks; uniform procedures to combat international financial crimes such as money laundering, drug trafficking, tax evasion, and bribery; regulations to control rapid, destabilizing inflows of money into or outflows of money from a country; and the avoidance of moral hazard. Moral hazard occurs when banks take excessive lending risks because a rescue mechanism, such as deposit insurance or international aid, will cover bank losses. Another recommendation is to halt capital flight. Capital flight is the excessive cross-border flow of financial capital, mainly from developing countries to more stable advanced countries. Reforms to reduce capital flight might include a more secure macroeconomic environment, enforceable private property rights, incentives to save in domestic financial institutions, or government restrictions on monetary outflows.

A third recommendation is to encourage grassroots financial initiatives. One promising financial reform is the explosion of microcredit. Microcredit institutions make small loans, perhaps less than $100, to local entrepreneurs. Recipients of microloans are the marginalized poor, those people who are unable to secure loans from established financial institutions. The Grameen Bank of Bangladesh is the preeminent microcredit institution in today's global economy. Muhammad Yunus began a microlending program in 1975, and founded the Grameen Bank in 1983. By 2004 the Grameen Bank had serviced 3.8 million borrowers, and conducted business operations in 46,000 villages in Bangladesh. Worldwide, thousands of microcredit institutions have been formed to serve the needs of the poor. In recent years, international organizations have jumped onto the microcredit bandwagon. The World Bank, United Nations, and regional development banks support microcredit projects throughout the world. The United Nations proclaimed 2005 the International Year of Microcredit to acknowledge the importance of microcredit to poverty reduction and economic development.

A fourth recommendation is to promote transparency and inclusion in the GFA. Transparency refers to the openness of financial transactions to public scrutiny. Governments, multilateral organizations, and transnational corporations must strive to share timely and accurate information with other stakeholders in the global economy. Transparency is a safeguard against cronyism and corruption in the public and private sectors. Similarly, policies of inclusion open the decision-making process to additional voices and perspectives. One positive step toward inclusion was the creation of the Group of Twenty, or G20 in 1999. The G20 brought emerging market and developing countries under the same roof with the G8 industrialized countries to discuss global issues. Today, the World Bank and regional development banks consult with NGOs,

CSOs, and local authorities when considering development projects in member countries.

A fifth recommendation is to increase the scope and effectiveness of foreign aid to the world's poorer regions. Foreign aid involves a cross-border transfer of money, capital equipment, goods or services, information, technology, or advisors to a recipient country. For some least developed countries (LDCs), foreign aid is the country's largest infusion of outside money, greater than the value of the country's exports, and greater than FDI inflows. In 2003, official development assistance (ODA) from the richer countries topped $68 billion, about one-quarter of one percent of the combined gross national income (GNI) of donor countries. Few countries have met the ODA target of ODA of 0.7 percent of GNI. Reforms in the global financial architecture must consider the foreign aid responsibilities of the wealthier countries. At the same time, mechanisms must be created to ensure that foreign aid is used for its intended purposes, rather than to line the pockets of corrupt officials.

See also **Capital Flight; Capital Markets; Financial Contagion; Foreign Aid; Global Economy; Good Governance; International Financial Institutions; International Monetary Fund; Microfinance Institutions; Non-Governmental Organizations; Regional Development Banks; World Bank Group; World Trade Organization.**

Further Reading

Akyuz, Yilmaz. *Reforming the Global Financial Architecture: Issues and Proposals.* New York: Zed Books, 2002.

Armijo, Leslie E. *Debating the Global Financial Architecture.* Albany, NY: State University of New York Press, 2002.

International Monetary Fund. *Global Financial Stability Report: Market Developments and Issues, April 2004.* Washington, DC: IMF, 2004.

Soederberg, Susanne. *The Politics of the New International Financial Architecture: Reimposing Neoliberal Domination in the Global South.* New York: Zed Books, 2005.

Vines, David, and Christopher L. Gilbert, eds. *The IMF and Its Critics: Reform of Global Financial Architecture.* New York: Cambridge University Press, 2004.

GLOBALIZATION

Globalization, in an economics context, refers to the freer cross-border movements of goods and services, labor, technology, real capital, and financial capital to create an integrated and interdependent global economy. The global economy represents the activities of individuals, businesses, multilateral organizations, and governments that make production, distribution, and consumption decisions in international markets. The pillars of economic globalization are international trade, foreign direct investment, and cross-border financial flows. Broadly speaking, globalization also deals with cross-border flows of ideas, political and social values, language, and other components of culture. Today, globalization is associated with the flow of Western economic, political, and social beliefs and institutions to other world regions.

Economic globalization has had its peaks and valleys over the past 150 years. The first peak, sometimes called the first age of globalization, spanned the

Great Britain spearheaded the first age of globalization from the mid-1800s to the outbreak of World War I in 1914.

Courtesy of Getty Images: Andrew Ward/Life File

period from 1850 to 1914. Great Britain, the dominant player during the first age of globalization, nurtured international trade and foreign investment throughout its sprawling empire. Technological advances supported global economic integration. During this age, steamships joined steam-powered locomotives to speed the transport of goods and people, while the telegraph and telephone increased the convenience of global communication. The first age of globalization crumbled under the destructive weight of World War I (1914–1918), the isolationism and protectionism of the 1920s, the global depression of the 1930s, and the carnage of World War II (1939–1945). The second age of globalization, led by the United States, rose out of the ashes of World War II. Post-war technologies in transportation and communications strengthened global business and financial linkages. Technological advances in high-speed railways, supertankers, supersonic aircraft, and motorized vehicles expanded opportunities for long-distance business enterprise. Similarly, the rapid growth of information and communications technologies (ICTs), such as fiber optics, microelectronics, computers, software, the Internet, and the World Wide Web, accelerated connectivity as the world raced toward the twenty-first century.

The World Bank and the International Monetary Fund (IMF), also called the Bretton Woods institutions, supported globalization's second age. The World Bank, which began operations in 1946, originally offered loans to reconstruct war-torn Europe. By the 1950s the World Bank's attention shifted to the developing world. Since the 1950s, the Bank's loans have targeted economic development in the world's poorer regions. The IMF, which also opened its doors for business in 1946, worked to stabilize the world's economic and financial system. The IMF extends short-term loans, called credits, to strengthen national currencies, and to help needy countries pay for imports or meet external debt payments. Complementing the Bretton Woods institutions was the General Agreement on Tariffs and Trade (GATT), which was founded in 1948. Under the auspices of GATT (1948–1994) and the World Trade Organization (1995–present), formal trade rounds reduced trade barriers and other impediments to free trade. Regional development banks, including the African Development Bank Group, the Asian Development Bank, the Inter-American Development Bank Group, and the European Bank for Reconstruction and Development, extended development loans to poorer nations in specific world regions. The institutions of the global economy, coupled with advanced technologies, strengthened the three pillars of globalization—international trade, FDI, and cross-border financial flows.

International trade is the cross-border exchange of goods or services. These exchanges occur when individuals, businesses, governments, or others import or export goods or services. The benefits of international trade are built on the principle of mutual benefit, and the theory of comparative advantage. The principle of mutual benefit emphasizes that both parties can be better off as a result of an informed, voluntary exchange. The theory of comparative advantage, popularized by British economist David Ricardo, calls for nations to specialize in the production of goods they can produce most efficiently relative to other countries. Since World War II, many of the world's leading economies have embraced free trade to stimulate production efficiency, product innovation, consumer choice, and higher living standards. In 2004, the World Trade Organization (WTO) reported that global exports reached $11 trillion. Today, the WTO administers the ground rules for international trade; monitors the global trading system for violations of its rules; and uses its dispute settlement authority to enforce its decisions.

A second pillar of globalization is foreign direct investment. Foreign direct investment (FDI) is a long-term cross-border investment in which one company gains ownership or control of production facilities in another country. The two types of FDI are mergers and acquisitions, and greenfield investments. Mergers and acquisitions (M&As) represent a legal joining of two existing companies under a single ownership. Today, M&As are the preferred method of FDI in advanced economies. Greenfield investments occur when transnational corporations (TNCs) construct new production facilities, such as factories or plantations, in a foreign country. Today, TNCs tend to favor greenfield investments in developing countries. In its *World Investment Report 2004* , the United Nations Conference on Trade and Development (UNCTAD) reported global FDI inflows of $560 billion, and global FDI outflows of $612 billion in 2003. The top five recipients of FDI inflows were Luxembourg, China, France, the United States, and Belgium. The top FDI outflows came from the United States, Luxembourg, France, the United Kingdom, and Belgium. UNCTAD also reported that 62,000 TNCs owned 927,000 foreign affiliate firms. In 2003, foreign affiliates employed 54 million workers, and had productive assets worth $30 trillion. In recent years liberalized investment regimes in most countries have encouraged FDI. Today, thousands of negotiated bilateral investment treaties (BITS) and double taxation treaties (DTTs), and thousands of export processing zones (EPZs), support FDI in the global economy.

Cross-border financial flows are the third pillar of globalization. Financial globalization weaves the world's banks, brokerage houses, stock and bond exchanges, and other financial institutions into highly integrated global capital markets. Financial globalization is supported by many of the same forces that stimulate FDI, such as sophisticated ICTs and liberalized investment regimes. Additional market participants and financial instruments, and the introduction of the flexible exchange rate system, expanded opportunities for short-term investments in the global financial system. For example, the switch from a fixed exchange rate system to a flexible exchange rate system in the early 1970s enabled foreign exchange trading, or forex trading. In 2004, $1.9 trillion in forex trading occurred each day in the global foreign exchange market.

The globalization juggernaut hit a few bumps during the 1990s and early 2000s. Under the umbrella of the "anti-globalization movement," disparate groups rejected the notion that globalization is desirable and inevitable. In the vanguard of the anti-globalization movement were non-governmental organizations (NGOs) and civil society organizations (CSOs). Key issues included the negative impact of globalization on human and worker rights, the environment, and people's quality of life. In 1999 a loose coalition of NGOs, CSOs, and others disrupted the WTO's ministerial conference in Seattle, Washington. The success of the Seattle protest against the WTO encouraged similar outbursts against the World Bank, IMF, World Economic Forum, and other pro-globalization institutions during the early 2000s.

In the early 2000s, NGOs and CSOs also embarked on a new strategy to affect global change—the social forum. A social forum is a mass meeting of NGOs and CSOs. The first World Social Forum was convened in Porto Alegre, Brazil, in 2001. Within a couple of years, annual social forums were attracting over 100,000 participants. The goal of a social forum is to bring attention to global issues such as poverty and environmental degradation, and to pressure governments and multilateral organizations to deal with growing global problems. Regional and thematic social forums complemented the successful World Social Forums. Hot issues in the early 2000s included global poverty reduction, health care, education, gender equity, and third world external debt.

Economic globalization faces other challenges. First, the specter of financial contagion hovers over the global economy. Financial contagion is the domino-like collapse of financial systems in an integrated, and largely unregulated, global financial system. In the late 1990s, financial crises in East Asia, Brazil, and Russia had far-reaching effects on the stability of other economies around the world. Second, protectionist trade policies threaten free trade. Today, backdoor protectionism, such as the excessive use of anti-dumping measures, is problematic. Protectionist trade policies invite retaliation by other countries. The trade war instigated by the U.S. Smoot-Hawley Tariff Act of 1930 is a grim reminder of past protectionism. Third, the growing income and development gap between the advanced countries and the least developed countries (LDCs) is a source of global instability. As the rich countries get richer and the poor get poorer, LDCs lose confidence in the empty promises of globalization. The digital divide, persistent trade restrictions on third world agricultural exports, irresponsible behaviors of some TNCs, and inadequate foreign aid, aggravate the development gap. Fourth, the localization movement challenges the economic wisdom of global connectivity. Localization favors small-scale community-based production, strict government controls on international trade and foreign direct investment, and respect for local cultures and traditions. Opponents of globalization believe that the benefits of globalization favor some and marginalize others. From a global perspective, many believe that globalization's feast should have a more inclusive guest list.

See also **Bretton Woods System; Civil Society Organizations; Financial Contagion; Foreign Direct Investment; Foreign Exchange Market; Global Culture; Global Economy; Global Financial Architecture; Information and Communications Technologies; International Financial Institutions; International Trade; Localization; Non-Governmental Organizations; Protectionism; Transnational Corporations. *See also in Volume 2,* Documents 9, 21, 27, 54.**

Further Reading

Bello, Walden. *Deglobalization: Ideas for a New World Order*. New York: Zed Books, 2005.

Bhagwati, Jagdish. *In Defense of Globalization*. New York: Oxford University Press, 2004.

Cavanagh, John, and Jerry Mander. *Alternatives to Economic Globalization: A Better World Is Possible*. 2d ed. San Francisco, CA: Berrett-Koehler Publishers, 2004.

Korten, David C. *When Corporations Rule the World*. 2d ed. San Francisco, CA: Berrett-Koehler Publishers, 2001.

Steger, Manfred B. *Globalization: A Very Short Introduction*. New York: Oxford University Press, 2003.

Stiglitz, Joseph. *Globalization and Its Discontents*. New York: W.W. Norton & Company, 2003.

GOOD GOVERNANCE

Good governance is the honest, competent administration of governments, businesses, civil society organizations, multilateral organizations, and other decision-making bodies in the global community. Good governance is characterized by decision making that is inclusive, efficient, transparent, and responsive to people's needs. At the core of good governance is respect for the rule of law. The rule of law requires all people to follow the same rules and regulations. In economics, the rule of law levels the playing field in business activity. Good governance is also built on a foundation of stable political institutions, which guarantee people's civil and human rights, and protect people from civil unrest or external aggression. Today, the United Nations, World Bank, International Monetary Fund (IMF) and other power brokers in the global economy have identified good governance as an important development goal for all economies.

Good governance promotes economic growth and development by creating a secure, predictable business environment for all participants in an economy. A sound business climate jump-starts the virtuous cycle of development by supporting entrepreneurship, research and development (R&D), savings and investment, and capital formation. A number of specific economic indicators signal good governance in action. One indicator of good governance is a sound legal environment that guarantees private property rights; enforces contracts; codifies bankruptcy procedures; and protects patents, copyrights, and trademarks. A second indicator is a fair regulatory regime that protects workers' rights, competitive markets, the environment, local cultures, and people's quality of life—including living conditions for minorities, women, and traditionally marginalized peoples. A third indicator is a fair tax system, devoid of corruption, cronyism, or other types of favoritism or preferences. A fourth indicator is the government's ability to form and implement appropriate stabilization policies. A favorable fiscal policy shows restraint in government spending, and limits federal budget deficits. A favorable monetary policy keeps the money supply in check, and avoids the debilitating effects of galloping inflation.

Good governance is the norm in the advanced countries, but is less apparent in the world's poorer regions. Stable political and economic institutions contribute to good governance in the advanced countries. Functioning democracies in the rich countries promote inclusive, efficient, and responsive institutions. Under democracy, corrupt or ineffective leaders are removed from office by the ballot or by the courts. An independent judiciary—a prominent feature of democratic systems—holds people accountable for unethical and illegal behaviors. A free press also promotes accountability through investigative reporting. The private sector, rather than the government, owns and operates the free press. The Freedom House, which monitors trends in democracy around the world, reported the highest concentrations of "free" and "partly free" countries were located in Western Europe and the Americas. Other regions recorded significantly lower levels of freedom.

Measurements of good governance are imprecise in today global economy. Recently, World Bank researchers evaluated good governance indicators in nearly 200 countries, and ranked countries and world regions by level of good governance. The World Bank research focused on six criteria: voice and accountability, political stability, government effectiveness, regulatory quality, rule of law, and control of corruption. The data suggest that good governance is highest in the rich countries of the Organization for Economic Cooperation and Development (OECD) and lower in other regions, as shown in Figure 15 (rankings in the figure do not reflect the official position of the World Bank, its executive directors, or member countries, and are subject to margins of error). In its *World Development Report, 2003*, the World Bank blamed "misguided policies and weak governance" over the past several decades for many of the world's current development woes such as environmental degradation, income disparities, and civil conflict.

Corporate governance became a front-burner issue during the early 2000s when a number of prominent U.S. corporations collapsed under the weight of corrupt business practices. Leading the parade was Enron, which filed for bankruptcy in December 2001. Top Enron executives were later convicted on charges of fraud, price gauging, and other unethical business practices. Top officials of Adelphia, Global Crossing, WorldCom, Tyco, and other corporate giants also felt the sting of investigations by the Securities and Exchange

High Level of Good Governance

Organization for Economic Cooperation and Development
Eastern Europe
Latin America and the Caribbean
East Asia
Middle East and North Africa
South Asia
Sub-Saharan Africa
Former Soviet Union

Low Level of Good Governance

FIGURE 15 **Good Governance in the World, 2002**
Source: Daniel Kaufmann and Aart Kraay, *Governance Matters 3: Governance Indicators for 1996–2002*, World Bank.

Commission (SEC), U.S. Department of Justice, congressional committees, and the media. Responding to public pressure, Congress soon passed the Sarbanes-Oxley Act (PL 107-204), which was signed into law by President George W. Bush on July 30, 2002. The Sarbanes-Oxley Act, also called SOX, was designed to restore public confidence in U.S. capital markets and expand management's responsibility in maintaining the integrity of corporate business practices.

See also **Advanced Economies; Civil Society Organizations; Corruption; Democracy; Developing Countries; Non-Governmental Organizations; Sustainable Economic Development.** ***See also in Volume 2,*** **Documents 5, 10, 14, 51, 52, 53, 58.**

Further Reading

Kaufmann, Daniel, and Aart Kraay. *Governance Matters III: Governance Indicators for 1996–2002*. Washington, DC: World Bank, 2003.
Neumayer, Eric. *The Pattern of Aid Giving: The Impact of Good Governance on Development Assistance*. New York: Routledge, 2003.
O'Brien, Robert et al., eds. *Contesting Global Governance: Multilateral Economic Institutions and Social Movements*. New York: Cambridge University Press, 2000.
Wilenson, Rorden, and Steve Hughes. *Global Governance: Critical Perspectives*. New York: Routledge, 2002.

GROSS DOMESTIC PRODUCT

The gross domestic product, or GDP, is the total dollar value of all newly produced final goods and services in an economy in a given year. A country's GDP includes all final goods produced by domestic and foreign firms within its borders. Final goods are products or services purchased for consumption rather than for further processing or resale. A similar measure of national output, the gross national product (GNP), tallies the value of output by a country's firms throughout the world, but excludes output produced by foreign firms that operate within its borders. The global GDP is the total output of the world's 208 economies. In 2004 the global GDP was $41 trillion using the traditional exchange rate, or Atlas, method of calculation. Adjusted for purchasing power parity (PPP), the global GDP was $56 trillion.

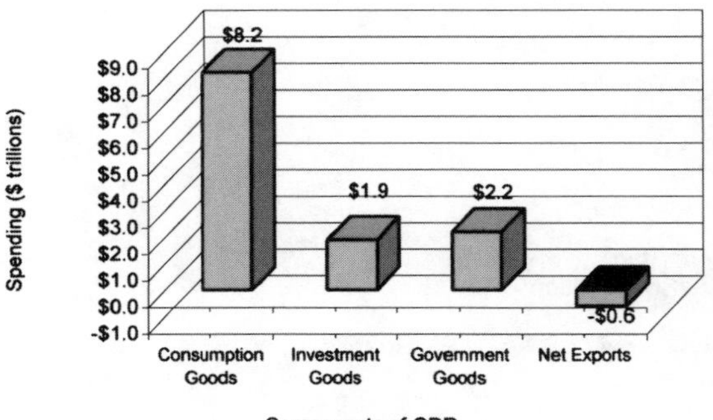

FIGURE 16 **Components of the U.S. GDP, 2004 ($ trillions)**

Source: Bureau of Economic Analysis, *BEA News*, April 28, 2005, 7.

The expenditures approach is the most common way to calculate a nation's GDP. The expenditures approach adds spending on consumption goods (C), investment goods (I), government goods (G), and net exports (Xn). Economists summarize the expenditures approach with the formula, C + I + G + Xn = GDP. The components of the U.S. GDP in 2004 are shown in Figure 16.

The dominant component in nations' GDP is consumption goods. Consumption goods include consumer durables such as furniture, household equipment, and automobiles; nondurable goods such as food, clothing, and heating oil; and services such as medical care, electricity, and recreation. In 2004, about two-thirds of all U.S. spending was on consumption goods. Investment goods include business structures, equipment, apartment buildings, and other housing. In the U.S. economy, most investment spending is on information and communications technologies (ICTs) such as computers and software. Investment spending accounted for 16 percent of U.S. spending in 2004. Government consumption spending and investment spending includes a variety of defense and non-defense public goods and services. Government spending at the national, state, and local levels accounted for nearly 18 percent of total U.S. spending in 2004. Net exports represents the difference between a nation's imports and exports. Net exports is a negative number when a nation incurs a trade deficit, and a positive number when a nation has a trade surplus. The U.S. trade deficit of more than $600 billion in 2004 indicates that Americans spent billions of dollars more foreign-made goods and services than foreigners spent on American-made products. Thus, net exports is a negative number, as shown in Figure 16.

Many types of transactions are excluded from a country's GDP. The GDP excludes intermediate goods and resources used in the production of a larger final good. For example, the value of a microprocessor is not included in a nation's GDP if it is used in the production of a computer. The exclusion of intermediate goods and resources from GDP avoids the problem of double counting, or counting the same item twice. Other transactions that are excluded from the GDP are the exchange of securities such as corporate stocks and bonds, or U.S. Treasury notes or bills; resale transactions such as items purchased at secondhand stores and flea markets; transactions made in the informal sector; and public transfer payments such as Social Security payments and welfare benefits.

$$\frac{\text{Nominal GDP}}{\text{Price Deflator}} \times 100 = \text{Real GDP}$$

$$\frac{\$11{,}735}{109} \times 100 = \text{Real GDP}$$

$$\$107.66 \times 100 = \$10{,}766$$

FIGURE 17 **Calculating the Real U.S. GDP, 2004 ($ billions)**

GDP is expressed in nominal and real terms. Nominal GDP is the value of national output expressed in current dollars, or dollars not adjusted for inflation. Real GDP is the value of national output expressed in constant dollars, or dollars that are adjusted for inflation. Real GDP is the most accurate measurement of a nation's total output. The real GDP is calculated using a GDP price deflator. The GDP price deflator is an index that tracks price level changes in an economy. A base year serves as a starting point for future comparisons of a currency's value. The current U.S. base year is 2000. Thus, in 2000, $1 was equal to $1, and the index was set at 100. Since 2000, the U.S. price level increased by about 2 percent per year, which raised the price index to 109 by 2004. Figure 17 converts the 2004 U.S. nominal GDP of $11.7 trillion to a real GDP of $10.8 trillion.

TABLE 56 **Global Gross Domestic Product, 2004**

Classification of Countries	Gross Domestic Product, Atlas Method ($ trillions)	Gross Domestic Product, PPP Method ($ trillions)
High income	$32.7	$31.0
Upper middle income	$3.0	$5.9
Lower middle income	$3.9	$13.8
Low income	$1.3	$5.3
World GDP	$40.9	$56.0

Source: World Bank, *World Development Indicators Database*, July 15, 2005.

In recent years, the GDP and many other types of economic data have been expressed in two forms—by traditional exchange rates (Atlas method) and by purchasing power parity (PPP). GDP data reported under the exchange rate system, or Atlas method, uses prevailing currency exchange rates to calculate and compare countries' total output. GDP data reported on a PPP basis considers the buying power of a currency in different countries. For instance, $1 can purchase more goods in a low-income country such as India than it can in a high-income country such as the United States.

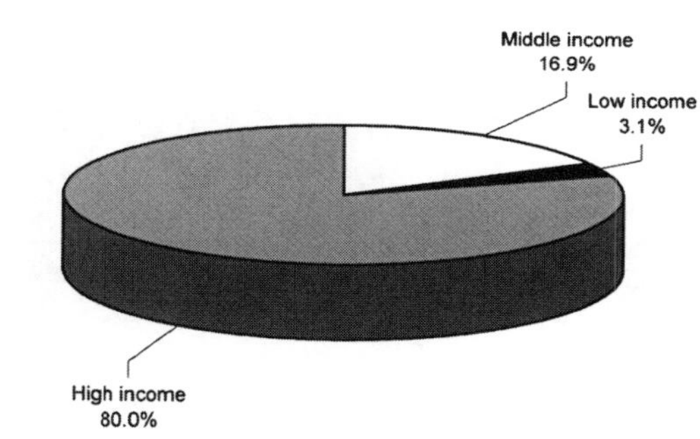

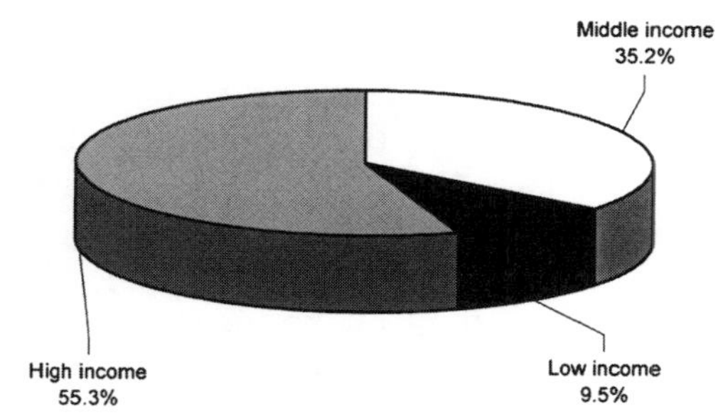

FIGURE 18 **Global GDP by Exchange Rate and PPP Calculations, 2004**

Source: World Bank, *World Development Indicators Database*, July 15, 2005.

The exchange rate GDP, and PPP GDP, paint strikingly different pictures about the relative size of economies in the global economy, as shown in Table 56. Under the exchange rate GDP, world output was $41 trillion in 2004, and high-income countries accounted for about 80 percent of the global GDP. Using PPP, world output was $56 trillion, and high-income countries produced just 55 percent of global GDP. Differences in the perceptions of world output are shown in Figure 18. Rival views about calculating GDP also affect perceptions about the size of individual economies. Using the exchange rate GDP, the world's five largest economies in 2004 were the United States, Japan, Germany, the United Kingdom, and France, respectively. Using the PPP figures, the world's five largest economies were the United States, China, Japan, India, and Germany, respectively.

See also **Advanced Economies; Developing Countries; Economic Growth; Gross National Income; Human Development; Kuznets, Simon; Poverty; Purchasing Power Parity; Quality of Life; Sustainable Economic Development.**

Further Reading

International Monetary Fund. *World Economic Outlook, April 2005*. Washington, DC: Author, 2004.

McMahon, Gary, and Lyn Squire, eds. *Explaining Growth: A Global Research Project*. New York: Palgrave Macmillan, 2003.

World Bank. *Global Economic Prospects 2004: Realizing the Development Promise of the Doha Agenda*. New York: Author, 2003.

———. *World Development Indicators 2005*. New York: United Nations and the Oxford University Press, 2005.

———. *World Development Report 2005: A Better Investment Climate for Everyone*. New York: World Bank and the Oxford University Press, 2004.

GROSS NATIONAL INCOME

Gross national income (GNI) is the broadest measure of national income. The GNI, previously called the gross national product (GNP), is the people's total income derived from domestic and foreign sources. Thus, GNI includes gross domestic product (GDP) plus the net receipt of income from abroad. The net receipt of income is the difference between income inflows and income outflows each year. The cross-border income flows stem mainly from wages or salaries, and property income. The GNI per capita states people's average annual income by dividing the GNI by the country's population. Since 2000, the World Bank has used the GNI and GNI per capita to classify countries, to assess the relative size and economic well-being of countries, and to determine eligibility for loans or other assistance. The gross domestic product (GDP) and GDP per capita measurements are also widely used to determine the relative size of economies and the economic well-being of people.

The World Bank classifies the world's 208 economies by GNI per capita. This classification scheme identifies four categories of countries: low-income, lower middle-income, upper middle-income, and high-income countries, as shown in Table 57. GNI per capita is not the sole criterion for determining a country's development status, however. Other development criteria include the size and sophistication of a nation's economic system. In 2004, all low-income and middle-income economies were classified as "developing countries or other emerging market economies." Some high-income economies, such as Bahrain, Brunei, Kuwait, Monaco, Qatar, Slovenia, and the United Arab

TABLE 57 **Classification of the World's Economies, 2004 ($US)***

Country	GNI per Capita	Average GNI per Capita (exchange rate method)	Number of Economies in the World	Average GNI per Capita (PPP method)
Low income	$825 or less	$510	59	$2,260
Lower middle income	$826–$3,255	$1,580	54	$5,640
Upper middle income	$3,256–$10,065	$4,770	40	$10,090
High income	$10,066 or more	$32,040	55	$30,970
World		$6,280	208	$8,760

*Classifications are based on the exchange rate method.
Source: World Bank, *World Development Report 2005*, 255–257; and World Bank, *Data and Statistics*.

Emirates, were also identified as developing countries or other emerging market economies because their economies lacked the size or sophistication to be considered advanced. Just twenty-nine high-income economies out of 208 total economies were classified as advanced.

In 2004 nearly 84 percent of the world's 6.4 billion people lived in low-income or middle-income countries. World population, by income status, is shown in Figure 19. Representative low-income countries include the Democratic Republic of Congo (annual GNI per capita of $120), Sierra Leone ($200), Cambodia ($320), Haiti ($390), Bangladesh ($440), and India ($620). Lower middle-income countries include Indonesia ($1,140), the Ukraine ($1,260), China ($1,290), Egypt ($1,310), Bulgaria ($2,740), and Brazil ($3,090). Upper middle-income countries include Russia ($3,410), Argentina ($3,720), Botswana ($4,310), Malaysia ($4,650), Poland ($6,090), Mexico ($6,770), and the Czech Republic ($9,150). High-income countries include the Republic of Korea ($13,980), Israel ($17,380), Canada ($28,390), Japan ($37,180), the United States ($41,400), and Switzerland ($48,230). Luxembourg's $56,230 GNI per capita was the world's highest in 2004.

Measuring income inequality in the global economy is a tricky business. Measurements that use the traditional exchange rate GNI per capita shown in Table 57 show that people in high-income economies ($32,040) had nearly seven times the average income of people living in the upper middle-income countries ($4,770), twenty times the income of people in lower middle-income countries ($1,580), and sixty-three times the income of people living in the low-income countries ($510). Measurements of GNI

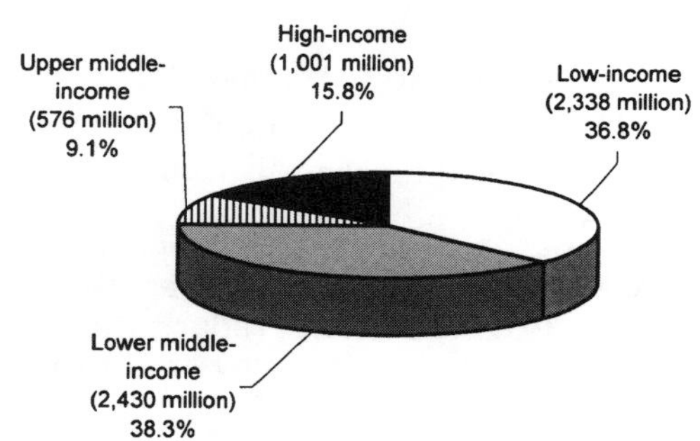

FIGURE 19 **World Population by Countries' Income Status, 2004**
Source: World Bank, *World Development Indicators Database*, July 15, 2005.

TABLE 58 **Income Distribution in Selected Countries***

Country	Share of Income or Consumption		Inequality Measures
	Poorest 20%	Richest 20%	Comparing Richest 20% to Poorest 20%
Advanced			
Canada	7.0%	40.4%	5.8 times
Japan	10.6%	35.7%	3.4 times
Germany	8.5%	36.9%	4.3 times
Israel	6.9%	44.3%	6.4 times
Emerging market			
Czech Rep.	10.3%	35.9%	3.5 times
Hungary	7.7%	37.5%	4.9 times
Poland	7.3%	42.5%	5.8 times
Russia	4.9%	51.3%	10.5 times
Developing			
Brazil	2.0%	64.4%	31.5 times
Guatemala	2.6%	64.1%	24.4 times
Nigeria	4.4%	55.7%	12.8 times
South Africa	2.0%	66.5%	33.6 times

*Income data are taken from selected years during the 1990s and early 2000s.
Source: United Nations Development Program (UNDP), *Human Development Report 2004*, 188–191.

per capita on a purchasing power parity (PPP) basis narrow the income gap between rich and poor nations. PPP accounts for differences in money's buying power around the world. The PPP GNI per capita shows that people living in high-income countries ($30,970) were just three times richer than people living in upper middle-income countries ($10,090), five times richer than people in lower middle-income countries ($5,640), and fourteen times richer than people in low-income countries ($2,260).

The GNI per capita offers a basis for national comparisons of economic well-being. Yet, there are limitations to this approach to national income accounting. First, national income data ignores most business activity in the informal sector. As a result, official GNI data often understate national income. Second, income data are often unreliable. In recent years, the International Monetary Fund (IMF), World Bank, and other multilateral organizations have extended technical assistance to strengthen data collection and analysis in the developing world. Third, GNI per capita does not assess the actual distribution of national income. The uneven distribution of income within nations is especially severe in African and Latin American countries, as shown in Table 58.

See also **Advanced Economies; Developing Countries; Emerging Market Economies; Gross Domestic Product; Human Development; Least Developed Countries; Poverty; Purchasing Power Parity; Quality of Life; Sustainable Economic Development.**

Further Reading

Bourguignon, Francois, Francisco H. G. Ferreira, and Nora Lustig. *The Microeconomics of Income Distribution Dynamics in East Asia and Latin America*. New York: World Bank Publications, 2004.

Firebaugh, Glenn. *The New Geography of Global Income Inequality*. Cambridge, MA: Harvard University Press, 2003.
United Nations Conference on Trade and Development. *Human Development Report 2004*. New York: Oxford University Press, 2004.
Wolfensohn, James D., and Rodrigo de Rato. *Global Monitoring Report 2004: Policies and Actions for Achieving the Millennium Development Goals and Related Outcomes*. New York: World Bank Publications, 2004.
World Bank. *World Development Report 2005: A Better Investment Climate for Everyone*. New York: World Bank and the Oxford University Press, 2004.

GROUP OF EIGHT

The Group of Eight (G8) is an organization of eight industrialized economies that discuss and form common policies on matters of global concern. The origins of the G8 date back to 1975, when the leaders of six industrialized countries held a summit meeting in Rambouillet, France. The six founding nations were France, Germany, Italy, Japan, the United Kingdom, and the United States. A year later, Canada, the seventh country to join the organization, completed the Group of Seven (G7). From 1976 to 1998, G7 membership was fixed at seven countries. Russia was invited to the G7's 1994 Naples Summit to participate in certain discussions. At the 1998 Birmingham (Alabama) Summit, Russia became a full member of the organization, giving birth to the Group of Eight (G8). Even after the formation of the G8, the G7 continued to meet separately to discuss certain economic and financial matters. In 2006, Russia will host the G8 summit, cementing Russia's status as a full member of the organization.

The G8 industrialized countries dominate global output. The Seattle, Washington, skyline symbolizes the prosperity of the major industrial countries.
Courtesy of CORBIS

TABLE 59 **Group of Eight (G8), 2003**

Country	Population (millions)	Real GDP ($ billions)	Percent of Global GDP	Per Capita GNI ($)
Canada	31.6	$834	2.3%	$23,930
France	59.7	$1,748	4.8%	$24,770
Germany	82.6	$2,401	6.6%	$25,250
Italy	57.6	$1,466	4.0%	$21,560
Japan	127.2	$4,326	11.9%	$34,510
Russian Federation	143.4	$433	1.2%	$2,610
United Kingdom	59.3	$1,795	4.9%	$28,350
United States	291.0	$10,882	29.9%	$37,610
G8 countries	851.9	$23,885	65.6%	n/a

Source: World Bank, *World Development Report 2005*, 256–257, 260–261.

The G8 is an economic powerhouse. In 2003, G8 countries produced $24 trillion in final goods and services, nearly two-thirds of the world's total output, as shown in Table 59. The original G7 countries were also high-income advanced economies. The high standard of living in the G7 is reflected in their gross national incomes (GNIs) per capita, which ranked among the highest in the world. In addition, the World Trade Organization (WTO) reported that G8 countries exported $4.9 trillion in goods and services in 2004, close to half of the $11 trillion in global trade.

Since 1975, leaders from the industrialized countries have met regularly to discuss economic and political issues that concern the global community. The annual summits bring the heads of state or government together to discuss international issues, to form common policies or responses to global problems, and to set a global agenda for the implementation of initiatives. Since 1977 the European Community (EC)—today the European Union (EU)—has also participated in the annual summits. In addition, regular ministerial meetings take place throughout the year. Foreign ministers, finance ministers, and others, participate in these meetings.

In the early years, most G7 discussions focused on economic growth and stability, international trade, and sustainable economic development. In more recent years, discussions expanded to a wide range of topics such as international crime (including drug trafficking and money laundering); foreign direct investment, transnational corporations, and corporate social responsibility; the environment, conservation, and sustainable consumption; good governance, the rule of law, and corruption; e-commerce and the information highway; energy; worker rights and human rights; armed conflict and civil unrest; and global terrorism. G8 leaders attending the July 2005 G8 summit in Gleneagles, Scotland, agreed to increase foreign aid to Africa. Staunch U.S. opposition to the Kyoto Protocol weakened global efforts to address global warming, however. In 1999, the G8 created the G20 to expand global participation in global decision making. The G20 consists of the G8 countries, plus finance ministers from a dozen key developing countries and other emerging market economies.

See also **Advanced Economies; Global Economy; Group of Twenty; Organization for Economic Cooperation and Development.**

Further Reading

Bayne, Nicholas. *Hanging in There: The G7 and G8 Summit in Maturity and Renewal.* Brookfield, VT: Ashgate Publishing Group, 2000.

DiRita, Lawrence T. *An Agenda for Leadership: The G-7 Summit in Naples.* Washington, DC: Heritage Foundation, 1994.

Kirton, John J., and Radoslava Stefanova, eds. *The G8, The United Nations, and Conflict Prevention.* Brookfield, VT: Ashgate Publishing Group, 2003.

Shafer, Byron E. *Postwar Politics in the G-7: Orders and Eras in Comparative Perspective.* Madison, WI: University of Wisconsin Press, 1996.

GROUP OF SEVENTY-SEVEN

The Group of Seventy-Seven (G77) is a coalition of 133 developing countries. The G77 was founded on June 15, 1964, by seventy-seven developing countries under the auspices of the United Nations Conference on Trade and Development (UNCTAD). In its 1964 Joint Declaration of the Seventy-Seven Developing Countries, the G77 declared its intension to create a "new and just world economic order." In 1967 the G77 held its first Ministerial Meeting, which adopted the Charter of Algiers. The Charter of Algiers laid the groundwork for the G77's organizational structure. The G77 is headquartered at the United Nations in New York City. The G77 chairmanship rotates among member nations. In 2005 the G77 Chairman was H. E. Stafford Neil, UN ambassador from Jamaica. The five G77 Chapters, each headed by a chairman, are located in Nairobi, Rome, Paris, Vienna, and Washington, DC. G77 conferences and programs are funded mainly by contributions from member and nonmember developing countries.

The annual Ministerial Meeting is the G77's most important forum for decision making. Since 1967, delegates to Ministerial Meetings have adopted numerous joint declarations, action programs, and other agreements. The G77 is the world's largest coalition of nations from the global South, and speaks for its membership on many topics related to sustainable economic development. In 2000 the G77's South Summit, the first-ever meeting of G77 heads of state and government, convened in Havana, Cuba. The South Summit produced the Havana Program of Action, which rekindled enthusiasm for South-South cooperation. The Havana Program of Action, the 2003 Ministerial Declaration of the G77 Foreign Ministers and China, and other G77 statements, also renewed calls for global economic justice. The G77 has consistently supported the UN Millennium Development Goals (MDGs), which have focused global development efforts since 2000.

The G77 supports the three pillars of globalization—international trade, foreign direct investment (FDI), and cross-border financial investments. Over the past forty years, the G77 has worked to narrow gross income and development disparities in the global economy, however. First, the G77 supports greater inclusion of developing countries, particularly the least developed countries

(LDCs), in the global trading system. Action plans call for expanded trade preferences for certain developing countries; the elimination of disguised protectionism, including arbitrary labor or environmental requirements that restrict exports from poorer regions; expanded South-South trade relationships; and an accelerated accession process for developing countries seeking membership into the World Trade Organization (WTO). Second, the G77 supports programs to attract foreign direct investment (FDI) to the global South. Action plans favor bilateral investment treaties (BITs), export processing zones (EPZs), and joint ventures between foreign and domestic firms. G77 initiatives also support entrepreneurship, including business activity in the informal sector; and technology transfers from transnational corporations (TNCs). Third, the G77 supports reforms in the global financial architecture. Action plans call for the creation of functional capital markets in the global South; greater access of poorer nations to global credit markets; expanded official development assistance (ODA); the reversal of capital flight; capital formation; the reduction of external debt and debt service obligations; and stronger ties between the global South and the Bretton Woods institutions—the World Bank and the International Monetary Fund (IMF).

See also **Developing Countries; Foreign Aid; Globalization; Group of Eight; Group of Twenty; Least Developed Countries; Poverty; South-South Cooperation; United Nations System.** ***See also in Volume 2,*** **Documents 20, 21, 54.**

Further Reading

Bhagwati, Jagdish N. *The New International Economic Order: The North-South Debate*. Cambridge, MA: MIT Press, 1977.

Ghosh, Pradip K., ed. *New International Economic Order: A Third World Perspective*. Westport, CT: Greenwood Press, 1984.

Rothstein, Robert L. *Global Bargaining: Unctad and the Quest for a New International Economic Order*. Princeton, NJ: Princeton University Press, 1979.

Williams, Marc. Third *World Cooperation: The Group of 77 in UNCTAD*. New York: St. Martin's Press, 1991.

GROUP OF TWENTY

The Group of Twenty (G20) is a forum comprised of advanced economies and other emerging market and developing economies. The G20 was founded in December 1999 in Berlin, Germany. The G20 is primarily concerned with strengthening the global financial architecture and promoting sustainable economic development. The founding of the G20 came on the heels of several financial crises around the world during the late 1990s—crises centered in East Asia, Russia, and Brazil. The G8 industrialized countries supplied much of the impetus to create the G20.

The fixed G20 membership includes the G8 countries, the European Union (EU), and major emerging market and developing economies from every populated continent, as shown in Table 60. Combined, G20 member countries produce about 90 percent of the world's total output, account for 80 percent of world's trade volume, and represent two-thirds of the world's population. The G20 has no permanent secretariat or headquarters. Instead, member countries host G20 meetings. Since the founding of the G20, host countries have included Canada (2000 and 2001), India (2002), Mexico (2003), Germany (2004), China (2005), and Australia (2006).

TABLE 60 **Group of Twenty (G20), 2005**

Region or Group	G20 Membership
Africa	South Africa
Americas	Argentina, Brazil, Mexico
Asia	China, India, Indonesia, South Korea
Middle East	Saudi Arabia, Turkey
Oceania	Australia
Europe	European Union
G8 countries	Canada, France, Germany, Italy, Japan, Russia, the United Kingdom, the United States

The G20 is an inclusive global forum. G20 members represent the interests of nations at different levels of economic development and from different world regions. The forum strives to gain consensus on important global topics, especially topics related to global financial security. Consensus building, rather than formal votes, guides forum discussions. G20 finance ministers and central bank governors meet annually to deal with hot global issues. Deputy ministers and other experts do much of the preparatory work for the ministerial meetings. The G20 has staunchly supported the creation of international codes and standards to support transparency and good governance, responsible fiscal and monetary policies, counter-terrorism initiatives, and stable international capital markets. Under China's presidency, the G20's 2005 theme was "Global Cooperation: Promoting Balanced and Orderly World Economic Development." The G20 is committed to multilateral decision making. It cooperates with all major multilateral organizations such as the International Monetary Fund (IMF), World Bank, the World Trade Organization (WTO), and the specialized agencies and programs within the United Nations System.

See also **Financial Contagion; Global Financial Architecture; Group of Eight; Group of Seventy-Seven; Sustainable Economic Development.**

Further Reading

Kaiser, Karl, John J. Kirton, and Joseph P. Daniels, eds. *Shaping a New International Financial System: Challenges of Governance in a Globalizing World*. Brookfield, VT: Ashgate Publishing Group, 2000.

Kirton, John J., Joseph P. Daniels, and Andreas Freytag. *Guiding Global Order: G8 Governance in the Twenty-First Century*. Brookfield, VT: Ashgate Publishing Group, 2001.

Siebert, Horst. *Global Governance: An Architecture for the World Economy*. New York: Springer, 2003.

H

HAYEK, FRIEDRICH A.

Friedrich August von Hayek (1899–1992) was an Austrian-born economist. A champion of economic freedom and laissez-faire capitalism, Hayek was born and raised in Vienna, Austria. He earned two doctorate degrees at the University of Vienna during the early 1920s. While a student at the University of Vienna, the young Hayek was influenced by Professor Ludwig von Mises, a celebrated free-market economist. In 1931 Hayek accepted a professorship at the prestigious London School of Economics, an institution he would call home for the next two decades. During his tenure at the London School of Economics, Hayek authored his best-known and most controversial book, *The Road to Serfdom* (1944). Since the 1940s, *The Road to Serfdom* has stood as a compelling defense of laissez-faire capitalism and the power of free markets. Later in his career, Hayek taught at the University of Chicago (1950–1962) and the University of Freiburg (1962–1968) in Germany. In 1974, thirty years after the publication of *The Road to Serfdom*, Hayek shared the Nobel Prize in Economics with Swedish economist Karl Gunnar Myrdal.

In *The Road to Serfdom* Hayek defended free markets as the most efficient means of allocating society's scarce resources. Hayek observed that knowledge about economic conditions is fragmented and dispersed among the general population. He reasoned that economic decision making must likewise be defused among private sector participants, mainly individuals and business firms. Hayek concluded that price signals and self-interest enabled people to answer the basic economic questions of what, how, and for whom to produce.

Hayek also warned of unwarranted government interventions in the economy. He was especially critical of central economic planning. Hayek argued that government meddling in economic activity was a prescription for economic collapse because central planners would distort price signals and misallocate scarce productive resources. In addition, Hayek argued that centralized decision making in the hands of a few government bureaucrats invited corruption, the destruction of personal freedoms, and other abuses of power. In his book, *The Fatal Conceit: The Errors of Socialism* (1988), Hayek critiqued the crumbling Soviet economy to illustrate the folly of central planning in the modern world.

Hayek was often caught in the twentieth century's shifting ideological currents. His free-market orientation during the 1920s was compatible with the laissez-faire spirit of the times. The economic turbulence caused by a global depression in the 1930s tested Hayek's free-market resolve, however. Depression-era economic debates pitted Hayek against John Maynard Keynes and other heavyweights who supported government intervention to reverse the global economic slump. Hayek's credibility was further eroded during the post–World War II era. From the mid-1940s to the 1970s, many western democracies turned toward democratic socialism; many newly independent countries in Asia and Africa adopted third world socialism; and countries in eastern and central Europe and the Far East turned to communism.

In 1947 Hayek, and long-time friend and colleague Ludwig von Mises, founded the Mont Pelerin Society. Since the late 1940s the Mont Pelerin Society has brought prominent people from academia and business together to discuss and debate global economic trends. The Mont Pelerin Society has consistently extolled the virtues of economic and political freedom, and the "fatal conceit" of governments that rely on central planning to guide economic activity. Since the 1980s the global economic pendulum has swung decisively toward free-market economics, restoring Hayek's credibility and influence. The collapse of most communist economies during the late 1980s and early 1990s, and the simultaneous demise of most of the democratic socialist and third world socialist governments, illustrate the contemporary world's preference for free-market economics.

See also **Basic Economic Questions; Capitalism; Command Economy; Communism; Democratic Socialism; Economic Freedom; Economic System; Market Economy; Transition Countries.**

Further Reading

Ebenstein, Alan. *Friedrich Hayek: A Biography*. Chicago: University of Chicago Press, 2003.

———. *Hayek's Journey: The Mind of Friedrich Hayek*. New York: Palgrave Macmillan, 2003.

Hayek, Friedrich A. *The Road to Serfdom*. 50th anniv. ed. Chicago: University of Chicago Press, 1994.

———, and W. W. Bartley, III, ed. *The Fatal Conceit: The Errors of Socialism*. Reprint ed. Chicago: University of Chicago Press, 1991.

Wood, John C., and Robert D. Wood. *Friedrich A. Hayek: Critical Assessments by Leading Economists*. New York: Routledge, 2004.

HEAVILY INDEBTED POOR COUNTRIES (HIPC) INITIATIVE

The Heavily Indebted Poor Countries (HIPC) Initiative is a debt relief program co-sponsored by the International Monetary Fund (IMF) and the World Bank. Debt relief under the HIPC Initiative involves the reduction of certain external debts owed by poorer countries to foreign creditors. The original HIPC Initiative was established in 1996. In 1999, the Enhanced HIPC Initiative made debt relief broader and deeper. The Enhanced HIPC Initiative identified thirty-eight severely indebted countries to participate in the program. By July 2004, twenty-seven of the thirty-eight countries had qualified for debt relief under HIPC. Over time, the external debt of these twenty-seven countries is expected to drop by two-thirds. HIPC's goal is not total debt forgiveness but instead debt reduction to a manageable level. Foreign creditors, including the World Bank, contribute to the debt relief initiative.

The thirty-eight countries targeted for debt relief under the HIPC Initiative are divided into three categories, as shown in Table 61. The first category is comprised of fourteen countries, which reached the completion point by July 2004. To reach the completion point, a country must successfully implement macroeconomic reforms; channel debt relief savings into poverty-reduction programs such as education and health care; and improve its overall business environment. Indicators of a pro-growth business environment include sound judicial and financial systems, and infrastructure. The second category is comprised of thirteen countries which reached the decision point. To reach the decision point, a country must make significant progress toward sound macroeconomic policies, and expand programs to improve people's quality of life. Countries at the decision point receive "interim relief" to help service external debt. Before advancing to the completion point, decision-point countries must write poverty-reduction strategy papers. These strategy papers outline a plan to build the necessary institutions for development. The third category is comprised of eleven countries, which have not instituted necessary financial reforms. The lack of progress by these eleven countries jeopardizes their eligibility for future debt relief.

The Heavily Indebted Poor Countries (HIPC) Initiative has sparked some controversy over the past decade. Critics argue that the limited scope of the HIPC Initiative hampers its effectiveness. During the 1990s, Jubilee 2000, a leading international non-governmental organization (NGO), rallied millions of people behind a more ambitious debt forgiveness platform. Debt forgiveness involves the elimination of external debt for severely indebted countries. Jubilee 2000 and other like-minded groups argued that external debt in many of the world's poorest countries was unsustainable, and could not be serviced without inflicting severe hardships on debtor nations and their people. Jubilee

TABLE 61 **Total Debt Relief under the HIPC Initiative, 2004**

Categories of Countries	Number	Total HIPC Debt Relief ($ billions)	Countries
Completion point	14	$29.4	Benin, Bolivia, Burkina Faso, Ethiopia, Guyana, Ghana, Mali, Mauritania, Mozambique, Nicaragua, Niger, Senegal, Tanzania, Uganda
Decision point	13	$24.3	Cameroon, Chad, Democratic Republic of Congo, The Gambia, Guinea, Guinea-Bissau, Honduras, Madagascar, Malawi, Rwanda, Sao Tome and Principe, Sierra Leone, Zambia
Future consideration	11	$0	Cote d'Ivoire, Burundi, Central African Republic, Comoros, Republic of Congo, Laos, Liberia, Myanmar, Somalia, Sudan, Togo
Potential HIPC recipients	38	$53.7	

Source: Staffs of the IMF and World Bank, *Heavily Indebted Poor Countries (HIPC) Initiative: Status of Implementation*, 7.

2000 and others recommended a more substantive overhaul of the global financial architecture to promote social and economic justice.

See also **Developing Countries; External Debt; Global Financial Architecture; International Monetary Fund; Poverty; Unsustainable Debt; World Bank Group.** ***See also in Volume 2,*** **Document 56.**

Further Reading

Birdsall, Nancy, John Williamson, and Brian Deese. *Delivering on Debt Relief: From IMF Gold to a New Aid Architecture*. Washington, DC: Institute for International Economics, 2002.

Gilbert, Christopher L. *The IMF and Its Critics: Reform of Global Financial Architecture*. New York: Cambridge University Press, 2004.

International Monetary Fund. *External Debt Statistics: Guide for Compilers and Users*. Washington, DC: Author, 2003.

Rieffel, Lex. *Restructuring Sovereign Debt: The Case for Ad Hoc Machinery*. Washington, DC: Brookings Institution Press, 2003.

HUMAN DEVELOPMENT

Human development refers to the realistic range of choices that people have to live happy and productive lives. There are many dimensions to human development. An adequate standard of living, usually measured by household income, is a key feature of human development. At its most basic level, an adequate standard of living guarantees access to the necessities of life, such as food, medical care, and shelter. A higher standard of living expands consumption possibilities and prospects for leisure activities. Good governance supports human development by protecting peoples' personal security, civil and human rights, cultural identity, and participation in the political process. Universal public education promotes human development by creating opportunities for people to explore their interests and develop their talents.

Education enhances human development by expanding people's opportunities, nurturing talents, and developing human capital.

Courtesy of Getty Images: Photodisc Collection

The level of human development varies widely among countries in the global economy. Since 1990, the United Nations Development Program (UNDP) has measured human development with

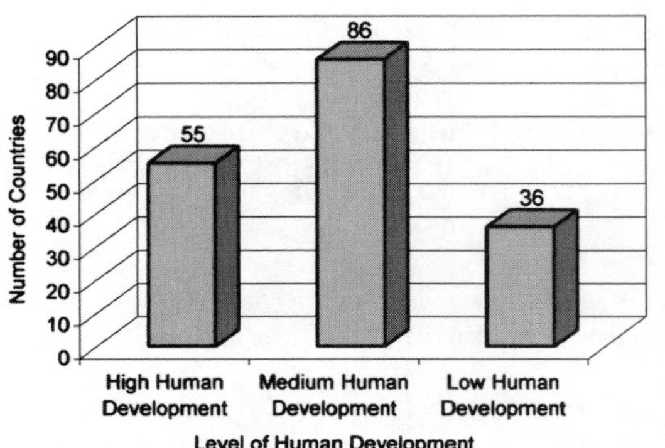

FIGURE 20 **Status of Human Development, 2002**

Source: United Nations Development Program, *Human Development Report 2004*, 139–142.

a Human Development Index (HDI). Life expectancy, adult literacy, school enrollment, and gross domestic product (GDP) per capita, are key indicators used in the HDI. The UNDP collects information from international organizations, governments, and other agencies to create an annual HDI ranking. The HDI ranking, and other topics related to human development, appear in the UNDP's flagship publication, the *Human Development Report.* The *Human Development Report 2004* noted that 31 percent of the 177 surveyed countries were classified as "high human development," 49 percent as "medium human development," and 20 percent as "low human development." The state of human development in 2002 is shown in Figure 20.

A high correlation exists between a country's GDP per capita and its human development status. High-income countries are most likely to be categorized as high human development, middle-income countries as medium human development, and low-income countries as low human development. Table 62 compares high, medium, and low human development countries by the four main HDI criteria: life expectancy, adult literacy rate, gross enrollment in public schools and colleges, and GDP per capita. High human development countries far outpace medium and low human development countries in all four categories. For example, people in high human development countries, on average, live ten years longer than people in medium human development countries, and twenty-eight years longer than people living in low human development countries. The average HDI score for high human development countries (.915 out of a possible 1.000) is significantly higher than medium human development (.695) and low human development (.438) countries. In 2002, the ten highest ranking countries in the HDI were high-income countries: Norway, Sweden, Australia,

TABLE 62 **Human Development Index, 2002**

HDI Categories	Life Expectancy at Birth (years)	Adult Literacy Rate (%)	Gross Education Enrollment (%)	GDP per Capita ($ PPP)	HDI Value
High human development	77.4	99.0%*	89%	$24,806	0.915
Medium human development	67.2	80.4%	64%	$4,269	0.695
Low human development	49.1	54.3%	40%	$1,184	0.438

*Most high human development countries have 99 percent adult literacy; some countries are lower than 99 percent.

Source: United Nations Development Program, *Human Development Report 2004*, 142.

Canada, the Netherlands, Belgium, Iceland, the United States, Japan, and Ireland, respectively. The ten lowest ranking countries were low-income countries: Democratic Republic of Congo, Central African Republic, Ethiopia, Mozambique, Guinea-Bissau, Burundi, Mali, Burkina Faso, Niger, and Sierra Leone, respectively.

See also **Advanced Economies; Developing Countries; Gross Domestic Product; Gross National Income; Least Developed Countries; Poverty; Quality of Life; Sustainable Economic Development.** ***See also in Volume 2*****, Documents 1, 2, 3, 33, 34, 35, 51, 55, 57, 59.**

Further Reading

Robinson-Pant, Anna. *Women, Literacy, and Development: Alternative Perspectives.* New York: Routledge, 2005.

Suarez-Orozco, Marcelo M., and Desiree B. Qin-Hilliard. *Globalization: Culture and Education in the New Millennium.* Berkeley, CA: University of California Press, 2005.

United Nations Development Program. *Human Development Report 2004: Cultural Liberty in Today's Diverse World.* New York: Author, 2004.

World Bank: *World Development Report 2005: A Better Investment Climate for Everyone.* New York: World Bank and the Oxford University Press, 2004.

IMPORT QUOTAS

An import quota is a type of trade barrier that limits the quantity of a product a government will allow into a country during a specified time period. An import quota specifies a quantity limit by number of items, weight, volume, or other measurement. In the United States, an import quota can be established by Congressional action or by Presidential decree. Over the past several decades, the United States has used import quotas to restrict the amount of sugar imported from Caribbean countries, lamb from New Zealand and Australia, automobiles from Japan, and clothing from China. The primary motive for imposing import quotas is to protect domestic industries, and jobs, from foreign competition. An import quota on a product tends to increase the price of the item in domestic markets.

The two main types of import quotas are absolute quotas and tariff rate quotas (TRQs). An absolute quota establishes a specific quantity of a good that can be imported into a country during a period of time, typically one year. An absolute quota can be bilateral or global. A bilateral quota sets a limit on the import of a good from a single country. In 1999 the United States imposed a bilateral quota on lamb from Australia, a quota that remained in effect until 2001. A global quota sets a limit on the import of a good from all foreign producers. In the early 1980s, the United States imposed a global quota on sugar imports from the Caribbean and other low-wage nations. The second type of import quota, the tariff rate quota (TRQ), permits the import of a specific quantity of a product at a reduced tariff rate during a period of time. Imports beyond the quota limit, however, face a higher tariff. The U.S. absolute quota on sugar evolved into a TRQ by the late 1980s, largely to comply with trade rules negotiated under the General Agreement on Tariffs and Trade (GATT).

Two types of "voluntary" restrictions also influence the flow of imports in the global economy. The voluntary export restraint (VER) is a bilateral agreement that limits the quantity of a product that can be exported from one country to another country. VERs are typically negotiated at the insistence of the importing country to reduce a surge of imports from the exporting country. For example, the United States negotiated a VER with Japan in 1981 to reduce the flow of Japanese automobiles to U.S. markets. The voluntary quota, initially set at 1.68 million automobiles, was raised to 1.85 million autos in 1984 and 2.3 million autos a year later. The VER was eliminated in the early 1990s. A second type of voluntary restriction is a voluntary import expansion (VIE). A VIE is a bilateral agreement that requires one country to purchase more of a certain product from another country. Often, VIEs are negotiated to counterbalance trade barriers that prevent fair trade between two nations. During the 1980s, the United States pressured Japan to voluntarily import a greater quantity of automobiles and auto parts, semiconductors, and other goods, a move that created tensions between the two economic titans. VERs and VIE were exempt from GATT rules and, thus, were a type of backdoor protectionism during the 1970s, 1980s, and early 1990s.

Among the most contentious import issues over the past half century was the use of VERs to limit textile and clothing exports from low-wage countries. In the 1950s, the United States and Japan negotiated the first textile VER to reduce the flow of Japanese cotton textiles to America. Within a decade, similar textile VERs were negotiated between the United States and other Asian nations, including South Korea and Chinese Taipei. European nations, under the umbrella of the European Economic Community (EEC), followed suit by negotiating VERs with low-wage Asian countries. In the early 1970s the hodgepodge of textile VERs were absorbed into a global Multi-Fiber Agreement (MFA), which set specific quantity restrictions on exports from the major textile-producing countries and listed specific import quotas for major textile-importing countries. Often referred to as a system of managed trade, the MFA stabilized the global textile and clothing trade for a couple of decades. At the close of the Uruguay round of GATT negotiations in 1994, the MFA was replaced with the Agreement on Textiles and Clothing (ATC). The ATC established a ten-year phase-out period for the complex network of VERs. On January 1, 2005, under the watchful eye of the World Trade Organization (WTO), all textile and clothing VERs in the global economy were terminated. Most experts agreed that the biggest winners in the global textile and clothing industry are China and other low-wage Asian economies. The biggest losers are textile and clothing producers in high-wage industrialized countries and in less efficient low-wage African and Latin American economies.

Multilateral organizations and regional trade agreements (RTAs) have promoted free trade and the reduction of trade barriers in recent decades. The core principles of the General Agreement on Tariffs and Trade (1948–1994) and the World Trade Organization (1995–present), such as most favored nation (MFN) and national treatment, have helped level the playing field in the global trading system. Many import quotas and other trade barriers on merchandise and commercial services have been reduced or eliminated. Under the WTO, new VERs were banned. WTO members also pledged to eliminate existing bilateral VERs by the late 1990s. Regional trading blocs such as the European Union (EU), North American Free Trade Agreement (NAFTA), and Southern Common Market (MERCOSUR), have significantly reduced or eliminated import quotas among member nations.

See also **Embargo; Exports; General Agreement on Tariffs and Trade; Imports; International Trade; New Protectionism; Protectionism; Regional Trade Agreements; Tariffs; Voluntary Quotas; World Trade Organization.**

Further Reading

Cline, William R. *Trade Policy and Global Poverty*. Washington, DC: Institute for International Economics, 2004.

Lusztig, Michael. *The Limits of Protectionism: Building Coalitions for Free Trade*. Pittsburgh: University of Pittsburgh Press, 2004.

McCillivray, Fiona. *Privileging Industry: The Comparative Politics of Trade and Industrial Policy*. Princeton, NJ: Princeton University Press, 2004.

Monnich, Christina. *Tariff Rate Quotas and Their Administration*. New York: Peter Lang Publishing, 2004.

IMPORTS

An import is any resource, intermediate good, or final good or service, that buyers in one country purchase from sellers in another country. Exports, on the other hand, are goods or services that are sold to another country. International trade involves the import and export of merchandise and commercial services. The most important categories of merchandise imports include capital goods, such as machinery and heavy equipment; industrial supplies and materials; automotive vehicles and auto parts; agricultural products, including animal feeds; and petroleum. The most important categories of commercial services include travel, passenger fares, transportation, and a variety of financial and professional services.

In 2004, global imports of merchandise and commercial services reached $11.3 trillion. Merchandise imports accounted for 81 percent of global imports, and commercial services accounted for the remaining 19 percent of imports. From 1994 to 2004 the value of imports in the global trading system roughly

Western Europe is the world's top importing region. The United States is the top importing country.

Courtesy of CORBIS

doubled, from $5.5 trillion to $11.3 trillion, as shown in Figure 21 (figure includes significant imports for re-export).

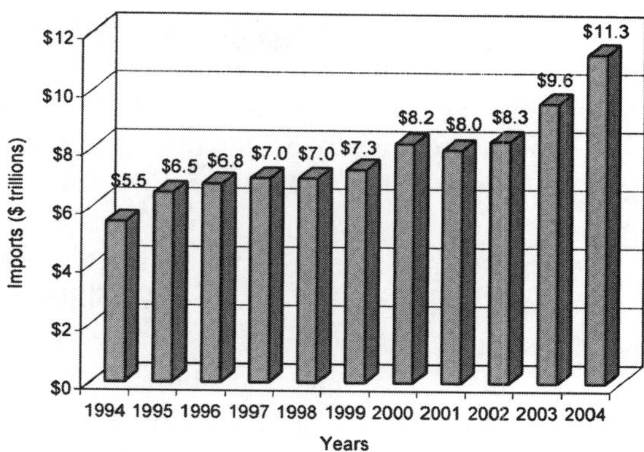

FIGURE 21 **Growth of World Imports, 1994 to 2004 ($ trillions)**

Source: World Trade Organization, *International Trade Statistics 2004*, 175–178, 182–184; World Trade Organization, *World Trade 2004, Prospects for 2005*, 13–14.

Three world regions accounted for the great majority of global imports in 2004. The World Trade Organization (WTO) identified Western Europe as the top importing region, accounting for 45.6 percent of global imports. Asia accounted for 24 percent of global imports, and North America, 20.8 percent. The remaining 9.6 percent of global imports flowed to Africa, Latin America, central and eastern Europe and the former Soviet Union, and the Middle East. Table 63 shows the world's six largest importers of goods and services. Combined, these six countries accounted for about 44 percent of all imports in the global economy.

Trade liberalization promotes the import and export of goods and services in the global economy. After World War II, the International Monetary Fund (IMF), World Bank, and the General Agreement on Tariffs and Trade (GATT) supported trade liberalization. Under the auspices of GATT, eight trade rounds progressively reduced tariff and non-tariff trade barriers between 1947 and 1994. Since 1995, GATT's successor organization, the World Trade Organization (WTO), has carried the free trade torch. In addition, regional trade agreements (RTAs) have reduced trade barriers. The Asia-Pacific Economic Cooperation (APEC), European Union (EU), North American Free Trade Agreement (NAFTA), Southern Common Market (MERCOSUR), and other trade blocs have negotiated reductions in traditional barriers to trade and cross-border investments. In 2003, the world's largest volume of intraregional imports occurred in APEC ($2,384 billion), the EU ($1,801 billion), and NAFTA ($631 billion).

TABLE 63 **The World's Leading Importing Countries, 2004 ($ billions)**

Rank	Country	Merchandise Imports ($ billions)	Commercial Services ($ billions)	Total Imports ($ billions)	Percent of World's Imports
1	United States	$1,526	$259	$1,785	15.5%
2	Germany	$718	$191	$909	7.9%
3	China	$561	$70	$631	5.5%
4	United Kingdom	$462	$135	$597	5.2%
5	Japan	$455	$134	$589	5.1%
6	France	$464	$95	$559	4.8%

Source: World Trade Organization, *World Trade 2004, Prospects for 2005*, 15, 17.

Imports satisfy certain consumer and producer needs in the global economy. Imports supply consumers with a greater variety of products, at competitive prices. The U.S. Commerce Department reported that in 2004 the United States imported nearly $1.8 trillion in goods ($1.5 trillion) and services ($0.3 trillion). About $600 billion of this total was for two categories of merchandise imports—consumer goods and automotive vehicles. For example, the United States purchased a significant amount of clothing from China and Indonesia, and a large number of automobiles from Japan and South Korea. Imports also supply businesses with resources, industrial supplies, and capital goods. In 2004, U.S. imports of industrial and capital goods topped $750 billion, about half of all U.S. merchandise imports. Businesses in resource-poor countries such as Japan are dependent on the import of resources such as petroleum, minerals, and timber.

Countries sometimes adopt trade policies to improve their trade position in the global economy. Shortly after World War II, many newly independent developing countries adopted an import substitution policy. Import substitution challenged domestic businesses to produce substitute goods for items normally imported. The goal of import substitution was to reduce dependence on foreign exports, especially manufactured items, and achieve a trade surplus. Import substitution was a dismal failure in most cases. Developing countries lacked the resources to produce and market sophisticated industrial goods. Expensive capital goods, inadequate research capabilities, an underdeveloped infrastructure, and an inexperienced labor force created roadblocks to industrialization. Government subsidies to domestic businesses, and high protective tariffs, only rewarded production inefficiencies. Over the past couple of decades, developing countries abandoned import substitution policies, favoring instead more stable export promotion strategies.

See also **Absolute Advantage; Balance of Payments; Balance of Trade; Comparative Advantage; Dumping; Exports; Import Quotas; International Trade; Localization; Mercantilism; Protectionism; Tariffs; Terms of Trade; Voluntary Quotas.**

Further Reading

Cline, William R. *Trade Policy and Global Poverty*. Washington, DC: Institute for International Economics, 2004.

United Nations Conference on Trade and Development. *Trade and Development Report, 2004*. New York: United Nations, 2004.

World Bank. *The Doha Round and the WTO: A New Agenda for Development*. Washington, DC: Author, 2005.

World Trade Organization. *World Trade Report 2004*. Geneva, Switzerland: WTO Secretariat, 2004.

INDUSTRIAL REVOLUTION

The Industrial Revolution was the economic transition from small-scale labor-intensive production to large-scale capital-intensive production in factories and mills. The Industrial Revolution began in England during the late 1700s, and spread to sections of Europe, North America, and Asia over the next century.

As Europe industrialized during the 1800s, its appetite for global resources and export markets increased. Supported by a simultaneous technological revolution, the Industrial Revolution helped pave the way for the first great age of globalization from the mid-1800s to 1914.

Great Britain led the charge toward industrialization and globalization during the 1800s. Several factors account for Britain's dominance. Britain was well-endowed with natural resources, such as iron ore and coal. It also had an abundant supply of inexpensive labor. Britain's vast colonial empire penetrated Africa, Asia, and the Americas, enabling the island nation to develop profitable trade relationships, foreign investments, and export markets. By the mid-1800s, Britain boldly pioneered free trade and capitalism. The resulting economic freedoms promoted entrepreneurship, competitive markets, technological advances, and business innovations. A stable, competent government also created a sound economic infrastructure, macroeconomic stability, and a powerful navy to protect its overseas interests.

Economic historians sometimes divide the early Industrial Revolution into two stages. During the first stage, which spanned the late 1700s to 1850, the factory system took hold in Great Britain's heavy industries such as textiles and iron. Technologies that harnessed the power of steam revolutionized production in many industries. The steam engine was a linchpin invention of the industrial age. By the late 1700s, James Watt's pioneering steam engines were used to drain water from mines, and power textile and iron mills. Over time, steam engines also powered locomotives and steamships. Across the Atlantic Ocean, American inventor Samuel F. B. Morse invented the telegraph (1838) and soon thereafter a communications code, called Morse code, to speed communications. By 1866 a transatlantic telegraph cable linked the United States and Europe. In agriculture, the McCormick reaper (1834) and John Deere's steel plow (1837) led to increased productivity on the farms.

During the second stage of the Industrial Revolution, which occurred from 1850 to 1914, industrialization spread quickly to the United States, Germany, Japan, and other countries. Once again, a technological revolution paralleled the budding Industrial Revolution. In America, the Bessemer process enabled the mass production of inexpensive, high-grade steel. In communications, the American Alexander Graham Bell invented the telephone in 1876, and in 1895, Italian Guglielmo Marconi successfully experimented with wireless communication—the precursor of the radio. The mass generation of electricity enabled telephone communications, lighting systems, mass transit systems, and the mass production of automobiles and other goods. German inventors, led by Nikolaus Otto, developed the first gasoline powered internal combustion engine in 1876, a technology that countrymen Gottleib Daimler and Karl Benz soon applied to the production of automobiles.

The Industrial Revolution established a new model for producing goods—the factory system. Under the factory system, large factory buildings were constructed, heavy machinery installed, and wage laborers recruited to work in manufacturing plants. The division of labor in factories was highly specialized.

Each worker was expected to perform a specific task in a larger production process. In the industrialized nations, the factory system increased national output, created a wealthy and powerful capitalist class, and laid the foundation for a rising middle class of industrial workers. The factory system also dehumanized the production process for many laborers. Lacking a strong labor union presence, men, women, and children endured sweatshop conditions in the factories, mills, and mines. A sweatshop is any industrial workplace characterized by unsanitary or unsafe working conditions, excessive working hours, low pay, and few protections for workers' rights. The factory system also contributed to harsh living conditions in urban slums and environmental degradation. Extractive industries, especially mining, degraded land resources in the industrialized countries and in resource-rich colonial possessions. Toxic pollutants emanating from factories also fouled the global commons, including the atmosphere and water bodies.

Great Britain maintained is dominant role as the torchbearer of industrialization and globalization during the 1800s and early 1900s. Under Britain's guiding hand cross-border flows of goods and services, investments, financial capital, and technology raced throughout the global economy. Underlying this complex web of economic relationships was the unifying force of global capitalism, an economic system that allowed self-interest to guide business decisions.

See also **Capitalism; Commercial Revolution; Globalization; Information and Communications Technologies.**

Further Reading

Brezina, Corona. *The Industrial Revolution in America: A Primary Source History of America's Transformation into an Industrial Society*. New York: Rosen Publishing Group, 2004.

Hobsbawm, E. J., and Chris Wrigley. *Industry and Empire: The Birth of the Industrial Revolution*. New York: New Press, 1999.

Hudson, Pat. *The Industrial Revolution*. New York: Oxford University Press, 2005.

Olson, Robert, and David Rejeski, eds. *Environmentalism and the Technologies of Tomorrow: Shaping the Next Industrial Revolution*. Washington, DC: Island Press, 2004.

Smil, Vaclav. *Creating the 20th Century*. New York: Oxford University Press, 2005.

INFLATION

Inflation is an increase in the overall price level in an economy. The two types of inflation are demand-pull and cost-push inflation. Demand-pull inflation results from excess demand in the economy. When aggregate demand exceeds aggregate supply, "too much money chases too few goods," and people tend to bid up the prices of products. Cost-push inflation is caused by an increase in the costs of production. Negotiated wage hikes and higher resource prices contribute to rising production costs. The oil-price shocks of the 1970s increased inflation throughout the global economy during the period.

Inflation reduces the purchasing power of money and imposes costs on different groups. Inflation erodes the real value of workers' wages, savers' deposits, and consumers' disposable income. Unanticipated inflation is especially severe for people on fixed incomes. For example, some U.S. public assistance programs, such as Temporary Assistance for Needy Families, are not indexed to the inflation rate. Over time, the real value of this public assistance is reduced. Unanticipated inflation also sours business investment. Businesses are reluctant to invest in new capital or hire additional workers when inflation dims prospects for macroeconomic stability.

The inflation rate measures the percentage increase in the overall price level over time. Creeping inflation is an annual inflation rate of a few percentage points, perhaps 1 percent to 3 percent. Creeping inflation is normal in a dynamic, growing economy. Over the past twenty years, most advanced countries have controlled inflation, keeping within the bounds of creeping inflation, as shown in Table 64. Galloping inflation and hyperinflation are more serious forms of inflation. Galloping inflation refers to an inflation rate of perhaps 20 percent, 50 percent, or even 100 percent. Over the past decade, most world regions experienced some galloping inflation. The Commonwealth of Independent States (24.3 percent average annual inflation rate), and the economies of central and eastern Europe (21.7 percent), suffered the worst bouts with galloping inflation during the 1996–2005 period. Hyperinflation refers to inflation rates that climb uncontrollably into the hundreds or thousands of percent. In the early 1990s, the Democratic Republic of Congo, Brazil, and Russia were ravaged by hyperinflation in excess of 1,000 percent. The IMF, the chief guardian of global financial security, reported greater global price stability in recent years. In fact, the average inflation rate for all world regions declined between 1996 and 2005.

Deflation, sometimes called negative inflation, occurs when the general price level in an economy decreases. Deflation is most often the result of insufficient aggregate demand in an economy. Deflation often occurs during a recession or depression, when unemployment rises and aggregate demand declines. The United States suffered from severe deflation during the post–World War I economic downturn in 1921 (−10.5 percent) and 1922 (−6.1 percent), and again a decade later when the Great Depression caused the price level to dip by nearly one-quarter between 1931 and 1933. Deflation sends negative signals to producers and consumers. Businesses respond to deflation by reducing production, a predictable response to the expectation of still lower prices in the future. Production cutbacks ripple through the economy, causing worker lay-offs and lower business investment. Job loss and

TABLE 64 **Inflation Rates by Development Status and Region, 1986 to 2005**

Classification of Country	1986–1995 Average	1996–2005 Average
Advanced economies	3.6%	1.9%
United States	3.5%	2.5%
Euro area	–	1.9%
Japan	1.4%	−0.1%
Other advanced	4.7%	2.0%
Other emerging market and developing countries	58.2%	8.8%
Africa	27.4%	12.3%
Central and Eastern Europe	59.2%	21.7%
CIS and Mongolia	–	24.3%
Middle East	17.7%	9.6%
Western Hemisphere	196.2%	9.1%

Source: International Monetary Fund, *World Economic Outlook, September 2004*, 210.

other economic uncertainties caused by deflation also discourage consumer spending, thus reducing aggregate demand. Deflation, which plagued the Japanese economy during most of the 1990s and early 2000s, contributed to the nation's lingering recession of the period.

Countries collect and analyze price information to determine changes in the overall price level. In the United States, the Consumer Price Index (CPI) is used to calculate the inflation rate. The CPI measures the percentage increase or decrease in the price of a uniform market basket of goods and services every month. The market basket in the United States consists of more than 200 categories of goods and services, which, in turn, are arranged into eight major groups: food and beverages, housing, apparel, transportation, medical care, recreation, education, and other goods. The starting point for the CPI is the base year, a point at which the government says $1 equals 100 percent of its value. At this point the CPI is set at 100. When the price of the market basket of goods increases, the CPI rises. Likewise, when the price of the market basket falls, the CPI declines. One commonly used base year is 1982–1984, a spread of three years. Government CPI data collected every month since 1982–1984 showed an increase in the CPI from 100 to 188.9 by 2004. This meant that it would take about $1.89 in 2004 to purchase the same amount of goods that $1.00 would have purchased twenty years earlier. The annual inflation rate is calculated by dividing the net change in CPI from year one to year two, by the CPI in year one. Figure 22 shows the net change in the CPI from 2003 to 2004 was 4.9 index points. Thus, the inflation rate for 2004 was 2.7 percent (4.9 divided by 184). A similar index, called the producer price index (PPI), measures price changes for raw materials, intermediate goods, and other items used in the production of goods and services.

$$\frac{\text{2004 CPI} - \text{2003 CPI}}{\text{2003 CPI}} = \text{Inflation Rate for 2004}$$

$$\frac{188.9 - 184.0}{184} = \frac{4.9}{184} = 2.7\%$$

FIGURE 22 **Calculating the U.S. Inflation Rate, 2004**

Source: U.S. Department of Labor, Bureau of Labor Statistics, "Consumer Price Index," February 20, 2005, 1.

Governments use stabilization policies to control inflation and other forms of macroeconomic instability such as unemployment and sluggish economic growth. Thus, macroeconomic stabilization deals with economic performance of the entire economy. The two main types of stabilization policy are monetary policy and fiscal policy. Monetary policy is typically administered through a nation's central bank. The central bank in the United States is the Federal Reserve System. Monetary policy regulates the nation's money supply and the cost of credit. To reduce inflation, a central bank employs a tight monetary policy, which withdraws money from the economy and increases the cost of borrowing. A tight monetary policy takes aim at the central problem of "too much money chasing too few goods." Fiscal policy is administered by elected officials, typically a national legislature and national executive. The national legislature in the United States is Congress, and the chief executive is the president. To reduce inflation, the government employs a restrictive fiscal policy, which increases taxes and decreases government spending. A restrictive fiscal policy, like a tight monetary policy, withdraws excess money from an overheated economy, and helps restore a balance between aggregate supply and aggregate demand. A tight monetary policy might also slow economic growth and increase unemployment, however.

See also **Gross Domestic Product; Gross National Income.**

Further Reading

Bernholz, Peter. *Monetary Regimes and Inflation: History, Economic and Political Relationships*. Northampton, MA: Edward Elgar Publishing, 2003.
Dalziel, Paul. *Money, Credit and Price Stability*. New York: Routledge, 2001.
Davidson, Paul, and Jan Kregel. *Full Employment and Price Stability in a Global Economy*. Northampton, MA: Edward Elgar Publishing, 1999.
International Monetary Fund. *Global Stability Report: Market Development and Issues, September 2004*. Washington, DC: Author, 2004.
———. *World Economic Outlook, September 2004*. Washington, DC: Author, 2004.

INFORMAL ECONOMY

The informal economy consists of business activity that is not reported to the government. Many other terms are used to describe unreported business activity, including underground economy, shadow economy, gray economy, and informal sector. Just as there are competing terms for the informal economy, there are also competing definitions. To some economists, the informal economy consists of legal types of transactions that take place in an extralegal business environment. For example, unlicensed street vendors conduct licit business in many urban areas throughout the world but for various reasons do not report business receipts or pay taxes to the government. Other economists include legal and illegal business enterprise in the informal economy. This broader definition accounts for financial and non-financial transactions of informal entrepreneurs, such as shopkeepers and craftsmen, and the criminal activities of drug traffickers, arms smugglers, and gambling rings.

Most informal economy business activity represents legal, if unreported productive enterprise. Business organization in the informal economy is diverse. One type of business structure is the informal own-account enterprise. Self-employed entrepreneurs, such as street vendors, taxicab drivers, or repairmen, own and operate own-account enterprises. These entrepreneurs sometimes work alone. Often these entrepreneurs rely on paid or unpaid assistance from family members to run the business, however. Many of these businesses are mobile, such as street vendors, or operate out of the entrepreneur's home. A second type of business structure is the microenterprise. A microenterprise typically employs several laborers on a regular basis. Employee compensation might include a wage or an in-kind benefit such as food or shelter. Auto repair shops and small-scale construction enterprises are sometimes organized as microenterprises. A third type of business structure is the established business firm that conducts a portion of its business in the informal economy. Production in the extralegal sector is usually a cost-cutting strategy. Low wages, tax avoidance, and the circumvention of government regulations motivate some established businesses to operate in the informal sector. In most parts of the world, people accept jobs in the informal sector to meet their subsistence needs for food, clothing, and shelter.

Informal economies operate beneath the layer of formal, reported business activity in all countries. The largest informal economies are found in the developing countries and emerging market economies. The smallest informal economies appear in the advanced economies. One recent study, conducted by economists Friedrich Schneider and Dominik H. Enste, quantified the size of the informal sectors of 110 countries by estimating the value of unreported business activity as a percent of gross national product (GNP). In *The Shadow Economy: An International Survey*, Schneider and Enste concluded the largest informal economies exist in Africa, South America, and the transition countries of eastern and central Europe, as shown in Figure 23. Smaller informal economies exist in North America, Oceania, and western Europe. The survey also noted tremendous variation within world regions. In Asia, for example, informal sector activity accounted for more than 40 percent of GNP in the Philippines, Sri Lanka, and Thailand, but less than 15 percent of GNP in China, Singapore, and Japan. Key factors that increase informal sector business activity include high business taxes, stifling business regulations, low worker education and skills, and dire poverty. Factors that reduce informal sector business activity include high national income, universal public education, good governance and the rule of law, and property rights.

The existence of informal economies in the global economy is well-documented. The magnitude of the informal sector has stimulated serious discussion about how to improve the lives of people working in the extralegal sector. Hernando de Soto, a noted Peruvian development economist, supports the extension of private property rights for the poor as a means to harness the power of the informal sector in his homeland. The World Bank supports improvements in the delivery of basic services to the marginalized poor, regulatory reform to remove barriers to business formation, worker training programs, and expanded access to credit for start-up firms. The International Labor Organization (ILO) stresses the development of human capital in countries. In 2000, the ILO formally proposed education and training of workers

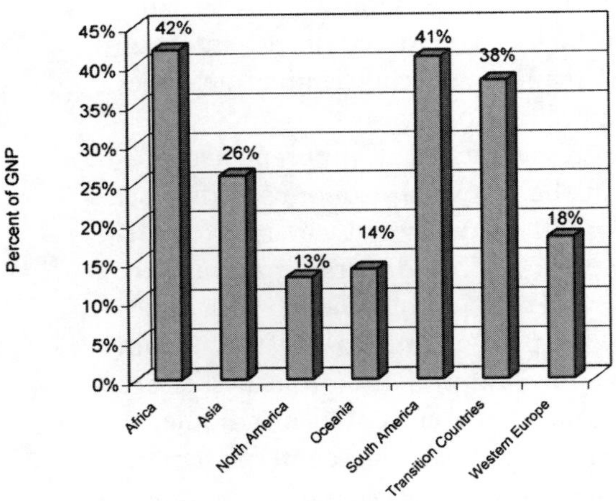

FIGURE 23 **Informal Economy by World Region, 1999/2000 (% of GNP)**

Source: Friedrich Schneider, "Size and Measurement of the Informal Economy in 110 Countries around the World," July 17, 2002, 6–18.

and managers in the informal economy. Improved knowledge and skills were viewed as necessary to improve workers' immediate standard of living and to create new opportunities for workers in the formal economy. Grassroots initiatives, such as the Movement of Landless Rural Workers (MST) in Brazil, pressure governments to redistribute idle agricultural land and to grant property rights to the poor.

See also **Developing Countries; Development Economics; Entrepreneurship; International Labor Organization; Soto, Hernando de.** ***See also in Volume 2,*** **Documents 8, 16, 55.**

Further Reading

Jhabvala, Renana, Ratna M. Sudarshan, and Jeemol Unni, eds. *Informal Economy Centre Stage: New Structures of Employment*. Thousand Oaks, CA: SAGE Publications, 2003.

Lund, Francie, and Jillian Nicholson. *Chains of Production, Ladders of Protection: Social Protection for Workers in the Informal Economy*. Washington, DC: World Bank Publications, 2004.

Schneider, Friedrich, and Dominik H. Enste. *The Shadow Economy: An International Survey*. New York: Cambridge University Press, 2003.

Soto, Hernando de. *The Mystery of Capital: Why Capitalism Triumphs in the West and Fails Everywhere Else*. New York: Basic Books, 2003.

Williams, Colin C. *Cash-in-Hand Work: The Underground Sector and the Hidden Economy of Favours*. New York: Palgrave Macmillan, 2004.

INFORMATION AND COMMUNICATIONS TECHNOLOGIES

Information and communications technologies (ICTs) are technological advances that increase people's ability to collect, store, retrieve, and share information. ICTs are the foundation of a recent transformation in global production, what some economists have called the information revolution. Some economists compare the information revolution to the epic Industrial Revolution, which began a couple centuries earlier. ICTs, such as computers and software, are highly integrated into today's evolving global economy. Global efforts to protect ICTs from international piracy are underway. International watchdogs include the World Intellectual Property Organization (WIPO), which administers the Patent Cooperation Treaty (PCT), and the World Trade Organization, which administers the Trade-Related Aspects of Intellectual Property (TRIPS) agreement. Many countries also protect ICTs and other innovations through national agencies, such as the U.S. Patent and Trademark Office.

Many ICTs are associated with the computer and software industries. Computer technology has progressed with lightning speed since World War II. In 1946, the Electronic Numerical Integrator and Calculator (ENIAC), the world's first functional electronic computer was invented by Americans John W. Mauchly and John P. Eckert, Jr. Since this time, technological advances have allowed the computer industry to evolve from the use of vacuum tubes to transistors, integrated circuits, and the microprocessor. Technology also broadened the appeal of computers, by expanding the market from large mainframe computers that were mainly used by big businesses, the government, and universities, to user-friendly personal computers. Complementing the rise of the computer was the production of sophisticated software. Advances in computers and software encouraged computer applications in homes, schools, and smaller businesses.

Microwave towers enhance communications and are an important feature of a country's economic infrastructure.

Courtesy of Getty Images: Russell Illig

The invention of the Internet in 1969 by the U.S. Department of Defense enabled computer networking. The use of the Internet, or "internetworking of networks," expanded during the 1970s and 1980s when a basic technological infrastructure was developed, and conveniences such as email were added. Tim Berners-Lee's invention of the World Wide Web (WWW) in 1989 opened the floodgates to Internet use. Through the World Wide Web, the information revolution accelerated, as people were able to communicate and share information through a global network that was both easy to use and inexpensive. By 2005 more than 800 million people in the global economy had ready access to the Internet. Other communications technologies, such as satellite communications, fiber optics, facsimile machines, and wireless telephone service also supported the growing ICT infrastructure.

In recent years ICTs have transformed business practices throughout the global economy, especially in the well-connected advanced economies. The Internet enables businesses to advertise their products, scan the planet for low-cost resources, and search for new markets or other business opportunities. Advanced ICTs encourage individualized marketing and distribution of goods. The cultivation of niche markets has proven successful for technology-savvy firms such as Amazon and eBay. Electronic record keeping has given birth to the virtual firm. The virtual firm, which conducts its business over the Internet, reduces many traditional costs of constructing retail or storage facilities. The growth of business-to-business (B2B) and business-to-consumer (B2C) electronic commerce in the global economy accounted for billions of dollars in business activity by the early 2000s. Further, ICTs streamlined research and development (R&D) and facilitated many types of transactions in services industries, including insurance, banking and financial services, and retail and wholesale trade. In the developing world the expansion of mobile phone networks has made an imprint on local business operations. Access to relatively inexpensive mobile phones has streamlined many local B2B and B2C transactions.

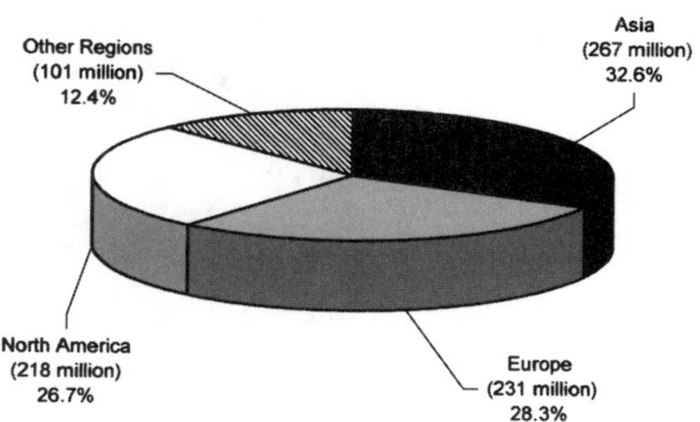

FIGURE 24 **Top Internet Users by World Region, 2005**

Source: Internet World Stats, "Internet Usage Statistics—The Big Picture," February 3, 2005 (www.internetworldstats.com).

The benefits of the ICT revolution are unevenly distributed in the global economy, giving rise to a severe digital divide. The digital divide is the ICT chasm between the advanced economies of the global North and the poorer developing countries of the global South. In its *2004 World Development Indicators*, the World Bank reported just 10 Internet users for every 1,000 people in the low-income countries in 2002. In that same year, there were 80 Internet users per 1,000 people in the middle-income countries, and 364 Internet users per 1,000 people in the high-income countries. The World Bank also reported just eight personal computers per 1,000 people in the low-income countries, compared to 467 personal computers per 1,000 people in the high-income countries. According to Internet World Stats, over 800 million people in the global economy were Internet users in 2005, with the heaviest concentrations of users in North America (66.7 percent of the population were Internet users), Oceania (47.4 percent), and Europe (31.6 percent). Lower percentages of people used the Internet in Latin America and the Caribbean (10.1 percent), Asia (7.4 percent), the Middle East (6.7 percent), and Africa (1.4 percent). Ranked by total number of Internet users, the top world regions were Asia, Europe, and North America, as shown in Figure 24.

The digital divide is one of the most important economic issues in today's global economy. It influences the pace of economic development—including people's quality of life—throughout the world. The digital divide creates an uneven playing field in international trade, foreign direct investment, and other types of global transactions. In *The Economist* 2005 e-readiness rankings, the top twenty-five countries were advanced economies. E-readiness measures countries' e-business environment, including broadband Internet access. By the early 2000s, many developing countries were becoming further marginalized by their lack of technological connectivity. In response, a number of international groups, such as the United Nations and the Group of Eight, pledged support to help bridge the digital divide.

See also **Advanced Economies; Developing Countries; Digital Divide; Globalization; Industrial Revolution; Trade-Related Aspects of Intellectual Property; World Intellectual Property Organization.**

Further Reading

Cohen, Daniel, Pietro Garibaldi, and Stephano Scarpetta. *The Ict Revolution: Productivity Differences and the Digital Divide.* New York: Oxford University Press, 2004.

Dutta, Soumitra, Bruno Lanvin, and Fiona Paua, eds. *The Global Information and Technology Report: 2003–2004: Towards and Equity Information Society.* New York: Oxford University Press, 2004.

———. *The Global Information and Technology Report 2004–2005.* New York: Palgrave Macmillan, 2005.

James, Jeffrey. *Bridging the Global Digital Divide.* Northampton, MA: Edward Elgar Publishing, 2003.

INTER-AMERICAN DEVELOPMENT BANK GROUP

The Inter-American Development Bank Group (IDB Group) is a regional development bank that serves Latin America and the Caribbean. It is one of four major regional development banks currently operating in the global economy. The IDB Group is comprised of three institutions: the Inter-American Development Bank (IDB), which was founded in 1959; the Inter-American Investment Corporation (IIC), which began operations in 1989; and the Multilateral Investment Fund (MIF), which was created in 1993. The three institutions within the IDB are autonomous but have complementary roles in promoting sustainable economic development in the Western Hemisphere. The organizational structures of these institutions vary. For example, a board of governors is the highest decision-making body in the IDB and IIC, while a donors committee coordinates the operations of the MIF. Member countries own and operate each of the three institutions of the Inter-American Development Bank Group. The headquarters for all three institutions of the IDB Group are located in Washington, DC.

The IDB is comprised of forty-seven member countries, twenty-six Latin American and the Caribbean countries, nineteen nonregional countries, the United States, and Canada. The Republic of Korea, the newest member country, joined the IDB and its sister institutions in November 2004. The Organization of American States (OAS) created the IDB in 1959 to "contribute to the acceleration of the process of economic and social development of the regional developing member countries, individually and collectively." To achieve this goal, the IDB provides loans, grants, guarantees, policy advice, and technical assistance to government and private sector decision makers. The chief policymaking group in the IDB is the board of governors, which delegates most of the bank's operations to a board of executive directors.

In recent years, the bank's priority areas have included support for poverty reduction and social equity, sustainable economic growth, modernization of the state, improving competitiveness, social sector reforms, regional and global economic integration, environmental protection, private sector development, and good governance. In 2003, the bank committed $6.8 billion to support its lending and other operations. Over 90 percent of this sum came from the bank's Ordinary Capital (OC), which financed fifty-nine loans ($6,147 million) and two guarantees ($85 million). Most loans granted by the bank are nonconcessional and carry interest rates appropriate to prevailing market conditions. An exception to this rule are loans granted through the bank's Intermediate Financing Facility (IFF), which offers lower interest rates to some low-income countries including the Dominican Republic, Ecuador, El Salvador, Guatemala, Jamaica, Paraguay, and Suriname. The bank can also "guarantee" the repayment of development loans granted through private financial institutions, thus encourage borrowing and productive investment in member countries. The bank's Fund for Special Operations (FSO) chipped in the remaining $578 million to finance twenty-three concessional loans. These concessional loans are designed to meet the needs of the region's poorest countries—Bolivia, Guyana, Haiti, Honduras, and Nicaragua. FSO loans typically carry an interest rate of less than 2 percent and have a repayment period of forty years. Since 1961, the three largest recipient countries—Argentina, Brazil, and Mexico—have garnered about one-half of all bank loans and guarantees, as shown in Table 65. The cumulative loans and guarantees offered by the IDB from 1961 to 2003 is $129 billion.

The Inter-American Investment Corporation (IIC) is the second institution of the IDB group. It is an autonomous multilateral organization comprised of forty-three countries—twenty-six borrowing countries from Latin America and the Caribbean, thirteen European countries, Japan and the Republic of Korea, Israel, and the United States. The IIC was established in 1989. It is headed by a board of governors, which delegates most of its authority to a board of executive directors to run the Corporation. According to its Establishing Agreement, the purpose of the IIC is "to promote the economic development of its regional developing member countries by encouraging the establishment, expansion, and modernization of private enterprises, preferably those that are small and medium-scale, in such a way as to supplement the activities of the Inter-American Development Bank." The IIC extends development loans, makes equity investments in private enterprises, and expands credit opportunities. IIC support for private businesses was designed to strengthen firms, create jobs, expand exports and regional integration, nurture productive domestic and foreign investment, and cultivate technological advance in regional developing countries. In 2003, the IIC approved $194 million to support twenty-six projects in fifteen countries, along with one regional project. These projects benefited nearly 3,000 small and medium-size firms, and created nearly 10,000 jobs. The IIC also supports co-financing, joint ventures, and other collaborative projects with international and local financial institutions, business firms, and other entities.

TABLE 65 **Cumulative IDB Loans and Guarantees, 1961 to 2003**

IDB Countries	Total Loans and Guarantees ($US in millions)	Percent of Total Loans and Guarantees
Argentina	$19,634	15.2%
Brazil	$26,134	20.3%
Mexico	$17,221	13.4%
Other 23 IDB countries and regions	$65,836	51.1%
Total	$128,857	100.0%

Source: Inter-American Development Bank, *Annual Report 2003*, 44.

The Multilateral Investment Fund (MIF) is the third institution of the IDB Group. The MIF is comprised of thirty-two member countries, which includes all of the twenty-six borrowing countries of the IDB. A donors committee governs MIF. Each of the thirty-two member countries is represented on the donors committee, with voting shares apportioned by the size of donors' contributions to the Fund. Because the United States and Japan have each contributed $500 million to the $1.2 billion Fund, these two countries dominate the voting shares. In practice, decisions about how to use the organization's funds are often by consensus rather than a formal vote. MIF is designed to support investment reforms to bolster private investment, including foreign direct investment (FDI); stimulate business activity and job creation; and encourage microenterprises and entrepreneurship. By supporting private investment and business creation the MIF also supports poverty reduction, economic growth, gender equity, human capital development, and responsible treatment of the natural environment. In 2003, the MIF approved seventy projects, at a cost of $70 million. Today, MIF's technical assistance also stresses project clusters, such as microfinance, environmental management, and information and communications technology. MIF financial resources are distributed through grants and investments, typically in conjunction with partners such as non-governmental organizations (NGOs), chambers of commerce, and public sector agencies. Between 1993 and 2003, MIF allocated $900 million to support nearly 600 projects in Latin America and the Caribbean.

Regional and sub-regional development banks are a major source of development loans and other development assistance in the global economy. The four main regional development banks are the African Development Bank Group, Asian Development Bank, European Bank for Reconstruction and Development, and the Inter-American Development Bank Group. Smaller, subregional development banks also dot the economic landscape, and include the Caribbean Development Bank, Central American Bank for Regional Integration, East African Development Bank, and West African Development Bank.

See also **African Development Bank Group; Asian Development Bank; European Bank for Reconstruction and Development; Regional Development Banks.**

Further Reading

Buvinic, Mayra, and Jacqueline Mazza, and Ruthanne Deutsch, eds. *Social Inclusion and Economic Development in Latin America*. Washington, DC: Inter-American Development Bank, 2004.

Devlin, Robert, Antoni Estevadordal, and Inter-American Development Bank, eds. *Bridges for Development*. Washington, DC: Inter-American Development Bank, 2004.

Inter-American Development Bank. *Annual Report 2003*. Washington, DC: Author, 2004.

———. *Unlocking Credit: The Quest for Deep and Stable Bank Lending*. Washington, DC: Author, 2005.

INTERNATIONAL BANK FOR RECONSTRUCTION AND DEVELOPMENT

The International Bank for Reconstruction and Development (IBRD) is a member-owned development institution that provides low-interest loans and technical assistance to middle-income developing countries. The overriding goals of the IBRD are global poverty reduction and sustainable economic development. IBRD was founded at the Bretton Woods Conference in 1944 and was operational by 1946. IBRD and the International Monetary Fund (IMF), which was also founded at the Bretton Woods Conference, are often referred as the Bretton Woods institutions. IBRD and the IMF are specialized agencies within the United Nations system. In 2005, IBRD consisted of 184 member countries. Paul Wolfowitz became the tenth president of the World Bank on June 1, 2005.

Today, IBRD is one of five institutions that comprise the World Bank Group. The other development institutions within the World Bank Group include the International Finance Corporation (IFC), the International Development Association (IDA), the International Centre for Settlement of Investment Disputes (ICSID), and the Multilateral Investment Guarantee Agency (MIGA). IBRD and its closest partner (the IDA) are called the World Bank. The work of the World Bank Group is coordinated by a board of governors and by the bank's executive directors. The bank is headquartered in Washington, DC. The bank also has country offices in over 100 member nations throughout the world.

The IBRD's overarching mission is to reduce poverty and promote sustainable economic development in the global economy. Thus, IBRD's mission is consistent with United Nations' Millennium Development Goals (MDGs). During the late 1940s and early 1950s, most IBRD loans were channeled toward the reconstruction of Europe, a continent devastated by World War II. Since the 1950s, most IBRD development loans, guarantees, and technical assistance have flowed to the more creditworthy middle-income developing countries. IBRD's partner institution, the IDA, extends loans and other assistance to the less creditworthy low-income developing countries.

IBRD's loans are divided into two categories, investment loans and development policy loans. Investment loans are long-term loans of five to ten years. Investment loans target infrastructure projects such as the construction of housing, schools, health clinics, and irrigation and sanitation systems. Investment loans also promote institution building and social reforms. Investment loans represent 75 percent to 80 percent of IBRD's total loans. Development policy loans are short-term loans of one to three years. Development policy loans, previously called adjustment lending, support policy reforms conducive to sustainable economic growth and development. These loans support good governance, the rule of law, privatization, and competitive markets, by reforming nations' financial systems, legal systems, tax and investment codes, civil service, social services, and trade policies. Between 1946 and 2004, IBRD's cumulative loans to member nations totaled $394 billion.

In fiscal 2004, IBRD loaned $11 billion to middle-income developing countries. About three-quarters of IBRD's loans were made to support four sectors, including law, justice, and public administration (24 percent of IBRD loans); transportation (23 percent); health and social services (16 percent); and finance

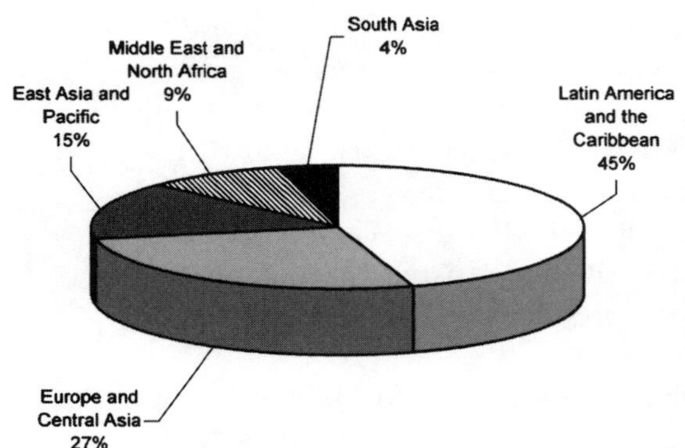

FIGURE 25 **IBRD Loans by World Region, 2004**

Source: World Bank, "Where Does the Money Go?" (www.worldbank.org)

(11 percent). The remaining loans were divided among industry and trade; water, sanitation and flood protection; agriculture, fishing and forestry; education; energy and mining; and information and communication. In 2004 IBRD loans financed eighty-seven projects in thirty-three countries. The dispersal of IBRD loans by world region is shown in Figure 25.

Most IBRD development loans are financed with World Bank Bonds. IBRD issues World Bank Bonds, which carry an AAA credit rating in global capital markets. In 2004, IBRD borrowed $13 billion from international investors through the issuance of World Bank Bonds. IBRD's secure position in the global financial system makes the bank's bonds an attractive investment. IBRD also earns limited revenues through interest payments on past loans. Unlike commercial banks and most other financial institutions, IBRD is not designed to earn profits. The bank's loans carry low interest rates compared with prevailing interest rates in global markets. Since 1946, quota subscriptions have also generated operating capital for IBRD. Each member nation is required to ante up a subscription payment in rough proportion to the size of its economy. The five largest subscription quotas were assigned to the United States (16.85 percent of all subscription payments), Japan (8.08 percent), Germany (4.60 percent), France (4.41 percent), and the United Kingdom (4.41 percent). The combined, subscriptions from these five countries have totaled $60 billion, nearly 40 percent of the world's total subscriptions of $157 billion.

The bank's 184 member countries own IBRD and the other four institutions of the World Bank Group. The voting power of each country is determined by the size of its economy. The United States, the world's largest economy, holds 16.39 percent of the bank's voting power, or 265,219 total votes. The small island nation of Palau, on the other hand, holds just .02 percent of the voting power, or 266 total votes. Member countries are often called shareholders in the bank, and the votes of member countries are called shares. The bank's highest decision-making group is the board of governors, which consists of the finance minister or other official of comparable rank from each member country. At its annual meeting, the board of governors establishes broad policies and sets priorities for the bank. The board of governors then delegates responsibility for running the bank to the executive directors, a twenty-four-member group. One executive director is selected by each of the five largest economies, including the United States (16.39 percent of the voting shares), Japan (7.86 percent), Germany (4.49 percent), France (4.30 percent), and the United Kingdom (4.30 percent). Member countries elect the remaining nineteen executive directors.

A staff of nearly 10,000 professionals assists in the implementation of bank policies, programs, and projects.

Over the years non-governmental organizations (NGOs), civil society organizations (CSOs), and other stakeholders in the global economy have criticized IBRD and the other institutions of the World Bank Group. Some critics cite flaws in past structural adjustment programs (SAPs). Critics argue that SAPs, guided by the bank's heavy market-oriented hand, undermined the authority of local governments and oversimplified the complex problems of the world's poor nations. Others critique the bank's structure, which they view as undemocratic, and self-serving for the rich nations of the global North. Many of the bank's critics view the bank as the top cheerleader of globalization. Some in the anti-globalization movement accuse the bank of being unresponsive to the abuse of workers, the environment, and indigenous peoples by powerful transnational corporations (TNCs). Anti-globalization demonstrations against the gatekeepers of the global economy—the World Bank, IMF, World Trade Organization—swelled during the early 2000s, especially after protestors successfully disrupted the WTO's 1999 ministerial meeting in Seattle, Washington.

See also **Bretton Woods System; International Centre for Settlement of Investment Disputes; International Development Association; International Finance Corporation; Multilateral Investment Guarantee Agency; World Bank Group. *See also in Volume 2,* Document 5.**

Further Reading

Buira, Ariel. *Challenges to the World Bank and IMF: Developing Country Perspectives*. London: Anthem, 2003.

Gill, Indermit S., and Todd Pugatch. *At the Frontlines of Development: Reflections from the World Bank*. Washington, DC: World Bank Publications, 2005.

Mallaby, Sebastian. *The World's Banker: A Story of Failed States, Financial Crises, and the Wealth and Poverty of Nations*. New York: Penguin Press HC, 2004.

McClure, Paul, ed. *A Guide to the World Bank*. Washington, DC: World Bank Publications, 2003.

Ritzen, Jozef, and Joseph E. Stiglitz. *A Chance for the World Bank*. London: Anthem, 2005.

INTERNATIONAL CENTRE FOR SETTLEMENT OF INVESTMENT DISPUTES

The International Centre for the Settlement of Investment Disputes (ICSID) is an autonomous international organization designed to help settle investment disputes between foreign investors and host governments. While ICSID exercises considerable independence in its dispute settlement role, the Centre is one of five institutions that comprise the World Bank Group. The four other institutions of the World Bank Group are the International Bank for Reconstruction and Development (IBRD), the International Development Association (IDA), the International Finance Corporation (IFC), and the Multilateral Investment Guarantee Agency (MIGA).

ICSID was established by the executive directors of the World Bank under the Convention on Settlement of Investment Disputes between States and

Nationals of Other States. This convention came into effect on October 14, 1966. The convention established a Secretariat and an Administrative Council to implement the dispute settlement process. The World Bank covers the modest costs of maintaining ICSID's administrative apparatus—a total of about $2.5 million in 2004. The two parties involved in a dispute are responsible for all other costs related to their case. Membership in ICSID is open to all World Bank member nations. In 2004, 140 nations had formally ratified the convention. ICSID is headquartered in Washington, DC.

ICSID's dispute settlement functions are a means to a desired end—the expansion of foreign direct investment (FDI) in the global economy. Arbitration and conciliation are the two mechanisms of dispute settlement under ICSID. Participation in arbitration or conciliation is based on voluntary consent by the foreign investor and the host government. Once proceedings have begun, however, neither party can unilaterally withdraw. Under arbitration, each side in an investment dispute selects up to four people from an existing Panel of Arbitrators. The ICSID Secretariat solicits arbitrators from member states to serve on this panel. ICSID can assign additional arbitrators to a case. Once the case is heard, and a decision is rendered, both parties are expected to abide by the ruling. Of the 159 total cases registered with ICSID between the 1960s and 2004, 155 have opted for arbitration. Under the lesser-used conciliation process, the two sides submit an investment dispute to a Panel of Conciliators. Just four conciliation cases have been registered with ICSID since the 1960s.

ICSID is neither judge nor jury in cases of arbitration or conciliation. Instead, ICSID provides a rules-based process for hearing investment disputes. Cases have been heard in ICSID's Washington, DC facility, and in other venues around the world including the Hague, Netherlands; Cairo, Egypt; Kuala Lumpur, Malaysia; Sydney, Australia; and elsewhere. ICSID disseminates legal information to governments and transnational corporations through a series of publications, most notably the *ICSID Review—Foreign Investment Law Journal*, and the regularly updated collections of *Investment Laws of the World* and *Investment Treaties*. ICSID procedures and rulings have also been a useful reference point for nations negotiating bilateral investment treaties (BITs) and other international agreements.

See also **Foreign Direct Investment; International Bank for Reconstruction and Development, International Development Association; International Finance Corporation; Multilateral Investment Guarantee Agency; World Bank Group.**

Further Reading

Crawford, James, and Karen Lee, eds. *ICSID Reports: Volume 6*. New York: Cambridge University Press, 2004.

Schreuer, Christoph H. *The ICSID Convention: A Commentary*. New York: Cambridge University Press, 2001.

Sornarajah, M. *The International Law on Foreign Investment*. New York: Cambridge University Press, 2004.

———. *The Settlement of Foreign Investment Disputes*. Norwell, MA: Kluwer Law International, 2000.

INTERNATIONAL COMMODITY AGREEMENTS

International commodity agreements (ICAs) are multilateral agreements between major producers and consumers of certain commodities in global markets. ICAs were established to stabilize commodity prices by balancing global supply and demand for items such as sugar and tin. Over the past half century a number of major ICAs were negotiated, including the International Sugar Agreement (ISA) in 1954, International Tin Agreement (ITA) in 1954, International Coffee Agreement (ICoA) in 1962, International Cocoa Agreement (ICCA) in 1972, and the International Natural Rubber Agreement (INRA) in 1980. These agreements, which were designed to bring long-term stability to commodities markets, had a mixed record of success. By 2005, just three major ICAs—the ISA, ICoA, and ICCA—remained, as shown in Table 66. Under recently negotiated revisions in their governing agreements, today's ICAs have little clout in shaping global pricing or output decisions.

The goal of ICAs is to create stable commodity markets. Unbalanced commodity markets and volatile commodity prices frustrated efforts to maintain macroeconomic stability in producer and consumer nations. Recurring commodity gluts plagued commodity-dependent developing countries. Gluts, or excess supply, resulted in chronic commodity surpluses in global markets. Surpluses depressed commodity prices, reduced export earnings, and stifled business expansion and jobs creation. Periodic commodity shortages, on the other hand, resulted in short-lived price spikes for certain commodities. Commodity-consuming nations balked at sudden, unanticipated price hikes for basic commodities. Elevated prices for rubber, sugar, copper, or tin meant higher consumer prices for a variety of related goods. During the 1950s and 1960s the impetus to stabilize commodities prices sparked interest in ICAs, which stressed cooperation between the largest producers and consumers of certain commodities. During the 1960s the United Nations Conference on Trade and Development (UNCTAD) assumed a leadership role in the negotiation of

TABLE 66 **International Commodity Agreements, 1954 to 2005**

Agreement Name	Date Founded	Current Status	Member Nations (number)
International Sugar Agreement (ISA)	1954	Active: International Sugar Agreement, 1992	71 countries (2005)
International Tin Agreement (ITA)	1954	Inactive: Decision to terminate in 1985	None
International Coffee Agreement (ICoA)	1962	Active: International Coffee Agreement, 2001	74 countries (2005)
International Cocoa Agreement (ICCA)	1972	Active: International Cocoa Agreement, 2001	39 countries (2003)
International Natural Rubber Agreement (INRA)	1980	Inactive: Decision to terminate in 1999	None

Sources: International Cocoa Organization, "Facts about the International Cocoa Organization (www.icco.org); International Sugar Organization, "ISO's New Strategic Direction," 1–2; International Coffee Organization, "History" (www.ico.org); International Rubber Organization, "Termination of the International Natural Rubber Agreement" (www.rubber-stichting.ind.tno.nl/art1nr16.html).

ICAs. The Group of Seventy-Seven (G77) and others in the global South applauded UN involvement in the creation of ICAs. Soon, ICAs were viewed as a cornerstone of the New International Economic Order.

ICAs have used different techniques to stabilize commodity markets. One type of ICA market intervention was the establishment of a buffer stock. Buffer stock stabilization involves storage of the excess supply of a commodity to prevent a market glut. Under a buffer stock arrangement, ICA members bear the cost of maintaining storage facilities for excess output. Over time, the International Tin Agreement (ITA), International Cocoa Agreement (ICCA), and International Natural Rubber Agreement (INRA), used buffer stocks to hold the global supply of tin, cocoa, and rubber in check. In the short term, buffer stocks had some success in keeping global prices within a certain range. Ultimately, the buffer stock stabilization failed due to high storage costs, the lack of market discipline by member nations, increased commodity production by non-member nations, and attempts to hold market prices at unrealistically high levels.

A second ICA stabilization approach was export controls. An export control is a type of quota, which limits the amount of a commodity each member nation is permitted to sell in global markets. Export controls represent a more aggressive approach to stabilization. Under export controls, the ICA behaves much like a producer cartel. However, unlike a producer cartel, which restricts membership to commodity producers, the ICA maintains ties between producer and consumer member countries. Export controls were used by the International Coffee Agreement (ICoA), International Sugar Agreement (ISA), and the International Tin Agreement (ITA). The failure of cartel-like export controls resulted from circumstances on the supply and demand sides of the market. Supply-side problems included pervasive cheating by producers who exceeded production quotas. New profit-seeking competitors from non-member countries also expanded the market supply of certain commodities. Demand-side troubles resulted from the introduction of lower-priced substitute goods in some commodity markets. For example, the switch from tin cans to aluminum cans in the beverage industry reduced the demand for tin, and sped the collapse of the ITA in the mid-1980s.

Today's ICAs lack the market power of earlier ICAs. By the early 2000s, neither buffer stocks nor export controls were used by ICAs to stabilize commodity markets. Yet, the restructured ICAs fill an important niche in global commodity markets. The ISA, ICoA, and ICCA foster intergovernmental communication in sugar, coffee, and cocoa markets. ICAs promote sustainable and balanced development of producer nations in the developing world. ICAs supply producers with pertinent research to improve the production and marketing of commodities. ICAs also support strategies to increase global consumption of commodities in order to stabilize prices. A number of multilateral study groups hold international conferences to discuss specific commodity markets. Conferences disseminate commodity-related information in industries producing copper, jute, nickel, olive oil, rubber, and other products. In addition, support for commodity producers is available from the Common Fund for

Commodities (CFC), an intergovernmental financial institution created under the auspices of the United Nations Conference on Trade and Development. The CFC was founded in 1989 and has supplied assistance to commodity-producing nations since the early 1990s. CFC-financed programs support research and development, technology transfers, economic diversification, marketing, product quality, and worker productivity.

See also **Cartel; Developing Countries; Terms of Trade.**

Further Reading

Akiyama, Takamasa, John Baffes, Donald Larson, and Panos Varangis. *Commodity Market Reforms: Lessons of Two Decades*. Washington, DC: World Bank Publications, 2001.

Dand, Robin. *The International Cocoa Trade*. New York: John Wiley & Sons, 1997.

Raffaelli, Marcelo. *Rise and Demise of Commodity Agreements: An Investigation into the Breakdown of International Commodity Agreements*. Lancaster, PA: Woodhead Publishing, Ltd., 1995.

United Nations. *International Producer-Consumer Cooperation in Commodities in the Mid-1990s: A Handbook on International Commodity Agreements, Arrangements and Study Groups*. Geneva, Switzerland: Author, 1998.

Viton, Albert. *The International Sugar Agreement: Promise and Reality*. West Lafayette, IN: Purdue University Press, 2004.

INTERNATIONAL CO-OPERATIVE ALLIANCE

The International Co-operative Alliance (ICA) is an autonomous, non-governmental organization that represents the interests of cooperatives in the global economy. The ICA was founded in London, in 1895 to promote cooperative enterprise, values, and principles around the world. A cooperative is a voluntary association of people who jointly own and control productive enterprises to meet the economic, social, or cultural needs of its membership. Cooperatives, or coops, take many forms. Health clinics, village banks, retail stores, fisheries, farms, and construction enterprises are often organized as coops. In 2004, ICA was the world's largest association of cooperatives. The ICA is comprised of 228 member organizations representing 760 million people in ninety countries. Most member organizations are located in Europe, followed by the Americas, Asia and the Pacific, and Africa.

The ICA's organizational structure consists of four governing bodies: the General Assembly, Regional Assemblies, the ICA Board, and the Audit and Control Committee. The General Assembly is the ICA's highest policymaking body. The General Assembly brings representatives from all member organizations together every two years to form policies, set global priorities, and approve the ICA budget. The Regional Assemblies also convene every two years, alternating with the biennial General Assembly meetings. Regional Assemblies take place in Africa, the Americas, Asia and the Pacific, and Europe. Regional Assemblies give a voice to coops in different world regions and advance the values and principles of the cooperative movement in the global community. The ICA Board attends to the overall operation of the International Co-operative

Alliance. It handles the ICA's administrative functions, proposes the ICA budget, and appoints the director-general. The Audit and Control Board reviews and reports on the ICA's financial status. Today, the ICA's head office is located in Geneva, Switzerland. Regional offices are located in Burkina Faso, which serves West Africa; Costa Rica, which serves the Americas; India, which serves Asia; and Kenya, which serves East, Central, and Southern Africa.

The ICA has nurtured cooperative values and principles for more than a century. In its *ICA Rules*, as approved in September 2003, the ICA renewed its commitment to seven core principles. First, cooperatives are voluntary associations, with membership open to all people regardless of gender, race, religion, or political beliefs. Second, cooperatives are democratic organizations controlled by their members. Third, members contribute to the economic sustainability of their cooperative. Fourth, cooperatives are autonomous associations that guarantee membership control over coop decision making. Fifth, cooperatives support education and training for members, who, in turn, behave responsibly and contribute to a positive public image. Sixth, cooperatives support other coops and the cooperative movement. Seventh, cooperatives promote sustainable development in local communities and regions.

The ICA has been the catalyst for the global cooperative movement. In 1946, the ICA was one of the first non-governmental organizations (NGOs) granted Consultative Status by the United Nations (UN). Today, the UN and other multilateral organizations recognize the ICA as a positive force in promoting responsible globalization. The World Commission on the Social Dimension of Globalization, an independent body formed by the International Labor Organization (ILO), commended the ICA in 2004 for its positive role in promoting good governance, local economic development, and corporate social responsibility in the global economy. The ICA supports the UN's Millennium Development Goals (MDGs), which have guided global poverty-reduction efforts since 2000. The United Nations celebrates a "UN International Day of Cooperatives" each year to acknowledge the work of the ICA and the cooperative movement.

See also **Corporate Social Responsibility; Democracy; Good Governance; United Nations System.** ***See also in Volume 2,*** **Document 31.**

Further Reading

Birchall, Johnston. *The International Co-Operative Movement*. New York: Manchester University Press, 1997.

International Cooperative Alliance. *ICA Rules, Policies, Procedures & Standing Orders*. Geneva, Switzerland: Author, 2003.

Lyons, Mark. *Third Sector: The Contributions of Nonprofit and Cooperative Enterprises in Australia*. St. Leonards, Australia: Allen & Unwin Academic, 2001.

Parnell, Edgar. *Reinventing the Co-operative: Enterprises for the 21st Century*. Oxford, UK: Plunckett Foundation, 1996.

Taimni, Krishan K. *Cooperatives in Asia: From Reform to Reconstruction*. Washington, DC: International Labor Office, 2001.

INTERNATIONAL DEVELOPMENT ASSOCIATION

The International Development Association (IDA) is a member-owned development institution that makes long-term interest-free loans and grants to the world's poorest countries. The IDA was founded in 1960 and began operations a year later. The IDA and the International Bank for Reconstruction and Development (IBRD) are more commonly called the World Bank. In 2004, the World Bank committed $20 billion to development assistance in low-income and middle-income developing countries—$9 billion through the IDA and $11 billion through IBRD. The IDA and IBRD share a common board of governors, which forms the bank's major policies, and an executive board that runs the bank's day-to-day operations. They also share a headquarters in Washington, DC. Today, the World Bank Group consists of five mutually supporting institutions including IBRD, the IDA, the International Finance Corporation (IFC), the International Centre for Settlement of Investment Disputes (ICSID), and the Multilateral Investment Guarantee Agency (MIGA). In 2005, IDA membership stood at 165 countries.

The IDA's central mission is to provide development assistance to low-income countries that are not eligible for IBRD loans or loans from commercial lenders in global capital markets. The IDA extends loans—called credits—and grants to the poorest countries to jump-start economic growth and improve people's quality of life. To be eligible for IDA loans or grants, a country's gross national income (GNI) per capita must be $865 or less. In all, eighty-one countries are eligible for IDA assistance. IDA loans are long term and interest free, although a small service charge of less than 1 percent is typically attached to loans. Recipient countries repay the principle of the loan over thirty-five to forty years, with a generous grace period that could extend repayment to fifty years. The IDA is often called the "soft loan window" of the World Bank because of the highly concessional terms of its loans. Between 1961 and 2004, the IDA extended $151 billion in loans and grants to low-income developing countries.

In fiscal 2004 the IDA committed $9 billion to finance 158 new development projects in sixty-two countries. Three-quarters of the IDA's loans and grants were made to support five sectors, including law, justice, and public administration (24 percent); health and other social services (14 percent); transportation (14 percent); education (13 percent); and water, sanitation, and flood protection (10 percent). The IDA also funded projects in agriculture, fishing and forestry; energy and mining; finance; industry and trade; and information and communications. Of the eighty-one countries eligible for IDA assistance, thirty-nine were located in sub-Saharan Africa, followed by East Asia and the Pacific (thirteen), Europe and Central Asia (ten), Latin American and the Caribbean (nine), South Asia (eight), and the Middle East and North Africa (two). In 2004, most of the $9 billion in IDA loans and grants were devoted to Africa and South Asia, the world's poorest regions, as shown in Figure 26 ("other regions" include Europe and Central Asia, Latin America and the Caribbean, and the Middle East and North Africa).

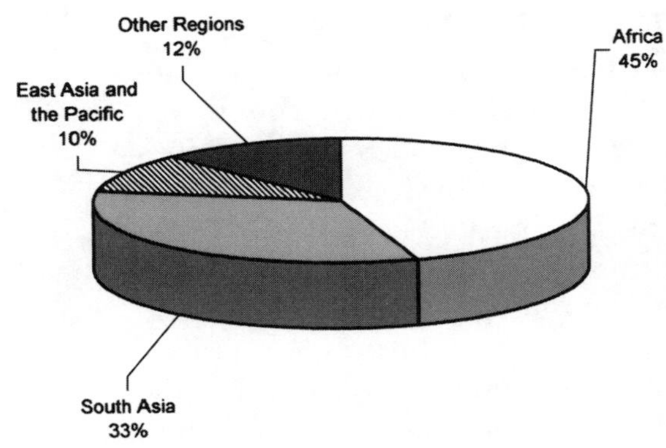

FIGURE 26 **IDA Loans and Grants by World Region, 2004**

Source: World Bank, "Where Does the Money Go?" (www.worldbank.org).

The IDA raises most of its funds through voluntary contributions called replenishments. Replenishments are negotiated every three years. Most replenishment funds come from donor countries. From 1960 to 2003, donor countries contributed $119 billion to IDA coffers. Over time the five largest IDA donor countries were Japan, the United States, Germany, the United Kingdom, and France, respectively. Other contributions come from IBRD and the regional development banks. The 13th replenishment, which concluded on June 2004, raised $23 billion to support IDA projects. The 14th replenishment, which spans the July 1, 2005 to June 30, 2008 period, provides an additional $34 billion to IDA coffers. In 2003, the top ten IDA borrowers were India, Bangladesh, the Democratic Republic of Congo, Uganda, Ethiopia, Vietnam, Pakistan, Tanzania, Sri Lanka, and Nigeria, respectively.

Non-governmental organizations (NGOs) and other stakeholders in the global economy have, at times, been critical of the IDA and the other institutions of the World Bank Group. Some criticism is directed at the structure of the World Bank Group, a structure that places the richer countries of the global North in the driver's seat. Others criticize the policies and practices of the World Bank and its affiliate institutions. For instance, mandated structural adjustment programs (SAPs) have been at the center of a global firestorm in recent years. Critics argue that inflexible SAPs have excluded local governments and members of civil society from key decisions that affect people's lives. Critics also contend that World Bank policies have advanced corporate interests over the interests of local workers, communities, and the natural environment.

See also **International Bank for Reconstruction and Development; International Centre for Settlement of Investment Disputes; International Finance Corporation; Multilateral Investment Guarantee Agency; World Bank Group.** ***See also in Volume 2,*** **Document 5.**

Further Reading

Ellerman, David. *Helping People Help Themselves: From the World Bank to an Alternative Philosophy of Development Assistance*. Ann Arbor, MI: University of Michigan Press, 2005.

Lele, Uma. *Addressing the Challenges of Globalization: An Independent Evaluation of the World Bank's Approach to Global Programs*. Washington, DC: World Bank Publications, 2005.

Paloni, Alberto. *Imf World Bank and Development*. New York: Routledge, 2005.

World Bank. *Africa and the World Bank: A Partnership for Development*. Washington, DC: Author, 2005.

———. *Young Person's Guide to the World Bank*. Washington, DC: Author, 2005.

INTERNATIONAL FINANCE CORPORATION

The International Finance Corporation (IFC) is a member-owned development institution that provides financing and technical assistance to private companies in the developing world. The IFC invests in commercially viable private firms to promote economic growth and sustainable economic development in the world's poorer regions. The IFC was founded in 1956, mainly to complement the development activities of the International Bank for Reconstruction and Development (IBRD). Today, the IFC, IBRD, the International Development Association (IDA), the International Centre for Settlement of Investment Disputes (ICSID), and the Multilateral Investment Guarantee Agency (MIGA) comprise the World Bank Group.

The IFC is a largely autonomous institution with its own articles of agreement, board of governors, and subscribed capital. Subscribed capital from donor countries totals $2.4 billion, nearly half of which comes from the United States, Japan, Germany, France, and the United Kingdom. IFC funds also come from interest payments on past loans and borrowing in international capital markets. The IFC's board of directors, which is comprised of IBRD's executive board, coordinates IFC activities with those of the World Bank Group. Between 1956 and 2005, IFC membership grew from 31 to 177 countries. IFC headquarters is located in Washington, DC, where a majority of its 2,200 staff is employed. The remainder of the IFC staff works in eighty-six field offices around the world.

The IFC supports private sector development in three main ways. First, the IFC provides direct financing to support start-up firms, and to facilitate business expansion of existing firms in developing countries. The IFC contributes up to one-quarter of the funds necessary for a project, relying on financial institutions, investors, and targeted firms to provide the remainder. IFC loans target businesses with high profit potential for investors, and high potential benefits for the host country. The IFC's private sector lending complements IBRD and IDA loans, which flow directly to governments. IFC financial commitments are normally in the $1 million to $100 million range.

The IFC also mobilizes other financial resources for businesses and offers technical advice to governments. IFC financing attracts additional domestic and foreign investors who, like the IFC, are constantly on the lookout for profitable investments. In addition, the IFC links local companies with lenders in global financial markets. IFC technical assistance helps businesses obtain financing, improve corporate governance, and advance the production, marketing, and distribution of the firm's output. IFC technical assistance helps governments create a sound business environment, develop local capital markets, privatize state-owned enterprises (SOEs), and attract foreign direct investment (FDI). In its *2004 Annual Report*, the IFC reported cumulative financial commitments to businesses totaling $44 billion since 1956. In addition, the IFC has helped firms tap into $23 billion in external financing. Since 1956, IFC financing has assisted over 3,000 companies in 140 developing countries.

In 2004, the IFC's total investment portfolio, which included all active loans and other financing throughout the developing world, totaled $18 billion. In

TABLE 67 **IFC Financial Commitments by World Region, 2004 ($ millions)**

World Region	New 2004 Commitments	Total Investment Portfolio
East Asia and the Pacific	$763	$2,897
Europe and Central Asia	$2,030	$4,554
Latin American and Caribbean	$1,593	$6,076
Middle East and North Africa	$236	$1,156
South Asia	$514	$1,529
Sub-Saharan Africa	$405	$1,603
Global*	$91	$124
World**	$5,633	$17,938

*Inter-regional commitments.
**Some rounding.
Source: International Finance Corporation, *2004 Annual Report*, 2.

2004 alone, the IFC made new financial commitments of $5.6 billion. Over 60 percent of the IFC's new 2004 commitments were dispersed to firms in five priority sectors, including finance and insurance (29.7 percent of all new commitments); utilities (13.1 percent); oil, gas, and mining (11.2 percent); information (5.5 percent); and industrial and consumer products (5.2 percent). Firms that operate in priority sectors tend to benefit large numbers of people, or offer significant spinoff benefits to other economic sectors. In addition, during the early 2000s, the IFC stepped up lending to firms in "frontier countries." Frontier countries are low-income developing countries or countries with low credit ratings. During the early 2000s, over 20 percent of IFC financing was earmarked for businesses in frontier countries. Table 67 summarizes the IFC's new 2004 commitments and its total active commitments in the global economy.

See also **International Bank for Reconstruction and Development; International Centre for Settlement of Investment Disputes; International Development Association; Multilateral Investment Guarantee Agency; World Bank Group.**

Further Reading

International Finance Corporation. *2004 Annual Report*. Washington, DC: Author, 2004.

———. *Scaling Up Private Sector Models for Poverty Reduction*. Washington, DC: Author, 2004.

———. *Sustainable Investment 2004*. Washington, DC: Author, 2004.

McClure, Paul, ed. *A Guide to the World Bank*. Washington, DC: World Bank Publications, 2003.

World Bank. *Assessing Development Assistance: Evaluation in the World Bank and the International Finance Corporation*. Washington, DC: Author, 1999.

INTERNATIONAL FINANCIAL INSTITUTIONS

International financial institutions (IFIs) are multilateral organizations and national agencies that use public funds to finance foreign investment, trade, and economic development. The three main categories of IFIs are the Bretton Woods institutions, regional development banks, and export credit agencies. The Bretton Woods institutions include the World Bank Group and the International Monetary Fund (IMF). The main regional development banks include the African Development Bank Group, Asian Development Bank, European Bank for Reconstruction and Development, and Inter-American Development Bank Group. All advanced economies, and some emerging market and developing economies have at least one government-controlled export credit agency (ECA) to promote foreign investment and trade. IFIs provide over $100 billion in loans, loan guarantees, grants, investment insurance, and other financing to governments and businesses each year.

The Bretton Woods institutions were established at the Bretton Woods Conference in 1944 to promote global economic growth and stability in the post–World War II period. The World Bank extends loans to support sustainable economic development. At its inception, the World Bank was a single institution called the International Bank for Reconstruction and Development (IBRD). The World Bank initially channeled development loans to war-ravaged Europe. The World Bank's mission changed course during the 1950s to accommodate the rising development needs of newly independent countries in Africa and Asia and other developing regions. Over time, IBRD spawned four affiliated institutions, collectively called the World Bank Group. Today, the five institutions of the World Bank Group make loans and grants and provide technical assistance and investment insurance to support the Millennium Development Goals (MDGs). The overarching MDG aim is global poverty reduction. IBRD loans money to creditworthy middle-income developing countries. IBRD's closest partner, the International Development Association (IDA), extends zero-interest, long-term loans to less creditworthy low-income and lower middle-income developing countries. The IBRD and IDA, which today comprise the World Bank, make development loans to governments. The World Bank's three affiliates also support the MDGs. The International Finance Corporation (IFC) makes loans to private businesses in the world's poorer regions. The International Centre for Settlement of Investment Disputes (ICSID) provides a mechanism for resolution of conflicts between foreign investors and host governments. The Multilateral Investment Guarantee Agency (MIGA) insures foreign investors from noncommercial losses that might be incurred in developing countries. The IFC, ICSID, and MIGA encourage private sector development, including foreign direct investment (FDI).

The International Monetary Fund (IMF) works to promote economic growth and stability in the global economy. The IMF's responsibilities are divided into three categories: financial assistance, technical assistance, and surveillance. Financial assistance includes IMF loans, known as credits, made to countries in need. IMF credits are used to help countries pay for imports, stabilize currencies, or service external debt. Technical assistance consists of policy advice the IMF offers to governments. Technical assistance promotes macroeconomic stability. IMF policy advice stresses good governance, institution building, banking regulation and supervision, and responsible monetary and fiscal policies. Surveillance deals with IMF consultations and oversight of nations' financial and economic policies. Surveillance seeks to identify weaknesses in public policies or institutions before serious problems arise. Surveillance assists the IMF in allocating its financial and technical assistance.

The second type of IFI is the regional development bank. A regional development bank extends development loans to poorer member countries within its region. Regional development banks are owned and operated by regional member countries and nonregional member countries. For example, the Asian

Development Bank consists of sixty-three member countries—forty-five regional member countries from Asia and the Pacific and eighteen nonregional countries from outside of Asia. The major regional development banks service the development needs of Africa, Asia, eastern and central Europe, and Latin American and the Caribbean.

A third type of IFI is the export credit agency (ECA). ECAs are typically government agencies that assist private companies finance trade or investment opportunities in other countries, especially the poorer countries. ECAs are bilateral agencies. That is, they deal one-on-one with foreign governments to encourage profitable export and investment venues for private firms. ECAs support export firms and transnational corporations (TNCs) through direct loans, loan guarantees, and investment insurance. All advanced economies, and some developing and emerging market economies, have ECAs to help domestic firms gain an upper hand in matters of trade or foreign investment. The amount of financial support that flows from nations' ECAs each year dwarfs the combined financial flows from the World Bank, IMF, and regional multilateral development banks. The Export-Import Bank of the United States, or Ex-Im Bank, is America's ECA. Over the past seventy years, the Em-Im Bank has financed export firms to the tune of $400 billion, $65 billion between 1999 and 2003 alone. Several other ECAs in the global economy include the Export Finance Insurance Corporation (Australia), Export Development Corporation (Canada), Hungarian Export-Import Bank (Hungary), Japan Bank for International Cooperation (Japan), Export Risk Guarantee (Switzerland), and the Export Credits Guarantee Department (United Kingdom). ECAs, like other IFIs, are highly controversial. Governments view ECAs as a way to stimulate foreign trade and investment and to protect domestic jobs. Opponents view ECAs, which often lack standards or stipulations for responsible corporate behaviors, as an invitation for business abuse of the environment, workers, and indigenous peoples.

See also **African Development Bank Group; Asian Development Bank; European Bank for Reconstruction and Development; Global Financial Architecture; Inter-American Development Bank Group; International Monetary Fund; Millennium Development Goals; Regional Development Banks; World Bank Group. *See also in Volume 2,* Document 7.**

Further Reading

Delphos, William A. *Inside the World's Export Credit Agencies*. Cincinnati, OH: South-Western Educational Pub, 2003.

International Business Publications USA. *US Export-Import Bank Handbook*. Washington, DC: Author, 2005.

McClure, Paul, ed. *A Guide to the World Bank*. Washington, DC: World Bank Publications, 2003.

Upton, Barbara. *The Multilateral Development Banks: Improving U.S. Leadership*. Westport, CT: Praeger, 2000.

Vreeland, James R. *The IMF and Economic Development*. New York: Cambridge University Press, 2003.

INTERNATIONAL INVESTMENT AGREEMENTS

An international investment agreement (IIA) is a bilateral or multilateral treaty that establishes the rules, procedures, or responsibilities of parties involved in a cross-border investment. Bilateral investment treaties (BITs) and double taxation treaties (DTTs) are the most common types of IIA.

BITs are mainly designed to promote FDI by protecting the assets and profits of transnational corporations (TNCs). BITs are negotiated between two countries, mainly to make foreign direct investments by TNCs more secure. The first BIT was negotiated between Germany and Pakistan in 1959. Most BITs have common provisions. First, BITs require equal treatment of foreign firms in host countries. The principle of national treatment prevents local governments from imposing discriminatory taxes or selective rules or regulations on foreign firms. Second, BITs guarantee the security of foreign investments from noncommercial losses. Host governments are responsible for financial losses that result from the nationalization of TNC properties, or from the ruinous effects of civil unrest or other forms of domestic violence. Third, BITs protect the right of TNCs to transfer corporate funds, including business profits from the host country to the home country. Fourth, BITs require international arbitration to settle investment disputes between a TNC and a host government. The International Centre for Settlement of Investment Disputes (ICSID), one of five institutions of the World Bank Group, is often selected to arbitrate investment disputes. The use of BITs accelerated during the 1980s, 1990s, and early 2000s. Initially, most BITs were negotiated between advanced economies and developing countries. The main goal was to protect the assets of TNCs in the poorer regions of the world. In more recent years, many developing countries have also negotiated BITs to develop profitable South-South commercial ties. South-South cooperation involves economic or financial relations among the countries of the global South. Between 1990 and 2003, the number of BITS quintupled, from 446 to 2,265, as shown in Figure 27.

Another type of bilateral investment treaty is the double taxation treaty (DTT). A DTT is negotiated between two governments to equitably tax the wealth or income generated by overseas investments. DTTs seek to avoid taxing the same money twice. The treatment of wages or salaries, dividend and interest income, capital gains, and royalty payments are often considered in DTTs. DTTs promote tax fairness in the global economy. They also encourage traditional FDI and investments in global financial markets. Between 1990 and 2003, the number of DTTs between nations nearly doubled, from 1,193 to 2,316, as shown in Figure 27.

Recent efforts to create a multilateral investment treaty have failed. The Organization for Economic Cooperation and Development (OECD), an organization that consists mainly of the advanced economies, initiated negotiations during the mid-1990s to frame a Multilateral Agreement on Investment (MAI). The goal of the proposed MAI was to establish a uniform investment regime that supported investment liberalization. The MAI was supported mainly by the advanced economies such as the United States, Canada, Japan, and the European

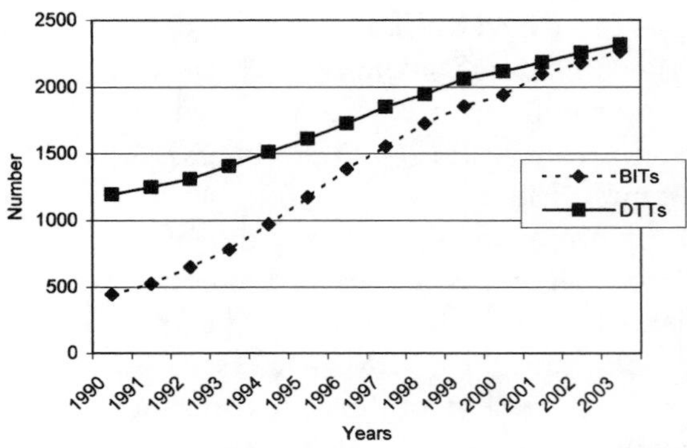

FIGURE 27 **BITs and DTTs in the Global Economy, 1990 to 2003**

Sources: United Nations Conference on Trade and Development (UNCTAD), BITs and DTT databases; UNCTAD, *World Investment Report 2004*, 6.

Union countries. The MAI pushed for national treatment, asset protections, profit repatriation, and international dispute settlement. Many emerging market and developing economies, and nongovernmental organizations (NGOs), opposed the MAI. Led by China, India, and Malaysia, developing countries and NGOs blocked the MAI. Poorer countries feared rigid MAI investment rules would restrict their ability to adapt investment policies to meet national development goals. NGOs opposed the special benefits extended to major TNCs. NGOs balked at the costs of investment liberalization, especially costs to the environment, workers, and local cultures. By the late 1990s, most serious discussions of a MAI were all but abandoned.

See also **Foreign Direct Investment; International Centre for Settlement of Investment Disputes; Transnational Corporations.**

Further Reading

Bennekom, Sander van. *The Multilateral Agreement on Investment (MAI)—Making the World Safe for Multinationals*. New York: Zed Books, 2000.

Crawford, James, and Karen Lee. *ICSIC Reports: Volume 6*. New York: Cambridge University Press, 2004.

Sornarajah, M. *The International Law on Foreign Investment*. New York: Cambridge University Press, 2004.

United Nations Conference on Trade and Development. *International Investment Agreements: Flexibility for Development*. New York: United Nations Publications, 2001.

World Bank. *World Development Report 2005: A Better Investment Climate for Everyone*. Washington, DC: Author, 2004.

INTERNATIONAL LABOR ORGANIZATION

The International Labor Organization (ILO) is an international organization that promotes worker rights and decent work in the global economy. The ILO is not an international labor union. Instead, the ILO is a specialized agency of the United Nations system. It brings workers, employers, and governments together to discuss ways to improve workers' quality of life. Collaboration among the three groups—workers, employers, and governments—is often called the ILO's tripartite partnership.

The ILO is the world's oldest and most recognized international authority on labor issues, and the most powerful voice for global justice for working men and women. The ILO was established in 1919 under the Treaty of Versailles, largely to support decent work for millions of workers in the post–World War I world. In 1946, the ILO became the first specialized agency within the new

United Nations system. Since this time, the ILO has initiated numerous conventions and recommendations to set global standards for workers' rights, and to influence labor laws and practices by companies and governments. From 1919 to 2005 ILO membership more than quadrupled from 42 to 178 countries. The ILO headquarters is located in Geneva, Switzerland. The ILO also maintains thirty-three field offices around the world.

The International Labor Organization promotes decent work for all laborers, skilled and unskilled.
Courtesy of Getty Images: John A. Rizzo

The Governing Body and the International Labor Conference are the ILO's two main decision-making groups. The Governing Body coordinates ILO programs and activities, assists countries develop labor laws, monitors compliance with labor standards, and disseminates the results of labor research to the global community. The Governing Body also advises the director-general, the ILO's chief executive. The Governing Body consists of forty-six members: fourteen representing workers, fourteen representing businesses, and twenty-eight representing governments. Some advanced economies hold permanent seats on the Governing Body. The annual International Labor Conference, or Conference, is a global decision-making forum. The Conference passes all conventions and recommendations. A convention is a formal, binding labor standard, right, or protection. Signatory nations are expected to uphold ILO conventions by passing legislation or imposing regulations to support labor standards. A recommendation is a less formal ILO statement. Recommendations set guidelines for desirable labor practices or conditions. Each of the 178 member nations has four delegates in the Conference—one worker representative, one employer representative, and two government representatives. Since 1919, the ILO has passed 184 conventions and numerous recommendations. In the early 2000s, the Governing Body was actively promoting just seventy-one conventions. Of the remaining 113 conventions, 5 were discarded and 108 were under review.

In the early 2000s, the ILO identified eight "fundamental conventions" as pivotal to workers' well-being in the global economy. These key conventions are listed in the ILO's *Promoting Better Working Conditions: A Guide to the International Labor Standards System* (2003). Conventions No. 87 and No. 98 protect workers' freedom of association and right to bargain collectively with employers. Conventions No. 29 and No. 105 prohibit forced labor as a form of punishment for workers' political views or labor activities, or as an expression of any form of discrimination. Conventions No. 100 and No. 111 ban discrimination in wages, employment, training, and working conditions based on race, gender, religion, or political views. Conventions No. 138 and No. 182 prohibit child labor, especially the more vile forms of child exploitation such as child prostitution. Four additional conventions were selected as "priority conventions" to strengthen key policy protocols. Priority conventions promote decent employment, global oversight of labor standards, and cooperative tripartite consultations among workers, employers, and governments.

The ILO's Declaration on Fundamental Principles and Rights at Work (1998) is the centerpiece for global labor reform. The principles outlined in the declaration are gleaned from earlier conventions, and include the right to free association and collective bargaining, and prohibitions against forced labor, child labor, and discrimination. Many corporate "codes of conduct" are rooted in the declaration's principles. Government labor laws and regulations are often based on ILO conventions. By 2004, governments had ratified over 7,000 ILO conventions. In addition, multilateral institutions are influenced by ILO conventions. Consultations with the United Nations Development Program, UNESCO, the World Bank, International Monetary Fund, and Organization for Economic Cooperation and Development, have spread the gospel of decent work throughout the global economy.

The goal of decent work for the global labor force is challenged by economic globalization, and by the unique political and economic environments in some countries. For example, globalization encourages trade and investment liberalization. Some of the world's poorest nations have relaxed labor and environmental standards to court foreign direct investment (FDI). Lower standards weaken worker rights and protections, particularly at the bottom of the supply chain where workers are most vulnerable. The ILO continues to monitor gross violations of labor rights in countries such as China, Colombia, Venezuela, and Myanmar (Burma). The ILO, labor organizations, and others, fear that substandard labor conditions in some countries could snowball into a more generalized global race to the bottom in the highly competitive global economy.

See also **Corporate Social Responsibility; Race to the Bottom; Supply Chains; Transnational Corporations; United Nations System.** ***See also in Volume 2,*** **Documents 29, 33, 34, 35, 36, 37, 38, 52, 53.**

Further Reading

Basu, Kaushik, Henrik Horn, Lisa Roman, and Judith Shapiro. *International Labor Standards: History, Theory, and Policy Decisions*. Malden, MA: Blackwell Publishers, 2003.

International Labor Organization. *Fair Globalization: The Role of the ILO*. Geneva, Switzerland: Author, 2004.

———. *A Future without Child Labour: ILO Global Report under the Follow-up to the Declaration on Fundamental Principles and Rights at Work*. Geneva, Switzerland: Author, 2002.

———. *Promoting Better Working Conditions: A Guide to the International Labor Standards System*. Washington, DC: ILO Washington Office, 2003.

La Cruz, Hector B., et al. *The International Labor Organization: The International Standards System and Basic Human Rights*. Boulder, CO: Westview Press, 1996.

INTERNATIONAL MONETARY FUND

The International Monetary Fund (IMF) is an international financial institution (IFI) designed to promote global economic stability, growth, and development. The IMF, often called the Fund, was founded at the Bretton Woods Conference, in New Hampshire, in the summer of 1944. The IMF's Articles of Agreement was approved in December of 1945, and the Fund's operations began in May 1946. The IMF and the World Bank, which was also founded at the Bretton Woods Conference, are often called the Bretton Woods institutions. The IMF and the World Bank became specialized agencies with the United Nations system in 1946. In 2005, the IMF consisted of 184 member nations. Its headquarters is located in Washington, DC, and its 2,700 employees live and work in over 100 countries. The IMF, World Bank, and World Trade Organization (WTO) are viewed as the Big Three international organizations that oversee the global economy.

The board of governors is the IMF's highest decision-making body. The board of governors is comprised of one governor from each member country. A governor is typically a country's finance minister or the head of its central bank. The board of governors convenes once each year at the joint IMF-World Bank Annual Meeting. Governors discuss IMF policies and priorities. The governors grant most decision-making authority to run the Fund to the executive board. The executive board consists of twenty-four members who meet regularly on IMF business. China, France, Germany, Japan, Russia, Saudi Arabia, the United Kingdom, and the United States, hold permanent seats on the executive board. The other sixteen seats are delegated to groupings of member nations. The managing director is the top official and spokesperson for the Fund, and is also the chairperson of the executive board. Most IMF decisions are made by consensus. If a formal vote is necessary, each member nation casts its votes. The number of votes each Fund member receives is in rough proportion to the size of its economy. In 2005, the United States held 17.1 percent of the IMF's voting power, or 371,743 total votes. The G8 countries, which include Canada, France, Germany, Italy, Japan, Russia, the United Kingdom, and the United States, controlled nearly one-half of all votes.

Most of the IMF's financial resources are raised through quota subscriptions, often called quotas. A quota is assigned to each Fund member. One-quarter of a member's quota is paid in a hard currency, such as the U.S. dollar or the euro, or in Special Drawing Rights (SDRs), the IMF's unit of account. The other three-quarters of the quota can be paid in the member's national currency. Quotas are assigned based on the size of an economy. Larger economies have higher quotas and smaller economies have lower quotas. The United States is the Fund's largest donor, contributing over $37 billion since 1946. The G8 countries account for about one-half of all subscribed capital. In February 2005, the Fund's total subscribed capital was $327 billion (SDR 213 billion). Interest payments on past IMF loans are a smaller component of IMF revenues. Revenues from interest payments are usually sufficient to cover the Fund's administrative costs. The Fund can also borrow money to cover budget shortfalls or crisis situations. Through its New Arrangements to Borrow (NAB), the Fund can quickly tap financial resources from twenty-six member nations.

IMF resources are used to stabilize the global economic and financial systems, and promote sustainable growth and development. The IMF pursues these goals in three ways—surveillance, technical assistance, and financial assistance. First, surveillance seeks to identify and address vulnerabilities in an economy. It involves consultations with local authorities and the monitoring of nations' domestic economic policies. Surveillance is mainly concerned with weaknesses in a nation's macroeconomic stabilization policies, currency stability, external debt, banking and financial systems, trade policy, and corporate governance. Second, technical assistance provides training, consultation, and other advice to strengthen nations' economic and financial institutions. Technical assistance is usually provided free of charge. It seeks to strengthen tax policies, monetary and fiscal policies, exchange rate policies, financial institutions, and data collection and analysis processes. Technical assistance can be short term, measured in weeks, or long term, measured in years. Third, financial assistance supplies money to economies plagued by balance of payments problems. IMF lending helps nations pay for imported goods, service foreign debt, or stabilize fragile currencies. Financial assistance also targets needed structural reforms in nations' financial or economic systems. IMF loans are dispersed in installments to ensure that necessary reforms are implemented over time.

The IMF is a major international financial institution (IFI) in today's global economy. In 2004, the Fund reported outstanding loans of $97 billion spread across eighty-four countries. Most of the $97 billion in outstanding loans were geared toward short-term balance of payments problems. Borrowers paid prevailing interest rates on these short-term non-concessional loans. In 2004, $87 billion in the IMF's total loan portfolio was comprised of non-concessional loans. In September 2004, these loans carried a 3.15 percent interest rate. Concessional loans were extended to certain low-income developing countries. Concessional loans have a lower interest rate and a longer maturity period than non-concessional loans. In 2004, the IMF's total outstanding loan portfolio included $10 billion in concessional lending, which was spread across fifty-nine countries. In September 2004, concessional loans carried a 0.5 percent interest rate.

The IMF and World Bank have co-sponsored the Heavily Indebted Poor Countries (HIPC) Initiative. The HIPC Initiative was established in 1996 and enhanced in 1999. It is designed to reduce the burden of external debt from the world's poorest economies. By 2004, twenty-seven low-income countries had qualified to receive debt relief under the HIPC Initiative—a sum expected to hit $54 billion over time. Eleven additional low-income countries had yet to meet IMF and World Bank requirements for debt relief. The HIPC Initiative has been controversial since its inception. Some non-governmental organizations (NGOs), such as Jubilee 2000, proposed debt forgiveness as an alternative strategy to remove the burden of unsustainable external debt from certain low-income nations.

The IMF has received its share of criticism in recent years. NGOs, civil society organizations (CSOs), and others have been critical of the Fund's structure, which puts most of the voting power into the hands of a few rich nations. Critics have questioned the IMF's staunch support for trade liberalization and other aspects of globalization. Some critics argue the IMF is ill-equipped to deal with major financial crises, such as the Asian Financial Crisis of 1997–1998, and unwilling to provide adequate debt relief for the world's poorest people. Anti-globalization demonstrations routinely targeted the leading symbols of globalization, including meetings of the IMF, World Bank, and World Trade Organization (WTO) during the early 2000s.

See also **Bretton Woods System; Civil Society Organizations; External Debt; Financial Contagion; Heavily Indebted Poor Countries (HIPC) Initiative; International Bank for Reconstruction and Development; International Development Association; International Financial Institutions; Non-Governmental Organizations; World Bank Group; World Trade Organization.**

Further Reading

Fischer, Stanley. *IMF Essays from a Time of Crisis: The International Financial System, Stabilization, and Development*. Cambridge, MA: MIT Press, 2004.

IMF Independent Evaluation Office. *Evaluation of Prolonged Use of Imf Resources*. Washington, DC: International Monetary Fund, 2003.

Paloni, Alberto. *Imf, World Bank and Development*. New York: Routledge, 2005.

Thirkell-White, Ben. *IMF and the Politics of Financial Globalization: From the Asian Crisis to a New International Financial Architecture*. New York: Palgrave Macmillan, 2005.

Vines, David, and Christopher L. Gilbert. *The IMF and Its Critics: Reform of Global Financial Architecture*. New York: Cambridge University Press, 2004.

INTERNATIONAL TRADE

International trade is the cross-border exchange of goods or services. International trade occurs when an individual, business, government, or other entity imports or exports products. An import is a product that is purchased from another country, while an export is a product that is sold to another country. The benefits of international trade are built on the principle of mutual benefit and the theory of comparative advantage. The principle of mutual benefit emphasizes the benefits received by both parties in a voluntary exchange. Trade expands the range of consumer choice, and also sparks technological advance, innovation, and entrepreneurship in competitive global markets. The theory of comparative advantage, which was popularized by David Ricardo nearly two centuries ago, stresses regional specialization to promote production efficiency. International trade is viewed as a major pillar of globalization in today's global economy. In 2004, total global trade, measured by global exports, was $11 trillion.

Since World War II, trade liberalization has encouraged international trade. Trade liberalization refers to the reduction or elimination of trade barriers such as import quotas, tariffs, and a variety of non-tariff trade barriers. Since the mid-1940s, the International Monetary Fund (IMF) and the World Bank, often called the Bretton Woods institutions, have supported free trade to stimulate global economic growth and stability. In addition, the General Agreement on Tariffs and Trade (GATT) worked to liberalize trade from 1948 to 1994. Eight GATT trade rounds dismantled many trade barriers during the period. The World Trade Organization (WTO), GATT's successor organization, has strengthened the institutional framework for free trade since 1995. The WTO's core principles include most favored nation (MFN), which extends a trade concession granted to one WTO member to all member nations; national treatment, which guarantees equal treatment of foreign and domestic goods in markets; and transparency, which requires the timely reporting of new or existing trade barriers.

Regional trade agreements have also encouraged free trade in the post-war global economy. A regional trade agreement (RTA) creates a trade bloc. Member countries within a trade bloc reduce or eliminate trade barriers. The WTO identified nearly 300 bilateral and multilateral RTAs in the global economy in 2005. The four types of RTAs include the free trade area (FTA),

Free trade policies promote international trade. Global exports reached $11 trillion in 2004.

Courtesy of Getty Images: Andy Sotiriou

customs union, common market, and economic and monetary union. An FTA is a trade bloc that eliminates trade barriers among member nations, but allows members to determine their own trade policies with non-member countries. The North American Free Trade Agreement (NAFTA) is the world's leading FTA. A customs union establishes an FTA and common trade policies, such as the common external tariff (CET), with non-member countries. The Andean Community is a customs union. A common market combines the qualities of a customs union with deeper economic integration among member nations, including free cross-border flows of resources and investments. An economic and monetary union is the highest form of economic integration. The European Union (EU) is an economic and monetary union with a common currency—the euro—and common policies on dealing with banking, labor, energy, foreign aid, foreign policy and security, and so on.

The global trading system represents the sum total of international trade and the institutions and practices that influence cross-border exchanges of goods and services. Exchanges in the global trading system increased dramatically in recent years. The WTO reported a doubling of global exports from 1994 to 2004, from $5.4 trillion to $11 trillion. In 2004, merchandise exports totaled $8.9 trillion and commercial services exports totaled $2.1 trillion. Ranked by value of exports, the top three world regions in the global trading system during the early 2000s were Western Europe, Asia, and North America, as shown in Figure 28 ("other" includes Africa, central and eastern Europe, the Commonwealth of Independent States, Latin America, and the Middle East). The world's top five exporting and importing nations are shown in Table 68.

The balance of trade measures the difference between the value of a country's imports and exports. A country's balance of trade rarely settles at a break-even point, a position in which the value of its imports and exports is equal. Instead, most countries experience a trade deficit or a trade surplus. A trade deficit occurs when the value of a country's imports is greater than its exports. A trade surplus occurs when the value of a country's exports is greater than its imports. The United States has incurred trade deficits since the mid-1970s. The U.S. Commerce Department reported a 2004 trade deficit of $617 billion. The overall U.S. trade deficit consisted of a $666 billion merchandise trade deficit, and a $49 billion trade surplus in commercial services ($666 billion − $49 billion = $617 billion). Other countries, such as Germany, Japan, and Russia, recorded significant trade surpluses in the early 2000s. Table 69 shows the trade balances of G8 countries in 2003.

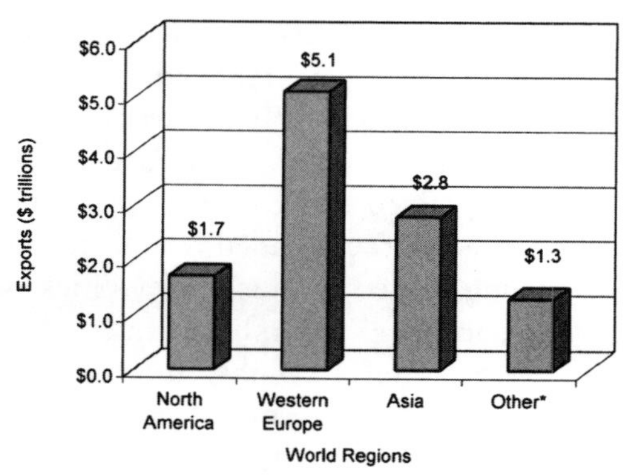

FIGURE 28 **International Trade (Exports) by World Region, 2004 ($ trillions)**

Source: World Trade Organization, *World Trade 2004, Prospects for 2005*, April 14, 2005, 13–14.

TABLE 68 **Top Exporting and Importing Nations, 2004**

Top Exporters			Top Importers		
Rank	Country	Value ($ billions)	Rank	Country	Value ($ billions)
1	United States	$1,138	1	United States	$1,785
2	Germany	$1,041	2	Germany	$909
3	Japan	$659	3	China	$631
4	China	$652	4	Britain	$597
5	France	$559	5	Japan	$589

Source: World Trade Organization, *World Trade 2004, Prospects for 2005*, 14 April 2005, 13–14.

TABLE 69 **Trade Deficits and Surpluses of the G8 Countries, 2003 ($ billions)**

G8 Countries	Total Exports	Total Imports	Trade Balance
Trade surplus			
Canada	$314.6	$295.0	+$19.6
France	$485.6	$474.2	+$11.4
Germany	$863.9	$772.5	+$91.4
Japan	$542.4	$493.2	+$49.2
Russia	$150.3	$100.7	+$49.6
Balanced trade			
Italy	$364.8	$364.8	–
Trade deficit			
United Kingdom	$448.0	$509.1	−$61.6
United States	$1,011.5	$1,531.6	−$520.1

Source: World Trade Organization, *International Trade Statistics 2004*, 19, 21.

Trade liberalization promotes sustainable growth and development in some countries. During the early 2000s, however, there were challenges to an equitable, universally accessible global trading system. First, the expanded use of anti-dumping measures restricted fair and free trade. Anti-dumping measures were often a form of backdoor protectionism designed to sidestep existing WTO prohibitions against tariffs and non-tariff trade barriers. Second, rising global competitiveness threatened decent work for low-skilled labor. Competitiveness depressed some wages, especially wages in the poorest countries, and contributed to the dreaded race to the bottom. Third, offshoring and production sharing shifted production facilities and jobs from high-wage countries to low-wage countries. Liberalized trade and investment regimes contributed to the export of capital and jobs, and lowered the standard of living for some households. Fourth, the terms of trade turned against producers of primary commodities such as sugar, natural rubber, cocoa, and coffee. Depressed commodity prices contributed to trade deficits, and balance of payments problems, in some poorer nations. Fifth, the lack of global connectivity in poorer world regions excluded the least developed countries (LDCs) from sharing in the benefits of globalization. To advance global prosperity for all countries, international trade must be fair and inclusive.

See also **Absolute Advantage; Andean Community; Balance of Payments; Balance of Trade; Bhagwati, Jagdish; Comparative Advantage; Dumping; European Union; Exports; General Agreement on Tariffs and Trade; Global Economy; Globalization; Imports; North American Free Trade Agreement; Offshoring; Protectionism; Race to the Bottom; Regional Trade Agreements; Ricardo, David; Terms of Trade; World Trade Organization.** ***See also in Volume 2,*** **Documents 9, 11, 12, 14, 17, 18, 19, 20, 21, 27, 50.**

Further Reading

Das, Dilip K. *Regionalism in Global Trade*. Northampton, MA: Edward Elgar Publishing, 2004.

Irwin, Douglas, A. *Free Trade under Fire*. 2d ed. Princeton, NJ: Princeton University Press, 2005.

Landau, Alice. *The International Trade System*. New York: Routledge, 2005.

Shafaeddin, Mehdi. *Trade Policy at the Crossroads: The Recent Experience of Developing Countries*. New York: Palgrave Macmillan, 2005.

World Trade Organization. *International Trade Statistics 2004*. Geneva, Switzerland: Author, 2004.

 J

JOSEPH, KEITH S.

Keith S. Joseph (1918–1994) was a leading British economist and champion of free-market economics. During the 1970s and 1980s, Joseph was instrumental in reversing the global drift toward democratic socialism. Joseph was born to a wealthy London family. The son of privilege, Joseph received a top-notch education, and graduated from Oxford College shortly before the outbreak of World War II. After the war, Joseph won election to a number of positions, including a seat in Parliament. Joseph's capable defense of conservatism, including merits of free enterprise, brought him into the national limelight during the 1970s. Teaming with another rising star, Margaret Thatcher, Joseph founded a free enterprise think-tank called the Centre for Policy Studies (CPS) in 1974. The CPS exposed the inherent weaknesses of democratic socialism, and advocated free-market solutions to the United Kingdom's growing economic problems. The election of Margaret Thatcher to the position of Prime Minister (1979), and the subsequent capitalist counterrevolution in Britain, was largely built on Joseph's ideas and presence.

Through the CPS, Joseph worked tirelessly to overcome three decades of statism, which he blamed for the nation's economic woes. Statism is an economic philosophy that supports aggressive government intervention in the economy. For decades, statism was the cornerstone of the Labour Party's political agenda, which included the nationalization of key industries, costly "cradle to grave" public welfare programs, and a bloated public sector. Joseph, Thatcher, and other Conservatives openly challenged Labour's economic policies and the oppressive tax system needed to finance these programs. Paralyzing labor strikes, double-digit inflation, and massive unemployment helped the Conservatives wrest control of the government from the ruling Labour Party by the late 1970s.

Joseph offered a free enterprise alternative to statism. As Prime Minister Thatcher's top economic advisor, Joseph was the chief architect of the capitalist counterrevolution of the 1980s. At the heart of the counterrevolution were supply-side theories advocating entrepreneurship, investment, and production. Joseph reasoned that more production meant more jobs, higher wages, and more profits for prudent investors. Joseph proposed government downsizing, dismantling the welfare state, tax cuts, privatization of state-owned industries, and containment of powerful labor unions. He believed these policies would restore incentives to work, save, invest, and produce. His policies also targeted Britain's pervasive dependency culture, a costly legacy of the welfare state.

Keith S. Joseph was a key figure in the economic transformation of the United Kingdom from democratic socialism to free-market capitalism during the final quarter of the twentieth century.

See also **Capitalism; Democratic Socialism; Market Economy; Pigou, Arthur C.**

Further Reading

Denham, Andrew, and Mark Garnett. *Keith Joseph*. Chesham, UK: Acumen, 2001.

Halcrow, Morrison. *Keith Joseph: A Single Mind*. London: MacMillan London, 1989.

Joseph, Keith. *Conditions for Fuller Employment*. London: Centre for Policy Studies, 1978.

———. *Stranded on the Middle Ground? Reflections on Circumstances and Policies*. London: Centre for Policy Studies, 1976.

K

KEYNES, JOHN MAYNARD

John Maynard Keynes (1883–1946) was an influential British economist, teacher, and author. Keynes is best known for his stabilization theories, and his leadership at the Bretton Woods Conference in 1944. Keynes was born to a prominent intellectual family in Cambridge, England. He attended Eton, and later graduated from Cambridge University. After graduation, Keynes pursued a number of careers in the British civil service and academia. By the 1920s, Keynes had already earned an international reputation, largely through his controversial *The Economic Consequences of Peace* (1919). In his most famous book, *The General Theory of Employment, Interest, and Money* (1936), Keynes proposed government intervention in an economy to counteract downturns in the business cycle. Keynes was also a dominant figure at the Bretton Woods Conference, which shaped the post–World War II global financial architecture.

The controversial Keynes published *The General Theory* during the depths of a global depression, called the Great Depression in the United States. In *The General Theory*, Keynes rejected orthodox laissez-faire economic doctrine, which maintained economic slumps were self-correcting. Instead, Keynes argued that economic downturns were the result of insufficient aggregate demand, and that market forces alone were not sufficient to end sluggish business investment and consumer spending. To Keynes, the solution to inadequate aggregate demand was government intervention in the economy. He proposed government injections of money into the economy, mainly through greater federal spending. Keynes supported government borrowing, and the resulting budget deficits, to jump-start aggregate demand and economic growth. Keynes's views reshaped the economic landscape in some industrialized countries. In the United States, President Franklin D. Roosevelt (FDR) embraced the Keynesian Revolution during the Great Depression. FDR increased federal spending on public works jobs, construction projects, and business subsidies to stimulate business activity.

Keynes was also a chief architect of the Bretton Woods System. Keynes led the British delegation at the Bretton Woods Conference in 1944. Keynes, and Harry D. White, who headed the U.S. delegation, dominated the proceedings. While there were differences between the American and British positions, Keynes and White shared a common vision for global stability and prosperity. The Bretton Woods sister institutions, the World Bank and the International Monetary Fund (IMF), were founded at the Conference. The World Bank and IMF were designed to support a more predictable, cooperative, and secure world economy. While each of the sister institutions conformed more to U.S. proposals than to the British view, Keynes saw the utility of each; the IMF as the main vehicle for exchange rate and balance of payments stability, and the World Bank as the vehicle for productive investment in needy countries.

The delegates to the Bretton Woods Conference also agreed on a fixed exchange rate system. Under the fixed exchange rate system, the value of the U.S. dollar was set at $35 per ounce of gold, and the value of national currencies were fixed to either the U.S. dollar or to gold. The fixed exchange rate system brought some financial order to world limping out of a global war. Keynes's consistent appeal for free trade, and a responsible multilateral approach to global economic problem solving, legitimized the work of the Conference. Keynes died in 1946, the same year the World Bank and IMF commenced their daunting task of post-war reconstruction.

See also **Bretton Woods System; Business Cycle; Capitalism; Foreign Exchange Market; Global Financial Architecture; International Bank for Reconstruction and Development; International Monetary Fund.** ***See also in Volume 2,*** **Document 17.**

Further Reading

Boughton, James M. *Why White, Not Keynes? Inventing the Postwar International Monetary System*. Washington, DC: International Monetary Fund, 2002.

Dow, Sheila C., and John Hillard. *Keynes, Uncertainty and the Global Economy: Beyond Keynes, Volume Two*. Northampton, MA: Edward Elgar Publishing, 2002.

Keynes, John M. *The End of Laissez-Faire, the Economic Consequences of Peace*. Amherst, NY: Prometheus Books, 2004.

———. *The General Theory of Employment, Interest, and Money*. Rev. ed. Amherst, NY: Prometheus Books, 1997.

Skidelsky, Robert. *John Maynard Keynes: Fighting for Freedom, 1937–1946*. New York: Penguin, 2002.

KRUGMAN, PAUL R.

Paul R. Krugman (1953–) is an American international economist and author. Krugman, and colleague Elhanan Helpman, developed the "new trade theory," a refinement of David Ricardo's famous theory of comparative advantage. Krugman was born in Long Island, New York, the only son of a middle-class family. He earned his bachelor's degree in economics from Yale University in 1974 and his doctorate from MIT in 1977. Krugman's first teaching position as a professional economist was at Yale, where the idea of the "new trade theory" began to crystallize. Krugman also taught at MIT, Stanford, and most recently at Princeton. Of the twenty books authored or co-authored by Krugman, none made a bigger splash than *Market Structure and Foreign Trade: Increasing Returns, Imperfect Competition, and the International Economy* (1985), and *Trade Policy and Market Structure* (1989), each co-authored by Elhanan Helpman.

In *Market Structure and Foreign Trade* (1985), Krugman and Helpman developed the "new trade theory," a theory that complements rather than replaces the Ricardo's time-honored theory of comparative advantage. The new trade theory stresses the role of economies of scale, and imperfect competition, in international trade. The new trade theory accents the benefits of economies of scale. Economies of scale occur when a large firm is able to lower its average production costs as the firm increases its rate of output. Nations that support research and development (R&D), innovation, and investment encourage large-scale production and economies of scale. Thus, even when nations have similar endowments of resources, and no apparent comparative advantage exists, economies of scale tilt the balance in favor of the high-volume producer. Economies of scale encourage specialization and make the high-volume producer more competitive in global markets.

The new trade theory also accounts for the reality of different market structures in the global economy. Krugman and Helpman recognized the importance of imperfectly competitive industries, including monopolistic competition and oligopoly, in the global arena. Imperfectly competitive industries, by definition, have some degree of market power due to product differentiation and significant barriers to entry. Product differentiation helps explain why producers of similar products, such as automobiles, engage in lively cross-border intra-industry trade. On a broader scale, the new trade theory explains why similar countries, particularly the advanced industrialized countries, trade with one another. The reality of imperfectly competitive markets distinguishes the new trade theory from traditional theories built around the single market structure of perfect competition.

In *Trade Policy and Market Structure* (1989), Krugman and Helpman identified policy implications for the new trade theory. First, given the realities of the global marketplace there may be instances in which "mild protectionism" could promote national economic objectives, such as rapid industrialization or economic growth. Mild protectionism might include temporary subsidies or tariffs to support selected industries. Second, the new trade theory supported free trade as the basis of international exchange. Krugman and Helpman warned against the misuse of the new trade theory to justify a reckless, self-serving protectionist agenda. The specter of retaliation by other countries is a check on inappropriate or excessive protectionism.

Since the 1980s, Krugman's interests have extended into other areas of public policy. In his books, and in columns for major publications such as *Fortune*, *Slate*, and *The New York Times*, Krugman plies his trade with vigor, offering viewpoints on a wide variety of topics. In 1991, Krugman earned the prestigious John Bates Clark Medal, a biennial honor bestowed by the American Economic Association to the nation's most gifted young economist.

See also **Comparative Advantage; International Trade; Protectionism; Ricardo, David.**

Further Reading

Helpman, Elhanan, and Paul R. Krugman. *Market Structure and Foreign Trade: Increasing Returns, Imperfect Competition, and the International Economy.* Cambridge, MA: MIT Press, 1985.

———. *Trade Policy and Market Structure.* Cambridge, MA: MIT Press, 1989.

Krugman, Paul R., and Maurice Obstfeld. *International Economics: Theory and Policy*. 7th ed. Reading, MA: Addison Wesley, 2005.

———, Alan Tonelson, and Charles R. Carlisle. *The New Trade Agenda*. New York: Council on Foreign Relations Press, 2001.

KUZNETS, SIMON

Simon Kuznets (1901–1985) was an American economist, widely recognized for his pioneering work in national income and product accounting and in development economics. Kuznets was born in Kharkiv, Russia. He immigrated to the United States in 1922, and earned his doctorate at Columbia in 1926. Kuznets's professional career integrated statistical research with teaching and writing. He joined the staff of the National Bureau of Economic Research (NBER) in 1927, a position he held for more than three decades. As a member of NBER, Kuznets was involved in the collection and analysis of macroeconomic data. Later in his career, Kuznets delved into the field of development economics. Kuznets held prestigious teaching positions at the University of Pennsylvania (1931–1954), Johns Hopkins University (1954–1960), and Harvard University (1960–1971).

Kuznets is renowned for the meticulous collection and analysis of statistical data related to national output and national income. His studies helped explain the process of economic growth and economic development, and the occurrence of business cycles in market economies. In his most famous book, *National Income and Its Composition, 1919–1938* (1941), Kuznets identified key features of national income and product accounts. He stressed "consistency and explicitness" in data collection. Even so, he recognized limitations in estimating aggregate output, or the gross national product (GNP). He excluded from GNP certain immeasurable goods and services provided outside of the market system, including the value of homemakers' labor and business activity in the informal economy. GNP calculations also excluded the value of leisure. Kuznets, the acknowledged father of GNP, established the primary framework for measuring nations' economic performance, identifying business cycles, and comparing relative well-being of people in different countries.

Kuznets's interest in the field of economic development broadened his contributions to economic science. He influenced "development economics," a strand of economic theory that was still in its infancy during the 1950s and 1960s. Development economics deals with the process of economic growth and sustainable development, mainly in the poorer world regions. Kuznets concluded that economic development was not a uniform process. He dismissed prevailing linear development theories, which argued that nations' must progress through a series of predetermined stages en route to development. Instead, Kuznets observed that unique economic circumstances influenced each nation's development strategy.

In *Economic Growth of Nations* (1971), Kuznets identified numerous obstacles to development in the developing world. Underdeveloped political and economic institutions, rapid population growth rates, inadequate natural resources, and a lack of appropriate technologies slowed poorer nations' journey toward modernization. For developing economies, Kuznets predicted slow progress toward development, with significant experimentation and struggle along the way. Meanwhile, Kuznets predicted continued economic progress for the advanced economies, which, over time, had developed the necessary institutions, practices, and attitudes for sustainable development. Kuznets won numerous awards for his contributions to the field of economics, including the Nobel Prize in Economic Science in 1971.

See also **Business Cycle; Development Economics; Economic Growth; Gross Domestic Product.**

Further Reading

Kuznets, Simon. *Economic Development, the Family, and Income Distribution: Selected Essays*. New York: Cambridge University Press, 2002.

———. *Economic Growth of Nations*. Cambridge, MA: Belknap Press, 1971.

———. *Growth, Population, and Income Distribution*. New York: W. W. Norton, 1980.

———. *National Income and Its Composition, 1991–1938*. 2 vols. New York: National Bureau of Economic Research, 1941.

———. *Toward a Theory of Economic Growth: With Reflections on the Economic Growth of Modern Nations*. New York: W. W. Norton, 1968.

L

LEAST DEVELOPED COUNTRIES

The least developed countries (LDCs) are among the world's poorest developing countries. Most LDCs are low-income developing countries. A few LDCs, mainly small island nations in the South Pacific, are categorized as lower middle income. Of the world's thirty landlocked developing countries (LLDCs), sixteen are classified as LDCs. Of the world's thirty-seven small island developing states (SIDS), twelve are also LDCs. In 2005, fifty countries in the global economy were classified as LDCs.

The Economic and Social Council of the United Nations uses three criteria to distinguish the least developed countries from other developing countries (see Table 70). First, to qualify as an LDC a country's gross national income (GNI) per capita must be less than $750. Second, LDCs share certain weaknesses in their human resources base. These weaknesses stem mainly from inadequate nutrition, health care, and education. Third, LDCs routinely experience many types of economic instability. Unstable commodity export prices, a reliance on subsistence agriculture, underdeveloped manufacturing and services sectors, susceptibility to natural disasters, and other weaknesses are considered. In addition, the UN standard excludes large economies and countries with a population of 75 million or more.

By the early 2000s, 700 million people lived in LDCs, or 11 percent of the world's population. In 2002 the average gross domestic product (GDP) per capita in LDCs was $281, compared to an average GDP per capita of $1,195 in all developing countries and an average GDP per capita of $28,388 in the advanced economies. Thus, the average GDP per capita in the advanced economies was 100 times the GDP per capita for people living in the LDCs.

LDCs are trapped in a vicious cycle of poverty. This vicious cycle stymies economic growth and sustainable economic development. The root causes of the vicious cycle of poverty are complex and intertwined. First, LDCs are unable to save sufficient money for investment in private physical capital, such as farm equipment, factories, or business computers. The lack of physical capital limits worker productivity and economic growth. In *The Least Developed Countries Report 2004*, the United Nations Conference on Trade and Development (UNCTAD) reported that LDCs, as a group, experienced negative growth from 1980 to 1990, and less than 1 percent annual growth from 1990 to 2000.

The vicious cycle of poverty in LDCs also stems from poor governance and scant public resources. Extreme poverty, inefficient or corrupt tax regimes, and weak institutions reduce the government's support for long-term investments in education, a necessary component in human capital development.

TABLE 70 **Least Developed Countries, 2005**

World Region	Number of Countries	Listing of Countries
Americas	1	Haiti
East and Southern Africa	16	Angola, Burundi, Comoros, Democratic Republic of the Congo, Eritrea, Ethiopia, Lesotho, Madagascar, Malawi, Mozambique, Rwanda, Somalia, Sudan, Uganda, Tanzania, Zambia
East Asia and the Pacific	9	Cambodia, Kiribati, Laos, Myanmar, Samoa, Solomon Islands, Timor-Lesté, Tuvalu, Vanuatu
Middle East	1	Yemen
North Africa	1	Djibouti
South Asia	5	Afghanistan, Bangladesh, Bhutan, Maldives, Nepal
West Africa	17	Benin, Burkina Faso, Cape Verde, Central African Republic, Chad, Equatorial Guinea, Gambia, Guinea, Guinea-Bissau, Liberia, Mali, Mauritania,Niger, Sao Tome and Principe, Senegal, Sierra Leone, Togo
Total	50	

Source: UN Office of the High Representative for the Least Developed Countries, Landlocked Developing Countries and Small Island Developing States, "List of Least Developed Countries," August 2, 2005.

UNCTAD reported that less than two-thirds of primary school age children were enrolled in school in LDCs. Only about one-quarter of secondary age students were enrolled. In addition, LDCs suffer from an inadequate infrastructure, which disconnects the world's poorest citizens from the national and global economy. In the early 2000s, more than 70 percent of all people in LDCs lived in rural areas, only 5 percent of the people had a television set, and just 1 percent of the people had a mainline telephone, cell phone, or access to the Internet. Other roadblocks to development include human rights abuses and horrific civil conflicts, which discouraged foreign investment, foreign trade, and foreign aid. In 2002, LDCs attracted just $5.2 billion in global FDI, over one-half of which was invested in just three countries—Angola, Chad, and the Sudan. From a global perspective, the fifty LDCs attracted less than 1 percent of the total FDI in 2002.

Sustainable economic development is concerned not only with economic growth, but also with people's quality of life. Indicators of a poor quality of life in LDCs abound. LDCs are plagued by extreme poverty, underdeveloped health and sanitation facilities, and low calorie intake. As a result, life expectancy is just fifty years. One out of every six children will die by age five. Over 13 million people in the LDCs were living with HIV/AIDS, and more than one-third of all children were not immunized against measles, diphtheria, and other preventable diseases. By 2005, UNCTAD estimated that only 56 percent of the adult population in LDCs was literate, less than 50 percent of all women. In the early 2000s, most LDCs were ranked "low human development" in the Human Development Index, an annual index published by the United Nations Development Program (UNDP).

Effective strategies to reverse the vicious cycle of poverty in LDCs have been elusive. Multilateral organizations have shouldered much of the responsibility for helping LDCs break the vicious cycle. The World Bank and regional development banks extend loans to support good governance, public and private capital formation, and human capital development. These international financial institutions (IFIs) also provide technical assistance to support institution building.

Most of the loans and grants earmarked for LDCs are made on concessional terms, often long term and interest free. The International Monetary Fund (IMF) extends loans to support financial and economic stability. IMF loans, like some World Bank loans, are contingent on nations' ability to show measurable progress in instituting governance and financial reforms. The joint World Bank-IMF Heavily Indebted Poor Countries (HIPC) Initiative supplies billions of dollars in external debt relief to some of the world's poorest nations. The United Nations' Millennium Development Goals (MDGs), which were established in 2000, provide direction to most multilateral development aid. The Development Assistance Committee (DAC), a group within the larger Organization for Economic Cooperation and Development (OECD), also funnels billions in official development assistance (ODA) from the rich countries to the poorer countries each year. In 2004, LDCs received $23.5 billion in ODA.

See also **Corruption; Developing Countries; Foreign Aid; Good Governance; Gross Domestic Product; Gross National Income; Heavily Indebted Poor Countries (HIPC) Initiative; Human Development; Poverty; Quality of Life; Sustainable Economic Development.** ***See also in Volume 2,*** **Documents 6, 11, 12, 20, 21, 51, 54, 55, 56, 57, 59.**

Further Reading

Cuffaro, Nadia. *Population, Economic Growth, and Agriculture in Less Developed Countries.* New York: Routledge, 2002.

United Nations. *Export Diversification and Economic Growth: The Experience of Selected Least Developed Countries.* New York: Author, 2005.

United Nations Conference on Trade and Development. *The Least Developed Countries Report 2004.* New York: United Nations, 2004.

World Bank. *Global Economic Prospects 2004.* Washington, DC: Author, 2004.

World Intellectual Property Organization. *Intellectual Property Profile of the Least Developed Countries.* Geneva, Switzerland: Author, 2002.

LEWIS, WILLIAM A.

Sir William Arthur Lewis (1915–1991) was a prominent British economist and specialist in the field of development economics. Arthur (his preferred name) Lewis was born in St. Lucia, a British possession in the West Indies. At age seventeen, Lewis won a scholarship to attend the London School of Economics, where he earned a Bachelor of Commerce degree in 1937 and a doctorate in Industrial Economics in 1940. The London School of Economics appointed Lewis to the position of lecturer in economics from 1938 to 1947, helping to break the color barrier that had long denied blacks the opportunity to advance in academia. In the years to come, Lewis served as an economics professor at other major universities including the University of Manchester (1947–1958) in England and Princeton University (1963–1968) in the United States. Lewis authored ten books, including *The Principles of Economic Planning* (1949), *Theory of Economic Growth* (1955), and *Development Planning* (1966).

Lewis was a pioneer in the field of development economics. He drew insights about the plight of the developing world from personal experiences, and from meticulous study of statistical data and economic history. Lewis concluded that many economies in the developing world operated on two different levels, one pushing toward modernity and growth, and the other clinging to traditional subsistence agriculture. Lewis argued that sustainable development was dependent on raising the domestic savings rate, investment in modern capital goods, aggressive export of agricultural and manufactured goods, and mutually beneficial foreign direct investment (FDI). Lewis also valued the role of education, and the transfer of knowledge from transnational corporations, to expand local entrepreneurial and management skills.

Lewis identified significant obstacles to development in the world's poorer regions. Inadequate domestic savings, low public investment in infrastructure, and an inexperienced business class—all stymied economic growth. A demographic shift, marked by rapid population growth and migrations from countryside to cities, created a labor glut in urban areas. Bloated labor markets depressed workers' wages, living standards, and quality of life. Unequal economic relations between rich and poor nations worsened the terms of trade between the industrial North and the agricultural South. Lewis argued that low agricultural productivity in developing countries reduced the value of commodity exports relative to the value of industrial imports, a circumstance that would inevitably cause balance of payments problems for the poorer countries.

While active in academic pursuits for much of his professional career, Lewis was also an agent of change in the developing world. Under the auspices of the United Nations, Lewis served as economic advisor to developing countries in the late 1950s. He also headed the University of the West Indies in the early 1960s, and founded the Caribbean Development Bank in the early 1970s. Lewis earned many honors during his career. Queen Elizabeth knighted Sir Arthur Lewis in 1963. In 1979, he shared the Nobel Prize in Economic Science with American economist Theodore W. Schultz.

See also **Developing Countries; Development Economics; Terms of Trade.**

Further Reading

Lewis, William A., Sir. *Development Planning: The Essentials of Economic Policy*. London: Allen & Unwin, 1966.

———. *The Evolution of the International Economic Order*. Princeton, NJ: Princeton University Press, 1978.

———. *Selected Economic Writings of W. Arthur Lewis*. New York: New York University, 1983.

———. *Theory of Economic Growth*. New York: Routledge, 2003.

LOCALIZATION

Localization is a system of economic and political activity that places most decision making in the hands of local authorities. In terms of the economy, localization favors small-scale production and consumption by self-reliant communities or regions. In terms of governance, localization favors full citizen participation by individuals, elements of civil society, and other local stakeholders. Economic localization, as a development strategy, is the antithesis of economic globalization. Globalization creates a more integrated and interdependent global economy by expanding cross-border flows of goods and services, investments, people, and ideas. Localization seeks to reverse the globalization juggernaut. Localization is a component of the anti-globalization crusade.

Economic localization is based on satisfying local needs with local resources. A community, nation, or even a regional cluster of nations, could be viewed as local decision makers. At the community level, localization supports policies that provide a favorable business environment for small-scale enterprises, including self-sustaining family farms. At the national level, localization favors government policies that discourage unfettered globalization. For example, a government trade policy based on the new protectionism is compatible with localization. The new protectionism favors trade barriers to restrict international trade; investment codes to restrict foreign direct investment (FDI) by powerful transnational corporations (TNCs); and government controls on financial flows between nations. Thus, localization opposes the liberalization of trade and investment policies of major multilateral organizations, such as the World Trade Organization (WTO), International Monetary Fund (IMF), and World Bank. In addition, localization favors the creation and enforcement of legal protections for labor and the environment in local, competitive markets. Localization supports the conservation of resources, use of renewable energy, local ownership of businesses, consumption of local output, and other conditions supportive of microenterprise. Localization supports limited, regulated commercial links between the local and the global, mainly to obtain goods not readily available in local markets. In addition, localization favors global cultural and technological linkages between peoples.

Localization seeks to reverse the globalization juggernaut. Localization requires the de-globalization of production and consumption decisions, and the restoration of local decision making. Localization rejects the premise that globalization is inevitable or desirable. Instead, globalization is viewed as an exploitative process that favors corporate profits over people's quality of life. Supporters of localization believe intense global competition inevitably leads to the race to the bottom. Signs of the race to the bottom include sweatshop conditions in some developing countries, environmental degradation, and other abuses of the global

Farmers in some regions of India support localization to keep local resources under local control.

Courtesy of Getty Images: Santokh Kochar

commons. In addition, localization opposes cultural homogenization, the process by which the planet's rich cultural diversity is trampled in the name of modernization. Supporters of localization argue national governments and multilateral organizations are generally distant, undemocratic, and unresponsive to people's needs.

Pockets of support for localization, or elements of the localization agenda, have emerged in the global economy. Labor unions in the United States and elsewhere press for restrictions on offshoring and production sharing in an effort to protect decent work, local jobs, and domestic production. Small businesses organize to resist the entry of retail giants, such as Wal-Mart and Home Depot, into certain geographic locations. Non-governmental organizations (NGOs) and civil society organizations (CSOs) campaign to protect local ecosystems, worker rights, human rights, and cultural diversity from aggressive TNCs. Microenterprises, in the formal and informal sectors, demonstrate the power of local business initiative to spark economic development. Microfinance institutions, such as the Grameen Bank of Bangladesh, empower local entrepreneurs. Small villages in India openly challenge large corporations over development rights to local resources. The International Labor Organization's Local Economic Development (LED) program offers technical assistance to small- and medium-sized enterprises (SMEs) in more than a dozen countries in Africa, Europe, and Latin America. The LED program is committed to local development and recognizes the potential for localization as a development strategy.

Critics of localization argue that de-globalization is an impractical path toward economic development. Large TNCs represent the hub of global production, supplying jobs to workers, profits to investors, tax revenues to governments, and a wide variety of goods and services to consumers. Localization undermines TNC business activity. Localization also rejects the types of efficiencies gained through regional specialization and economies of scale. Critics conclude that small-scale local production is inadequate to the task of supplying a growing world population with the necessities of life. Further, critics point to the unlikelihood of a global about-face, and the systematic dismantling of the attitudes and institutions of global capitalism.

See also **Development Economics; Global Culture; Globalization; International Trade; New Protectionism; Race to the Bottom; Schumacher, Ernst F.; Supply Chains; Sustainable Economic Development.**

Further Reading

Almas, Reidar, and Geoffrey Lawrence. *Globalization, Localization and Sustainable Livelihoods*. Brookfield, VT: Ashgate Publishing, 2003.

Cavanagh, John, and Jerry Mander. *Alternatives to Economic Globalization: A Better World Is Possible*. 2d ed. San Francisco, CA: Berrett-Koehler Publishers, 2004.

Hines, Colin. *Localization: A Global Manifesto*. Washington, DC: Earthscan Publications, 2000.

Mander, Jerry, and Edward Goldsmith, eds. *The Case against the Global Economy and for a Turn toward the Local*. San Francisco, CA: Sierra Club Books, 1997.

M

MALTHUS, THOMAS R.

Thomas Robert Malthus (1766–1834) was a controversial English economist, whose theories on global population painted a grim future for humanity. Malthus was born to an intellectual family. In 1784, Malthus entered Jesus College in Cambridge, England. Four years later he was ordained a minister of the Church of England. While still a young man, Malthus penned his most famous work, *An Essay on the Principle of Population as It Affects the Future Improvement of Society* (1798). This pessimistic essay foretold of a future filled with misery and poverty as population growth outpaced food production. It also gave rise to the Malthusian Doctrine, which, even today, warns of global catastrophe if population growth is not checked.

Over time, *An Essay on the Principle of Population* evolved into a lengthier and more sophisticated book. First, Malthus theorized that population, if unchecked by conscious actions or other circumstances, would double every twenty-five years. Hence, population growth would occur in geometrical progression—from one, two, four, eight, sixteen, and so on. Second, he theorized growth in food production would occur in arithmetical progression—from one, two, three, four, five, and so on. Malthus concluded that population growth would outpace food production and that the human condition would therefore deteriorate. Malthus introduced two types of checks on human population. First, preventive checks, such as abstinence from sexual activity and marrying later in life, represented a form of population control based on personal choice. Preventive checks focused mainly on reducing the birth rate to control population growth. Malthus had little confidence in people's self-discipline, however, and he doubted preventive checks would stabilize population growth. Second, positive checks offered a gruesome array of ways to limit population growth, including war, famine, and disease. Positive checks doomed the world to persistent human misery and despair, and to an existence perched precariously on the edge of subsistence. Positive checks focused mainly on increasing the death rate to reduce overpopulation. Malthus's gloomy forecasts colored his views on domestic policies in his native England. For example, Malthus opposed most forms of public assistance to the poor, believing that even modest provisions for food or housing would only encourage the poor to multiply. Soon after Malthus's famous essay was published, economics was dubbed the dismal science.

An Essay on the Principle of Population was published in the early years of the Industrial Revolution. His doomsday predictions did not anticipate the enormity of technological advances during the industrial age. Over time, the Industrial Revolution expanded the production of goods and services, and improved people's standard of living in many countries. Advances in agricultural productivity, including the technologies of the green revolution, vastly expanded global food output. In effect, new technologies and advanced capital goods accelerated the production of food and other goods to meet the consumption needs of a growing world population.

Today, some development economists and demographers view with discomfort the quadrupling of global population from 1900 to 2000, from 1.6 billion to 6 billion people. Current projections for a 3 billion person increase in the world's population by 2050—an increase that will occur almost exclusively in the developing world—is another cause for concern.

See also **Developing Countries; Industrial Revolution; Least Developed Countries; Population; Quality of Life; Sustainable Economic Development.** ***See also in Volume 2,*** **Documents 1, 2, 3.**

Further Reading

Brown, Lester R., Gary Gardner, and Brian Halweil. *Beyond Malthus: Nineteen Dimensions of the Population Challenge.* New York: W. W. Norton & Company, 1999.

Heilbroner, Robert L. *The Worldly Philosophers: The Lives, Times and Ideas of the Great Economic Thinkers.* 7th rev. ed. New York: Touchstone, 1999.

Malthus, Thomas R. *An Essay on the Principle of Population.* 2d ed. New York: W.W. Norton & Company, 2003.

Peterson, Wilham. *Malthus: Founder of Modern Demography.* Piscataway, NJ: Transaction Publishers, 1998.

Winch, Donald. *Malthus.* New York: Oxford University Press, 1987.

MAQUILADORAS

Maquiladoras are duty-free assembly plants located mainly in Mexico and some Latin American countries. Most maquiladoras are located on the Mexican side of the U.S.-Mexico border. Major maquila industries include clothing and textiles, electronics, and auto parts. Maquiladoras were created in 1965 under Mexico's Border Industrialization Program, later renamed the Maquiladora Program. The Border Industrialization Program replaced the earlier Bracero Program, which for years allowed Mexican laborers to work in the United States. Foreign interest in maquiladoras spiked in the 1980s after Mexico joined the General Agreement on Tariffs and Trade (GATT), and again in the 1990s after Mexico joined Canada and the United States in the North America Free Trade Agreement (NAFTA). The maquila sector of Mexico's economy is often referred to as an export processing zone (EPZ).

Transnational corporations (TNCs) build maquiladora plants in host countries to minimize production costs. Foreign-owned maquiladoras are a type of foreign direct investment (FDI), called greenfield investment. Greenfield investment involves the construction of an entirely new production facility. The United Nations Conference on Trade and Development (UNCTAD) reported that FDI inflows to Mexico's maquila industries peaked in 2000, as shown in

Table 71. Foreign TNCs set up shop in Mexico, and other low-wage Latin American countries, to reduce production costs. Maquiladoras also offer duty-free import and export of resources, semi-finished goods, and final goods. After sustained growth in the number of Mexican maquiladoras during the 1990s, UNCTAD reported a significant drop in the early 2000s. In 2000, 3,703 maquila plants operated in Mexico, compared to just 2,820 plants in 2004. The exodus of maquila plants from Mexico was mainly due to even lower-cost labor, and a friendlier business environment, in several Asian economies. In the 1990s and early 2000s, large concentrations of maquiladoras were located in and around Ciudad Juarez, Mexicali, and Tijuana.

TABLE 71 **Mexico's Maquila Industries: FDI Inflows, 1996 to 2003**

Year	FDI Inflows ($ billions)	Maquila FDI Inflows (% of total FDI inflows)
1996	$1.42	14.2%
1997	$1.68	11.8%
1998	$2.11	17.2%
1999	$2.78	21.1%
2000	$2.98	18.1%
2001	$2.17	8.2%
2002	$2.04	15.4%
2003	$1.96	20.8%

Source: United Nations Conference on Trade and Development, *World Investment Report 2004*, 61.

The maquiladora program is controversial, mainly because there are significant costs and benefits to the program. Supporters of maquiladoras argue that the benefits far outweigh the costs. First, FDI creates jobs in Mexico and other low-wage Latin American economies. Supporters say these jobs offer comparable pay, better working conditions, and more comprehensive fringe benefits than other jobs in the domestic economy. Second, supporters argue that FDI accelerates industrialization, modernization, and economic development. TNCs build and maintain sophisticated plants, employ advanced capital goods, and infuse the latest technology and management techniques into production. Third, supporters argue that production sharing—the assembly of products in stages and in different countries—promotes competitiveness. Maquiladoras involved in production sharing generate profits for TNCs and lower prices for buyers in global markets.

Opponents stress the costs of maquila enterprise. TNC relocation of plants to low-wage countries results in the loss of jobs, plant closures, and a weakened tax base for communities in high-wage countries. Maquila production in Mexico, coupled with trade liberalization under NAFTA, also contributes to growing U.S. trade deficits with Mexico—a trade deficit that hit $45 billion in 2004. The costs to Mexico and other host countries are also substantial. Opponents argue maquiladoras are modern-day sweatshops, plagued by unsafe working conditions, long work hours, abusive bosses, low pay, and the absence of union representation. In addition, opponents argue that the expansion of maquiladoras has degraded the local environment, strained limited water resources, stretched social services, and damaged the quality of life for workers and their families.

See also **Corporate Social Responsibility; Export Processing Zone; Foreign Direct Investment; North American Free Trade Agreement; Production Sharing; Race to the Bottom; Supply Chains; Transnational Corporations.** ***See also in Volume 2,*** **Documents 26, 28, 38.**

Further Reading

Gravey, Altha J. *Women and Work in Mexico's Maquiladoras.* Lanham, MD: Rowman & Littlefield Publishers, 1998.

Kamel, Rachael, and Anya Hoffman, eds. *The Maquiladora Reader: Cross-Border Organizing since NAFTA.* Philadelphia, PA: American Friends Service Committee, 1999.

Mendez, Jennifer B. *From Revolution to the Maquiladoras: Gender, Labor, and Globalization in Nicaragua.* Durham, NC: Duke University Press, 2005.

Prieto, Norma I. *Beautiful Flowers of the Maquiladora: Life Histories of Women Workers in Tijuana.* Austin, TX: University of Texas Press, 1997.

MARKET ECONOMY

A market economy is a type of economic system in which the private sector owns and controls the factors of production—natural resources, human resources, and capital goods. The private sector consists of individuals and business firms. In a market economy, the private sector answers the basic economic questions of what to produce, how to produce, and for whom to produce. English economist Adam Smith outlined the basic structures and practices of a market economy in his famous book, *An Inquiry into the Nature and Causes of the Wealth of Nations* (1776).

A market economy represents one extreme along a continuum of economic systems, an extreme marked by decentralized decision making in all realms of economic activity. A pure command economy represents the opposite extreme along the economic continuum. In a pure command economy, the government, rather than the private sector, owns essential resources and answers the basic economic questions. Both the market economy and the command economy are

Street vendors in the developing world respond to market incentives by supplying goods that people are willing to buy.
Courtesy of CORBIS

considered economic models. In reality, no economy meets the standards set by either model. Instead, the world's 208 economies tend to lean toward one model or the other, but are a mixture of each. Since the 1980s most economies in the global economy have drifted toward the market model.

In today's global economy, the term "market economy" is used to describe the "mixed economies" that lean heavily toward the market model. Examples of market economies are the United States, Japan, and the United Kingdom. Broadly speaking, the world's twenty-nine advanced economies are market economies. The International Monetary Fund (IMF) classifies many other economies as emerging market economies. Emerging market economies are economies that have made significant progress toward creating market institutions and the conditions that support sustainable economic development. Examples of emerging market economies are Chile, Hungary, Malaysia, Poland, and South Africa.

Underpinning market economies are a number of informal institutions, including private property, economic freedom, profit incentives, and competitive markets. Consumers exercise freedom of choice when they purchase goods and services. Businesses exercise freedom of enterprise when they decide how to use resources in production. The market model places strict guidelines on the role of government in the economy. Under the market model, the government protects the country from foreign aggression and civil unrest, enforces laws, and collects taxes. Today's mixed economies have expanded on these basic functions of government. Governments in mixed economies generally redistribute income and wealth through social programs; stabilize the economy through monetary and fiscal policies; and regulate business activity through environmental laws and protections for workers, consumers, savers, and other stakeholders.

See also **Advanced Economies; Basic Economic Questions; Capitalism; Command Economy; Emerging Market Economies; Transition Countries.** ***See also in Volume 2,*** **Document 13.**

Further Reading

Fulcher, James. *Capitalism: A Very Short Introduction.* New York: Oxford University Press, 2004.

Lindblom, Charles E. *The Market System: What It Is, How It Works, and What to Make of It.* New Haven: Yale University Press, 2001.

McMillan, John. *Reinventing the Bazaar: A Natural History of Markets.* New York: W. W. Norton & Company, 2003.

Smith, Adam. *The Wealth of Nations.* New York: Bantam Classics, 2003.

Smith, Roy. *Adam Smith and the Origins of American Enterprise.* New York: St. Martin's Griffin, 2004.

MARX, KARL H.

Karl Heinrich Marx (1818–1883) was a German-born historian, economist, philosopher, and revolutionary. Marx founded modern communism, an economic theory that contended with capitalism for global dominance during the twentieth century. Marx was born to a comfortable middle-class family in

Trier, Germany. He entered the University of Berlin in 1836 and earned a doctorate in philosophy from the University of Jena in 1841. His association with radical groups and thinkers during the 1830s and 1840s provided fertile ground for original thinking about economics, economic history, and the plight of the industrial worker during the industrial age. Marx concluded that all history involved conflict between an exploited class and an exploiter class. But it was precisely the inevitable conflict between economic classes that brought change—the progression of history from one stage to the next—a process Marx called dialectical materialism. Marx collaborated with his friend Friedrich Engels to bring this theory to life in *The Communist Manifesto* (1848).

Marx's radicalism often brought him into conflict with the authorities. During the 1840s, he contributed articles and editorials to newspapers, wrote inflammatory pamphlets, and joined secret organizations such as the Communist League. The Communist League commissioned Marx and Engels to co-author the *Communist Manifesto* in the winter of 1847–1848. Marx's revolutionary activities did not go unnoticed, however. He was banished from a number of countries including France, Belgium, and Prussia (now Germany). He, his wife Jenny, and his growing family took refuge in London, England, in 1849. Marx lived in poverty for much of the 1850s and 1860s.

While in London, Marx's international reputation grew. In the mid-1860s, he assumed a leadership role in the Communist International, an organization dedicated to worldwide communism. Meanwhile, he labored on his most important work, *Das Kapital*, or *Capital*. Volume I of *Das Kapital* was published in 1867 and was immediately hailed by the Communist International as the bible of the laboring classes. *Das Kapital* eventually grew to three volumes. Volumes II and III were edited by Engels and published in 1883, shortly after Marx's death. In *Das Kapital*, Marx vigorously critiqued the brutality of capitalist production. He predicted competition among the capitalists would result in even lower wages for workers, who had nothing to sell except their labor. He believed that intense competition would also encourage capitalists to invest in labor-saving equipment, causing massive unemployment for wage laborers and economic instability for nations. He concluded that intolerable economic conditions would inevitably spark a bloody revolution led by the proletariat, the exploited class of urban industrial workers. The proletarian revolution would topple the oppressive capitalist class and create a new economic system based on the principles of scientific socialism. At the time of Marx's death in 1883, his ideas were narrowly circulated among radical groups, mainly in Europe.

Vladimir I. Lenin, Mao Zedong, Fidel Castro, and other revolutionaries successfully toppled governments and established communist regimes during the twentieth century. Communism expanded after World War II, penetrating deeply into Eastern and Central Europe, East Asia, and the developing world. By the late 1940s, the Cold War pitted totalitarian communist nations against democratic capitalist nations. The resulting ideological battleground reshaped the global economic landscape. Communist governments were generally inward-looking, developing commercial contacts among themselves but shunning most economic relations with other countries. The lack of global connectivity, and the inefficiencies of central planning, undermined most communist economies by the late 1980s and early 1990s. Facing economic collapse, the Soviet Union, the leader of the communist world, dissolved in 1991. The dissolution of the Soviet Union sparked an epic economic transition among twenty-eight countries of eastern and central Europe and Western Asia, away from their communist past and toward a more capitalist and democratic future.

See also **Command Economy; Communism; Transition Countries.**

Further Reading

Blumenberg, Werner, and Scott Douglas. *Karl Marx: An Illustrated Biography*. Rev. ed. New York: Verso, 1998.

Evans, Michael. *Karl Marx*. New York: Routledge, 2004.

Marx, Karl, and Friedrich Engels. *The Communist Manifesto*. New York: Washington Square Press, 1964.

McLellan, David. *Karl Marx: Selected Writings*. New York: Oxford University Press, 2000.

Uchida, Hiroshi, ed. *Marx for the 21st Century*. New York: Routledge, 2005.

MERCANTILISM

Mercantilism, or the mercantile system, rests on the belief that the accumulation of specie, mainly gold and silver, is the wellspring of a nation's wealth and prosperity. Mercantilism stresses the importance of international trade to increase a nation's hoard of specie. During the 1600s and 1700s, mercantilism was an entrenched dogma in major European countries. Thomas Mun (1571–1641), a merchant from London, England, was mercantilism's most eloquent spokesman. Mun's *Discourse on England's Treasure by Foreign Trade* (1664), published after his death, remains the world's most articulate defense of mercantilism.

The mercantilists were mainly merchants and manufacturers. The mercantilists allied themselves with ambitious monarchs to shift political and economic power away from the backward-looking landed aristocracy. To support commercial profits, and to fill national treasuries, governments created trade policies to achieve a favorable balance of trade. A favorable balance of trade, or trade surplus, occurs when the value of a nation's exports is greater than the value of its imports. Leading European nations including Great Britain, France, Spain, and Prussia embraced mercantilism during the 1600s and 1700s.

Trade policies created a favorable business climate for merchants and manufacturers. Governments created trade barriers, such as import tariffs and quotas, to discourage or prohibit certain foreign imports. Governments subsidized domestic industries, and granted trade monopolies, to encourage production and the export of surpluses. Governments built vast colonial empires to support business activity in the mother country. Under mercantilism, colonies were expected to supply the mother country with inexpensive raw materials, and then purchase the finished products produced by manufacturers in the mother country.

The mercantilists viewed the world through a narrow lens, which, invariably, supported the interests of the commercial class and the monarchy. The mercantilists neglected other growth factors in the realms of agricultural production, human capital development, technological advance, and so on. The mercantilists also embraced a narrow view of trade, seeing exchanges in terms of winners and losers rather than as business transactions from which both parties could benefit. Further, mercantilism heaped lavish financial rewards on the merchants, manufacturers, and supportive monarchs. The common people, however, were viewed as little more than cheap labor, a market for industrial output, and an endless supply of soldiers to carry out the monarch's global ambitions.

The mercantilists also jump-started the global economy during the 1600s and 1700s. Mercantilists were the vanguard of the commercial revolution that swept across the European continent. They forged global commercial networks. They helped solidify the power of monarchs, who created national unity, built an economic infrastructure, and wrestled power from the traditional landed nobility. The mercantilists also nurtured capitalist ideas such as the sanctity of private property, and the importance of profit incentives, entrepreneurship, and innovation. While enriching themselves and their kings, the mercantilists laid the groundwork for the emergence of capitalism.

See also **Balance of Trade; Capitalism; Commercial Revolution; Industrial Revolution; International Trade; Mun, Thomas; Protectionism.**

Further Reading

Ekelund, Robert B., and Robert D. Tollison. *Politicized Economies: Monarchy, Monopoly, and Mercantilism.* College Station, TX: Texas A&M University Press, 1997.

Magnusson, Lars. *Mercantilism.* 4 vols. New York: Routledge, 1996.

Mun, Thomas. *England's Treasure by Foreign Trade.* New York: Augustus M. Kelly Publishers, 1986.

Ormrod, David et al., eds. *The Rise of Commercial Empires: England and the Netherlands in the Age of Mercantilism, 1650–1770.* New York: Cambridge University Press, 2003.

Wallerstein, Immanuel M. *Modern World System II: Mercantilism and the Consolidation of the European World-Economy, 1600–1750.* San Diego, CA: Academic Press, 1997.

MERCOSUR

MERCOSUR, or *Mercado Comun del Sur*, is a four-nation regional trade association. The *Mercado Comun del Sur*, or Southern Common Market, consists of Argentina, Brazil, Paraguay, and Uruguay. Chile and Bolivia are associate members. The Treaty of Asuncion established MERCOSUR in 1991. The Treaty began a formal phase-in of policies to integrate the four-nation economic region. By the early 2000s, MERCOSUR had evolved from a free trade area to a customs union.

View of La Paz, Bolivia. Bolivia is an associate member of MERCOSUR.
Courtesy of Getty Images: Adalberto Rios Szalav/Sexto Sol

As a customs union, MERCOSUR eliminated most trade barriers among member nations, and established a common trade policy with non-member nations. MERCOSUR's common external tariff (CET) is its most visible sign of regional unity. Its common trade policy also synchronizes member nations' policies on import quotas, licensing requirements, and responses to unfair trade practices such as dumping. The Treaty of Ouro Preto in 1994 strengthened MERCOSUR's institutional framework and its resolve to create a comprehensive common market modeled on the European Union (EU) by 2006. The Committee on Permanent Representatives and the Dispute Settlement Court were both established in 2003. The creation of these institutions was hailed as a positive step toward further economic integration.

MERCOSUR's organizational structure rests on two main institutions, the Common Market Council and the Common Market Group. The Common Market Council is MERCOSUR's highest authority. It is responsible for maintaining the momentum toward full economic integration among member countries. The Council consists of member nations' top ministers of economic and foreign affairs. It meets at least once every year, and its decisions are made by consensus. The second tier in MERCOSUR's organizational structure is the Common Market Group. The Common Market Group implements the policy directives of the Common Market Council. The Group also has the authority to devise and implement its own policies to further the goal of economic integration. The Group consists of representatives of member nations' central banks, and economic and foreign affairs ministries. The Group meets regularly, but at least once every three months. Decision making by the Group is also based on consensus. The administrative office, and numerous advisory and working groups, handle MERCOSUR's day-to-day operations.

Trade liberalization within MERCOSUR, and between MERCOSUR and other regional trade agreements (RTAs), has increased members' international

TABLE 72 **MERCOSUR Exports, 1990 to 2003 ($ billions)**

Year	Intra-MERCOSUR Exports	Exports to Other Regions	Total MERCOSUR Exports
1990	$4,127	$42,292	$46,419
2003	$12,614	$93,307	$105,921

Source: World Trade Organization, *International Trade Statistics 2004*, 54.

trade since the early 1990s. In its *International Trade Statistics 2004*, the World Trade Organization (WTO) reported intra-MERCOSUR trade tripled from 1990 to 2003, while trade between MERCOSUR nations and other world regions more than doubled, as shown in Table 72. In 2003, MERCOSUR, as a region, recorded a trade surplus of $37 billion in merchandise and commercial services. Still, MERCOSUR remains a work in progress. Challenges include promoting greater intraregional cooperation, expanding trade relationships with the EU and other partners, and pondering the implications of the proposed Free Trade Area of the Americas (FTAA).

See also **European Union; Free Trade Area of the Americas; North American Free Trade Agreement; Regional Trade Agreements. *See also in Volume 2,* Document 26.**

Further Reading

Behar, Jaime. *Cooperation and Competition in a Common Market: Studies on the Formation of MERCOSUR*. Heidelberg, Germany: Physica-Verlag, 2000.

Dominguez, Francisco, and Marcos Guedes de Oliveira. *Mercosur: Between Integration and Democracy*. New York: Peter Lang Publishing, 2003.

Porrata-Doria, Rafael. *Mercosur: The Common Market of the Southern Cone*. Durham, NC: Carolina Academic Press, 2005.

Roetti, Riordan, ed. *Mercosur: Regional Integration, World Markets*. Boulder, CO: Lynne Rienner Publishers, 1999.

MICROFINANCE INSTITUTIONS

Microfinance institutions (MFIs) are organizations that provide a range of financial services to the poor, mainly in the developing world. MFIs accept savers' deposits, extend loans, transfer money, and sell insurance to clients. The MFI's most important financial service is to make microcredit loans. Microcredit loans, or microloans, are small loans, perhaps $50 to $100, made to small businesses called microenterprises. Microenterprises use microloans to finance business start-ups or to grow existing businesses. Common microenterprises include repair shops, bakeries, farms, and handicraft shops. MFIs are sometimes formal financial institutions such as rural banks, credit unions, or even commercial banks. Most MFIs are less formal organizations, including nongovernmental organizations (NGOs) and private voluntary organizations (PVOs). Thousands of MFIs provide financial services to millions of low-income entrepreneurs in the global economy.

MFIs generally share certain common characteristics. Most MFIs are nonprofit organizations, mainly NGOs and PVOs. Many MFIs provide microloans and a variety of microfinance services. MFIs require repayment of microloans, plus interest. The high interest rates charged by MFIs, sometimes more than a

50 percent annual rate, are necessary to cover the high costs of processing large numbers of small loans. MFI interest rates are considerably lower than rates charged by moneylenders in the informal economy, however. Microloans are short term, usually less than one year. Microloan repayments of principal and interest are often made in weekly installments. Collateral is not required to obtain microloans. Instead, peer supervision by assigned peer groups of five to eight people monitor compliance. In some cases, peer groups are collectively responsible for the repayment of microloans should the borrower default. Most borrowers are women entrepreneurs. MFIs obtain initial start-up funds from a variety of sources, including governments; multilateral donors, such as regional development banks; or bilateral donors, such as the United States Agency for International Development (USAID).

The Grameen Bank in Bangladesh is the world's largest MFI. Muhammad Yunus experimented with microloans in the mid-1970s. In 1983, special legislation was passed to formally establish the Grameen Bank. Yunus's goal was to supply financial resources to the poor on reasonable terms. He reasoned that microloans could bring millions of marginalized people, which had been shunned by commercial lenders, into the economic mainstream. In 1976, Yunus dispersed just $498 in microloans. In 2003, the Grameen Bank made $369 million in loans. Since its founding, the Grameen Bank has extended $4.2 billion in microloans to 3.8 million borrowers in Bangladesh. Ninety-six percent of all microloan recipients were women. By 2004, the Grameen Bank provided services to 46,620 villages and employed 12,500 workers at the bank's 1,277 branches.

MFI resources and visibility have increased since the 1990s. The success of the Grameen Bank in Bangladesh, and greater financial inflows from multilateral institutions and other donors, established microfinance as a priority development strategy. The Inter-American Development Bank's (IDB) Small Project Program pioneered microfinance lending as early as the 1970s. By the mid-1990s, the Small Project Program had assisted hundreds of thousands of microenterprises, which accounted for more than a million new jobs. In 1997, the IDB introduced its MICRO 2001 initiative, a $500 million microenterprise development program. The African Development Bank Group and the Asian Development Bank also initiated microfinance support programs. The UNCDF Microfinance program, which is administered by the United Nations Capital Development Fund, is another recent microenterprise development initiative. The UNCDF Microfinance program funds MFIs and related support services in the least developed countries (LDCs). Since 1997, the UNCDF has also teamed with the United Nations Development Program (UNDP) in the MicroStart program. Today, the MicroStart program provides funding and technical assistance MFIs in twenty additional developing countries. MFIs are an important component in a larger global poverty-reduction strategy. The mission of MFIs is supportive to the UN Millennium Development Goals (MDGs), which puts poverty reduction at the center of the global development agenda. The United Nations proclaimed 2005 the Year of Microcredit.

See also **Entrepreneurship; Informal Economy, Inter-American Development Bank Group; Localization; Poverty; Sustainable Economic Development; Yunus, Muhammad.** ***See also in Volume 2,*** **Document 8.**

Further Reading

Klobuchar, Jim, and Susan C. Wilkes. *The Miracles of Barefoot Capitalism: A Compelling Case for Microcredit*. Minneapolis, MN: Kirk House Publishers, 2003.

Morduch, Jonathon, and Beatriz Armendriz de Aghion. *The Economics of Microfinance*. Cambridge, MA: MIT Press, 2005.

Robinson, Marguerite. *The Microfinance Revolution: Sustainable Finance for the Poor*. Washington, DC: World Bank Publications, 2001.

Weber, Heloise, and Caroline Thomas. *The Politics of Microcredit: Global Governance and Poverty Reduction*. London: Pluto Press, 2004.

Yunus, Muhammad. *Banker to the Poor: Micro-Lending and the Battle against World Poverty*. Washington, DC: Public Affairs, 2003.

MILLENNIUM DEVELOPMENT GOALS

The Millennium Development Goals (MDGs) consists of eight specific objectives for human and economic development in the global economy. The MDGs was a key component in the Millennium Declaration, a more inclusive document that received unanimous approval from the United Nations' 189 member states in 2000. The Millennium Declaration established a series of broad commitments to guide the planet toward a more prosperous and secure future. UN member nations pledged to promote peace, security, and disarmament; economic development and poverty reduction (the Millennium Development Goals); responsible environmental standards; human rights, democracy, and good governance; respect for vulnerable groups; constructive assistance to Africa; and a stronger United Nations system. The MDGs are the world's most recognized roadmap toward sustainable economic development.

The MDGs roadmap consists of eight mutually supporting goals. Accompanying each development goal is at least one target. The target establishes a standard by which success or failure is measured. For example, the first MDG is to "eradicate extreme poverty and hunger" by 2015. To achieve success, two targets must be met. First, the proportion of people living on less than $1 per day must be cut in half. Second, the proportion of people who suffer from hunger must be cut in half. Similar targets are set for the other seven MDGs, as shown in Table 73.

The MDGs sharpened the development strategies of nations, and focused economic assistance from the World Bank and the regional development banks. Progress toward achieving the MDGs is mixed. For example, the World Bank reported there were 100 million fewer people living in extreme poverty in 2000 than in 1990, and rapid progress was being made to reduce extreme poverty in East Asia and the Pacific, Europe, and Central Asia. Extreme poverty in South Asia and sub-Saharan Africa was still rampant, however. Uneven global progress in the prevalence of extreme poverty and hunger dimmed global prospects for meeting MDG number one by 2015. According to World Bank projections,

TABLE 73 **Millennium Development Goals**

Millennium Development Goals		Targets (number)	Measurable Outcomes by 2015
1	Eradicate extreme poverty and hunger	1, 2	Halve the proportion of people whose daily income is less than $1, and who suffer from hunger
2	Achieve universal public education	3	All children will complete primary school
3	Promote gender equity and empower women	4	End gender disparity in primary and secondary education by 2005; end all gender disparities in education by 2015
4	Reduce child mortality	5	Reduce under-five child mortality by two-thirds
5	Improve maternal health	6	Reduce maternal mortality ratio by three-quarters
6	Combat HIV/AIDS, and other diseases	7, 8	Reverse the spread of HIV/AIDS, malaria, and other diseases
7	Ensure environmental sustainability	9, 10, 11	Reverse the loss of environmental resources; halve the proportion of people without safe drinking water and sanitation; improve the quality of life for 100 million slum dwellers by 2020
8	Develop a global partnership for development	12, 13, 14, 15, 16, 17, 18	Improve trading and financial system; address needs of least developed, landlocked and small island countries; address external debt burdens; promote decent work for the youth; increase access to medicine, and new technologies

Source: The World Bank Group (www.developmentgoals.org/About_the_goals.htm).

a similar story unfolds for the other MDGs. Global progress has been uneven in achieving educational goals, gender equity, health care improvements, disease prevention, and environmental sustainability. Particularly vulnerable were the least developed countries (LDCs), where the crushing burden of poverty weakened nations' prospects for sustainable development.

See also **Developing Countries; Foreign Aid; Human Development; Least Developed Countries; Poverty; Quality of Life; Sustainable Economic Development; United Nations System; World Bank Group.** ***See also in Volume 2,*** **Documents 4, 5, 7, 12.**

Further Reading

Miller, Margaret J., ed. *Implementing the Millennium Development Goals*. Washington, DC: World Bank, 2005.

Sachs, Jeffrey D., ed. *Investing in Development: A Practical Guide to Achieve the Millennium Development Goals*. New York: United Nations Development Project, 2005.

United Nations Development Program. *Human Development Report 2003: Millennium Development Goals, a Compact among Nations to End Human Poverty*. New York: Oxford University Press, 2003.

Wolfensohn, James D. *Global Monitoring Report 2004: Policies and Actions for Achieving the Millennium Development Goals and Related Outcomes.* Washington, DC: World Bank Publications, 2004.

MOORE, MIKE

Mike Moore (1949–) is a prominent political figure from New Zealand, and former director-general of the World Trade Organization (WTO). Moore is a staunch defender of globalization, and policies of inclusion, to promote sustainable economic development. Moore was born in the small town of Whakatane, New Zealand, the son of working class parents. In his youth, Moore held manual jobs in construction and meatpacking. Soon his interests turned to trade unionism and politics. In 1972, at the age of twenty-three, Moore was elected to the New Zealand Parliament. Moore remained active in New Zealand's Labour Party and, in 1990, was elected Prime Minister. In the late 1990s, Moore and Thailand's Supachai Panitchpakdi were locked in a contentious election for the position of WTO director-general. Eventually, a compromise divided the director-general term between the two candidates, enabling each to serve in the WTO's top spot for three years. Moore's term ran from September 1, 1999, to August 31, 2002; Panitchpakdi's term from September 1, 2002, to August 31, 2005.

As WTO director-general, Moore consistently supported trade liberalization. Trade liberalization involves the dismantling of trade barriers such as tariffs and import quotas. Moore argued that open trade among nations creates business opportunities, jobs, and an environment conducive to economic growth and development. Conversely, Moore argued the rejection of globalization meant isolation and marginalization for the world's poorer countries. Moore worked to include additional countries in the rules-based WTO system. During his tenure, ten new members joined the WTO, most notably the People's Republic of China and Chinese Taipei.

Moore's tenure as WTO chief was not without controversy. The failure of the WTO's third ministerial meeting, hosted by Seattle, Washington in November 1999, underscored significant opposition to globalization, the WTO, and Moore. Thousands of anti-globalization protesters, mostly representing nongovernmental organizations (NGOs) and civil society organizations (CSOs), converged on the Washington State Convention and Trade Center in Seattle to disrupt the ministerial meeting. Equally troubling was a more subtle rebellion among WTO delegates from some developing countries. These delegates demanded greater transparency and a larger voice in global decision making.

In the aftermath of the failed conference, Moore instigated changes in the WTO's structure and direction. He reformed the WTO Secretariat to make it more efficient, transparent, and accountable to member nations and other stakeholders—including NGOs and CSOs. Moore also shifted the organization's direction to devote more attention to economic development. The WTO's fourth ministerial meeting, hosted by Doha, Qatar in 2001, emphasized economic development. The main outcome of the conference was the Doha Development Agenda (DDA), which committed member nations to a new round of trade talks and reaffirmed certain preferential treatment for poorer countries in the global trading system.

In *A World without Walls: Freedom Development, Free Trade and Global Governance* (2003), Moore remained an unabashed proponent of free trade. The book made a compelling connection between globalization and economic growth, sustainable development, and good governance. Moore highlighted the need for inclusion, transparency, and accountability to heal the wounds incurred in Seattle and to advance the WTO's credibility with stakeholders. The success of the Doha ministerial meeting of 2001 was, in large measure, a testament to the internal reforms initiated by Moore. Moore also supported the retention of decision-making authority by member states. In Moore's view, NGOs, CSOs, and other global voices should contribute to discussions and debates about global issues. Member countries, however, should remain the ultimate decision makers in the WTO and in other multilateral organizations.

See also **Bretton Woods System; Economic Growth; General Agreement on Tariffs and Trade; Globalization; International Trade; New Protectionism; Protectionism; World Trade Organization. *See also in Volume 2,* Document 18.**

Further Reading

Evenett, Simon J., and Bernard M. Hoekman. *The Doha Round and the Wto: A New Agenda for Development*. Washington, DC: World Bank Publications, 2005.

Moore, Mike. *A World without Walls: Freedom, Development, Free Trade and Global Governance*. New York: Cambridge University Press, 2003.

———, ed. *Doha and Beyond: The Future of the Multilateral Trading System*. New York: Cambridge University Press, 2004.

Thomas, Janet. *The Battle in Seattle: The Story Behind and Beyond the WTO Demonstrations*. Golden, CO: Fulcrum Publishing, 2000.

MULTILATERAL ENVIRONMENTAL AGREEMENTS

Multilateral environmental agreements (MEAs) are formal protocols, conventions, treaties, or declarations negotiated by countries to protect or restore the natural environment. Over the past few decades, hundreds of MEAs have been negotiated. At times, MEAs deal with regional environmental problems. The 2003 ASEAN Agreement on Transboundary Haze Pollution, for example, was negotiated and implemented by the ten-member Association of Southeast Asian Nations. Other MEAs deal with global environmental concerns, especially threats to the global commons. The 1987 Montreal Protocol, for example, took aim at ozone-depleting substances that threatened the planet's protective ozone shield. In 2005, the UN Millennium Ecosystem Assessment (MA) highlighted the rapid degradation of ecosystems by human populations and warned that current production and consumption practices were unsustainable. MEAs offer some guidelines for the responsible use of nature's gifts in today's global economy.

The Montreal Protocol on Substances that Deplete the Ozone Layer (1987) is an MEA designed to reverse the depletion of the ozone layer of the earth's atmosphere. This protocol followed on the heels of research that showed a gaping hole in the ozone layer over Antarctica. The Montreal Protocol required countries to reduce and eventually eliminate the production and consumption of ozone-depleting substances (ODS), such as chlorofluorocarbons (CFCs), carbon tetrachloride, and methyl chloroform. Other ODS, such as bromochloromethane, were banned by later amendments to the Montreal Protocol. The advanced countries took the lead in the phase-out of ODS. The production and consumption of some items, such as certain aerosol sprays and packaging materials, were banned. The industrialized countries also established the Multilateral Fund for the Implementation of the Montreal Protocol in 1991 to assist developing countries comply with emissions standards. By 2004, the fund had dispersed $1.6 billion to support 4,600 projects in 134 countries. Projects are overseen by United Nations agencies, such as the United Nations Environment Program (UNEP) and the United Nations Development Program (UNDP), and by the World Bank. Widespread compliance with the provisions of this agreement resulted in reduced ODS contamination, and a reversal in ozone destruction. In fact, five adjustments were made in the protocol between 1990 and 1999 to accelerate planned ODS phase-outs. The Montreal Protocol was signed by 172 countries, and is widely viewed as the world's most successful MEA.

Multilateral environmental agreements regulate pollution, especially toxic wastes that foul the global commons.
Courtesy of Getty Images: Kent Knudson/PhotoLink

The UN Framework Convention on Climate Change (1992) is an MEA designed to address global warming. The convention was an important outcome of the 1992 Earth Summit in Rio de Janeiro, Brazil. The convention stressed controls on emissions of greenhouse gases such as carbon dioxide, nitrous oxide, and methane to slow global warming. 180 countries signed the convention. Its voluntary emissions standards, which asked the advanced countries to hold emissions to 1990 levels, were largely ignored, however. The Kyoto Protocol (1997) strengthened the original 1992 convention. The Kyoto Protocol, which was negotiated in Kyoto, Japan, established binding emissions targets for the advanced economies. The protocol required a 5.2 percent reduction in greenhouse gas emissions during the first commitment period, from 2008 to 2012. Developing countries were exempted from the first commitment period. In 1998 the Kyoto Protocol was ready to collect signatures. To come into force, the protocol required ratification by at least fifty-five countries accounting for at least 55 percent of developed country emissions. In October 2004, Russia ratified the controversial protocol. Russia's ratification enabled the protocol to meet the 55 percent emissions threshold. In all, 128 countries signed the protocol. On February 15, 2005, the Kyoto Protocol entered into force. Conspicuously missing from the list of signatory nations was the United States, the world's largest source of greenhouse gas emissions, and Australia. The George W. Bush administration had removed the United States from the Kyoto Protocol in 2001, favoring a voluntary emissions control plan instead.

Over time, other conventions addressed specific environmental issues. The UN Convention on the Law of the Sea (1982) established broad protections for the oceans. This convention stressed sustainable harvesting and conservation of sea resources and protections against pollution. The Convention on the Law of the Sea gathered 148 signatory nations by 2005. The Convention on Biological Diversity (1992) focused on balancing the planet's economic and ecological needs. The convention stressed maintenance of biological diversity, which includes the wide variety of plants, animals, and microorganisms, as well as natural ecosystems such as forests, deserts, wetlands, and so on; the responsible use of nature's resources; and an equitable distribution of the benefits of the world's genetic resources. Currently, 168 have signed the Convention on Biological Diversity. The UN Convention to Combat Desertification (1994) addressed the problem of land degradation mainly in dry rural areas. This convention encouraged programs and projects that promote effective land and water management in desert regions such as the Sahel in Africa. In 2004, the Convention to Combat Desertification was in force in 191 countries.

Broadly interpreted, MEAs also include umbrella environmental declarations or statements made under the auspices of the United Nations or other multilateral institutions. *Agenda 21*, which was approved at the 1992 Earth Summit in Rio de Janeiro, is the world's most comprehensive action plan for sustainable development and environmental protection. *Agenda 21* pledged to protect the global commons, including the atmosphere and oceans; combat environmental degradation, including desertification and deforestation; promote land management and sustainable agriculture; and regulate the production, transports, and dispersal of hazardous wastes. The Rio Declaration on Environment and Development, also approved at the Rio Earth Summit in 1992, affirmed all nations' responsibility to protect the integrity of the Earth's ecosystems and promote sustainable consumption and production. The UN's Global Compact (1999) built on the spirit of the Rio Earth Summit. The Global Compact challenged nations to take preemptive steps to avoid looming environmental catastrophes, to promote fair and sustainable production and consumption habits, and to share environmentally friendly technologies and knowledge. The UN's Millennium Declaration (2000) stressed respect for nature. It also reaffirmed the UN's commitment to the environmental goals outlined in the landmark *Agenda 21*.

See also **Corporate Social Responsibility; Energy Resources; Environmental Degradation; Millennium Development Goals; Sustainable Consumption; Sustainable Economic Development.** ***See also in Volume 2,*** **Documents 39, 40, 41, 42, 43.**

Further Reading

Clapp, Jennifer, and Peter Dauvergne. *Paths to a Green World: The Political Economy of the Global Environment*. Cambridge, MA: MIT Press, 2005.

Kiss, Alexandre, Dinah Shelton, and Kanami Ishibashi, eds. *Economic Globalization and Compliance with International Environmental Agreements*. Cambridge, MA: Kluwer Law International, 2003.

Robinson, Nicholas A. *Strategies toward Sustainable Development: Implementing Agenda 21*. Dobbs Ferry, NY: Oceana, 2004.

Sands, Philippe. *Principles of International Environmental Law*. 2d ed. New York: Cambridge University Press, 2003.

United Nations. *Agenda 21 Earth Summit: United Nations Program of Action from Rio*. New York: Author, 1992.

MULTILATERAL INVESTMENT GUARANTEE AGENCY

The Multilateral Investment Guarantee Agency (MIGA) is an international organization that supports foreign direct investment (FDI) in emerging market and developing countries. MIGA encourages FDI by issuing risk insurance, called guarantees, to transnational corporations (TNCs) that set up shop in other countries. MIGA is one of five institutions that comprise the World Bank Group. The other four institutions of the World Bank Group are the International Bank for Reconstruction and Development (IBRD), International Development Association (IDA), International Finance Corporation (IFC), and International Centre for Settlement of Investment Disputes (ICSID). In 2005, MIGA consisted of 164 member countries.

MIGA was established in 1988 to improve the investment climate in the world's poorer regions. MIGA's main tool to promote FDI is risk insurance, or guarantees, that protect foreign investments from noncommercial losses. To qualify for MIGA's guarantees, the FDI must be long term (at least three years). Guarantees cover business start-ups, expansions, and the privatization of existing firms. Rarely does risk insurance extend beyond fifteen years. MIGA guarantees also target enterprises that offer collateral benefits to the host economy, such as jobs creation and economic growth. In recent years, MIGA expanded loan guarantees to higher-risk regions, such as post-conflict areas and low-income countries. Examples of MIGA-insured projects include infrastructure construction projects in the West African states of Benin, Mali, Senegal, and Togo; telecommunications in Syria; water treatment and distribution in China; banking in Bosnia and Herzegovina; power transmission lines in Brazil; and a computer database system in Kenya. Since 1988, MIGA has issued 650 guarantees that covered projects in eighty-five poorer countries. In addition, cumulative loan guarantees of $13.5 billion have generated roughly four times this amount in additional FDI in host countries. MIGA currently caps the amount of risk insurance coverage available to any one country at $420 million.

A regional distribution of MIGA's $5.3 billion in outstanding loan guarantees in is shown in Figure 29.

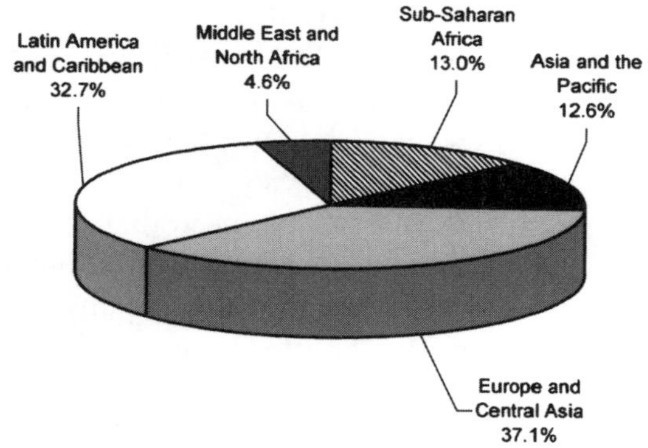

FIGURE 29 **MIGA Loan Guarantees by Region, 2004**

Source: Multilateral Investment Guarantee Agency, "Regional Activities" (www.miga.org).

MIGA guarantees cover four types of noncommercial risk. First, guarantees protect investors from government expropriations. Expropriation is the government seizure of private physical assets, such as plant or equipment, or financial assets such as savings. Second, guarantees protect investors from breach of contract. Breach of contract occurs when the host government reneges on the terms of a business agreement. Refusal to pay for goods or services is an example of a breach of contract. Third, guarantees protect investors from losses that result from civil conflicts, revolutions, sabotage, and terrorism. Fourth, guarantees protect investors from losses that result from the non-convertibility of a local currency. A non-convertible currency is one that cannot readily be converted into a more widely accepted form of foreign exchange, such as the U.S. dollar or the euro.

In addition to guarantees, MIGA offers technical assistance and advisory services. MIGA's technical and advisory support is designed to create and maintain an attractive investment climate for transnational corporations (TNCs). Technical assistance is offered to businesses, governments, and other stakeholders. It promotes good governance, and the creation of appropriate labor and environmental standards. MIGA's legal expertise is also tapped to mediate differences that may arise between TNCs and host governments. MIGA has undertaken hundreds of technical assistance activities since 1988. MIGA programs are financed mainly by contributions from member countries and from the World Bank.

See also **Foreign Direct Investment; International Bank for Reconstruction and Development; International Centre for Settlement of Investment Disputes; International Development Association; International Finance Corporation; World Bank Group.**

Further Reading

Baker, James C. *Foreign Direct Investment in Less Developed Countries: The Role of ICSID and MIGA*. Westport, CT: Quorum Books, 1999.

Moran, Theodore H. *International Political Risk Management: The Brave New World*. Washington, DC: World Bank Publications, 2003.

———, ed. *International Political Risk Management: Exploring New Frontiers*. Washington, DC: World Bank Publications, 2001.

West, Gerald T., and Ethel I. Tarazona. *Investment Insurance and Developmental Impact: Evaluating Miga's Experience*. Washington, DC: World Bank Publications, 2001.

MUN, THOMAS

Thomas Mun (1571–1641) was a prominent merchant, and spokesman for the mercantile and manufacturing classes during the early 1600s. Mun was born to a wealthy merchant family in England. At a young age, Mun's business dealings in Italy, Turkey, and elsewhere tuned his skills in the art of commerce. Mun was soon convinced that international trade was a potential goldmine for merchants, manufacturers, and his nation. In 1615, Mun became a director of the British East India Company, a private corporation to which the English government granted monopoly power in certain traded commodities. Mun's views on trade policy, manufacturing, and government intervention in the economy influenced the economic development of England and Europe for the next two centuries. Mun is viewed as the most influential mercantilist of his age.

Mun's *Discourse on England's Treasure by Foreign Trade* (1664) is the world's most recognized treatise on mercantilism and its benefits. Later economists coined the term "mercantilism," to describe Mun's perception of a mercantile system. According to Mun, international trade and manufacturing were vital to the accumulation of national wealth. He stressed the importance of maintaining a favorable balance of trade, or trade surplus, which occurs when the value of a nation's exports is greater than the value of its imports. A favorable balance of trade enriches merchants, manufacturers, and kings. Mun also identified the perfect merchant as an expert in accounting; currency conversion; shipping; navigation; and foreign laws, languages, and cultures.

In *Discourse on England's Treasure by Foreign Trade*, Mun prescribed policies to promote a favorable balance of trade. First, Mun supported trade restriction to limit certain imports, especially expensive luxury goods. Mun reasoned that the purchase of high-priced foreign imports would drain England's wealth. Mun favored the duty-free import of inexpensive resources, such as spices, that could be profitably re-exported, however. Second, Mun supported the reduction or elimination of English duties on exports. The elimination of export duties would lower the price of English manufactured goods, and, thus, make English products more competitive in global markets. Third, Mun supported the creation of monopolies, such as the British East India Company. Monopoly status protected domestic manufacturers and merchants from destructive domestic competition. Fourth, Mun favored government subsidies to support domestic production, particularly export industries whose surpluses could be sold abroad.

Over time, the views of Thomas Mun, Antonio Serra in Italy, Jean-Baptiste Colbert in France, and other mercantilists influenced the trade and industrial policies of leading European nations. The mercantilists viewed global commercial relations through a narrow lens, a lens that favored commercial interests and nation building above all else. The alliance between merchants, manufacturers, and kings created wealth and power for these groups. The costs of mercantilist policies were severe for other groups, however. Industrial and agricultural laborers earned subsistence wages in exchange for their backbreaking toil. Low-wage labor was viewed as a necessity if England was to be competitive in world markets. Overseas colonial possessions were obliged to serve the mother country's interests, often at the expense of indigenous peoples and local resources.

By the late 1700s and early 1800s, the idea of free trade was challenging mercantilist dogma in the western world. Adam Smith, author of the classic *An Inquiry into the Nature and Causes of the Wealth of Nations* (1776), spearheaded the assault on mercantilism.

See also **Capitalism; Commercial Revolution; Industrial Revolution; International Trade; Mercantilism.**

Further Reading

Blaug, Mark, ed. *Early Mercantilists: Thomas Mun.* Northampton, MA: Edward Elgar Publishing Company, 1991.

Mun, Thomas. *Discourse on Trade, from England unto the East-Indies.* New York: Augustus M. Kelly Publishers, 1971.

———. *England's Treasure by Foreign Trade.* New York: Augustus M. Kelly Publishers, 1986.

Wallerstein, Immanuel M. *Modern World System II: Mercantilism and the Consolidation of the European World-Economy, 1600–1750.* San Diego, CA: Academic Press, 1997.

MYRDAL, KARL G.

Karl Gunnar Myrdal (1898–1987) was a prominent Swedish sociologist, politician, and development economist. Myrdal advocated economic planning to focus the development efforts of poorer countries. Myrdal was born in Gustafs, a small village in Sweden, the son of working class parents. In 1927, Myrdal earned a doctorate in economics from Stockholm University. Myrdal's colorful professional career combined scholarship, teaching, and public service. In Sweden, he served as an economics professor at Stockholm University, as a senator, and as a commerce secretary. His international reputation grew during a decade-long stint as secretary-general of the United Nations Economic Commission for Europe, a post he held from 1947–1957. In 1957, Myrdal published his first book in the field of development economics, *Rich Lands and Poor: The Road to World Prosperity.* In that same year, he began a ten-year research project on economic conditions in the developing world. His results were published in a three-volume tome, *Asian Drama: An Inquiry into the Poverty of Nations* (1968).

Myrdal's highly acclaimed *Asian Drama* rekindled interest and debate about development strategies for the world's poorer countries. His keen observations—observations that begged for policy reforms—and meticulous research identified many obstacles to development. Myrdal was attentive to key elements in the vicious cycle of poverty. He analyzed the complex and interdependent web of forces that blocked sustainable economic development in poorer regions, a dilemma he referred to as cumulative causation. Long an advocate of economic planning, Myrdal argued that the governments in the developing world must control rising populations, expand basic services in education and health care, and reform land tenure laws to guarantee private ownership and economic inclusion of the poor. Myrdal challenged developing countries to reform legal codes which, historically, protected the narrow interests of the ruling elite and stymied human development. He also challenged the advanced countries to increase foreign aid, extend trade preferences to poorer nations, and curtail unsustainable consumption in their own countries. Other elements in Myrdal's prescription for prosperity included improvements in labor productivity, the application of appropriate technologies, good governance, protections for the natural environment, and public works jobs for the unemployed.

Myrdal viewed economic development as a complex process. He shunned narrow interpretations of economic development that focused on a single major remedy, such as capital accumulation or human capital development. He supported economic planning, a widely accepted development strategy during the post–World War II period. He believed that the market mechanism, a system of resource allocation based solely on price signals, was not equipped to handle the overwhelming development needs of poorer countries. During his lifetime, Myrdal received many honors and awards in recognition of his groundbreaking work in development economics. In 1974, Gunnar Myrdal was selected co-recipient of the Nobel Prize in Economic Science, an honor he shared with Friedrich August von Hayek.

See also **Developing Countries; Development Economics; Development Plan; Poverty; Sustainable Economic Development.**

Further Reading

Bok, Sissela, Stellan Andersson, and Richard Litell, eds. *The Essential Gunnar Myrdal*. New York: New Press, 2005.

Dostaler, Gilles. *Gunnar Myrdal & His Works*. Eugene, OR: Harvest House Publishers, 1992.

Myrdal, Gunnar. *Asian Drama: An Inquiry into the Poverty of Nations*. New York: Pantheon Books, 1968.

———. *Beyond the Welfare State: Economic Planning and Its International Implications*. Westport, CT: Greenwood Press, 1982.

N

NEWLY INDUSTRIALIZED ECONOMIES

The newly industrialized economies (NIEs) are the four Asian economies that recently joined the ranks of the advanced economies. In 2005, the global economy consisted of twenty-nine advanced economies, and 179 emerging market and developing economies. The NIEs include Chinese Taipei, Hong Kong Special Administrative Region (SAR), Singapore, and South Korea. NIEs are often called the newly industrialized Asian economies, or the Asian Tigers. All NIEs are high-income countries, with highly sophisticated economic sectors. According to the International Monetary Fund (IMF), NIEs accounted for 3.3 percent of global output and 9.3 percent of global exports in 2003. Table 74 summarizes NIE output and income data.

NIEs, like other advanced economies, have benefited from the virtuous cycle of economic development. High national savings and investment rates underpin NIEs' virtuous cycle. Heavy investment in new capital goods increased the NIEs' capital stock, the total amount of productive capital in each nation. The growth of NIEs' capital stock, in turn, supported capital deepening. Capital deepening occurs when the amount of real capital per worker increases. High investment in capital goods, human capital, and social capital paved the way for economic growth and development in the NIEs. From 1986 to 1995, worker productivity in NIEs increased by 7.3 percent per year, more than double the rate of the major advanced economies. From 1996 to 2005, the 5.6 percent annual rise in NIE productivity was more than 50 percent higher than productivity growth in the major advanced economies. In addition, growth in the volume of NIE trade far outpaced that of the major advanced economies. From 1986 to 1995, NIE exports increased by 13.4 percent per year, compared to 5.5 percent in the major advanced economies. From 1996 to 2005, NIE exports increased at an 8.2 percent annual clip, compared to 5.1 percent in the major advanced economies. Table 75 compares the economic performance of NIEs with the major advanced economies over the past decade.

NIEs are among the most competitive economies in the world. Competitive economies nurture sound public and private institutions, pursue responsible macroeconomic policies, and promote productivity gains through investments in human capital, research and development (R&D), information and communications technologies (ICTs), entrepreneurship, and other growth factors. Leading competitiveness reports give NIEs high marks for their competitiveness in global markets. The International Institute for Management Development's *IMD World Competitiveness Yearbook 2004* ranked the

Raffles Place, in downtown Singapore, symbolizes successful economic development in the newly industrialized Asian economies.
Courtesy of CORBIS

competitiveness of sixty major economies. NIEs captured three of the top twelve spots in this ranking, including Singapore (2), Hong Kong SAR (6), and Chinese Taipei (12). South Korea was thirty-fifth. The World Economic Forum's *Global Competitiveness Report 2004–2005* reported similar results with Chinese Taipei (4) leading the way, followed by Singapore (7), Hong Kong SAR (21), and South Korea (29).

NIEs also score well in economic freedom. Economic freedom, a core principle of capitalism, rests on people's ability to use private property as they see fit. Institutions and policies that support personal choice, individual initiative, good governance and the rule of law, macroeconomic stability, private property rights, and market incentives tend to support economic freedom. Global rankings of economic freedom put NIEs at the top of the pack. In the Heritage Foundation/Wall Street Journal *Index of Economic Freedom* for 2005, Hong Kong SAR (1) and Singapore (2), topped the ranking, followed by Chinese Taipei (27) and South Korea (45). In the Fraser Institute's *Economic Freedom of the World 2004 Annual Report*, Hong Kong SAR and Singapore again gained the top two spots, followed by Chinese Taipei (22) and South Korea (31).

TABLE 74 **Newly Industrialized Economies: Output and Income Data, 2003**

Country	Gross Domestic Product ($ billions)	Gross National Income per Capita	Gross National Income per Capita (PPP)
Chinese Taipei*	$282	$13,320	$23,400
Hong Kong SAR	$159	$25,430	$28,810
Singapore	$91	$21,230	$24,180
South Korea	$605	$12,020	$17,930

*Chinese Taipei's (Taiwan) GDP data is for 2002; Chinese Taipei's $23,400 is GDP per capita rather than GNI per capita.
Source: World Bank, *World Development Report 2005*, 256–257, 260–261; *Taipei Times*, *Taiwan Yearbook 2004*.

TABLE 75 **NIEs Comparisons by Selected Performance Indicators, 1986 to 2005**

Performance Indicators (annual)	Newly Industrialized Economies		Major Advanced Economies	
	1986–1995	1996–2005	1986–1995	1996–2005
Real GDP growth	8.1%	4.3%	2.7%	2.6%
Growth in real GDP per capita	7.0%	3.4%	2.1%	2.1%
Unemployment rate	2.4%	4.0%	6.7%	6.3%
Growth in employment	2.7%	1.3%	1.0%	0.9%

Source: International Monetary Fund, *World Economic Outlook September 2004*, 200, 203–204.

See also **Advanced Economies; Competitiveness; Economic Freedom; Economic Growth; Sustainable Economic Development.**

Further Reading

Chow, Peter C. Y., ed. *Taiwan in the Global Economy: From Agrarian Economy to an Exporter of High-Tech Products*. Westport, CT: Praeger Publishers, 2002.

Kim, Eun Mee. *The Four Asian Tigers: Economic Development & the Global Political Economy*. San Diego, CA: Academic Press, 1999.

Nelson, Richard R., and Linsu Kim, eds. *Technology, Learning, and Innovation: Experiences of Newly Industrializing Economies*. New York: Cambridge University Press, 2000.

Rowen, Henry S., ed. *Behind East Asian Growth: The Political and Social Foundation of Prosperity*. New York: Routledge, 1998.

Stiglitz, Joseph, and Shahid Yusuf, eds. *Rethinking the East Asian Miracle*. New York: World Bank Publications, 2001.

NEW PROTECTIONISM

The new protectionism refers to policies that restrict international trade, foreign direct investment (FDI), and cross-border flows of financial capital. The goals of the new protectionism are to make local economies more secure, improve people's quality of life, and democratize decision making. The new protectionism is intertwined with the localization movement, which supports small-scale production and sustainable consumption by self-reliant communities or regions. The new protectionism, like localization, is a component of the anti-globalization movement.

The new protectionism perceives most long-distance exchanges in the global economy as detrimental to people's economic and social well-being. From the standpoint of the new protectionists, the globalization juggernaut has trampled local economies, disrupted local cultures, and robbed local decision makers of their authority to rule. The overlords of globalization include giant transnational corporations (TNCs), multilateral organizations such as the World Bank and World Trade Organization (WTO), and powerful governments.

The new protectionists oppose most long-distance international trade and investment in today's highly competitive global marketplace. The new protectionists argue TNCs, always on the prowl for low-cost resources in the global economy, make production and investment decisions based solely on anticipated profits. TNCs invest in developing countries to exploit low-wage labor, lax labor standards, and unenforceable environmental regulations. In the process, foreign direct investment (FDI) by TNCs destroys smaller, less competitive domestic firms, and reduces the diversity of business enterprise in poorer nations. Free trade compounds the damage by encouraging the export of low-priced products to high-wage countries. The influx of low-priced imported goods undermines production and worker security in high-wage countries. Manufacturers in high-wage countries cannot compete with low-priced imports from countries such as China, India, or Bangladesh. As a result, manufacturers in high-wage countries shut down, or relocate. Unemployment and underemployment offer two unattractive possibilities for displaced workers. New protectionists also oppose unfettered cross-border financial flows. They argue unregulated transfers of money across national borders destabilize local economies. The herd behavior of investors in Thailand, Indonesia, South Korea, and other East Asian economies during the East Asian Financial Crisis (1997–1998) demonstrated the need for restrictions on international financial flows.

The new protectionist agenda proposes a reversal of trade and investment liberalization, and the creation of policies that discriminate in favor of local production and consumption. The new protectionists support trade barriers, such as import quotas and tariffs, to discourage most foreign trade, especially long-distance trade. The new protectionists favor policies that help local economies meet local production and consumption needs with local resources. The new protectionists support strict limits on FDI. FDI guidelines would require a long-term commitment to the region, and guarantees that most output would be sold in local markets. Other FDI requirements could mandate positive technology transfers, human capital development, the training of local managers, and limits on the repatriation of corporate profits. The new protectionists favor policies that distribute the benefits of foreign enterprises more equitably, and restore decision-making authority to local officials.

Critics warn that protectionism, new or old, stifles prospects for global growth and sustainable economic development. Critics of the new protectionism argue that trade barriers and investment restrictions impose artificial restrictions on people's economic freedom, retard incentives, and reduce production efficiency. Small-scale production also eliminates the benefits of the economies of scale, which, traditionally, have lowered production costs and consumer prices for many mass-produced items. Critics also contend that the reversal of economic globalization is impractical. It would require a universal commitment to localized production, sustainable consumption, and a redistribution of global wealth through foreign aid or other transfer programs.

See also **Foreign Direct Investment; International Trade; Globalization; Localization; Protectionism; Schumacher, Ernst F.; Sustainable Economic Development.**

Further Reading

Bhagwati, Jagdish. *Free Trade, Fairness & the New Protectionism: Reflections on an Agenda for the World Trade Organization*. Philadelphia, PA: Coronet Books, 1995.

Cavanagh, John, and Jerry Mander. *Alternatives to Economic Globalization: A Better World Is Possible*. 2d ed. San Francisco, CA: Berrett-Koehler Publishers, 2004.

Hines, Colin. *Localization: A Global Manifesto*. Washington, DC: Earthscan Publications, 2000.

Hudgins, Edward L., ed. *Freedom to Trade: Refuting the New Protectionism*. Washington, DC: Cato Institute, 1997.

NON-GOVERNMENTAL ORGANIZATIONS

A non-governmental organization (NGO) is a special interest group that conducts research, disseminates information, and advocates for change at the national and international levels. In recent years, NGOs have also been services providers, sometimes in partnership with multilateral organizations such as the World Bank and United Nations. Most NGOs maintain branches in, and solicit membership from, more than one country. An international non-governmental organization (INGO) is a NGO with cross-border affiliations. INGOs often promote activist agendas in areas that transcend nationality, such as human rights, global poverty, and the environment. NGOs represent an important element within civil society. Civil society is a catchall term used to describe the volunteerism of individuals who work for the common good. Civil society organizations (CSOs) are groups, including NGOs, which promote positive economic, social, and political change. NGOs are organized along democratic lines to express the collective will of members. The London-based Center for Civil Society and Center for the Study of Global Governance estimated that nearly 50,000 NGOs operated in the local and global arenas during the early 2000s.

NGOs, at the national and international levels, give a voice to marginalized, distressed, and powerless groups of people in the global economy. In recent years, NGO voices have become more powerful for a variety of reasons. First, NGOs benefited from new information and communications technologies (ICTs), such as the Internet, email, and the World Wide Web (WWW). ICTs boosted cross-border communications, and facilitated organization building by NGOs. Second, NGOs benefited from democratization. The rise of democratic political systems in eastern and central Europe and elsewhere expanded freedom of expression, including the freedom to dissent. Third, NGOs benefited from policies of inclusion by multilateral organizations, including the World Bank, International Monetary Fund (IMF), World Trade Organization (WTO), and the specialized agencies and programs of the United Nations system. Inclusion increased the visibility of NGOs and legitimized their role as change agents. Kofi Annan, secretary-general of the United Nations, called NGOs "indispensable partners" in global decision making. Fourth, NGOs benefited from more generous flows of financial resources since the 1970s. Individuals, foundations, transnational corporations (TNCs), and multilateral organizations supplied billions of dollars to NGOs during the early 2000s. Fourth, NGOs showed a record of accomplishment. NGOs linked people with essential services, many financed by governments, multilateral organizations, and other agencies. NGOs also advocated for change through mass protests. NGO demonstrations at the World Trade Organization's ministerial meeting in Seattle, Washington, in 1999, and at other global forums in subsequent years, were expressions of this newfound power.

NGOs are typically organized around a common cause, which is outlined in the group's mission statement. Today, many NGOs are devoted to protecting human rights, preserving peace, reducing poverty and hunger, preventing environmental degradation, promoting good governance, and a host of other causes related to economic and human development. Among the world's largest NGOs are Amnesty International and Human Rights Watch, which advocate for human rights; CIVICUS and Transparency International, which promote good governance; Friends of the Earth and the Nature Conservancy, which support environmentalism; Oxfam International and Save the Children, which promote poverty reduction and food aid; and Eurodad and ActionAid, which deal with issues related to sustainable economic development. Increasingly, governments, multilateral organizations, and TNCs solicit NGO advice to form policies.

See also **Civil Society Organizations; Corporate Social Responsibility; Sustainable Economic Development.** ***See also in Volume 2,*** **Documents 40, 42, 53, 56, 59.**

Further Reading

Anheier, Helmut K., Mary H. Kaldor, and Marlies Glasius, eds. *Global Civil Society 2004/5*. Thousand Oaks, CA: SAGE Publications, 2004.

Boli, John, and George M. Thomas, eds. *Constructing World Order: International Nongovernmental Organizations Since 1875*. Stanford, CA: Stanford University Press, 1999.

Fowler, Alan. *The Virtuous Spiral: A Guide to Sustainability for NGOs in International Development*. Washington, DC: Earthscan, 2001.

Lewis, David. *Management of Non-Governmental Development Organizations: An Introduction*. New York: Routledge, 2001.

Lindenberg, Marc, and Coralie Bryant. *Going Global: Transforming Relief and Development Ngos*. West Hartford, CT: Kumarian Press, 2001.

NORTH AMERICAN FREE TRADE AGREEMENT

The North American Free Trade Agreement (NAFTA) is a comprehensive regional trade agreement (RTA) between Canada, Mexico, and the United States. Negotiations to establish NAFTA were initiated shortly after the creation of the U.S.-Canada Free Trade Agreement (1988). NAFTA negotiations were successfully concluded in the early 1990s, and the Agreement took effect on January 1, 1994. The Agreement created a free trade area (FTA) to eliminate trade barriers among member nations and pave the way for expanded cross-border foreign direct investment (FDI). NAFTA did not require a unified trade or

TABLE 76 **NAFTA Members: A Profile, 2003**

Country	Population (millions)	GDP ($ billions)	GNI per Capita	GNI per Capita (PPP)
Canada	31.9	$834.4	$23,930	$29,740
Mexico	106.2	$626.1	$6,230	$8,950
United States	293.6	$10,881.6	$37,610	$37,500
NAFTA Totals	431.7	$12,342.1	–	–

Source: Population Reference Bureau, *2004 World Population Data Sheet*, 7; World Bank, *World Development Report 2005*, 256–257, 260–261.

investment policy with non-member nations, however. NAFTA consists of more than 400 million people with a combined gross domestic product (GDP) of more than $12 trillion—roughly one-third of the world's total GDP. Members' development status and gross national income (GNI) per capita vary considerably. A profile of NAFTA members is shown in Table 76.

The two main institutions of NAFTA include the NAFTA Secretariat and the NAFTA Commission. The NAFTA Secretariat is an agency mainly responsible for administering the agreement's dispute settlement mechanisms. It is divided into three sections, one in Canada, one in Mexico, and one in the United States. A national secretary heads each section. The NAFTA Commission is mainly responsible for implementing the three main components of the agreement. It consists of three commissions, the Free Trade Commission, Commission for Labor Cooperation, and Commission for Environmental Cooperation. The Free Trade Commission deals with the implementation of the complex web of trade agreements among the three signatory nations. It is comprised of the trade ministers, or an appointed trade representative, from each member nation. The Commission for Labor Cooperation monitors labor conditions in the member nations to ensure compliance with accepted labor standards. It is comprised of the nations' labor ministers or their designees. The Commission for Environmental Cooperation is responsible for enforcing the environmental safeguards outlined in the agreement. It is comprised of environmental ministers, or representatives, from each member nation. Numerous specialized committees and working groups assist the NAFTA Secretariat and NAFTA Commission in the operation of the agreement.

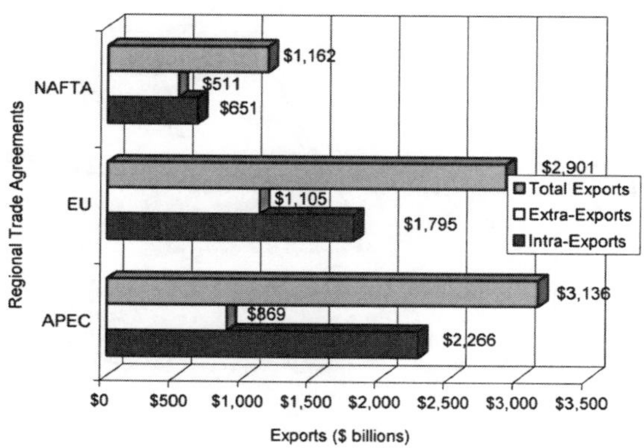

FIGURE 30 **Merchandise Exports: APEC, EU (15), and NAFTA, 2003**

Source: World Trade Organization, *International Trade Statistics 2004*, 24.

NAFTA is the world's largest RTA, measured by total GDP. It is the world's third largest RTA measured by volume of merchandise exports. In

2003, NAFTA followed the twenty-one-member Asia-Pacific Economic Cooperation (APEC), and the fifteen-member European Union (EU), in total merchandise exports, as shown in Figure 30 (some rounding in the figure). The majority of NAFTA exports were "intra-exports," which traveled from one NAFTA country to another. Intra-exports of merchandise between Canada, Mexico, and the United States totaled $651 billion in 2003, compared to a total of $511 billion in "extra-imports" to other regions of the world. Similarly, intra-exports dominated merchandise trade within APEC and the EU.

NAFTA has sparked controversy since its inception in 1994. Supporters argue that the agreement benefits consumers, who enjoy a wider variety of low-priced goods and services due to liberalized trade and investment. Second, supporters argue that NAFTA creates more and better paying jobs. Job creation was mainly the result of brisk business activity within the FTA. The Office of the U.S. Trade Representative reported that trade volume among members more than doubled from 1993 to 2003, and that cumulative FDI totaled nearly $300 billion. Third, supporters claim that the NAFTA Commissions adequately protect the environment, workers' rights, and fair trade within the economic region. Fourth, supporters credit NAFTA with stimulating economic growth in the three member nations. According to the U.S. Trade Representative, the U.S. economy grew by 38 percent during NAFTA's first decade, followed by Canada (31.9 percent growth) and Mexico (30 percent growth).

Opponents paint a different picture of NAFTA's impact on the economies and people of member nations. Opponents argue the elimination of trade barriers hurts the U.S. trade position with Canada and Mexico. Growing U.S. trade deficits with each trading partner illustrate the deteriorating U.S. trade position with its NAFTA partners. Since 1994, the small U.S. trade surplus with Mexico has become a $45 billion trade deficit. During this same time period, the U.S. trade deficit with Canada has climbed by nearly 400 percent, from $14 billion in 1994 to $66 billion in 2004. The annual Canadian and Mexican trade surpluses with the United States are shown in Figure 31. Second, opponents claim that working people, mainly in the United States and Mexico, are hurt by NAFTA. Plant closures in the United States, the "export" of U.S. jobs to Mexico, and the exploitation of inexpensive labor in Mexico's maquila industries, are indicators of NAFTA's failure. Third, opponents note that environmental degradation has accelerated since NAFTA's inception. Heavy foreign investment in maquiladoras, and the resulting population boom along the

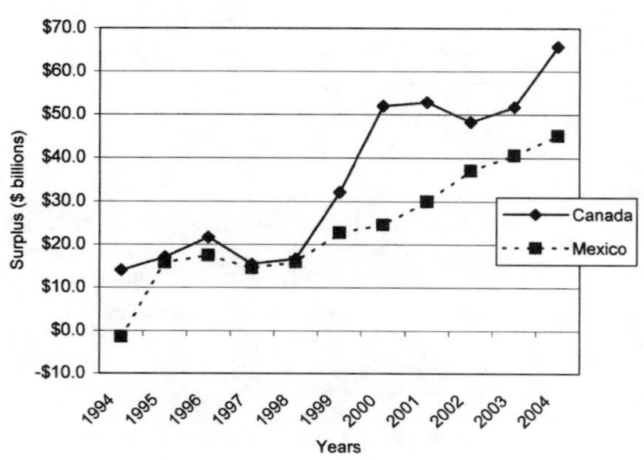

FIGURE 31 **Annual Canadian and Mexican Trade Surpluses with the United States, 1994 to 2004 ($ billions)**

Source: U.S. Census Bureau, Foreign Trade Division, *Foreign Trade Statistics*.

U.S.-Mexico border, has strained water supplies and sanitation facilities. Pressure to cut production costs has also encouraged the illegal disposal of toxic wastes, mainly in Mexico.

See also **Asia-Pacific Economic Cooperation; Corporate Social Responsibility; European Union; Foreign Direct Investment; International Trade; Maquiladoras; MERCOSUR; Production Sharing; Regional Trade Agreements.** ***See also in Volume 2,*** **Documents 24, 26, 27, 28.**

Further Reading

Bacon, David. *The Children of NAFTA: Labor Wars on the U.S./Mexico Border.* Berkeley, CA: University of California Press, 2005.

Hufbauer, Gary C., Jeffrey J. Schott, and Diana Orejas. *NAFTA: A Seven Year Appraisal.* Washington, DC: Institute for International Economics, 2005.

Kennedy, Kevin C., ed. *The First Decade of NAFTA: The Future of Free Trade in North America.* Piscataway, NJ: Transaction Publishers, Inc., 2004.

Nevaer, Louis, E. V. *NAFTA's Second Decade: Assessing Opportunities in the Mexican and Canadian Markets.* Cincinnati, OH: South-Western, 2004.

Weintraub, Sidney, ed. *Nafta's Impact on North America: The First Decade.* Washington, DC: Center for Strategic & International Studies, 2004.

NYERERE, JULIUS K.

Julius K. Nyerere (1922–1999) was a prominent Tanzanian educator and political leader. He was also the most influential supporter of African socialism during the post–World War II era. Nyerere was born the son of a Zanaki chief in the former British colony of Tanganyika. He earned his teaching certificate in 1945 from Makerere University in Kampala, Uganda, and a Master of Arts degree in the early 1950s from the University of Edinburgh, Scotland. In 1952, Nyerere returned to Tanganyika, founded the Tanganyika African National Union (TANU), and led Tanganyika's peaceful transition from British colony to independent nation. In 1961, Tanganyika gained its independence. A year later, Nyerere was elected president. He successfully negotiated the unification of Tanganyika and Zanzibar into the United Republic of Tanzania. Nyerere served as president of Tanzania from 1964 to his retirement in 1985.

Nyerere's vision of African socialism was based on traditional African communalism and a doctrine of self-reliance. He rejected neocolonial dependence on Western powers. He nationalized key industries and collectivized agriculture. Rural development was the centerpiece of his development strategy. In the Arusha Declaration (1967), Nyerere committed Tanzania to *ujamaa* socialism. *Ujamaa*, often translated as "familyhood," was based on cooperative agricultural enterprise. He believed communal effort, modeled on the structures of the traditional extended family, was the fairest way to share the workload and distribute society's output. *Ujamaa* required the forced relocation of millions of peasants from their private plots of land to village cooperatives during the late 1960s and early 1970s. By the mid-1970s, most of Tanzania's population was resettled in rural *ujamaa* villages.

Nyerere's experiment in African socialism was largely unsuccessful. Peasants resented the forced relocation program and refused to work long hours for the collective welfare of *ujamaa* villages. Inefficient central planning misallocated resources. Poorly planned *ujamaa* villages were often located on land unsuitable for permanent agriculture. Central plans, which called for greater production of cash crops such as tobacco, also cut into the nation's production of food staples. The state's production targets were rarely met, and Tanzania remained one of the world's poorest countries. Even billions of dollars in foreign aid during the 1970s and 1980s, mainly from the sympathetic Scandinavian nations, was unable to prop up Tanzania's failing economy.

After Julius Nyerere stepped down from the presidency in the mid-1980s, Tanzania adopted a more market-oriented approach to economic development. Nyerere witnessed the dismantling of central planning, rural collectivization, price controls, and other features of *ujamaa* socialism. During the 1990s and early 2000s, Tanzania also instituted policies to privatize state-owned enterprises (SOEs), liberalize its trade and investment regimes, and restore profit incentives.

See also **Democratic Socialism; Developing Countries; Development Plan; Third World Socialism.**

Further Reading

Assensoh, A. B. *African Political Leadership: Jomo Kenyatta, Kwame Nkrumah, and Julius K. Nyerere*. Melbourne, FL: Krieger Publishing Company, 1998.

Du Bois, Shirley G. *Julius K. Nyerere: Teacher of Africa*. Parsippany, NJ: Julian Messner, 1975.

McDonald, David A., and Eunice N. Sahle. *The Legacies of Julius Nyerere: Influences on Development Discourse and Practice in Africa*. Lawrenceville, NJ: Africa World Press, 2002.

Nyerere, Julius K. *Nyerere on Socialism*. New York: Oxford University Press, 1985.

———. *Ujamaa—Essays on Socialism*. New York: Oxford University Press, 1968.

O

OFFSHORE FINANCIAL CENTERS

Offshore financial centers (OFCs) are jurisdictions that offer financial and regulatory advantages to individuals and business firms. Many host jurisdictions are small island nations, or island territories or dependencies of larger countries. Examples of island OFCs include the Cayman Islands, Aruba, and Barbados in the Caribbean; the Maldives and Seychelles in the Indian Ocean; the Cook Islands, Samoa, and Tonga in the South Pacific; and Guernsey and the Isle of Man in the North Atlantic. Other OFCs are small "onshore" jurisdictions, such as Liechtenstein, Gibraltar, and Monaco in Europe; Belize and Panama in Central America; and Liberia in Africa. OFCs host many types of financial and business institutions, such as offshore banks and international business corporations (IBCs). OFCs are often called tax havens to accent the special tax advantages they offer.

Financial institutions, businesses, even wealthy individuals locate in OFCs to hide or protect assets, avoid taxes, or engage in illegal activities such as money laundering and other forms of international crime. OFCs offer offshore banks and other foreign clients a largely unregulated business environment, low taxes, and the tax-free movement of financial assets in and out of the jurisdiction. The accounts, transactions, and other dealings of offshore banks and other clients are highly secretive. Most offshore banks allow individual or corporate clients to hide different forms of income-generating assets, such as dividends, interest, and capital gains. Similarly, international business corporations establish corporate headquarters in OFCs to conceal corporate ownership, disguise or hide assets, avoid taxes, and circumvent existing business regulations in their home countries. Table 77 shows several major OFCs operating in the global economy.

OFCs have come under intense scrutiny in recent years. Public attention was drawn to OFCs for a number of reasons. First, new technologies sped legal and illegal financial transactions. The electronic transfer of funds aided criminal activity, such as drug trafficking and money laundering. Second, OFCs sparked well-publicized trade battles between nations. For example, the European Union (EU) condemned the heavy use of OFCs by U.S. corporations during the early 2000s as an unfair trade practice. The EU argued that OFCs were tax havens for U.S. firms, which gave American exports a competitive advantage in global markets. Third, the September 11, 2001, terrorist attacks on the World Trade Center in New York City, and the Pentagon in Washington, DC, increased concerns about the origin and destination of secret OFC money flows. Many

Offshore financial centers have instituted reforms to become more accountable and transparent.
Courtesy of CORBIS

felt the rapid, untraceable transfer of funds gave terrorists an unacceptable advantage over law enforcement officials. Fourth, OFCs were embroiled in the issue of tax fairness. Tax avoidance by the rich increased the tax burden on the middle class and the poor. The tax fairness issue was particularly sensitive in the developing world where capital flight, which included assets pilfered by corrupt officials and ruthless dictators, was aided by offshore banks and businesses. Fifth, the size of financial flows through offshore banks, insurance companies, and other OFC clients startled the general public. Conservative estimates placed annual OFC money flows in the trillions of dollars.

Since the late 1990s, international organizations and governments have pressured OFCs to become more accountable, transparent, and cooperative with law enforcement agencies. Leading the charge for OFC reform was the Organization for Economic Cooperation and Development (OECD), a group comprised mainly of the world's leading industrialized countries. Throughout the 1990s and early 2000s, the OECD's Financial Action Task Force (FATF) investigated money-laundering schemes. In 2000, the OECD released a list of OFCs, and identified specific nations and territories it deemed "uncooperative tax havens." Numerous global agencies joined the campaign to introduce banking and financial reforms for OFCs, and to remove the shield of secrecy that had protected OFC clients for generations. The OECD's major allies in this drive for accountability and transparency were the International Monetary Fund (IMF), Basel Committee on Banking, World Bank, and United Nations. In addition, new legislation in the United Kingdom and the United States, two of the financial hubs of the global economy, clamped down on OFCs. In the United States, the Patriot Act (2001) required stricter

TABLE 77 **Offshore Financial Centers, 2003**

Jurisdictions	Offshore Banks (number)	International Business Companies (number)
Bahamas	301	47,040
British Virgin Islands	13	360,000
Cayman Islands	580	30,000
Panama	34	370,000
Cyprus	29	57,600
Liechtenstein	17	75,000
Luxembourg	200	68,000
Switzerland	500	n.a.
Hong Kong	n.a.	500,000

Source: U.S. Department of State, *International Narcotics Control Strategy Report*, March 2004, 4–5.

surveillance of offshore banking, particularly money-laundering activity. Threats of economic sanctions under U.S. and U.K. laws increased OFC compliance with reform measures.

See also **Capital Flight; Capital Markets; Corruption; International Financial Institutions; Organization for Economic Cooperation and Development.** ***See also in Volume 2,*** **Document 58.**

Further Reading

Cornez, Arnold. *The Offshore Money Book: How to Move Assets Offshore for Privacy, Protection, and Tax Advantage.* 2d ed. New York: McGraw-Hill, 2000.
Lilley, Peter. *Dirty Money: The Untold Truth about Global Money Laundering, International Crime and Terrorism.* 2d ed. Dover, NH: Kogan Page, 2003.
Neal, Terry L. *The Offshore Solution.* Sandy, OR: Mastermedia Publishing, 2001.
Starchild, Adam. *Using Offshore Havens for Privacy & Profit.* Rev. ed. Boulder, CO: Paladin Press, 2001.

OFFSHORING

Offshoring occurs when a producer from one country outsources production to another country. The two types of offshoring are "captive offshoring" and "offshore outsourcing." Captive offshoring, also called intra-firm offshoring, occurs when a producer in one country transfers production to one of its affiliates in a second country. Offshore outsourcing occurs when a producer in one country transfers production to an unaffiliated local company in the second country. Not all "outsourcing" is connected with "offshoring." In fact, most outsourcing occurs between companies in the same country. For example, U.S. corporations often outsource peripheral services, such as tax preparing and legal consulting, to other American businesses. Liberalized trade and investment regimes, and advanced information and communications technologies (ICTs), have accelerated offshoring in recent years.

Offshoring is a political hot potato in some advanced economies. In the United States and Australia, heated debates rage about offshoring the "export of jobs" to low-wage countries. Public reaction to offshoring, especially was far milder among the countries of the European Union. During the 1990s, offshoring mainly affected manufacturing in industries such as textiles and clothing, motor vehicles and auto parts, and electronics. By the early 2000s, many services-producing industries were also offshored, a shift that widened interest in the topic of offshoring. Low-skill offshored services included call centers, and data entry services; medium-skill services included accounting, basic computer programming, and bill collecting; and high-skill services included architectural, engineering, and medical services. Popular destinations for offshored production in manufacturing were Mexico, China, and other low-wage countries in Latin America and Asia. In the early 2000s, the most popular offshoring destinations for the services-producing industries were Ireland, India, Canada, and Israel.

Offshoring provides a variety of benefits to home and host economies. Lower production costs is the top reason for offshoring. Lower wages and favorable tax regimes are two common types of cost savings. In some cases, outsourced production also results in improved product quality, lower consumer prices, and higher corporate profits. Companies hold some corporate profits as retained earnings for future investment. Companies distribute the remaining profits to shareholders in the form of dividends. Benefits to host, or recipient, countries include job creation, capital formation, technology transfers, and expanded global connectivity. The infusion of foreign investment into host countries expands physical, social, and human capital, key building blocks in the process of sustained economic development.

Host and recipient countries also experience offshoring-related costs. Home countries risk job loss in manufacturing and service industries and downward pressure on wages in some labor markets. Offshoring causes some corporate downsizing and cross-border plant relocations, reduces tax revenues for communities, and forces cuts in public services. Recipient countries face adjustment issues related to employment, industrial production, and the environment. For example, offshored production in Mexico's maquila region creates low-skill assembly jobs for women, degrades local ecosystems, and strains public services such as water and sanitation systems. By the early 2000s, the maquila sector also experienced sharp declines in the number of maquila plants and jobs as "foot-loose" foreign firms relocated to China and other low-wage East Asian countries. The ease of cross-border capital movements raised concerns about the sustainability of economic gains from offshoring in recipient countries.

See also **Foreign Direct Investment; Maquiladoras; Production Sharing; Supply Chains; Transnational Corporations.** ***See also in Volume 2,*** **Documents 37, 38.**

Further Reading

Brittain-Catlin, William. *Offshore: The Dark Side of the Global Economy*. New York: Farrar, Straus and Giroux, 2005.

Carmel, Erran, and Paul Tjia. *Offshoring Information Technology: Sourcing and Outsourcing to a Global Workforce*. New York: Cambridge University Press, 2005.

Corbett, Michael F. *The Outsourcing Revolution: Why It Makes Sense and How to Do It Right*. Chicago, IL: Dearborn, A Kaplan Professional Company, 2004.

Davies, Paul. *What's This India Business? Offshoring, Outsourcing, and the Global Services Revolution*. Naperville, IL: Nicholas Brealey International, 2004.

Nandu, Thondavadi, and George Albert. *Offshore Outsourcing: Path to New Efficiencies in IT and Business Practices*. Bloomington, IN: Authorhouse, 2004.

ORGANIZATION FOR ECONOMIC COOPERATION AND DEVELOPMENT

The Organization for Economic Cooperation and Development (OECD) is a thirty-member intergovernmental organization that collects and analyzes statistical data, discusses global trends and issues, and forms binding and nonbinding economic and social policies. The OECD, originally called the Organization of European Economic Cooperation (OEEC), was established in 1947. The OEEC's primary mission was to administer the Marshall Plan, a massive

U.S. and Canadian aid package designed to rebuild Europe after World War II. In 1961, the Organization for Economic Cooperation and Development (OECD) replaced the OEEC. The original OECD consisted of twenty signatory nations. The OECD charter identified key goals for member nations, including sustainable economic growth and employment, international trade, rising living standards, financial stability, and economic development. The OECD charter also pledged support for policies to promote the process of economic development in non-member countries. The OECD headquarters, and secretariat, are located in Paris, France.

OECD membership consists of thirty countries. OECD member countries are required to maintain a functioning market economy and democratic political institutions. Originally, the OECD was comprised exclusively of advanced economies. In recent years, membership has expanded to include a number of emerging market and developing economies from Asia, Latin America, and eastern and central Europe. The current OECD membership is shown in Table 78. OECD member states hold a dominant position in the global economy. The combined gross domestic product (GDP) of OECD countries totaled $32.7 trillion in 2004, more than 60 percent of global output, according to the OECD's *Main Economic Indicators*. OECD member nations also accounted for 59 percent of the world's gross national income (GNI) and 75 percent of world trade, according to the *OECD Annual Report 2005*.

The OECD is a global forum for discussion and policymaking on issues or problems broadly related to sustainable economic development. The OECD, often in consultation with non-member countries, devises binding agreements and nonbinding agreements. OECD members are required to comply with binding agreements. Examples of binding agreements include the OECD Anti-Bribery Convention, the OECD Code of Liberalization of Capital Movements, and the agreement on National Treatment for Foreign Controlled Enterprises. OECD members are expected, but not required, to adhere to the organization's nonbinding agreements. One important nonbinding agreement is the OECD Guidelines for Multinational Enterprises. This document outlines certain expectations for transnational corporations in the areas of business ethics, human and labor rights, transparency, fair competition, respect for the

TABLE 78 **Organization for Economic Cooperation and Development, 2005**

World Region	Number	Member Countries
Asia and the Pacific	4	Australia, Japan, South Korea, New Zealand
Western Europe	19	Austria, Belgium, Denmark, Finland, France, Germany, Greece, Iceland, Ireland, Italy, Luxembourg, the Netherlands, Norway, Portugal, Spain, Sweden, Switzerland, Turkey, the United Kingdom
North America	3	Canada, Mexico, the United States
Eastern and Central Europe	4	Czech Republic, Hungary, Poland, Slovak Republic

Source: Organization for Economic Cooperation and Development.

environment, and other areas of corporate social responsibility. Nonbinding agreements are sometimes called "soft" agreements because compliance is voluntary. Multilateral surveillance and peer pressure are the most significant enforcement mechanisms for member and non-member countries that sign OECD agreements. The OECD's binding and nonbinding agreements help define "best practice" in today's rules-based global economy.

The OECD also promotes sustainable economic development through its twenty-three member Development Assistance Committee (DAC). The DAC coordinates foreign aid from twenty-two major donor countries and the Commission of the European Communities. Neither the OECD, nor the DAC, collects money or extends loans or grants to recipient nations. In 2003, DAC members contributed $76 billion in foreign aid to 188 countries and territories throughout the world. The two types of DAC aid are official development assistance (ODA) and official aid (OA). ODA is dispersed to developing countries. ODA totaled $69 billion in 2003. OA is dispersed to countries in eastern and central Europe and western Asia. OA totaled $7 billion in 2003. Most of the DAC foreign aid was distributed in the developing world to support pro-growth programs and projects, which ranged from peacekeeping activities to infrastructure construction. In 2003, the largest flows of DAC assistance came from the United States, Japan, France, Germany, and the United Kingdom, respectively. Underpinning DAC aid is the understanding that recipient nations, ultimately, must accept responsibility for their own development.

See also **Advanced Economies; Developing Countries; Foreign Aid; Group of Eight; Sustainable Economic Development. *See also in Volume 2,* Document 30.**

Further Reading

Armingeon, Klaus, and Michelle Beyeler, eds. *The OECD and European Welfare States*. Northampton, MA: Edward Elgar Publishing, 2004.

Henry, Miriam, et al., eds. *The OECD: Globalization and Education Policy.* New York: Pergamon Press, 2001.

Organization for Economic Cooperation and Development. *OECD in Figures*. Paris: International Energy Agency, 2004.

———. *Oecd Principles of Corporate Governance 2004*. Paris: Author, 2005.

———. *The Sources of Economic Growth in OECD Countries*. Paris: Author, 2003.

ORGANIZATION OF PETROLEUM EXPORTING COUNTRIES

The Organization of Petroleum Exporting Countries (OPEC) is an eleven-member producer cartel comprised of major petroleum-producing countries. A producer cartel is a formal agreement or organization of producers, in this case oil producers, which coordinates and harmonizes production decisions by member states. OPEC was founded in 1960. Since 1982, the OPEC cartel has increased or decreased the supply of petroleum by assigning each member country a production quota, or production ceiling. OPEC's collusive behavior increased its power to influence the price of petroleum in global petroleum markets. In March 2000 the OPEC oil ministers established a price range of $22 to $28 per barrel as the official target price for a "basket" of seven crude oils. The announced OPEC basket price range, and the assignment of subsequent production quotas, attempted to stabilize the volatile oil market. The OPEC basket price range was abandoned in January 2005 as prices soared, topping $70 per barrel in August 2005. According to the U.S. Energy Information Agency, OPEC controls about two-thirds of the world's proven petroleum reserves. A profile of OPEC's member nations is shown in Table 79.

The composition of OPEC has changed over the past several decades. OPEC was formed on September 24, 1960, in Baghdad, Iraq. OPEC's five Founding Members were Iran, Iraq, Kuwait, Saudi Arabia, and Venezuela. OPEC was established mainly to present a united front against giant oil companies, which, up to 1960, dictated oil prices to the oil-producing nations. By the mid-1970s, OPEC membership peaked at thirteen nations, with the addition of Qatar (1961), Indonesia and Libya (1962), the United Arab Emirates (1967), Algeria (1969), Nigeria (1971), Ecuador (1973), and Gabon (1975). Ecuador and Gabon withdrew from OPEC in 1992 and 1995, respectively, leaving the cartel with eleven full members. Membership is open to countries that are capable of exporting petroleum in quantity, and that share certain core values and interests with existing member nations.

OPEC's organizational structure consists of the OPEC Conference, a board of governors, a secretariat, and a number of committees and commissions. The conference is OPEC's highest authority. At its semi-annual meetings, the conference forms the cartel's policies and acts on other recommendations made by the board of governors. The conference consists of delegations from member nations, each headed by the nation's oil minister, or minister of oil,

TABLE 79 Organization of Petroleum Exporting Countries: A Profile, 2003

Region/Country	Population (millions)	Gross Domestic Product ($ millions)	GDP per Capita	Production Quota (barrels per day, 1000s)
Africa				
Algeria	31.8	$56.2	$1,766	782
Libya	5.7	$23.0	$4,064	1,312
Nigeria	124.4	$55.8	$448	2,018
Asia				
Indonesia	217.0	$208.3	$960	1,270
Middle East				
Iran	67.1	$134.7	$2,010	3,597
Iraq	25.2	$19.9	$789	n.a.
Kuwait	2.4	$43.6	$17,942	1,966
Qatar	0.6	$20.4	$32,945	635
Saudi Arabia	22.7	$211.4	$9,327	7,963
United Arab Emirates	3.1	$75.6	$24,244	2,138
South America				
Venezuela	25.7	$89.0	$3,463	2,819
OPEC totals (excl. Iraq)	525.6	$938.0	$1,785	24,500

Source: Organization of Petroleum Exporting Countries, *OPEC Annual Statistical Bulletin 2003*, xiii, 1–3, 5.

mines, and energy of member countries. The board of governors is the second tier in OPEC's structure. The board of governors attends to the day-to-day operation of OPEC and implements the policies and resolutions of the conference. The board of governors also proposes the annual budget and makes recommendations to the conference on matters of concern to the cartel. The board of governors consists of representatives from each member nation. The secretariat is OPEC's administrative and research hub. The secretariat serves as the cartel's headquarters, and is located in Vienna, Austria. The secretary-general heads the secretariat. The secretariat is funded by mandatory contributions from each member nation.

The OPEC cartel has been a dominant player in global petroleum markets for decades. Over the years, the use of production quotas has successfully bolstered oil prices, especially when members complied with agreed upon production ceilings. OPEC has also used oil as a political weapon. For example, OPEC slapped an oil embargo on the United States in 1973–1974 in protest over U.S. support for Israel during the Yom Kippur War. The power of OPEC has wavered over the years, however. Cracks in the cartel's armor appeared regularly. Most breakdowns in OPEC's unity stemmed from faltering oil prices and subsequent cheating on assigned production quotas. Over time, volatile oil prices created periods of boom and bust, which aggravated underlying tensions among member nations. Disputes over production quotas, for example, contributed to the withdrawal of Gabon and Ecuador from OPEC during the 1990s. Rumblings of dissatisfaction were also heard in Indonesia and Nigeria in the early 2000s. Cheating by member nations in the late 1990s contributed to oil's free fall in 1999 when the price dipped to just $11 per barrel. In contrast, greater OPEC unity and rising demand for petroleum increased the price of oil to more than $70 per barrel in the summer of 2005.

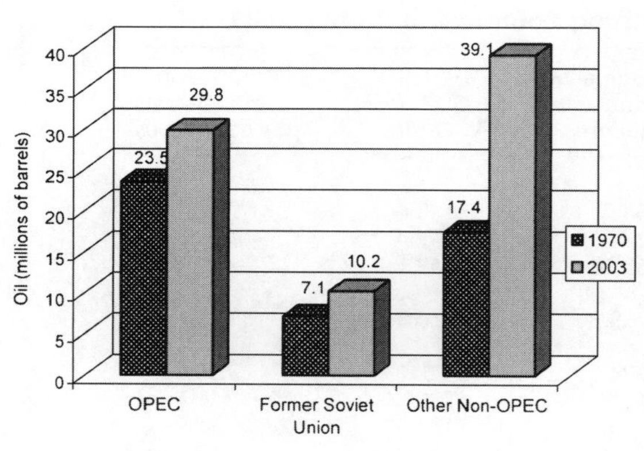

FIGURE 32 **Daily OPEC and Non-OPEC Oil Production, 1970 and 2003 (millions of barrels)**

Source: World Bank, *Global Economic Prospects 2004*, 274.

Despite the oil-price spike in 2005, long-term projections indicated a moderating in oil prices. Checks on OPEC's power include the availability of substitute primary energy sources, such as natural gas and coal; new, less expensive extractive technologies; increased production capacities among OPEC members; and the rise of additional non-OPEC oil production in West Africa, Russia, the Caspian Sea, deepwater areas in the Atlantic Ocean, and elsewhere. From 1970 to 2003, OPEC's share of global oil production fell from 49 percent to 38 percent. A snapshot comparison of global petroleum output in 1970 and 2003 is shown in Figure 32.

See also **Cartel; Energy Resources.** ***See also in Volume 2,*** **Document 44.**

Further Reading

Amuzegar, Jahangir. *Managing the Oil Wealth: OPEC's Windfalls and Pitfalls*. Rev. ed. New York: I. B. Tauris, 2001.

Citino, Nathan J. *From Arab Nationalism to OPEC: Eisenhower, King Sa'ud, and the Making of U.S.-Saudi Relations*. Bloomington, IL: Indiana University Press, 2002.

Organization of Petroleum Exporting Countries, *OPEC Annual Statistical Bulletin 2003*. Vienna, Austria: Author, 2004.

Simmons, Matthew R. *Twilight in the Desert: The Coming Saudi Oil Shock and the World Economy*. New York: John Wiley & Sons, 2005.

P

PEACE CORPS OF THE UNITED STATES

The Peace Corps of the United States is an independent agency within the executive branch of the U.S. government. President John F. Kennedy established the Peace Corps by signing Executive Order 10924 on March 1, 1961. Initially, the Peace Corps was a pilot program. On September 22, 1961, Congress gave its stamp of approval by passing the Peace Corps Act, solidifying the Peace Corps' status as an agency of the federal government. The Peace Corps' mission was to advance the cause of peace and to improve the quality of life for people in the developing world. The Peace Corps was also designed as a cultural bridge between American volunteers and the international community.

Between 1961 and 2004, 178,000 Peace Corps volunteers have lived and worked in 138 countries. In 2004 alone, more than 7,700 Peace Corps volunteers worked in seventy-two countries. Volunteers served in three general regions: Africa (35 percent of all volunteers), the Mediterranean and Asia (32 percent), and Inter-America and the Pacific (33 percent). The Peace Corps sends volunteers only to countries that request assistance. In recent years, larger Peace Corps budgets have spawned new initiatives. Congress authorized $317 million for Peace Corps activities in fiscal year 2005. The operation of the Peace Corps is the responsibility of a director and deputy director, each of whom are appointed by the president of the United States and confirmed by the senate. The Senate Foreign Relations Committee and the House Committee on International Relations also monitor Peace Corps activities and programs.

The Peace Corps has maintained a commitment to peace, human progress, and international understanding, yet its priorities have evolved over time. In recent years, the Peace Corps has increased the flow of resources to rural development, mainly to improve agricultural practices in some of the world's poorest regions. The Peace Corps also extends emergency assistance to people in distress. For example, the Peace Corps created a Crisis Corps to aid tsunami relief efforts in Thailand after the massive tsunami of December 2004 ravaged coastal regions of the country. The Crisis Corps was comprised former Peace Corps volunteers, many of whom served in Thailand in the past.

The Peace Corps responds to new challenges. For example, HIV/AIDS education and prevention is a top priority on the Peace Corps agenda. The Peace Corps identified the HIV/AIDS crisis as the most serious humanitarian challenge of the modern age. Today, all Peace Corps volunteers working in Africa are trained in HIV/AIDS prevention, education, and care. The Peace Corps supports human capital development. For example, the Peace Corps provides information technology (IT) education programs throughout the developing world to bridge the digital divide. Volunteers teach computer literacy skills, such as word processing, Internet use, and Web page design. Instruction also highlights applications of IT technologies, such as distance learning in education, and e-commerce in business. In 2005, Peace Corps volunteers' primary work areas included education (34 percent of all volunteers), health and HIV/AIDS (20 percent), environment (16 percent), business (16 percent), agriculture (6 percent), youth (3 percent), and other areas (5 percent). The Peace Corps' poverty-reduction efforts complement the work of multilateral development organizations, and are consistent with the UN Millennium Development Goals (MDGs).

See also **Developing Countries; Digital Divide; Foreign Aid; Human Development; Quality of Life; Sustainable Economic Development.**

Further Reading

Banerjee, Dillon. *So You Want to Join the Peace Corps: What to Know before You Go*. Berkeley. CA: Ten Speed Press, 2000.

Collins, Joseph, Stefano Dezerega, and Zahara Heckscher. *How to Live Your Dream of Volunteering Overseas*. New York: Penguin Books, 2002.

Erdman, Sarah. *Nine Hills to Nambonkaha: Two Years in the Heart of an African Village*. New York: Henry Holt and Company, 2003.

Rice, Gerald T. *The Bold Experiment: JFK's Peace Corps*. Notre Dame, IN: University of Notre Dame Press, 1985.

Vandegrift, Tom. *24 New Moons*. Seattle, WA: Infinity Publishing, 2003.

PIGOU, ARTHUR C.

Arthur C. Pigou (1877–1959) was a British economist and educator. Pigou is widely recognized as the founder of welfare economics, a branch of economics that favors an expanded role for government in promoting social and economic justice. Pigou's ideas attacked the prevailing laissez-faire doctrine of the early twentieth century. Later, his ideas underpinned the welfare state concept. Pigou was born on the Island of Wight, England, received his early education at Harrow, and his higher education at King's College, Cambridge. In 1902, Pigou was appointed a lecturer at Cambridge and, in 1908, succeeded the venerable Alfred Marshall as chair of political economy at the college. While chair of the political economy department, a position he held until his retirement in 1943, Pigou wrote *Wealth and Welfare* (1912) and *The Economics of Welfare* (1920).

The Economics of Welfare, an expanded version of his earlier *Wealth and Welfare*, supported additional government intervention in the economy to relieve the human suffering of the poor. He reasoned that under capitalism, self-interest guided the allocation of resources by individuals and firms. He also recognized that the winners in a capitalist economy were rewarded lavishly, while the poor were left to fend for themselves. Pigou concluded that because society sanctioned certain economic inequities, the government should assume some responsibility for the plight of the poor. He also reasoned that the redistribution of some income from the rich to the poor would increase the well-being of society. Pigou proposed public assistance programs to provide housing, health care, and other necessities to the poor. He also proposed the creation of a system of "labor exchanges" to help workers find jobs; higher wages to promote economic justice; and public works programs to create jobs during recessions or depressions. Economists often look to *The Economics of Welfare* as the birth of welfare economics, a branch of economics that deals with the redistribution of society's income and wealth to promote people's economic well-being.

By the 1920s, Pigou's groundbreaking work in the field of welfare economics directly challenged the entrenched laissez-faire doctrine. Laissez-faire economics viewed most government intervention in the economy as unwarranted and counterproductive. Pigou's work also laid the philosophical foundation for the creation of the welfare state. In a welfare state, the government assumes a central role in promoting the general well-being of citizens through extensive social insurance and public assistance programs, free public education, and other programs. After World War II, Sweden, Norway, and other democratic socialist nations in Western Europe instituted programs compatible with Pigou's welfare-state concept. Critics argued that cradle-to-grave security under the welfare state destroys work incentives, and retards economic efficiency and growth.

See also **Capitalism; Democratic Socialism; Economic Freedom.**

Further Reading

Ambrosi, Gerhard M. *Keynes, Pigou and Cambridge Keynesians: Authenticity and Analytical Perspective on the Keynes-Classics Debate.* New York: Palgrave Macmillan, 2004.

Blaug, Mark. *Arthur Pigou (1877–1959).* Northampton, MA: Edward Elgar Publishing, 1992.

Little, Ian M. D. *A Critique of Welfare Economics.* 2d ed. New York: Oxford University Press, 2003.

Pigou, A. C. *The Economics of Welfare.* Piscataway, NJ: Transaction Publishers, 2002.

POPULATION

Population refers to the number of people living within a region, such as a city, country, or the world. In August 2005, for example, the population of the United States was 297 million people, while the population of the world stood at 6.5 billion people. Economists, demographers, and others study population to better understand how population affects economic and human development.

Two important global population trends are readily observable. First, the world's total population will continue to grow well into the twenty-first century. Historically, it wasn't until 1850 that the world's population hit its first billion people. In 2000, 6 billion people inhabited the planet. By 2050 the world's population will jump to nearly 9 billion people. The rapid population

Street in Windhoek, Namibia. Population growth in poorer countries will swell world population to 9 billion people by 2050.
Courtesy of CORBIS

growth over the past 150 years was due mainly to progressively lower mortality rates and a higher life expectancy for people in many world regions. Access to modern medicine and health care facilities, improved nutrition, knowledge about hygiene and sanitation, and better communications and transportation networks contributed to lower mortality rates and a longer life span for people in most countries. While death rates fell, fertility rates among women remained relatively high, however, especially in the developing world. The world's population will climb by nearly 3 billion people between 2000 and 2050, as shown in Figure 33.

The second global population trend illustrates the divergent paths of more developed and less developed countries. The population outlook for the more developed countries is one of stability over the next fifty years. The population trend for the less developed countries is for continued growth, as shown in Figure 33. In 1950, 32 percent of the global population lived in the more developed countries in Europe and North America, and in Japan, Australia, and New Zealand. The remaining 68 percent of the world's people lived in the less developed regions of Africa, Asia, and

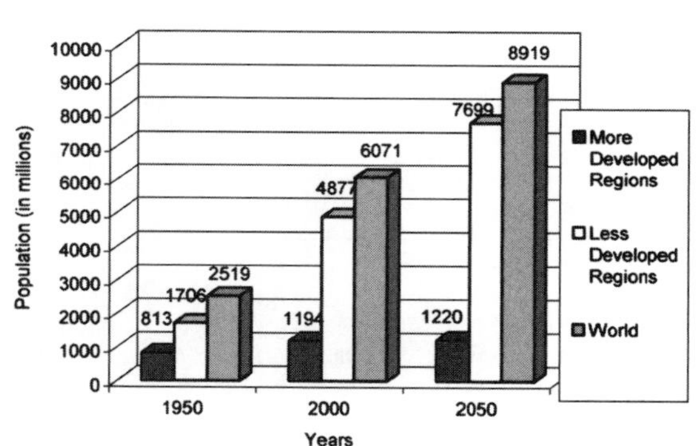

FIGURE 33 **World Population Growth, 1950 to 2050 (in millions)**

Source: United Nations Department of Economic and Social Affairs, Population Division, *World Population to 2300*, 14.

the Pacific, and Latin America and the Caribbean. The population gap between richer and poorer countries widened by 2000, when the percentage of people living in more developed countries shrunk to 20 percent, compared to 80 percent in the less developed countries. By 2050, just 14 percent of the world's people will reside in the more developed countries, and 86 percent will live in less developed countries. According to the United Nations, 99 percent of the world's population growth will occur in the less developed regions. In addition, population growth in the fifty least developed countries (LDCs) will roughly triple from 2000 to 2050, rising to 1.7 billion people. In contrast, the populations of many developed countries will decline by the mid-twenty-first century. The population of the United States will continue to climb, however, topping 400 million by 2050. In the United States, a relatively high fertility rate, and immigration, will account for most of the country's population boom. A comparison of the world's largest countries from 1950 to 2050 illustrates the population shift toward the less developed countries. This population shift is shown in Table 80.

Rapid population growth is a major challenge to sustainable economic development, especially in the world's poorest regions. Population pressures perpetuate the vicious cycle of poverty, which plagues billions of people in the developing world. Rising populations in low-income developing countries strain fragile ecosystems as larger numbers of people compete for dwindling supplies of fresh water, arable land, and energy resources. In addition, resources devoted to people's rudimentary survival needs such as food, clothing, and shelter weaken national savings and investment in new capital goods, research and development (R&D), and technology. Prospects for breaking the cycle of poverty are further dimmed by an underdeveloped and overburdened social infrastructure, which cannot support a quality educational system, health care, and other social services. Table 81 shows glaring disparities in selected indicators of human development by world region.

In 1994, the United Nations convened the International Conference on Population and Development (ICPD) to address population issues. The ICPD, which

TABLE 80 **World's Largest Countries: 1950 to 2050 (millions of people)**

Ranking in 1950		Ranking in 2000		Ranking in 2050	
Country	Population	Country	Population	Country	Population
China	555	China	1,275	India	1,531
India	358	India	1,017	China	1,395
United States	158	United States	285	United States	409
Russia	103	Indonesia	212	Pakistan	349
Japan	84	Brazil	172	Indonesia	294
Indonesia	80	Russia	146	Nigeria	259
Germany	68	Pakistan	143	Bangladesh	255
Brazil	54	Bangladesh	138	Brazil	233
United Kingdom	50	Japan	127	Ethiopia	171
Italy	47	Nigeria	115	Congo, DR	152

Source: United Nations Department of Economic and Social Affairs, Population Division, *World Population to 2300*, 42.

TABLE 81 **Selected Population Data by World Region, 2004**

World Region	Population (millions)	Rate of Natural Increase	Total Fertility Rate (per 1000)	Infant Mortality Rate (per 1000)	Life Expectancy (years)
Africa	885	2.4	5.1	90	52
Asia	3,875	1.3	2.6	54	67
Europe	728	−0.2	1.4	7	74
Latin America and Caribbean	549	1.6	2.6	29	72
N. America	326	0.5	2.0	7	78
Oceana	33	1.0	2.1	26	75
World	6,396	1.3	2.8	56	67

Source: Population Reference Bureau, *2004 World Population Data Sheet*, 5–12.

took place in Cairo, recognized the link between population growth and the vicious cycle of poverty in the developing world. The ICPD adopted a twenty-year Program of Action, which created a global blueprint for reducing the population growth rate, and advancing social and human development. The UN General Assembly strengthened the blueprint five years later (ICPD + 5). First, the blueprint called for educational reform to equalize opportunities between male and female children. Second, the blueprint proposed legal reforms to protect women's rights in employment, property ownership, and inheritance. Expanded protections against gender-based violence were also included. Third, the blueprint stressed women's reproductive rights, including the right to choose the number and spacing of children. Fourth, the blueprint proposed expanded family planning services to reduce unwanted or mistimed pregnancies. Family planning services require skilled medical personnel, adequate health care facilities, family counselors, and access to contraceptives.

By 2004, ten years after the ICPD Program of Action was approved, the United Nations Population Fund (UNFPA) issued a progress report on the state of human population in the world. The UNFPA identified promising developments in integrating population policies with countries' development plans, expanding reproductive health programs and women's rights initiatives, strengthening HIV/AIDS education programs, and improving access to family planning services. Significant challenges remained, however. Topping the list were relatively high fertility rates and maternal mortality rates in many of the world's least developed countries (LDCs); the spread of the HIV/AIDS epidemic in Africa, the Caribbean, and other world regions; and gaps in program coverage for traditionally marginalized peoples such as the rural poor, urban slum dwellers, and refugees. The United Nations Department of Economic and Social Affairs predicted the global population will plateau at roughly 9 billion people by the mid-twenty-first century.

See also **Developing Countries; Human Development; Least Developed Countries; Malthus, Thomas R.; Poverty; Quality of Life; Sustainable Economic Development.** ***See also in Volume 2,*** **Documents 1, 2, 3, 49.**

Further Reading

Population Reference Bureau. *2004 World Population Data Sheet.* Washington, DC: Author, 2004.

United Nations. *Review and Appraisal of the Progress Made in Achieving the Goals and Objectives of the Programme of Action of the International Conference on Population and Development: The 2004 Report.* New York: Author, 2004.

United Nations Department of Economic and Social Affairs, Population Division. *World Population to 2300.* New York: United Nations, 2004.

United Nations Population Fund. *UNFPA State of World Population 2004.* New York: Author, 2004.

World Bank. *Improving Health, Nutrition and Population Outcomes in Sub-Saharan Africa: The Role of the World Bank.* Washington, DC: Author, 2005.

POVERTY

Poverty is a human condition in which people lack the material goods necessary for a minimal standard of living. Essential material goods include food, clothing, and shelter. The most common measurement of poverty is level of income or consumption. In 1990, the World Bank introduced the $1 per person per day income standard to distinguish the poor from the non-poor in the developing world. The $1 per person per day poverty line is measured in purchasing power parity (PPP) prices to reflect different costs of living in different countries. Over time, the $1 per person per day standard has become the world's most universally accepted poverty line, or poverty threshold. In the early 2000s, 1.1 billion people in the global economy subsisted on less than $1 per day, and 2.7 billion people lived on less than $2 per day.

Extreme poverty refers to people who fall beneath the World Bank's $1 per day poverty line. The poverty rate, also called poverty incidence, is the percentage of a country's total population that lives in extreme poverty. In some of the world's poorest countries—including Burundi, the Central African Republic, Mali, Niger, Nigeria, Sierra Leone, and Zambia—more than half the entire population lives in extreme poverty. Table 82 shows World Bank estimates of extreme poverty in the developing world from 1990 to 2015. According to World Bank, extreme poverty will drop by about one-half, or 600 million

TABLE 82 **Extreme Poverty in the Developing World by Region, 1990 to 2015***

Region	Extreme Poverty (1990)	Extreme Poverty (2001)	Extreme Poverty (2015)
East Asia and the Pacific	472	271	19
Europe and Central Asia	2	17	2
Latin America and Caribbean	49	50	43
Middle East and North Africa	6	7	4
South Asia	462	431	216
Sub-Saharan Africa	227	313	340
Developing world	1,218	1,089	622

*Extreme poverty counts people living on less than $1 per day.
Source: World Bank, *Global Economic Prospects 2005*, 21.

people, between 1990 and 2015. The number of people living in extreme poverty will decline in all regions except sub-Saharan Africa.

Many countries in the developing and developed world have established their own measurements of poverty. In developing countries, the national poverty line typically falls between $1 and $2 per person per day. In the advanced economies, however, the $1 per person per day standard is unrealistically low. In the United States, for example, the U.S. Census Bureau uses a household's money income, size, and composition to distinguish the poor from the non-poor. In 2003, a household consisting of two people was poor if its money income dipped below $12,015; a household of four was poor if its income fell below $18,810; and a household of nine or more persons was poor if its income fell below $37,656. As was the case with developing countries, the income or consumption level that separates the poor from the non-poor is called the poverty line, or poverty threshold. In the United States the government calculates the poverty line by multiplying a typical household's annual food budget times three. Thus, the poverty line inches upward each year as price levels rise. Over the past three decades the number of Americans falling below the poverty line ranged from a low of 23 million in 1973 to a high of 39 million in 1993. In 2003, about 35.9 million people were considered poor, and the poverty rate, which measures the percentage of Americans living in poverty, was 12.5 percent.

Glaring disparities in income and consumption exist between nations and within nations. In 2002, for example, 700 million people lived in the least developed countries (LDCs). The average gross domestic product (GDP) per capita in LDCs was just $281 per year. In contrast, the GDP per capita of people living in the advanced economies averaged $28,388. Disparities in income and consumption also exist within countries. Sometimes income inequality is severe within developing countries. Table 83 compares income inequality in representative developing countries. The level of inequality is based on the amount of

TABLE 83 **Income Distribution in Selected Developing Countries**

	Share of Income or Consumption		Inequality Measures
Country	Poorest 20%	Richest 20%	Comparing Richest 20% to Poorest 20%
High degree of inequality			
Botswana	2.2%	70.3%	31.5 times
Brazil	2.0%	64.4%	31.5 times
Namibia	1.4%	78.7%	56.1 times
Sierra Leone	1.1%	63.4%	57.6 times
Low degree of inequality			
Bangladesh	9.0%	41.3%	4.6 times
Egypt	8.6%	43.6%	5.1 times
Ethiopia	9.1%	39.4%	4.3 times
India	8.9%	41.6%	4.7 times

Source: United Nations Development Program, *Human Development Report 2004*, 188–191.

income or consumption by the richest and poorest 20 percent of the population in each country. In Brazil, Botswana, Namibia, and Sierra Leone, the income of the top 20 percent of the population is more than thirty times the amount of the bottom 20 percent. Lower income inequality was recorded in Bangladesh, Ethiopia, Egypt, and India, however.

Income and consumption inequality is less severe in the advanced economies than in many developing countries. In the United States, for example, the richest 20 percent of the population has about eight times the income of the poorest 20 percent. The income inequality in Norway, Sweden, Japan, and Finland is less than half that of the United States. There are many reasons for the income disparity between the different economic classes in the U.S. economy. Income distribution is influenced by the compensation workers receive in labor markets, as well as income derived from interest payments, dividends, capital gains, rents, entrepreneurial profits, and a variety of public transfer payments. The U.S. Census Bureau reported a widening income gap between America's richest and poorest citizens over the past quarter century. Stricter regulations on public assistance for the poor, stagnant or declining real wages for many middle-class wage earners, and higher incomes for the highly educated and well-connected professional classes helped account for the growing income gap.

Income and consumption are the most widely used measures of poverty. Some economists view monetary measures as narrow and inadequate, however. These economists favor the inclusion of a broader spectrum of factors related to the human condition. Broader measures of poverty not only include people's income, but also daily calorie intake, level of educational attainment, personal health and security, and degree of inclusion in the economic and political mainstream. Some experts suggest that a broader, multidimensional approach to defining poverty enables the government to identify and address specific problems of the poor.

By the early 2000s, poverty reduction was the overriding goal of the international community. The Millennium Development Goals (MDGs), which was approved by the United Nations in 2000, solidified the world's commitment to poverty reduction. The MDG's first goal, to "eradicate extreme poverty and hunger" is the centerpiece of global efforts to establish a more just and secure global economy. The World Bank, International Monetary Fund (IMF), regional development banks, specialized agencies and programs of the United Nations system, and other major institutions in the global economy have hopped onto the poverty-reduction bandwagon.

See also **Advanced Economies; Developing Countries; Foreign Aid; Gross National Income; Human Development; International Monetary Fund; Least Developed Countries; Millennium Development Goals; Purchasing Power Parity; Quality of Life; Regional Development Banks; Sachs, Jeffrey D.; Ward, Barbara M.; World Bank Group.** ***See also in Volume 2,*** **Documents 4, 5, 7, 8, 9, 32, 38, 39, 50, 51, 59.**

Further Reading

Cline, William R. *Trade Policy and Global Poverty*. Washington, DC: Institute for International Economics, 2004.

Kerbo, Harold R. *World Poverty: Modern World System and the Roots of Global Inequality*. New York: McGraw-Hill, 2005.
Milanovic, Branko. *Worlds Apart: Measuring International and Global Inequality*. Princeton, NJ: Princeton University Press, 2005.
Prahalad, C. K. *The Fortune at the Bottom of the Pyramid: Eradicating Poverty through Profits*. Philadelphia, PA: Wharton School Publishing, 2004.
Smith, Stephen C. *Ending Global Poverty: A Guide to What Works*. New York: Palgrave Macmillan, 2005.

PRIVATIZATION

Privatization is the process of converting state-owned assets, production facilities, or service-delivery systems to the private sector. Since the 1980s, many countries in the global economy have privatized government assets and enterprises. Privatization accompanied the global shift toward market-oriented economies over the past quarter century. The transfer of goods-producing and services-producing enterprises from the public to the private sector was designed to increase production efficiency, improve product quality, create domestic and foreign investment opportunities, and stimulate entrepreneurial activity. Privatization also addressed structural reforms in national economies. Privatization helped reduce bloated government bureaucracies, dismantle ineffective state planning agencies, and end expensive subsidy programs. Further, privatization generates a one-time revenue windfall for governments. A recent International Monetary Fund (IMF) report concluded that privatization raised $1.1 trillion for governments between 1985 and 1999. Privatization revenues, by region, are shown in Figure 34 ("other" in the figure includes Eastern Europe and Central Asia, Middle East and North Africa, Southeast Asia, and sub-Saharan Africa).

Governments privatize companies and other assets in a variety of ways. The most common privatization approach is the issuance of shares of stock in the enterprise. The issue of new stocks is called an initial public offering (IPO). Shares of stock are sold to individuals, workers, financial institutions, local businesses, transnational corporations (TNCs), and other investors. Often, the government holds some of the shares in the privatized enterprise. Another approach to privatization is the issuance of "vouchers." Vouchers dominated the early years of Russia's privatization from 1992 to 1994. Under the voucher system, the government issued vouchers to the Russian people. Vouchers gave citizens the right to buy small enterprises or buy shares of newly privatized corporations at public auction. Russia's

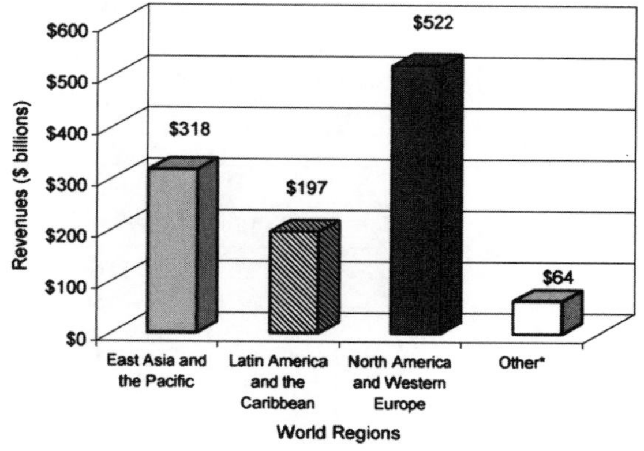

FIGURE 34 **Global Privatization Revenues, 1985 to 1999 (in constant 1985 $US)**

Source: Nancy Brune, Geoffrey Garrett, and Bruce Kogut, "The International Monetary Fund and the Global Spread of Privatization," *IMF Staff Papers*, vol. 51, no. 2, 2004, 197.

privatization has gone through additional phases since the mid-1990s. Some privatization occurs through simple asset sales. The purchase of government assets by TNCs illustrates this type of asset transfer. Privatization, broadly interpreted, also occurs when the government retains ownership in an enterprise but hires a private firm to manage the facility. Management contracts are common in larger facilities such as airports and convention centers.

Privatization swept through the global economy during the 1980s, 1990s, and early 2000s. Governments in Latin America and the Caribbean launched extensive privatization initiatives earlier than most world regions. From the mid-1980s to the early 2000s, governments privatized key services such as banking and telecommunications, and features of the economic infrastructure such as water and transportation systems. In Europe, the United Kingdom was in the vanguard of privatization. From 1979 to 1990, Conservative British Prime Minister Margaret Thatcher aggressively privatized key industries, including telecommunications, coal, and some railway operations. France, under the leadership of Prime Minister Jacques Chirac, carried the privatization torch to the European mainland. Between 1990 and 2001, the fifteen European Union (EU) countries privatized more than half a trillion dollars worth of government assets. The largest privatization revenues, by country and world region, are shown in Table 84.

Since the early 1990s, privatization has been a centerpiece in the epic shift from communism to capitalism for twenty-seven transition economies in eastern and central Europe and central Asia. The pace of privatization varied significantly, however. Most transition economies successfully privatized small- and medium-sized enterprises (SMEs). SMEs include retail stores, construction firms, and personal and professional services. The privatization of large state-owned enterprises (SOEs), such as mines and heavy industries, was less successful. The European Bank for Reconstruction and Development (EBRD) provides development loans and privatization assistance to transition economies. EBRD reported significant progress in most countries' privatization. In 2004, the private sector accounted for at least half of the gross domestic product (GDP) in all but four transition economies. EBRD gave most transition economies high marks for their privatization efforts. In terms of small-scale privatization, nineteen transition countries, including Russia, earned a "market economy" designation. Just nine transition countries earned market economy status for the more difficult privatization of large SOEs. Reforms in eight transition countries were insufficient to meet the market economy standard in either privatization category.

TABLE 84 **Privatization Revenues by Country and Region, 1985 to 1999 (in constant 1985 $US)**

Region	Top Countries	Revenues ($ billions)
East Asia and the Pacific	Japan	$164
	Australia	$69
	China	$22
Latin America and the Caribbean	Brazil	$73
	Argentina	$43
	Mexico	$40
North America and Western Europe	United Kingdom	$130
	Italy	$102
	France	$89

Source: Nancy Brune, Geoffrey Garrett, and Bruce Kogut, "The International Monetary Fund and the Global Spread of Privatization," *IMF Staff Papers*, vol. 51, no. 2, 2004, 214–216.

Privatization has sparked controversy around the world. In Latin America, for example, price hikes resulting from the privatization of key services, such as water supplies and transportation, created a storm of protest. The 2000 privatization of the water supply in Cochabamba, Bolivia was reversed after mass demonstrations and strikes destabilized the country's third largest city. People throughout Latin American also blamed privatization for rising unemployment and the widening income gap between the rich and poor. People resented the highly favorable terms extended to foreign transnational corporations (TNCs) by national governments. Discontent with privatization also stems from the process of transferring ownership or control to private interests. Russia's voucher system, for example, was criticized for giving unfair advantages to the traditional power elite. In some countries, privatized firms have been re-acquired by the government to ensure a reliable supply of a product at a reasonable price.

See also **Communism; Democratic Socialism; European Bank for Reconstruction and Development; Foreign Direct Investment; Transition Countries; Transnational Corporations.**

Further Reading

Finger, Matthias, Oran R. Young, and Ernst U. Von Weizsacker, eds. *Limits to Privatization: When a Solution Becomes a Problem*. Washington, DC: Earthscan Publications, 2005.

Hoffman, David E. *The Oligarchs: Wealth and Power in the New Russia*. New York: Public Affairs Books, 2004.

Kessides, Ioannis. *Reforming Infrastructure: Privatization, Regulation, and Competition*. Washington, DC: World Bank Publications, 2004.

MacArov, David. *What the Market Does to People: Privatization, Globalization and Poverty*. Atlanta, GA: Clarity Press, 2003.

Megginson, William L. *The Financial Economics of Privatization*. New York: Oxford University Press, 2005.

PRODUCTION SHARING

Production sharing occurs when a business produces a good or service in stages in different countries. Production sharing is sometimes referred to as the internationalization of production. International production sharing enables a business to employ low-cost resources in an overseas production facility. The overseas facility might be owned and operated by a parent transnational corporation (TNC), or be run by a local company. Lower production costs in the overseas facility lower the price of the final good and, thus, increases the firm's global competitiveness. Production sharing in the manufacture of goods requires an efficient transportation system to carry resources and goods from one location to the next. Production sharing in services often requires sophisticated information and communications technologies (ICTs).

Production sharing has evolved since World War II. During the 1950s and 1960s, businesses in the advanced economies imported basic commodities, such as rubber, cocoa, and tin from developing countries. The advanced economies processed these commodities into final goods, which were then sold in domestic and international markets. Production sharing during this early stage involved little more than the extraction or harvesting of primary commodities for export to the industrialized countries. Over the past few decades, the concept of production sharing expanded to include the offshore outsourcing of goods-producing and services-producing enterprises. Initially, TNCs or local subcontractors built assembly plants to reap the benefits of low-wage labor. Assembly plants assembled low-end goods such as toys, clothing, and some electrical goods. In more recent years, some production sharing has involved the use of advanced physical capital and a skilled work force. Examples include the manufacture of sophisticated office equipment, computers and software, and other high-tech export goods. Offshore-outsourced business, technology, and medical services have added yet another twist to production sharing since the early 2000s. Production sharing in high-end export goods and services is concentrated in middle-income and high-income developing countries.

Production sharing benefits from trade and investment liberalization, the introduction of new technologies, and other features of globalization. Free trade enables businesses to ship resources, components, and semi-finished goods across national borders for assembly. The General Agreement on Tariffs and Trade (GATT), the World Trade Organization (WTO), and hundreds of regional trade agreements (RTAs) support trade liberalization. Foreign direct investment (FDI) by TNCs encourages the construction of assembly plants in regions with low production costs and a favorable investment climate. The rapid expansion of bilateral investment treaties (BITS) and double taxation treaties (DTTs) favor production sharing, as does the creation of export processing zones (EPZs) and investment promotion agencies (IPAs). New technologies in the transport and storage of goods, and in information and communications technologies (ICTs), encourage TNCs to set up shop in different world regions.

Production sharing underlies manufacturing in Mexico's maquiladoras. Maquiladoras are the duty-free assembly plants that produce many types of export goods. Most of Mexico's maquiladora plants are owned by American firms, which locate south of the Rio Grande River to employ low-cost Mexican labor. Production in Mexico's maquila industries is controversial. Supporters argue that maquiladoras provide competitive jobs, teach business and management skills, and build Mexico's manufacturing sector—all key features of sustainable economic development. Opponents counter that maquiladoras exploit low-wage labor, degrade the local environment, and have a ruinous effect on employment in the TNC's home country. Opponents conclude that any benefits derived from production sharing are short-lived. In the early 2000s, production sharing in Mexico's maquila industries became a political hot potato in the larger debate over the proposed Free Trade Area of the Americas (FTAA).

See also **Foreign Direct Investment; Free Trade Area of the Americas; Globalization; International Investment Agreements; International Trade; Maquiladoras; Offshoring; Race to the Bottom; Supply Chains; Terms of Trade; Transnational Corporations. *See also in Volume 2,* Documents 37, 38.**

Further Reading

Feenstra, Robert C. *Global Production Sharing and Rising Inequality: A Survey of Trade and Wages*. Cambridge, MA: National Bureau of Economic Research, 2001.

Kamel, Rachael, and Anya Hoffman, eds. *The Maquiladora Reader: Cross-Border Organizing since NAFTA*. Philadelphia, PA: American Friends Service Committee, 1999.

Yeats, Alexander J. *Just How Big Is Global Production Sharing?* Washington, DC: World Bank, 1998.

Yusuf, Shahid, M. Anjum Altaf, and Kaoru Nabeshima. *Global Production Networking and Technological Change in East Asia*. Washington, DC: World Bank Publications, 2004.

PROTECTIONISM

Protectionism is the government's use of import controls and export subsidies to distort the free movement of merchandise and commercial services between countries. The main goal of protectionism is to protect domestic businesses and workers from foreign competition. Since World War II, trade and investment liberalization have weakened protectionist sentiments in the global economy. Under the auspices of the General Agreement on Tariffs and Trade (GATT), eight trade rounds were negotiated to dismantle countries' protectionist trade policies. Since 1995 the World Trade Organization (WTO), GATT's successor organization, has carried the free trade torch. Under the WTO, a ninth trade round commenced in 2001. Often called the Doha Round, formal negotiations centered on creating a fair global trading system and promoting economic development.

Protectionism involves the use of tariff and non-tariff trade barriers to restrict foreign imports into a country, or expand exports to another country. The main import controls are tariffs, import quotas, voluntary quotas, and embargoes. Tariffs are federal taxes on imported goods or commercial services. A tariff increases the price of a foreign import. Tariffs discourage the consumption of imported goods, and encourage the consumption of similar domestically produced goods. An import quota limits the quantity of an imported product by number of items, weight, volume, or other measurement. A voluntary quota, also called a voluntary export restraint (VER), is a bilateral agreement that sets a "voluntary" limit on the quantity of an export from another country. In practice, there is little difference between an import quota and a VER. An embargo stops imports from and exports to another country. A comprehensive embargo stops all trade with the targeted country, while a selective embargo bans trade in one or several key products. Often, embargoes are politically motivated, designed to pressure another government to change an offensive domestic or international policy.

Export subsidies represent a second type of protectionist trade policy. An export subsidy is a government payment to a domestic firm. The subsidy defrays certain production costs and, thus, enables the firm to sell its output at lower, more competitive prices in global markets. Agricultural subsidies are particularly contentious in today's global economy. Many advanced economies pump billions of dollars into agricultural subsidies to encourage domestic production and enhance producers' global competitiveness. Developing countries, on the other hand, view massive subsidies in the global North as an unfair trade practice that stacks the deck against agricultural exports from the global South. In the early 2000s, direct subsidies to farmers were relatively high in the European Union (EU) countries and the United States, and relatively low in Australia and New Zealand. Controversial subsidies in the industrial sector also create conflicts in the global trading system. In 2005 the United States and European Union (EU) traded charges of unfair government subsidies to rival commercial aircraft companies, Airbus (EU) and Boeing (US). The United States and EU each submitted formal requests to the World Trade Organization in 2005 to establish a dispute settlement panel to resolve the dispute.

A number of arguments support protectionism. First, the infant industries' argument supports trade barriers to temporarily protect younger, vulnerable industries in an economy. Once the infant industry matures, the trade barriers are removed. Second, the diversification argument supports trade restrictions to prevent overspecialization in an economy. Excessive specialization, especially in the production of primary commodities, could create a cycle of boom and bust in volatile international markets. Third, the anti-dumping argument supports trade barriers, such as tariffs, to counterbalance dumping. Dumping is an unfair trade practice in which foreign merchandise is sold at a price below its costs of production. Fourth, the sensitive industries argument supports trade protections for specific industries vital to national defense or homeland security. Fifth, the new protectionism supports trade barriers to create self-reliant, localized economies. The new protectionists oppose most long-distance trade and foreign direct investment.

Compelling arguments oppose protectionism. First, protectionism stifles free trade, a wellspring of global economic growth. Free trade encourages countries to specialize in the production of goods in which they have a comparative advantage, and exchange surpluses in global markets. Second, protectionism hurts business efficiency. By restricting foreign competition, trade barriers remove incentives for domestic producers to innovate and become more productive. Third, protectionism limits consumer choice. Trade barriers reduce or exclude certain items from domestic markets and raise the price of many other items. Fourth, protectionism invites retaliation, even trade wars. The Smoot-Hawley Tariff (1930) set off a global trade war during the early years of the global depression. The trade war hindered the global economy's recovery from the global economic downturn.

See also **Comparative Advantage; Embargo; General Agreement on Tariffs and Trade; Globalization; Import Quotas; International Trade; New Protectionism; Tariffs; Voluntary Quotas; World Trade Organization.**

Further Reading

Barfield, Claude E. *High-Tech Protectionism: The Irrationality of Antidumping Laws.* Washington, DC: American Enterprise Institute Press, 2003.

Dormois, Jean-Pierre. *Classical Trade Protectionism: 1815–1914*. New York: Routledge, 2005.
Lusztig, Michael. *The Limits of Protectionism: Building Coalitions for Free Trade*. Pittsburgh, PA: University of Pittsburgh Press, 2004.
Neumayer, Eric. *Greening Trade and Investment: Environmental Protection without Protectionism*. Washington, DC: Earthscan Publications, 2001.
Roberts, Russell D. *The Choice: A Fable of Free Trade and Protectionism*. Rev. ed. Paramus, NJ: Prentice Hall, 2000.

PURCHASING POWER PARITY

Purchasing power parity (PPP) is an approach to converting national currencies in the global economy. The PPP method of currency conversion considers the buying power of a nation's currency within its domestic economy. PPP is an alternative to the traditional exchange rate approach to currency conversion. The exchange rate approach states the relative value of currencies in foreign exchange markets. The exchange rate approach does not consider the actual purchasing power of money within countries, however. The PPP conversion acknowledges that $1 buys more goods in a low-income developing country than in a high-income country. The difference in purchasing power stems from lower prices for food, clothing, housing, personal services, and other goods in poorer countries. Today, major international organizations, such as the World Bank and the International Monetary Fund (IMF), use PPP to make cross-border comparisons of gross domestic product (GDP), standard of living, and poverty.

The International Comparison Program (ICP) was founded in 1968 to collect international price data for statistical analyses. Over time, the ICP developed and improved PPP measures for use by governments, multilateral organizations, researchers, and other stakeholders in the global economy. Initially, the ICP was co-sponsored by the United Nations (UN) and a special statistical unit at the University of Pennsylvania. The ICP piloted its first international price surveys in 1970. The 1970 surveys covered just ten countries. Today, the World Bank coordinates ICP data collection in the emerging market and developing economies. Data collection is enhanced by the World Bank's partner organizations such as the United Nations, regional development banks, and other statistical agencies. The Organization for Economic Cooperation and Development (OECD) and the Statistical Office of the European Union (Eurostat) organize data collection for the OECD countries. Price data for about 150 countries is collected and analyzed. The PPP exchange rate is determined by comparing the market price of a uniform "basket" of commonly consumed goods and services in different countries. The "basket" of commonly consumed items includes consumer goods and services, government services, physical capital, public utilities, and so on. PPP is calculated in three- to five-year cycles, depending on world region.

PPP measures of GDP, gross national income (GNI) per capita, and other price data enable more reliable international comparisons of national output,

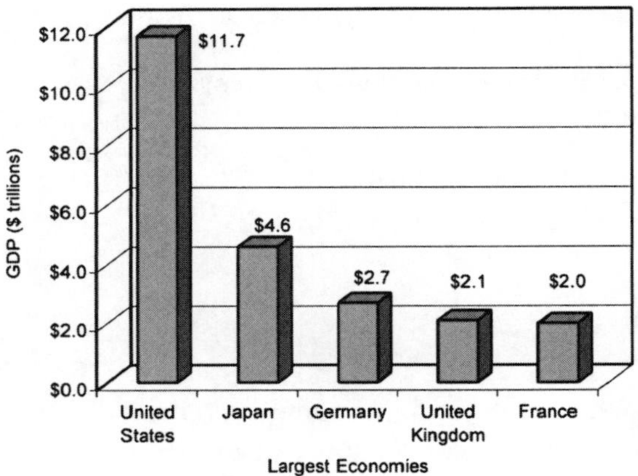

FIGURE 35 **World's Largest Economies: Exchange Rate (Atlas) Method, 2004 ($ trillions)**

Source: World Bank, *World Development Bank Database*, July 15, 2005.

consumption, and living standards. For example, in 2004, the global GDP totaled $41 trillion using the traditional exchange rate calculation, also known as the Atlas method. Of this total, high-income countries produced $32.7 trillion in new goods and services (80 percent of global output), middle-income countries produced $6.9 trillion (16.9 percent), and low-income countries produced $1.3 trillion (3.1 percent). After adjusting output data for purchasing power parity, global GDP in 2004 jumped to $56 trillion, with middle-income and low-income developing countries contributing larger shares of the world's total output. Using PPP calculation of the 2004 global GDP, high-income countries produced $31 trillion in new goods and services (55.3 percent of global output), middle-income countries produced $19.7 trillion (35.2 percent), and low-income countries produced $5.3 trillion (9.5 percent). The use of PPP calculations also adjusts the relative size of individual economies, adding significantly to the position of low-income and middle-income countries where $1 is able to purchase more goods than in high-income countries. Figure 35 and Figure 36 compare the world's largest economies using the Atlas and PPP calculations.

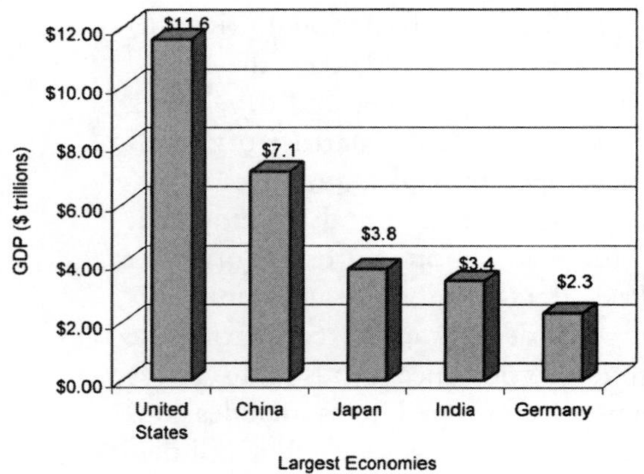

FIGURE 36 **World's Largest Economies: PPP Method, 2004 ($ trillions)**

Source: World Bank, *World Development Bank Database*, July 15, 2005.

Estimates of nations' GNI per capita, a leading indicator of living standards, are also influenced by PPP. For example, the World Bank reported India's 2004 GNI per capita was just $620 using the Atlas calculation. India's PPP measurement of GNI per capita was $3,100, however, about five times its Atlas method total. India's PPP GNI per capita accounts for the greater purchasing power of $1 in this poorer country. Conversely, Japan's 2004 GNI per capita was $37,180 using the Atlas calculation. PPP adjustments lowered Japan's GNI per capita to just $30,040 to reflect the high cost of living in Japan.

See also **Advanced Economies; Developing Countries; Gross Domestic Product; Gross National Income.**

Further Reading

Cashin, Paul. *An Unbiased Appraisal of Purchasing Power Parity*. Washington, DC: International Monetary Fund, Research Department, 2001.

Chang-Tai Hsieh. *Relative Prices and Relative Prosperity*. Cambridge, MA: National Bureau of Economic Research, 2003.

Li Lian Ong. *The Big Mac Index: Applications of Purchasing Power Parity*. New York: Routledge, 2003.

Organization for Economic Cooperation and Development. *Purchasing Power Parities and Real Expenditures: 2002 Benchmark Year*. Paris: Author, 2005.

Q

QUALITY OF LIFE

Quality of life refers to the overall conditions under which people live. Quality of life is concerned with people's level of consumption and other factors related to economic well-being. Quality of life also deals with people's social, political, and cultural environment. It is difficult to measure quality of life or to make cross-border quality-of-life comparisons. Instead, government leaders, development economists, and others tend to examine a broad range of economic, social, and political indicators of human development. Measurable indicators show that people in high-income countries have a higher quality of life than people in middle-income and low-income countries. Improving the quality of life for people in the world's poorer regions is a crucial component in achieving sustainable economic development.

Many quality-of-life issues fall within the purview of the United Nations' Millennium Development Goals (MDGs), which was adopted by the UN General Assembly in 2000. The overarching MDG is to "eradicate extreme poverty and hunger." Quality-of-life indicators such as gross national income (GNI) per capita, and access to food and clean water, are used to assess progress toward poverty reduction. Quality-of-life indicators also consider educational opportunities, occupational training, and employment, regardless of gender; the adequacy of public services in health care, transportation, and personal security; governance issues related to citizen participation; and respect for civil and human rights.

Major multilateral organizations, such as the World Bank the United Nations Development Program (UNDP), collect and publish data about people's quality of life. The UNDP's annual *Human Development Report* offers the most comprehensive set of data on quality-of-life indicators. In its Human Development Index (HDI), the UNDP ranks countries by level of human development. The HDI considers quality-of-life indicators such as life expectancy, adult literacy, educational attainment, and gross domestic product (GDP) per capita. In 2002, the HDI identified fifty-five high human development countries, eighty-six medium human development countries, and thirty-six low human development countries. Table 85 compares and contrasts selected quality-of-life indicators for low-income, middle-income, and high-income countries. Significant inequalities in income and wealth between countries and within countries complicate analyses of people's overall quality of life.

Access to food is among the most important quality-of-life concerns in today's global economy. A recent study by the Food and Agriculture Organization (FAO) of the United Nations reported that more than 800 million people

TABLE 85 **Selected Quality-of-Life Indicators, 2002–2004**

Indicators	Low-income Countries	Middle-income Countries	High-income Countries
Income			
GNI per capita (2004)	$510	$2,190	$32,040
GNI per capita, PPP (2004)	$2,260	$6,480	$30,970
Health			
Life expectancy (years)	59	70	78
Undernourished people (%)	22%	10%	n/a
Infant mortality (per 1000)	80	30	5
Under-five mortality (per 1000)	120	37	7
Population			
Total population (millions)	2,561	2,721	941
Urban population (%)	31%	53%	78%
Annual population growth rate, 1975 to 2001	2.1	1.4	0.7
Fertility rate (per woman)	3.7	2.1	1.7
Education			
Adult literacy (%)	64%	90%	99%
Internet users (per 1000)	13	60	446

Source: United Nations Development Program (UNDP), *Human Development Report 2004,* 139–142, 152–155, 168–171, 180–183; and World Bank, *World Development Report 2005*, 256–257; World Bank, *World Development Indicators Database*, July 15, 2005, 4.

were undernourished in the early 2000s. Undernourishment was most severe in sub-Saharan Africa, where one-third of the entire population suffered from an inadequate diet. The FAO report noted 17 percent of all people living in the developing world were undernourished. More than 60 percent of the population of Burundi, Comoros, the Democratic Republic of Congo, and Eritrea were malnourished. The largest numbers of malnourished people lived in India (250 million people, 24 percent of the population), China ($142 million people, 11 percent of the population), Bangladesh (43 million people, 30 percent of the population), Ethiopia (31 million people, 46 percent of the population), and Pakistan (29 million people, 20 percent of the population).

See also **Advanced Economies; Developing Countries; Economic Growth; Gross Domestic Product; Gross National Income; Human Development; Least Developed Countries; Population; Poverty; Sustainable Economic Development.** ***See also in Volume 2,*** **Documents 1, 2, 3, 14, 33, 34, 35, 38, 51, 57, 59.**

Further Reading

Cornia, Giovanni A. *Inequality, Growth, and Poverty in an Era of Liberalization and Globalization*. New York: Oxford University Press, 2004.

Prescott-Allen, Robert. *The Wellbeing of Nations: A Country-by-Country Index of Quality of Life and the Environment*. Washington, DC: Island Press, 2001.

Seligson, Mitchell A., and John T. Passe-Smith, eds. *Development and Underdevelopment: The Political Economy of Global Inequality*. 3d ed. Boulder, CO: Lynne Rienner Publishers, 2003.

Shek, Daniel T. L., Ying-keung Chan, and Paul S. N. Lee, eds. *Quality of Life Research in Chinese, Western and Global Contexts*. New York: Springer, 2005.

United National Development Program. *Human Development Report 2004: Cultural Liberty in Today's Diverse World*. New York: Author, 2004.

R

RACE TO THE BOTTOM

Race to the bottom refers to the deterioration of labor and environmental standards that result from cross-border investments by transnational corporations (TNCs). According to the race-to-the-bottom theory, governments, mainly in the developing world, compete aggressively for foreign direct investment (FDI) by TNCs. To attract FDI, host governments relax labor standards and environmental regulations. Governments also establish export processing zones (EPZs), eliminate bureaucratic obstacles to investment, provide an economic and technological infrastructure, and offer tax breaks and other financial incentives to lure FDI to their shores. Government policies sweeten the investment climate to promote economic growth and sustainable economic development. The race-to-the-bottom theory contends that workers, local communities, and the local environment are sacrificed on the altar of corporate profits.

The term "race to the bottom" came into common usage during the 1990s. It accompanied the liberalization of international trade, FDI, and other cross-border business activity. The race-to-the-bottom theory is hotly debated. On one side of the debate are multilateral organizations such as the World Trade Organization (WTO) and World Bank, most national governments, TNCs, and other institutions that support globalization. Together, these economic and political institutions have dismantled barriers to international trade, FDI, and cross-border financial flows. On the other side of the debate are many nongovernmental organizations (NGOs), labor unions, environmental groups, and individuals. These groups believe unbridled globalization creates unjust and unsustainable patterns of production and consumption, which, inevitably, harm the planet and its peoples.

Race-to-the-bottom theorists argue that negotiations between TNCs and host governments are tilted in favor of the foreign firms. The TNC's main advantage is the high mobility of physical and financial capital. That is, the TNC is free to choose a location for its FDI. The other factors of production—labor and natural resources—are less mobile, however. Intense competition for billions of dollars in FDI obliges governments to offer highly favorable labor and environmental concessions to TNC. As a result, some TNCs (or their subcontractors) exploit workers in sweatshops, deplete natural resources, and lay waste to fragile ecosystems in order to reduce production costs. Harsh working conditions in Mexico's maquiladoras, and in China's emerging industrial sector, illustrate worker exploitation. Environmental nightmares associated with foreign extractive industries, such as mining and lumbering, illustrate the pillage of the natural environment. In addition, the offshore outsourcing of jobs to low-wage countries puts downward pressure on wages and working conditions in the advanced economies. Many participants in the massive antiglobalization protests, and the global social forums of the early 2000s, subscribed to the race-to-the-bottom theory.

Spillover costs, such as pollution, occur when production damages the natural environment or other people's quality of life.
Courtesy of Getty Images: Doug Menuez

Other economists believe the race to the bottom is a myth. These economists argue the benefits of globalization far outweigh the costs. They note FDI in the developing world creates jobs that offer competitive wage rates and decent working conditions. They contend that corporate codes of conduct, the International Labor Organization's (ILO) Declaration on Fundamental Principles and Rights at Work, and other internationally recognized labor standards protect workers' rights. They argue that FDI has spillover benefits for local economies, including technology transfers, the infusion of management skills, global connectivity, and the introduction of best practices in the world of business. Critics of the race-to-the-bottom theory conclude that weak labor and environmental standards are not the primary determinants of foreign investment. Instead, TNC investment decisions are based mainly on the sophistication of an economy's infrastructure, the stability of its economic and political institutions, and its commitment to legal protections for private property rights.

See also **Corporate Social Responsibility; Foreign Direct Investment; Globalization; Human Development; International Labor Organization; International Trade; Maquiladoras; Quality of Life; Supply Chains; Sustainable Economic Development; Transnational Corporations.** ***See also in Volume 2,*** **Documents 28, 29, 30, 31, 33, 34, 35, 36, 37, 38, 39.**

Further Reading

Hackett, John T. *Race to the Bottom*. Bloomington, IN: Authorhouse, 2004.
Hira, Ron, and Anil Hira. *Outsourcing America: What's behind Our National Crisis and How We Can Reclaim American Jobs*. New York: AMACOM, 2005.
Kernaghan, Charles. *Bangladesh: Ending the Race to the Bottom*. Collingdale, PA: DIANE Publishing Company, 2004.

Tonelson, Alan. *The Race to the Bottom: Why a Worldwide Worker Surplus and Uncontrolled Free Trade Are Sinking American Living Standards*. Boulder, CO: Westview Press, 2002.

REGIONAL DEVELOPMENT BANKS

A regional development bank (RDB) is a member-owned, not-for-profit multilateral lending and development institution. Regional member banks are also called multilateral development banks. Regional member countries are located within the world geographic region serviced by the RDB. Nonregional member countries, which are comprised mainly of richer advanced economies, are located outside of the serviced geographic region. The overarching goal of RDBs in today's global economy is poverty reduction through sustainable economic development.

RDBs extend loans and provide technical assistance to regional member nations. Loanable funds are derived from three sources: monetary contributions from member nations, interest payments from past loans, and borrowing from global financial institutions. Regional development banks loan money to regional member nations at favorable rates. The poorest member countries are often eligible for concessional loans. Concessional loans are normally interest free and are repaid over several decades.

RDBs and sub-regional development banks service clusters of emerging market and developing economies around the world. The world's four main RDBs include the African Development Bank Group, which serves the continent

TABLE 86 **Regional Development Banks: An Overview**

Regional Development Bank	Established (year)	Cumulative Loans and Assistance ($ billions)	Affiliated Institutions
African Development Bank (ADB) Group (77 members)	1964	$36	African Development Bank African Development Fund Nigeria Trust Fund
Asian Development Bank (ADB) (63 members)	1966	$105	Asian Development Bank Asian Development Fund Technical Assistance Special Fund Japan Special Fund ADB Institute Special Fund
European Bank for Reconstruction and Development (EBRD) (60 members)	1990	23 (euro)*	European Bank for Reconstruction and Development
Inter-American Development Bank (IDB) Group (47 members)	1959	$129	Inter-American Development Bank Inter-American Investment Corporation Multilateral Investment Fund

*In billions.

Sources: African Development Bank Group, *Compendium of Statistics on Bank Group Operations*, vol. 27, 2004, 6, 18, 32, 46; Asian Development Bank, *Annual Report 2003*, vi; European Bank for Reconstruction and Development, *Annual Report 2003*, 4; Inter-American Development Bank, *Annual Report 2003*, 44.

of Africa; the Asian Development Bank, which serves most of Asia; the European Bank for Reconstruction and Development, which serves the transition economies of eastern and central Europe and central Asia; and the Inter-American Development Bank Group, which serves Latin America. An overview of the four main RDBs is shown in Table 86. Over time, the four main RDBs have extended loans, grants, and other assistance in excess of $300 billion to support economic development in the global economy. Sub-regional development banks service smaller clusters of countries. Sub-regional development banks include the Caribbean Development Bank, the Central American Bank for Economic Integration, the East African Development Bank, and the West African Development Bank.

See also **African Development Bank Group, Asian Development Bank, European Bank for Reconstruction and Development, Inter-American Development Bank Group, International Financial Institutions.** ***See also in Volume 2,*** **Documents 4, 7, 10, 32.**

Further Reading

African Development Bank. *African Development Report 2004*. New York: Oxford University Press, 2004.
Asian Development Bank. *ADB Annual Report 2003*. Manila: Author, 2004.
Bronstone, Adam. *The European Bank for Reconstruction and Development*. Manchester, UK: Manchester University Press, 1999.
Devlin, Robert, Antoni Estevadordal, and the Inter-American Development Bank, eds. *Bridges for Development*. Washington, DC: Inter-American Development Bank, 2004.
Mule, Harris M., and E. Philip English. *The Multilateral Development Banks: The African Development Bank*. Boulder, CO: Lynne Rienner Publishers, 1996.

REGIONAL TRADE AGREEMENTS

A regional trade agreement (RTA) is an agreement that creates preferential trade concessions among member countries. The most common form of trade preference is the reduction or elimination of tariffs. RTAs promote regional economic integration by dropping trade barriers. Many RTAs also promote regional integration by establishing common standards or protocols governing labor rights, environmental protection, foreign investment, and fair competition. RTAs include multilateral and bilateral trade agreements. In many cases, RTAs establish a trade bloc, which cements preferential trade and investment concessions among members. Membership in a trade bloc is often limited to countries located in a certain geographic region, such as Europe, North America, South America, or Southeast Asia. The World Trade Organization (WTO) identified about 300 RTAs in the world economy by the close of 2005. Representative RTAs, by world region, are shown in Table 87. Intraregional trade among countries belonging to RTAs accounts for about 40 percent of the world's total merchandise trade.

RTAs are categorized by level of economic integration. The World Bank identifies four RTA categories including the free trade area, customs union, common market, and economic and monetary union.

TABLE 87 **Representative Regional Trade Agreements by Region, 2004**

World Region	Representative RTAs	Member Nations (number)
Africa	East African Community	3
	Economic Community of West African States	15
	Southern African Customs Union	5
Americas	Andean Community	5
	MERCOSUR (Southern Common Market)	4
	North American Free Trade Agreement	3
Asia	ASEAN Free Trade Area	10
	Asia Pacific Economic Cooperation	21
	South Asian Free Trade Area	7
Europe	Central European Free Trade Area	7
	European Free Trade Association	4
	European Union	25
Middle East and North Africa	Euro-Mediterranean Free Trade Area	13
	Greater Arab Free Trade Area	18
	Gulf Cooperation Council	6

Source: World Bank, *Global Economic Prospects 2005*, xxiii–xxv.

A free trade area is a trade bloc that eliminates trade barriers among members, but permits individual members to devise their own restrictions on imports from non-member nations. Many regional trade blocs are organized as free trade areas. Examples of free trade areas include the North American Free Trade Agreement (NAFTA), ASEAN Free Trade Area (AFTA), and Economic Community of West African States (ECOWAS). Steps toward creating a U.S.-Central American Free Trade Agreement (CAFTA), and an even more expansive Free Trade Area of the Americas (FTAA) among the thirty-four democracies of the Western Hemisphere, were also underway during the early 2000s. Ranked by combined gross domestic product, NAFTA, which is comprised of Canada, Mexico, and the United States, is the world's largest free trade area.

A customs union creates a free trade zone for members and a common external trade policy with non-member countries. The common external tariff (CET) is a custom union's most visible external trade policy. A CET requires RTA members to levy the same import tariffs on goods entering the customs union. Examples of a customs union include the Southern Common Market (MERCOSUR) and the Andean Community, each of which evolved from a free trade area to a customs union in the early 2000s. MERCOSUR is comprised of Argentina, Brazil, Paraguay, and Uruguay. The Andean Community is comprised of Bolivia, Colombia, Ecuador, Peru, and Venezuela. All Andean Community member nations, except Peru, implemented a CET in 2004.

The final two categories of RTA require progressively larger degrees of economic integration. A common market expands on the common internal and external trade policies of the custom union by opening national borders to other resource flows—especially labor and capital. An economic and monetary union completes the process of regional economic integration by establishing a common currency and a variety of common policies related to banking and finance, investment, labor standards and mobility, agriculture, energy, tourism, foreign aid, and other economic activity. Over time, the European Union (EU) evolved from a free trade area, to a customs union, to a common market, and finally to an economic and monetary union. Today, the EU is the most highly integrated RTA in the global economy. In 2002, the euro replaced the national currencies of twelve of fifteen EU countries. On May 1, 2004, an EU enlargement brought ten more countries into the EU family, expanding the EU15 to the EU25.

The number of RTAs operating in the global economy increased from about fifty in 1990 to nearly 300 by 2005. The causes of RTA growth were varied. One factor was the reintegration of former Soviet republics and eastern bloc countries into the global economy. Another was the explosion of RTAs among different classifications of countries, such as North-North agreements, North-South, and South-South. Nearly every country in the global economy belongs to at least one RTA. Developing countries, on average, belong to five RTAs. The web of RTAs is complex, even cumbersome, for some countries. RTAs have also stirred some controversy because trade and investment preferences in RTAs are inherently discriminatory against non-member countries. Yet, the World Trade Organization (WTO), the global guardian of free and fair trade, tolerates certain trade and investment preferences. The WTO's Article 24 permits preferential trade arrangements among members as long as RTAs do not impose additional trade restrictions on non-member nations.

See also **Andean Community; Asia-Pacific Economic Cooperation; Association of Southeast Asian Nations; Caribbean Community; Central American Common Market; Economic Community of West African States; European Free Trade Association; European Union; Free Trade Area of the Americas; MERCOSUR; North American Free Trade Agreement; World Trade Organization. *See also in Volume 2*, Documents 23, 24, 25, 26, 27, 28, 46.**

Further Reading

Dinan, Desmond. *Ever Closer Union: An Introduction to European Integration.* Boulder, CO: Lynne Rienner Publishers, 2005.

Mathis, James H., and Jagdish Bhagwati. *Regional Trade Arrangements in the GATT/WTO: Article XXIV and the Internal Trade Requirement.* New York: Cambridge University Press, 2002.

Schiff, Maurice, and Alan L. Winters. *Regional Integration and Development.* Washington, DC: World Bank Publications, 2003.

Schott, Jeffrey J. *Free Trade Agreements: US Strategies and Priorities.* Washington, DC: Institute for International Economics, 2004.

World Bank. *Global Economic Prospects 2005: Trade, Regionalism, and Development.* Washington, DC: Author, 2005.

RICARDO, DAVID

David Ricardo (1772–1823) was a leading nineteenth-century British economist. His theory of comparative advantage revolutionized thinking in international trade, and provided a theoretical justification for a more integrated and interdependent global economy. Ricardo was born to a prominent family. In his youth, Ricardo gained valuable experience in the world of finance at the London

Stock Exchange. Ricardo's financial acumen made him fabulously wealthy. At the age of forty-one, he retired and wrote extensively on controversial economic issues. As a member of the British Parliament, Ricardo supported the laissez-faire and free trade doctrines. These themes were featured in Ricardo's most famous book, *The Principles of Political Economy and Taxation* (1817).

In *The Principles of Political Economy and Taxation* Ricardo introduced the theory of comparative advantage, an economic theory that justified free trade. The theory of comparative advantage supported regional specialization, efficient production, and international trade. Ricardo used the wine and bread trade between Portugal and England to illustrate the benefits of comparative advantage. Ricardo demonstrated that even if Portugal had an absolute advantage in the production of both wine and bread, it was in both countries' best interest to specialize in the product in which it enjoyed its greatest advantage, or at least the lesser disadvantage. Ricardo believed regional specialization would create a more interdependent and prosperous global economy.

Ricardo pressured Britain to dismantle its protectionist trade policies. As a leading intellectual and member of Parliament, he rallied opposition to England's Corn Laws. The Corn Laws, which severely restricted the import of low-priced grains to protect inefficient domestic grain producers, were eventually repealed in 1846. The repeal of the Corn Laws encouraged Britain to reallocate resources toward more profitable enterprises in manufacturing and commerce. Ricardo's free trade doctrine also influenced Britain's trade policies. Free trade stimulated production of raw materials and semi-finished goods in foreign mines, plantations, and other businesses throughout the vast British Empire. Over the next 100 years, Great Britain became the hub of the global economy, and torchbearer for the first age of globalization. Even today Ricardo's theory of comparative advantage is the most recognized defense of free trade.

See also **Absolute Advantage; Comparative Advantage; Globalization; International Trade; Smith, Adam. *See also in Volume 2,* Document 19.**

Further Reading

Henderson, John P., and John B. Davis. *Life and Economics of David Ricardo.* Norwell, MA: Kluwer Academic Publishers, 1997.

Peach, Terry, ed. *David Ricardo: Critical Responses*. New York: Routledge, 2003.

Ricardo, David, and F. W. Kolthammer. *The Principles of Political Economy and Taxation.* Mineola, NY: Dover Publications, 2004.

Ricardo, David, and J. R. McCulloch. *The Works of David Ricardo*. Stockton, CA: University of the Pacific, 2002.

Weatherall, D. *David Ricardo: A Biography*. Norwell, MA: Kluwer Academic Publishers, 1976.

ROSTOW, WALT W.

Walt W. Rostow (1916–2003) was a prominent American development economist and economic historian. He pioneered the linear stages theory of economic development and staunchly supported free enterprise solutions to development problems. Rostow was born in New York City, the son of Russian immigrants.

After earning his doctorate from Yale University (1940), Rostow began a distinguished career in teaching and public service. Rostow taught economics at Columbia University, the Massachusetts Institute of Technology, and the University of Texas. He also served as a top advisor to former U.S. presidents Kennedy and Johnson. Rostow's most influential book, *The Stages of Growth: A Non-Communist Manifesto* (1960) was written during his tenure at MIT.

In *The Stages of Economic Growth: A Non-Communist Manifesto*, Rostow identified five development stages. As an economic historian, Rostow generalized about countries' linear progression from one stage of economic development to the next. He recognized, however, that unique features within countries could disrupt an orderly progression toward economic development. Underpinning Rostow's linear model was a premise that free markets, self-interest, and profit incentives would set developing countries on the right path toward modernization. Rostow offered his linear development model as an alternative to Marxist theory, which stressed class struggle as the impetus for economic change.

Rostow's five stages of development included the traditional society, preconditions for take-off, take-off, drive to maturity, and age of high mass consumption. The first stage, traditional society, was dominated by small-scale subsistence agriculture. Limited technology and capital goods, and parochial attitudes, blocked substantive gains in productivity and economic growth. The second stage, preconditions for take-off, featured advances in technology, capital formation, entrepreneurship, institution building, and commerce. Business activity during this transitional stage grew parallel to, but did not replace, society's dominant agricultural base. The third stage, take-off, was defined by industrialization, technological advance, aggressive entrepreneurship, and expanded commercial opportunities. Modernization and economic growth dominated the take-off stage. The fourth stage, drive to maturity, widened scientific and technological advances to all realms of economic activity. Entrepreneurs, motivated by profit incentives, expanded production to meet society's rising wants and needs. The fifth stage, the age of mass consumption, was marked by capital-intensive enterprise, rising productivity, and higher real incomes. Higher incomes and expanded social programs improved people's standard of living. The journey toward economic development could take hundreds of years to complete.

Interest in linear development theories faded over time. Later development economists dismissed the linear model as being too rigid. Instead, they searched for underlying obstacles to economic development and strategized about how to speed progress toward economic growth and human development. However, Rostow's pioneering work in the field of development economics jump-started a wider, ongoing development debate.

See also **Development Economics.**

Further Reading

Mookherjee, Dilip, and Debraj Ray, eds. *Readings in the Theory of Economic Development*. Malden, MA: Blackwell Publishers, 2000.

Rihani, Samir. *Complex Systems Theory and Development Practice: Understanding Non-Linear Realities*. New York: Zed Books, 2002.

Rostow, Walt. W. *Rich Countries and Poor Countries: Reflections on the Past, Lessons for the Future*. Boulder, CO: Westview Press, 1987.

———. *The Stages of Growth: A Non-Communist Manifesto*. Rev. ed. New York: Cambridge University Press, 1971.

S

SACHS, JEFFREY D.

Jeffrey D. Sachs (1954–) is a leading American economist, author, and consultant in the field of development economics. He has influenced development and stabilization policies in Africa, Asia, central and eastern Europe, and Latin America. Sachs was born in Detroit, Michigan, the son of a prominent lawyer. Sachs attended Harvard University, where he earned a bachelor's degree (1976), master's degree (1978), and doctorate (1980). Sachs joined the Harvard faculty in 1980 and earned the rank of full professor three years later. From 1998 to 2002, Sachs served as director of The Center for International Development (CID) at Harvard. In July 2002, Sachs moved to Columbia University, where he is director of The Earth Institute and a professor of sustainable development. Sachs is also the special advisor to the UN Secretary-General Kofi Annan, and director of the UN Millennium Project.

Sachs is a leading authority in the field of development economics. During the 1980s, he was an economic consultant for numerous governments in the developing world. Much of Sachs' work dealt with macroeconomic stabilization. His prescription for economic stability stressed fiscal discipline within countries and the rescheduling of external debt with foreign creditors. In recent years, Sachs has held leadership positions in organizations that support sustainable development. As director of the CID at Harvard, Sachs dealt with development issues related to disease prevention, overpopulation, environmental decay, bio-diversity, international poverty, and climate change. In 2002, UN Secretary-General Kofi Annan appointed Sachs as his special advisor on the UN Millennium Development Goals (MDGs). The MDGs, which consists of eight global poverty-reduction initiatives, help coordinate the development efforts of the World Bank, UN specialized agencies and programs, and other multilateral organizations. In July 2002, Sachs became the director of The Earth Institute at Columbia University. In this capacity, he explored global problems related to economic growth, human health, good governance, and the environment. In his most recent book, *The End of Poverty: Economic Possibilities for Our Time* (2005), Sachs offered a comprehensive blueprint for economic development in the world's poorer regions. His "Big Plan" involved a complex web of solutions to extreme poverty. His Big Plan also challenged richer countries to ante up significantly greater amounts of financial aid during the coming decades.

Sachs is also known for his "shock therapy" prescription for growth and stability in the transition economies of eastern and central Europe. Shock therapy required a radical restructuring of the former communist economies during the 1990s. Its overriding goal was to replace inefficient command structures with market institutions and incentives. Sachs proposed internal reforms to privatize businesses, protect competitive markets and private property rights, and abolish subsidies, government wage and price controls, and other distortions in the price system. He encouraged trade and investment liberalization to enable transition economies to "rejoin Europe." Sachs also proposed external debt rescheduling, and other foreign assistance, to ease the transition toward capitalism. Sachs orchestrated Poland's largely successful economic restructuring during the early 1990s and monetary reforms in Estonia and Slovenia. His reform initiatives were less successful in Russia.

See also **Development Economics; Emerging Market Economies; External Debt; Foreign Aid; Millennium Development Goals; Poverty; Privatization; Sustainable Economic Development; Transition Countries.**

Further Reading

Sachs, Jeffrey D. *Development Economics*. Malden, MA: Blackwell Publishers, 2003.

———. *The End of Poverty: Economic Possibilities for Our Time*. New York: Penguin Press, 2005.

———. *Poland's Leap to the Market Economy*. Cambridge, MA: MIT Press, 1993.

———, and Katharina Pistor, eds. *The Rule of Law and Economic Reform in Russia*. Boulder, CO: Westview Press, 1997.

———, Ashutosh Varshney, and Nirupan Bajpai, eds. *Indian in the Era of Economic Reform*. New York: Oxford University Press, 2000.

SCHUMACHER, ERNST F.

Ernst Friedrich (E. F.) Schumacher (1911–1977) was a British development economist and reformer. The cornerstones of his formula for sustainable economic development were localized production and appropriate technology. Schumacher was born in Bonn, Germany. In 1930, he was selected a Rhodes scholar, and continued his studies at Oxford in England. Schumacher and his young family immigrated to Great Britain in 1936 to escape the horrors of Nazism, which had taken hold in Germany. Soon after World War II, Schumacher became a British citizen and served in a number of important government posts. In the 1950s, Schumacher traveled to Burma as a United Nations' economic consultant. He was influenced by the simplicity of the Burmese lifestyle. Over time, he rejected the Western model for economic development, a model that favored industrialization regardless of the human or environmental costs. In the mid-1960s Schumacher founded the Intermediate Technology Development Group (ITDG) to research and disseminate information about appropriate technologies for small-scale enterprises in the third world.

In his most influential book, *Small Is Beautiful: Economics as if People Mattered* (1973), Schumacher defended localized production, appropriate technology, and sustainable consumption as the basis for human and economic development. For the economies of the developing world, appropriate technology lay somewhere between the modern capital-intensive methods employed by the West and the traditional indigenous techniques, a middle path that Schumacher called intermediate technology. To suit local needs, intermediate technologies were simple, understandable, and repairable. Schumacher opposed new labor-saving technologies that tossed workers into involuntary idleness. To Schumacher, unemployment was a curse on the human condition and a potentially explosive force in the developing world. He viewed intermediate technology as a source of business and job creation.

During the 1960s and 1970s, Schumacher's development strategy ran contrary to the economic mainstream, which tended to glorify technological advance, specialization and a division of labor, and the economics of bigness. He was highly critical of unbridled economic growth, and of the destructive forces that underpinned globalization. He was especially critical of self-serving transnational corporations (TNC) and inept government officials who ignored the human and environmental costs of large-scale business activity.

Today's localization movement, which rests on small-scale production, sustainable consumption, and localized decision making, is compatible with Schumacher's vision of economic development. Schumacher continues to influence development economics through his books, and the work of the ITDG.

See also **Development Economics; Localization; Sustainable Consumption; Sustainable Economic Development.**

Further Reading

Pearce, Joseph. *Small Is Still Beautiful.* News York: HarperCollins, 2001.
Schumacher, Ernst F. *Small Is Beautiful: Economics as if People Mattered.* New York: Harper & Row, 1973.
———, and Peter N. Gillingham. *Good Work.* Rev. ed. New York: HarperCollins, 1980.
Wood, Barbara. *E. F. Schumacher, His Life and Thought.* New York: Harper & Row, 1984.

SCHUMPETER, JOSEPH A.

Joseph A. Schumpeter (1883–1950) was a prominent economic historian, author, and teacher. His theory of "creative destruction" described the evolutionary nature of modern capitalism and underscored the role of entrepreneurs in innovation and economic growth. Schumpeter was born in Triesch in the former Austria-Hungary (now the Czech Republic). His studies at Vienna University culminated in a Doctor of Law degree in 1906. Law, teaching, authorship, and government service occupied Schumpeter's early career. In the 1920s, he settled into teaching, first at the University of Bonn (1925–1932), Germany, and later at Harvard University (1932–1950). Schumpeter authored ten books in the fields of economic growth theory, business cycles, economic systems, and economic history. His most famous work, *Capitalism, Socialism, and Democracy* (1942) was written during Schumpeter's Harvard years.

Schumpeter made significant contributions to growth theory and the evolutionary nature of capitalism. While teaching at the University of Graz, Schumpeter penned the *Theory of Economic Development* (1911). This book stressed the central role of entrepreneurs in economic growth and development. In his classic *Capitalism, Socialism, and Democracy* (1942) Schumpeter coined the term, "creative destruction," to explain the role of innovation in an economy. According to Schumpeter, capitalism was built on entrepreneurial innovations. Innovation improved product quality and production methods and expanded commercial opportunities in new markets. Innovation also rendered some older industries and jobs obsolete. Hence, the creation of some new enterprises involved the destruction of older ones. Schumpeter concluded that entrepreneurship and innovation were the engines of long-run economic growth. He also concluded that innovation and growth would occur in irregular spurts over time.

Schumpeter believed capitalism was a dynamic economic system, capable of adaptation. He credited creative destruction with increasing the availability of consumer goods and improving production methods. Creative destruction also changed the underlying principles of capitalism. For instance, Schumpeter predicted the capitalist principle of limited government would eventually embrace a broader range of social services for the poor and needy. In fact, Schumpeter believed that as capitalism evolved, it would take on more features of socialism.

See also **Capitalism; Democratic Socialism; Development Economics; Economic Growth; Entrepreneurship; Sustainable Economic Development.**

Further Reading

Marz, Eduard. *Joseph Schumpeter: Scholar, Teacher, and Politician.* Rev. ed. New Haven: Yale University Press, 1991.

Schumpeter, Joseph A. *Capitalism, Socialism, and Democracy.* New York: Harper & Row, 1942.

———. *Essays: On Entrepreneurs, Innovations, Business Cycles, and the Evolution of Capitalism.* Piscataway, NJ: Transaction Publishers, 1989.

Swedberg, Richard. *Joseph A. Schumpeter.* Princeton, NJ: Princeton University Press, 1991.

SEN, AMARTYA K.

Amartya Kumar Sen (1933–) is a prominent Indian economist, who specializes in welfare and development economics. Sen is often called the "conscience of economics" in recognition of his steadfast advocacy for the world's poorest citizens. Sen was born in Shantiniketan, West Bengal, India, to an intellectual family. He earned bachelor's degrees from Calcutta University in India and the University of Cambridge in the United Kingdom, and a doctorate from Cambridge in 1959. Over the years, Sen served as a professor of economics at a number of universities, including the Delhi School of Economics during the 1960s, the London School of Economics during the 1970s and 1980s, and Harvard University during the late 1980s and 1990s. In 1998 Sen accepted a position as the Master of Trinity College at Cambridge. Recent books in the field of development economics are *Inequality Reexamined* (1995) and *Development as Freedom* (2000).

Human welfare and human development dominate Sen's work in the field of development economics. His books examine the plight of the desperately poor and the effects of income inequalities on health care, education, and other aspects of the human condition. Sen argues that human misery could be reduced if food and other resources were distributed more equitably. He also observed that economic development means more than growth in a nation's gross domestic product (GDP). Sen proposed a broader view of economic development, a view that embraced widespread human progress and the expansion of people's freedoms.

As a social activist, Sen stressed normative economics. Normative economics considers "what should be" rather than simply describing "what is." In *Development as Freedom* (2000), Sen linked people's freedoms with sustainable economic development. He advocated for broader participation by the poor in the economic, social, and political decisions that affect developing countries. Sen also argued that free markets, and government intervention, can co-exist in pursuit of freedom and development. Free markets stimulate business activity and modernization. Government policies promote social justice and human welfare. To expand people's range of choices, Sen favored public policies that enhanced universal public education, nutrition programs, health care, and other programs that promote inclusion. He also supported democratic institutions, including a free press and an independent judiciary, to protect personal freedoms. In 1998 Sen was awarded the Nobel Prize in Economic Science in recognition of his contributions to development and welfare economics.

See also **Development Economics; Human Development; Poverty; Quality of Life; Sustainable Economic Development.**

Further Reading

Alkire, Sabina. *Valuing Freedoms: Sen's Capability Approach and Poverty Reduction.* New York: Oxford University Press, 2002.

Nussbaum, Martha, and Amartya Sen, eds. *The Quality of Life.* New York: Oxford University Press, 1993.

Sen, Amartya. *Development as Freedom.* New York: Anchor Books, 2000.

———. *Inequality Reexamined.* Cambridge, MA: Harvard University Press, 1995.

SMITH, ADAM

Adam Smith (1723–1790) was a prominent Scottish economist and philosopher. His defense of free enterprise and free trade radically altered economic thinking and paved the way for a more interdependent global economy. Smith was born in Kirkcaldy, Scotland. He was educated at Glasgow University in Scotland and Oxford University in England. After six years in England, Smith returned to his native Scotland, first as lecturer at Edinburgh University and later as a professor of philosophy at Glasgow University. From 1762 to 1766, Smith tutored the Duke of Buccleuch. During his travels with the young duke, Smith rubbed shoulders with prominent European scholars. Smith devoted the next ten years to writing *An Inquiry into the Nature and Causes of the Wealth of Nations* (1776), a free-market treatise that changed the economic landscape of the world.

The Wealth of Nations was a staunch defense of laissez-faire economics. The laissez-faire doctrine opposed most forms of government intervention in the economy. In matters of international trade, Smith favored free trade. He believed that nations should specialize in the production of goods in which they had an absolute advantage, and then exchange their surpluses in global markets. Voluntary exchanges in international markets would benefit buyers and sellers under these conditions. Smith also supported specialization of labor, called division of labor, in business enterprise. He argued that regional specialization, the division of labor, and trade promoted greater efficiency and productivity within nations and greater total output in the global economy.

In *The Wealth of Nations* Smith openly challenged the powerful mercantilists. The mercantilists clung to the belief that government regulation of businesses encouraged a favorable balance of trade and the inflow of specie—gold and silver—into the nation. Smith believed government should dismantle its web of special privileges and restraints on commerce, which catered to the narrow interests of the merchants and manufacturers. He condemned import quotas and tariffs, trade barriers that discouraged the inflow of less expensive foreign goods into Britain. He also opposed export subsidies. Export subsidies were government payments to export industries. Export subsidies were designed to reduce the price of British exports in world markets. Smith argued trade restrictions reduced competition, raised consumer prices, limited consumer choice, and misallocated society's resources. Instead, Smith proposed that business activity and commerce be guided by an "invisible hand," a hand guided by self-interest in competitive domestic and global markets.

Adam Smith is often called the founder of modern economics. His observations of markets, recorded in *The Wealth of Nations*, elevated the study of economics into an academic discipline. Smith challenged Great Britain to unchain the power of free markets. His support for private profits, competitive markets, voluntary exchange, and self-interest, helped set the pillars of capitalism in Great Britain and other Western nations. Smith's bold defense of the laissez-faire doctrine helped define the role of government in economic activity for the next 150 years.

See also **Absolute Advantage; Capitalism; International Trade; Market Economy; Mercantilism; Protectionism. *See also in Volume 2,* Document 19.**

Further Reading

Haldane, Richard. *Life of Adam Smith*. Kila, MT: Kessinger Publishing, 2005.
Kennedy, Gavin. *Adam Smith's Lost Legacy*. New York: Palgrave Macmillan, 2005.
Ross, Ian S. *The Life of Adam Smith*. New York: Clarendon Press, 1995.
Smith, Adam. *An Inquiry into the Nature and Causes of the Wealth of Nations*. New York: Oxford University Press, 1976.
Weinstein, Jack R. *On Adam Smith*. Belmont, CA: Wadsworth Publishing, 2000.

SOLOW, ROBERT M.

Robert M. Solow (1924–) is a prominent American economist, teacher, and author. His work in economic growth theory has influenced mainstream thinking in the field of development economics for decades. Solow was born and raised in New York City. He entered Harvard University in 1940. After serving in the U.S. military during World War II, he returned to Harvard, where he earned a doctorate in 1951. In 1950, Solow accepted an assistant professorship at the nearby Massachusetts Institute of Technology (MIT), an institution that he would call home for his entire professional career. While at MIT, Solow penned many articles and books, including *Growth Theory: An Exposition* (1970), a classic text that was revised and republished in 2000.

In *Growth Theory: An Exposition*, Solow examined the complexities of production, a process that relied on the skillful use of productive resources and technology. He concluded that technological development, more than any other factor, was the true engine of long-run economic growth. He noted that technological advances and innovation progressed at uneven intervals over time. Yet, in the long run, technology and innovation bolstered the capabilities of physical capital and the productivity of labor and stimulated economic growth. Solow's emphasis on technological advance as the primary determinant of economic growth departed from mainstream economic thought. Traditional growth theory rested on an inflexible set of growth conditions related to national savings, the labor supply, and physical capital. Solow created a more flexible growth model, which permitted adjustments for new technologies and other variables. Solow's theories created a new economic mainstream in the field of growth and development.

Over time, Solow's work branched out to other aspects of economic growth and sustainable economic development. For instance, Solow explored the long-neglected economics of natural resources. These studies considered the impact of economic growth on the natural environment and on the supply of finite resources. Solow also acknowledged the necessity of international trade and foreign direct investment (FDI) in sustaining economic growth and development. He was highly critical of the uneven distribution of wealth wrought by globalization, however, preferring instead greater inclusion of marginalized nations and peoples in the global trading system. In recognition of Solow's groundbreaking contributions to growth theory, he was awarded the prestigious Nobel Prize in Economic Science in 1987.

See also **Development Economics; Economic Growth; Gross Domestic Product; Gross National Income.**

Further Reading

McMahon, Gary, and Lyn Squire, eds. Robert M. Solow (Introduction). *Explaining Growth: A Global Research Project*. New York: Palgrave Macmillan, 2003.

Solow, Robert M. *Growth Theory: An Exposition*. 2d ed. New York: Oxford University Press, 2000.

———, ed. *Landmark Papers in Economic Growth*. Northampton, MA: Edward Elgar Publishing, 2001.

———. *Structural Reform and Economic Policy*. New York: Palgrave Macmillan, 2005.

SOTO, HERNANDO DE

Hernando de Soto (1941–) is among the world's most influential development economists. Soto was born in Peru, but received much of his early education in Switzerland. He pursued his university studies in Lima, Peru, and completed his graduate work in Geneva, Switzerland. In 1980 he returned to Peru. Soto's attention soon turned to reforming the dysfunctional Peruvian economy. During the early 1980s he laid the groundwork for the Institute for Liberty and Democracy (ILD), which was up and running by 1984. Today, based in Lima, ILD is one of the world's most influential think-tanks. In his books, *The Other Path: The Invisible Revolution in the Third World* (1989) and *The Mystery of Capital: Why Capitalism Triumphs in the West and Fails Everywhere Else* (2000), Soto examined Peru's development problems and described the untapped potential of "dead capital." Dead capital refers to the productive assets and business enterprises that exist in an economy's informal, or extralegal sector. Soto argued that the integration of dead capital into Peru's economic mainstream was the key to sustainable economic development.

Soto's work in the field of development economics stresses capital formation, the process of increasing the nation's total supply of productive capital resources. To advance capital formation, Soto highlights the need to combine nations' dual economies, the informal and the formal, into a single competitive market. His research confirmed that the informal sector accounted for most of Peru's business activity. He argued that the country's prospects for sustainable development hinged on the infusion of dead capital into the formal economy and the extension of credit and other services to the poor. By the mid-1980s, Soto and the ILD sponsored groundbreaking policy changes to level the playing field between the rich propertied class and the poor. His reform agenda, sometimes called "poor people's capitalism," recommended streamlining business regulations and expanding property rights to people working in the extralegal sector. He emphasized policies to promote inclusion and to harness the productive power of dead capital and the entrepreneurial spirit that workers in the informal sector embody. Working with government leaders in Peru, Soto's ideas became public policy. As a result of ILD initiatives during the late 1980s and early 1990s, over 1 million households were awarded titles to their homes in rural and urban areas. The goal of capital formation, the wellspring of sustainable economic growth, increased as hundreds of thousands of businesses emerged from the shadows of the informal sector. The reform package reduced corruption and black market activity and increased government tax receipts. Legal ownership of assets also expanded opportunities for the poor, including access to credit and public services. Other ILD initiatives worked toward good governance, tax fairness, financial stability, and improved education.

The success of Soto's development strategy in Peru soon gained international attention. In 1990 the ILD went global. Under Soto's leadership, the ILD grew to be one of the world's most influential think-tanks during the 1990s and early 2000s. Governments in Africa, Asia, Eastern Europe, Latin America, and the Middle East, sought development advice from Soto and the ILD. Soto's prescription for economic development featured a five-pronged, sequentially organized plan of action. This action plan is uniform in approach but tailored to meet the individual needs of different countries. First, the "awareness" stage puts private property rights and policies of inclusion at the center of the client's development agenda. Second, the "diagnosis" stage investigates the current status of property law and the functioning of extralegal business activity within the country. Third, the "reform design" rewrites the legal codes regarding property rights to ease the transition from extralegal to legal business activity. Fourth, the "implementation" creates the necessary physical and human infrastructure to explain, publicize, monitor, and enforce legal reforms. Finally, the "capital formation and good governance" stage promotes business linkages within and between countries, develops capital markets, and solidifies the rule of law within the client country.

In recent years, Soto's prescription for prosperity has received financial and other support from the World Bank, the U.S. Agency for International Development (USAID), and prominent individuals including UN Secretary-General Kofi Annan and former U.S. President Bill Clinton. In Soto's native Peru, expanded property rights and other legal reforms have already generated more than half a million new jobs, and brought 300,000 enterprises into the formal sector. Around the world no fewer than nineteen countries have solicited the development advice of the ILD, including giants such as China and Brazil. Soto's ultimate goal is to bring the world's 4 billion economically disenfranchised people into the global market system. In recognition of his work, and that of the ILD, Soto has received numerous awards including The Freedom Prize, the Adam Smith Award, the CARE Canada Award for Outstanding Development Thinking, and the OECD Best Practices Award.

See also **Capital Formation; Capitalism; Developing Countries; Development Economics; Entrepreneurship; Informal Economy.** ***See also in Volume 2,*** **Document 55.**

Further Reading

Honohan, Patrick. *Financial Sector Policy and the Poor: Selected Findings and Issues.* New York: World Bank Publications, 2004.

Portes, Alejandro, Manuel Castells, and Lauren A. Benton. *The Informal Economy: Studies in Advanced and Less Developed Countries.* Baltimore, MD: Johns Hopkins University Press, 1989.

Prahalad, C. K. *The Fortunes at the Bottom of the Pyramid: Eradicating Poverty through Profits.* Philadelphia: Wharton School Publishing, 2004.

Soto, Hernando de. *The Mystery of Capital: Why Capitalism Triumphs in the West and Fails Everywhere Else.* Rev. ed. New York: Basic Books, 2003.

———. *The Other Path: The Invisible Revolution in the Third World.* New York: Harper & Row, 1989.

———. *The Other Path: The Economic Answer to Terrorism*. Cambridge, MA: Perseus Books Group, 2002.

SOUTH-SOUTH COOPERATION

South-South cooperation refers to the coordinated actions among the world's developing countries to promote sustainable economic development. The term South, in this context, refers to the developing nations of the "global South." South-South cooperation seeks to tap the internal strengths and resources within the developing world, and also strengthen the voice of the world's poorer countries in the global economy. The Group of Seventy-Seven (G77) is the most significant voice of South-South cooperation. The G77 is a coalition of 133 developing countries. The G77 was founded in 1964 by seventy-seven developing countries under the auspices of the United Nations Conference on Trade and Development (UNCTAD). The first Joint Declaration of the Seventy-Seven Developing Countries (1964) called for the creation of a "new and just world economic order" to speed the development process in the world's poorer regions. Since 1964, the G77 has articulated the development needs of the developing world, and has established South-South cooperation as a top priority in this mission.

South-South cooperation takes many forms. Regional trade agreements (RTAs) among developing countries represent one manifestation of South-South cooperation. RTAs reduce or eliminate tariff and non-tariff trade barriers among member states. The primary goal of RTAs is to support economic development by building mutually beneficial trade relationships. Examples of RTAs in the developing world include the Andean Community, ASEAN Free Trade Area, Economic Community of West African States (ECOWAS), and the Southern Common Market (MERCOSUR). Some RTAs also support other forms of regional cooperation, such as liberalized cross-border investment privileges, and common policies to protect workers' rights, the environment, and local cultures.

Another indicator of South-South cooperation is the growing number of bilateral investment treaties (BITs) and double taxation treaties (DTTs) between developing countries. BITs remove obstacles to cross-border investment, called foreign direct investment (FDI). Most BITs guarantee equal treatment of products produced by foreign firms in host-country markets, and protections against noncommercial losses due to expropriation or civil unrest. The double taxation treaty (DTT) establishes equitable tax rules for foreign workers and investors to avoid the double taxation of income by home and host governments. DTTs cover different forms of income such as wages, dividends, capital gains, and royalties. Thus, DTTs remove some financial barriers to FDI. In addition, South-South cooperation was instrumental in the defeat of the proposed Multilateral Agreement on Investment (MAI) during the late 1990s. The MAI, which was drafted by the Organization for Economic Cooperation and Development (OECD) in the mid-1990s, was opposed by many developing nations. Nations of the global South feared the MAI's rigid investment rules would retard unique national development efforts and favor the interests of transnational corporations (TNCs) from the global North.

The G77's Havana Program of Action is the global South's most comprehensive agenda for global action. The Havana Program of Action was adopted by the Group of Seventy-Seven South Summit, which was held in Havana, Cuba, April 10–14, 2000. The Havana Program of Action acknowledged the widening development gap between the advanced economies of the global North and the developing economies of the global South. The heads of state and government called for greater participation by poorer countries in global decision making, a stronger UN presence in global development, a respect for cultural diversity, and an expansion of technology and human capital development in the global South. The Havana Program of Action addressed specific goals for South-South cooperation, including greater South-South trade and investment, monetary and financial cooperation, and exchanges to improve social services in health care, education, and population planning. The Action Program also called for the global North to remove trade barriers in agriculture and textiles, expand foreign aid, and devise strategies to more equitably distribute the benefits of globalization.

See also **Advanced Economies; Developing Countries; Globalization; Group of Seventy-Seven; International Investment Agreements; International Trade; Least Developed Countries; Poverty; Regional Trade Agreements; Sustainable Economic Development.** ***See also in Volume 2,*** **Documents 20, 21, 54.**

Further Reading

Hudson, Michael. *Global Fracture: The New International Economic Order*. 2d ed. London: Pluto Press, 2005.

Sidaway, James D. *Imagined Regional Communities: Integration and Sovereignty in the Global South*. New York: Routledge, 2001.

Soederberg, Susanne. *The Politics of the New International Financial Architecture: Reimposing Neoliberal Domination in the Global South*. New York: Zed Books, 2005.

Thomas-Slayter, Barbara P. *Southern Exposure: International Development and the Global South in the Twenty-First Century*. West Hartford, CT: Kumarian Press, 2003.

STIGLITZ, JOSEPH E.

Joseph E. Stiglitz (1943–) is an influential American economist. His controversial views on economic development, and the role of multilateral organizations in the development process, ignited constructive debate about the benefits of globalization in the world's poorer regions. Stiglitz was born in Gary, Indiana, to a comfortable middle-class family. His undergraduate studies at Amherst College and MIT sparked an interest in economics. In 1967, he earned a doctorate in economics from MIT. Stiglitz held professorships at Yale, Princeton, Stanford, MIT, and is currently at Columbia University. He was appointed to the Council of Economic Advisors (CEA) by President Bill Clinton and served from 1993 to 1997. He chaired the CEA from 1995 to 1997. He also served as chief economist and senior vice president of the World Bank from 1997 to 2000. Stiglitz was named co-recipient of the Nobel Prize in Economic Science in 2001, the same year he joined the faculty at Columbia University. His breadth of experience in academia and in the inner circles of the U.S. government and World Bank make Stiglitz a powerful voice in the ongoing globalization debate.

Stiglitz stoked the fires in the debate over globalization with the publication of *Globalization and Its Discontents* (2001). This controversial book acknowledged the potential benefits of globalization, but was highly critical of current policies that skewed the benefits of globalization toward richer countries and powerful corporate interests. Stiglitz was particularly distressed by the ill-advised policies of the International Monetary Fund (IMF), which mandated rigid structural economic reforms and a shock therapy approach to the liberalization of trade, foreign direct investment (FDI), and cross-border capital flows. Stiglitz argued that IMF rigidity failed to consider the unique histories, cultures, and economic conditions that existed in the developing world and transition countries of eastern and central Europe. As chief economist of the World Bank, Stiglitz openly criticized the IMF and other institutions for unwise policies, and for the lack of transparency in the decision-making process. His gradualist approach to liberalization was placed on the back burner, however.

Stiglitz was particularly alarmed about the pace of liberalization in financial flows between countries during the 1990s. The liberalization of financial flows encouraged investors to make highly speculative, short-term financial investments in the global economy. The sophisticated electronic trading infrastructure, along with largely unregulated global financial markets, was a prescription for global financial instability. He questioned how financial liberalization helped poorer countries achieve economic growth and sustainable development. The subsequent financial crises in East Asia, Russia, and Brazil added tinder to the disputes between Stiglitz, the IMF, and powerful officials in the U.S. government. Stiglitz was also critical of the IMF's initial response—policies that required government fiscal restraint in economies that teetered on collapse—to the flurry of financial crises. Under pressure from the IMF and other agencies, Stiglitz ended his tenure at the World Bank in 2000.

Today, Stiglitz is a university professor and executive director of the Initiative for Policy Dialogue (IPD) at Columbia University. Stiglitz co-founded the IPD in 2000. The IPD provides an alternative source of policy advice to developing and transition countries, apart from the technical assistance offered by the IMF and other multilateral organizations. The IPD stresses wider civic participation in economic policymaking. Today, the IPD is a global network of more than 200 economists and other stakeholders in economic development.

See also **Developing Countries; Economic Growth; Financial Contagion; Globalization; International Financial Institutions; International Monetary Fund; Sustainable Economic Development; World Bank Group.**

Further Reading

Meier, Gerald M., and Joseph E. Stiglitz, eds. *Frontiers of Development Economics: The Future in Perspective*. New York: Oxford University Press, 2000.

Stiglitz, Joseph E. *Globalization and Its Discontents*. New York: W. W. Norton & Company, 2003.

———. *The Roaring Nineties: A New History of the World's Most Prosperous Decade*. New York: W. W. Norton & Company, 2004.

———, and Ha-Joon Chang, eds. *The Rebel Within: Joseph Stiglitz and the World Bank*. London: Anthem Press, 2002.

SUPPLY CHAINS

A supply chain is a network of businesses that are collectively responsible for the production and distribution of a product. The supply chain network includes businesses involved in the procurement of raw materials, the transformation of resources into an intermediate good or a finished product, the transport and storage of the good, and the distribution of the good to customers.

Global supply chains are cross-border business networks that contribute to the production and distribution of a product. At times, a single transnational corporation (TNC) dominates a global supply chain by owning or controlling foreign subsidiaries, joint ventures, or subcontractors. In other cases, independent firms network with one another to form a supply chain. Production sharing is intimately connected with supply chains. Production sharing occurs when the production of a good takes place in stages and in different countries. Supply chains are a more inclusive process, dealing with the production and distribution of goods. Predictable, timely, and efficient flows of resources, components, and final goods are crucial to a supply chain. Advances in transportation and communications technologies, and the liberalization of trade and investment regimes, have advanced the efficiency of global supply chains.

The storage and transport of goods is a key feature in global supply chains.
Courtesy of CORBIS

The composition of a supply chain depends on the good that is produced. The supply chain for casual wear might begin with the procurement of cotton from a plantation in India. The cotton might be processed in a textile mill in Bangladesh, and re-exported to a maquiladora in Mexico for "assembly" into a final good such as a shirt or pants. Wholesalers, who buy items in bulk, assist in the distribution of the clothing to retailers, such as Wal-Mart or Sears in the United States or elsewhere. The cotton, fabric, and articles of clothing are likely stored in warehouses and transported within and between countries by train, truck, ship, or airplane. Firms that provide storage and transportation services are key components in the supply chain for goods and services.

The operation of global supply chains is highly controversial. The controversy stems from the exploitation of workers and the degradation of the natural environment at the bottom of the supply chain. This human and environmental exploitation is often referred to as the race to the bottom. In many cases, unskilled women laborers occupy the lowest rung in the supply chain. The intense competition in global markets is one cause of worker abuse and environmental degradation. Price-conscious consumers pressure retailers to sell inexpensive items. Retailers, in turn, pressure manufacturers and their subcontractors to cut costs. Eventually, workers at the bottom of the supply chain feel the financial pinch. Employers reduce wages, extend work hours, evade benefits, and discourage union representation to cut costs and meet production schedules. Employers also sidestep environmental standards. Chronic abuse of workers and the environment is aggravated by inadequate government regulation, ineffective corporate "codes of conduct," and weak labor organizations.

Supply chains marred by corporate misconduct and the deterioration of people's quality of life have instigated a global uproar in recent years. Multilateral organizations, corporations, non-governmental organizations, and other elements of civil society have banded together to structure more effective guidelines to protect workers and the environment. For example, the Fair Labor Association in the United States, and the Ethical Trading Initiative in the United Kingdom, have worked to protect workers from abusive employers. Another promising labor initiative is Social Accountability 8000, which recognizes businesses for compliance with core labor standards. In addition, the International Labor Organization (ILO), a specialized agency within the United Nations system, has redoubled its efforts to promote "decent work" for all people in the global economy.

See also **Corporate Social Responsibility; Developing Countries; Foreign Direct Investment; Globalization; International Labor Organization; Maquiladoras; Production Sharing; Quality of Life; Race to the Bottom; Transnational Corporations.** ***See also in Volume 2,*** **Documents 28, 29, 30, 31, 33, 34, 35, 36, 37, 38.**

Further Reading

Fold, Niels, and Bill Pritchard. *Cross-continental Agro-food Chains: Structures, Actors and Dynamics in the Global Food System*. New York: Routledge, 2005.

Mamic, Ivanka. *Implementing Codes of Conduct: How Businesses Manage Social Performance in Global Supply Chains*. Washington, DC: International Labor Office, 2005.

Neef, Dale. *The Supply Chain Imperative: How to Ensure Ethical Behavior in Your Global Suppliers*. New York: AMACOM, 2004.

New, Steve, and Roy Westbrook. *Understanding Supply Chains: Concepts, Critiques, and Futures*. New York: Oxford University Press, 2004.

Raworth, Kate. *Trading Away Our Rights: Women Working in Global Supply Chains*. London: Oxfam International, 2004.

SUSTAINABLE CONSUMPTION

Sustainable consumption is the ability to satisfy people's present consumption needs without undermining the world's capacity to meet the consumption needs of future generations. Sustainable consumption applies to the purchase or use of resources, such as water or petroleum, as well as final goods such as food, household appliances, and motor vehicles. It also applies to the decisions made by all consumptive units, including households, businesses, and governments. The overriding objective of sustainable consumption is to guarantee a high and sustainable quality of life for all people, today and in the future.

The movement toward sustainable consumption in the global economy was bolstered by a number of international agreements during the 1990s. The landmark *Agenda 21*, which was adopted by the Rio Earth Summit in 1992, propelled sustainable consumption into the international limelight. *Agenda 21* made a compelling link between unsustainable consumption and production on the one hand, and global poverty and environmental degradation on the other. *Agenda 21* recommended a global shift in lifestyles and consumption patterns, particularly in the industrialized countries. *Agenda 21* noted that richer countries accounted for the lion's share of global consumption. *Agenda 21* called for more efficient and "green" production methods, the use of new and renewable energy resources, the development and sharing of green technologies, the creation of recycling and waste reduction programs, and the dissemination of information about ethical consumption through education, public awareness programs, advertising, or other means.

Sustainable consumption was formally added to the UN Guidelines for Consumer Protection in 1999. Consumers International (CI), a nonprofit federation of

One goal of sustainable consumption is to reduce waste, particularly in the industrialized countries.
Courtesy of Getty Images: Doug Menuez

consumer groups and non-governmental organizations (NGOs), was instrumental in framing the sustainable consumption addendum to the UN Guidelines. Under the revised Guidelines for Consumer Protection, the United Nations challenged consumers, governments, businesses, labor organizations, environmental groups, and other stakeholders to join in common cause behind sustainable consumption. The revised Guidelines also called for governments to provide a suitable environment for sustainable consumption through appropriate regulations, prohibitions, and incentives to achieve desired results. The Guidelines asked governments to lead by example by introducing sustainable consumption practices into their own operations, financing green research and development (R&D), ending subsidies to wasteful or inefficient producers, and forcing businesses to pay for external production costs such as pollution.

The goal of sustainable consumption requires a significant change in attitudes and lifestyles, particularly in the richer industrialized countries. In the early 2000s, the United Nations Environment Program (UNEP) reported slow progress in implementing the sustainable consumption recommendations outlined in the UN Guidelines for Consumer Protection. A UNEP survey cited high compliance with sustainable consumption guidelines in Australia, Belgium, Brazil, the Czech Republic, Denmark, Hungary, Korea, Mexico, Nicaragua, Sri Lanka, and Sweden. Lower compliance with the UN Guidelines was recorded in Bulgaria, Burundi, Costa Rica, Cote d'Ivoire, Cyprus, Ecuador, Haiti, Kenya, and Zambia.

See also **Consumers International; Environmental Degradation; Quality of Life; Sustainable Economic Development; United Nations System.** ***See also in Volume 2,*** **Documents 40, 43, 44, 45, 46, 47, 48, 49.**

Further Reading

Princen, Thomas, Michael F. Maniates, and Ken Conca, eds. *Confronting Consumption*. Cambridge, MA: MIT Press, 2002.

Reisch, Lucia A., and Inge Ropke, eds. *The Ecological Economics of Consumption*. Northampton, MA: Edward Elgar Publishing, 2005.

Southerton, Dale, Heather Chappelle, and Bas Van Vliet, eds. *Sustainable Consumption*. Northampton, MA: Edward Elgar Publishers, 2005.

United Nations. *Agenda 21 Earth Summit: United Nations Program of Action for Rio*. New York: Author, 1992.

Worldwatch Institute. *State of the World 2004: A Worldwatch Institute Report on Progress toward a Sustainable Society*. New York: W. W. Norton & Company, 2004.

SUSTAINABLE ECONOMIC DEVELOPMENT

Sustainable economic development occurs when an economy achieves sustained economic growth and substantive improvements in people's quality of life. Economic growth results from increases in a country's total output of goods and services over time. The two most common measurements of economic growth are the gross domestic product (GDP) and the GDP per capita. Quality of life deals with the overall conditions under which people live. Quality-of-life indicators consider people's consumption levels; access to education, health, and social services; degree of personal security; and respect for civil and human rights.

The concept of sustainable economic development has expanded in recent years. The landmark *Agenda 21* was an important outcome of the 1992 United Nations Conference on Environment and Development, also called the Rio Earth Summit. *Agenda 21* is one of the world's most authoritative statements on sustainable development. *Agenda 21* embraced a broad view of sustainable economic development, which included economic growth and a series of protections for the natural environment, worker and human rights, and indigenous cultures. UN's *Millennium Declaration* solidified the link between sustainable economic development and global poverty reduction (2000). The *Millennium Declaration* established eight Millennium Development Goals (MDGs), which rallied global support for poverty reduction, universal primary education, gender equity, health care, the natural environment, and partnerships for development.

Economists often classify countries by level of economic development. The most recent International Monetary Fund (IMF) classification established two broad categories of economies. The twenty-nine advanced economies, also called the developed countries, are the rich industrialized economies. The remaining 179 economies are considered emerging market and developing economies. A country's level of economic development is determined partly by its income status. All of the twenty-nine advanced economies, for example, are high-income countries. Development status also considers the size and sophistication of the economy's three economic sectors: agricultural, goods producing, and services producing. The advanced economies have well-developed economic sectors, typically dominated by services-producing industries. Less developed countries are obliged to devote more resources to agriculture and goods-producing industries to satisfy society's basic needs.

A convergence of many mutually supporting economic, political, and social factors is necessary if the virtuous cycle of development is to replace the vicious cycle of poverty in the developing world. The effective management of productive resources—natural resources, human resources, and capital goods—is one important step toward creating the virtuous cycle. The sustainability of natural resources is enhanced by policies to reduce environmental degradation, increase the use of renewable resources, and apply the principles of sustainable consumption. Human resources, or labor, is enhanced by education, job training, adequate food and fresh water, and health care. Investments in human resources expand society's human capital. Policies to reverse the brain drain, and nurture domestic entrepreneurship, are also essential to human capital development. Finally, the accumulation of capital goods increases the productivity of labor and prospects for economic growth. Capital deepening, the expansion of real capital per worker, is a key feature of sustainable development.

The virtuous cycle of development is also enhanced by a pro-growth business climate. A favorable business climate includes stable, transparent, and inclusive economic and political institutions and practices. A favorable economic environment relies on a well-developed economic infrastructure, a respect for private property and market institutions, and macroeconomic stability. A well-developed economic infrastructure includes transportation and communications systems, basic services in sanitation and water supply, health and educational facilities, and a system of justice capable of enforcing contracts and administering the rule of law. The infrastructure also includes institutions to attend to the specific needs of the poor and other marginalized segments of society. Respect for market institutions provides incentives to work, save, invest, and produce goods. Macroeconomic stabilization policies foster price stability, full employment, and growth.

A stable political environment is based on good governance. Good governance refers to honest and competent public service by government officials. Democratic practices and the rule of law underpin good governance. Good governance supports equal opportunity and protects private property rights and profits. Good governance has proven elusive for many developing countries, particularly those victimized by extreme poverty, dictatorship, corruption, and civil conflict. In recent years, international development institutions such as the World Bank and the IMF have extended financial and technical assistance to promote good governance. In addition, governments and multilateral organizations have encouraged participation by non-governmental organizations (NGOs) and civil society organizations (CSOs) to help devise and monitor compliance with the principles of good governance.

Foreign aid is another ingredient in attaining sustainable economic development. Foreign aid refers to cross-border grants, loans, technical assistance, and emergency aid. Foreign governments and multilateral organizations provide most economic assistance. Other sources of assistance include transnational corporations, non-governmental organizations (NGOs), civil society organizations (CSOs), and individual philanthropists. The five most important sources of economic assistance include the five mutually supporting institutions of the World Bank Group; the regional development banks and sub-regional banks; the International Monetary Fund; the Development Assistance Committee (DAC), within the Organization for Economic Cooperation and Development; and the specialized agencies and programs of the United Nations system. Today, the network of multilateral institutions is increasingly attentive to economic and human development in the world's poorer regions.

See also **Advanced Economies; Capital Formation; Developing Countries; Development Economics; Economic Growth; Economic Sectors; Emerging Market Economies; Entrepreneurship; Factors of Production; Foreign Aid; Good Governance; Human Development; Quality of Life; Sustainable Consumption.** ***See also in Volume 2,*** **Documents 1, 2, 3, 4, 5, 6, 7, 9, 10, 11, 12, 13, 14, 15, 16, 21, 32, 39, 40, 41, 43, 44, 45, 47, 48, 49, 50, 51, 54.**

Further Reading

Elliot, Jennifer A. *An Introduction to Sustainable Development*. 3d ed. New York: Routledge, 2005.

Jolly, Richard, Louis Emmerij, and Dharam Ghai. *UN Contributions to Development Thinking and Practice*. Bloomington, IN: Indiana University Press, 2004.
Munasinghe, Mohan. *Towards Sustainomics: Making Development More Sustainable*. Northampton, MA: Edward Elgar Publishing, 2005.
Rogers, Peter, Kazi F. Jalal, and John A. Boyd. *An Introduction to Sustainable Development*. Cambridge, MA: Harvard University Press, 2005.
Soubbotina, Tatyana P. *Beyond Economic Growth: An Introduction to Sustainable Development*. 2d ed. New York: World Bank Publications, 2004.

T

TARIFFS

A tariff, or customs duty, is a federal tax on an imported good or service. The two main types of tariffs are protective tariffs and revenue tariffs. A protective tariff is designed to protect domestic businesses and jobs by increasing the price of an imported product. In this way, a protective tariff discourages the consumption of the imported product and encourages the consumption of a domestically produced substitute. A revenue tariff is designed to raise money for the federal government. During the 1800s, revenue tariffs were the main source of U.S. government receipts. Over the past century, protective tariffs have been an important policy tool for protectionists around the world. Protectionism refers to the government's use of tariffs and other import controls to restrict the inflow of foreign goods into a country. Free trade, the opposite of protectionism, favors the elimination of tariffs and non-tariff barriers to trade. Since World War II, a trend toward free trade has resulted in the dismantling of many tariffs and other protectionist policies.

Tariffs are levied in one of two ways. First, a duty can be levied on a specific quantity of an imported good. Weight, volume, size, and number are common types of quantity measurements. For instance, a country could assign a $1 duty on each gallon of imported wine, or a $100 duty on each ton of imported sugar. Second, an ad valorem duty is levied as a percentage of the imported good's market price. Ad valorem duties are more complex because a change in the imported good's price likewise changes the amount of the duty. Normally, ad valorem duties rise when the price of an imported good falls. The automatic increase in the tariff is designed to keep the price of the imported good artificially high. Conversely, ad valorem duties tend to fall when the price of the imported good rises. The decrease in the tariff acknowledges that the higher priced import will probably not attract as many buyers, hence the duty is less necessary to protect domestic producers. Today, ad valorem duties are the most popular form of tariff.

National governments, and regional associations of countries, establish tariffs. In the United States, for example, congress or the president can establish a tariff. Congress established the Smoot-Hawley Tariff in 1930 to protect failing American industries at the outset of the Great Depression. More recently, President George W. Bush enacted a temporary tariff on foreign steel. The tariff, which commenced in March 2002, was lifted in December 2003 under pressure from the World Trade Organization (WTO) and important trading partners such as the European Union (EU) and Japan. Regional associations of countries also impose tariffs. The world's most integrated regional association of countries, the EU, has a common external tariff (CET) for the twenty-five-nation region. Similarly the Andean Community, a five-nation customs union in South America, recently established a common external tariff.

Tariffs and other trade barriers have fallen in recent years. One reason for the decline in tariffs is the rise of regional trade agreements (RTAs) and other regional associations of countries. Tariffs among members of the EU, Southern Common Market (MERCOSUR), North American Free Trade Agreement (NAFTA), and other regional associations have been eliminated. International agreements have also dismantled tariffs and other trade barriers in the wider global economy. For example, the General Agreement on Tariffs and Trade (GATT) sponsored eight trade rounds from 1947 to 1994 to liberalize global trade. Under GATT's most-favored-nation (MFN) principle, a trade concession granted to one member nation automatically applied to all GATT members. GATT's successor organization, the World Trade Organization (WTO), also adopted the MFN principle. The World Bank and the International Monetary Fund (IMF), commonly called the Bretton Woods institutions, support trade liberalization to smooth the path toward global poverty reduction and sustainable economic development. Average tariffs for most countries have declined in recent years, as shown in Table 88.

Significant tariff issues linger in the global economy. For example, retaliatory tariffs have become a popular anti-dumping measure in recent years. Dumping is an illegal trade practice that involves the sale of foreign imports at a price below the product's true costs of production. The 2002–2003 U.S. tariff on foreign steel was framed as an anti-dumping measure. By the early 2000s, more than 1,000 anti-dumping cases were pending, awaiting WTO action. Another contentious tariff issue involved trade restrictions on agricultural output from developing countries. The lack of market access for third world agricultural products to lucrative markets in the developed world sharpened the North-South divide.

TABLE 88 **Simple Mean Tariffs: Representative Countries, 1980s to 2003**

	Simple Mean Tariff			
Category of Country	Year	Percent	Year	Percent
Developing economies				
Brazil	1989	43.5%	2002	14.9%
China	1992	41.6%	2001	15.1%
India	1990	76.6%	2001	31.0%
Emerging market economies				
Chile	1992	11.0%	2002	7.0%
Hungary	1991	12.0%	2002	8.3%
Poland	1991	11.8%	2003	4.0%
Advanced economies				
European Union	1988	2.6%	2002	3.1%
Japan	1988	4.0%	2002	2.9%
United States	1989	5.9%	2002	4.1%

Source: World Bank, *2004 World Development Indicators*, 322–325.

See also **Bretton Woods System; Embargo; General Agreement on Tariffs and Trade; Import Quotas; Imports; International Trade; Protectionism; Regional Trade Agreements; Voluntary Quotas; World Trade Organization.**

Further Reading

Barfield, Claude E. *High-Tech Protectionism: The Irrationality of Antidumping Laws*. Washington, DC: American Enterprise Institute Press, 2003.

Ingco, Merlinda D. *Agriculture and the WTO: Creating a Trading System for Development*. Washington, DC: World Bank Publications, 2005.

Irwin, Douglas A. *Free Trade under Fire*. Princeton, NJ: Princeton University Press, 2003.

Lusztig, Michael. *The Limits of Protectionism: Building Coalitions for Free Trade*. Pittsburgh, PA: University of Pittsburgh Press, 2004.

TERMS OF TRADE

Terms of trade is a measure of the relative prices of a country's exports and imports. The terms of trade is expressed as a ratio of a country's export price index to its import price index. These price indexes are linked to a 1980 base year. In the base year the terms of trade index is set at 100. A favorable movement in a country's terms of trade occurs when the terms of trade index rises above 100. A favorable movement indicates the price of a country's exports has risen relative to the price of imported goods. A country's terms of trade deteriorates when the index falls below 100. This occurs when the price of its exports has fallen relative to the price of imported goods. Table 89 shows the terms of trade index for representative countries in the global economy.

Unstable markets for cotton and other commodities worsen the terms of trade for many poorer commodity-producing countries.

Courtesy of CORBIS

For decades the terms of trade has been a major trade issue in the global economy. It is particularly contentious in trade relations between the nations of the global South and the global North. The World Bank and other multilateral institutions have encouraged developing countries to specialize in the production of goods in which they have a comparative advantage. Poorer countries responded by specializing in the production of basic commodities such as cocoa, coffee, cotton, rubber, sugar, or tobacco. An economy's over-reliance on one crop, or several crops, contributes to unbalanced growth and economic instability, however. When a certain commodity is in oversupply, its price plummets in global markets. When there is a shortage of the commodity, its price rises. Over time, the price of exported commodities from many developing countries, especially the least developed countries (LDCs), has fallen relative to the price of imported

TABLE 89 **Terms of Trade Index: Selected Countries, 2001 (1980 = 100)**

Advanced Countries	Terms of Trade	Emerging Market and Developing Countries	Terms of Trade
Australia	86	Argentina	81
Canada	93	Brazil	136
Germany	106	Chile	39
Israel	122	Dominican Republic	58
Italy	125	Egypt	46
Japan	126	Haiti	45
Norway	123	Hungary	85
South Korea	84	India	136
United Kingdom	100	Mexico	33
United States	114	Poland	285

Source: United Nations Development Program, *Human Development Report 2004*, 192–195.

manufactured goods from the advanced countries. The deterioration in the terms of trade for these commodity-reliant countries often means that export earnings decline, and trade deficits rise. The Group of Seventy-Seven (G77) and other voices from the developing world have expressed concerns about the worsening terms of trade, lack of access to markets in the industrialized world, and other trade issues.

The terms of trade index, by itself, cannot be used as the sole measure of a country's strength in the global trading system. For example, the deterioration of a country's terms of trade could reflect greater production efficiency in export industries. Greater efficiency by domestic producers could lower the average price of exported goods and vastly increase the quantity of exports sold in global markets. The terms of trade measures the average price of exports but does not measure the volume of exports or the reasons for an increase or decrease in the terms of trade index. Conversely, a favorable movement in a country's terms of trade could mean nothing more than higher priced exports are being offered for sale in global markets. The higher prices, however, may reduce the demand for these exported goods.

See also **Absolute Advantage; Advanced Economies; Balance of Trade; Comparative Advantage; Developing Countries; Exports; Group of Seventy-Seven; Imports; International Commodity Agreements; International Trade. *See also in Volume 2,* Documents 6, 50.**

Further Reading

Akiyama, Takamasa. *Commodity Market Reforms: Lessons of Two Decades*. Washington, DC: World Bank Publications, 2001.

Ingco, Merlinda D. *Agriculture and the WTO: Creating a Trading System for Development*. Washington, DC: World Bank Publications, 2005.

United Nations. *Export Diversification and Economic Growth: The Experience of Selected Least Developed Countries*. New York: Author, 2005.

———. *Returning to an Eternal Debate: The Terms of Trade for Commodities in the Twentieth Century*. New York: Author, 2003.

THIRD WORLD SOCIALISM

Third world socialism refers to the application of socialist principles to developing economies. Most experiments in third world socialism spanned a forty-year period between the mid-1940s and the mid-1980s. Key features of the socialist agenda included the redistribution of society's wealth and central economic planning, each designed to promote economic justice and sustainable economic development. Interest in third world socialism faded during the 1980s, as unmet development objectives pushed developing countries toward market-oriented strategies.

Third world socialism faced many obstacles, most of which were associated with countries' low level of economic development. The success or failure of socialism became intertwined with the success or failure of nations' development efforts. Economic development was stymied by economic factors, including underdeveloped productive resources, infrastructure, and social services; political factors, including ineffective tax and regulatory regimes, rampant corruption, and political instability; and cultural factors, including population issues, tribal or clan conflict, and conflicting perceptions of modernity. Countries that embraced third world socialism typically offered development plans based on land reform, nationalization, and central planning.

Land reform involved a change in ownership or control of productive farmland from a landed aristocracy to village groups. Land reform was viewed as pivotal to the socialist agenda due to the centrality of agriculture in developing economies. Tanzanian President Julius K. Nyerere initiated one bold experiment in land reform in the late 1960s when he introduced the "villagization" process, called *ujamaa*. Under *ujamaa*, tracts of land were transformed into community-based farming collectives. Clusters of families jointly worked the collectives and shared the output. Under the banner of "African socialism," Tanzania and other African countries sought to capitalize on the traditional, communal concept of land tenure that had existed in some pre-colonial African societies. Unfortunately, in Tanzania and elsewhere, collectivized agriculture failed to increase crop yields or the self-reliance of the people. At the same moment in time, a similar socialist experiment was underway in the South American country of Chile. Under legislation sponsored by the Socialist and Communist parties, the Chilean government expropriated uncultivated lands and established peasant cooperatives to work them. Expropriation is the government seizure of private property without compensation to the previous owner. Plans to expand Chile's agrarian reform during the early 1970s were cut short when, in 1973, Socialist President Salvador Allende was killed in a military *coup d'etat*.

A second feature of the socialist agenda was the seizure of the economy's commanding heights. The commanding heights of an economy include essential industries, such as transportation, communications, energy resources and production facilities, financial services, and so on. Government seizures of property, through nationalization or expropriation, were intended to advance economic justice. After India gained its independence from Great Britain in

1947, the newly elected government of socialist Prime Minister Jawaharlal Nehru instituted large-scale nationalization of mining, heavy industries, transportation, communications, and financial services. Egypt, under the leadership of Gamal Abdel Nasser, undertook an aggressive program of nationalization during the 1950s and 1960s. Nasser brought most major industrial and financial enterprises under the control of the government. Similar government seizures occurred in the North African nations of Tunisia and Algeria during the 1950s, Chile in the early 1970s, and dozens of other countries during the post-colonial era. The state-owned enterprises in the developing countries encountered predictable problems, such as poor work incentives, distorted price signals, and bloated bureaucracies.

A third feature of the socialist agenda was central economic planning. The scope and rigidity of economic plans varied. For example, India's indicative plans guided the nation's economic development, but did not dictate production quotas or resource use for all industries. In fact, Indian five-year plans barely touched the agricultural sector, which remained in private hands and employed the vast majority of all workers in the country. More rigid five-year plans were formed in the one-party states and those run by military dictatorships. Socialist planning in these states more closely resembled that of the authoritarian socialists such as the former Soviet Union. Central plans, usually called "development plans," stressed the collectivization of agriculture and large-scale nationalization or expropriation of major industries to jump-start modernization. Economic planning also solidified the government's control over a country. One-party or military governments in the socialist camp were led by President Julius K. Nyerere in Tanzania, President Kwame Nkrumah in Ghana, President Gamal Abdel Nassar in Egypt, and President Sekou Toure in Guinea. Socialist economic planning was largely unsuccessful in the developing world. It was plagued by inaccurate or unreliable economic data, poor coordination of programs, and unrealistic expectations for progress.

In the early 2000s third world socialism surfaced in Venezuela, an upper middle-income developing country. Under the elected President Hugo Chavez, Venezuelan socialism embraced workers' cooperative enterprises and expanded social programs and universal public education. Venezuela's "socialism for the twenty-first century" features a strong government presence in the economy. Government interventions include the creation of state-owned enterprises (SOEs) in transportation, communications, and other key industries; limited expropriation of undeveloped land from large estates; some restrictions on private enterprise; and control over Petroleos de Venezuela (PDVSA), the state-owned oil monopoly. In 2005 President Chavez demanded a restructuring of some foreign transnational corporations (TNCs) into joint ventures, a proposal designed to increase the voice of the government in the local operations of ChevronTexaco (U.S.), BP (UK), and other TNCs. Revenues from Venezuela's petroleum exports help fund President Chavez's socialist agenda.

Venezuela's recent experimentation with socialism has done little to reverse the pendulum swing away from command-oriented socialist approaches and toward market-oriented development strategies. Exemplars of successful market-based economic development include the newly industrialized economies (NIEs) of East Asia—Chinese Taipei, Hong Kong SAR, Singapore, and South Korea. Significant progress along the development continuum has also been made by the other emerging market economies, including Chile, the Czech Republic, Hungary, Poland, Slovenia, and the former Soviet republics of Estonia, Latvia, and Lithuania.

See also **Advanced Economies; Command Economy; Democratic Socialism; Developing Countries; Development Plan; Emerging Market Economies; Market Economy; Newly Industrialized Economies; Nyerere, Julius K.**

Further Reading

Batley, Richard, and George Larbi. *The Changing Role of Government: The Reform of Public Services in Developing Countries*. New York: Palgrave Macmillan, 2004.

Brundenius, Claes, and John Weeks, eds. *Globalization and Third-World Socialism: Cuba and Vietnam*. New York: Palgrave Macmillan, 2001.

Muravchik, Joshua. *Heaven on Earth: The Rise and Fall of Socialism*. San Francisco: Encounter Books, 2002.

Nyerere, Julius K. *Freedom and Development*. New York: Oxford University Press, 1985.

TRADE-RELATED ASPECTS OF INTELLECTUAL PROPERTY

The Trade-Related Aspects of Intellectual Property (TRIPS) agreement is an international agreement designed to protect intellectual properties in global markets. The TRIPS agreement was negotiated during the Uruguay Round (1986–1994) of trade talks, the eighth trade round conducted under the auspices of the General Agreement on Tariffs and Trade (GATT). The formal agreement, officially called the Agreement on Trade-Related Aspects of Intellectual Property Rights, came into effect on January 1, 1995. The World Trade Organization (WTO), GATT's successor organization, administers TRIPS.

TRIPS is the world's most comprehensive set of protections for intellectual property rights (IPR). The agreement outlines minimum standards for the protection of intellectual properties from unauthorized duplication, broadcast, or other forms of intellectual piracy. Specific protections guard against the pirating of copyrighted materials, including computer programs, software, books, scripts, broadcasts, movies, and music; trademarks, including signs or symbols, personal names, letters, numbers, or color combinations that are registered to businesses; industrial designs; patents on new inventions, whether products or processes, in the realm of technology; and other innovations such as the layout designs of integrated circuits. The agreement also establishes specific procedures for monitoring compliance with TRIPS rules, settling disputes, and enforcing the ruling of the WTO. Noncompliance with TRIPS could result in the imposition of WTO trade sanctions.

The agreement is binding on WTO member nations. Compliance with the terms of the TRIPS agreement was phased in during the 1990s and early 2000s.

Advanced countries were required to make the necessary adjustments to national regulations and legislation by 1996. In most cases, the IPR spelled out in the TRIPS agreement were already in effect in the advanced economies. A transition period for emerging market and developing countries mandated compliance by 2000. Some of the world's least developed countries (LDCs) were given until 2006 to fulfill the terms of the agreement. The TRIPS agreement also respected the past work of the World Intellectual Property Organization (WIPO), a specialized agency within the United Nations system. WIPO administers twenty-three international treaties that deal with the protection of intellectual properties. In 2004, WIPO's Patent Cooperation Treaty (PCT) recorded its one millionth patent filing.

Economists view protections for patents and copyrights as essential to invention, innovation, and the spirit of entrepreneurship in the global economy. Violations of IPR, on the other hand, reduce business profits and investments and cheat governments out of legitimate tax revenues. The United States initiated several legal actions related to TRIPS in recent years, mainly against piracy of copyrighted materials in other advanced economies. In 2005, the biggest IPR showdown was emerging between the United States and China, however. High-level negotiations between the economic giants resulted in assurances that rampant IPR piracy in China would be curtailed by improved legal rules, enforcement, and a national education campaign. The George W. Bush administration pledged to monitor the piracy issue vigorously under its Strategy Targeting Organized Piracy (STOP) initiative.

See also **General Agreement on Tariffs and Trade; Information and Communications Technologies; World Intellectual Property Organization; World Trade Organization.**

Further Reading

Drahos, Peter, and John Braithwaite. *Information Feudalism.* New York: W. W. Norton & Company, 2003.

Drahos, Peter, and Ruth Mayne. *Global Intellectual Property Rights: Knowledge, Access, and Development.* New York: Palgrave Macmillan, 2002.

Rao, M. B., and Manjula Guru. *Understanding TRIPS: Managing Knowledge in Developing Countries.* Thousand Oaks, CA: SAGE Publications, 2003.

Richards, Donald G. *Intellectual Property Rights and Global Capitalism: The Political Economy of the Trips Agreement.* Armonk, NY: M. E. Sharpe, 2004.

TRANSITION COUNTRIES

The transition countries, or transition economies, are the twenty-eight countries of eastern and central Europe and central Asia that are in the process of transforming from communism to capitalism, and from totalitarianism to democracy. The epic transition began in the late 1980s in Poland and Hungary, and accelerated after the collapse of the Soviet Union in December 1991. National strategies to achieve a transition toward free-market economies and democracy differed. For example, Poland and Russia adopted shock therapy in the early 1990s to jump-start the transition to capitalism. Shock therapy

TABLE 90 **Transition Countries by Region, 2005**

Region	Countries (number)	Countries
Baltic States	3	Estonia, Latvia, Lithuania
Central and Eastern Europe	12	Albania, Bosnia and Herzegovina, Bulgaria, Croatia, the Czech Republic, the FYR of Macedonia, Hungary, Poland, Romania, Slovakia, Slovenia, Federal Republic of Yugoslavia (Serbia/Montenegro)
Commonwealth of Independent States*	13	Armenia, Azerbaijan, Belarus, Georgia, Kazakhstan, Kyrgyz Republic, Moldova, Mongolia, Russia, Tajikistan, Turkmenistan, Ukraine, Uzbekistan

*Mongolia is not a member of the Commonwealth of Independent States (CIS), but shares common characteristics with CIS members.
Source: European Bank for Reconstruction and Development, *Building Prosperity*, 3.

advocated rapid, comprehensive market reforms to break from communism. Other countries, such as the Ukraine, opted for a more gradualist transition.

The term "transition countries" has fallen out of favor in recent years. The International Monetary Fund (IMF) and other international agencies introduced a new country classification scheme in 2004. The new classification identifies two broad categories of countries: the twenty-nine advanced economies, and 179 emerging market and developing economies. Table 90 identifies the transition countries.

The pillars of economic transition include privatization, limited government, competitive markets, and the liberalization of trade and investment regimes. Privatization transferred state-owned productive properties such as farms, factories, mines, and retail stores to the private sector. Privatization was most successful in the small- and medium-sized enterprises (SMEs), mainly in light industries, services, construction, and retail trade. More problematic was the privatization of large, inefficient state-owned enterprises (SOEs) and the collective farms. Second, limited government reduced many types of state intervention in resource allocation, pricing, and output decisions. Market reforms focused on creating a legal framework to protect private property rights, profits, and business activity; dismantling central planning agencies; and building institutions compatible with good governance and the rule of law. Third, competitive markets required individuals and businesses to respond to the invisible signals of the price system. Price signals, rather than government decree, would henceforth direct consumption and production decisions. Fourth, the liberalization of trade and investment enabled countries to rejoin the global economy and share in the benefits of globalization. Liberalization, in combination with other economic and political reforms, also opened new doors to foreign aid from multilateral and bilateral sources. Since 1991, the European Bank for Reconstruction and Development (EBRD) has approved over 1,000 loans, worth 23 billion euros for economic development in the transition countries. Table 91

TABLE 91 **Comparing Transition, Advanced, and Developing Countries***

Economic Indicators	Transition Economies	Advanced Economies	Developing Economies
Number of countries (2002)	28	29	125
World population (% of world total, 2002)	6.4%	15.4%	78.2%
Real GDP growth rate (1985–1994)	−2.1%	3.0%	5.2%
Real GDP growth rate (1995–2004)	2.8%	2.7%	5.1%
Annual GDP per capita (1985–1994)	−2.6%	2.4%	3.2%
Annual GDP per capita (1995–2004)	3.0%	2.1%	3.5%
Real GDP (% of world total, 2002, PPP)	6.3%	55.7%	38.1%
Annual inflation rate (1985–1994)	146.4%	3.9%	9.5%
Annual inflation rate (1995–2004)	12.9%	2.1%	5.2%
Total Exports (% of world total, 2002, PPP)	4.8%	74.8%	20.3%
External debt ($ billions, 2004)	$453.5	n.a.	$2,211.6
External debt payments ($ billions, 2004)	$107.1	n.a.	$314.9

*Some rounding. Some countries omitted from the data due to economy size or unreliable data. Data for 2004 are IMF estimates.
Source: International Monetary Fund, *World Economic Outlook, September 2003*, 164, 173, 184, 228.

compares the transition countries with other categories of countries by selected indicators.

Recent EBRD research pointed to a number of economic successes and challenges for the transition countries by the early 2000s. In 2003–2004, EBRD noted positive signs of macroeconomic stability, including robust economic growth and low inflation, on average. Eight transition countries were formally admitted to the European Union (EU) in May 2004, an acknowledgment of their successful transition. The eight countries included the Czech Republic, Estonia, Latvia, Lithuania, Hungary, Poland, Slovenia, and Slovakia. However, progress has been irregular and pitted with setbacks. Key economic problems included rising federal budgetary deficits, trade deficits, and external debt payments. EBRD also expressed concern about the implementation of poverty-reduction programs, and the lack of diversification in the resource-based economies of the CIS. The democratization process, including the creation of good governance and the rule of law, has stumbled in some countries. Strained democratic institutions in Russia, the largest transition country, were cause for concern by the early 2000s.

See also **Advanced Economies; Capitalism; Communism; Developing Countries; Emerging Market Economies; European Bank for Reconstruction and Development; Privatization.**

Further Reading

Jackson, John E., et al., eds. *The Political Economy of Poland's Transition: New Firms and Reform Governments*. New York: Cambridge University Press, 2005.

Kiggundu, Moses N. *Managing Globalization in Developing Countries and Transition Countries: Building Capacities for a Changing World*. Westport, CT: Quorum Books, 2002.

Kolodko, Grzegorz. *Globalization and Catching-Up in Transition Economies*. Rochester, NY: University of Rochester Press, 2002.

Macey, David A. J., William Pyle, and Stephen K. Wegren, eds. *Building Market Institutions in Post-Communist Agriculture: Land, Credit, and Assistance*. Lanham, MD: Lexington Books, 2004.

Winiecki, Jan. *Transition Economies and Foreign Trade*. 2d ed. New York: Routledge, 2002.

TRANSNATIONAL CORPORATIONS

A transnational corporation (TNC) is a company that is based in one country, but owns or controls other companies, called affiliates, in one or more additional countries. From its headquarters in one country, the parent company exercises direct control over the policies of its affiliates, including policies related to the production and distribution of goods. The ownership of TNCs might be private, public, or some mixture of the two. TNCs, which are also called multinational corporations (MNCs) or multinationals, have strengthened the economic web that binds the global economy. The United Nations Conference on Trade and Development (UNCTAD) reported that about 62,000 TNCs, with 927,000 foreign affiliates operated in the global economy by the early 2000s. In 2003, TNCs' foreign affiliates employed 54 million workers, and controlled assets in excess of $30 trillion. Figure 37 shows the distribution of the 62,000 parent corporations in the global economy (the newly industrialized economies of East Asia are included as advanced economies).

Ranked by total revenues, Wal-Mart Stores was the world's largest TNC in 2004, with sales receipts of $288 billion, according to *Fortune's* Global 500 List of the World's Largest Corporations. Wal-Mart was also the world's largest corporate employer, with 1.7 million employees. Wal-Mart is a privately owned U.S. company. Its corporate headquarters is located in Bentonville, Arkansas. The corporation's primary business is retail trade, which encompasses four main divisions: Wal-Mart Stores, Wal-Mart Supercenters, SAM's Clubs, and Wal-Mart Neighborhood Markets. Since the opening of the first Wal-Mart store in 1962, the retail empire has focused on high-volume, low-margin retailing to guarantee low prices for consumers. In recent years, Wal-Mart has come under increased scrutiny for exerting pressure on producers in global supply chains to reduce production costs, regardless of the impact on low-wage foreign labor. In 2004, about 5,000 Wal-Mart retail outlets operated in nine countries, including Argentina, Brazil, Canada, China, Germany, Korea, Mexico, the United Kingdom, and the United States. Table 92 shows the world's top ten TNCs,

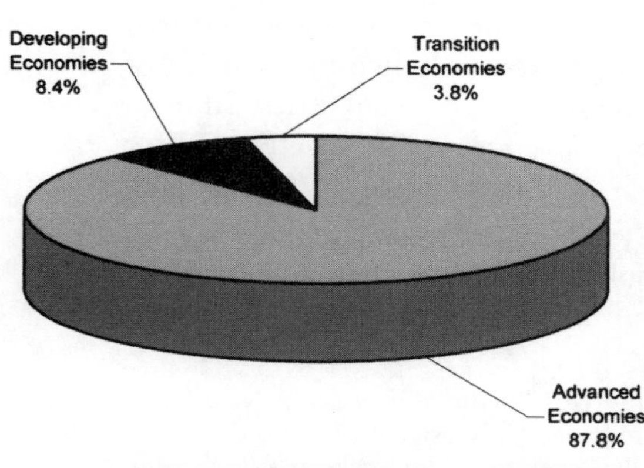

FIGURE 37 **Parent Corporations in the Global Economy**

Source: United Nations Conference on Trade and Development, *World Investment Report 2004*, 273–274.

TABLE 92 **Top Transnational Corporations by Revenues, 2004**

Rank	Corporation	Home Country	Total Revenues ($ billions)	Employees
1	Wal-Mart Stores	United States	$288	1,700,000
2	BP	Britain	$285	103,700*
3	Exxon Mobil	United States	$271	88,300*
4	Royal Dutch/Shell	Britain/Netherlands	$269	119,000*
5	General Motors	United States	$194	324,000
6	DaimlerChrysler	Germany	$177	384,723
7	Toyota Motor	Japan	$173	265,753
8	Ford Motor	United States	$172	324,864
9	General Electric	United States	$153	307,000
10	Total	France	$152	110,783*

*2003 data.
Source: "Global 500 World's Largest Corporations," *Fortune*, July 25, 2005, 119, 139; and "Fortune 500 Largest U.S. Corporations," *Fortune*, April 18, 2005, F-33.

ranked by total revenues in 2004. All but four of the world's top 100 corporations are headquartered in the advanced economies.

Ranked by the number of employees, Wal-Mart was again the world's top corporation in 2004, with 1.7 million employees. China National Petroleum (1,133,985 employees), the U.S. Postal Service (807,596 employees), Sinopec (774,800 employees), and State Grid (729,327 employees), round out the top five employers in the global economy. Thus, government corporations occupy four of the top five spots in this ranking. China National Petroleum and Sinopec, which are owned and operated by the government of China, produce petroleum and petrochemicals. The U.S. Postal Service is a largely self-sustaining, autonomous agency of the federal government. State Grid is China's dominant state-owned electricity generating and power transmission company.

TNCs are also ranked by the dollar value of their foreign assets. Foreign assets include manufacturing or assembly plants, warehouses, equipment, and so on. According to the *World Investment Report 2004*, General Electric held the largest stock of foreign assets, as shown in Table 93. Ranked by foreign assets, 99 of the top 100 TNCs hailed from advanced economies. Heavily represented in the top 100 TNCs were firms headquartered in European Union countries (52 percent of the top TNCs), North America (30 percent), and East Asia and the Pacific (12 percent). The United States entered twenty-six TNCs on the top 100 list, the largest total for a single country. The lone developing country penetrating the top 100 was Mexico, with Cemex S.A. occupying the 87th position in the ranking.

Some TNCs are conglomerates. A conglomerate is a highly diversified corporation. For example, Unilever is one of the world's most diverse conglomerates. Unilever was founded in 1930 and is headquartered in the United Kingdom and the Netherlands. During the 1960s, Unilever acquired numerous firms in areas such as food, home care, and personal care. During the 1990s, Unilever reversed course by divesting itself of certain brand names and discontinuing

TABLE 93 **World's Top TNCs by Foreign Assets, 2002 ($ billions)**

Rank	Corporation	Country	Foreign Assets ($ billions)	Foreign Sales ($ billions)	Foreign Employees
1	General Electric	United States	$229	$45	150,000
2	Vodafone	Britain	$208	$34	56,667
3	Ford Motor	United States	$165	$54	188,453
4	British Petroleum	Britain	$126	$146	97,400
5	General Motors	United States	$108	$48	101,000
6	Royal Dutch/Shell	Britain/Neth.	$94	$114	65,000
7	Toyota Motor	Japan	$79	$72	85,057
8	Total	France	$79	$77	68,554
9	France Telecom	France	$73	$18	102,016
10	Exxon Mobil	United States	$61	$141	56,000

Source: United Nations Conference on Trade and Development, *World Investment Report 2004*, 276.

others. In its *Annual Report and Accounts 2004*, Unilever reported total revenues of about $50 billion in 2004. Unilever earned its highest revenues in Europe (43 percent of total sales), followed by North America (22 percent), Asia and the Pacific (16 percent), Latin America (11 percent), and Africa and the Middle East (8 percent). Unilever maintains facilities in about 100 countries and employs 223,000 workers. Several popular Unilever-owned brands in U.S. markets include Ben & Jerry's ice cream, Slim Fast diet products, Lipton tea and soft drinks, Birds Eye frozen foods, Bertolli Mediterranean cuisine, Wish-Bone salad dressing, Dove soaps, and Pond's skin creams.

TNCs are a favorite target of anti-globalization activists, non-governmental organizations, and other elements of civil society. Activists argue TNCs put corporate profits ahead of corporate social responsibilities. In the process, TNCs sacrifice people's quality of life by lowering workers' wages, ruining local environments, and disrespecting local cultures. In effect, anti-globalization activists view trade and investment liberalization as an invitation for TNCs to exploit human and natural resources at the bottom of the supply chain. Pro-globalization forces, including major multilateral organizations and TNCs, counter that TNC investment and other cross-border business activity stimulate job and business creation. Pro-globalization forces also note the positive impact of TNC investment on technology transfers, capital formation, and the infusion of modern management skills to economies in the developing world. TNCs conclude that foreign investment is an important engine of economic growth and sustainable economic growth.

See also **Capital Formation; Corporate Social Responsibility; Economic Growth; Foreign Direct Investment; Localization; Maquiladoras; Non-Governmental Organizations; Offshoring; Race to the Bottom; Supply Chains. *See also in Volume 2*, Documents 29, 30, 31, 32, 33, 35, 36, 37, 38, 52.**

Further Reading

Cuyvers, Ludo, and Filip DeBeule, eds. *Transnational Corporations and Economic Development: From Internalisation to Globalization*. New York: Palgrave Macmillan, 2005.

Gillies, Grazia I. *Transnational Corporations and International Production: Concepts, Theories and Effects*. Northampton, MA: Edward Elgar Publishing, 2005.

Giorgio, Barba N, and Anthony J. Venables. *Multinational Firms in the World Economy*. Princeton, NJ: Princeton University Press, 2004.

Suter, Keith. *Curbing Corporate Power: How Can We Control Transnational Corporations?* New York: Zed Books, 2005.

United Nations Conference on Trade and Development. *World Investment Report 2004: The Shift towards Services*. New York: United Nations, 2004.

U

UNITED NATIONS SYSTEM

The United Nations System consists of the six branches of the United Nations (UN), and twenty-five autonomous specialized agencies, programs, and funds. The United Nations System promotes world peace, sustainable economic development, and human rights. In 2000, the UN adopted the Millennium Development Goals (MDGs) to focus the energy of the United Nations System and other international organizations on poverty reduction, sustainable economic development, and related objectives.

The UN was born in 1945 when fifty-one countries formally adopted the UN Charter at the San Francisco Conference. Membership climbed during the post–World War II era, as newly independent countries from the developing world joined the UN. The largest membership increase occurred during the 1960s when forty-four nations, mainly from Africa, joined the UN. In 2005, the UN was comprised of 191 countries. The growth in UN membership is shown in Figure 38. The secretary-general is the UN's leading official. Since 1945 the UN has had seven secretary-generals. Kofi Annan, a native of Ghana, is the current secretary-general. Annan entered his first term of office on January 1, 1997, and his second term of office on January 1, 2002. Annan's second term will end on December 31, 2006.

The six principal branches, or organs, of the UN protect the personal and economic security of the world's peoples. UN branches include the General Assembly, Security Council, Economic and Security Council, Trusteeship Council, International Court of Justice, and Secretariat. Table 94 summarizes the function of each branch. Five UN branches are located in New York City. The sixth, the International Court of Justice, or World Court, is located in the Hague, Netherlands.

The United Nations System also consists of fifteen specialized agencies, and ten special programs and funds. These institutions of the UN family are autonomous, self-financing bodies. Yet, the specialized agencies, programs, and funds are linked to the UN through formal agreements and a shared mission to improve the human condition. Many institutions of the UN family are directly involved in promoting sustainable economic development. Key specialized agencies within the UN family include:

- **World Bank Group**: The World Bank Group works to reduce world poverty and promote sustainable economic development. Through its five complementary institutions, the World Bank Group makes development

The United Nations headquarters is located in New York City. The United Nations System promotes world peace, economic development, and human rights.
Courtesy of CORBIS

loans, provides technical assistance, and supports foreign investment in developing countries.

- **International Monetary Fund (IMF):** The IMF promotes financial and monetary stability and economic growth in developing countries. Its main policy tools are financial assistance, technical assistance, and financial and monetary surveillance.
- **World Health Organization (WHO):** WHO sets global health standards, and supplies technical and financial assistance to strengthen nations' health programs. WHO assistance is vital to human capital development in the world's poorer regions.
- **International Labor Organization (ILO):** The ILO establishes and monitors core labor standards to safeguard workers' rights and improve working conditions and wages. The ILO's labor standards set a benchmark for acceptable labor practices in the global economy.
- **United Nations Educational, Scientific and Cultural Organization (UNESCO):** UNESCO promotes

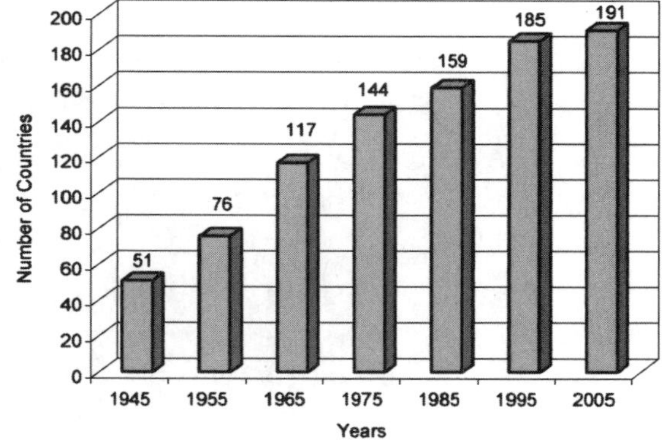

FIGURE 38 **Growth in United Nations Membership, 1945 to 2005**
Source: United Nations, "Growth in United Nations Membership, 1945–2005," April 2005.

TABLE 94 **Principal Branches of the United Nations, 2005**

UN Branches	Membership (number of countries)	Main Functions
General Assembly	191	Discusses and debates key issues related to peace and security, human development, and economic development. Adopts "resolutions" on the one nation one vote principle.
Security Council	15	Discusses threats to peace and is empowered to secure peace through mediation, peacekeeping missions, economic sanctions, and, if necessary, collective military action against aggressors.
Economic and Social Council	54	Coordinates the economic and social policies of the UN System, especially actions that promote economic and human development.
Trusteeship Council	5	Prepared colonial possessions for independence and self-government. Suspended operations in 1994 when Palau, the final UN Trust Territory, gained its independence.
International Court of Justice	15	Hears legal cases and settles disputes between countries. Parties that agree to participate in the court's proceedings are obliged to comply with its decisions.
Secretariat	Staff (15,000)	Provides administrative support to the principal branches of the UN. Facilitates implementation of UN resolutions, policies, and programs.

Source: United Nations, "Membership of Principal Unified Nations Organs in 2005," *Fact Sheet 25*, March 2005.

educational opportunity, scientific collaboration, and cultural preservation and development. Its mission directly supports human development in the developing world.

- **Food and Agriculture Organization (FAO)**: The FAO strives to improve people's standard of living and quality of live by boosting agricultural productivity, mainly in the developing world. Agriculture is the backbone of many of the world's least developed countries (LDCs).
- **World Intellectual Property Organization (WIPO)**: WIPO protects copyrights, trademarks, patents, and other forms of intellectual property in the global economy. The protection of intellectual property encourages invention, innovation, and entrepreneurship.

A number of autonomous UN programs and funds also support global poverty reduction and sustainable economic development. Key programs and funds include:

- **United Nations Development Program (UNDP)**: The UNDP sponsors development projects, especially those directly related to the overriding goal of poverty reduction. Projects reverse desertification, advance education and training for women, and promote agricultural development, technology sharing, and infrastructure construction.
- **United Nations Environment Program (UNEP)**: The UNEP promotes environmentally sound programs and sustainable economic development in the developing world. UNEP projects expand access to clean

water, reverse local environmental degradation, and introduce appropriate technologies. Globally, the UNEP works to reduce global warming, ozone depletion, desertification, deforestation, acid rain, and threats to the world's bio-diversity.

- **United Nations Children's Fund (UNICEF):** UNICEF provides a number of basic services to the developing world to improve people's quality of life. UNICEF programs improve nutrition and health care, sanitation systems, education, and other social services for women and children. UNICEF also responds to people's needs after natural disasters and other crises.
- **World Food Program (WFP):** The WFP provides food aid, mainly to alleviate human suffering in crisis situations. WFP food aid reaches refugees and others dislocated by civil strife, warfare, or other human calamity. The WFP is the world's largest food aid organization.
- **United Nations Population Fund (UNFPA):** The UNFPA supports programs to improve reproductive health, a precondition for sustainable economic development. Specific initiatives help young people plan their families, avoid sexually transmitted diseases, and stop violence against women.

The United Nations has also sponsored major international conferences, approved global resolutions, and used its prestige to promote positive change in the global economy. For example, in 1992, the United Nations Conference on Environment and Development, more commonly called the Rio Earth Summit, produced *Agenda 21*—the world's most comprehensive statement on sustainable production, worker and human rights, and protections for the natural environment and indigenous peoples. In 1999, the UN's Global Compact garnered international support for corporate social responsibility in the realms of human rights, worker rights, and environmental protection. In 2000, the UN's Millennium Development Goals (MDGs) gave focus to global development efforts. Today, the work of multilateral institutions such as the World Bank Group and the International Monetary Fund is guided by measurable objectives listed in the MDGs.

See also **Annan, Kofi; Developing Countries; International Labor Organization; International Monetary Fund; Millennium Development Goals; Poverty; Sustainable Economic Development; World Bank Group; World Health Organization; World Intellectual Property Organization.** ***See also in Volume 2,*** **Documents 4, 6, 21, 29, 33, 34, 35, 39, 40, 45, 48, 50, 51, 52, 53, 54, 57, 58.**

Further Reading

Alger, Chadwick, and Mildred Vasan, eds. *The United Nations System: A Reference Handbook*. Santa Barbara, CA: ABC-Clio, 2005.

Drakulich, Angela, ed. *A Global Agenda: Issues before the 59th General Assembly of the United Nations, 2004–2005 Edition*. Lanham, MD: Bernan Press, 2004.

Schlesinger, Stephen. *Act of Creation: The Founding of the United Nations: A Story of Superpowers, Secret Agents, Wartime Allies and Enemies, and Their Quest for a Peaceful World*. Boulder, CO: Westview Press, 2004.

United Nations, *Basic Facts about the United Nations*. New York: United Nations Department of Public Information, 2004.
Weiss, Thomas G. *UN Voices: The Struggle for Development and Social Justice*. Bloomington, IN: Indiana University Press, 2005.

UNSUSTAINABLE DEBT

Unsustainable debt refers to a country's inability to service, or make payments on, its external debt without decimating its domestic economy. External debt, also called foreign debt, is money owed by a country to a foreign government or commercial bank, a multilateral organization such as the World Bank or International Monetary Fund (IMF), or other creditor. Unsustainable debt is a problem faced by many developing countries. During the 1990s and early 2000s, developing countries and other emerging market economies accumulated massive external debts. From 1996 to 2005, the IMF estimated total external debt climbed from $2.2 trillion to $3 trillion, an increase of nearly 40 percent. During this same period of time, debt service payments rose from $312 billion to $475 billion, a 52 percent increase, as shown in Figure 39 (data for 2005 are IMF estimates).

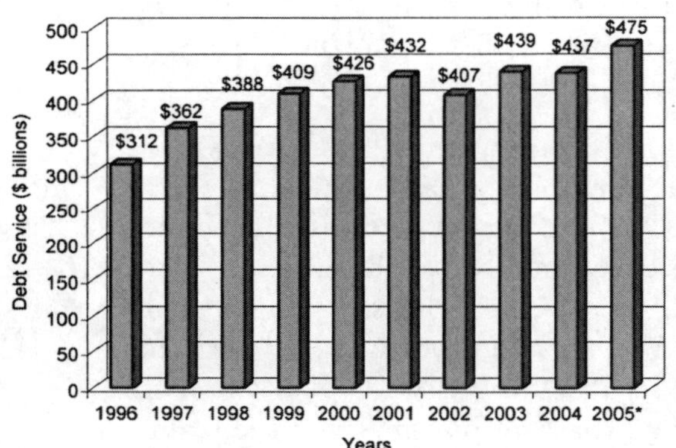

FIGURE 39 **Increase in External Debt Service, 1996 to 2005 ($ billions)**
Source: International Monetary Fund, *World Economic Outlook*, April 2005, 262.

Unsustainable debt disrupts poorer countries' ability to achieve sustainable economic development. Debt payments strain the already shallow stream of revenues flowing to governments in the world's poorest regions. Thus, governments in the severely indebted countries are forced to choose between honoring debt obligations to foreign creditors, and providing essential social services to their own people. According to the World Bank, fifty-two countries were "severely indebted" in

TABLE 95 **Severely Indebted Countries, 2005**

Country Classification	Number	Severely Indebted Countries
Low-income	28	Angola, Bhutan, Burundi, Central African Republic, Chad, Comoros, Democratic Republic of Congo, Cote d'Ivoire, Eritrea, Gambia, Guinea, Guinea-Bissau, Indonesia, Kyrgyz Republic, Laos, Liberia, Malawi, Myanmar, Republic of Congo, Rwanda, Sao Tome and Principe, Sierra Leone, Somalia, Sudan, Tajikistan, Togo, Zambia, Zimbabwe
Lower middle-income	10	Brazil, Bulgaria, Ecuador, Guyana, Kazakhstan, Jordan, Peru, Samoa, Serbia and Montenegro, Syria
Upper middle-income	14	Argentina, Belize, Croatia, Dominica, Estonia, Gabon, Grenada, Latvia, Lebanon, Panama, Seychelles, St. Kitts and Nevis, Turkey, Uruguay

Source: World Bank, "Country Groups," *Data and Statistics*, 2005.

2005, mostly in developing Africa and Asia. Most of the severely indebted countries were low-income countries, as shown in Table 95.

International efforts to address the problem of unsustainable debt increased during the 1990s and early 2000s. Today, debt relief is considered an essential component of the world's poverty-reduction strategy. For example, the Heavily Indebted Poor Countries (HIPC) Initiative was initiated by the World Bank and the International Monetary Fund (IMF) in 1996, and expanded in 1999, to coordinate a global response to mounting external debt in the world's poorest countries. By 2004, more than two dozen countries had met eligibility requirements for external debt assistance. Over time, debt relief to the severely indebted countries will top $50 billion. One condition of debt relief under the HIPC Initiative is that government money not spent on debt service payments must be funneled to social programs such as education and health care.

Other groups in the global economy have waged an aggressive campaign favoring debt forgiveness rather than debt relief. For example, Jubilee 2000, an international non-governmental organization (NGO), spearheaded a global debt forgiveness campaign during the 1990s. The Jubilee 2000 campaign brought the issue of unsustainable debt into the limelight, and pressured governments and multilateral organizations to step up debt relief efforts.

See also **Developing Countries; External Debt; Foreign Aid; Heavily Indebted Poor Countries (HIPC) Initiative; International Monetary Fund; Least Developed Countries; Non-Governmental Organizations; Poverty; World Bank Group.** ***See also in Volume 2*, Documents 5, 6, 56.**

Further Reading

Ajayi, S. I., and Mohsin S. Khan. *External Debt and Capital Flight in Sub-Saharan Africa*. Washington, DC: International Monetary Fund, 2000.

Hertz, Noreena. *The Debt Threat: How Debt Is Destroying the Developing World*. New York: HarperBusiness, 2005.

Pettifor, Ann. *The Real World Economic Outlook 2003: The Legacy of Globalization, Debt and Deflation*. New York: Palgrave Macmillan, 2003.

Rieffel, Lex. *Restructuring Sovereign Debt: The Case for Ad Hoc Machinery*. Washington, DC: Brookings Institution Press, 2003.

V

VOLUNTARY QUOTAS

A voluntary quota is a bilateral trade agreement that limits the import of a specific good, or expands the export of a certain good. Thus, a voluntary quota is a type of trade barrier. A voluntary quota is an alternative to imposing an import quota by law or decree. Once a voluntary quota is negotiated, the terms are binding. Voluntary quotas were often viewed as a type of backdoor protectionism. That is, for decades voluntary quotas sidestepped free trade pledges made under the General Agreement on Tariffs and Trade (GATT) and the World Trade Organization (WTO). The two types of voluntary quotas are voluntary export restraint and voluntary import expansion agreements.

The voluntary export restraint (VER) is a bilateral agreement that restricts the quantity of a product that can be exported from one country to another. Weight, number, volume, and other units are used to measure the quantity of an exported good. The United States negotiated a VER with Japan during the early 1980s to protect the ailing U.S. auto industry from a surge of Japanese auto imports. The VER set a number limit of 1.68 million Japanese auto imports in 1981. The VER was raised to 1.85 million Japanese autos in 1984, and 2.3 million autos in 1985. This VER was eventually removed in the early 1990s. During the 1950s and 1960s many other VERs were negotiated between the advanced countries, and East Asian countries such as South Korea and Chinese Taipei, in the textile, clothing, and footwear industries.

A second type of voluntary quota is voluntary import expansion (VIE). VIE is a bilateral agreement that requires one country to accept additional imports from a second country. VIEs are sometimes negotiated to level the playing field in international trade by counteracting non-tariff trade barriers in the first country. Non-tariff trade barriers include licensing and excessive product-testing requirements. In the mid-1990s, the United States negotiated a VIE agreement which required Japan to open its doors to additional U.S.-produced automobiles and auto parts. VIE agreements might also be negotiated to help correct a severe trade imbalance between two countries.

Voluntary quotas, like other trade barriers, are a form of trade protectionism. VERs, for example, were used extensively by advanced economies over the past fifty years to restrict imports of clothing and textiles from low-wage developing countries. During the 1950s and 1960s the United States and the European Economic Community (EEC) negotiated VERs with emerging Asian economies to limit their clothing and textile exports. Later, many VERs were absorbed into multilateral agreements, such as the Multi-Fiber Agreement in the early 1970s and the Agreement on Textiles and Clothing in the mid-1990s. The World Trade Organization (WTO), which began operations on January 1, 1995, banned new VERs, and set in motion a phaseout of existing VERs. The Agreement on Textiles and Clothing was formally terminated in January 2005. In May 2005 President George W. Bush invoked the "safeguard clause" to limit the annual growth of some Chinese imports to the United States. Under the safeguard clause, which was built into China's World Trade Organization (WTO) accession agreement, the president can restrict the growth of certain imports to 7.5 percent per year. The safeguard clause offers some protection for U.S. industries threatened by imports from China.

For decades voluntary quotas limited textile and clothing imports to the United States and Europe.
Courtesy of Getty Images: Jan Suttle/Life File

See also **Embargo; Exports; General Agreement on Tariffs and Trade; Import Quotas; Imports; International Trade; Protectionism; Tariffs; World Trade Organization.**

Further Reading

Berry, Steven. *Voluntary Export Restraints on Automobiles: Evaluating a Strategic Trade Policy*. Cambridge, MA: National Bureau of Economic Research, 1995.

Lusztig, Michael. *The Limits of Protectionism: Building Coalitions for Free Trade*. Pittsburgh: University of Pittsburgh Press, 2004.

Monnich, Christina. *Tariff Rate Quotas and Their Administration*. New York: Peter Lang Publishing, 2004.

Suh, Joon H. *"Voluntary" Export Restraints and Their Effects on Exporters and Consumers: The Case of Footwear Quotas*. St. Louis, MO: Center for the Study of American Business, Washington University, 1981.

WARD, BARBARA M.

Barbara M. Ward (1914–1981) was an influential British development economist, lecturer, journalist, and teacher. Her pioneering work in the field of sustainable economic development called for greater cooperation between the rich and poor nations, and a more equitable distribution of the world's resources. Barbara Ward was born in York, England, to an upper-class educated family. Later, she studied at the Sorbonne in France and at Oxford in England. After the publication of her first book, *The International Share-Out* (1938), Ward was invited to join the staff of the *Economist*, a prominent British newspaper. Her position as foreign editor of the *Economist* deepened her interest in the developing world, its peoples, and the prerequisites for economic growth and development. For much of the 1950s, 1960s, and 1970s, Ward traveled the developing world and penned numerous books on the subject. During the late 1960s and early 1970s she also taught development economics at Columbia University in New York City.

Ward was a prolific author in the field of development economics. She championed the cause of economic justice for all nations in the global economy. Ward argued economic justice must be based on international cooperation and on a more equitable distribution of the world's precious resources. To achieve economic justice, rich countries had a responsibility to increase foreign aid and to otherwise facilitate poor countries' economic transition from colonial dependencies to full partners in an interdependent global economy. Ward believed gross disparities in income and wealth between the have and have-not nations was a prescription for global instability. She also believed a generalized prosperity, built on capitalist foundations, was the surest path toward global peace and security. The theme of economic justice dominated Ward's early books such as *Faith and Freedom* (1954), *The Rich Nations and the Poor Nations* (1962), *Spaceship Earth* (1966), *The Lopsided World* (1968), and *The Widening Gap* (1971).

During the 1970s, Ward explored a second theme related to sustainable economic development, the need to protect and preserve the natural environment. In 1972 Ward, and co-author Rene Dubos, wrote *Only One Earth: The Care and Maintenance of a Small Planet*. This book was commissioned by the United Nations as a background report for the UN Conference on the Human Environment, sometimes called the Stockholm Conference. *Only One Earth* accented the trade-offs between economic growth and environmental protection and the responsibilities of nations to protect natural habitats. The

Stockholm Declaration, a main outcome of the Stockholm Conference, is still considered a key statement on the need to preserve and enhance the human environment. In *Progress for a Small Planet* (1979), Ward offered hope that progress toward a sustainable future was possible.

See also **Advanced Economies; Developing Countries; Development Economics; Environmental Degradation; Multilateral Environmental Agreements; Poverty; Quality of Life; Sustainable Economic Development.** ***See also in Volume 2,*** **Document 39.**

Further Reading

Ward, Barbara. *The Lopsided World.* New York: W. W. Norton & Company, 1968.
———. *Progress for a Small Planet.* New York: W. W. Norton & Company, 1979.
———. *The Rich Nations and the Poor Nations.* New York: W. W. Norton & Company, 1962.
———. *Who Speaks for the Earth?* New York: W. W. Norton & Company, 1973.

WOLFENSOHN, JAMES D.

James D. Wolfensohn (1933–) is an international investment banker and former president of the World Bank Group. During his ten-year tenure as World Bank president, Wolfensohn framed a new people-centered development agenda, which placed global poverty reduction as the Bank's top priority. Wolfensohn was born in Australia, and later became a naturalized U.S. citizen. He earned his BA and LLB degrees from the University of Sydney, Australia, and his MBA from the Harvard Graduate School of Business. He held top spots in major financial companies such as Salomon Brothers in New York and Schroders in London, before establishing his own investment firm, James D. Wolfensohn, Inc., in 1981. Wolfensohn became the ninth president of the World Bank Group on June 1, 1995. The Bank's board of executive directors reappointed Wolfensohn to a second five-year term of office, which began on June 1, 2000. On June 1, 2005, Wolfensohn's successor, Paul Wolfowitz, assumed the presidency of the World Bank Group.

Wolfensohn's decade at the helm of the World Bank Group sharpened the Bank's focus on poverty reduction. Wolfensohn was a key proponent of the Heavily Indebted Poor Countries (HIPC) Initiative in 1996, a joint undertaking by the World Bank and the International Monetary Fund (IMF). The HIPC Initiative, a comprehensive external debt reduction program, was expanded in 1999. By 2004, tens of billions of dollars were committed to debt relief for qualifying countries. Wolfensohn was also an enthusiastic supporter of the UN Millennium Development Goals (MDGs). The MDGs placed the eradication of extreme poverty and hunger at the top of the global development agenda. The MDGs also supported universal primary education, gender equity, improvements in health care, environmental sustainability, and the creation of global partnerships for development. By the early 2000s, Wolfensohn noted with dismay the growing income and technological gap between the rich and poor nations and called for a "new global balance" to improve the human condition in the developing world.

Wolfensohn also transformed the World Bank Group's approach to poverty reduction and economic development. Under Wolfensohn's leadership, the World Bank adopted the Comprehensive Development Framework (CDF) in 1999. The CDF stressed the creation of partnerships among stakeholders to jointly devise and implement World Bank programs. Within developing countries, the World Bank forged partnerships with local governments, religious groups, non-governmental organizations, and other elements of civil society. In *A New Development Agenda: The Transformation of the World Bank Under James D. Wolfensohn, 1995–2005* (2005), Wolfensohn highlighted the value of coalition-building to achieve global development goals. Broad-based coalitions should include reform governments, multilateral development organizations such as the World Bank, the entire United Nations system, regional development banks, transnational corporations, local businesses, NGOs, and civil society. What Wolfensohn suggested was the creation of a focused, inclusive, and dynamic development architecture to transform the vision of poverty reduction and sustainable economic development into a reality.

Wolfensohn, as head of the World Bank Group, also received severe criticism for the Bank's past performance. For example, NGOs, such as Jubilee 2000 critiqued the HIPC Initiative as an inadequate response to the problem of unsustainable external debt. The World Bank, and its sister organization the IMF, were criticized for the rigidity of certain structural reforms imposed on developing countries; reforms that failed to consider the unique circumstances of countries. Anti-globalization activists also targeted Wolfensohn for Bank projects viewed as harmful to workers, local communities, or the environment.

See also **Heavily Indebted Poor Countries (HIPC) Initiative; International Monetary Fund; Millennium Development Goals; Poverty; Quality of Life; World Bank Group.**

Further Reading

Goldman, Michael. *Imperial Nature: The World Bank and Struggles for Social Justice in the Age of Globalization*. New Haven, CT: Yale University Press, 2005.

Marquette, Heather. *Corruption, Politics and Development: The Role of the World Bank*. New York: Palgrave Macmillan, 2004.

Wolfensohn, James D. *A New Development Agenda: The Transformation of the World Bank under James D. Wolfensohn, 1995–2005*. Washington, DC: World Bank Publications, 2005.

———. *Voice for the World's Poor: Selected Speeches and Writings of World Bank President James D. Wolfensohn, 1995–2005*. Washington, DC: World Bank Publications, 2005.

———, and Rodrigo de Rato (Foreword). *Global Monitoring Report 2004: Policies and Actions for Achieving the Millennium Development Goals and Related Outcomes*. Washington, DC: World Bank Publications, 2004.

WORLD BANK GROUP

The World Bank Group is a multilateral development organization, which consists of five mutually supporting institutions: the International Bank for Reconstruction and Development (IBRD), International Development Association

(IDA), International Finance Corporation (IFC), International Centre for Settlement of Investment Disputes (ICSID), and the Multilateral Investment Guarantee Agency (MIGA).

The overriding goal of the World Bank Group is global poverty reduction through sustainable economic development. The World Bank Group promotes economic growth and development through loans and technical assistance to developing countries. It also supports the liberalization of international trade and foreign direct investment to expand the benefits of globalization to all world regions. The World Bank Group is one of the Big Three international organizations designed to oversee economic relations among countries, joining the International Monetary Fund (IMF) and the World Trade Organization (WTO). In 2005, 184 countries were members of the World Bank. The World Bank Group's headquarters is located in Washington, DC. Current World Bank President Paul Wolfowitz began his five-year term of office on June 1, 2005.

The World Bank Group traces its origins to the Bretton Woods Conference, which convened at Bretton Woods, New Hampshire, from July 1–20, 1944. The Bretton Woods Conference brought representatives from forty-four countries together to plan for a more secure and prosperous post–World War II world. The conference supported multilateral cooperation rather than the bilateralism that plagued the pre-war years. Two multilateral organizations were founded at the Bretton Woods Conference: the International Bank for Reconstruction and Development (IBRD) or World Bank, and the International

TABLE 96 **World Bank Group at a Glance, 2004**

Institutions of the World Bank Group	Founded (year)	Member Nations (number)	Cumulative Loans ($ billions)	Functions
International Bank for Reconstruction and Development (IBRD)	1944	184	$394	Provides long-term investment loans and short-term development policy loans to more creditworthy developing countries.
International Finance Corporation (IFC)	1956	176	$44	Provides direct and indirect financing, and technical assistance, to firms with high profit potential.
International Development Association (IDA)	1960	165	$151	Provides long-term, interest-free loans (concessional loans) to poorer, less creditworthy developing countries.
International Centre for the Settlement of Investment Disputes (ICSID)	1966	140	none	Provides a forum for the settlement of investment disputes between investors and host governments. Encourages FDI.
Multilateral Investment Guarantee Agency (MIGA)	1988	164	$13.5	Insures investments of transnational corporations (TNCs) from noncommercial losses. Encourages FDI.

Source: The World Bank Group, "The World Bank Group," *Annual Report 2004*.

Monetary Fund (IMF). Combined, the IBRD and the IMF are called the Bretton Woods institutions. IBRD and the IMF soon signed on as specialized agencies within the newly formed United Nations System. Both IBRD and the IMF were operational by 1946. Today, IBRD and its closest partner organization, the International Development Association (IDA), are referred to as the World Bank. The World Bank Group is comprised of IBRD, IDA, IFC, ICSID, and MIGA. An outline of the five World Bank Group institutions is shown in Table 96.

See also **Bretton Woods System; International Bank for Reconstruction and Development; International Centre for Settlement of Investment Disputes; International Development Association; International Finance Corporation; Multilateral Investment Guarantee Agency; Wolfensohn, James D.** ***See also in Volume 2,*** **Documents 4, 5, 10, 12.**

Further Reading

Ellerman, David. *Helping People Help Themselves: From the World Bank to an Alternative Philosophy of Development Assistance.* Ann Arbor, MI: University of Michigan Press, 2005.

Gill, Indermit S., and Todd Pugatch, eds. *At the Frontlines of Development: Reflections from the World Bank.* Washington, DC: World Bank Publications, 2005.

Pleskovic, Boris, and Francois Bourguignon, eds. *Annual World Bank Conference on Development Economics 2005: Lessons of Experience.* Washington, DC: World Bank Publications, 2005.

Ritzen, Josef. *A Chance for the World Bank.* London: Anthem Press, 2005.

Wolfensohn, James D. *A New Development Agenda: The Transformation of the World Bank under James D. Wolfensohn, 1995–2005.* Washington, DC: World Bank Publications, 2005.

WORLD ECONOMIC FORUM

The World Economic Forum (WEF) is a nonprofit foundation committed to improving people's quality of life and the state of the world. WEF members and partners come from the global business community. Today, WEF consists of about 1,200 member companies, mostly large transnational corporations (TNCs). Partner companies share WEF's commitment to building a stronger, more prosperous global economy. Members and partners work closely with other stakeholders in economic growth and development. Key stakeholders include governments, academics, non-governmental organizations (NGOs), and civil society organizations (CSOs). WEF's headquarters is located in Cologny, Switzerland. The Forum's largest meeting, the Annual Meeting, is held in Davos, Switzerland.

Klaus Schwab, a business professor at the University of Geneva, founded WEF in 1971. Schwab created the European Management Forum, the precursor to WEF, after hosting a successful conference comprised of business leaders. The name switch to World Economic Forum occurred in 1987, largely to reflect the more global outlook of the organization. WEF provides a forum for communication among leaders in the private and public sectors of the global economy. WEF members, partners, and other invited leaders discuss issues related to the business and investment climate, and sustainable growth and development. Recent discussions have focused on the importance of good governance and the rule of law, gender equity in education, entrepreneurship, and environmental protection. The 2005 Annual Meeting proposed measures to reduce global poverty, including improved foreign aid delivery systems, reduced trade barriers, and strengthened anti-corruption partnerships.

Through its publications, WEF's research staff complements the work conducted at meetings and summits. WEF research on global competitiveness identifies strengths and weaknesses in nations' economies. WEF's flagship publication, *The Global Competitiveness Report*, is among the world's most authoritative statements on the competitiveness of nations. Businesses, scholars, governments, labor organizations, multilateral organizations, and aid agencies use WEF's research to form policies in the public and private sectors. The two barometers of competitiveness shown in the annual report are the Growth Competitiveness Index and the Business Competitiveness Index. The Growth Competitiveness Index is mainly concerned with macroeconomic stability and the strength of nations' public institutions and infrastructure. The Business Competitiveness Index is mainly concerned with microeconomic indicators such as business management and corporate strategies. Combined, the indexes paint a portrait of hospitable and inhospitable economic environments under which economic activity occurs in the global economy. The advanced economies are clustered at the top of each index ranking, and the poorer developing countries are clustered near the bottom.

In recent years, WEF has come under fire by a number of NGOs and others opposed to globalization and the dominance of the industrial North over the poorer regions of the global South. Critics point out that membership in WEF is highly selective, not elected, and not representative of the diverse interests of the peoples of the world. Critics argue that the WEF is more concerned with the profits of transnational corporations (TNCs) than with improving people's quality of life. During the early 2000s, anti-globalization demonstrations targeted WEF Annual Meetings in Davos, and WEF's regional meetings. Similar protests disrupted summits, conferences, and meetings of the World Trade Organization (WTO), International Monetary Fund (IMF), and the World Bank during the period.

See also **Civil Society Organizations; Competitiveness; Globalization; Non-Governmental Organizations; Poverty; Quality of Life; Transnational Corporations. *See also in Volume 2,* Documents 52, 53.**

Further Reading

Dutta, Soumitra, Bruno Lanvin, and Fiona Paua. *The Global Information Technology Report 2004–2005* (World Economic Forum Reports). New York: Palgrave Macmillan, 2005.

Houtart, Francois, and Francois Polet. *The Other Davos: The Globalization of Resistance to the World Economic Order*. New York: Zed Books, 2001.

Porter, Michael E., Klaus Schwab, Xavier Sala-I-Martin, and Augusto Lopez-Claros. *The Global Competitiveness Report 2004–2005*. New York: Palgrave Macmillan, 2004.

Schwab, Klaus, ed. *Overcoming Indifference: Ten Key Challenges in Today's Changing World.* New York: New York University Press, 1995.

WORLD HEALTH ORGANIZATION

The World Health Organization (WHO) is a multilateral organization dedicated to improving the health of all people. Under the WHO Constitution, human health is defined as "a state of complete physical, mental and social well-being and not merely the absence of disease or infirmity." The WHO Constitution also establishes human health as a "fundamental right" to which all people are entitled.

WHO was founded on April 7, 1948, as a specialized agency within the United Nations System. The main goals of WHO are to provide guidance for nations on health issues, to set global health standards, to strengthen nations' health programs, and to develop and share new health technologies with the peoples of the world. Between 1948 and 2005, WHO membership grew from the original twenty-six signatory countries to 192 countries. The World Health Assembly (WHA) is the supreme decision-making body for WHO. The WHA consists of representatives from all member nations. It meets once each year to establish priorities and policies. The WHA also elects the director-general, WHO's top official, and approves the biennial budget. WHO's current Director-General, LEE Jong-wook of South Korea, began his five-year term of office on July 21, 2003. Numerous boards and commissions convene throughout the year to implement WHO policies—a process supported by 3,500 administrative staff. WHO's Secretariat is located in Geneva, Switzerland.

WHO has helped eradicate diseases such as smallpox and yaws. It has led successful campaigns to reduce other diseases such as leprosy, guinea-worm disease, and river blindness. Currently, the major challenges for the WHO are the global epidemic of HIV/AIDs, which had claimed more than 20 million lives by the early 2000s; a resurgence of tuberculosis (TB); the perennial battle with malaria; and periodic outbreaks of ebola and Severe Acute Respiratory Syndrome (SARS).

The WHA approves a biennial budget, called a Program Budget, every second year. In its Proposed Budget Program for 2006–2007, the WHA has allocated $3.3 billion to attend to its global health commitments. Only 30 percent of the WHA funds are generated from assessed contributions from member states. The remaining 70 percent of all funds are derived from voluntary contributions. The biennial budget for 2006–2007 allocated roughly half of all funds to "essential health interventions," which

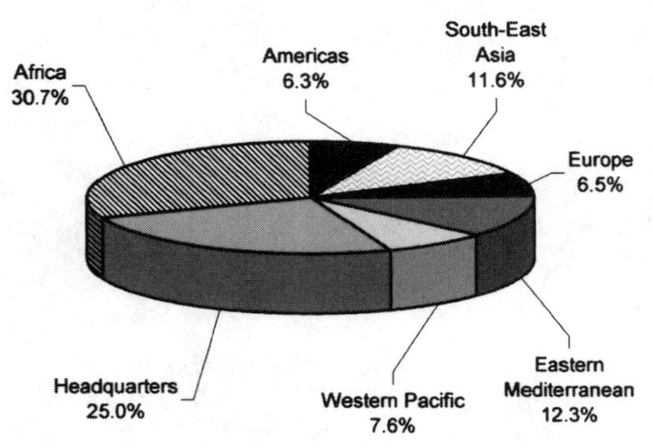

FIGURE 40 **World Health Organization Spending by Region, 2006–2007**

Source: World Health Organization, *Proposed Program Budget, 2006–2007*, 10–12.

is mainly concerned with the prevention and treatment of diseases. The remaining funds were allocated to research, the dissemination of health information, health personnel, food safety, administrative costs, and other programs. The distribution of WHO's spending, by region, is shown in Figure 40.

See also **Developing Countries; Economic Growth; Human Development; Poverty; Quality of Life; Sustainable Economic Development; United Nations System.**

Further Reading

Burci, Gian L., and Claude-Henri Vignes. *World Health Organization.* Norwell, MA: Kluwer Law International, 2004.

Powell, Jillian. *World Health Organization.* Danbury, CT: Franklin Watts, 2000.

World Health Organization. *Proposed Program Budget, 2006–2007.* Geneva, Switzerland: Author, 2005.

———. *The World Health Report 2004: HIV/AIDS—Changing History.* Geneva, Switzerland: Author, 2004.

———. *The World Health Report 2005: Make Every Mother and Child Count.* Geneva, Switzerland: Author, 2005.

WORLD INTELLECTUAL PROPERTY ORGANIZATION

The World Intellectual Property Organization (WIPO) is an international organization that protects intellectual property rights in the global economy. Intellectual property, broadly defined, includes human endeavors that reach beyond existing accomplishments in the realms of science, technology, and artistic expression. The Convention Establishing the World Intellectual Property Organization was signed in Stockholm, Sweden, on July 14, 1967, and the provisions of the agreement went into force in 1970. In the WIPO Convention, Contracting Parties expressed a desire "to encourage creative activity, [and] to promote the protection of intellectual property throughout the world." WIPO was established as an autonomous specialized agency within the United Nations system. In 2005, WIPO consisted of 182 member states and administered twenty-three international intellectual property treaties. WIPO membership is open to countries within the United Nations System and to countries invited to join by the WIPO General Assembly. WIPO's headquarters is located in Geneva, Switzerland.

Protecting intellectual property from piracy is a cornerstone of an orderly global economy.
Courtesy of Getty Images: Ryan McVay

One million international patent applications were filed under WIPO's Patent Cooperation Treaty (PCT) by 2004, mainly by individuals and businesses from the world's major advanced economies. In 2004, 126 countries were signatories to the PCT. Of the 120,000 patent filings in 2004, filings from the United States topped the list (34.9 percent of all filings), followed by Japan (16.6 percent), Germany (12.4 percent), France (4.4 percent), and the United Kingdom (4.2 percent). Filings from the developing world, which, according to WIPO data, included the newly industrialized economies (NIEs) of Asia, represented 6.3 percent of the global total. The top ten corporations filing for international patent protection in 2004 were Philips Electronics N.V. (Netherlands), Matsushita (Japan), Siemens (Germany), Nokia (Finland), Bosch (Germany), Intel (United States), BASF (Germany), 3M (United States), Motorola (Germany), and Sony (Japan). Many countries also offer patent protection. The U.S. Patent and Trademark Office, an agency in the U.S. Department of Commerce, processes thousands of patent and trademark applications each year.

The protection of intellectual property predates the founding of WIPO. The Paris Convention (1883) and the Berne Convention (1886) were created to protect industrial property and copyrights more than a century ago. In 1893, these Conventions united into the United International Bureau for the Protection of Intellectual Property and, in 1960, relocated from Berne, Switzerland to Geneva. With the creation of WIPO in 1967 the Swiss government, which had supervisory authority over the Bureau, was relieved of its responsibilities. Today, as a specialized agency of the United Nations, WIPO is governed by member nations through its principal organs: the General Assembly, the Conference, the Coordination Committee, and the Secretariat. The director-general, who is appointed by the General Assembly, is WIPO's leading official.

WIPO is an important intergovernmental organization in the rules-based global economy. It promotes fair use of people's creative endeavors. WIPO classifies intellectual property under two headings, industrial property and copyrights, much like the Paris and Berne conventions had done in the 1880s. Industrial property includes protections for patented products or processes, trademarks, and industrial designs. Copyrights protect literary and artistic works such as movies, novels, poems, scripts, music, drawings and paintings, photographs, architectural designs, and other artistic expression. The explosion of new information and communications technologies (ICTs) over the past two decades expanded creative enterprise, and increased the need to protect industrial property and copyrights from piracy. Today, the work of WIPO is reinforced by the Trade-Related Aspects of Intellectual Property (TRIPS) agreement. TRIPS was negotiated under the General Agreement on Tariffs and Trade (GATT), came into force in January 1995, and is administered by the World Trade Organization (WTO).

WIPO has helped developing countries create appropriate legal regimes to protect intellectual property. WIPO's Cooperation for Development Program conducts courses, workshops, and seminars to familiarize people with international agreements. During the early 2000s, thousands of participants attended WIPO programs in the developing world. Participants included the owners of intellectual property such as artists and inventors. Other participants represented governments, research institutions, and businesses. WIPO also expanded its outreach to the least developed countries (LDCs) through the WIPO Worldwide Academy and other programs. Among the most important topics of concern for the developing countries was the protection of traditional knowledge and genetic resources. WIPO helps developing countries draft enforceable intellectual property laws. An appropriate legal regime is a key step toward meeting countries' development goals and complying with the provisions of the TRIPS agreement.

See also **Entrepreneurship; General Agreement on Tariffs and Trade; Globalization; Information and Communications Technologies; Trade-Related Aspects of Intellectual Property; United Nations System; World Trade Organization.**

Further Reading

Choate, Pat. *Hot Property: The Stealing of Ideas in an Age of Globalization.* New York: Alfred A. Knopf, 2005.

Einhorn, Michael A. *Media, Technology and Copyright: Integrating Law and Economics.* Northampton, MA: Edward Elgar Publishing, 2005.

George, Alexandra. *Globalization and Intellectual Property.* Brookfield, VT: Ashgate Publishing Company, 2005.

World Intellectual Property Organization. *Intellectual Property Profile of the Least Developed Countries.* Geneva, Switzerland: Author, 2002.

WORLD TRADE ORGANIZATION

The World Trade Organization (WTO) is an international organization that oversees the operation of the rules-based multilateral trading system. The WTO is based on a series of trade agreements negotiated during the Uruguay Round (1986–1994), the eighth and final trade round conducted under the General Agreement on Tariffs and Trade (GATT). The Treaty of Marrakesh established the WTO at the close of the Uruguay Round in 1994. The WTO began operations on January 1, 1995. In 2005, the WTO was comprised of 148 members. The organization's operating budget for 2005 was about $150 million. The WTO is one of the Big Three international organizations that oversee economic relations among nations, joining the International Monetary Fund (IMF) and the World Bank. The WTO's headquarters is located in Geneva, Switzerland. Pascal Lamy of France, current WTO director-general, began a four-year,

TABLE 97 **Directors-General of GATT and the WTO, 1948 to 2009**

Director-General	Term of Office	GATT/WTO	Home Country
Sir Eric Wyndham White	1948–1968	GATT	United Kingdom
Olivier Long	1968–1980	GATT	Switzerland
Arthur Dunkel	1980–1993	GATT	Switzerland
Peter Sutherland	1993–1995	GATT/WTO	Ireland
Renato Ruggiero	1995–1999	WTO	Italy
Mike Moore	1999–2002	WTO	New Zealand
Supachai Panitchpakdi	2002–2005	WTO	Thailand
Pascal Lamy	2005–2009	WTO	France

Source: World Trade Organization, *Understanding the WTO*, 3d ed., 15.

renewable term of office on September 1, 2005. A chronology of directors-general of GATT and the WTO is shown in Table 97.

The WTO's main function is to monitor and enforce trade rules in the global economy. The WTO administers the complex trade agreements listed in the WTO agreement. Article 1 of the WTO agreement, the General Agreement on Tariffs and Trade, deals with rules of merchandise trade. The General Agreement on Tariffs and Trade in Article 1 is often called GATT 1994 to distinguish it from the original GATT agreement of 1947. Article 2, the General Agreement on Trade in Services (GATS), pertains to the trade of commercial services. Article 4, the Agreement on Trade-Related Aspect of Intellectual Property (TRIPS), provides uniform legal protections for scientific, technological, and artistic achievements. In addition, the WTO is a forum for trade negotiations, a dispute settlement mechanism, a source of technical expertise on trade and development for the world's poorer countries and a sister organization to the World Bank and IMF. Unlike the World Bank and IMF, the WTO does not make loans to countries.

The WTO inherited many of GATT's guiding principles. These fundamental principles are incorporated in the numerous agreements that comprise the Agreement Establishing the World Trade Organization. In its *Understanding the WTO* (2003), the World Trade Organization identified five core principles. The first principle is "trade without discrimination," which involves most-favored-nation (MFN) status and national treatment. MFN states that a trade concession granted to one WTO member automatically applies to all members. National treatment guarantees equal treatment of imported goods with domestically produced output in nations' markets. The second principle is freer trade through the progressive liberalization of trade regimes. The third principle is the predictability of trade rules. Predictability, in this context, prevents governments from arbitrarily raising existing tariffs or non-tariff trade barriers. The fourth principle is fair competition. Fair competition attempts to level the playing field in international trade and minimize the market distortions caused by export subsidies, dumping, and other disruptive trade practices. The fifth principle is economic development through trade. Economic development for the world's poorer countries should be enhanced by trade assistance and increased market access through preferential trade arrangements.

The WTO's dispute settlement process is the enforcement arm of the organization. The WTO's apparatus for dispute settlement is stronger and more defined than GATT's dispute settlement procedures. The WTO's dispute settlement process is the essence of multilateralism. That is, a country or group of countries can air trade grievances in a global forum. A trade complaint is made to the WTO's Dispute Settlement Body (DSB), which consists of the entire WTO membership. The DSB, in turn, establishes a panel of three to five experts to hear the evidence and render a ruling. The panel's ruling can only be reversed by a unanimous vote of the DSB. Under normal conditions, the entire process takes one year or less to complete. One or both sides in the dispute can appeal the panel's decision, however. A seven-member Appellate Body considers an appeal and renders a decision. Again, only a unanimous vote of the DSB can reverse the Appellate Body's ruling. The appellate process could add as much as three months to the dispute settlement process. A member country found guilty breaking WTO trade rules is required to correct the violation with due speed. The DSB is empowered to initiate retaliatory tariffs or other trade sanctions for noncompliance with a WTO ruling.

Since 1995, the WTO's dispute settlement process has been dotted with successes and failures. About 300 trade disputes have been brought before the WTO, about 100 of which entered formal review by WTO panels. Many cases were settled through informal consultations. Some high-profile disputes illustrate the inherent challenges of dispute settlement, however. In 1999–2001, the European Union (EU) rejected a WTO ruling that called for an end to EU trade restrictions on bananas from Latin America. In response, the WTO authorized stiff U.S. retaliatory tariffs on selected EU products. The EU and United States quietly came to terms in 2001. Similarly, in 2003, the WTO ruled that the United States must drop tariffs on imported steel from the EU, Japan, and other important trading partners. Threats of retaliation influenced President George W. Bush's decision to remove the tariffs, which had been imposed in 2002 to protect U.S. steel producers.

The WTO has also had confrontations with elements within the anti-globalization movement. The most publicized conflict occurred at the WTO's 1999 ministerial conference in Seattle, Washington. The Seattle conference was intended to launch the Millennium Round of trade negotiations, the ninth trade round under the GATT/WTO structure. Instead, the ill-fated four-day conference turned into a battlefield outside the convention center and within the conference halls. Tens of thousands of demonstrators, many representing non-governmental organizations (NGOs) or other civil society organizations (CSOs), jammed the streets of Seattle to protest perceived injustices associated with globalization—violations of human rights, abuse of workers, environmental degradation, the destruction of local cultures, and other issues. The WTO, a main symbol and proponent of globalization, was a lightening rod for anti-globalization sentiments. Discord inside the Washington State Convention and Trade Center pitted poorer countries against richer ones. Delegates from developing countries complained they were systematically excluded from key discussions and decisions. Some delegates from poorer countries threatened to boycott the conference. The collapse of the Seattle ministerial conference stalled the ninth WTO trade round. The failure of the conference was also a stark reminder that significant differences existed among nations in the multilateral trading system.

The WTO's fourth ministerial conference was hosted by Doha, Qatar, in November 2001. The conference jump-started a ninth trade round, often called the Doha Round. WTO delegates in Doha proposed the Doha Development Agenda (DDA). The DDA revitalized the WTO's commitment to create a fair multilateral trading system and to promote economic development in the global South. The DDA pledged to further liberalize international trade. It also pledged support for Special and Differential Treatment (SDT) to benefit developing countries, especially the least developed countries (LDCs). SDT includes special trade rights such as expanded access to markets in advanced countries, greater technical assistance to develop trade opportunities, and extended time periods to implement WTO agreements. The implementation of the DDA hit some snags in the early 2000s, including the collapse of the WTO's ministerial meeting in Cancun, Mexico, in September 2003. Signs of compromise, and renewed commitments to a streamlined version of the DDA, were in evidence as member nations prepared for the WTO's Hong Kong SAR ministerial meeting, scheduled for December 2005.

See also **Balance of Payments; Bretton Woods System; Exports; General Agreement on Tariffs and Trade; Imports; International Commodity Agreements; International Monetary Fund; International Trade; Protectionism; Terms of Trade; Trade-Related Aspects of Intellectual Property; World Bank Group.** ***See also in Volume 2,*** **Documents 11, 12, 17, 18, 27.**

Further Reading

Guha-Khasnobis, Basudeb, ed. *The WTO, Developing Countries, and the Doha Development Agenda: Prospects and Challenges for Trade-Led Growth*. New York: Palgrave Macmillan, 2004.

Katrak, Homi, and Roger Strange, eds. *The WTO and Developing Countries*. New York: Palgrave Macmillan, 2004.

Matsushita, Mitsuo, Thomas J. Schoenbaum, and Petros C. Mavroidis. *The World Trade Organization: Law, Practice, and Policy*. New York: Oxford University Press, 2005.

Wallach, Lori, Patrick Woodall, and Ralph Nader. *Whose Trade Organization? A Comprehensive Guide to the World Trade Organization*. 2d ed. New York: New Press, 2004.

World Trade Organization, *Understanding the WTO*. 3d ed. Geneva, Switzerland: Author, 2003.

Y

YUNUS, MUHAMMAD

Muhammad Yunus (1940–) is a prominent Bangladeshi development economist and social reformer. Yunus, the founder of the Grameen Bank in Bangladesh, introduced microcredit as a viable antipoverty and development strategy. Yunus was born in Chittagong, Bengal, India. In 1947, Chittagong became part of East Pakistan, and, in 1971, part of an independent Bangladesh. Yunus exhibited exceptional intellectual abilities as a child. Born to a middle-class family, Yunus attended the best schools. He earned a BA (1960) and MA (1961) from Dhaka University. Yunus traveled to the United States for his advanced studies in development economics and earned a PhD from Vanderbilt University in 1970. From the United States, Yunus supported East Pakistan's independence movement and eventual break from West Pakistan. Soon after independence was achieved, and Bangladesh established, Yunus returned to his homeland to teach and to initiate radical reform in the country's rural development.

As a social scientist, Yunus was committed to finding solutions to development problems. After Yunus returned to Bangladesh in the early 1970s, he accepted a position in government service in Dhaka, and an economics professorship at Chittagong College, neither of which satisfied his desire to bring positive change to his desperately poor country. In 1976, Professor Yunus developed the concept of microcredit to fit local conditions in Bangladesh. On a small scale, microcredit had existed in other world regions for decades. Yunus argued that microcredit could accelerate the pace of rural development by jump-starting entrepreneurship on the farms and in the small villages. Microloans of $50 or $100 could start a new business enterprise, and improve the quality of life for an entire household.

Yunus based his microcredit program on several key principles. First, microloans would be made mainly to landless, marginalized peoples who did not qualify for conventional commercial loans. Second, microloans were loans, not grants. Repayment of principal plus interest was required in weekly installments. Third, most microloans would be made to women, mainly to develop this untapped reservoir of entrepreneurial talent. Fourth, small groups of borrowers would take collective responsibility for microloans. The success or failure of each borrower would directly affect future loans to other group members. The experiment in microfinance expanded rapidly, spurred on by near-perfect loan repayments, and outside assistance from international donors such as the International Fund for Agricultural Development and the Ford Foundation. In September 1983, Yunus officially established the

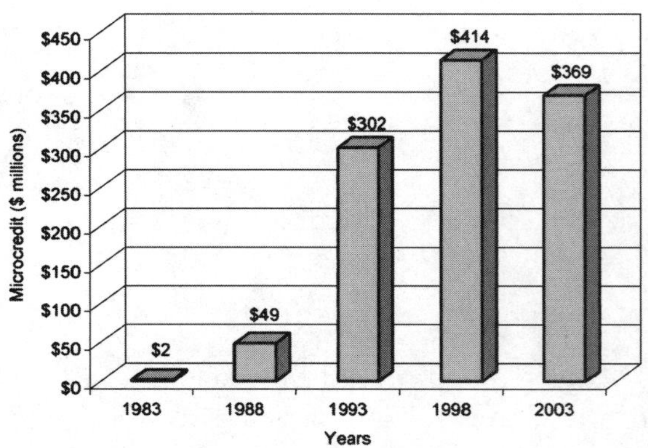

FIGURE 41 **Microcredit and the Grameen Bank, 1983 to 2003 ($ millions)**

Source: Grameen Bank, *Grameen Bank Historical Data Series*, 1980–2003.

Grameen Bank, jointly owned by private shareholders and the government of Bangladesh.

Today, the Grameen Bank is the world largest microfinance institution (MFI). In 2004, the Grameen Bank's 1,277 branches provided banking and other financial services to people in 47,000 Bangladeshi villages. Nearly 4 million borrowers have obtained microloans since the bank was founded. The Grameen Bank's annual lending between 1983 and 2003 increased from $2.3 million to $369 million, as shown in Figure 41. In addition, Yunus's experiment in microcredit inspired the creation of microfinance institutions throughout the developing world. Over time, multilateral organizations, including the World Bank and regional development banks, embraced microcredit as a viable development strategy. The United Nations proclaimed 2005 the Year of Microcredit.

Microcredit is widely acclaimed as a success story in Bangladesh and in other countries of the developing world. Some criticisms have been leveled at microcredit practices, however. One criticism is that microcredit, which often carries a high interest rate, creates additional debt for the world's poorest citizens. Second, some research suggests microcredit obtained by women sometimes ends up in the hands of their husbands. Third, some experts suggest microfinance institutions are inherently unstable. The financial challenges face by the Grameen Bank after the devastating 1998 floods in Bangladesh illustrate the pitfalls of collateral-free loans. The impact of microcredit on households' financial security and on economic development will be fertile ground for research in the coming years.

See also **Capital Markets; Global Financial Architecture; Microfinance Institutions; Sustainable Economic Development.** ***See also in Volume 2,*** **Document 8.**

Further Reading

Fernando, Jude L. *Microfinance: Perils and Prospects*. New York: Routledge, 2005.

Rahman, Aminur. *Women and Microcredit in Rural Bangladesh: An Anthropological Study of Grameen Bank*. Boulder, CO: Westview Press, 2001.

Yunus, Muhammad. *Banker to the Poor: Micro-Lending and the Battle against World Poverty*. Washington, DC: Public Affairs, 2003.

———, and Alan Jolis. *Banker to the Poor: The Autobiography of Muhammad Yunus, Founder of Grameen Bank*. New York: Oxford University Press, 2001.

Glossary of Selected Terms

Absolute advantage. Occurs when a nation or other economic region is able to produce a good or service more efficiently than a second nation or region.

Acquisition. Occurs when one firm buys controlling interest in a target firm; acquisitions of foreign firms by transnational corporations are an important form of foreign direct investment.

Advanced economies. The twenty-nine richer, more industrialized countries in the world; also called the developed countries.

Advertising. A paid announcement by a business, designed to inform consumers about a good or service and to persuade people to buy the product.

Affiliate. A company that has been formed or purchased by another company; transnational corporations operated over 900,000 foreign affiliates in the early 2000s.

African Development Bank Group (ADB Group). A regional development bank that serves the continent of Africa.

Agenda 21. A landmark document that established guidelines for global sustainable economic development; *Agenda 21* was adopted at the Rio Earth Summit in 1992.

Agricultural sector. An economic sector comprised of farms, dairies, poultry and livestock farms, forestry, and fishing and shellfish industries.

Andean Community. A five-nation sub-regional organization, which promotes regional integration, economic development, and social progress in South America.

Annan, Kofi (1938–). The seventh secretary-general of the United Nations; supporter of globalization to promote economic development.

Asian Development Bank (ADB). A regional development bank that serves Asia and the Pacific region.

Asia-Pacific Economic Cooperation (APEC). The world's largest forum designed to promote economic growth, regional cooperation, and free trade and investment.

Association of Southeast Asian Nations (ASEAN). A regional association of ten countries designed to foster regional economic growth, cultural development, social progress, and peace among member states.

Balance of payments (BOP). A record of one country's transactions with the rest of the world in a given period of time.

Balance of trade. The difference between the value of a nation's total imports and total exports in a given period of time.

Bank for International Settlements (BIS). An international organization designed to promote international monetary and financial cooperation among central banks, and serve as a bank for central banks and international organizations.

Basic economic questions. The universal questions that all economies, past and present, have answered, including what, how, and for whom to produce.

Bhagwati, Jagdish (1934–). A prominent Indian-born academic economist and one of the world's most recognized supporters of globalization.

Big Three. The dominant multilateral organizations that oversee economic relations among countries—the International Monetary Fund, World Bank, and World Trade Organization.

Bilateral investment treaty (BIT). A formal agreement between two countries designed to protect and promote foreign direct investment.

Brain drain. The migration of skilled professionals from one country to another country for an extended period of time; the brain drain is often an outflow of skilled workers from developing countries to the advanced countries.

Bretton Woods System. The institutions and operation of the international monetary system from 1946 to 1973.

Business cycle. A recurring, but irregular pattern of upswings and downswings in economic activity on the national, or global levels.

Capital deepening. Occurs when the real capital per worker increases in a country over time.

Capital flight. The excessive cross-border transfers of financial capital, often an outflow of funds from developing countries to more stable advanced economies.

Capital formation. The process of increasing the amount of capital goods in a country; capital formation stems from savings and productive investments.

Capital goods. The items that are designed to produce other goods; a factor of production.

Capital-intensive production. A method of producing goods and services that relies on the use of sophisticated capital goods, often associated with production in the advanced economies.

Capitalism. A type of economic system based on the private ownership and control of the factors of production—natural resources, human resources, and capital goods.

Capital markets. The institutions that channel surplus money into medium- and long-term productive investments, investments of at least one year in duration.

Capital stock. The total amount of capital goods in a country.

Caribbean Community. A fifteen-nation multilateral organization that promotes economic development and social progress in the Caribbean region.

Cartel. A formal agreement or organization that coordinates the production decisions of independent producers or suppliers of a similar or identical product in order to influence the product's global supply and price.

Cash crops. Agricultural output produced for sale in domestic or global markets rather than for the household's consumption; examples are cotton, rubber, coffee.

Central American Common Market (CACM). A five-nation regional trade organization.

Civil society organizations (CSOs). A variety of non-governmental and nonprofit groups, or citizens' associations, that work to improve society and the human condition.

Collusion. An agreement among producers to limit the supply, market share, and price of a good; used by producer cartels.

Command economy. A highly centralized economic system in which the government owns or controls the factors of production—natural resources, human resources, and capital goods; viewed as an economic model.

Commercial revolution. The dramatic increase in international trade, and the underlying forces that supported these commercial relationships, during the late fifteenth century through the eighteenth century.

Common external tariff (CET). The uniform customs duties that some regional trade blocs place on imports from non-member countries.

Common market. A type of regional trade agreement that creates a free trade area, uniform external trade policy, and other types of regional economic integration.

Commonwealth of Independent States (CIS). A loose confederation of twelve former Soviet republics, now independent countries.

Communism. An economic system based on government ownership and control of the factors of production—and on the theories of Karl Marx.

Comparative advantage. Occurs when a nation or economic region is able to produce a product at a lower opportunity cost compared to another nation or region.

Competition. The economic rivalry that exists among producers of a similar product.

Competitiveness. The factors that influence economic performance in a nation's macroeconomy and microeconomy.

Concessional terms. Favorable credit terms on loans, including a low interest rate and extended repayment period; offered by some multilateral development institutions to the poorest developing countries.

Conglomerate. A highly diversified corporation.

Consumer price index (CPI). Measures the percentage change in the price of a uniform market basket of goods and services every month; the CPI is used to calculate the inflation rate.

Consumers International (CI). An independent, nonprofit federation of consumer groups and non-governmental organizations (NGOs).

Cooperative. A voluntary association of people who jointly own and control a productive enterprise to satisfy the economic, social, or cultural needs of members; also called a co-op.

Corporate code of conduct. A set of rules established by a corporation to guide its business practices and behaviors; codes of conduct focus on fair treatment of workers.

Corporate social responsibility (CSR). The responsibilities that corporations, including transnational corporations (TNCs), have to workers and their families, consumers, investors, host governments, and indigenous peoples.

Corporate state. An economy that places firms, workers, and other aspects of business activity under the control of the government; private enterprise exists, but under the direction of the government. The corporate state existed under twentieth-century fascist regimes.

Corporation. A type of business that is owned by stockholders, but typically run by professional managers.

Corruption. The abuse of the public trust for personal gain.

Cultural homogenization. The process by which local cultures are transformed or absorbed by a dominant outside culture.

Customs union. A type of regional trade agreement that establishes a free trade area, and a common external trade policy with non-member countries.

Default. Occurs when a government refuses to make scheduled payments on its debts.

Deflation. The overall decline in the price level in an economy; also called negative inflation.

Deforestation. The clearing of timber and brush from a region; a type of environmental degradation.

Democracy. A type of political system in which political authority is derived from the people, either directly or through freely elected representatives.

Democratic socialism. A type of economic system in which core socialist beliefs guide national economic policy, and democratic institutions govern the nation.

Deng Xiaoping (1904–1997). An important Chinese revolutionary, leader and reformer.

Depression. A severe, prolonged economic downturn characterized by a drop in a country's national output and investment, and higher unemployment and business failures.

Desertification. The transformation of fertile land into desert, usually caused by a combination of human actions and natural forces; a type of environmental degradation.

Devaluation. A government action that lowers the value of its currency relative to other countries' currencies.

Developing countries. The poorer, less industrialized countries in the global economy.

Development Assistance Committee (DAC). A twenty-three member group within the Organization for Economic Cooperation and Development that coordinates official development assistance, and official aid, to developing and emerging market economies.

Development economics. A specialized field of study in economics that deals with the topic of sustainable economic development.

Development plan. A country's strategy to promote sustainable economic development.

Digital divide. The information and communications technologies (ICTs) gap between the "have" and "have not" countries.

Doha Development Agenda (DDA). A 2001 World Trade Organization statement pledging support for fair trade and sustainable economic development.

Dumping. An illegal trade practice that occurs when a company from one nation sells its output in a second country at a price lower than its production costs, or lower than the price charged in its own domestic market.

Economic and monetary union. The highest form of regional economic integration consisting of a free trade area, common external trade policy, and highly integrated regional economy.

Economic Community of West African States (ECOWAS). A fifteen-member multilateral organization designed to promote regional economic integration, sustainable growth and development, and political stability in West Africa.

Economic freedom. The ability of individuals and businesses to freely choose how to use their private property in an economy.

Economic growth. Occurs when the value of a nation's output increases over time; economic growth can be measured by the growth of national output over time, or by the growth of national output per person over time.

Economic infrastructure. The physical capital that underpins economic growth and development; examples include transportation and communications systems, public utilities, and courts.

Economics. The study of how people choose to use scarce resources to satisfy their wants and needs; the study deals with production, consumption, and distribution decisions.

Economic sanctions. Any restrictions on trade, investment, or foreign aid that are intended to pressure a country to change a policy or action.

Economic sectors. The three main areas of production in a country—the services-producing sector, goods-producing (industrial) sector, and agricultural sector.

Economic system. Represents all economic activity in a country; different types of economic systems answer the basic economic questions in different ways.

Economies of scale. The decline in the average cost of producing a good as the rate of output rises; highlights the advantages of bigness.

Ecosystems. Systems consisting of organic and inorganic matter and natural forces that interact and change; basic ecosystems include grasslands, forests, agricultural areas, freshwater, and coastal.

Embargo. A type of economic sanction often designed to influence a domestic or international policy in a second country; embargoes can be comprehensive or selective.

Emerging market economies (EMEs). Refers to countries that have made significant strides toward capitalism and sustainable economic development.

Energy resources. The fuel for most production in the global economy; the main categories include oil, natural gas, coal, nuclear, and other.

Entrepreneur. A person who starts a new business, develops a new product, or devises a new way to produce a product; a risk-taker and innovator.

Entrepreneurship. The actions of entrepreneurs in developing new businesses, products, or processes.

Environmental degradation. A wide variety of human-induced and naturally occurring stresses on the natural environment.

Euro. The common currency of the European Union; the euro replaced the national currencies of twelve EU countries in 2002.

European Bank for Reconstruction and Development (EBRD). A regional development bank that serves twenty-seven transition countries.

European Economic Area (EEA). An economic region comprised of the European Union and the European Free Trade Agreement (with the exception of Switzerland).

European Free Trade Association (EFTA). An intergovernmental organization that promotes free trade among Iceland, Liechtenstein, Norway, and Switzerland.

European Monetary Union (EMU). The twelve European Union countries that have adopted the euro as their sole currency; also called the euro zone.

European Union (EU). A unique intergovernmental organization that coordinates economic, foreign, security, and judicial policies among its twenty-five member nations.

Exchange rates. The value of one currency compared to a second currency.

Export credit agency (ECA). A government agency that assists private companies finance trade or investment opportunities in other countries; a type of international financial institution.

Export processing zone (EPZ). An industrial area that offers special incentives to attract foreign direct investment, and in which export industries produce products.

Export promotion. A trade strategy designed to increase the export of goods; government incentives, such as tax breaks and subsidies, support export industries.

Exports. A resource, intermediate good, or final good or service that producers in one country sell to buyers in another country.

Expropriation. The government's seizure of private physical assets or financial assets without compensation to the previous owner.

External debt. The money owed by a nation to a foreign government or commercial bank, a multilateral organization, or other creditor; also called foreign debt.

Extreme poverty. Refers to people who fall beneath the $1 per day, per person poverty line in the developing world; about 1.1 billion people live in extreme poverty.

Factors of production. The resources used to produce goods or services, including natural resources, human resources, and capital goods; entrepreneurship is often considered a fourth factor of production; also called productive resources.

Financial contagion. The spread of a financial crisis from one country or region to other countries or regions.

Five-year plan. A government economic plan that outlines economic goals, production targets, and resource allocation; commonly associated with communist economies.

Fixed exchange rate system. A system of converting nations' currencies at a rate tied to gold or to the U.S. dollar; the fixed exchange rate system was an important feature of the Bretton Woods System from 1946 to 1973.

Foreign aid. A grant of money, technical assistance, food, capital equipment, or other assistance from one country to another.

Foreign direct investment (FDI). A cross-border investment that results in one company gaining ownership or control of productive facilities in another country.

Foreign exchange market. A network of commercial banks, investment banks, brokerage houses, and other financial institutions that buy and sell currencies for profit; also called the forex market.

Foreign reserves. The value of a country's holdings of foreign currencies, gold, and IMF special drawing rights (SDRs); the reserve is sometimes tapped to make international payments.

Free trade. Refers to international trade that is not restricted by trade barriers—such as tariffs and import quotas—or other distortions such as subsidies.

Free trade area. A type of regional trade agreement that eliminates trade barriers among members.

Free Trade Area of the Americas (FTAA). A proposed free trade area for thirty-four democracies in the Western Hemisphere.

General Agreement on Tariffs and Trade (GATT). A multilateral agreement that established rules for international trade from 1948 to 1994.

Glasnost. A political reform program initiated by Soviet Premier Mikhail Gorbachev in the mid-1980s; Glasnost stressed a more open political environment in the USSR.

Global commons. World resources in which people have an equal interest, such as the atmosphere and the oceans; the degradation of the global commons is a major environmental concern.

Global Compact. A UN document designed to promote corporate social responsibility.

Global culture. The standardization of people's attitudes and beliefs, behaviors, social norms, and institutions around the world; associated with the globalization process.

Global economy. The international network of individuals, businesses, governments, and multilateral organizations, which collectively make decisions about the production, consumption, and distribution of goods and services.

Global financial architecture (GFA). The structures and practices of international financial institutions and other multilateral organizations, governments, businesses, and others involved in economic or financial transactions in the global economy.

Globalization. The freer cross-border movements of goods and services, labor, technology, real capital, and financial capital to create an integrated and interdependent global economy.

Global warming. The gradual warming of world surface temperatures over time, due mainly to the greenhouse effect.

Good governance. The honest, competent administration of governments, businesses, civil society organizations, multilateral organizations, and other decision-making bodies in the global community.

Goods-producing sector. The economic sector that supplies tangible items in the economy such as final goods, intermediate goods, and resources; the goods-producing sector is comprised of manufacturing, construction, and mining.

Gradualism. A cautious approach to economic transition, based on experimentation and the gradual infusion of successful market reforms.

Greenfield investments. A type of foreign direct investment that involves the construction of new production facilities such as factories, plantations, or office buildings.

Greenhouse effect. The result of gases—such as carbon dioxide and chlorofluorocarbons—trapped in the earth's atmosphere, which holds in some of the heat that normally would have radiated back into space; the greenhouse effect is responsible for global warming.

Green revolution. Agricultural techniques used to increase crop yields; employs mechanization, hybrid seeds, pesticides and fertilizers, and scientific planting methods.

Green technologies. Environmentally friendly technologies that promote the efficient use of resources and reduce waste and pollution.

Gross domestic product (GDP). The total dollar value of all newly produced final goods and services in an economy in a given year.

Gross national income (GNI). The people's total income derived from domestic and foreign sources; the broadest measure of national income; previously called the gross national product (GNP).

Group of Eight (G8). An organization of eight industrialized economies that discuss and form common policies on matters of global concern; comprised of the G7 plus Russia.

Group of Seven (G7). An organization of the world's most advanced economies, which meet to discuss and form common policies on matters of global concern.

Group of Seventy-Seven (G77). A coalition of 133 developing countries; originally formed to promote economic justice in the global economy.

Group of Twenty (G20). A forum comprised of advanced economies, and emerging market and developing countries; designed to strengthen the global financial architecture and promote sustainable economic development.

Hard currency. The currency of a major advanced economy, such as the U.S. dollar, Japanese yen, or EMU euro; used in many types of international transactions.

Hayek, Friedrich A. (1899–1992). An Austrian-born economist and champion of economic freedom and laissez-faire capitalism.

Heavily Indebted Poor Countries (HIPC) Initiative. A debt relief program co-sponsored by the International Monetary Fund (IMF) and the World Bank.

Herd mentality. A rush to buy or sell securities, or to make other types of financial investments, based on the buy or sell transactions of other investors; the herd mentality is a main cause of financial contagion in the largely unregulated global financial system.

High-income country. A country with a per capita gross national income of $10,066 or more in 2004.

Human capital. Workers whose abilities and skills have been enhanced by education, training, apprenticeships, or other means.

Human development. Reflects the realistic range of choices that people have to live happy and productive lives.

Human Development Index (HDI). An index of people's well-being; an annual HDI is published by the United Nations Development Program.

Human resources. The people involved in production; human resources is a factor of production.

Hyperinflation. An annual inflation rate that rises into the hundreds or thousands of percent.

Import quota. A type of trade barrier that limits the quantity of a product a government will allow into a country during a specified time period.

Imports. Any resource, intermediate good, or final good or service that buyers in one country purchase from sellers in another country.

Import substitution. A trade strategy that challenges domestic businesses to produce substitute goods for items normally imported; designed to reduce the country's dependence on foreign goods.

Indicative planning. A collaborative, inclusive economic planning process employed by some democratic socialist economies.

Industrial Revolution. The economic transition from small-scale labor-intensive production to large-scale capital-intensive production in factories and mills; the Industrial Revolution began in Great Britain during the 1700s.

Infant industry. A newly formed industry in a country; the infant industry argument is used to defend protectionist trade policies, such as tariffs and import quotas.

Inflation. An increase in the overall price level in an economy; two types of inflation are demand-pull and cost-push inflation.

Inflation rate. Measures the percentage increase in the overall price level over time.

Informal economy. Refers to business activity that is not reported to the government.

Information and communications technologies (ICTs). Refers to technological advances that increase people's ability to collect, store, retrieve, and share information.

Innovation. The process of converting scientific discoveries and technological advances into profitable business ventures, products, or production processes.

Intellectual property rights. Refers to legal codes and structures to protect people's creative endeavors, including industrial property and copyrights.

Inter-American Development Bank Group (IDB Group). A regional development bank that serves Latin America and the Caribbean.

International Bank for Reconstruction and Development (IBRD). A member-owned development institution that provides low-interest loans and technical assistance mainly to middle-income developing countries; part of the World Bank Group.

International Centre for Settlement of Investment Disputes (ICSID). An autonomous international organization designed to help settle investment disputes between foreign investors and host governments; part of the World Bank Group.

International commodity agreement (ICA). A multilateral agreement between major producers and consumers of certain commodities in global markets.

International Co-operative Alliance (ICA). An autonomous, non-governmental organization that represents the interests of cooperatives in the global economy.

International Development Association (IDA). A member-owned development institution that makes long-term interest-free loans and grants to the world's poorest countries; part of the World Bank Group.

International Finance Corporation (IFC). A member-owned development institution that provides financing and technical assistance to private companies in the developing world; part of the World Bank Group.

International financial institutions (IFIs). Refers to multilateral organizations and national agencies that use public funds to finance foreign investment, trade, and economic development.

International investment agreement (IIA). A bilateral or multilateral treaty that establishes the rules, procedures, or responsibilities of parties involved in a cross-border investment.

International Labor Organization (ILO). A specialized agency of the United Nations that promotes worker rights and decent work in the global economy.

International Monetary Fund (IMF). An international financial institution (IFI) designed to promote global financial and economic stability, growth and development; a specialized agency in the United Nations System.

International trade. The cross-border exchange of goods or services; occurs when an individual, business, government, or other entity imports or exports products.

Investment goods. Items not designed for present consumption, including capital goods, inventories, and residential housing.

Investment promotion agency (IPA). A government agency that recruits foreign direct investment from transnational corporations through tax breaks, subsidies, or other incentives.

Joint venture. A business agreement between two or more companies to produce or sell a product; usually short-term in nature.

Joseph, Keith S. (1918–1994). A leading British economist and champion of free-market economics; Joseph was instrumental in reversing the global drift toward democratic socialism during the 1970s and 1980s.

Keynes, John M. (1883–1946). An influential British economist, teacher, and author; Keynes is best-known for his stabilization theories, and his leadership at the Bretton Woods Conference in 1944.

Krugman, Paul R. (1953–). An American international economist and author, and proponent of the new trade theory.

Kuznets, Simon (1901–1985). An American economist, widely recognized for his pioneering work in national income and product accounting and development economics.

Labor force. Consists of individuals of employable age, who have a job or are actively seeking employment

Labor-intensive production. A method of producing goods or services that relies on physical labor; often associated with production in the developing countries.

Labor union. A formal association of workers empowered by members to negotiate labor contracts with management; a union's main power stems from collective bargaining.

Least developed countries (LDCs). Refers to fifty of the world's poorest developing countries; most low-income developing countries are LDCs.

Lewis, Sir William A. (1915–1991). A prominent British economist and specialist in the field of development economics.

Localization. A system of economic and political activity that places most decision making in the hands of local authorities.

Lower middle-income country. A country with a per capita gross national income between $826 and $3,255 in 2004.

Low-income country. A country with a per capita gross national income of $825 or less in 2004.

Malthus, Thomas R. (1766–1834). A controversial English economist, whose theories on global population growth painted a grim future for humanity.

Managed exchange rate system. A system of converting nations' currencies that includes selective government interventions to stabilize currency values.

Maquiladoras. The duty-free assembly plants located mainly in Mexico and in some other Latin American countries.

Market economy. A type of economic system in which the private sector owns and controls the factors of production—natural resources, human resources, and capital goods; viewed as an economic model.

Market mechanism. The interaction of supply and demand in free markets to determine prices and allocate resources without government intervention.

Marx, Karl H. (1818–1883). A German-born historian, economist, philosopher, and revolutionary; founder of modern communism.

Marxism. An economic doctrine that stems from the theories of Karl H. Marx; Marxism, also called communism, has been adapted by revolutionaries during the twentieth century to meet local objectives.

Mercantilism. The belief that the accumulation of specie, mainly gold and silver, is the wellspring of a nation's wealth and prosperity.

MERCOSUR (*Mercado Comun del Sur*). A four-nation regional trade association that consists of Argentina, Brazil, Paraguay, and Uruguay; also called the Southern Common Market.

Merger. Occurs when two or more firms combine their assets, or equity, to form a single larger firm; mergers of firms headquartered in different countries is a type of foreign direct investment.

Mergers and acquisitions (M&As). Occur when two existing companies are legally joined under single ownership; M&As are a type of foreign direct investment.

Microfinance institutions (MFIs). The organizations that provide a range of financial services, including microloans, to the poor.

Millennium Development Goals (MDGs). The eight specific objectives for human and economic development in the global economy; established by the United Nations in 2000.

Ministry of International Trade and Industry (MITI). A quasi-public institution in Japan designed to promote export industries through a variety of incentives; replaced by the Ministry of Economy, Trade and Industry in 2001.

Mixed economy. An economy that combines features of the market economy and command economy models; in common usage, mixed economies refer to economic systems that lean toward the market model.

Moore, Mike (1949–). A former director-general of the World Trade Organization and staunch supporter of free trade and globalization.

Most favored nations (MFN). Agreement that a trade concession granted by one World Trade Organization member to another member automatically applies to all members; a basic principle of the General Agreement on Tariffs and Trade and the WTO.

Multilateral environmental agreements (MEAs). The formal protocols, conventions, treaties, or declarations negotiated by countries to protect or restore the natural environment.

Multilateral Investment Guarantee Agency (MIGA). An international organization that supports foreign direct investment (FDI) by insuring transnational corporations from certain non-commercial losses; part of the World Bank Group.

Mun, Thomas (1571–1641). A prominent merchant, and spokesman for the mercantile and manufacturing classes during the early 1600s.

Myrdal, Karl G. (1898–1987). A prominent Swedish sociologist, politician, and development economist; favored economic planning to promote economic development.

National debt. The accumulated debt of the federal government; also called the federal debt.

Nationalization. The government's seizure of private productive assets with compensation to the previous owner.

National treatment. A principle of trade that requires countries to treat imported goods in the same way as domestically produced goods; an important principle underlying the GATT/WTO agreements; also called equal treatment.

Natural resources. The gifts of nature that are used in production, such as natural forests and rivers; natural resources is a factor of production.

Newly industrialized economies (NIEs). The four Asian economies that recently joined the ranks of the advanced economies.

New protectionism. Refers to policies that restrict international trade, foreign direct investment (FDI), and cross-border flows of financial capital; policies are designed to make local economies more secure, improve people's quality of life, and democratize decision making.

Nominal gross domestic product. A country's gross domestic product not adjusted for inflation.

Non-concessional terms. Credit terms on loans at prevailing market rates.

Nonconvertible currency. A currency that cannot be exchanged for other currencies due to its uncertain value; nonconvertible currencies are rarely used in international trade or other cross-border transactions.

Non-governmental organization (NGO). A special interest group that conducts research, disseminates information, and advocates for change at the national and international levels.

Nonrenewable resources. Resources that are consumed during production and cannot be replenished, such as oil and natural gas.

North. Refers to the advanced economies; also called the global North.

North American Free Trade Agreement (NAFTA). A comprehensive regional trade agreement between Canada, Mexico, and the United States.

Nyerere, Julius K. (1922–1999). A prominent Tanzanian educator, political leader, and supporter of African socialism during the post–World War II era.

Official aid (OA). Foreign aid mainly to transition countries; OA is coordinated by the Development Assistance Committee of the OECD.

Official development assistance (ODA). Foreign aid to developing countries; ODA is coordinated by the Development Assistance Committee of the OECD.

Offshore financial centers (OFCs). Refers to jurisdictions that offer financial and regulatory advantages to individuals and business firms.

Offshoring. Occurs when a producer from one country outsources production to another country.

Organization for Economic Cooperation and Development (OECD). A thirty-member intergovernmental organization that collects and analyzes statistical data, discusses global trends and issues, and forms binding and nonbinding economic and social policies.

Organization of Petroleum Exporting Countries (OPEC). An eleven-member producer cartel comprised of major petroleum-producing countries.

Peace Corps of the United States. An independent aid agency within the executive branch of the U.S. government.

Perestroika. An economic restructuring in the Soviet Union, initiated by Soviet Premier Mikhail Gorbachev during the mid-1980s; the restructuring stressed market-oriented reforms.

Pigou, Arthur C. (1877–1959). An influential British economist and educator, and founder of a branch of economic study called welfare economics.

Population. The number of people living within a region, such as a city, country, or the world.

Poverty. A human condition in which people lack the material goods necessary for a minimal standard of living.

Preferential trade agreement (PTA). Special trade advantages extended mainly to developing countries to promote inclusion in the global trading system; also called preferential trade arrangements.

Private property. Any good, resource, or other asset that is owned and controlled by an individual or business firm.

Private property rights. The legal codes and other protections that guarantee people's right to own, control, buy, sell, and profit from private property.

Private sector. The sector of the economy comprised of business firms and individuals; the non-governmental sector.

Privatization. The process of converting state-owned assets, production facilities, or service delivery systems to the private sector.

Producer price index (PPI). Measures the percentage change in the prices of raw materials, intermediate goods, and other items used in production.

Production sharing. Occurs when a business produces a good or service in stages in different countries.

Productivity. Measures a change in output per unit of input; productivity usually measures a change in output per unit of labor input.

Protectionism. The government's use of import controls, such as tariffs and import quotas, and export subsidies to protect local industries and jobs.

Public sector. The sector of the economy comprised of government at the local, state, and national levels.

Purchasing power parity (PPP). An approach to converting national currencies in the global economy, which considers the buying power of a nation's currency within its domestic economy.

Quality of life. The overall conditions under which people live.

Race to the bottom. The deterioration of labor and environmental standards that result from intense competition in global markets, and resulting cost-cutting production decisions by transnational corporations.

Real gross domestic product. A country's gross domestic product adjusted for inflation.

Recession. A relatively short-term economic downturn in economic activity, marked by a drop in national output and investment, and higher unemployment and business failures.

Regional development bank. A member-owned, not-for-profit multilateral lending and development institution.

Regional trade agreement (RTA). An agreement that creates preferential trade concessions among member countries.

Remittances. Money earned by foreign-born or immigrant workers in one country but sent to family, friends, business associates, or others in the home country; sometimes viewed as a type of foreign aid.

Renewable resources. Resources that can be replenished, such as sunlight and forests.

Ricardo, David (1772–1823). A leading nineteenth-century British economist and supporter of free trade; popularized the theory of comparative advantage.

Rio Earth Summit. A landmark United Nations–sponsored meeting in 1992 that created guidelines for sustainable economic development in the global economy.

Rostow, Walt W. (1916–2003). A prominent American development economist and economic historian; championed linear development theory.

Rule of law. Refers to the fair and uniform application of the law to all participants in a country.

Sachs, Jeffrey D. (1954–). A leading American economist, author, and consultant in the field of development economics.

Schumacher, Ernst F. (1911–1977). A British development economist, reformer, and supporter of appropriate technology in economic development.

Schumpeter, Joseph A. (1883–1950). A prominent economic historian, author, and teacher; stressed the role of entrepreneurs and innovation in economic growth.

Sen, Amartya K. (1933–). A prominent Indian economist, who specializes in welfare and development economics.

Services-producing sector. An economic sector that supplies productive activities; includes companies connected with transportation, communication, retail trade, and other services.

Smith, Adam (1723–1790). A prominent Scottish economist and philosopher, and defender of free enterprise and free trade; founder of modern economics.

Social capital. A country's broad infrastructure; social capital is provided by the government for the collective welfare of the people.

Socialism. A type of economic system based on public ownership and control of key resources and industries; strands range from democratic socialism to communism.

Solow, Robert M. (1924–). A prominent American economist, teacher, and author; stressed the role of technology as the primary engine of economic growth.

Soto, Hernando de (1941–). An influential Peruvian development economist, who advocated the infusion of productive capital from the informal economy into the formal economy.

South. Refers to the developing countries; also called the global South.

South-South cooperation. The coordinated actions of developing countries to promote sustainable economic development.

Special Drawing Rights (SDR). The International Monetary Fund's unit of account, roughly comparable to the European Union's euro, the U.S. dollar, or other national unit of account.

Statism. An economic philosophy that supports active government intervention in the economy, including the nationalization of key industries.

Stiglitz, Joseph E. (1943–). An influential American economist and advocate for reform of the global financial architecture.

Subcontractor. A company that is contracted by a second company to produce a good, or a component of a good.

Subsidy. A government payment to a business, mainly to support domestic producers; viewed as a type of protectionism in international markets.

Subsistence agriculture. An agricultural system designed to satisfy the personal consumption needs of households rather than to produce surpluses for export.

Supply chain. A network of businesses that are collectively responsible for the production and distribution of a product.

Sustainable consumption. The ability to satisfy people's present consumption needs without undermining the world's capacity to meet the consumption needs of future generations.

Sustainable economic development. Occurs when an economy achieves sustained economic growth and substantive improvements in people's quality of life.

Tariff. A federal tax on an imported good or service; the two types of tariffs are protective tariffs and revenue tariffs; also called a customs duty.

Technology transfer. The sharing of advanced technology between transnational corporations and their affiliates or other related firms.

Terms of trade. A measure of the relative prices of a country's exports and imports.

Third world socialism. The application of socialist principles to developing economies.

Trade barrier. Government policies designed to discourage or prohibit imports, such as import tariffs and import quotas.

Trade deficit. Occurs when the value of a country's imports is greater than its exports.

Trade liberalization. Refers to government policies that result in freer trade; includes the removal of trade barriers and business subsidies.

Trade-Related Aspects of Intellectual Property (TRIPS). An international agreement designed to protect intellectual properties in global markets; administered by the World Trade Organization.

Trade surplus. Occurs when the value of a country's exports is greater than its imports.

Traditional economy. An economic system that relies on custom or tradition to answer the basic economic questions.

Transition countries. The twenty-eight countries of eastern and central Europe and central Asia that are in the process of transforming from communism to capitalism, and from totalitarianism to democracy; also called transition economies.

Transnational corporation (TNC). A company that is based in one country, but owns or controls other companies, called affiliates, in one or more additional countries.

Transparency. Refers to a free flow of information; transparency promotes accountability of governments, transnational corporations, multilateral organizations, and others; it also promotes inclusion of the marginalized in global decision making.

Underemployment. Occurs when workers are employed at jobs beneath their skill level, at jobs that do not fully utilize their skills, or at jobs that offer insufficient work hours.

United Nations System. The six branches of the United Nations, and its twenty-five autonomous specialized agencies, programs, and funds.

Unsustainable debt. A country's inability to service, or make payments on, its external debt without decimating its domestic economy.

Upper middle-income country. A country with a per capita gross national income of between $3,256 and $10,065 in 2004.

Urbanization. The process of becoming more urban; the shift of population and economic activity from rural areas to cities.

Venture capital. Money invested to create new businesses; also called risk capital.

Venture initiation. The creation of a new business through entrepreneurial activity.

Virtuous cycle. Occurs when national savings and investment jump-start economic growth and development.

Voluntary quota. A bilateral trade agreement that limits the import of a specific good, or expands the export of a certain good.

Ward, Barbara M. (1914–1981). An influential British development economist, lecturer, journalist, and teacher; stressed cooperation and economic justice in the global economy.

Welfare economics. The branch of economics that deals with the redistribution of society's wealth or income to improve people's economic well-being.

Wolfensohn, James D. (1933–). An international investment banker, author, and former president of the World Bank Group.

World Bank Group. A multilateral development organization, which consists of five mutually supporting institutions: the International Bank for Reconstruction and Development (IBRD), International Development Association (IDA), International Finance Corporation (IFC), International Centre for Settlement of Investment Disputes (ICSID), and the Multilateral Investment Guarantee Agency (MIGA).

World Economic Forum (WEF). A nonprofit foundation committed to improving people's quality of life and the state of the world.

World Health Organization (WHO). A multilateral organization dedicated to improving the health of all people; a specialized agency of the United Nations.

World Intellectual Property Organization (WIPO). An international organization that protects intellectual property rights in the global economy; a specialized agency of the United Nations.

World Trade Organization (WTO). An international organization that oversees the operation of the rules-based multilateral trading system.

World Wide Web. Links documents and files on the Internet.

Yunus, Muhammad (1940–). A prominent Bangladeshi development economist, social reformer; a proponent of microcredit as a viable development strategy.

Key Global Economy Web Sites

African Development Bank Group, www.afdb.org
Andean Community, www.comunidadandina.org/endex.htm
Asian Development Bank, www.adb.org
Asia-Pacific Economic Cooperation, www.apecsec.org
Association of Southeast Asian Nations, www.asean.or.id
Bank for International Settlements, www.bis.org
Bureau of Economic Analysis (U.S.), www.bea.gov
Caribbean Community, www.caricom.org
Economic Community of West African States, www.ecowas.int/
Energy Information Administration (U.S.), www.eia.doe.gov
European Bank for Reconstruction and Development, www.ebrd.com
European Commission to the U.S., www.eurunion.org
European Free Trade Association, www.efta.int
European Union, http://europa.eu.int/
Freedom House, www.freedomhouse.org
Free Trade Area of the Americas, www.ftaa-alca.org/alca_e.asp
G8 Information Centre, www.g8.utoronto.ca
G20, www.g20.org
Global Entrepreneurship Monitor, www.gemconsortium.org
Global Policy Forum (UN), www.globalpolicy.org
Grameen Bank, www.grameen-info.org
Greenpeace, www.greenpeace.org
Group of Seventy-Seven, www.g77.org
Institute for Liberty and Democracy, www.ild.org
Inter-American Development Bank, www.iadb.org
International Bank for Reconstruction and Development, www.worldbank.org
International Centre for Settlement of Investment Disputes, www.icsid.org
International Co-operative Alliance, www.coop.org
International Development Association, www.ida.org
International Finance Corporation, www.ifc.org
International Labor Organization, www.ilo.org
International Monetary Fund, www.imf.org
International Trade Administration (U.S.), www.ita.doc.gov
International Trade Commission (U.S.), www.usitc.gov
Millennium Development Goals, www.developmentgoals.org
Multilateral Investment Guarantee Agency, www.miga.org
North American Free Trade Agreement, www.nafta-sec-alena.org
Organization for Economic Cooperation and Development, www.oecd.org
Organization of Petroleum Exporting Countries, www.opec.org
Oxfam International, www.oxfaminternational.org
Partnership in Statistics for Development, www.paris21.org
Peace Corps of the United States, www.peacecorps.gov
Population Reference Bureau, www.prb.org

Transparency International, www.transparency.org
United Nations, www.un.org
UN Children's Fund, www.unicef.org
UN Conference on Trade and Development, www.unctad.org
UN Development Program, www.undp.org
UN Educational, Scientific and Cultural Organization, www.unesco.org
UN Environment Program, www.unep.org
UN Population Fund, www.unfpa.org
U.S. Agency for International Development, www.usaid.gov
World Bank, www.worldbank.org
World Economic Forum, www.weforum.org
World Health Organization, www.who.org
World Intellectual Property Organization, www.wipo.int
World Resources Institute, www.wri.org
World Trade Organization, www.wto.org
Worldwatch Institute, www.worldwatch.org
World Wide Web Consortium, www.w3.org/Consortium

Selected Bibliography

Akiyama, Takamasa, John Baffes, Donald Larson, and Panos Varangis. *Commodity Market Reforms: Lessons of Two Decades*. Washington, DC: World Bank Publications, 2001.

Akyuz, Yilmaz. *Reforming the Global Financial Architecture: Issues and Proposals*. New York: Zed Books, 2002.

Albritton, Robert, John R. Bell, and Shannon Bell, eds. *New Socialisms: Futures beyond Globalization*. New York: Routledge, 2004.

Alger, Chadwick, and Mildred Vasan, eds. *The United Nations System: A Reference Handbook*. Santa Barbara, CA: ABC-Clio, 2005.

Almas, Reidar, and Geoffrey Lawrence. *Globalization, Localization and Sustainable Livelihoods*. Brookfield, VT: Ashgate Publishing, 2003.

Anderson, Sarah, John Cavanagh, and Thea Lee. *Global Economy: Field Guide*. New York: New Press, 2005.

Anheier, Helmut K., Mary H. Kaldor, and Marlies Glasius, eds. *Global Civil Society 2004/5*. Thousand Oaks, CA: SAGE Publications, 2004.

Armingeon, Klaus, and Michelle Beyeler, eds. *The OECD and European Welfare States*. Northampton, MA: Edward Elgar Publishing, 2004.

Bacon, David. *The Children of NAFTA: Labor Wars on the U.S./Mexico Border*. Berkeley, CA: University of California Press, 2005.

Baker, James C. *The Bank for International Settlements: Evolution and Evaluation*. Westport, CT: Quorum Books, 2002.

Bank for International Settlements. *Triennial Central Bank Survey of Foreign Exchange and Derivatives Market Activity in April 2004*. Basel, Switzerland: Author, 2004.

Basu, Kaushik, Henrik Horn, Lisa Roman, and Judith Shapiro. *International Labor Standards: History, Theory, and Policy Decisions*. Malden, MA: Blackwell Publishers, 2003.

Bello, Walden. *Deglobalization: Ideas for a New World Order*. New York: Zed Books, 2005.

Benioff, Marc, and Karen Southwick. *Compassionate Capitalism: How Corporations Can Make Doing Good an Integral Part of Doing Well*. Franklin Lakes, NJ: Career Press, 2004.

Benn, Denis, and Kenneth Hall. *The Caribbean Community: Beyond Survival*. Concord, MA: Ian Randle Publishers, 2002.

Bennekom, Sander van. *The Multilateral Agreement on Investment (MAI)—Making the World Safe for Multinationals*. New York: Zed Books, 2000.

Bhagwati, Jagdish N. *Free Trade Today*. Princeton, NJ: Princeton University Press, 2003.

———. *In Defense of Globalization*. New York: Oxford University Press, 2004.

Birchall, Johnston. *The International Co-Operative Movement*. New York: Manchester University Press, 1997.

Birdsall, Nancy, John Williamson, and Brian Deese. *Delivering on Debt Relief: From IMF Gold to a New Aid Architecture*. Washington, DC: Institute for International Economics, 2002.

———. *What Role for Regional Development Banks in Financing for Development?* Washington, DC: Institute for International Economics, 2003.

Black, John. *A Dictionary of Economics*. 2d ed. New York: Oxford University Press, 2003.

Blustein, Paul. *The Chastening: Inside the Crisis That Rocked the Global Financial System and Humbled the Imf*. Cambridge, MA: Public Affairs/Perseus, 2003.

Bok, Sissela, Stellan Andersson, and Richard Litell, eds. *The Essential Gunnar Myrdal*. New York: New Press, 2005.

Boughton, James M. *Why White, Not Keynes? Inventing the Postwar International Monetary System*. Washington, DC: International Monetary Fund, 2002.

Brenner, Robert. *Merchants and Revolution: Commercial Change, Political Conflict, and London's Overseas Traders, 1550–1653*. New York: Verso, 2003.

Brittain-Catlin, William. *Offshore: The Dark Side of the Global Economy*. New York: Farrar, Straus and Giroux, 2005.

Brooks, Douglas H. and Hall Hill, eds. *Managing FDI in a Globalizing Economy: Asian Experiences*. New York: Palgrave Macmillan, 2004.

Brundenius, Claes, and John Weeks, eds. *Globalization and Third-World Socialism: Cuba and Vietnam*. New York: Palgrave Macmillan, 2001.

Burci, Gian L., and Claude-Henri Vignes. *World Health Organization*. Norwell, MA: Kluwer Law International, 2004.

Burki, Shahid J., and Danile P. Erikson, eds. *Transforming Socialist Economies: Lessons for Cuba and Beyond*. New York: Palgrave Macmillan, 2005.

Burnell, Peter, and Oliver Morrissey. *Foreign Aid in the New Global Economy*. Northampton, MA: Edward Elgar Publishing, 2004.

Carmel, Erran, and Paul Tjia. *Offshoring Information Technology: Sourcing and Outsourcing to a Global Workforce*. New York: Cambridge University Press, 2005.

Cavanagh, John, et al. *Alternatives to Economic Globalization: A Better World Is Possible*. San Francisco, CA: Berrett-Koehler Publishers, 2004.

Chang-Tai Hsieh. *Relative Prices and Relative Prosperity*. Cambridge, MA: National Bureau of Economic Research, 2003.

Chisholm, Andrew. *An Introduction to Capital Markets: Products, Strategies, Participants*. New York: John Wiley & Sons, 2002.

Choate, Pat. *Hot Property: The Stealing of Ideas in an Age of Globalization*. New York: Alfred A. Knopf, 2005.

Clapp, Jennifer, and Peter Dauvergne. *Paths to a Green World: The Political Economy of the Global Environment*. Cambridge, MA: MIT Press, 2005.

Cline, William R. *Trade Policy and Global Poverty*. Washington, DC: Institute for International Economics, 2004.

Cohen, Daniel, Pietro Garibaldi, and Stefano Scarpetta. *The Ict Revolution: Productivity Differences and the Digital Divide*. New York: Oxford University Press, 2004.

Collins, Joseph, Stefano Dezerega, and Zahara Heckscher. *How to Live Your Dream of Volunteering Overseas*. New York: Penguin Books, 2002.

Cornia, Giovanni A. *Inequality, Growth, and Poverty in an Era of Liberalization and Globalization*. New York: Oxford University Press, 2004.

Cuyvers, Ludo, and Filip DeBeule, eds. *Transnational Corporations and Economic Development: From Internalisation to Globalization*. New York: Palgrave Macmillan, 2005.

Das, Dilip K. *Financial Globalization and the Emerging Market Economies*. New York: Routledge, 2004.

———. *Regionalism in Global Trade*. Northampton, MA: Edward Elgar Publishing, 2004.

Delphos, William A. *Inside the World's Export Credit Agencies*. Cincinnati, OH: South-Western Educational Pub, 2003.

De Mooij, Marieke. *Global Marketing and Advertising: Understanding Global Paradoxes*. 2d ed. Thousand Oaks, CA: SAGE Publications, 2005.

Deng Rong. *Deng Xiaoping and the Cultural Revolution: A Daughter Recalls the Critical Years*. New York: Doubleday, 2005.

Devlin, Robert, Antoni Estevadordal, and Inter-American Development Bank, eds. *Bridges for Development*. Washington, DC: Inter-American Development Bank, 2004.

Dinan, Desmond. *Ever Closer Union: An Introduction to European Integration.* Boulder, CO: Lynne Rienner Publishers, 2005.

Dormois, Jean-Pierre. *Classical Trade Protectionism: 1815–1914.* New York: Routledge, 2005.

Downing, Sandra L. *Asia Pacific Economic Cooperation Apec: Current Issues and Background.* Huntington, NY: Nova Science Pub Inc., 2003.

Drahos, Peter, and John Braithwaite. *Information Feudalism.* New York: W. W. Norton & Company, 2003.

Duesterberg, Thomas J., and Ernest H. Preeg, eds. *U.S. Manufacturing: The Engine for Growth in a Global Economy.* Westport, CT: Praeger Publishers, 2003.

Dutta, Soumitra, Bruno Lanvin, and Fiona Paua, eds. *The Global Information and Technology Report: 2003–2004: Towards and Equity Information Society.* New York: Oxford University Press, 2004.

Easterly, William. *The Elusive Quest for Growth: Economists' Adventures and Misadventures in the Tropics.* Cambridge, MA: MIT Press, 2002.

Ebenstein, William, Edwin Fogelman, and Alan Ebenstein. *Today's ISMS: Socialism, Capitalism, Fascism, Communism, and Libertarianism.* 11th ed. Paramus, NJ: Prentice Hall, 1999.

Economic Report of the President: 2004. Washington, DC: United States Government Printing Office, 2004.

Ellerman, David. *Helping People Help Themselves: From the World Bank to an Alternative Philosophy of Development Assistance.* Ann Arbor, MI: University of Michigan Press, 2005.

Elliot, Jennifer A. *An Introduction to Sustainable Development.* 3d ed. New York: Routledge, 2005.

Epstein, Gerald A. *Capital Flight and Capital Controls in Developing Countries.* Northampton, MA: Edward Elgar Publishers, 2005.

Erdman, Sarah. *Nine Hills to Nambonkaha: Two Years in the Heart of an African Village.* New York: Henry Holt and Company, 2003.

Estevadeordal, Antoni, Dani Rodrik, Alan M. Taylor, and Andres Velasco. *Integrating the Americas: FTAA and Beyond.* Cambridge, MA: Harvard University Press, 2004.

Feenstra, Robert C. *Global Production Sharing and Rising Inequality: A Survey of Trade and Wages.* Cambridge, MA: National Bureau of Economic Research, 2001.

Fernando, Jude L. *Microfinance: Perils and Prospects.* New York: Routledge, 2005.

Finger, Matthias, Oran R. Young, and Ernst U. Von Weizsacker, eds. *Limits to Privatization: When a Solution Becomes a Problem.* Washington, DC: Earthscan Publications, 2005.

Fischer, Stanley. *IMF Essays from a Time of Crisis: The International Financial System, Stabilization, and Development.* Cambridge, MA: MIT Press, 2004.

Fulcher, James. *Capitalism: A Very Short Introduction.* New York: Oxford University Press, 2004.

Garelli, Stephanie. *IMD World Competitiveness Yearbook 2004.* Lausanne, Switzerland: International Institute for Management Development, 2004.

Garlake, Teresa. *Global Debt: The Impact on Our Lives.* Austin, TX: Raintree, 2003.

George, Alexandra. *Globalization and Intellectual Property.* Brookfield, VT: Ashgate Publishing Company, 2005.

Gilbert, Christopher L. *The IMF and Its Critics: Reform of Global Financial Architecture.* New York: Cambridge University Press, 2004.

Gill, Indermit S., and Todd Pugatch. *At the Frontlines of Development: Reflections from the World Bank.* Washington, DC: World Bank Publications, 2005.

Gillies, Grazia I. *Transnational Corporations and International Production: Concepts, Theories and Effects.* Northampton, MA: Edward Elgar Publishing, 2005.

Gilpin, Robert. *The Challenge of Global Capitalism: The World Economy in the 21st Century.* Princeton, NJ: Princeton University Press, 2002.

Goldman, Michael. *Imperial Nature: The World Bank and Struggles for Social Justice in the Age of Globalization*. New Haven, CT: Yale University Press, 2005.

Goodhart, C. A. E., and Gerhard Illing. *Financial Crises, Contagion, and the Lender of Last Resort*. New York: Oxford University Press, 2002.

Gotthelf, Philip. *Currency Trading: How to Access and Trade the World's Biggest Market*. New York: Wiley, 2002.

Guangwen Meng. *The Theory and Practice of Free Economic Zones: A Case Study of Tianjin/ The People's Republic of China*. New York: Peter Lang Publishing, 2003.

Guha-Khasnobis, Basudeb, ed. *The WTO, Developing Countries, and the Doha Development Agenda: Prospects and Challenges for Trade-Led Growth*. New York: Palgrave Macmillan, 2004.

Gwartney, James, and Robert Lawson. *Economic Freedom of the World: 2004 Annual Report*. Vancouver, Canada: The Fraser Institute, 2004.

Hacker, R. Scott, B. Johansson, and Charlie Karlsson. *Emerging Market Economies and European Economic Integration*. Northampton, MA: Edward Elgar Publishing, 2005.

Hackett, John T. *Race to the Bottom*. Bloomington, IN: Authorhouse, 2004.

Haney, Patrick J., and Walt Vanderbush. *The Cuban Embargo: The Domestic Politics of an American Foreign Policy*. Pittsburgh, PA: University of Pittsburgh Press, 2005.

Harrison, Graham, ed. *Global Encounters: The International Political Economy, Development and Globalization*. New York: Palgrave Macmillan, 2005.

Hartman, Laura P., Denis G. Arnold, and Richard E. Wokutch. *Rising above Sweatshops: Innovative Approaches to Global Labor Challenges*. Westport, CT: Praeger Publishers, 2003.

Hayek, Friedrich A., and W. W. Bartley, III, eds. *The Fatal Conceit: The Errors of Socialism*. Rev. ed. Chicago: University of Chicago Press, 1991.

Helpman, Elhanan. *The Mystery of Economic Growth*. Cambridge, MA: Belknap Press, 2004.

———, and Paul R. Krugman. *Trade Policy and Market Structure*. Rev. ed. Cambridge, MA: MIT Press, 1989.

Hertz, Noreena. *The Debt Threat: How Debt Is Destroying the Developing World*. New York: HarperBusiness, 2005.

Hines, Colin. *Localization: A Global Manifesto*. Washington, DC: Earthscan Publications, 2000.

Hoekman, Bernard, and Michael Kostecki. *The Political Economy of the World Trading System: From Gatt to Wto*. 2d ed. New York: Oxford University Press, 2001.

Hopkins, Michael. *The Planetary Bargain: Corporate Social Responsibility Matters*. Washington, DC: Earthscan Publications, 2003.

Houtart, Francois, and Francois Polet. *The Other Davos: The Globalization of Resistance to the World Economic Order*. New York: Zed Books, 2001.

Hudgins, Edward L., ed. *Freedom to Trade: Refuting the New Protectionism*. Washington, DC: Cato Institute, 1997.

Hudson, Michael. *Global Fracture: The New International Economic Order*. 2d ed. London: Pluto Press, 2005.

Hudson, Pat. *The Industrial Revolution*. New York: Oxford University Press, 2005.

Ingco, Merlinda D. *Agriculture and the WTO: Creating a Trading System for Development*. Washington, DC: World Bank Publications, 2005.

International Confederation of Free Trade Unions. *Export Processing Zones—Symbols of Exploitation and a Development Dead-End*. Brussels, Belgium: Author, 2003.

International Labor Organization. *Fair Globalization: The Role of the ILO*. Geneva, Switzerland: Author, 2004.

International Monetary Fund. *Balance of Payments Statistics Yearbook 2003*. Washington, DC: Author, 2003.

———. *World Economic Outlook, April 2005*. Washington, DC: Author, 2005.

Irwin, Douglas A. *Free Trade under Fire*. Princeton, NJ: Princeton University Press, 2003.

Isaak, Robert A. *The Globalization Gap: How the Rich Get Richer and the Poor Get Left Further Behind*. Paramus, NJ: Prentice Hall Financial Times, 2004.

Ito, Takatoshi, and Andrew K. Rose, eds. *Growth and Productivity in East Asia*. Chicago: University of Chicago Press, 2004.

James, Jeffrey. *Bridging the Global Digital Divide*. Northampton, MA: Edward Elgar Publishing, 2003.

Johansson, B., and Charlie Karlsson. *Regional Policies and Comparative Advantage*. Northampton, MA: Edward Elgar Publishers, 2002.

Kaldor, Mary, Helmut Anheier, and Marlies Glasius. *Global Civil Society 2003*. New York: Oxford University Press, 2003.

Karatnycky, Adrian. *Freedom in the World 2004: The Annual Survey of Political Rights and Civil Liberties*. New York: Freedom House, 2004.

Kaufmann, Daniel, and Aart Kraay. *Governance Matters III: Governance Indicators for 1996–2002*. Washington, DC: World Bank, 2003.

Kennedy, Gavin. *Adam Smith's Lost Legacy*. New York: Palgrave Macmillan, 2005.

Kennedy, Kevin C., ed. *The First Decade of NAFTA: The Future of Free Trade in North America*. Piscataway, NJ: Transaction Publishers, Inc., 2004.

Kerbo, Harold R. *World Poverty: Modern World System and the Roots of Global Inequality*. New York: McGraw-Hill, 2005.

Kiggundu, Moses N. *Managing Globalization in Developing Countries and Transition Countries: Building Capacities for a Changing World*. Westport, CT: Quorum Books, 2002.

Kiss, Alexandre, Dinah Shelton, and Kanami Ishibashi, eds. *Economic Globalization and Compliance with International Environmental Agreements*. Cambridge, MA: Kluwer Law International, 2003.

Klobuchar, Jim, and Susan C. Wilkes. *The Miracles of Barefoot Capitalism: A Compelling Case for Microcredit*. Minneapolis, MN: Kirk House Publishers, 2003.

Korten, David C. *When Corporations Rule the World*. 2d ed. San Francisco, CA: Berrett-Koehler, 2001.

Krugman, Paul R. *The Return of Depression Economics*. New York: W. W. Norton & Company, 2000.

Krugman, Paul R., and Maurice Obstfeld. *International Economics: Theory and Policy*. 7th ed. Reading, MA: Addison Wesley, 2005.

Kuznets, Simon. *Economic Development, the Family, and Income Distribution: Selected Essays*. New York: Cambridge University Press, 2002.

Landau, Alice. *The International Trade System*. New York: Routledge, 2005.

Leonard, Dick. *Guide to the European Union*. 9th ed. Princeton, NJ: Bloomberg Press, 2005.

Li Lian Ong. *The Big Mac Index: Applications of Purchasing Power Parity*. New York: Routledge, 2003.

Lilley, Peter. *Dirty Money: The Untold Truth about Global Money Laundering, International Crime and Terrorism*. 2d ed. Dover, NH: Kogan Page, 2003.

Lindblom, Charles E. *The Market System: What It Is, How It Works, and What to Make of It*. New Haven, CT: Yale University Press, 2001.

Lindenberg, Marc, and Coralie Bryant. *Going Global: Transforming Relief and Development Ngos*. West Hartford, CT: Kumarian Press, 2001.

Lindstrom, Martin, and Patricia B. Seybold. *Brandchild: Remarkable Insights into the Minds of Today's Global Kids & Their Relationships with Brands*. Rev. ed. Dover, NH: Kogan Page, 2004.

Little, Ian M. D. *A Critique of Welfare Economics*. 2d ed. New York: Oxford University Press, 2003.

Lund, Francie, and Jillian Nicholson. *Chains of Production, Ladders of Protection: Social Protection for Workers in the Informal Economy*. Washington, DC: World Bank Publications, 2004.

Lusztig, Michael. *The Limits of Protectionism: Building Coalitions for Free Trade.* Pittsburgh: University of Pittsburgh Press, 2004.

Mallaby, Sebastian. *The World's Banker: A Story of Failed States, Financial Crises, and the Wealth and Poverty of Nations.* New York: Penguin Press HC, 2004.

Mamic, Ivanka. *Implementing Codes of Conduct: How Businesses Manage Social Performance in Global Supply Chains.* Washington, DC: International Labor Office, 2005.

Marquette, Heather. *Corruption, Politics and Development: The Role of the World Bank.* New York: Palgrave Macmillan, 2004.

Marx, Karl, and Friedrich Engels. *The Communist Manifesto.* New York: Washington Square Press, 1964.

Masey, Douglas S., and J. Edward Taylor. *International Migration: Prospects and Policies in a Global Market.* New York: Oxford University Press, 2004.

Mathews, Gordon. *Global Culture: Searching for Home in the Cultural Supermarket.* New York: Routledge, 2000.

Matsushita, Mitsuo, Thomas J. Schoenbaum, and Petros C. Mavroidis. *The World Trade Organization: Law, Practice, and Policy.* New York: Oxford University Press, 2005.

McClure, Paul, ed. *A Guide to the World Bank.* Washington, DC: World Bank Publications, 2003.

McDonald, David A., and Eunice N. Sahle. *The Legacies of Julius Nyerere: Influences on Development Discourse and Practice in Africa.* Lawrenceville, NJ: Africa World Press, 2002.

McGillivray, Fiona. *Privileging Industry: The Comparative Politics of Trade and Industrial Policy.* Princeton, NJ: Princeton University Press, 2004.

McMillan, John. *Reinventing the Bazaar: A Natural History of Markets.* New York: W. W. Norton & Company, 2003.

Megginson, William L. *The Financial Economics of Privatization.* New York: Oxford University Press, 2005.

Mendez, Jennifer B. *From Revolution to the Maquiladoras: Gender, Labor, and Globalization in Nicaragua.* Durham, NC: Duke University Press, 2005.

Milanovic, Branko. *Worlds Apart: Measuring International and Global Inequality.* Princeton, NJ: Princeton University Press, 2005.

Miles, Marc, Edwin J. Feulner, Mary Anastasia O'Grady, Ana Isabel Eiras, and Aaron Schavey. *2005 Index of Economic Freedom.* Washington, DC: Heritage Books, 2005.

Miller, Margaret J. *Implementing the Millennium Development Goals.* Washington, DC: World Bank, 2003.

Monnich, Christina. *Tariff Rate Quotas and Their Administration.* New York: Peter Lang Publishing, 2004.

Moore, Mike. *A World without Walls: Freedom, Development, Free Trade and Global Governance.* New York: Cambridge University Press, 2003.

Munasinghe, Mohan. *Towards Sustainomics: Making Development More Sustainable.* Northampton, MA: Edward Elgar Publishing, 2005.

Muravchik, Joshua. *Heaven on Earth: The Rise and Fall of Socialism.* San Francisco: Encounter Books, 2002.

Nederveen, Pieterse. *Globalization and Culture.* Lanham, MD: Rowman & Littlefield, 2003.

Neef, Dale. *The Supply Chain Imperative: How to Ensure Ethical Behavior in Your Global Suppliers.* New York: AMACOM, 2004.

Nelson, Richard R., and Linsu Kim, eds. *Technology, Learning, and Innovation: Experiences of Newly Industrializing Economies.* New York: Cambridge University Press, 2000.

Neumayer, Eric. *Greening Trade and Investment: Environmental Protection Without Protectionism.* Washington, DC: Earthscan Publications, 2001.

Nyerere, Julius K. *Ujamaa—Essays on Socialism.* New York: Oxford University Press, 1968.

O'Brennan, John. *The Eastern Enlargement of the European Union*. New York: Routledge, 2005.

Obstfeld, Maurice, and Alan M. Taylor. *Global Capital Markets: Integration, Crisis, and Growth*. New York: Cambridge University Press, 2004.

O'Connor, David E. *The Basics of Economics*. Westport, CT: Greenwood Press, 2004.

———. *Demystifying the Global Economy*. Westport, CT: Greenwood Press, 2002.

———, and Christopher Failles. *Basic Economic Principles: A Guide for Students*. Westport, CT: Greenwood Press, 2000.

Olson, Robert, and David Rejeski, eds. *Environmentalism and the Technologies of Tomorrow: Shaping the Next Industrial Revolution*. Washington, DC: Island Press, 2004.

Ormrod, David, et al., eds. *The Rise of Commercial Empires: England and the Netherlands in the Age of Mercantilism, 1650–1770*. New York: Cambridge University Press, 2003.

Pendergast, Sara, and Tom Pendergast, eds. *Worldmark Encyclopedia of National Economies*. Vols. 1–4. Farmington Hills, MI: Gale Group, 2002.

Pettifor, Ann. *The Real World Economic Outlook 2003: The Legacy of Globalization, Debt and Deflation*. New York: Palgrave Macmillan, 2003.

Piano, Aili, and Arch Puddington. *Freedom in the World 2004: The Annual Survey of Political Rights and Civil Liberties*. New York: Freedom House, 2004.

Poot, Jacques. *On the Edge of the Global Economy*. Northampton, MA: Edward Elgar Publishers, 2005.

Porrata-Doria, Rafael. *Mercosur: The Common Market of the Southern Cone*. Durham, NC: Carolina Academic Press, 2005.

Porter, Michael E., Klaus Schwab, Xavier Sala-I-Martin, and Augusto Lopez-Claros. *The Global Competitiveness Report 2004–2005*. New York: Palgrave Macmillan, 2004.

Prahalad, C. K. *The Fortunes at the Bottom of the Pyramid: Eradicating Poverty through Profits*. Philadelphia: Wharton School Publishing, 2004.

Raworth, Kate. *Trading Away Our Rights: Women Working in Global Supply Chains*. London: Oxfam International, 2004.

Reid, T. R. *The United States of Europe: The New Superpower and the End of American Supremacy*. New York: Penguin Press, 2004.

Reisch, Lucia A., and Inge Ropke, eds. *The Ecological Economics of Consumption*. Northampton, MA: Edward Elgar Publishing, 2005.

Reynolds, Paul D., William D. Bygrave, and Erkko Autio. *GEM 2003 Global Report*. Babson Park, MA: Babson College and the London Business School, 2003.

Rhee, Chase C. *Principles of International Trade (Import and Export): The First Step toward Globalization*. Bloomington, IN: 1st Books Library, 2003.

Ricardo, David. *The Principles of Political Economy and Taxation*. New York: E. P. Dutton & Company, Inc., 1911.

———, and J. R. McCulloch. *The Works of David Ricardo*. Stockton, CA: University of the Pacific, 2002.

Richards, Donald G. *Intellectual Property Rights and Global Capitalism: The Political Economy of the Trips Agreement*. Armonk, NY: M. E. Sharpe, 2004.

Ritzen, Jozef, and Joseph E. Stiglitz. *A Chance for the World Bank*. Palo Alto, CA: Anthem, 2005.

Rivoli, Pietra. *The Travels of a T-Shirt in the Global Economy: An Economist Examines the Markets, Power, and Politics of World Trade*. New York: John Wiley & Sons, 2005.

Robinson, Nicholas A. *Strategies toward Sustainable Development: Implementing Agenda 21*. Dobbs Ferry, NY: Oceana, 2004.

Robinson-Pant, Anna. *Women, Literacy, and Development: Alternative Perspectives*. New York: Routledge, 2005.

Rogoff, Kenneth S. *Evolution and Performance of Exchange Rate Regimes*. Washington, DC: International Monetary Fund, 2004.

Rostow, W. W. *The Stages of Economic Growth: A Non-Communist Manifesto*. New York: Cambridge University Press, 1960.

Ruland, Jurgen, Eva Manske, and Werner Draguhn. *Asia-Pacific Economic Cooperation (Apec): The First Decade*. London: Curzon Press, 2002.

Sachs, Jeffrey D. *Development Economics*. Malden, MA: Blackwell Publishers, 2003.

———. *The End of Poverty: Economic Possibilities for Our Time*. New York: Penguin Press, 2005.

———, ed. *Investing in Development: A Practical Guide to Achieve the Millennium Development Goals*. New York: United Nations Development Project, 2005.

Sacquet, Anne-Marie. *World Atlas of Sustainable Development: Economic, Social and Environmental Data*. London: Anthem, 2005.

Sarno, Lucio, and Mark P. Taylor. *The Economics of Exchange Rates*. New York: Cambridge University Press, 2003.

Schneider, Friedrich, and Dominik H. Enste. *The Shadow Economy: An International Survey*. New York: Cambridge University Press, 2003.

Schott, Jeffrey J. *Free Trade Agreements: US Strategies and Priorities*. Washington, DC: Institute for International Economics, 2004.

Schrattenholzer, Leo, and Asami Miketa. *Achieving a Sustainable Global Energy System*. Northampton, MA: Edward Elgar Publishing, 2005.

Schumacher, Ernst F. *Small Is Beautiful: Economics as if People Mattered*. New York: Harper & Row, 1973.

Schumpeter, Joseph A. *Capitalism, Socialism, and Democracy*. New York: Perennial, 1962.

Schwartz, Benjamin, John K. Fairbanks, and Conrad Brandt. *A Documentary History of Chinese Communism*. New York: Routledge, 2004.

Sen, Amartya K. *Development as Freedom*. New York: Anchor Books, 2000.

Shafaeddin, Mehdi. *Trade Policy at the Crossroads: The Recent Experience of Developing Countries*. New York: Palgrave Macmillan, 2005.

Shamah, Shani B. *A Foreign Exchange Primer*. New York: John Wiley & Sons, 2003.

Shek, Daniel T. L., Ying-keung Chan, and Paul S. N. Lee, eds. *Quality of Life Research in Chinese, Western and Global Contexts*. New York: Springer, 2005.

Siebert, Horst. *Global Governance: An Architecture for the World Economy*. New York: Springer, 2003.

Simmons, Matthew R. *Twilight in the Desert: The Coming Saudi Oil Shock and the World Economy*. New York: John Wiley & Sons, 2005.

Smart, Alan, and Josephine Smart. *Petty Capitalists and Globalization: Flexibility, Entrepreneurship, and Economic Development*. New York: Suny Press, 2005.

Smith, Adam. *An Inquiry into the Nature and Causes of the Wealth of Nations*. New York: Oxford University Press, 1976.

Smith, Stephen C. *Ending Global Poverty: A Guide to What Works*. New York: Palgrave Macmillan, 2005.

Soederberg, Susanne. *The Politics of the New International Financial Architecture: Reimposing Neoliberal Domination in the Global South*. New York: Zed Books, 2005.

Sogge, David. *Give and Take: What's the Matter with Foreign Aid?* New York: Zed Books, 2002.

Solow, Robert M., ed. *Landmark Papers in Economic Growth*. Northampton, MA: Edward Elgar Publishing, 2001.

Sornarajah, M. *The International Law on Foreign Investment*. New York: Cambridge University Press, 2004.

Soto, Hernando de. *The Mystery of Capital: Why Capitalism Triumphs in the West and Fails Everywhere Else*. New York: Basic Books, 2000.

———. *The Other Path: The Invisible Revolution in the Third World*. New York: Harper & Row, 1989.

Soubbotina, Tatyana P. *Beyond Economic Growth: An Introduction to Sustainable Development*. 2d. ed. New York: World Bank Publications, 2004.

Southerton, Dale, Heather Chappelle, and Bas Van Vliet, eds. *Sustainable Consumption*. Northampton, MA: Edward Elgar Publishers, 2005.

Stearns, Peter N. *Consumerism in World History: The Global Transformation of Desire*. New York: Routledge, 2001.

Steffen, W. L., et al. *Global Change and the Earth System: A Planet under Pressure*. New York: Springer-Verlag, 2004.

Steger, Manfred B. *Globalization: A Very Short Introduction*. New York: Oxford University Press, 2003.

Stiglitz, Joseph E. *Globalization and Its Discontents*. New York: W.W. Norton & Company, 2003.

———, and Ha-Joon Chang, eds. *The Rebel Within: Joseph Stiglitz and the World Bank*. London: Anthem Press, 2002.

Suter, Keith. *Curbing Corporate Power: How Can We Control Transnational Corporations?* New York: Zed Books, 2005.

Sykes, Michael, ed. *Understanding Economic Growth*. New York: Palgrave Macmillan and the Organization for Economic Cooperation and Development, 2004.

Thirkell-White, Ben. *IMF and the Politics of Financial Globalization: From the Asian Crisis to a New International Financial Architecture*. New York: Palgrave Macmillan, 2005.

Thirlwall, A. P. *Trade, The Balance of Payments and Exchange Rate Policy in Developing Countries*. Northampton, MA: Edward Elgar Publishing, 2004.

Thomas-Slayter, Barbara P. *Southern Exposure: International Development and the Global South in the Twenty-First Century*. West Hartford, CT: Kumarian Press, 2003.

Tonelson, Alan. *The Race to the Bottom: Why a Worldwide Worker Surplus and Uncontrolled Free Trade Are Sinking American Living Standards*. Boulder, CO: Westview Press, 2002.

Transparency International. *Global Corruption Report 2005, Special Focus: Corruption in Construction and Post-Conflict Reconstruction*. London: Pluto Press, 2005.

Uchida, Hiroshi, ed. *Marx for the 21st Century*. New York: Routledge, 2005.

United Nations. *Agenda 21 Earth Summit: United Nations Program of Action for Rio*. New York: Author, 1992.

———. *Export Diversification and Economic Growth: The Experience of Selected Least Developed Countries*. New York: Author, 2005.

———. *Returning to an Eternal Debate: The Terms of Trade for Commodities in the Twentieth Century*. New York: Author, 2003.

———. *Review and Appraisal of the Progress Made in Achieving the Goals and Objectives of the Programme of Action of the International Conference on Population and Development: The 2004 Report*. New York: Author, 2004.

United Nations Conference on Trade and Development. *The Least Developed Countries Report 2004*. New York: United Nations, 2004.

———. *Trade and Development Report 2004*. New York and Geneva: United Nations, 2004.

United Nations Development Program. *Human Development Report 2004: Cultural Liberty in Today's Diverse World*. New York: Oxford University Press, 2004.

United Nations Economic and Social Affairs Department. *World Population to 2300*. New York: United Nations Publications, 2004.

United Nations Population Fund. *UNFPA State of World Population 2004*. New York: Author, 2004.

U.S. Agency for International Development. *Foreign Aid in the National Interest: Promoting Freedom, Security, and Opportunity*. Washington, DC: Author, 2003.

Van Rooy, Alison. *The Global Legitimacy Game: Civil Society, Globalization and Protest*. New York: Palgrave Macmillan, 2004.

Van Til, Jon. *Growing Civil Society: From Nonprofit Sector to Third Space*. Bloomington, IN: Indiana University Press, 2000.

Vines, David, and Christopher L. Gilbert, eds. *The IMF and Its Critics: Reform of Global Financial Architecture*. New York: Cambridge University Press, 2004.

Vizentini, Paulo, and Marianne Wiesebron, eds. *Free Trade for the Americas? The US Push for the FTAA Agreement*. New York: Zed Books, 2004.

Wallach, Lori, Patrick Woodall, and Ralph Nader. *Whose Trade Organization? A Comprehensive Guide to the World Trade Organization*. 2d ed. New York: New Press, 2004.

Ward, Barbara. *The Rich Nations and the Poor Nations*. New York: W. W. Norton & Company, 1962.

Weintraub, Sidney, ed. *Nafta's Impact on North America: The First Decade*. Washington, DC: Center for Strategic & International Studies, 2004.

Weiss, Thomas G. *UN Voices: The Struggle for Development and Social Justice*. Bloomington, IN: Indiana University Press, 2005.

Williams, Marc. *Third World Cooperation: The Group of 77 in UNCTAD*. New York: St. Martin's Press, 1991.

Wilson, Ernest J., III. *The Information Revolution and Developing Countries*. Cambridge, MA: MIT Press, 2004.

Winiecki, Jan. *Transition Economies and Foreign Trade*. 2d ed. New York: Routledge, 2002.

Wolf, Martin. *Why Globalization Works*. New Haven, CT: Yale University Press, 2004.

Wolfensohn, James D. *A New Development Agenda: The Transformation of the World Bank under James D. Wolfensohn, 1995–2005*. Washington, DC: World Bank Publications, 2005.

———, and Rodrigo de Rato. *Global Monitoring Report 2004: Policies and Actions for Achieving the Millennium Development Goals and Related Outcomes*. New York: World Bank Publications, 2004.

World Bank. *Doing Business in 2005: Obstacles to Growth*. Washington, DC: Author, 2004.

———. *Global Economic Prospects 2004*. Washington, DC: Author, 2004.

———. *2004 World Development Indicators*. New York: Oxford University Press, 2004.

———. *World Development Report 2005: A Better Investment Climate for Everyone*. Washington, DC: Author, 2004.

———. *Young Person's Guide to the World Bank*. Washington, DC: Author, 2005.

World Economic Forum. *The Global Competitiveness Report: 2004*. New York: Oxford University Press, 2004.

World Resources Institute. *World Resources 2000–2001, People and Ecosystems: The Fraying Web of Life*. Washington, DC: World Resources Institute, United Nations Development Program, United Nations Environment Program, World Bank, 2000.

World Trade Organization. *International Trade Statistics 2004*. Geneva: Author, 2004.

———. *Understanding the WTO*. 3d ed. Geneva, Switzerland: Author, 2003.

———. *World Trade Report 2004*. Geneva, Switzerland: Author, 2004.

Worldwatch Institute. *State of the World 2004: A Worldwatch Institute Report on Progress toward a Sustainable Society*. New York: W. W. Norton & Company, 2004.

Xiaolan Fu. *Exports, Foreign Direct Investment and Economic Development in China*. New York: Palgrave Macmillan, 2005.

Yergin, Daniel, and Joseph Stanislaw. *The Commanding Heights: The Battle for the World Economy*. Rev. ed. New York: Free Press, 2002.

Yi Feng, *Democracy, Governance, and Economic Performance*. Cambridge: MIT Press, 2005.

Ying Huang, Robert McCormick, and Lawrence J. McQuillan. *U.S. Economic Freedom Index: 2004 Report*. San Francisco, CA: Pacific Research Institute, 2004.

Yunus, Muhammad, and Alan Jolis. *Banker to the Poor: The Autobiography of Muhammad Yunus, Founder of Grameen Bank*. New York: Oxford University Press, 2001.

Zetter, Roger, and Mohamed Hamza. *Market Economy and Urban Change: Impacts in the Developing World*. Washington, DC: Earthscan Publications, 2004.

Index

Note: **Boldface** indicates the volume number; *italic* page locators lead to a main encyclopedia entry. The letters "t" and "f" in parentheses following a page locator refers to a table or figure, respectively.

About the Author

DAVID E. O'CONNOR is a nationally recognized economics teacher at the Edwin O. Smith High School in Storrs, Connecticut. He has earned many state and national honors in the fields of economic education and social studies, including the Connecticut Council on Economic Education's Distinguished Service Award, the Connecticut Council for the Social Studies Honor and Service awards, and the University of Connecticut's Excellence in Teaching Alumni Award. He has served as a College Board consultant in economics, president of the Connecticut Council for the Social Studies, and economics instructor at the Taft Summer Institute for Teachers. He has conducted over 100 teacher workshops at state and national conferences. He has also worked in assessment with the Educational Testing Service, Psychological Corporation/Harcourt Educational Measurement, and the American Institutes for Research.

Mr. O'Connor has authored or co-authored eighteen books or teacher's manuals in the fields of economics, ethnic history, and world history. His most recent books include *The Basics of Economics* (Greenwood, 2004), *Demystifying the Global Economy* (Greenwood, 2002), and *Basic Economic Principles: A Guide for Students* (Greenwood, 2000). During the early 2000s he authored a series of teacher's manuals and reference materials on the global economy for the University of Connecticut's Center for International Business Education and Research (CIBER). O'Connor also participated in a number of international economics grants. He was an instructor in a two-year USAID market economics program in Poland during the early 1990s, a participant in a Fulbright scholar program in the Peoples Republic of China in 2002, and co-coordinator for a high school sister schools project with the Linqu Experimental Middle School in China in 2004.